TORT:
CASES AND MATERIALS

AUSTRALIA
Law Book Co.
Sydney

CANADA AND USA
Carswell
Toronto

HONG KONG
Sweet & Maxwell Asia

NEW ZEALAND
Brookers
Wellington

SINGAPORE and MALAYSIA
Sweet & Maxwell Asia
Singapore and Kuala Lumpur

TORT: CASES AND MATERIALS

SECOND EDITION

By

GEOFFREY SAMUEL

LONDON
SWEET & MAXWELL
2008

First edition, *Cases and Materials on Torts* by Geoffrey Samuel,
published 2006 by Law Matters Publishing.
Second edition 2008

Published in 2008 by
Sweet & Maxwell Limited of 100 Avenue Road,
http://www.sweetandmaxwell.co.uk
Typeset by LBJ Typesetting Ltd of Kingsclere
Printed and bound in Great Britain by
Ashford Colour Press Ltd, Gosport, Hants

No natural forests were destroyed to make this product;
only farmed timber was used and re-planted.

British Library Cataloguing in Publication Data

A CIP catalogue record for this book
is available from the British Library

ISBN 978-184703-448-9

©
Sweet & Maxwell
2008

DEDICATION

This book is dedicated to my sister, and to her courage and humour, whose life would have been devastated had it not been for the devotion of our parents and the great skill of Sir Alexander Fleming

PREFACE TO THE SECOND EDITION

This casebook is an updated edition of the one that I published in 2006 with LawMatters. The purpose of this book is to provide a relatively solid introduction to the main areas of undergraduate tort law through the words of a range of those who are responsible for the modern development of the subject. Such an introductory sourcebook should be valuable when used alongside tort lectures, but it ought not to replace the library (or Internet) research which, of course, remains the essential foundation for success in the subject. It will, then, hopefully act as a stimulating *passerelle* between classroom and library source material. If any specific characteristics are to be associated with this sourcebook, perhaps (as with my *Contract Law: Cases and Materials*, Sweet & Maxwell, 2007), the European orientation and the emphasis on method might be the ones to gain attention. They have been my guides.

In the Preface of my contract casebook I record my thanks to a number of friends and colleagues and to my wife. I would like to extend that paragraph to the present casebook. In addition I would like to thank Bernard Rudden who has provided me with stimulating comments and criticisms with regard both to the first edition of this book and to my contract casebook (which hopefully will complement and interrelate with this new edition). Finally I must sincerely thank not just Sweet & Maxwell for agreeing to take on and publish this second edition but equally the firm's editorial team. They have been most supportive and helpful.

The book is dedicated to my sister and, through her, to the late Sir Alexander Fleming and to the artist Ethel Gabain. In 1944 Sir Alexander Fleming took on Gillian as a test patient for a new drug that he was developing; penicillin saved her leg and the lives and limbs of millions of others. While undergoing treatment my sister was the subject of a painting by Ethel Gabain, then working as a government war artist, and the picture is entitled *A Child Bomb-Victim Receiving Penicillin Treatment* (1944). What makes the painting relevant for this present book is that Gillian was not in fact the victim of a bomb but of a traffic accident. The painting, which was rediscovered by us only a few years ago, can be seen at the Imperial War Museum (London).

Geoffrey Samuel
Kent Law School
May 2008

CONTENTS

ABBREVIATIONS

AC	Appeal cases (Third Series)
AJCL	American Journal of Comparative Law
All ER	All England Law Reports (Butterworths & Co)
App Cas	Appeal Cases (Second Series)
BGB	Burgerliches Gesetzbuch (German Civil Code)
C	Code of Justinian
CA	Court of Appeal
C&MC	G Samuel, *Contract: Cases and Materials* (Sweet & Maxwell, 2007)
CC	Code civil (French Civil Code)
Ch	Chancery Division (Third Series)
Ch D	Chancery Division (Second Series); Chancery Division (High Court)
CLJ	Cambridge Law Journal
CLP	Current Legal problems
CLR	Commonwealth Law Reports
D	Dalloz (also Digest of Justinian)
EHRR	European Human Rights Reports
ER	English Reports
Ex Ch	Court of Exchequer Chamber
FLR	Family Law Reports
G	Institutes of Gaius
HL	House of Lords
ICLQ	International and Comparative Law Quarterly
IECL	International Encyclopedia of Comparative Law
J	Institutes of Justinian/Justice (High Court)
JCP	Jurisclasseur periodique (La Semaine Juridique)
KB	King's Bench (Third Series)
LC	Lord Chancellor
LJ	Lord Justice (Court of Appeal)
LJCP	Law Journal Common Pleas
LJ Ex	Law Journal Exchequer
LJQB	Law Journal Queen's Bench
Ll Rep	Lloyd's List Law Reports
LQR	Law Quarterly Review
LR. . .CP	Common Pleas Cases (First Series)
LR. . .Eq	Equity Cases (First Series)
LR. . .Ex	Exchequer Cases (First Series)
LR. . .HL	English and Irish Appeals (First Series)
LR. . .QB	Queen's Bench Cases (First Series)
LS	Legal Studies
LT	Law Times Reports
MLR	Modern Law Review

NILQ	Northern Ireland Legal Quarterly
OJLS	Oxford Journal of Legal Studies
OUP	Oxford University Press
P	Probate Division (Third Series)
PC	Privy Council
PECL	Principles of European Contract Law
PETL	Principles of European Tort Law
PL	Public Law
QB	Queen's Bench (Third Series)
QBD	Queen's Bench (Second Series); Queen's Bench Division (High Court)
UC&TO	G Samuel, *Understanding Contractual and Tortious Obligations* (LawMatters, 2005)
WLR	Weekly Law Reports

ACKNOWLEDGMENTS

Grateful acknowledgment is made to the following authors and publishers for permission to quote from their works:

Birks, Peter: "Equity in the Modern Law: An Exercise in Taxonomy", 26 *The University of Western Australia Law Review* 1, (1996) pp.5–6.

Cane, Peter: *The Anatomy of Tort Law* (Hart Publishing, 1997), p.1. Reproduced by permission of Hart Publishing.

Cane, Peter: *Tort Law and Economic Interests* (2nd edn, Oxford University Press, 1996), pp.3–5, 427–429. Reproduced by permission of Oxford University Press.

Conaghan, Joanne & Mansell, Wade: *The Wrongs of Tort* (2nd edn, Pluto Press, 1999), p.3. Reproduced by permission of Pluto Press.

Demichel, Andre & Lalumiere, Pierre: *Le Droit Public* (7th edn, Presses Universitaires de France, 1996) pp.6–11. Reproduced by permission of Presses Universitaires de France.

Fleming, John G.: *An Introduction to the Law of Torts* (2nd edn, Oxford University Press, 1986), p.1. Reproduced by permission of Oxford University Press.

Honore, A.M.: "Causation and Remoteness of Damage", International Encyclopedia of Comparative Law Volumes (Brill NV, 1971), Vol. XI, Ch. 7. Reproduced by permission of Brill NV.

Ibbetson, David: *A Historical Introduction to the Law of Obligations* (Oxford University Press, 1999), p.159. Reproduced by permission of Oxford University Press.

Jones, Michael A.: *Textbook on Torts* (Oxford University Press, 2002), pp.20–21. Reproduced by permission of Oxford University Press.

Jolowicz, J.A.: "Liability for Accidents", *Cambridge Law Journal* 50, p.50.

Justinian I: *The Digest of Justinian* (Cambridge University Press, 1904), Vol.1. Reproduced by permission of Cambridge University Press.

Lewis, Richard: "Insurance and the Tort System", *Legal Studies* 2005, Vol. 25, 85 pp. 86, 89, 116.

Moreau, Jacques: *La Responsabilite administrative* (Presses Universitaires de France, 1996) pp.108–110. Reproduced by permission of Presses Universitaires de France.

Rudden, Bernard: *The Battle of Manywells Spring* (London Review of Books, 2003), p.24. Reproduced by permission of the London Review of Books.

Samuel, Geoffrey: *Understanding Contractual and Tortious Obligations* (Law Matters, 2008) pp.98–104. Reproduced by permission of Law Matters.

Samuel, Geoffrey: "Notion of an Interest as a Formal Concept in English and in Comparative Law" originally appeared in Guy Canivet, Mads Andenas and Duncan Fairgrieve (eds) *Comparative Law Before the Courts* (London, BIICL 2004), and is reprinted with the permission of the British Institute of International and Comparative Law.

Stone, Ferdinand: "Liability for Damage caused by things" in *International Encyclopedia of Comparative Law Volumes* (Brill NV, 1983), Vol.XI Chapter 5, pp.5–6 and 5–19. Reproduced by permission of Brill NV.

Tunc, Andre: "Introduction" in *International Encyclopedia of Comparative Law Volumes*, (Brill NV, 1983), Vol.XI p.6. Reproduced by permission of Brill NV.

Von Bar, Christian: *Common European Law of Torts,* Vol.II (Oxford University Press, 2000), pp.4, 6–7. Reproduced by permission of Oxford University Press.

Waddams, Stephen: *Dimensions of Private Law* (Cambridge University Press, 2003), pp.12–14, 222–223, 231 and 233. Reproduced by permission of Cambridge University Press.

Wainwright v United Kingdom (2006) © The Times/NI Syndication

Weir, Tony.: *Introduction to Tort Law* (2nd edn, Oxford University Press, 2006), p.ix. Reproduced by permission of Oxford University Press.

Weir, Tony.: "Recent Developments in Causation in English Tort Law" in B. Fauvarque-Cosson, E. Picard & A. Voinnesson (eds) *De tous horizons: Melanges Xavier Blanc Jouvan* (Societe de Legislation Comparee, 2005), pp.883, 890.

Weir, Tony.: "Governmental Liability" in *Public Law* 40 [1989], pp.62–63.

Weir, Tony.: *A Casebook on Tort* (10th edn, Sweet & Maxwell, 2004), p.6.

Winfield, Sir Percy Henry: *The Province of the Law of Tort* (Cambridge University Press, 1931), pp.32, 229 and 231. Reproduced by permission of Cambridge University Press.

Grateful acknowledgment is made to The European Group on Tort Law for permission to quote from their work. Grateful acknowledgment is also made to The Incorporated Council of Law Reporting for England and Wales and LexisNexis Butterworths for permission to quote from a number of their works.

While every care has been taken to establish and acknowledge copyright and contact copyright owners, the publishers tender their apologies for any accidental infringement. They would be pleased to come to a suitable arrangement with the rightful owners in each case.

Table of Cases

1

Definition and scope of the law of tort

The purpose of this first chapter is to look at attempts to define the law of tort (or torts) in the common law world. This is an exercise that does not prove easy, partly because it can be approached from a variety of perspectives each of which tends to result in a rather different definition. There is also a danger here for those keen to draw comparisons with the legal systems of the UK's continental EU partners. Although the law of torts can be seen as roughly equivalent to delictual or civil liability, such comparison can mask as much as it can reveal since differences of structure, mentality and methodology profoundly affect the perception, role and context of tort vis-à-vis non-contractual liability in the European codes.

1.1 Historical considerations

The first perspective from which tort can be viewed (and to an extent defined) is that of history. In the civil law world the history of the fundamental legal categories is tied up with the history of Roman law; the forms of legal thinking had been determined and defined by the great classical jurists and these categories were transported to the modern world in Justinian's *Institutes*. Liability was *ex contractu*, *quasi ex contractu*, *ex delicto* or *quasi ex delicto*. In the common law there was no such blue print. Both the system of courts and the system of liability developed in a haphazard fashion according to the empirical needs of the time. The result was a structural foundation—in effect a list or personal actions—very different to that of Roman law.

1.1.1 Forms of action

The historical basis of liability in the common law is to be found in a series of writs which were in effect a list of categories of personal action into which one had to fit one's claim. These writs were not "based on substantive legal categories or any legal plan"; and if "there was a plan behind it all, it was merely to create an adequate royal remedy for a number of very common wrongs, which upset society and with which the existing courts dealt in too slow, cumbersome and incalculable a way" (RC van Caenegem, 'History of European Civil Procedure', IECL, (Tubingen: JCB Mohr, 1971) Volume XVI, Chapter 2, para.22). Very simply, the English 'law of obligations' (a Roman category now in vogue in English law) was not divided up into contract and tort, but into trespass, debt, detinue, trover, nuisance and so on. A useful overview is to be found in the extract from one of Lord Goff's judgments.

Henderson v Merrett Syndicates Ltd **[1995] 2 A.C. 145, HL**

(For facts see p.18)

Lord Goff: "... The situation in common law countries, including of course England, is exceptional, in that the common law grew up within a procedural framework uninfluenced by Roman law. The law was categorised by reference to the forms of action, and it was not until the abolition of the forms of action by the Common Law Procedure Act 1852 (15 & 16 Vict c 76) that it became necessary to reclassify the law in substantive terms. The result was that common lawyers did at last separate our law of obligations into contract and tort, though in so doing they relegated quasi-contractual claims to the status of an appendix to the law of contract, thereby postponing by a century or so the development of a law of restitution. Even then, there was no systematic reconsideration of the problem of concurrent claims in contract and tort. We can see the courts rather grappling with unpromising material drawn from the old cases in which liability in negligence derived largely from categories based upon the status of the defendant. In a sense, we must not be surprised; for no significant law faculties were established at our universities until the late 19th century, and so until then there was no academic opinion available to guide or stimulate the judges . . ."

NOTES

1. One reason why English law is different to continental law is, as Lord Goff observes, the lack of law faculties before (for the most part) the 20th century. As Sir John Baker has noted: "Had the early Tudor authorities insisted upon an academical law degree before call to the Bar, that might indeed have revolutionized the history of English law and achieved what books alone could not" (*The Oxford History of the Laws of England: Volume VI 1483–1558*, (Oxford: OUP, 2003), p.12). The absence of such law faculties meant that legal knowledge was in the hands of practitioners and judges rather than academics; and practitioners, unlike academics, are often little interested in order and system (see Lord Macmillan in *Read v Lyons* (1947), below p.209).

2. Another reason why the idea of a 'law of obligations' is misleading is that English law does not rigidly distinguish between real rights (in rem) and personal rights (in personam), the former being the objects of the law of property and the latter objects of the law of obligations. The action of debt, for example, was as much a proprietary claim as 'contractual' (D. Ibbetson, *A Historical Introduction to the Law of Obligations* (Oxford: OUP, 1999) p.18). Equally many 'torts' like trover or detinue (although detinue even in the 19th century was being seen as more 'contractual' in nature) were not really, from a Romanist viewpoint, dealing with relations between persons. They were part of the law of property. The forms of action were abolished in 1852 (as Bramwell L.J. indicates in the next extract) and this had the effect of opening up the system in as much as it became much easier for a substantive law to free itself from the procedural forms which had dominated legal thinking in the common law.

Bryant v Herbert **(1877) 3 C.P.D. 389, CA**

Bramwell L.J.: "... [The Common Law Procedure Acts 1852–1860] did not abolish forms of action in words. The Common Law Commissioners recommended that: but it was supposed that, if adopted, the law would be shaken to its foundations; so that all that could be done was to provide as far as possible that, though forms of actions remained, there never should be a question what was the form. This was accomplished save as to this very question of costs in actions within the county court jurisdiction. Until the passing of the statute [County Courts Act] we are discussing, it was necessary to see if an action was *assumpsit*, case &c. But the Common Law Procedure Act having passed, and the forms of actions being practically abolished, the legislature pass this Act dropping the words '*assumpsit*, case', &c., and using the words 'founded on contract', 'founded on tort'. This shows to me that the substance of the matter was to be looked at. One may observe there is no middle term; the statute supposes all actions are founded either on contract or on tort. So that it is tort, if not contract, contract if not tort. . . ."

NOTE

Lawyers throughout Europe distinguish today between jurisdiction, procedure and substantive rights. What one has to remember, with regard to the forms of action, is that they did not make these distinctions; each form defined whether or not a common law court had jurisdiction, the procedure that attached to a claim and the 'right' in issue. For a list of the some of the main forms of action see the extract from Richard Garde in C&MC, pp.510–511.

1.1.2 Causes of action

The effect of the abolition of the forms of action was not to dispense with centuries of legal thinking overnight. The old forms of personal action at common law became causes of action; that is to say they moved from being procedural structures that obliquely defined substantive ideas to become a list of substantive ideas underpinning liability. Thus, while debt and *assumpsit* got swallowed up by a general theory of contract (although not completely), trespass, nuisance, trover (conversion), detinue and the like became 'torts'. They became little more than 'wrongs' that could not be accommodated by the category of contract. Tort, in other words, is not in its origin some rationally conceived category of liability; it is, or was, simply a category into which claims which could not be classified elsewhere were housed (or dumped). As the next case indicates, history is still in the making.

Letang v Cooper **[1965] 1 Q.B. 232, CA**

Mrs Letang brought an action for damages against Mr Cooper after she had been run over by the latter while sunbathing in a hotel car park. However, as the action was brought more than three years after the accident, there was a problem with respect to the limitation period. Statute states that 'in the case of actions for damages for negligence, nuisance or breach of duty', where the damage consists of 'personal injuries', the limitation period is three years (instead of six with respect to other kinds of damage). Mrs Letang tried to get around this limitation bar by pleading the case in trespass to the person, claiming that the statute did not apply to trespass. This argument was rejected by the Court of Appeal (Lord Denning M.R., Danckwerts L.J. and Diplock L.J.).

Lord Denning M.R.: ". . . The truth is that the distinction between trespass and case is obsolete. We have a different sub-division altogether. Instead of dividing actions for personal injuries into trespass (direct damage) or case (consequential damage), we divide the causes of action now according as the defendant did the injury intentionally or unintentionally. If one man intentionally applies force directly to another, the plaintiff has a cause of action in assault and battery, or, if you so please to describe it, in trespass to the person. 'The least touching of another in anger is a battery,' per Holt CJ in *Cole v Turner*. If he does not inflict injury intentionally, but only unintentionally, the plaintiff has no cause of action today in trespass. His only cause of action is in negligence, and then only on proof of want of reasonable care. If the plaintiff cannot prove want of reasonable care, he may have no cause of action at all. Thus, it is not enough nowadays for the plaintiff to plead that 'the defendant shot the plaintiff.' He must also allege that he did it intentionally or negligently. If intentional, it is the tort of assault and battery. If negligent and causing damage, it is the tort of negligence.

The modern law on this subject was well expounded by Diplock J in *Fowler. Lanning* with which I fully agree. But I would go this one step further: when the injury is not inflicted intentionally, but negligently, I would say that the only cause of action is negligence and not trespass. If it were trespass, it would be actionable without proof of damage; and that is not the law today.

In my judgment, therefore, the only cause of action in the present case, where the injury was unintentional, is negligence and is barred by reason of the express provision of the statute. . . .

Diplock L.J.: . . . A cause of action is simply a factual situation the existence of which entitles one person to obtain from the court a remedy against another person. Historically, the means by which the remedy was obtained varied with the nature of the factual situation and causes of action were divided into categories according to the 'form of action' by which the remedy was obtained in the particular kind of factual situation which constituted the cause of action. But that is legal history, not current law . . . The Judicature Act, 1873 abolished forms of action. It did not affect causes of action; so it was convenient for lawyers and legislators to continue to use, to describe the various categories of factual situations which entitle one person to obtain from the court a remedy against another, the names of the various 'forms of action' by which formerly the remedy appropriate to the particular category of factual situation was obtained. But it is essential to realise that when, since 1873, the name of a form of action is used to identify a cause of action, it is used as a convenient and succinct description of a particular category of factual situation which entitles one person to obtain from the court a remedy against another person. To forget this will indeed encourage the old forms of action to rule us from their graves . . ."

QUESTION

Can a defendant in a negligence case raise the defence that he caused the harm intentionally? If not, why distinguish between trespass and negligence?

NOTE

As a category tort 'provided few answers to the substantive questions that might have been asked' (Ibbetson, *A Historical Introduction to the Law of Obligations*, p.57) and this is still true today. 'Tort' (unlike contract) is not itself the basis of a cause of action; it is only a generic category containing a list of specified causes of action and before liability in tort can be established a claimant must base his claim on one of these causes, as the next case illustrates.

Esso Petroleum Co Ltd v Southport Corporation **[1953] 3 W.L.R. 773, Q.B.D., [1954] 2 Q.B. 182, CA, [1956] A.C. 218, HL**

Southport Corporation brought an action for damages against an oil company in respect of a tanker that had run aground and whose cargo of oil, when deliberately released from the stricken ship by the captain in order to avoid endangering his crew, had polluted the Corporation's beaches. The Corporation pleaded the following causes of action: (i) trespass; (ii) private nuisance; (iii) public nuisance; and (iv) negligence of the captain (for which the employer would be vicariously liable). Devlin J. at first instance held that the oil company was not liable since the captain had not acted negligently. This decision was reversed in the Court of Appeal. The oil company then appealed to the House of Lords (Earl Jowitt, Lords Normand, Morton, Radcliffe and Tucker), but in turn the Corporation tried to add a further cause of action to the list, namely that the oil company were in breach of a direct duty to the plaintiff in putting to sea an unseaworthy ship. The Corporation were not allowed to add this new cause of action and the oil company was held not to be liable.

> **Denning L.J.** (Court of Appeal): "This is one of those cases, rare nowadays, where much depends on ascertaining the proper cause of action, particularly with regard to the burden of proof. . . . The judge seems to have thought that it did not matter much what was the proper cause of action; it all came back in the end to the universal tort of negligence. . . I do not share this view,. . .
>
> (1) *Trespass to land.* . . . I am clearly of opinion that the Southport Corporation cannot here sue in trespass. This discharge of oil was not done directly on to their foreshore, but outside in the estuary. It was carried by the tide on to their land, but that was only consequential, not direct. Trespass, therefore, does not lie.
>
> (2) *Private nuisance.* In order to support an action on the case for a private nuisance the defendant must have used his own land or some other land in such a way as injuriously to affect the enjoyment of the plaintiffs' land. 'The ground of responsibility', said Lord Wright in *Sedleigh-Denfield v O'Callaghan*, 'is the possession and control of the land from which the nuisance proceeds'. Applying this principle, it is clear that the discharge of oil was not a private nuisance, because it did not involve the use by the defendants of any land, but only of a ship at sea.
>
> (3) *Public nuisance.* The term 'public nuisance' covers a multitude of sins, great and small . . . Suffice it to say that the discharge of a noxious substance in such a way as to be likely to affect the comfort and safety of Her Majesty's subjects generally is a public nuisance . . .
>
> Applying the old cases to modern instances, it is, in my opinion, a public nuisance to discharge oil into the sea in such circumstances that it is likely to be carried on to the shores and beaches of our land to the prejudice and discomfort of Her Majesty's subjects. It is an

5

offence punishable by the common law. Furthermore, if any person should suffer greater damage or inconvenience from the oil than the generality of the public, he can have an action to recover damages on that account, provided, of course, that he can discover the offender who discharged the oil. This action would have been described in the old days as an action on the case, but it is now simply an action for a nuisance . . .

(4) *Burden of proof*. One of the principal differences between an action for a public nuisance and an action for negligence is the burden of proof. In an action for a public nuisance, once the nuisance is proved and the defendant is shown to have caused it, then the legal burden is shifted on to the defendant to justify or excuse himself. If he fails to do so, he is held liable, whereas in an action for negligence the legal burden in most cases remains throughout on the plaintiff. In negligence, the plaintiff may gain much help from provisional presumptions like the doctrine of *res ipsa loquitur*, but, nevertheless, at the end of the case the judge must ask himself whether the legal burden is discharged. If the matter is left evenly in the balance, the plaintiff fails. But in public nuisance, as in trespass, the legal burden shifts to the defendant, and it is not sufficient for him to leave the matter in doubt. He must plead and prove a sufficient justification or excuse.

(5) *Justification or excuse*. The defendants seek to justify themselves by saying that it was necessary for them to discharge the oil because their ship was in danger. She had been driven by rough seas on to the revetment wall, and it was necessary to discharge the oil in order to get her off. If she had not done so, lives might have been lost. This is, no doubt, true at that stage in the story, but the question is, how came she to get upon the wall? If it was her own fault, then her justification fails, because no one can avail himself of a necessity produced by his own default. Where does the legal burden rest in this respect? Must the Southport Corporation prove that the ship was at fault in getting on to the wall, or must the ship prove that she herself was not at fault? In my opinion the burden is on the ship. She does not justify herself in law by necessity alone, but only by unavoidable necessity, and the burden is on her to show it was unavoidable.

Public nuisance is, in this respect, like unto a trespass, as to which it was said by the Court of King's Bench as long ago as 1616 in *Weaver v Ward*, that no man shall be excused 'except it may be judged utterly without his fault' . . .

Those were, it is true, cases in trespass; but the same principle applies to cases of public nuisance. That is shown by *Tarry v Ashton*, where a lamp which projected over the Strand fell on to a passer-by. This was described by Lord Wright as private action for a public nuisance: see *Sedleigh-Denfield v O'Callaghan*. Another example is *Wringe v Cohen*, where the gable of a house next the highway was blown down in a storm (which was treated by this court as a public nuisance). In both cases the defendant was held liable because his premises were in a defective state. He did not know of the defect, and he was not negligent in not knowing, but, nevertheless, he was liable because he did not prove any sufficient justification or excuse. He did not prove inevitable accident . . ."

Earl Jowitt (House of Lords): ". . . In the present case every allegation of negligence has been answered by the finding of the judge, and there was no allegation of unseaworthiness. That being so, I do not think that the present appellants, the owners of the *Inverpool*, can be held responsible because they did not negative some possible case which had never been alleged against them in the pleadings or made against them in the course of the trial. . . ."

Lord Radcliffe (House of Lords): "My Lords, I think that this case ought to be decided in accordance with the pleadings. If it is, I am of opinion, as was the trial judge, that the respondents failed to establish any claim to relief that was valid in law. If it is not, we might do better justice to the respondents -- I cannot tell, since the evidence is incomplete -- but I am certain that we should do worse justice to the appellants, since in my view they were entitled to conduct the case and confine their evidence in reliance upon the further and better particulars of the statement of claim which had been delivered by the respondents. It seems to me that it is the purpose of such particulars that they should help to define the issues and to indicate to the party who asks for them how much of the range of his possible evidence will be relevant and how much irrelevant to those issues. Proper use of them shortens the hearing and reduces costs. But if an appellate court is to treat reliance upon them as pedantry or mere formalism, I do not see what part they have to play in our trial system . . ."

NOTES

1. Although Denning L.J.'s judgment was overturned in the House of Lords it remains very valuable from a methodological point of view. Liability in tort is a matter of going through the various heads of liability and applying each one to the facts in order to see if there is a 'fit'. If one does fit the facts, the defendant is liable; if not, then there is no liability in tort. According to this approach, tort consists of distinct causes of action with the result that one takes an alphabetical approach to liability (B Rudden, 'Torticles' (1991–92) 6/7 *Tulane Civil Law Forum* 105; and see **1.7**, below).

2. Note also how the law of procedure was instrumental in preventing the Corporation from succeeding in its tort claim. Had it been allowed to add the fifth cause of action, the oil company may well have been liable on the basis that they were in breach of a direct duty owed to the claimant not to put to sea an unseaworthy ship. This is where Denning L.J.'s approach was most perceptive: he effectively achieved the same result through his interpretation of the tort of public nuisance.

3. Damage arising from oil contamination at sea is now covered by statute and, to an extent, by a voluntary scheme: see Cane, *Tort Law and Economic Interests*, 2nd edn (Oxford: OUP, 1996), pp.433–435.

QUESTIONS

1. Read the case of *Benjamin v Storr* (1874). Could this case have been of help to the Corporation? Should the Corporation's lawyers have impressed it on the House of Lords in their arguments? Can you draft such an argument using the case?

2. Procedure was reformed in 1998 (see Civil Procedure Rules 1998). Would these new rules now allow a new cause of action to be added at an appeal stage?

Sterman v E W & W J Moore Ltd **[1970] 1 Q.B. 596, CA**

Lord Denning M.R.: ". . . Here was a plaintiff who issued his writ and served it on the defendants well within the period of limitation. They knew perfectly well that the plaintiff was claiming damages for his fall from the trestle because it was their fault. Yet they seek to bar him on the most technical consideration -- just because he omitted the words 'for negligence and breach of statutory duty'. I do not think that we should allow this technical objection to prevail . . . [W]e should allow the plaintiff to amend the writ so as to state in terms that his claim is for damages 'for negligence and breach of statutory duty'. I see no harm in adding the further claim for damages for 'breach of agreement' . . ."

Salmon L.J.: "I agree. I would emphasise that it is highly desirable that the indorsement to the writ should plainly set out the cause of action on which the plaintiff relies. It may be that it is sufficient . . . if the writ merely gives a concise statement of the nature of the relief or remedy required by the plaintiff; but the disadvantage of confining the indorsement of the writ to a concise statement of the relief or remedy required (as the plaintiff has done in the present case) is that the plaintiff may find himself in considerable difficulty when he comes to deliver his statement of claim. It seems to me, although I am expressing no concluded view on the point, that the provisions of [the Rules of Supreme Court] preclude the plaintiff from including any cause of action in his statement of claim which is not mentioned in the writ. . ."

NOTE

See *Goode v Martin* (2002).

QUESTION

Causes of action must be set out by the claimant in the statement of claim (pleadings). But what are the principal causes of action in tort? (cf. **1.7.**)

1.1.3 General principles of liability

The abolition of the forms of action did open up the common law to the development of forms of liability based upon general principles and this is a process that is still continuing. At the end of the 19th century a general principle of liability was established in respect of physical harm intentionally caused (*Wilkinson*) and this was extended to negligently caused physical harm during the early part of the 20th century (*Donoghue*). One can, now, more or less say that any *physical* damage (personal injury and actual damage to property) intentionally or negligently caused will give rise to tortious liability (*Letang*).

Wilkinson v Downton [1897] 2 Q.B. 57, QBD

Wright J.: "In this case the defendant, in the execution of what he seems to have regarded as a practical joke, represented to the plaintiff that he was charged by her husband with a message to her to the effect that her husband was smashed up in an accident, and was lying at The Elms at Leytonstone with both legs broken, and that she was to go at once in a cab with two pillows to fetch him home. All this was false. The effect of the statement on the plaintiff was a violent shock to her nervous system, producing vomiting and other more serious and permanent physical consequences at one time threatening her reason, and entailing weeks of suffering and incapacity to her as well as expense to her husband for medical attendance. These consequences were not in any way the result of previous illhealth or weakness of constitution; nor was there any evidence of predisposition to nervous shock or any other idiosyncrasy . . .

. . . The defendant has, as I assume for the moment, wilfully done an act calculated to cause physical harm to the plaintiff -- that is to say, to infringe her legal right to personal safety, and has in fact thereby caused physical harm to her. That proposition without more appears to me to state a good cause of action, there being no justification alleged for the act. This wilful injuria is in law malicious, although no malicious purpose to cause the harm which was caused nor any motive of spite is imputed to the defendant . . ."

QUESTION

Is this a trespass or a negligence case? (cf. *Wainwright v Home Office* (2004) at § 47.)

NOTE

The development of general principles continued during the 20th century as the next extracts indicate.

Donoghue v Stevenson [1932] A.C. 562, HL(Sc)

(See p.131)

Lord Goff, *The Search for Principle, Maccabaean Lecture in Jurisprudence, 1983*

". . . [P]erhaps . . . one of Lord Denning's principal contributions will be perceived to have been his loosening of the reins of a doctrine of precedent which had become too strict. When I was a student, there appeared to exist some judges who saw the law almost as a deductive science, a matter of finding the relevant authorities and applying them to the facts of the particular case. This is no longer so; and there is now a readiness among judges, not of course to disregard or ignore precedents by which they are bound, but, where they are at liberty to do so, to adopt or qualify them—not simply to achieve a personally desired result, but to ensure that principles are so stated as to embrace the legally just result on facts possibly not foreseen by those who had previously formulated them. . . ."

NOTE

It would be a mistake to think that the old categories of liability have disappeared, even if the onward march of negligence, with its empirical notion of reasonable behaviour, is infecting the law of tort as a whole (T Weir, The Staggering March of Negligence, in P Cane & J Stapleton eds, *The Law of Obligations: Essays in Celebration of John Fleming*, (Oxford: OUP, 1998), pp.97–138). Trespass, nuisance, defamation, conversion, the rule in *Rylands v Fletcher* and so on remain distinct causes of action with the result that one can still take an alphabetical approach to the law of torts (see Rudden,). What is important, however, about this movement towards general principle is that it poses a question about whether common lawyers should be talking about a law of 'torts' or a law of 'tort'.

European Group on Tort Law, Principles of European Tort Law (2003)

"Art. 1:101. Basic norm

(1) A person to whom damage to another is legally attributable is liable to compensate that damage.
(2) Damage may be attributed in particular to the person

    a) whose behaviour constituting fault has caused it; or
    b) whose abnormally dangerous activity has caused it; or
    c) whose auxiliary has caused it within the scope of his functions."

QUESTION

Read the case of *Bradford Corporation v Pickles* (1895) (p.72). If art.1:101 became part of English tort law would *Bradford*, if it arose again, have to be decided differently?

1.2 Definitional approaches

When one tries to rise above history, there are, very broadly, two main approaches to defining tort and these can be expressed in two questions. What *is* the law of tort? And what does the law of tort *do*? The first question approaches the subject from what might be called a formalist viewpoint and thus invites a formalist definition (for example: 'the law of tort arises from a breach of duty. . .'). The second question is one that goes to the *function* of the law of tort and, accordingly, attracts functional definitions (for example: 'the law of tort is about obtaining a remedy for harm caused. . .'). Formalism and functionalism are not, however, absolute or alternative categories; they are schemes of approach or understanding. They are broad templates for viewing an object called 'tort'. Not only may some definitions display both formalist and functionalist tendencies, but formalism and functionalism hide a range of other analytical templates of analysis.

1.2.1 Formalist definitions

Perhaps the leading formalist definition is the one fashioned by Winfield.

Percy Winfield, *The Province of the Law of Tort*, Cambridge University Press, 1932, pp.32, 229, 231

"Tortious liability arises from the breach of a duty primarily fixed by the law: such duty is towards persons generally and its breach is redressible by an action for unliquidated damages. . . .

The words 'primarily fixed by the law' serve to distinguish liability in tort from that arising on breach of contract, and from breach of bailment.

The statement that the duty is 'towards persons generally' marks off tort from contract, bailment, and quasi-contract. . . .

The last requisite in the definition is that tort is remediable by 'an action for unliquidated damages'. This distinguishes it from crime and from breach of trust, though. . . trusts are more conveniently separated from the law of tort by the historical gulf which lies between them and the Common Law rather than by the narrow line of a particular legal remedy. . . .

Of course, an action for damages is not the only remedy for tort. Other remedies are self help, injunctions, and actions for the specific restitution of property. . . ."

NOTE

1. Winfield's definition of tort is now seen by many as either obsolete or circular, yet it remains valuable as an example of a definition based on a structural or systems approach. The category of 'tort' is identified in terms of its relations with other categories of law such as 'contract', 'bailment' and 'crime'. It is part of a 'system' of law. This view of law is in many ways more than just a view; a systems approach is an essential part of legal knowledge itself and has roots going back to Roman law (thus see D.44.7.4 for a Roman definition of liability for wrongs). The Romans structured their law around the three focal points of 'persons', 'things' and 'actions' and each of these three generic categories was in turn divided into sub-categories. Areas of law became part of a grand system— subsequently given expression on the continent by civil codes—and this system provided one means of definition.

2. Winfield's definition is also valuable because it emphasises two other important aspects of legal knowledge, namely 'duty' and 'remedy'. In fact it now seems that he may have been over-optimistic in trying to reduce all of tort law to a matter of duty (*Stubbings v Webb* (1993), at p.508), although more recently there have been more encouraging noises from the judges (see *A v Hoare* (2008)). As we have seen (*Merrett Syndicates*, above p.2) if one replaces 'duty' by 'obligation' one captures the general normative (what one *ought* to do) dimension to civil liability. Tort law is part of the 'law of obligations'.

Peter Cane, *The Anatomy of Tort Law*, Hart Publishing, 1997, 1

"As its name implies, this book is about the structure of tort law. Its starting point is the proposition that the law of tort can be viewed as a system of ethical rules and principles of personal responsibility for conduct. This approach is in contrast to the traditional one of seeing tort law as made up of a number of discrete 'torts', that is, legal formulae which can be used to obtain remedies from courts or as bargaining counters in out-of-court negotia-tions. I see tort law as a collection of causes of action (or 'heads of liability') each made up of three main components: an interest protected by the law, some conduct which the law sanctions, and a remedy or sanction by which the interest is protected and the conduct is sanctioned. The structure of causes of action in tort is 'correlative'; that is, every cause of action in tort is a two-sided affair made up of elements relating to the plaintiff and elements relating to the defendant. . . ."

NOTES

1. Cane is a leading and respected contemporary commentator on tort law and although he is not attempting a formal definition as such, his 'starting point' is valuable in that it emphasises what one might call an 'actionist' and 'causal' approach to tort. It focuses on

11

the individual in society (actor) and analyses damage in terms of a relationship between an individual who suffers damage and an actor who causes it. Of course this causal relation is often not enough in itself to establish liability and thus the harmed individual may well have to establish some ethical reason as to why the actor should be liable. From Roman law times, one central ethical reason is *fault*; an actor is liable if his culpable behaviour causes damage.

2. In fact, in English (and for example German) law, damage, fault and cause are not enough to establish liability in tort (but cf. French law: CC art.1382). Something more is required, as Cane indicates. The damage must also amount to the invasion of a legally protected 'interest'. Accordingly certain types of damage such as pure economic loss or psychological harm, if caused negligently, may not give rise to liability (see, e.g. *Customs and Excise Commissioners v Barclays Bank Plc* (2007), below p.137). This notion of an 'interest' is particularly useful as an analytical tool in tort law, but it is equally a very subversive word in that it appears to be purely *descriptive* (factual). That is to say, unlike 'duty' or 'right', it seemingly carries no *normative* (ought) implication. In practice it often proves to be a more subtle analytical and reasoning tool (see **Chapter 11**).

3. Cane also makes use of a 'structural' scheme of analysis when he relates 'heads of liability' to the claimant and to the defendant. He is attempting to define tort by its internal structure. As one will see, this proves necessary in that there are occasions when even damage, fault, cause and interest prove inadequate to explain certain cases. A further concept, either a 'right' or a 'duty', will need to be brought into the structural scheme of tort elements to explain cases like *Bradford v Pickles* (1895) (p.72) (*damnum sine injuria*: damage without any legal wrong) or those cases where proof of damage is unnecessary (e.g. defamation) (*injuria sine damno*: legal wrong without damage). Thus the great value of the Winfield and the Cane view is that the former provides an *external* structural definition while the latter provides an *internal* structural view. Cane sees tort liability as involving the interplay of a number of elements, notions and concepts. Persons, ethical principles, interests, rights, duties, causes of action and remedies are key elements when it comes to analysing factual problems and the student should try to identify them in every tort case (note for example the interplay of ethics or 'practical justice', interest, damage, duty and remedy in *White v Jones* (1995), below p.289).

1.2.2 Functional definitions

A functional approach defines a system or category of knowledge, not so much in terms of the internal structure of the system or category, but in respect of its *purpose*. Perhaps it is misleading to describe the extracts that follow below as definitional, but they do indicate how tort can be approached and understood as a category of legal knowledge through reference to its purpose. These aims and objectives are probably more important than pure formal definitions, although if one sees tort law in terms of the pursuit of 'justice', the position becomes more complex since justice can attach to the internal and (or) external mechanisms of a category of law.

John G Fleming, *An Introduction to the Law of Torts*, 2nd edn (Oxford: OUP, 1985), p.1 (footnotes omitted)

"The toll on life, limb, and property exacted by today's industrial operations, methods of transport, and many another activity benignly associated with the 'modern way of life' has reached proportions so staggering that the economic cost of accidents represents a constant and mounting drain on the community's human and material resources. The task of the law of torts is to play an important regulatory role in the adjustment of these losses and the eventual allocation of their cost. . . ."

Michael A Jones, *Textbook on Torts*, 8th edn (Oxford: OUP, 2002), p.1

"The law of tort is primarily concerned with providing a remedy to persons who have been harmed by the conduct of others. In any society conflicts of interest are bound to lead to the infliction of losses, a process that, not surprisingly, tends to increase with the level of social interaction. The allocation, and in some instances the prevention, of these losses is the principal function of tort law. . . ."

Tony Weir, Governmental Liability [1989] *Public Law* 40, pp.62–63

"We have had several compendious theories as to the law of tort. Lynx-eyed predecessors who noticed that a tort suit often resulted in a transfer of funds from the defendant to the plaintiff inferred that it was the purpose of tort law to effect such transfers: the more transfers the better, or tort was being false to its purpose. This was especially true if the defendant could spread the loss, very thinly like jam so that no one could taste it. . . .

An appropriate basis for discriminating between plaintiffs would be according to whether they were the victims of misfortune or of mismanagement, of bad luck or of bad behaviour, that is, whether they have just a pain or a grievance as well, whether we can say of them that, the world being what it is, they should not have been hurt . . . The purpose of fault would be to determine not who must pay but who may claim, to distinguish between plaintiffs rather than between defendants. And we would also distinguish according to the nature of the harm in issue, and make the law reflect society's proper value-judgments by letting people recover more easily in respect of personal injury than financial harm, and for property damage only if it also represented financial loss to them . . ."

NOTE

The purpose and policy of the law of torts will be pursued in a separate chapter (**Chapter 2**). Suffice it to stress here, once again, that a too rigid separation between definition and function can be both helpful and misleading. Schemes of analysis can focus on individual things (e.g. acts of individuals) or on holistic elements (activities like driving or manufacturing). If one says that the law of tort is concerned only with acts, it is likely that key elements of liability will be behaviour, duty, right, responsibility and the like. But if tort were to focus on activities—for example driving and industry (see Fleming, above)—it could well be that a rather different set of liability elements will come into play such as risk, costs and loss-spreading. Justice, as we shall see, can attach to act or activity and that is why there can be definitional and functional tension even at the moral level. There is no right answer, just different schemes of analysis and different types of justice.

1.2.3 **Definitional scepticism**

The sceptical approach to defining tort has one great strength: it reflects the historical construction of the subject that, as we have seen, is a matter of different forms of action. These forms of action, before the 19th century, were not categorised under the labels of 'contract' and 'tort'. This classification did not happen until the abolition of the forms of action in 1852 (see *Bryant v Herbert*, above p.3; Garde, extracted in C&MC, pp 510–511). Perhaps the dialectical scheme is the appropriate one here in as much as tort is the result of the development of a general theory of 'contract'; any 'form' (later 'cause') of action for damages that could not be categorised under 'contract' usually had to be put into the open-ended category of 'tort'. If it is not contract it must be tort. And this is why the next writer is able to describe tort as a 'ragbag'.

Tony Weir, *Introduction to Tort Law*, 2nd edn (Oxford: OUP, 2006), p.ix (Preface)

". . . The Dean of an American Law School once asked me over lunch 'And what is your normative theory of tort?' It was rather a poor lunch and, as I thought, a very stupid question. Tort is what is in the tort books, and the only thing holding it together is the binding. In contract matters the courts may be predominantly a debt-collecting agency (it can now be done on the Internet), but, in tort they function as a complaints department—though the claimant, unlike the customer, is not always right. The complaints are of such different kinds that very different reactions may be appropriate, and though there are horses for courses, the tort course sports quite a lot of horses, and they are of very different breeds and speeds. In any case before producing a 'normative theory' or even discussing the purpose of 'tort', it is surely desirable to become familiar with what that ragbag actually contains: otherwise we shall be like adolescents spending all night discussing the meaning of life before, perhaps instead of, experiencing it. . . ."

NOTE

Some writers adopt a more political orientation.

Joanne Conaghan & Wade Mansell, *The Wrongs of Tort*, 2nd edn (London: Pluto Press, 1999), p.3

"Conventional texts such as *Winfield & Jolowicz on Tort* proceed on the basis that tort law consists of a basically uncontentious and apolitical body of principles. This encourages a view of tort law as 'largely common sense' and often corresponds closely with many students' perception of what is just and fair. This tendency to take the common sense of tort for granted impedes the development of a reflective and critical approach to the subject. Tort law appears apolitical because it is experienced as largely uncontentious and because it is uncontentious we do not tend to question its politics. But the politics are there. It is vital to understand that tort, its texts and its syllabuses, are inherently political and this is no less true because the politics are hidden. The foundation of tort law reflects a particular ideological and philosophical perspective (essentially captured by the principle of individual rather than societal responsibility for the misfortune of others) which is, in our view, highly contentious. . . ."

NOTE

Perhaps an example of this kind of 'apolitical' thinking is to be found in the next extract.

Read v J Lyons & Co **[1947] A.C. 156, HL**

(For facts see p.209)

> **Lord Simonds:** ". . . Here is an age-long conflict of theories which is to be found in every system of law. 'A man acts at his peril', says one theory. 'A man is not liable unless he is to blame', answers the other. It will not surprise the students of English law or of anything English to find that between these theories a middle way, a compromise, has been found. . . . There is not one principle only which is to be applied with rigid logic to all cases. To this result both the infinite complexity of human affairs and the historical development of the forms of action contribute. . . . Yet I would venture to say that the law is that, subject to certain specific exceptions which I will indicate, a man is not in the absence of negligence liable in respect of things, whether they are called dangerous or not, which he has brought or collected or manufactured upon his premises, unless such things escape from his premises. . ."

QUESTION

In the Court of Appeal Scott L.J. stated that 'our law of torts is concerned not with activities but with acts' ((1945) at p.228). Is this an ideological statement? Having digested the cases in this and the following chapters, consider how our law of tort might be different if its concern had been with activities rather than acts.

1.3 Liability and remedies

It is easy to think that in any one situation there is just one rule (or set of rules) that will apply to the facts (cf C&MC, pp.87–105). But legal knowledge is more complex because rules attach to particular institutions which, as the Roman lawyers observed, were threefold. Rules could attach to *persons*, to *things* or to *actions* (remedies) and it is this plurality of possibilities that Lord Denning exploits in the next case.

Miller v Jackson **[1977] Q.B. 966, CA**

This was an appeal by a cricket club against the granting of an injunction by a High Court judge ordering the club not to play cricket on a piece of land adjacent to the claimants' house. The claimants had sought the injunction because at weekends, when cricket was played, cricket balls sometimes landed in their garden; the fear of injury from the balls resulted in the claimants being unable to use their garden on days when there were matches. A majority of the Court of Appeal (Lord Denning M.R. and Cumming-Bruce L.J.; Geoffrey Lane L.J. dissenting) allowed the appeal.

> **Lord Denning M.R.:** ". . . The case here was not pleaded by either side in the formulae of the 19th century. The plaintiffs did not allege trespass . . . The case was pleaded in negligence or alternatively nuisance . . .

The tort of nuisance in many cases overlaps the tort of negligence . . . But there is at any rate one important distinction between them. It lies in the nature of the remedy sought. Is it damages? Or an injunction? If the plaintiff seeks a remedy in damages for injury done to him or his property, he can lay his claim either in *negligence* or in *nuisance*. But, if he seeks an injunction to stop the playing of cricket altogether, I think he must make his claim in nuisance. The books are full of cases where an injunction has been granted to restrain the continuance of a nuisance. But there is no case, so far as I know, where it has been granted so as to stop a man being negligent. At any rate in a case of this kind, where an occupier of a house or land seeks to restrain his neighbour from doing something on his own land, the only appropriate cause of action, on which to base the remedy of an injunction, is nuisance . . . He must have been guilty of the fault, not necessarily of negligence, but of the unreasonable use of land. . .

I would, therefore, adopt this test: is the use by the cricket club of this ground for playing cricket a reasonable use of it? To my mind it is a most reasonable use. . .

On taking the balance, I would give priority to the right of the cricket club to continue playing cricket on the ground, as they have done for the last 70 years. It takes precedence over the right of the newcomer to sit in his garden undisturbed. After all he bought the house four years ago in mid-summer when the cricket season was at its height. He might have guessed that there was a risk that a hit for six might possibly land on his property. If he finds that he does not like it, he ought, when cricket is played, to sit in the other side of the house or in the front garden, or go out; or take advantage of the offers the club have made to him of fitting unbreakable glass, and so forth. Or, if he does not like that, he ought to sell his house and move elsewhere. I expect there are many who would gladly buy it in order to be near the cricket field and open space. At any rate he ought not to be allowed to stop cricket being played on this ground.

This case is new. It should be approached on principles applicable to modern conditions. There is a contest here between the interest of the public at large and the interest of a private individual. The *public* interest lies in protecting the environment by preserving our playing fields in the face of mounting development, and by enabling our youth to enjoy all the benefits of outdoor games, such as cricket and football. The *private* interest lies in securing the privacy of his home and garden without intrusion or interference by anyone. In deciding between these two conflicting interests, it must be remembered that it is not a question of damages. If by a million-to-one chance a cricket ball does go out of the ground and cause damage, the cricket club will pay. There is no difficulty on that score. No, it is a question of an injunction. And in our law you will find it repeatedly affirmed that an injunction is a discretionary remedy. In a new situation like this, we have to think afresh as to how discretion should be exercised . . . As between their conflicting interests, I am of opinion that the public interest should prevail over the private interest . . . In my opinion the right exercise of discretion is to refuse an injunction; and, of course, to refuse damages in lieu of an injunction. Likewise as to the claim for past damages. The club were entitled to use this ground for cricket in the accustomed way. It was not a nuisance, nor was it negligence . . . So if the club had put it to the test, I would have dismissed the claim for damages also. But as the club very fairly say that they are willing to pay for any damage, I am content that there should be an award of £400 to cover any past or future damage. . . ."

NOTE

The tort of nuisance, as we shall see (**Chapter 6**), attaches to a thing (land) and this land rule favoured the claimants (although Lord Denning, unlike the other two judges, thought that it did not). However the two majority judges out-flanked this rule by putting the accent on the rule that attached to the *remedy*, namely the injunction (cf. **Chapter 11**). This discretion rule allowed Lord Denning to bring into the analysis the notion of a 'public interest' which he can play off against the 'private interest'. This is a classic piece of legal reasoning, even if, in the end, it is wrong (since the tort of private nuisance by definition tends to put the private interest before the public: *Kennaway v Thompson* (1981)). In addition it shows how important the remedy can be in the establishment of liability (cf. **Chapter 11**). In any contract and tort case the reader should always ask: what remedy is the plaintiff seeking?

QUESTION

If one of the claimants had been hit on the head by a cricket ball could he or she have sued the club for damages? (Read Lord Denning's judgment in full in the law reports.)

1.4 Province and scope of tort

A structural or systems approach to tort sees this category as being defined by its relationship with other legal categories. Winfield talked in terms of the province of the law of tort: "no clear-cut exclusive definition of tort is possible until the complementary task of settling the limits of other fields of the law has been accomplished" (*The Province of the Law of Tort*, (Cambridge: CUP, 1931), at p.6). These relations are particularly difficult in the common law tradition because no category of law is either clearly defined as a matter of internal theory or properly systematised one with another as a matter of legal (that is say Romanist) legal science. In fact, in no European legal system, can tort or its equivalent be considered these days in isolation of contract, crime, property and public law. There is another reason for examining tort in relation to contract, crime, property and public law. These areas now impact on the law of tort—or one should say impact upon sets of facts categorised as primarily falling within tort—in such a way that they cannot be ignored as a matter of tort law itself.

1.4.1 Tort and contract

Given the central role of the remedy of damages in tort law, one ought perhaps to start with the subject's relationship with the other great area where damages are important, the law of contract (although perhaps one should bear in mind that statistically most actions in contract are in debt). Indeed tort liability was once defined in terms of its not being contractual (*Bryant v Herbert* (1877), p.3).

Henderson v Merrett Syndicates Ltd **[1995] 2 A.C. 145, HL**

This was an action for damages brought by underwriting members at Lloyd's (known as 'names') against underwriting agents. The former claimed that the latter had been negligent in the handling of their affairs. Some of the names had specific contractual relationships with the defendants while others did not; and the question arose, on a preliminary issue, as to whether a duty of care was owed in tort by all the defendants, even where there was a specific contractual regime in place. The question was important because of the more liberal limitation period in tort. The lower courts held that concurrent contract and tort duties were owed and an appeal to the House of Lords (Lords Keith, Goff, Browne-Wilkinson, Mustill and Nolan) was dismissed.

Lord Goff: ". . . All systems of law which recognise a law of contract and a law of tort (or delict) have to solve the problem of the possibility of concurrent claims arising from breach of duty under the two rubrics of the law. Although there are variants, broadly speaking two possible solutions present themselves: either to insist that the claimant should pursue his remedy in contract alone, or to allow him to choose which remedy he prefers. . . . France has adopted the former solution in its doctrine of non cumul, under which the concurrence of claims in contract and tort is outlawed (see Tony Weir in XI Int.Encycl.Comp.L., ch. 12, paras. 47–72, at paragraph 52). The reasons given for this conclusion are (1) respect for the will of the legislator, and (2) respect for the will of the parties to the contract (see paragraph 53). The former does not concern us; but the latter is of vital importance. It is however open to various interpretations. For such a policy does not necessarily require the total rejection of concurrence, but only so far as a concurrent remedy in tort is inconsistent with the terms of the contract. It comes therefore as no surprise to learn that the French doctrine is not followed in all civil law jurisdictions, and that concurrent remedies in tort and contract are permitted in other civil law countries, notably Germany (see paragraph 58). I only pause to observe that it appears to be accepted that no perceptible harm has come to the German system from admitting concurrent claims. . . .

I think it is desirable to stress at this stage that the question of concurrent liability is by no means only of academic significance. Practical issues, which can be of great importance to the parties, are at stake. Foremost among these is perhaps the question of limitation of actions. If concurrent liability in tort is not recognised, a claimant may find his claim barred at a time when he is unaware of its existence. This must moreover be a real possibility in the case of claims against professional men, such as solicitors or architects, since the consequences of their negligence may well not come to light until long after the lapse of six years from the date when the relevant breach of contract occurred. Moreover the benefits of the Latent Damage Act 1986, under which the time of the accrual of the cause of action may be postponed until after the plaintiff has the relevant knowledge, are limited to actions in tortious negligence. This leads to the startling possibility that a client who has had the benefit of gratuitous advice from his solicitor may in this respect be better off than a client who has paid a fee. Other practical problems arise, for example, from the absence of a right to contribution between negligent contract-breakers; from the rules as to remoteness of damage, which are less restricted in tort than they are in contract; and from the availability of the opportunity to obtain leave to serve proceedings out of the jurisdiction. It can of course be argued that the principle established in respect of concurrent liability in contract and tort should not be tailored to mitigate the adventitious effects of rules of law such as these, and that one way of solving such problems would no doubt be to rephrase such incidental rules as have to remain in terms of the nature of the harm suffered rather than the nature of the liability asserted (see Tony Weir, XI Int Encycl Comp L ch.12, para 72). But this is perhaps crying for the moon; and with the law in its present form, practical considerations of this kind cannot sensibly be ignored.

Moreover I myself perceive at work in these decisions not only the influence of the dead hand of history, but also what I have elsewhere called the temptation of elegance. Mr Tony Weir (XI Int Encycl Comp L ch.12, para 55) has extolled the French solution for its elegance; and we can discern the same impulse behind the much-quoted observation of Lord Scarman when delivering the judgment of the Judicial Committee of the Privy Council in *Tai Hing Cotton Mill Ltd v Liu Chong Hing Bank Ltd* [1986] AC 80, 107. . .

It is however my understanding that by the law in this country contracts for services do contain an implied promise to exercise reasonable care (and skill) in the performance of the relevant services; indeed, as Mr Tony Weir has pointed out (XI Int Encycl Comp L. ch. 12, para 67), in the 19th century the field of concurrent liabilities was expanded 'since it was impossible for the judges to deny that contracts contained an implied promise to take reasonable care, at the least, not to injure the other party.' My own belief is that, in the present context, the common law is not antipathetic to concurrent liability, and that there is no sound basis for a rule which automatically restricts the claimant to either a tortious or a contractual remedy. The result may be untidy; but, given that the tortious duty is imposed by the general law, and the contractual duty is attributable to the will of the parties, I do not find it objectionable that the claimant may be entitled to take advantage of the remedy which is most advantageous to him, subject only to ascertaining whether the tortious duty is so inconsistent with the applicable contract that, in accordance with ordinary principle, the parties must be taken to have agreed that the tortious remedy is to be limited or excluded. . . .''

NOTES

1. *Definition*. Several points emerge from the relationship. Tort and contract have been distinguished not only in the common law but equally by statute, in particular the old County Court Acts; this legislation forced the courts to state whether an action was 'founded on contract' or 'founded upon tort' (*Taylor v MS & LR Co* (1895), at p.138). When forced to choose between the two, contract was said to be based on a breach of promise (*assumpsit*) whereas tort became based on a 'wrong' (see e.g. *Danby v Lamb* (1861))

2. *Absence of a rule of non-cumul*. The frontier between the two never became rigid. In the 19th century the courts and Bar accepted that parties could often choose between the two forms of liability on many sets of facts (see *Alton v Midland Ry* (1865)). And today an action for damages arising out of a single set of facts can still be based either on a breach of contract or on say the tort of negligence (*Henderson v Merrett*). It may well be however that the courts will not allow tort to be used to undermine well established contractual structures in certain types of commercial situations (*Marc Rich & Co v Bishop Rock Marine Co Ltd* (1996), below p.324).

3. *Adjunct to contract*. In other situations the courts may use tort to fill certain gaps in the law of contract. Thus the absence of consideration in support of a statement that causes

19

damage will not necessarily mean that an action for damages will fail; if the relationship between the parties is close then the statement might give rise to tortious liability (*Hedley Byrne v Heller* (1964), below p.134; and see e.g. *Lennon v Comr of Police for the Metropolis* (2004)). Another area where tort has aided contract was (statute has now intervened) where the rule of privity of contract prevented a third party from suing (*White v Jones* (1995), below p.289).

4. *Strict liability and negligence*. One area where the frontier between contract and tort can be important is where a single set of facts discloses both a liability based on negligence and a stricter liability based on breach of an implied term to warrant a result (similar to the *obligation de moyens* and *obligation de résultat* dichotomy in French law; and see UNIDROIT art.5.4). In the case of a contract for services, negligence can indifferently give rise to liability in contract (Supply of Goods and Services Act 1982 s.13) and in the tort of negligence; but in contracts to supply goods there may be a stricter form of liability (e.g. under Sale of Goods Act 1979 s.14) and this will bring into play different rules as to remoteness of damage and contributory negligence (see **Chapter 10**).

5. *Complex liabilities*. Contract and tort can intertwine in situations where there are multiple grounds of claim, not just in respect of one party (concurrence), but where two or more parties may have claims against a single other party or vice-versa (see **11.5**). This produces inherent complexity (Weir, *Complex Liabilities*, IECL, Vol XI, Chap 12, § 73). The growth of liability insurance (contract) and subrogation (restitution) have been a major factor in this development of complex liabilities since it is usually insurance companies, subrogated to the rights of parties, that are behind the recourse actions; these (contractual) actions in turn can, on occasions, undermine the loss-spreading aim of the law of tort (see e.g. *Lister v Romford Ice & Cold Storage Co* (1957), below p.63).

6. *Damage*. The distinction between a cause of action in tort and one in contract can be important with respect to some types of damage. In the tort of negligence both pure economic loss and psychological injury are interests that are not so well protected as personal injury and physical damage. Indeed, with respect to mental distress, anxiety and depression it is generally true to say that these interests are not protected in a tort of negligence claim. However they may be protected if the claim can be framed in contract, as the next extract indicates:

Rothwell v Chemical & Insulating Co Ltd **[2007] 3 W.L.R. 876, HL**

(See also p.92)

Lord Hope: ". . . 59 I share the regret expressed by Smith LJ that the claimants, who are at risk of developing a harmful disease and have entirely genuine feelings of anxiety as to what they may face in the future, should be denied a remedy. But they have not yet sustained an injury for which the law can give them a remedy in damages. The question whether employees might have a remedy against their employers in contract has not been explored in the present context, as my noble and learned friend, Lord Scott of Foscote, points out. There may be room for development of the common law in this area. In that connection it is worth noting a recent assessment of the potential for the development of contractual remedies for employees against their employers by Matthew Boyle, 'Contractual Remedies of Employees at Common Law: Exploring the Boundaries' [2007] JR 145. But, for the reasons Lord Scott gives, it would not be appropriate to attempt such a difficult and uncertain exercise in these cases. . . ."

NOTE

See C&MC, pp.542–549.

1.4.2 Tort and crime

The relationship between tort and crime is also difficult because the two were not easily distinguished in early Roman and common law. The distinction today is, from a practical point of view, based on entirely separate procedures: the criminal process involves one set of courts, the civil process another. However there are various points at which the two areas meet and interrelate.

Arthur J.S Hall & Co v Simons **[2002] 1 A.C. 615, HL**

A series of claims (and counter-claims) for damages were brought by clients against firms of solicitors for negligence. The judge at first instance decided that in all of the actions the solicitors enjoyed advocate's immunity and struck out the claims. The Court of Appeal restored the claims and an appeal to the House of Lords (Lords Steyn, Browne-Wilkinson, Hoffmann, Hope, Hutton, Hobhouse and Millett) was dismissed. All of the Law Lords agreed that the public interest no longer required that advocates should have immunity from negligence claims and a majority (Lords Hope and Hobhouse dissenting) concluded that immunity was not required where the disputed proceeding were criminal.

> **Lord Hobhouse** (dissenting in part): ". . . All of your Lordships are in favour of dismissing the appeals; the solicitors are not entitled to the immunity which they claim in the present cases. Your Lordships agree that on any view the immunity claimed in these cases falls outside the recognised immunity afforded to advocates. The Court of Appeal arrived at the right conclusion. Further, all your Lordships would be prepared to arrive at the same conclusion on the basis that there is no longer an adequate justification for continuing to recognise a general immunity for advocates engaged in civil litigation.
>
> But that is the limit of the unanimity. Some of your Lordships would be prepared to declare that the immunity should also no longer be recognised for advocates engaged in criminal litigation. Other of your Lordships, among whom I number myself, would not be prepared to take that step on the present appeals. . . .
>
> *The civil process*
>
> . . . The character of civil litigation is that it involves the assertion by one party that the other has infringed his rights; he seeks a remedy, normally a monetary remedy but sometimes a remedy of declaration of right or specific implement. The court, therefore, has essentially to make a decision between two conflicting parties and determining their respective rights inter se. It is primarily the provision by the state of a service similar to the

provision of arbitration services. The public interest does not normally come into it save in so far as the provision of a system of civil dispute resolution and the enforcement of civil rights is a necessary part of a society governed by the rule of law not by superior force.

It is a system of relative justice. It exists in economic terms. The plaintiff complains that he has suffered loss and damage; he claims that the defendant should be required to pay monetary damages to compensate him; the remedy is a redistribution of wealth between the parties. Or he may assert a property right and ask that the court should assist him enforce it against the defendant. . . .

The Criminal Process

Even though the criminal process is formally adversarial, it is of a fundamentally different character to the civil process. Its purpose and function are different. It is to enforce the criminal law. The criminal law and the criminal justice system exists in the interests of society as a whole. It has a directly social function. It is concerned to see that the guilty are convicted and punished and those not proved to be guilty are acquitted. Anyone not proved to be guilty is to be presumed to be not guilty. It is of fundamental importance that the process by which the defendant is proved guilty shall have been fair and it is the public duty of all those concerned in the criminal justice system to see that this is the case. This is the public interest in the system.

The criminal trial does not exist to protect private interests. It exists as part of the enforcement of the criminal law in the public interest. Those who take part in the trial do so as a public duty whether in exchange for remuneration or the payment of expenses. The purpose of all is, or should be, to see justice done and to play their appropriate part in achieving that end. . . .

It follows from these fundamentals that the salient features of this procedure exist to serve the public interest, not to serve any private interest. . . .

The legitimate interest of the citizen charged with a criminal offence is that he should have a fair trial and only be convicted if his guilt has been proved. It is not an economic interest. His interest like his potential liability under the criminal law stems from his membership of the society to which he belongs - his citizenship. If the charge against him has not been proved, he should be acquitted. If he has been wrongly convicted, his appeal against conviction should be allowed. If he has been wrongly or excessively sentenced, his punishment should be remitted or reduced. His only remedy lies within the criminal justice system. This is appropriate. The civil courts do not have any part to play in such matters. The relevance of what the advocate does during the criminal trial is to the issues at that trial, not the remoter economic consequences of the outcome of that trial. . . .''

NOTES

1. *Introduction*. Although Lord Hobhouse's judgment is a dissenting one (at least on the criminal proceedings point), it is extracted here because it is instructive in the way it exhaustively distinguishes between civil and criminal proceedings. See also Lord Scott in *Ashley v Chief Constable of Sussex Police* (2008), paras 16–20 (read in law report and see below p.466).

2. *Action civile*. There is no equivalent to the French *action civile* in English law whereby a victim can use the criminal proceedings to pursue a civil remedy (see *Black v Yates*

(1992)). The victim of, say, a theft can sue in conversion and/or trespass to goods while the victim of an attack will sue in trespass to the person (assault); the victim of fraud can sue in deceit. But this civil process has to be pursued quite separately from the criminal proceedings (although there is statutory power to make compensation orders in criminal proceedings; and see Proceeds of Crime Act 2002).

3. *Public nuisance*. At the level of substance the relationship between tort and crime can be more complex because certain crimes can also be torts if they cause damage to an individual. One important tort here is public nuisance which is not just a crime but also a tort if any individual suffers special damage (*Campbell v Paddington Corporation* (1911)).

4. *Breach of statutory duty*. Another crime which can, in certain circumstances, amount to a tort is where a person causes damage in breach of a statutory provision. Not all breaches will give rise to torts and this is why this area is complex; but the general principles have been set out by Lord Browne-Wilkinson in the *X (Minors)* case (see below p.178).

5. *Trespass*. Facts which give rise to the tort of trespass to the person will often equally give rise to the crime of assault (or causing bodily harm) (see *Ashley v Chief Constable of Sussex Police* (2008)). However unlike public nuisance and breach of statutory duty it is not the crime itself which gives rise to the tort; the facts which constitute the crime also constitute the tort and thus may be the subject of two quite different processes (see e.g. *A v Hoare* (2008), at para.26; and see generally *Ashley v Chief Constable of Sussex Police* (2008)). One might note that the standard of proof is not so high in the civil courts and thus failure to establish the crime of assault in the criminal court will not necessarily mean that a claim in the civil court for damages for trespass will fail (*Ashley v Chief Constable of Sussex Police* (2008)). (Authoritarian Home Secretaries dream of introducing the civil standard of proof into the criminal process, which, were it ever to be successful, would no doubt fill the prisons with ever more, possibly innocent, people.)

6. *Evidence*. However if a defendant is successfully convicted of a crime whose facts also constitute a tort (for example driving without due care and attention, assault, theft), the conviction can be used as evidence in the civil proceedings (Civil Evidence Act 1968 s.11).

7. *Defence of illegality*. The criminal law can also be of importance when it comes to defences in tort: if the claimant was involved in a criminal act when he suffered tortious damage he may be prevented from suing by the defence of illegality (see e.g. *Pitts v Hunt* (1991), p.370). This rule ex turpi causa non oritur actio was originally a rule that applied only to contractual liability, but it has been adopted in more recent years by the law of tort.

8. *Injunctions*. One might note that the remedy of an injunction can play a role in respect of certain kinds of behaviour that are not in themselves tortious but which may be unlawful according to the criminal law. Even if the unlawful behaviour does not give rise to the tort of breach of statutory duty, the court may nevertheless issue an injunction (*Burris v Azadani* (1995), p.421); once issued the case could become a precedent establishing a new tort. Sometimes statute might intervene to confirm both the crime and the tort (see Protection from Harassment Act 1997).

9. *Anti-social behaviour*. These injunctions for anti-social behaviour are now supplemented by public law remedies which are quasi-criminal in nature. That is to say they are

23

remedies that are civil in form but essentially criminal in substance (*R (McCann) v Crown Court at Manchester* (2001)). Thus the victim of a nuisance can ask a local authority to act against either the things (Noise Act 1996 s.10(2)) or the persons causing the nuisance (Crime and Disorder Act 1998 s.1).

10. *Criminal injuries compensation.* A person who suffers personal injury as a result of a crime can of course sue the criminal in tort for damages. But the victim can also claim compensation from the state under a government scheme (Criminal Injuries Compensation Act 1995 and regulations made under it). Such a scheme was once as generous as damages in tort, but this is no longer true. The scheme does not cover property damage and thus if a victim (or his insurance company) want compensation they will have to use the law of tort (see e.g. *Home Office v Dorset Yacht Co* (1970), below p.254).

EXERCISE

Compare and contrast in *Arthur Hall* the different types of interest employed in the analysis: (i) public interest; (ii) private interest; (iii) legitimate interest; (iv) interests of society; (v) economic interests.

1.4.3 **Tort and property**

Tort also provides causes of action and remedies for the protection of property and thus the borderline between tort and property is another area of difficulty. These difficulties, it must be stressed again, are not just academic; they can create structural problems which then emerge in the reasoning of judges and in questions of the existence, the non-existence and (or) the level of any duty. The problem is often one between 'owning' and 'owing' or between obligation and right: does an owner of an expensive car who carelessly leaves his keys in the vehicle while purchasing some fancy fresh pasta owe a duty of care to any subsequent good faith acquirer who might obtain it after it has been stolen by an opportunist thief? Here the tort of negligence finds itself confronting the rights of ownership (*Moorgate Mercantile Ltd v Twitchings* (1977)). Or take the local authority that gratuitously agrees to look after the claimant's property which is subsequently stolen by an employee of the authority. If one applies rules of tort it might well be arguable that an employer should not be liable for an act which does not form part of the employee's duties; the law of property might take a different view (*Mitchell v Ealing LBC* (1979)). As Diplock L.J. explains in the next case, bailment creates its own duties that are independent of the law of tort. Where tort is relevant is in respect of the remedies used by a bailor against a bailee (the tort of detinue up until 1977 and now the tort of conversion).

Morris v CW Martin & Sons Ltd **[1966] 1 Q.B. 716, HL**

The owner of a mink stole brought an action against a firm of cleaners for its value. She had sent it to Beder, a furrier, for cleaning and Beder, with the owner's consent, sent it to the defendants for the actual cleaning. The defendants' employee who was supposed to clean it stole it instead. The trial judge held the defendants not liable, but an appeal to the Court of Appeal (Lord Denning M.R., Diplock L.J. and Salmon L.J.) was allowed.

Diplock L.J.: ". . . Duties at common law are owed by one person to another only if there exists a relationship between them which the common law recognises as giving rise to such duty. One of such recognised relationships is created by the voluntary taking into custody of goods which are the property of another. By voluntarily accepting from Beder the custody of a fur which they knew to be the property of a customer of his, they brought into existence between the plaintiff and themselves the relationship of bailor and bailee by sub-bailment. The legal relationship of bailor and bailee of a chattel can exist independently of any contract, for the legal concept of bailment as creating a relationship which gives rise to duties owed by a bailee to a bailor is derived from Roman law and is older in our common law than the legal concept of parol contract as giving rise to legal duties owed by one party to the other party thereto. The nature of those legal duties, in particular as to the degree of care which the bailee is bound to exercise in the custody of the goods and as to his duty to redeliver them, varies according to the circumstances in which and purposes for which the goods are delivered to the bailee. But we are concerned here with conversion. This is a breach of a particular duty common to all classes of bailment. While most cases of bailment today are accompanied by a contractual relationship between bailee and bailor which may modify or extend the common law duties of the parties that would otherwise arise from the mere fact of bailment, this is not necessarily so—as witness gratuitous bailment or bailment by finding . . .

One of the common law duties owed by a bailee of goods to his bailor is not to convert them, ie not to do intentionally in relation to the goods an act inconsistent with the bailor's right of property therein. (See *Caxton Publishing Co Ltd v Sutherland Publishing Co*, per Lord Porter.) This duty, which is common to all bailments as well as to other relationships which do not amount to bailment, is independent of and additional to the other common law duty of a bailee for reward to take reasonable care of his bailor's goods. Stealing goods is the simplest example of conversion; but, perhaps because in his classic judgment in *Coggs v Bernard* Sir John Holt CJ discusses the circumstances in which bailees are liable to their bailors for the loss of goods stolen not by the servant of the bailee but by a stranger, some confusion has, I think, arisen in later cases through failure to recognise the co-existence of the two duties of a bailee for reward; to take reasonable care of his bailor's goods and not to convert them—even by stealing.

If the bailee in the present case had been a natural person and had converted the plaintiff's fur by stealing it himself, no one would have argued that he was not liable to her for its loss. But the defendant bailees are a corporate person. They could not perform their duties to the plaintiffs to take reasonable care of the fur and not to convert it otherwise than vicariously by natural persons acting as their servants or agents. It was one of their servants to whom they had entrusted the care and custody of the fur for the purpose of doing work upon it who converted it by stealing it. Why should they not be vicariously liable for this breach of their duty by the vicar whom they had chosen to perform it? Sir John Holt, I think, would have answered that they were liable 'for seeing that someone must be the loser by this deceit it is more reason that he who employs and puts a trust and confidence in the deceiver should be the loser than a stranger': *Hern v Nichols*. . ."

NOTE

The use and enjoyment of land equally raises questions about the relationship between the exercise of property rights and any damage this exercise might cause to others. A person who *unreasonably* uses his land will normally be liable for any harm that this unreasonable use causes to his neighbour's use and enjoyment of property (*Hollywood Silver Fox Farm v Emmett* (1936), below p.93); but the *unreasonable* exercise of an actual property *right* could well result in no liability, English law having no general principle of an abuse of a right (*Bradford Corporation v Pickles* (1895), below p.72).

1.4.4 Tort and restitution

Another frontier that can cause problems, again because of the traditional law of remedies approach, is the one between tort and unjust enrichment. Until relatively recently the only two categories of liability were contract and tort, but the House of Lords has now recognised the law of restitution as a separate category (*Kleinwort Benson Ltd v Glasgow CC* (1999)). Restitution differs from tort in that its focal point is the defendant's *enrichment* rather than the claimant's *harm* and consequently liability in restitution is not measured by the claimant's loss. Where there is overlap between tort and restitution is in the area of profits arising out of wrongs and this can give rise to a conflict of purpose. Should the court be focusing on the claimant's loss or the defendant's profit? Sometimes this can have very real practical effects, as the next case illustrates.

Inverugie Investments Ltd v Hackett **[1995] 1 W.L.R. 713, PC**

Lord Lloyd: "This is in form an ordinary claim for mesne profits, that is to say a claim for damages for trespass to land. But the facts are unusual, since the land consists of 30 specified apartments in a much larger hotel. The hotel is owned by the defendants, Inverugie Investments Ltd. The plaintiff, the late Mr Richard Hackett, was the lessee of the apartments under a lease dated 5 June 1970 for a term of 99 years. On 25 November 1974 the plaintiff was ejected by the defendants. On 6 March 1975 he brought proceedings for possession. Those proceedings culminated on 19 December 1984 when the Board dismissed the defendants' appeal against a decision of the Court of Appeal of the Commonwealth of the Bahamas in favour of the plaintiff. Despite a further order granted by Malone J on 23 June 1986 requiring the defendants to give up possession forthwith, they did not do so until 12 April 1990. The trespass thus lasted for a continuous period of 15 years. The question for decision is the appropriate measure of damages. . . . .

Before stating their own conclusions on the facts, their Lordships should say a brief word on the law. The cases to which they have already referred establish, beyond any doubt, that a person who lets out goods on hire, or the landlord of residential property, can recover damages from a trespasser who has wrongfully used his property whether or not he can show that he would have let the property to anybody else, and whether or not he would have used the property himself. . . .

It is sometimes said that these cases are an exception to the rule that damages in tort are compensatory. But this is not necessarily so. It depends how widely one defines the 'loss' which the plaintiff has suffered. As the Earl of Halsbury LC pointed out in *Mediana (Owners of Steamship) v Comet (Owners of Lightship)* [1900] AC 113, 117, it is no answer for a wrongdoer who has deprived the plaintiff of his chair to point out that he does not usually sit in it or that he has plenty of other chairs in the room.

In *Stoke-on-Trent City Council v WJ Wass Ltd* [1988] 1 WLR 1406 Nicholls LJ called the underlying principle in these cases the 'user principle.' The plaintiff may not have suffered any actual loss by being deprived of the use of his property. But under the user principle he is entitled to recover a reasonable rent for the wrongful use of his property by the trespasser. Similarly, the trespasser may not have derived any actual benefit from the use of the property. But under the user principle he is obliged to pay a reasonable rent for the use which he has enjoyed. The principle need not be characterised as exclusively compensatory, or exclusively restitutionary; it combines elements of both.

If this is the correct principle, how does it apply to the facts of the present case?. . .

The point is not altogether easy. But their Lordships have concluded that Mr Mowbray's argument is to be preferred. If a man hires a concrete mixer, he must pay the daily hire, even though he may not in the event have been able to use the mixer because of rain. So also must a trespasser who takes the mixer without the owner's consent. He must pay the going rate, even though in the event he has derived no benefit from the use of the mixer. It makes no difference whether the trespasser is a professional builder or a do-it-yourself enthusiast.

The same applies to residential property. In the present case the defendants have had the use of all 30 apartments for 15 years. Applying the user principle, they must pay the going rate, even though they have been unable to derive actual benefit from all the apartments for all the time. The fact that the defendants are hotel operators does not take the case out of the ordinary rule. The plaintiff is not asking for an account of profits. The chance of making a profit from the use of the apartments is not the correct test for arriving at a reasonable rent.

It follows that their Lordships cannot agree with the judgment of the majority in the court below. . . ."

NOTE

Perhaps one difference between tort and restitution is to be found in the distinction between obligations and property as the next extract suggests. However the nature of the remedy is another focal point of distinction.

Attorney-General v Blake [2001] 1 A.C. 268, HL

Lord Hobhouse (dissenting): ". . . The concepts of restitution and compensation are not the same though they will on occasions fulfil the same need. Restitution is analogous to property: it concerns wealth or advantage which ought to be returned or transferred by the defendant to the plaintiff. It is a form of specific implement. Its clearest form is an order for the return or transfer of property which belongs in law or in equity to the plaintiff. Property includes an interest in property. Then there are rights recognised in equity such as those which arise from a fiduciary relationship. These rights give rise to restitutionary remedies including the remedy of account which, depending on the circumstances, could also derive from a common law relationship such as agency. Then, again, there are the rights now grouped under the heading of the law of restitution or unjust enrichment. These are still truly restitutionary concepts leading to restitutionary remedies. Typically they require the payment of money by the person unjustly enriched to the person at whose expense that enrichment has taken place. In so far as the appropriate remedy is the payment of money or the delivery up of a chattel or goods is concerned the common law could provide it; insofar as it required some other remedy or the recognition of an equitable right, the chancery jurisdiction had to be invoked.

The essential of such rights and their enforcement was the procuring by the courts of the *performance* by the defendant of his obligations. The plaintiff recovers what he is actually entitled to not some monetary substitute for it. If what the plaintiff is entitled to is wealth expressed in monetary terms, the order will be for the payment of money but this does not alter the character of the remedy or of the right being recognised. He gets the money because it was his property or he was in some other way entitled to it. It is still the enforced performance of an obligation. The same is the case where an injunction is granted or a decree of specific performance or the ordering of an account."

QUESTION

"If a wrongdoer has made use of goods for his own purpose, then he must pay a reasonable hire for them, even though the owner has in fact suffered no loss . . . The claim for a hiring charge is . . . not based on the loss to the plaintiff, but on the fact that the defendant has used the goods for his own purposes. It is an action against him because he has had the benefit of the goods. It resembles, therefore, an action for restitution, rather than an action of tort" (Denning L.J. in *Strand Electric & Engineering Ltd v Brisford Entertainments Ltd* (1952), at pp.254–255). Given that damages are designed to compensate for loss, would it not be better to see an action for a hiring charge, or sometimes an action for damages in trespass, as a claim in debt? Would the equitable remedy of account of profits (mentioned by Lord Lloyd in *Inverugie*) be a more suitable remedy? (cf. *Att-Gen v Blake* (2001).)

1.4.5 Tort and constitutional law

We have already seen that tort (especially trespass and conversion) plays an important role in protecting property rights and as a result tort and property law overlap. The same is true for constitutional law since trespass (and other torts) can be used against the police or any other local or central government agency that assaults or imprisons a person, or deliberately damages property, without legal justification (see **Chapter 9**). Thus where a house owner saw his home, built without planning permission, knocked down without notice by the local Board of Works, the owner succeeded in trespass against the Board (*Cooper v Wandsworth Board of Works* (1863)).

R v Governor of Brockhill Prison, Ex p. Evans (No 2) [2001] 2 A.C. 19, HL

(See also p.96)

Lord Steyn: "My Lords, the applicant was kept in prison for 59 days longer than she should have been. The Governor was blameless. He relied on a Home Office explanation of the legal position of prisoners in the position of the applicant. The Home Office was also blameless. The Home Office view of the position was founded on a clear line of Divisional court decisions, starting with *Reg v Governor of Blundeston Prison, Ex parte Gaffney* [1982]

W.L.R. 696. But the courts had erred. On the applicant's application for judicial review the Divisional court overruled the earlier decisions: *Reg v Brockhill Prison, Ex parte Evans* [1997] QB 443. It was held that the applicant was unlawfully detained. The governor immediately released the applicant. The applicant pursued claim for false imprisonment against the Governor. Collins J dismissed the claim but in the event that he was wrong, assessed damages at £2,000. By a majority the Court of Appeal allowed the appeal of the applicant, and increased the assessment to £5,000: [1999] QB 1043. The majority (Lord Woolf, MR and Judge LJ) took the view that a defendant may be liable for false imprisonment of a plaintiff in circumstances where the defendant acts in good faith on a view of the law which appears to be settled by precedent but which subsequently turns out to have been wrong. . . .

On balance I think the arguments of the applicant outweigh those of the Solicitor-General. In *Eshugbayi Eleko v Officer Administering the Government of Nigeria* [1931] AC 662, a habeas corpus case, Lord Atkin observed, at p. 670, that 'no member of the executive can interfere with the liberty or property of a British subject except on the condition that he can support the legality of his action before a court of justice.' Recently, with the approval of other members of the House, I cited Lord Atkin's observation in the *Eleko* case: *Boddington v British Transport Police* [1999] 2 AC 143, 173F. It represents the traditional common law view. It points to a decision in the present case that the respondent is entitled to recover compensation of the ground of false imprisonment where the executive can no longer support the lawfulness of the detention. . . ."

[Lords Slynn, Browne-Wilkinson, Hope and Hobhouse agreed that the defendant was liable for false imprisonment.]

NOTE

The Human Rights Act 1998, which 'incorporated' the European Convention for the Protection of Human Rights and Fundamental Freedoms, creates a direct legislative connection between tort and constitutional law. However the Act does not necessarily import directly into English law Convention rights.

Wainwright v Home Office **[2004] 2 A.C. 406, HL**

This was an action for damages by a mother and her son against the Home Office in respect of a prison visit during which they were both strip-searched. The searches were not conducted according to prison rules, and were thus not covered by statutory authority, and both claimants alleged that they had been humiliated and stressed. In addition the son, who had physical and learning difficulties, claimed damages for post-traumatic stress disorder. The damages claims were based upon trespass to the person and upon infringement of the right of privacy (subsequently protected by article 8 of the European Convention for the Protection of Human Rights and Fundamental Freedoms). The trial judge found that the touching of the son's penis during the search amounted to a battery and awarded the son damages. The judge also found that the authorities were liable under a form of trespass extended by the principle of *Wilkinson v Downton* (1897) and accordingly awarded damages to the mother as well. The Court of Appeal considered that the prison authorities had not committed any trespass save the battery to the son and thus reduced the damages to the son and quashed those awarded to the mother. The House of Lords (Lords Bingham, Hoffmann, Hope, Hutton and Scott) dismissed an appeal and asserted that there was no tort of an invasion of privacy.

Lord Hoffmann: ". . . **7** The conclusion of both the judge and the Court of Appeal was. . . that the searches were not protected by statutory authority. But that is not enough to give the Wainwrights a claim to compensation. The acts of the prison officers needed statutory authority only if they would otherwise have been wrongful, that is to say, tortious or in breach of a statutory duty. People do all kinds of things without statutory authority. So the question is whether the searches themselves or the manner in which they were conducted gave the Wainwrights a cause of action. . . ."

Lord Scott: ". . . **62** The important issue of principle is not, in my opinion, whether English common law recognises a tort of invasion of privacy. As Lord Hoffmann has demonstrated, whatever remedies may have been developed for misuse of confidential information, for certain types of trespass, for certain types of nuisance and for various other situations in which claimants may find themselves aggrieved by an invasion of what they conceive to be their privacy, the common law has not developed an overall remedy for the invasion of privacy. The issue of importance in the present case is whether the infliction of humiliation and distress by conduct calculated to humiliate and cause distress, is without more, tortious at common law. I am in full agreement with the reasons that have been given by Lord Hoffmann for concluding that it is not. Nor, in my opinion, should it be. Some institutions, schools, university colleges, regiments and the like (often bad ones) have initiation ceremonies and rites which newcomers are expected to undergo. Ritual humiliation is often a part of this. The authorities in charge of these institutions usually object to these practices and seek to put an end to any excesses. But why, absent any of the traditional nominate torts such as assault, battery, negligent causing of harm etc, should the law of tort intrude? If a shop assistant or a bouncer or barman at a club is publicly offensive to a customer, the customer may well be humiliated and distressed. But that is no sufficient reason why the law of tort should be fashioned and developed with a view to providing compensation in money to the victim.

63 Whether today, the Human Rights Act 1998 having come into effect, conduct similar to that inflicted on Mrs Wainwright and Alan Wainwright, but without any element of battery and without crossing the line into the territory of misfeasance in public office, should be categorised as tortious must be left to be decided when such a case arises. It is not necessary to decide now whether such conduct would constitute a breach of article 8 or of article 3 of the Convention. . . ."

(For further extracts see pp.77, 95)

QUESTION

Do you think the European Court of Human Rights would hold that the claimant had not suffered a human right abuse?

Wainwright v United Kingdom (2006) *The Times* October 3, 2006, EctHR

"**45.** In the case of these applicants, it has been found by the domestic courts that the prison officers who carried out the searches had failed to comply with their own regulations and had demonstrated "sloppiness". In particular, it appears that the prison officers did not provide the applicants with a copy of the form which set out the applicable procedure to be followed before the search was carried out, and which would have put them on notice of what to expect and permitted informed consent; they also overlooked the rule that the person to be searched should be no more than half-naked at any time and required the second applicant to strip totally and the first applicant to be in a practically equivalent state at one instant. It also appears that the first applicant was visible through a window in breach of paragraph 1.2.7 of the applicable procedure (see paragraph 28 above). The Government have not contradicted her assertion in that respect, saying that she should have asked for the blinds to be drawn. It is however for the authorities, not the visitor, to ensure the proper procedure is followed.

46. The Court notes that although there was a regrettable lack of courtesy there was no verbal abuse by the prison officers and, importantly, there was no touching of the applicants, save in the case of the second applicant. That aspect was found to be unlawful by the domestic courts which gave damages for the battery involved; the second applicant cannot claim any longer to be victim of this element and it is excluded from the Court's assessment. The treatment undoubtedly caused the applicants distress but does not, in the Court's view, reach the minimum level of severity prohibited by Article 3. Rather the Court finds that this is a case which falls within the scope of Article 8 of the Convention and which requires due justification under the second paragraph of Article 8 (see paragraph 29 above).

47. As regards the criteria of 'in accordance with the law' and 'legitimate aim', the Court is not persuaded by the applicants that these were not complied with. The domestic courts found that the breach of internal procedure did not disclose any unlawfulness (battery aside) and the Court does not perceive any basis for finding unlawfulness in the broader Convention sense. It has accepted above that the search pursued the aim of fighting the drugs problem in the prison, namely the prevention of crime and disorder.

48. On the other hand, it is not satisfied that the searches were proportionate to that legitimate aim in the manner in which they were carried out. Where procedures are laid down for the proper conduct of searches on outsiders to the prison who may very well be innocent of any wrongdoing, it behoves the prison authorities to comply strictly with those safeguards and by rigorous precautions protect the dignity of those being searched from being assailed any further than is necessary. They did not do so in this case.

49. Consequently, the Court finds that the searches carried out on the applicants cannot be regarded as 'necessary in a democratic society' within the meaning of Article 8 paragraph 2 of the Convention. There has been, accordingly, a breach of Article 8 of the Convention in that regard. . . .

54. In light of the finding of a violation of Article 8 above, the complaint is clearly arguable. The question which the Court must therefore address is whether the applicants had a remedy at national level to 'enforce the substance of the Convention rights . . . in whatever form they may happen to be secured in the domestic legal order' (see *Vilvarajah and Others v. the United Kingdom*, judgment of 30 October 1991, Series A no. 215, pp. 38–40, §§ 117–27).

55. ile it is true that the applicants took domestic proceedings seeking damages for the searches and their effects they had on them, they were unsuccessful, save as regards the instance of battery on the second applicant. As stated above, the Court considers that the finding of unlawfulness of that action and the provision of compensation deprived the second applicant of victim status for the purposes of Article 8 in that regard; it finds no basis, under Article 13 of the Convention, to consider that the amount of compensation awarded by the domestic courts was so derisory as to raise issues of the effectiveness of the redress. As regards the other objectionable elements of the strip searches, the Court observes that the House of Lords found that negligent action disclosed by the prison officers did not ground any civil liability, in particular as there was no general tort of invasion of privacy. In these circumstances, the Court finds that the applicants did not have available to them a means of obtaining redress for the interference with their rights under Article 8 of the Convention.

56. There has therefore been a violation of Article 13 of the Convention.

FOR THESE REASONS, THE COURT UNANIMOUSLY

1. *Holds* that there has been no violation of Article 3 of the Convention;

2. *Holds* that there has been a violation of Article 8 of the Convention;

3. *Holds* that there has been a violation of Article 13 of the Convention;"

QUESTION

Was it not obvious that the UK was going to lose this case before the European Court of Human Rights?

1.4.6 Tort and administrative law

In tort itself there is no formal distinction between public and private bodies (cf. **Chapter 9**). A local authority can be just as liable as the manufacturer of ginger beer in the tort of negligence, nuisance, trespass or whatever. Equally the local authority can sue the private person or commercial corporation for damages under one of these heads (*Esso v Southport* (1954), above p.5). Nevertheless at the level of remedies tort claims must be distinguished from actions for judicial review.

X (Minors) v Bedfordshire County Council **[1995] 2 A.C. 633, HL**

Lord Browne-Wilkinson: ". . . The question is whether, if Parliament has imposed a statutory duty on an authority to carry out a particular function, a plaintiff who has suffered damage in consequence of the authority's performance or non-performance of that function has a right of action in damages against the authority. It is important to distinguish such actions to recover damages, based on a private law cause of action, from actions in public law to enforce the due performance of statutory duties, now brought by way of judicial review. The breach of a public law right by itself gives rise to no claim for damages. A claim for damages must be based on a private law cause of action. The distinction is important because a number of earlier cases (particularly in the field of education) were concerned with the enforcement by declaration and injunction of what would now be called public law duties. . . ."

NOTE

Probably only when it comes to defamation will there be a restriction on a government body's right to sue (*Derbyshire CC v Times Newspapers* (1993)). Sometimes an aggrieved citizen might well decide to sue in private law for damages rather than to seek the quashing of a decision in administrative law; and unless this procedure amounts to an abuse of process (*O'Reilly v Mackman* (1983)) it will be perfectly valid (see e.g. *Blackpool & Fylde Aero Club Ltd v Blackpool BC* (1990) C&MC, p.177). There is, however, one very important qualification to this right to sue. Although in form a public body like a local authority or the police can be sued for negligence (see *Rigby v Chief Constable of Northamptonshire* (1985), p.371), in substance the judges have a number of weapons that they can use to protect a public authority. To succeed in negligence the claimant must establish a duty of care and so a court can simply declare that no such duty exists, say on the ground that the claimant or the damage is unforeseeable or that there are policy reasons against the existence of a duty (see **Chapter 9**).

1.4.7 Tort and equity

The frontier between tort and equity is to be found mainly (but not exclusively) at the level of remedies. The common law remedy of damages needs to be distinguished not just from the equitable remedy of injunction (see *Miller v Jackson* (1977), p.15 and *Burris v Azadani* (1995), p.421) but also from the equitable remedy of account of profits (*English v Dedham Vale Properties* (1978); *Att-Gen v Blake* (2001)) (cf. C&MC, pp.549–557). However just to complicate things further there is also an equitable form of damages which, thanks to statute, can be awarded in lieu of an injunction (see generally *Jaggard v Sawyer* (1995) C&MC, p.557). Equitable ideas can also influence tort thinking: see e.g. *Hedley Byrne v Heller* (1964), p.134.

1.5 Tort and methodology

It was once believed, at least on the continent, that the application of a rule was merely a matter of syllogistic logic: the judge was little more than a computer mechanically applying legal rules (major premise) to sets of facts (minor premise), the solution flowing deductively from the juxtaposition of the two premises. This methodology was shown to be a myth even before it was discovered that one cannot produce a computer programme that thinks like a judge. All the same, if we assume (in fact a dangerous assumption) that having knowledge of a particular area of law is knowing the rules said to fall within that area, then tort rules come in two sorts. There are those arising out of legal precedents and those set out in statutes.

1.5.1 Tort and precedent

Knowing the rules is not, however, enough. The tort lawyer must know how to discover their scope and extent and how to apply them to particular factual situations. When the rule has its source in case-law, what counts is the ratio decidendi. But what exactly is the ratio of a case in which there are several judgments each one saying something slightly different? And what role does the facts of a precedent play when applying such a precedent to a new situation? Statute might appear less ambiguous in that the rule is clearly stated in writing; however it may not be clearly expressed (see e.g. Animals Act 1971 s.2(2), p.200) with the result that applying it to certain sets of facts can be extremely problematic. In fact, knowing tort law is knowing how to reason like a tort lawyer and in this sense the whole subject could be said to be one of method rather than rules (cf. **11.8**). Accordingly there are a number of methodological points that can be usefully absorbed at this introductory and definitional stage. These are set out in the following extracts.

> *Home Office v Dorset Yacht Co Ltd* **[1970] A.C. 1004, HL**
>
> (For facts and further extracts see p.254)
>
> > **Lord Diplock**: "... The method adopted at this stage of the process is analytical and inductive. It starts with an analysis of the characteristics of the conduct and relationship involved in each of the decided cases. But the analyst must know what he is looking for; and this involves his approaching his analysis with some general conception of conduct and relationships which ought to give rise to a duty of care. This analysis leads to a proposition which can be stated in the form: 'In all the decisions that have been analysed a duty of care has been held to exist wherever the conduct and the relationship possessed each of the characteristics A, B, C, D etc, and has not so far been found to exist when any of these characteristics were absent.'
> >
> > For the second stage, which is deductive and analytical, that proposition is converted to: 'In all cases where the conduct and relationship possess each of the characteristics A, B, C, D etc., a duty of care arises.' The conduct and relationship involved in the case for decision is then analysed to ascertain whether they possess each of these characteristics. If they do the conclusion follows that a duty of care does arise in the case for decision.
> >
> > But since *ex hypothesi* the kind of case which we are now considering offers a choice whether or not to extend the kinds of conduct or relationships which give rise to a duty of care, the conduct or relationship which is involved in it will lack at least one of the characteristics A, B, C, or D etc. And the choice is exercised by making a policy decision ... which ... will be influenced by the same general conception of what ought to give rise to a duty of care as was used in approaching the analysis. The choice to extend is given effect to by redefining the characteristics in more general terms so as to exclude the necessity to conform to limitations imposed by the former definition which are considered to be inessential ...
> >
> > Inherent in this methodology, however, is a practical limitation which is imposed by the sheer volume of reported cases. The initial selection of previous cases to be analysed will itself eliminate from the analysis those in which the conduct or relationship involved possessed

characteristics which are obviously absent in the case for decision. The proposition used in the deductive stage is not a true universal. It needs to be qualified so as to read: 'In all cases where the conduct and relationship possess each of the characteristics A, B, C and D etc, but do not possess any of the characteristics Z, Y or X etc, which were present in the cases eliminated from the analysis, a duty of care arises.' But this qualification, being irrelevant to the decision of the particular case, is generally left unexpressed . . ."

QUESTION

What do you think is the most important focal point in Lord Diplock's analysis of legal reasoning: (i) induction; (ii) deduction; or (iii) policy?

NOTE

It is very tempting to think that legal method is a question of inducing a rule or principle out of a set of previous cases and then applying this rule in a deductive manner whereby the rule acts as the major premise, the facts of the case to be decided as the minor premise, the solution seemingly following as a matter of syllogistic logic (cf. C&MC, pp.88–92). However legal method is not so simple, as indeed Lord Diplock indicated with his reference to policy (cf. C&MC, pp.92–105). The next extract shows how even the formal reasoning method is more complex than just induction and deduction.

Lupton v FA & AB Ltd [1972] A.C. 634, HL

Lord Simon: ". . . A judicial decision will often be reached by a process of reasoning which can be reduced into a sort of complex syllogism, with the major premise consisting of a pre-existing rule of law (either statutory or judge-made) and with the minor premise consisting of the material facts of the case under immediate consideration. The conclusion is the decision of the case, which may or may not establish new law—in the vast majority of cases it will be merely the application of existing law to the facts judicially ascertained. Where the decision does constitute new law, this may or may not be expressly stated as a proposition of law: frequently the new law will appear only from subsequent comparison of, on the one hand, the material facts inherent in the major premise with, on the other, the material facts which constitute the minor premise. As a result of this comparison it will often be apparent that a rule has been extended by an analogy expressed or implied. I take as an example . . . *National Telephone Co v Baker* [1893] 2 Ch 186. Major premise: the rule in *Rylands v Fletcher* (1866) LR 1 Exch 265, (1868) LR 3 HL 330. Minor premise: the defendant brought and stored electricity on his land for his own purpose; it escaped from the land; in so doing it injured the plaintiff's property. Conclusion: the defendant is liable in damages to the plaintiff (or would have been but for statutory protection). Analysis shows that the conclusion establishes a rule of law, which may be stated as 'for the purpose of the rule in *Rylands v Fletcher* electricity is analogous to water' or 'electricity is within the rule in *Rylands v Fletcher*'. That conclusion is now available as the major premise in the next case, in which some substance may be in question which in this context is not perhaps clearly analogous to water but is clearly analogous to electricity. In this way, legal luminaries are constituted which guide the wayfarer across uncharted ways."

NOTE

Although Lord Simon puts the emphasis on the syllogism, the real key to the solution in *National Telephone* is reasoning by analogy: electricity is analogous to water. This technique of analogy is fundamental to tort law as the next cases show.

Goodwill v British Pregnancy Advisory Service [1996] 1 W.L.R. 1397, CA

The claimant brought an action for damages, in respect of her unwanted pregnancy, against an organisation which had arranged a vasectomy for a man with whom the claimant subsequently had sexual relations which resulted in the pregnancy. The Court of Appeal (Peter Gibson L.J. and Thorpe L.J.) held that the action should be struck out.

> **Peter Gibson L.J.:** "The law of negligence, and in particular that part relating to the recovery of damages for economic loss caused by negligent statements or advice, has undergone a number of shifts in direction. The attempt in *Anns v Merton London Borough Council* [1978] AC 728 to lay down a principle of general applicability did not find favour for long. Instead, whilst certain key ingredients of the tort, such as foreseeability, proximity, assumption of responsibility and reliance have been identified, it has been held that the law should develop incrementally by reference to or analogy with established categories of situations where the law has recognised that a duty of care arises and a plaintiff may recover for his loss. The situation in the present case, it is accepted on behalf of the plaintiff, does not fall within an established category, but, it is suggested, it requires only a modest step from an established category and one which should on the favoured incremental approach now be taken to afford the plaintiff a remedy in tort. That is challenged by the defendants who say that it requires a giant and impermissible leap from an established category and that not even arguably was any duty of care owed by these defendants to this plaintiff in the circumstances of this case. . . .
>
> Miss Booth also relied on *White v Jones* [1995] 2 AC 207 as providing an example of an analogous situation in which a duty of care has been recognised. In that case a solicitor who was instructed to prepare a will but delayed in carrying out his instructions was held to owe a duty of care to the intended beneficiaries. She submitted that a woman who had a sexual relationship with Mr MacKinlay is in an analogous position to the intended beneficiaries under the will, because just as the solicitor was employed to confer a benefit (in the form of bequests) on a particular class of people (the beneficiaries), so the doctor is employed to confer a benefit (not getting pregnant) on a particular class of people (women who have sexual relationships with Mr MacKinlay). I admire the ingenuity of the suggested analogy, but I have to say that I am wholly unpersuaded that the analogy is real. . . ."

NOTES

1. Principles are never to be abstracted from the particular factual situations of the precedents in which they are latent. For "what constitutes binding precedent is the ratio decidendi of a case and this is almost always to be ascertained by an analysis of the material facts of the case—that is, generally, those facts which the tribunal whose decision is in question itself holds, expressly or implicitly, to be material" (Lord Simon in *Lupton*). Precedent, therefore, is as much a question of analogy between factual situations as induction and deduction from some pre-existing proposition of law. Previous

cases can always be 'distinguished' (avoided) on their facts. As Lobban has observed of the early 19th century, "precedents were not absolute, nor did they create precise rules. Rather, they acted as a source of legal analogy. . . . Since precedent was unclear, and worked only by rough analogies from decided cases, the law could be favourable to flexibility and certainty at the same time" (Lobban, *The Common Law and English Jurisprudence 1760–1850*, (Oxford: OUP, 1991), pp.83, 86).

2. Lord Hoffmann has observed that the "common law develops from case to case in harmony with statute" and its "principles are generalisations from detailed rules, not abstract propositions from which those rules are deduced" (*In re McKerr* (2004), § 71).

Esso Petroleum Co Ltd v Southport Corporation **[1953] 3 W.L.R. 773, Q.B.D., [1954] 2 Q.B. 182, CA, [1956] A.C. 218, HL**

(See p.5)

Devlin J. (Queen's Bench Division): ". . . [I]f one seeks an analogy from traffic on land, it is well established that persons whose property adjoins the highway cannot complain of damage done by persons using the highway unless it is done negligently: . . . These cases amplify the principle in *Holmes v Mather* which dealt with collisions on the highway itself and which is the foundation of the modern practice whereby a plaintiff in a running-down action sues for negligence and not for trespass . . ."

NOTE

Denning L.J. in the Court of Appeal (see above p.5) drew quite a different analogy. The discharge of oil into the sea was analogous to an adjoining neighbour's horses polluting the street and harming the claimant's café business (*Benjamin v Storr* (1874)). A difference of analogy led to a difference of result (although not for long since the House of Lords reinstated Devlin J.'s decision) (cf. C&MC, pp.94–96).

1.5.2 Tort and statute

The foundational source of the law of torts is the common law (precedent). However legislative intervention and the methods that attach to the interpretation of statutes cannot now be ignored in tort even if the intervention is relatively modest. In the remedial field of damages the intervention is such that the texts have become one starting point in personal injury claims (see Fatal Accidents Act 1976, Damages Act 1996, Social Security (Recovery of Benefits) Act 1997 etc.). And in the area of liability for defective premises (occupiers' liability) the foundation is almost entirely statutory as will be seen in a later chapter. Animals in tort are now governed by a statutory regime as the next case illustrates.

Animals Act 1971 (c.22)

(For extract see p.200)

Mirvahedy v Henley **[2003] 2 A.C. 491, HL**

This was an action for damages brought by a car driver against the owner of a horse that had escaped from a field in a panic and collided with the claimant's car causing him severe personal injury. The trial judge found that the escape had not been due to any negligence on the part of the defendant and the sole question, therefore, was whether liability could be established under the Animals Act 1971 s.2(2). A majority of the House of Lords (Lords Nicholls, Hobhouse and Walker; Lords Slynn and Scott dissenting) held that there was liability.

> **Lord Hobhouse**: ". . . 69. Horses are not normally in a mindless state of panic nor do they normally ignore obstacles in their path. These characteristics are normally only found in horses in circumstances where they have been very seriously frightened. It is only in such circumstances that it becomes likely that, due to these characteristics, the horse will cause severe damage. This case clearly comes within the words of s.2(2)(b). There is no ambiguity either about the facts of this case or about the meaning of paragraph (b). . . .
>
> **72.** The statute, in this respect following the recommendation of the Law Commission, had to reflect a choice as to the division of risk between the keeper of an animal and members of the general public. Neither is blameworthy but it is the member of the public who suffers the injury or damage and it is the keeper who knows of the characteristics of the animal which make it dangerous and liable to cause such injury or damage. The element of knowledge makes the choice a coherent one but it, in any event, was a choice which it was for the Legislature to make. . . ."
>
> **Lord Scott** (dissenting): ". . . 130. A clear answer to the question as to the proper construction of paragraph (b) cannot, in my opinion, be obtained from the actual language of the provision, nor from a perusal of Hansard, nor from examining the contents of the Law Commission Report of 1967 on which the 1971 Act was in part based. The answer depends upon identifying what Parliament appears to have been trying to achieve. It seems to me that Parliament was trying to draw a distinction between animals that in normal circumstances behaving normally are dangerous and those that in normal circumstances behaving normally are not. As to the former, they belong to a dangerous species and there was to be strict liability for damage; as to the latter they do not belong to a dangerous species and strict liability was to be limited to damage caused by the animal displaying abnormal characteristics that it was known by its keeper to possess. This seems to me to be a coherent policy. In respect of damage for which no strict liability was imposed, a remedy in negligence would always be available if the keeper of the animal had failed to exercise reasonable care to see that the animal did not cause damage. The keeper's knowledge of the circumstances in which and times at which the animal might be likely to become dangerous and cause damage would, of course, be highly relevant in determining the standard of care required to be observed by the keeper. A standard of care can, in appropriate circumstances, be placed so high as to require the person subject to it to become virtually an insurer against damage. . . ."

(See also extracts on pp.199, 203)

NOTES

1. The methods applied to the interpretation and application of statutory texts are traditionally seen as being rather different from the application of precedents since the starting point is not analogy with pre-existing factual situations. The method is 'hermeneutical' in the more traditional sense of working directly on a text (signifier) to discover what Parliament 'intended' (signified) (cf. C&MC, pp.97–103). But this 'intention' is normally to be gauged only from the words of the text and reasoning by analogy is excluded (see T Weir, *Introduction to Tort Law*, 2nd edn (Oxford: OUP, 2006), p.10). Thus the s.2(1) strict liability under the Animals Act 1971 cannot be extended by analogy from a dangerous animal to a dangerous non-living thing.

2. In the past the approach towards statutes was often quite literal, the judges stopping at the text itself and not considering the contextual situation (see e.g. *Haigh v Charles W Ireland* (1973)). It is not what the legislature aims at but what it hits that counts (*St Aubyn v Att-Gen* (1952) at p.32; Weir, *Introduction to Tort Law*, p.8). But among some judges (although not all) the approach has become more flexible in recent years (see Lord Nicholls in *Ex p Spath Holme Ltd* (2001)). Thus where the statute is ambiguous the judges have abandoned their rule that they could never look at the *travaux préparatoires* (see the Court of Appeal judgment in *Mirvahedy v Henley* at § 24).

3. In addition, where human rights are involved, the judges are now under a statutory duty to interpret in such a way that, if at all possible, the Act in question is compatible with European Convention rights (Human Rights Act 1998 s.3; cf. *Ghaidan v Godin-Mendoza* (2004)). However, artificial distinctions are still to be found especially in cases where, for example, the judges feel they are being forced to make policy decisions which would be better made by Parliament, especially if there are huge financial implications (*Birmingham CC v Oakley* (2001)). Moreover traditional distinctions such as those between physical and mental injury (cf. *Morris v KLM Royal Dutch Airlines* (2002)) and physical and pure economic damage (*Merlin v British Nuclear Fuels Plc* (1990)) can, sometimes at least, still influence the way texts are interpreted.

1.5.3 Tort and policy

Legal theorists in the UK, as we have said, tend to present law as a body of rules. Yet the actual case law perhaps tells a rather different story from those presented by rule-theorists. Thus one finds in the judgments comments such as the common law often prefers pragmatism to logic (see e.g. *Ex p King* (1984), at p.903). Direct appeals to policy are now particularly prevalent in the law of tort.

***Hill v Chief Constable of West Yorkshire* [1989] A.C. 53, HL**

This was an action for damages brought against the police by the estate of the last victim of the notorious 'Yorkshire Ripper' (Peter Sutcliffe). The claimant alleged in the writ that the police had been negligent in failing to apprehend the murderer thus leaving him free to murder the claimant. The judge ordered that the claim should be struck out and a final appeal to the House of Lords (Lords Keith, Brandon, Templeman, Oliver and Goff) was dismissed.

Lord Keith: ". . . [I]n my opinion there is another reason why an action for damages in negligence should not lie against the police in circumstances such as those of the present case, and that is public policy. . . . Potential existence of such liability may in many instances be in the general public interest, as tending towards the observance of a higher standard of care in the carrying on of various different types of activity. I do not, however, consider that this can be said of police activities. The general sense of public duty which motivates police forces is unlikely to be appreciably reinforced by the imposition of such liability so far as concerns their function in the investigation and suppression of crime. From time to time they make mistakes in the exercise of that function, but it is not to be doubted that they apply their best endeavours to the performance of it. In some instances the imposition of liability may lead to the exercise of a function being carried on in a detrimentally defensive frame of mind. The possibility of this happening in relation to the investigative operations of the police cannot be excluded. Further it would be reasonable to expect that if potential liability were to be imposed it would be not uncommon for actions to be raised against police forces on the ground that they had failed to catch some criminal as soon as they might have done, with the result that he went on to commit further crimes. While some such actions might involve allegations of a simple and straightforward type of failure - for example that a police officer negligently tripped and fell while pursuing a burglar - others would be likely to enter deeply into the general nature of a police investigation, as indeed the present action would seek to do. The manner of conduct of such an investigation must necessarily involve a variety of decisions to be made on matters of policy and discretion, for example as to which particular line of inquiry is most advantageously to be pursued and what is the most advantageous way to deploy the available resources. Many such decisions would not be regarded by the courts as appropriate to be called in question, yet elaborate investigation of the facts might be necessary to ascertain whether or not this was so. A great deal of police time, trouble and expense might be expected to have to be put into the preparation of the defence to the action and the attendance of witnesses at the trial. The result would be a significant diversion of police manpower and attention from their most important function, that of the suppression of crime. Closed investigations would require to be reopened and retraversed, not with the object of bringing any criminal to justice but to ascertain whether or not they had been competently conducted. I therefore consider that Glidewell LJ, in his judgment in the Court of Appeal [1988] QB 60, 76 in the present case, was right to take the view that the police were immune from an action of this kind on grounds similar to those which in *Rondel v Worsley* [1969] 1 AC 191 were held to render a barrister immune from actions for negligence in his conduct of proceedings in court."

QUESTIONS

1. Ought judges to be concerned with policy reasons or should they confine themselves only to legal rights and duties?

2. The judges have now recognised that the blanket immunity given to advocates by *Rondel v Worsley* (1969) is no longer acceptable (see *Arthur Hall*, above p.21). Do you think that one day the same will be said of the immunity given to the police? Is there any actual empirical evidence to support Lord Keith's opinions or is much of what he says simply his own intuitive feelings? (cf. *Brooks v Comr of Police for the Metropolis* (2005).)

NOTE

Policy was used as one of the main reasons behind the economic loss rule in the tort of negligence (see *Spartan Steel* (1973), p.159). It would appear, however, that there are limits to policy reasoning as the next extract powerfully shows.

Vellino v Chief Constable of Greater Manchester Police [2002] 1 W.L.R. 218, CA

This was an action for damages against the police in respect of serious injuries sustained by the claimant while attempting to escape from arrest. The claimant alleged that the police, in permitting him to jump from a bedroom window, had been in breach of the duty of care that they owed to arrested persons. The trial judge dismissed the action on the basis that there was no duty of care and that the defence of ex turpi causa was applicable. A majority of the Court of Appeal (Schiemann L.J. and Sir Murray Stuart-Smith; Sedley L.J. dissenting) dismissed an appeal.

Schiemann L.J.: ". . . 19 To suggest that the police owe a criminal the duty to prevent the criminal from escaping, and that the criminal who hurts himself while escaping can sue the police for the breach of that duty, seems to me self-evidently absurd. No policy reason has been suggested for the law adopting such a course. Mr Stockdale expressly disavowed this way of putting his case. . . ."

Sedley L.J. (dissenting): ". . . 60 The House of Lords in *Tinsley v Milligan* [1994] 1 AC 340 rejected the 'public conscience' test articulated by Hutchison J in *Thackwell v Barclays Bank plc* [1986] 1 All ER 676 as a filter on claims with a criminal dimension. We are not now required, in other words, to look over our shoulders at what we fear the press will make of our decisions in this already difficult field. The public conscience, an elusive thing, as often as not turns out to be an echo-chamber inhabited by journalists and public moralists. To allow judicial policy to be dictated by it would be as inappropriate as to let judges dictate editorial policy. It is not difficult, for example, to visualise how some sections of the media would choose to report a decision along the lines which I have proposed. The Law Commission's scholarly and constructive working paper has so far been reported under the headline 'Law paves way for thugs to sue victims' (*Daily Express*, 30 June 2001) and has earned the Law Commission the soubriquet 'Enemy of the people' (*Sunday Times*, 1 July 2001). In a free society such comment is perfectly permissible and its influence on public opinion no doubt considerably greater than that of a judgment or a Law Commission paper. The public may one day have to decide through the democratic process whether it wants the law to legitimise the use of firearms against intruders in a society which at present has a gun homicide rate 150 times lower than the United States. But to expect a judiciary to modify its decisions as to what the law and justice require because of what it fears the media would make of them is to ask for the surrender of judicial independence. The 'fair, just and reasonable' test is now the established judicial control on ground-breaking in tort. If the law were ever to revert to an exogenous test, it should be one which gauges the response of people who actually know what the court's reasoning is; and no court which has confidence in its own reasoning should be worried about that. . . ."

QUESTION

What do you think is the difference between the 'public conscience' test and the 'fair, just and reasonable' test? Are they both not tests rooted in what the public are imagined to perceive as what is 'just'?

1.5.4 **Tort and argumentation**

Several other methodological points need to be stressed. One important point is that it is not just the judges who are the sources of law; they make their decisions on the basis of arguments presented to them by the parties' barristers. Indeed, the judges rely on the barristers to research the law. The presentation of these arguments is itself dialectical because of the nature of the legal process; thus nearly all English judgments consider in turn the arguments presented first by the claimant's counsel and then by the defendant's. The judge then decides between them, sometimes after a lengthy analysis of the precedents (and/or the statutory provisions) and (or) sometimes after a detailed consideration of the factual context.

Tony Weir, 'Recent Developments in Causation in English Tort Law', in B Fauvarque-Cosson, E Picard & A Voinnesson (eds), *De tous horizons: Mélanges Xavier Blanc Jouvan*, **Société de Législation Comparée, 2005, pp.883, 890**

"The importance in the common law of the arguments of counsel is frequently overlooked by comparative lawyers. They are important because of the way our judges are selected. Until very recently all our senior judges had spent most of their lives as barristers. Now whereas barristers are successful enough to be appointed judges only if they specialise in a particular area of law, once they are raised to the bench they instantly become generalists having to deal with cases of all kinds. . . Consequently the judges are often not at all familiar with the area of law being discussed before them by the barristers: in England the maxim *curia novit jura* is more a joke than a principle. . . It may perhaps be added that in difficult cases counsel are tempted to try every argument at all plausible, and that the judges who have to respond to them are sometimes less dismissive of feeble arguments than they might be, perhaps out of deference to their future colleagues. Again it may happen that the spokesman for the party that ought to win on the merits may not adduce the best arguments in their client's favour, with the effect that the judges, who usually reach the correct result, may not be able to give the best reasons for it."

QUESTION

What if a barrister fails to present to the court an accurate account of the law?

Copeland v Smith **[2000] 1 W.L.R. 1371, CA**

Buxton L.J.: ". . . Although the matter does not arise for decision because it is now conceded, I cannot draw back from expressing my very great concern that the judge was permitted by those professional advocates to approach the matter as if it were free from authority when there was a recently reported case in this court directly on the point, which was reported not in some obscure quarter but in the official law reports. It is, of course, not only extremely discourteous to the judge not to inform him properly about the law, but it has also been extremely wasteful of time and money in this case, because not only did the judge have to deal with the matter, but it has also formed an issue in the appeal to this court. I have, I fear, to say that the advocates who appeared below did not discharge their duty properly to the court in that they apparently failed to be aware of the existence of that authority. . . ."

> **Brooke L.J.:** ". . . The English system of justice has always been dependent on the quality of the assistance that advocates give to the bench. This is one of the reasons why, in contrast to systems of justice in other countries, English judges are almost invariably in a position to give judgment at the end of a straightforward hearing without having to do their own research and without the state having to incur the cost of legal assistance for judges because they cannot rely on the advocates to show them the law they need to apply. . . ."

NOTE

Decisions are often supported by a series of justifications (arguments) that may use reasoning internal to the law (e.g. the interpretation and application of a precedent or text) or external to strict positive law (e.g. arguments of policy or morality: see *Hill v Chief Constable*, above). Recourse to metaphor is not unusual (see e.g. *Spartan Steel* (1973) below p.452); and in one recent tort case the majority based its decision on the notion of 'practical justice' (*White v Jones* (1995), below p.289).

1.6 European considerations

European law, in the sense of law having its direct or indirect source in continental Europe, impacts on tort law in three main ways. First, there is EU law which finds expression in regulatory texts, European Directives and in European Court of Justice decisions. UK courts must have regard to this law (European Communities Act 1972); and failure to implement a Directive may give an individual the right to sue in tort. Secondly, there is human rights law where the UK courts are under a statutory duty to 'take into account' any decisions of the European Court of Human Rights or opinion or decision of the Commission (Human Rights Act 1998 s.2(1)). Thirdly there are the continental legal systems themselves which produce not just their own legal decisions on 'tort' problems but much academic writing on the law of obligations within the member states of the EU. These court decisions are in no way binding on UK courts, but judges sometimes take note of developments in the civil law systems (see e.g. *Fairchild v Glenhaven Funeral Services Ltd* (2003), below p.45). In addition, several unofficial groups of (mainly) continental jurists are working on the codification of tort law (*Principles of European Tort Law*) and, while these codes are unlikely to replace English law in the foreseeable future, they ought not to be ignored by today's UK law student.

1.6.1 **European union**

One important European source is the Directive. These are texts that are not as such directly enforceable as a statute and thus they need to be implemented. One such implementation that is of importance to tort lawyers is the Consumer Protection Act 1987 (see p.184) which implements the Council Directive of July 25, 1985 on liability for defective products. However failure to implement a Directive can give rise to a tort on behalf of individuals.

R v Transport Sec, Ex p Factortame Ltd (No 7) **[2001] 1 W.L.R. 942, Q.B.D.**

This was an action for damages brought by Spanish fishermen against the United Kingdom for breach of European Community law. On a preliminary issue a question arose as to whether certain new parties and new claims could be added to the proceedings or whether they were statute-barred under the Limitation Act 1980. A further question arose as to whether the claimants were entitled to damages for injury to feelings and distress. The judge held that the new parties and claims were statute-barred and that damages were limited strictly to economic losses.

Judge John Toulmin Q.C.: ". . . **56**. It was not until the *Francovich* case [1995] ICR 722 that the European Court of Justice gave a right to individuals to recover damages against the state for the state's failure to implement a directive, provided the appropriate conditions were fulfilled.

57. The court said, at p 772, para 41: 'Those conditions are sufficient to give rise to a right on the part of individuals to obtain reparation, a right founded directly on Community law.'

58. This finding must be read in the light of the explanation given in *Factortame 4* [1996] QB 404, 455, at para 42, that individuals derive their rights from Community law, but the means of enforcing those rights are derived from the principle that an unlawful act or omission of the member states gives rise to an obligation to make good the damage caused. . . .

145. An action for breach of English statutory duty is properly classified as an action founded on tort. It is argued that this can be properly extended to breaches of Community law by the government in these circumstances. The breach relied on in relation to breaches of the Treaty is the government's breach of its obligations under section 2(1) of the European Communities Act 1972, which requires domestic law to give effect to all rights, powers, liabilities, obligations and restrictions arising out of the Treaties and provides that where there is an enforceable Community right it should be enforceable as a matter of domestic law. . . .

148. [The authorities do] not address the fundamental problem of whether or not an action by an individual against a government for breach of Community law can properly be described as an action founded on tort. Nevertheless, giving the statute the widest construction in accordance with its purpose, a combination of a breach of article 52 of the Treaty (now article 43 EC) and section 2(1) of the European Communities Act 1972 does amount to a breach of statutory duty which is within section 2 of the Limitation Act 1980.

149. This does not absolve me from answering the fundamental question. I start from the fact that the term 'action founded on tort' is not defined in section 2 of the 1980 Act and that it is within the purpose of the Act that the words should be given a wide construction.

150. Following the approach suggested by Lord Hoffmann in the *Banque Bruxelles Lambert* case [1997] AC 191, 211, I define a tort as a breach of non-contractual duty which gives a private law right to the party injured to recover compensatory damages at common law from the party causing the injury.

151. This covers not only the present case but those few torts in English law where violation of a plaintiff's interest without proof of actual damage is sufficient to found a claim in tort. . . ."

NOTES AND QUESTIONS

1. Note (in para.50) the formalist definition of tort based on duty, right and remedy.

2. It is one thing for the European Court of Justice to declare that an individual is entitled to sue for damages for a state's failure to implement a Directive and another thing to fashion a cause of action for such a claim in domestic English law. The English courts could have done one of two things. They could have created a new cause of action or tort such as 'Failure to implement a Directive' and such a head of liability could be added to the list set out in the last section of this chapter (see **1.7**). Alternatively they could try to fit the claim within an existing head of liability. Which alternative did the court choose?

1.6.2 Human rights

The 'incorporation' of the European Convention of Human Rights and Fundamental Freedoms into English law by the Human Rights Act 1998 (see p.126) is a constitutional event of immense importance to the law of tort (there is some argument whether 'incorporation' is the correct term). The Convention and Act impact on English law in a direct (vertical) way in as much as the Act creates a new form of liability (Human Rights Act 1998 s.6(1)) which will give rise to "such relief or remedy. . . as [a court] considers just and appropriate" (s.8(1)). However such a claim is *not* actually an action in tort (see **11.4.7**). The Act and Convention also impact in an indirect (horizontal) way in as much as the Convention rights—together with decisions of the European Court of Human Rights—are modifying existing areas of tort law such as negligence, nuisance and defamation. *Z v United Kingdom* (2001) is a good example of the importance of the European Court jurisprudence on the English tort of negligence (see *Barrett v Enfield LBC* (2001)). Another decision that ought in principle to be of importance both to tort and to constitutional law is *Steel & Morris v UK* (2005) (see p.300).

1.6.3 Influence of civil law

Finally, mention must be made of the indirect influence of European law on English tort. In this context 'European law' refers not just to the case law (jurisprudence) of France, Germany and other continental systems but also Roman law (see e.g. the full judgment of Lord Rodger in the case extracted below—read in the law report).

Fairchild v Glenhaven Funeral Services Ltd **[2003] 1 A.C. 32, HL**

(For facts see p.386)

Lord Bingham: ". . . 32. . . . Development of the law in this country cannot of course depend on a head-count of decisions and codes adopted in other countries around the world, often against a background of different rules and traditions. The law must be developed coherently, in accordance with principle, so as to serve, even-handedly, the ends of justice. If, however, a decision is given in this country which offends one's basic sense of justice, and if consideration of international sources suggests that a different and more acceptable decision would be given in most other jurisdictions, whatever their legal tradition, this must prompt anxious review of the decision in question. In a shrinking world (in which the employees of asbestos companies may work for those companies in any one or more of several countries) there must be some virtue in uniformity of outcome whatever the diversity of approach in reaching that outcome. . . ."

Lord Rodger: ". . . 156. I derive support for that conclusion from what has been done in other legal systems. In the course of the hearing counsel for both sides referred to authorities from a number of different jurisdictions. It would be impossible to do justice to all of them in this opinion. Broadly speaking, they appear to me to demonstrate two things: first, that other systems have identified the need to adopt special rules or principles to cope with situations where the claimant cannot establish which of a number of wrongdoers actually caused his injury; secondly, that there are considerable divergences of view and indeed uncertainty as to the proper area within which any such special rules or principles should apply. I have simply selected a few among the many authorities cited by counsel. . . ."

NOTE

It might be tempting to think that this judicial interest in Europe is a recent phenomenon. It is not. Over a century ago, particularly after the abolition of the forms action in 1852, the English judges seriously started to look over the Channel for guidance in particular areas of private law (see e.g. *Taylor v Caldwell* (1863); C&MC, p.464; and see generally G Samuel, 'Civil Codes and the Restructuring of the Common Law', in D Fairgrieve (ed), *The Influence of the French Civil Code on the Common Law and Beyond*, (British Institute of International and Comparative Law, 2007), 91). The World Wars discouraged this process, but the impact of these events are receding, at least in the minds of some, with the result that a number of common lawyers are interesting themselves once again with Europe and with comparative law.

1.7 Foundations of liability

We saw near the beginning of this chapter (see *Esso v Southport* (1954), p.5) how liability in tort is traditionally founded upon causes of action. Thus knowledge of the subject is in one sense simply a knowledge of the list of the various causes of action available (see extract from Weir, above p.14). In fact tort knowledge is more complex than this and, as we have also seen, involves recourse to a range of other concepts in addition to causes of action. Nevertheless the starting point is the cause of action and, as Professor Rudden has shown (see above p.7), these can be presented in list form using only the alphabet as a guide. A list of some of the main causes of action in tort is presented in the next extract along with brief summaries of the elements of liability that attach to each of them.

Geoffrey Samuel, Understanding Contractual and Tortious Obligations, (Exeter: Law Matters, 2005), pp.98–104

"The nature of the damage is one important key, then, when it comes to harm intentionally caused. Yet despite movements towards some kind of general principle with respect both to physical and to economic loss, the only safe approach to liability is via specific existing torts (*Wainwright v Home Office* (2003)). Some of the principal torts dealing with intentionally (or maliciously) caused harm thus need to be examined in outline. As there is no common denominator, save a particular state of mind, the torts are arranged alphabetically

7.3.3.1 Abuse of civil (and criminal) process

Abuse of the criminal process can give rise, as we shall see (at 7.3.3.10), to the tort of malicious prosecution. Abuse of the civil process is also now to be a tort and one that seems to be an extension by analogy of malicious prosecution (see 7.3.3.10, below). Whereas malicious prosecution lies only in respect of criminal proceedings, the tort of abuse of process extends across the whole spectrum of civil proceedings. The foundational modern case is *Speed Seal Products v Paddington* (1985) which in some ways is a rather weak authority being only a striking out action (whether a claimant has an arguable case). Nevertheless there have been subsequent first instance decisions that fall under this heading of abuse of process and the whole developmental logic of the law of tort would suggest that this is an established head of liability. One such (relatively) recent decision is *Gibbs v Rea* (1998) which establishes that the malicious procurement of a search warrant is actionable if four conditions are fulfilled. These conditions, set out in a recent case, are: '(1) a successful application for a search warrant, (2) lack of reasonable and probable cause to make the application, (3) malice and (4) resultant damage arising from the issue or execution of the warrant' (*Keegan v Chief Constable of Merseyside* (2003), § 13 per Kennedy LJ). What is interesting about this tort is that it seems to be a cause of action independent of malicious prosecution, abuse of public office and even perhaps abuse of civil process (although for convenience it is listed here under this more general heading), thus confirming that an alphabetical list of causes of action is still the approach when it comes to intentional damage.

7.3.3.2 Abuse of public office (misfeasance in public office)

Another 'administrative' tort in some ways analogous to malicious prosecution and abuse of civil process is abuse of public office. This tort can be brought by an individual against a public officer who has intentionally or recklessly damaged the claimant. The history and the requirements of the tort have been fully explored recently by the House of Lords in *Three Rivers DC v Bank of England* (2003) where Lord Steyn set out the conditions for liability (191ff). These are that there must be an abusive exercise of power by a public officer aimed at the claimant, or a class of persons in which the claimant belongs, and the claimant him or herself must have a 'sufficient interest' in the action which will no doubt be fulfilled if serious economic loss (or other damage) is suffered. The abuse must also be the cause of the claimant's loss. As Lord Millet observed, the 'tort is an intentional tort which can be committed only by a public official' and from 'this two things follow.' The 'tort cannot be committed negligently or inadvertently' and, secondly, the 'core concept is abuse of power' which 'in turn involves other concepts, such as dishonesty, bad faith, and improper purpose'

(235). This emphasis on abuse of power by a public official means that the victim of abuse may well be able to sue even if he or she cannot prove substantial physical or economic harm; an invasion of a constitutional right might be enough to found a claim which could result in exemplary damages (*Watkins v Home Secretary* (2005)).

7.3.3.3 Conversion

Where one person aims his intention to injure not directly at the claimant but at the claimant's tangible property there is the possibility of the defendant being liable for wrongful interference with goods. This notion of wrongful interference is possibly not a tort in itself but a statutory creation which includes trespass, negligence and conversion (Torts (Interference with Goods) Act 1977 s 1). Trespass to goods involves a direct interference with *possession*, and thus a defendant will be liable if, for example, he deliberately rides off on the claimant's bicycle simply to annoy him. If the defendant were to sell the bicycle claiming it as his own, the claimant would have an action in conversion, a tort remedying interference with *title*. Lord Nicholls has recently stated that conversion of goods 'can occur in so many different circumstances that framing a definition of universal application is well nigh impossible.' However he said that there are in general three basic features to the tort:

(a) that the defendant's conduct was inconsistent with the owner's rights or other person entitled to possession;
(b) that the conduct was deliberate and not accidental; and
(c) that 'the conduct was so extensive an encroachment on the rights of the owner as to exclude him from the use and possession of the goods'.

Lord Nicholls then added that these requirements are to be contrasted with lesser acts of interference such as trespass or negligence (*Kuwait Airways v Iraqi Airways* (2002), § 39). Conversion, then, can truly be an intentional tort, although it can also be committed even in situations where the defendant is innocent of any fault (see eg *Willis & Son v British Car Auctions* (1978)). Finally, it seems that the tort of conversion applies only to goods and cannot be extended to a chose in action (*OGB Ltd v Allan* (2005)).

7.3.3.4 Deceit

'For a plaintiff to succeed in the tort of deceit', said Hobhouse LJ, 'it is necessary for him to prove that (1) the representation was fraudulent, (2) it was material and (3) it induced the plaintiff to act (to his detriment).' And a 'representation is material when its tendency, or its natural and probable result, is to induce the representee to act on the faith of it in the kind of way in which he is proved to have in fact acted.' And, he added, the 'test is objective' (*Downs v Chappell* (1997), 433). This is an old tort and is the basis of most actions for damages where the loss arises from the defendant's fraud. Accordingly it can often have a role in situations involving contracts that have been entered into as a result of one party's fraudulent misrepresentation. The main difficulty facing claimants is that they must prove fraud. However, thanks to statute, any misrepresentation that induces a contract will now be actionable in tort without the claimant having to prove fraud; the defendant can escape liability only by proving the absence of fault (Misrepresentation Act 1967 s 2(1)).

7.3.3.5 Defamation

Defamation occurs when one person publishes an untrue statement that is calculated to injure the reputation of another, and it is very easily incurred even in situations where the writer and (or) publisher had no intention of defaming the claimant. It is, therefore, a central tort against a person who deliberately sets out to damage another through the publication of statements. Although easily incurred—almost any statement critical of another will be defamatory provided it is published (defamation is strictly a three party tort)—there are three important defences:

(a) justification (truth);
(b) fair comment; and
(c) privilege.

As a result of the Human Rights Act 1998, this last defence has been extended in recent years to cover the 'reasonable journalist' who reports in good faith a story in the public interest that turns out to be untrue (*Reynolds v Times Newspapers* (1999); cf *Jameel (Mohammed) v Wall Street Journal* (2005)).

7.3.3.6 Harassment

If one moves from the business interest to what might be called the individual interest of freedom from a deliberately caused mental distress, a number of established torts can be relevant. As we shall see below, threats of violence might be a trespass and deliberate harassment of a neighbour can amount to a private nuisance. However, although there is no general tort of harassment (or privacy) at common law (confirmed in *Wainwright v Home Office* (2003)), there is now a statutory one in which damages can be obtained for anxiety and any financial loss arising from the harassment (Protection from Harassment Act 1997 s 3; and see *Majrowski v Guy's & St Thomas's NHS Trust* (2005)). It is possible, in equity, that a court might issue an injunction on the basis of preventing a person from being tempted to commit an existing tort, such as trespass or public nuisance, in situations where the problem is one of harassment and the claimant has a clear interest in need of protection (*Burris v Azadani* (1995)).

7.3.3.7 Human rights

Even if there were no 1997 Act against harassment (see 7.3.3.6, above), it is possible that certain forms of conduct falling within it would also now amount to an invasion of a right protected by the European Convention of Human Rights and Fundamental Freedoms, now part of English law thanks to the Human Rights Act 1998. The 1998 Act impacts on tort in two main ways. First it has a vertical effect in declaring unlawful any act by a 'public authority' which is 'incompatible with a Convention right' (s 6) and granting the victim a remedy in damages against such an authority (s 8). Secondly, it has a horizontal effect in introducing into English law some new rights, for example privacy, which were not available at common law. It may be that if these rights are invaded by a private body or individual there will be no action for damages as such (*Wainwright v Home Office* (2003)). However equity, whose jurisdiction is wider and encompasses all established legal rights, might well be prepared to grant one its remedies to the victim of an invasion. It should perhaps be added that, strictly speaking, an action for damages under the 1998 Act is not a claim in the law of tort (*R (Greenfield) v Home Secretary* (2005), § 19).

7.3.3.8 Inducing a breach of contract (economic torts)

Intentionally causing damage in the world of business is, as we have seen, a particularly difficult area for the law of tort since commercial competition is regarded as healthy and justified. This attitude was even extended to trade unions. If, in encouraging its members to go on strike, a union official committed no civil or criminal wrong, then such an official could not be liable in tort (*Allen v Flood* (1898)). However it had been established earlier in the 19th century that if one person induced another to break his or her contract with a third party the third party would have an action in tort against the person who induced the breach (*Lumley v Gye* (1853)). In the later 20th century this tort was seemingly extended to include any interference (rather than actual breach) by one person with a contract between two others and thus the scope of the tort of inducing a breach of contract is now more uncertain (*Torquay Hotel v Cousins* (1969); cf *OBG Ltd v Allan* (2005)).

In addition to this particular tort, the courts have developed others, such as civil conspiracy, that are both separate yet analogous; and one tort, in particular, that is of importance with respect to intention to injure is the tort of intimidation. 'So long as the defendant only threatens to do what he has a legal right to do he is on safe ground', said Lord Reid. Provided that 'there is no conspiracy he would not be liable to anyone for doing the act, whatever his motive might be, and it would be absurd to make him liable for threatening to do it but not for doing it.' However Lord Reid then asserted 'that there is a chasm between doing what you have a legal right to do and doing what you have no legal right to do, and there seems to me to be the same chasm between threatening to do what you have a legal right to do and threatening to do what you have no legal right to do' (*Rookes v Barnard* (1964), 1168–1169).

7.3.3.9 Malicious falsehood

Malicious falsehood is a separate tort from defamation (see 7.3.3.5, above), although the two may overlap, in that it protects a person's business interest rather than reputation interest (*Joyce v Sengupta* (1993)). It is available where one person maliciously publishes a falsehood about another's trade or business. The claimant does not have to prove loss if the damage to the business was intentional and the publication is in a permanent form (Defamation Act 1952 s 3). More recently the tort has been used in circumstances where one person has deliberately set out to blacken another's name and, although damages may be modest (because the damage must be to a person's business interest rather than reputation), it can be useful to a claimant who wishes to clear his or her name (*Khodaparast v Shad* (2000)).

7.3.310 Malicious prosecution

In *Martin v Watson* (1996), 80) Lord Keith quoting *Clerk & Lindsell on Torts* said this (at 80):

> "In an action of malicious prosecution the plaintiff must show first that he was prosecuted by the defendant, that is to say, that the law was set in motion against him on a criminal charge; secondly, that the prosecution was determined in his favour; thirdly, that it was without reasonable and probable cause; fourthly, that it was malicious."

Further, he said, the 'onus of proving every one of these is on the plaintiff'.

One might note here that malicious intention is not enough; the prosecution itself must be unreasonable. However although the tort is, in practice, one that is used mainly against the police, and is thus an aspect of what a civil lawyer would call administrative liability, it can also be brought against private individuals if such an individual is the person who 'set the law in motion' (Lord Keith).

7.3.3.11 Passing off

Where a defendant interferes with another's intangible property by passing off his goods as those of another, this will also amount to a tort. According to Lord Diplock, five characteristics which must be present:

in order to create a valid cause of action for passing off: (1) misrepresentation, (2) made by a trader in the course of his trade, (3) to prospective customers of his or ultimate consumers of the goods and services supplied by him, (4) which is calculated to injure the business or goodwill of another trader (in the sense that this is a reasonably foreseeable consequence) and (5) which causes actual damage to a business or goodwill of the trader. (*Erven Warnink BV v J Townend & Sons* (1979), 742)

From the defendant's position it is a kind of *deceit* practised on the public while from the claimant's position it is an invasion of a particular *commercial interest* bordering on a property right. It is, accordingly, a tort that can be put alongside malicious falsehood and the economic torts in as much as it is an action founded mainly on intentional wrongdoing which invades another's business or professional interests.

7.3.3.12 Private nuisance

Where one neighbour carries out an activity on his land with the sole purpose of intentionally annoying his neighbour this may amount to the tort of private nuisance if the behaviour is regarded as an unreasonable use of land. Private nuisance is available where a defendant has unreasonably 'used his own land or some other land in such a way as injuriously to affect the enjoyment of the plaintiffs' land' (Denning LJ in *Esso v Southport Corporation* (1954), 196 CA). Intention to injure is important here because this of itself can turn a reasonable activity into an unreasonable one. Thus where one land owner set off shotguns on his land deliberately to cause injury to his neighbour's silver foxes this amounted to a nuisance (*Hollywood Silver Fox Farm v Emmett* (1936)).

7.3.3.13 Public nuisance

Public nuisance, although it may on some occasions arise out of the same facts as private nuisance, is conceptually a quite distinct tort from private nuisance. It arises out of the crime of public nuisance and generates a claim in tort for any person who suffers special damage, a term which includes pure economic loss. Public nuisance is difficult to define—it 'covers a multitude of sins, great and small' (Denning LJ in *Esso*, 196)—but can be summed up as 'any nuisance. . . which materially affects the reasonable comfort and convenience of life of a class of Her Majesty's subjects' (Romer LJ in *Att-Gen v PYA Quarrries* (1957), 184). Any person who intentionally intends to cause annoyance or harm through behaviour that injuriously affects a section of the public at large (for example a demonstration on the highway) risks being sued for damages in public nuisance from any individual who suffers damage over and above the rest of the community. One might also note that indulging in criminal or unsocial activity, such as running a brothel, could well result in an action for an injunction based on public nuisance brought by an irate neighbour (*Thompson-Schwab v Costaki* (1956)), although no doubt many victims will now seek an Anti-Social Behaviour Order (Crime and Disorder Act 1998, s 1).

7.3.3.14 Trespass

The tort of trespass comes in several forms depending upon the type of invasion. Direct violence to the person is assault and battery, while the unlawful restraint of a person is false imprisonment. Invasion of a person's possession of land or a chattel amounts to trespass to land or to goods. The main requirement is that the defendant directly invades the defendant's person or property without lawful authority.

In theory the mere intentional touching of another is a battery, and thus if D pushes C into a swimming pool and C is badly injured as a result, D will be liable in trespass. But merely bumping into someone in a school playground, supermarket or busy street, even if it causes injury, might be different because there is an implied consent to this type of behaviour ('we live in a crowded world') (*Wilson v Pringle* (1987)).

In false imprisonment, the defendant must be directly responsible for the imprisonment (*Harnett v Bond* (1925)) and there must be no means of escape (*Bird v Jones* (1845)). But technically speaking the claimant does not necessarily have to be aware of the imprisonment (*Murray v Ministry of Defence* (1988)).

Consent is a defence to trespass and this can be implied in for example cases of necessity (*In re F* (1990)) or where various persons indulge in sport or even in horseplay (*Blake v Galloway* (2004))."

NOTES

1. The list set out in the above extract is not complete because it is dealing only with torts in respect of intentionally caused damage. Accordingly several (many?) other causes of action must be added (on which see B. Rudden, "Torticles" above, p.7). Some of these are set out in the following notes:

2. *Animals*. Damage caused by animals is now governed by statute: see **5.5**. Much depends on the animal in question and thus the Animals Act 1971 sets out different conditions of liability depending on the type of animal and the nature of the damage. The main categories are: (a) damage done by animals which belong to a dangerous species; (b) damage done by animals which belong to a non-dangerous species; (c) damage done by dogs to livestock; (d) damage done by trespassing cattle. One French professor once described this Act as an exercise in animal character studies. See generally *Mirvahedy v Henley* (2003) (pp.38, 199, 203).

3. *Breach of contract*. The failure to perform a contractual promise will give rise to liability in damages if the failure (breach) causes damage to the other party. In other words

breach of contract is a cause of action in itself. The interesting question is whether a breach of contract is, in itself, also a tort (cf. *Hedley Byrne v Heller & Partners*, below p.134).

4. *Breach of statutory duty*. Liability for a breach of statutory duty can arise in situations where an individual suffers damage as a result of an act or omission of another which amounts to a breach of a statute (cf. **1.4.2**). However not all breaches of statute will give rise to tort claims as Lord Browne-Wilkinson explains in *X (Minors) v Bedfordshire CC* (1995) (below p.178). The tort is of major importance with regard to accidents at work and (along with negligence) is one of the foundations of employers' liability.

5. *Negligence*. By far the most important head of liability in the whole of the law of tort is negligence which became an independent cause of action in 1932 with the decision in *Donoghue v Stevenson* (1932) (below p.131). There are normally three elements of liability: (a) duty of care; (b) breach of duty; and (c) causation (see Lord Scott in *Barker v Corus UK Ltd* (2006) at § 51). A considerable part of the rest of this book will be concerned with this tort.

6. *Privacy and confidential information*. Reference should also be made to privacy since this is a right specifically protected by the European Convention (article 8). Now privacy is *not* recognised as a cause of action in itself; there is, in other words, no tort of privacy (see **2.4.2**). However it is protected *indirectly* by torts such as defamation, trespass and sometimes conversion. In addition Equity has been prepared to use its remedies to protect confidential information; but whether misuse of confidential is actually a cause of action in tort, as opposed to the breach of an equitable duty, is still unclear: see *Douglas v Hello! Ltd (No 3)* (2007) (p.69).

7. *Rylands v Fletcher*. The case of *Rylands v Fletcher* (1866–68) (below p.243) established an independent cause of action with respect to damage done by a dangerous thing brought onto land and which escapes and does damage. See **6.4.1** and in particular the decision in *Transco v Stockport MBC* (2004) (below p.246) where the present status of this tort has been reviewed by the House of Lords.

8. *Statutory torts*. In addition to the various torts existing at common law, the legislator can create new causes of action such as the action for damages for misrepresentation (Misrepresentation Act 1967 s.2(1)). The breach of intellectual property rights has also been described as a statutory tort (Lord Walker in *Revenue & Customs v Total Network* (2008), § 99). However, the statutory action for damages in the Human Rights Act 1998 is not an action in tort.

9. *Vicarious liability*. Strictly speaking vicarious liability is not in itself a cause of action. However it is a central form of liability in tort law and can be summed up by the rule itself. An employer will be liable for torts by his employee committed during the course of his employment. See generally **7.2**.

2 Purpose and policy of tort

A major definitional perspective of the law of tort is, as we have seen, from the position of its function. The category having been established as an historical fact, one can ask what are its aims or what is its purpose. In truth this may involve a number of different viewpoints within functionalism depending upon differences of method, philosophy and (or) policy.

2.1 Aims and philosophy of the law of tort

Yet defining tort from the position of its purpose and function is by no means easy. The subject's fragmentary basis in a wide range of old forms (now causes) of action is at the heart of the problem since this fragmentation is equally reflected in its functions (cf. **1.7**). Moreover the lack of any formal distinction between public and private law—between administrative and civil liability—means that tort ends up playing an important administrative and constitutional law role (cf. **Chapter 9**). This constitutional role has become increasingly acute, and in some ways more complex, with the incorporation of the European Convention for the Protection of Human Rights and Fundamental Freedoms into English Law (Human Rights Act 1998). The absence of any strict divisions, at the level of remedies at any rate, between property and obligations, and between personal and patrimonial rights, results in yet further roles for tort. It ends up as the category providing remedies for the 'vindication' of property rights and of personal rights such as privacy (to the extent that it actually protects this interest). This said, it must be remembered that statistically the great majority of tort claims are for personal injury arising out of accidents on the road or in the factory. Personal injury thus dominates the purpose and policy dimension. All these differing aims and functions have created, as the next extract suggests, an atmosphere of 'crisis'.

André Tunc, 'Introduction', Torts, *International Encyclopedia of Comparative Law*, **Volume XI, Chapter 1 (footnotes omitted)**

"1. . . . The law of tort . . . is in a state of crisis. It may have reached its zenith; at the very moment where it occupies a position without precedent, it is impregnated and surrounded by institutions which deeply modify its traditional working and put into question its functions and its domain. Inherited from a time when there was neither social security nor insurance, it is now threatened by the rise of these institutions of loss distribution. Furthermore, it has been designed to govern individuals and it now mainly applies to private and public enterprises. The notions according to which western societies have lived for centuries are no longer true: it is no longer true that we are liable for the harm we have done by a tort, since it is likely that we will be either employed or insured; by reason of social security it is no longer true that no-one can recover for the damage he suffers as a consequence of his own fault. In certain respects man is more responsible than ever; his power to cause harm (as is his power to help his fellow men) is multiplied by increased industrialization and by the general development of technology. In other respects, as a result of the emergence of social security and insurance, his responsibility disappears.

Clearly, the law of tort needs a deep reconsideration. . . ."

QUESTION

These words were written well over thirty years ago. Why is it that the law of tort seems, to date, not to have been subject to any serious reconsideration?

NOTE

In a famous article published half a century ago professor Glanville Williams identified a number of differing aims of the law of tort ((1951) 4 CLP 137; and see also Glanville Williams & Hepple, *Foundations of the Law of Tort*, 2nd edn (London: Butterworths, 1984), pp.27–30). The most important of these aims are: (i) compensation; (ii) deterrence; and (iii) protecting constitutional rights. Other aims include (iv) protecting expectation interests, (v) preventing unjust enrichment and (vi) determining status. Behind these aims is, as the next extract suggests, the philosophy of justice, the major dichotomy being that between distributive and corrective justice.

McFarlane v Tayside Health Board [2000] 2 A.C. 59, HL

This was an action for damages by a husband and wife to recover the cost of bringing up a healthy and normal child born to the wife. The couple alleged they followed negligent advice on the effect of a vasectomy performed on the husband. The House of Lords (Lords Slynn, Steyn and Hope; Lords Millett and Clyde dissenting in part) rejected the claim.

Lord Steyn: "My Lords, A surgeon wrongly and negligently advised a husband and wife that a vasectomy had rendered the husband infertile. Acting on his advice they ceased to take contraceptive precautions. The wife became pregnant and gave birth to a healthy child. The question is what damages, if any, the parents are in principle entitled to recover. . . .

It is possible to view the case simply from the perspective of corrective justice. It requires somebody who has harmed another without justification to indemnify the other. On this approach the parents' claim for the cost of bringing up Catherine must succeed. But one may also approach the case from the vantage point of distributive justice. It requires a focus on the just distribution of burdens and losses among members of a society. If the matter is approached in this way, it may become relevant to ask commuters on the Underground the following question: Should the parents of an unwanted but healthy child be able to sue the doctor or hospital for compensation equivalent to the cost of bringing up the child for the years of his or her minority, i.e. until about 18 years? My Lords, I am firmly of the view that an overwhelming number of ordinary men and women would answer the question with an emphatic 'No.' And the reason for such a response would be an inarticulate premise as to what is morally acceptable and what is not. Like Ognall J in *Jones v Berkshire Area Health Authority* (unreported) 2 July 1986 they will have in mind that many couples cannot have children and others have the sorrow and burden of looking after a disabled child. The realisation that compensation for financial loss in respect of the upbringing of a child would necessarily have to discriminate between rich and poor would surely appear unseemly to them. It would also worry them that parents may be put in a position of arguing in court that the unwanted child, which they accepted and care for, is more trouble than it is worth. Instinctively, the traveller on the Underground would consider that the law of tort has no business to provide legal remedies consequent up upon the birth of a healthy child, which all of us regard as a valuable and good thing.

My Lords, to explain decisions denying a remedy for the cost of bringing up an unwanted child by saying that there is no loss, no foreseeable loss, no causative link or no ground reasonable restitution is to resort to unrealistic and formalistic propositions which mask the real reasons for the decisions. And judges ought to strive to give the real reasons for their decision. It is my firm conviction that where courts of law have denied a remedy for the cost of bringing up an unwanted child the real reasons have been grounds of distributive justice. That is, of course, a moral theory. It may be objected that the House must act like a court of law and not like a court of morals. That would only be partly right. The court must apply positive law. But judges' sense of the moral answer to a question, or the justice of the case, has been one of the great shaping forces of the common law. What may count in a situation of difficulty and uncertainty is not the subjective view of the judge but what he reasonably believes that the ordinary citizen would regard as right. . . .

In my view it is legitimate in the present case to take into account considerations of distributive justice. That does not mean that I would decide the case on grounds of public policy. On the contrary, I would avoid those quick sands. Relying on principles of distributive justice I am persuaded that our tort law does not permit parents of a healthy unwanted child to claim the costs of bringing up the child from a health authority or a doctor. If it were necessary to do so, I would say that the claim does not satisfy the requirement of being fair, just and reasonable.

This conclusion is reinforced by an argument of coherence. . . ."

QUESTIONS

1. How does Lord Steyn in *McFarlane* know what people on the underground might think? Is this a helpful or useful way of deciding cases?

2. Lord Steyn in *McFarlane* denies that he is deciding the case on ground of public policy. Do you agree? (cf. C&MC, pp.103–104.)

3. What do you consider to be the most powerful motivating reason behind the decision in *McFarlane*: (i) the 'no business' thesis of the traveller on the underground; (ii) distributive justice theory; (iii) the discomfort felt by the judges that the NHS should be paying out to families with healthy children; (iv) practical justice? Would you classify (iii) as a policy argument?

4. The judgment of Lord Steyn in *McFarlane* has been deliberately cut off after his opening paragraph statement about coherence. What do you imagine this coherence argument to be about?

NOTES

1. See now *Rees v Darlington Memorial Hospital NHS Trust* (p.423).

2. Another form of justice, namely 'practical justice', has also been identified by the English judiciary.

***Attorney-General v Blake* [2001] 1 A.C. 268, HL**

> **Lord Steyn**: ". . . I bear in mind that the enduring strength of the common law is that it has been developed on a case-by-case basis by judges for whom the attainment of practical justice was a major objective of their work. It is still one of the major moulding forces of judicial decision-making. These observations are almost banal: the public would be astonished if it was thought that judges did not conceive it as their prime duty to do practical justice whenever possible. A recent example of this process at work is *White v Jones* [1995] 2 AC 207 where by a majority the House of Lords held that a solicitor who caused loss to a third party by negligence in the preparation of a will is liable in damages. Subordinating conceptual difficulties to the needs of practical justice a majority, and notably Lord Goff of Chieveley, at pp.259G-260H, upheld the claim. . . ."

QUESTION

How does 'practical justice' differ from other forms of justice? Do the public have a well-developed notion of practical justice? If they do, do you think this accords with the judicial view of practical justice?

NOTE

In addition to the doctrinal work on the purpose, policy and aims of the law of tort, there is a huge body of literature, especially American, devoted to the theory and philosophy behind tort liability (see e.g. Owen, *Philosophical Foundations of Tort Law*, (Oxford OUP, 1995). Indeed, there is enough to fill a whole course on the subject. Some theories are based directly on particular notions of justice; thus an emphasis on individual *corrective justice* usually focuses on the balance between individuals in society and the moral imperative behind the obligation to pay damages. Theories of *distributive justice* often emphasise the statistical cost (human and economic) of certain activities and the unrealistic nature of moral imperatives in a legal structure where most defendants are insured and accidents statistics are predictable. These theories motivate the debate between fault and no-fault liability. In the USA the law and economics school has been particularly active in the area of tort law (see **2.3**), but old ideas about individual responsibility and freedom to act are by no means dead as the next extracts indicate.

***Read v J Lyons & Co Ltd* [1947] A.C. 156, HL**

(For facts see p.209)

> **Lord Macmillan**: ". . . In my opinion the appellant's statement of claim discloses no ground of action against the respondents. The action is one of damages for personal injuries. Whatever may have been the law of England in early times I am of opinion that as the law now stands an allegation of negligence is in general essential to the relevancy of an action of reparation for personal injuries. The gradual development of the law in the matter of civil liability is discussed and traced by the late Sir William Holdsworth with ample learning and lucidity in his *History of English Law*, vol 8, pp.446 et seq, and need not here be rehearsed.

Suffice it to say that the process of evolution has been from the principle that every man acts at his peril and is liable for all the consequences of his acts to the principle that a man's freedom of action is subject only to the obligation not to infringe any duty of care which he owes to others. The emphasis formerly was on the injury sustained and the question was whether the case fell within one of the accepted classes of common law actions; the emphasis now is on the conduct of the person whose act has occasioned the injury and the question is whether it can be characterized as negligent. I do not overlook the fact that there is at least one instance in the present law in which the primitive rule survives, namely, in the case of animals ferae naturae or animals mansuetae naturae which have shown dangerous proclivities. The owner or keeper of such an animal has an absolute duty to confine or control it so that it shall not do injury to others and no proof of care on his part will absolve him from responsibility. But this is probably not so much a vestigial relic of otherwise discarded doctrine as a special rule of practical good sense. At any rate, it is too well established to be challenged. But such an exceptional case as this affords no justification for its extension by analogy. . . ."

Lord Simonds: ". . . Here is an age-long conflict of theories which is to be found in every system of law. 'A man acts at his peril,' says one theory. 'A man is not liable unless he is to blame,' answers the other. It will not surprise the students of English law or of anything English to find that between these theories a middle way, a compromise, has been found. . . ."

NOTE

Given the discursive nature of common law judgments, the policy, aims and philosophy questions remain important in the understanding of the case law itself. Different judgments can reveal differing theoretical perspectives. However the judges themselves do tend to agree on one thing; that English tort law has committed itself to no single theory.

Broome v Cassell & Co Ltd [1972] A.C. 1027, HL

Lord Wilberforce (dissenting): ". . . English law does not work in an analytical fashion;. . . That is why the terminology used is empirical and not scientific. And there is more than merely practical justification for this attitude. For particularly over the range of torts for which punitive damages may be given (trespass to person or property, false imprisonment and defamation being the commonest) there is much to be said before one can safely assert that the true or basic principle of the law of damages in tort is compensation, or, if it is, what the compensation is for (if one says that a plaintiff is given compensation because he has been injured, one is really denying the word its true meaning) or, if there is compensation, whether there is not in all cases, or at least in some, of which defamation may be an example, also a delictual element which contemplates some penalty for the defendant. It cannot lightly be taken for granted, even as a matter of theory, that the purpose of the law of tort is compensation, still less that it ought to be, an issue of large social import, or that there is something inappropriate or illogical or anomalous (a question-begging word) in including a punitive element in civil damages, or, conversely, that the criminal law, rather than the civil law, is in these cases the better instrument for conveying social disapproval, or for redressing a wrong to the social fabric, or that damages in any case can be broken down into the two separate elements. As a matter of practice English law has not committed itself to any of these theories: it may have been wiser than it knew. . . .

. . . Take a common case: a man is assaulted, or his land is trespassed upon, with accompanying circumstances of insolence or contumely. He decides to bring an action for damages, he need not further specify the claim. Is he suing for compensation, for injury to his feelings, to teach his opponent a lesson, to vindicate his rights, or 'the strength of the law,' or for a mixture of these things? Most men would not ask themselves such questions, many men could not answer them. If they could answer them, they might give different answers. The reaction to a libel may be anything from 'how outrageous' to 'he has delivered himself into my hands.' The fact is that the plaintiff sues for damages, inviting the court to take all the facts into consideration, and, if he wins, he may ascribe his victory to all or any of the ingredients. . . ."

QUESTION

Is Lord Wilberforce not in truth committing himself to a theory?

2.2 Compensation and loss spreading

One broad way of defining tort in terms of its purpose and policies is through the remedies associated with this category (cf. **Chapter 11**). By far the most important of these is damages; only the equitable remedy of injunction has any other real claim and this remedy is more or less limited to certain specific torts (*Miller v Jackson* (1977), p.15). However the deterrence effect of forcing a defendant to pay damages is now in question.

Reid v Rush & Tompkins Plc [1990] 1 W.L.R. 212, CA

This was an action for damages by an employee against his employer. The facts are well-summarised by Ralph Gibson L.J.: "The plaintiff on 26 January 1984 suffered severe injuries while driving the defendant's Landrover vehicle on a road in Ethiopia in the course of his employment by the defendant as a quarry foreman on the Armati Diversion Project. His injuries were caused by a collision between the Landrover and a lorry which was being driven along the road in the opposite direction by some person whose identity is not known. The defendant was in no way responsible for the happening of the accident of which the sole cause was the negligence of the lorry driver. The plaintiff has alleged that the defendant was in breach of its duty of care as employer in failing either to insure the plaintiff so as to provide suitable benefits to him in the event of his being injured, as a result of the negligence of a third party, in such a traffic accident or to advise the plaintiff to obtain such insurance cover for himself. His case is that if he had been so advised he would have obtained personal accident cover". The Court of Appeal (Ralph Gibson L.J., May L.J. and Neill L.J.) held the employer not liable.

Ralph Gibson L.J.: ". . . The defendant, apart from submitting that the law leaves to employees the responsibility for deciding whether they need personal accident insurance, has not contended that the special risk is not sufficiently special or unusual to provide an arguable case for the plaintiff if he can surmount the legal barriers which, on the defendant's submissions, justify striking out his claim. The defendant recognises, rightly in my view, that assessment of the nature and extent of the risk, for the purposes of the plaintiff's case, must be made, if the case is to proceed, when the evidence is before the court. It was for that reason that detailed submissions were not made by either side as to the extent of the risk in this country of suffering injury which may go uncompensated. Nevertheless, before considering the points of law raised in the submissions before the court, it is useful to describe, and to put into context, the special risk upon which the plaintiff's case depends.

It is, of course, not the case under the law of this country that in respect of all injuries, caused by the fault of another, a claimant will be able actually to recover the compensation which the law would award in respect of his injuries. The person responsible may have no money. For some 50 years the law has dealt with one of the most common causes of serious injury by the requirement of compulsory third party insurance in respect of the use on the public roads of a motor vehicle. Effective cover, in the event of the driver in breach of the law having no insurance cover, was provided by means of the Motor Insurers' Bureau agreement in 1946, and was extended to the case of the untraced driver in 1969. A description of the terms and of the wording of the MIB agreements can be found in *Charlesworth & Percy on Negligence*, 7th ed (1983), c 17, pp.1036–1042. Effective cover, however, is by no means complete even for traffic accidents: a pedestrian or a cyclist may be solely to blame for an accident in which a driver or other persons are seriously hurt and there is no compulsory insurance or scheme like that of the MIB to cover such accidents. Further the MIB is not liable where the accident occurred in some place which was not a public road: see *Buchanan v Motor Insurers' Bureau* [1955] 1 WLR 488.

As to accidents which a servant may suffer in the course of his employment as a result of the fault of the master, or of a fellow servant, actual recovery of the compensation to which the servant was in law entitled was for many years not certain because the master might have no money and no insurance to cover his liability. Compulsory insurance against liability to employees was required by the Employers' Liability (Compulsory Insurance) Act 1969—which came into force on 1 January 1972—but the requirement applies only to 'liability for bodily injury or disease sustained by his employees, and arising out of and in the course of their employment in Great Britain': see section 1(1). Insurance for liability for 'injury or disease suffered or contracted outside Great Britain' is only compulsory when required by regulations. According to the note to the Act of 1969 in *Halsbury's Statutes of England and Wales*, 4th ed., vol 16 (1986), p.181, the Act of 1969 has been applied to employers of persons working on or from off-shore installations in designated areas of the continental shelf and territorial waters by the Offshore Installation (Application of the Employers' Liability (Compulsory Insurance) Act 1969) Regulations 1975 (S.I. 1975 No. 1289) made under the Mineral Workings (Off-Shore Installations) Act 1971. Failure to insure as required by the Act of 1969 is a criminal offence: see section 5. There is, however, no scheme equivalent to that of the MIB to ensure recovery of compensation by a servant in respect of injury suffered in this country if, in breach of law, the employer has failed to take out insurance cover.

Next, it is to be noted that the insurance required by the Act of 1969 applies only to liability to employees. Liability to members of the public is, I think, usually covered by a public liability policy in the case of responsible employers whose activities expose members of the public to risk of injury but the law imposes no statutory duty to have such insurance cover and serious injury might be suffered without compensation by a servant in the course of his employment as a result of the wrongdoing of a third party not concerned with the use of a motor vehicle on a public road.

Another common form of injury for which the victim cannot normally recover substantial compensation from the wrongdoer is criminal injury. The Criminal Injuries Compensation Scheme, which came into operation in 1964, enabled the Criminal Injuries Compensation Board to make ex gratia payments in respect of personal injury directly attributable to a crime of violence, to an arrest of an offender, to the prevention of an offence, or to the giving of help to a constable engaged on making an arrest or preventing an offence. Details of the current scheme as revised in 1979 are now contained in the 21st Report of the Board (Cmnd. 9684). Two matters must be noted: first, the scheme applies only to injuries suffered in this country or upon a British ship or aircraft and not to criminal injuries suffered abroad, and, secondly, the scheme provides no compensation for property or economic loss caused by crime save for such loss resulting from a criminal injury within the scheme.

From this limited survey it can be seen that in a number of cases it is possible for someone to suffer personal injury in this country, caused by the wrongdoing of another, for which the victim may well not recover the compensation which the law would award. Further, in respect of injury suffered or disease contracted outside this country by a person normally resident here, or employed abroad by an employer based in this country, there is in general no protection of compulsory employers' insurance and, in respect of the special claims of injury arising from road accidents or criminal activity, there is no protection from any body such as the MIB or the Criminal Injuries Compensation Board. . . ."

NOTES

1. Viewed from the position of damages one can talk of the law of tort as being concerned with compensation, but several qualifications must be made here. First, to talk in terms of compensation is to view tort from the position of the claimant; tort can, and must, equally be viewed from the position of the defendant. From this position tort can be seen in terms of freedom of action; or, put another way, tort equally aims to promote initiative and risk-taking, important to the economic welfare of society (cf. Compensation Act 2006 s.1, below p.140). Thus one might add that tort can equally be viewed from the perspective of society and from this perspective a number of conflicting aims come into play.

2. Secondly, the rise of insurance has impacted on tort (and contract) in a number of ways. It goes far in undermining the deterrence aim in as much as the wrongdoer is not the one who must shoulder the burden of the damages. Yet it also provides a means of loss spreading. See **2.6**.

3. Thirdly, an award of damages in tort is not the only means of securing help and compensation for harm. Private insurance, social security, criminal injuries compensation, family support, charity and of course the National Health Service (NHS) are other support systems. Tort needs to be considered in relation to these other systems and not just because this contextual perspective is an accepted part of any tort course. These other systems are also of importance because they can directly influence the actual reasoning and decisions of the judges (see e.g. *Wadey v Surrey CC* (2000), p.440).

4. Fourthly, damages as a remedy has a variety of aims and functions not all of which are compensatory (see **Chapter 11**). These differing functions are directly reflected back into

the causes of action that give rise to the remedy and thus compensation has to be distinguished, for example, from restitution and from deterrence (cf. Proceeds of Crime Act 2002). In other words damages as a common law monetary remedy needs to be distinguished from other monetary claims such as an action for debt, an action for account or a claim for damages in equity. Indeed, some claims for 'damages' are in substance really 'debt' (see e.g. *The Stonedale (No 1)* (1956); *Yorkshire Electricity Board v British Telecom* (1986)) or account actions (see e.g. *Att-Gen v Blake* (2001)) and as a result they belong in substantive categories different from tort (for further information on debt claims see C&MC, pp.514–519).

QUESTION

Do the courts always fully appreciate these differing aims and functions of the law of tort?

Lister v Romford Ice & Cold Storage Co Ltd [1957] A.C. 555, HL

This was an action in damages and (or) debt by an insurance company, subrogated to the rights of an assured employer, against an employee who had, while driving a lorry, negligently injured a fellow-employee. The fellow-employee had obtained damages, paid by the insurance company, on the basis that the employer was vicariously liable for the fault of its lorry driving employee. The insurance company based their claims on breach of an implied term of the employee's contract of employment (damages) and (or) on statutory rights of contribution and indemnity (debt). A majority of the House of Lords (Viscount Simonds, Lord Morton and Lord Tucker; Lords Radcliffe and Somerville dissenting) gave judgment for the insurance company.

Viscount Simonds: ". . . [referring to Denning LJ's dissenting judgment in the Court of Appeal] . . . [H]e says: 'This shows that there is an implied term in these cases whereby, if the employer is insured, he will not seek to recover contribution or indemnity from the servant.'

It will be observed that the implied term which thus commended itself to the learned Lord Justice is limited in its scope. The driver is to be relieved from liability if his master is covered by insurance against the claim. If he is not covered, for instance, because the accident takes place not on a road but on private premises and the law does not require him to insure against such a risk, and he has not done so, then under this plea the driver must bear the consequences of his negligence if he is himself sued. This consideration led counsel to yet another variation of the plea. This was that the driver was entitled to be indemnified not only if the employer was in fact insured or was required by law to be insured, but also if he ought, as a reasonable and prudent man, to have been insured against the risk in question . . .

My Lords, undoubtedly there are formidable obstacles in the path of the appellant . . . First, it is urged that it must be irrelevant to the right of the master to sue his servant for breach of duty that the master is insured against its consequences. As a general proposition it has not, I think, been questioned for nearly 200 years that in determining the rights *inter se* of A and B the fact that one or other of them is insured is to be disregarded . . . And this general proposition no doubt, applies if A is a master and B his man. But its application to a case or class of case must yield to an express or implied term to the contrary, and, as the question is whether that term should be implied, I am not constrained by an assertion of the general proposition to deny the possible exception. Yet I cannot wholly ignore a principle so widely applicable as that a man insures at his own expense for his own benefit and does not thereby suffer any derogation of his rights against another man . . .

Here, it was said, was a duty alleged to arise out of the relation of master and servant in this special sphere of employment which was imposed by the common law. When, then, did it first arise? Not, surely, when the first country squire exchanged his carriage and horses for a motor car or the first haulage contractor bought a motor lorry. Was it when the practice of insurers against third-party risk became so common that it was to be expected of the reasonable man or was it only when the Act of 1930 made compulsory and therefore universal what had previously been reasonable and usual? . . ."

Lord Radcliffe (dissenting): ". . . Now, the insurance policy required [by the Road Traffic Act 1930] could not come into existence of its own motion. One of the two parties, employer and employed, had to assume responsibility for taking it out or keeping it running and for paying up the necessary premiums to buy the cover. To which of them ought we to attribute that responsibility, having regard to the relationship of the parties? In my view, to the employer. I cannot suppose that, short of special stipulation, any other answer would be given in such a case . . .

Then it is sought to show that the term in question cannot exist in law because it has never been heard of before this case. When did it first enter into the relations of employer and employed? Could it really have existed since the Road Traffic Act, 1930, if it did not exist before it? My Lords, I do not know because I do not think that I need to know. After all we need not speak of the master's action against his servant for negligence as if it had been common fare at the law for centuries. Economic reasons alone would have made the action a rarity. If such actions are now to be the usual practice I think it neither too soon nor too late to examine afresh some of their implications in a society which has been almost revolutionised by the growth of all forms of insurance . . ."

Lord Somerville (dissenting): ". . . Romer LJ [in the Court of Appeal], at the end of his judgment said that it was not in the public interest that drivers should be immune from the financial consequences of their negligence. The public interest has for long tolerated owners being so immune, and it would, I think, be unreasonable if it was to discriminate against those who earned their living by driving. Both are subject to the sanction of the criminal law as to careless or dangerous driving. The driver has a further sanction in that accidents causing damage are likely to hinder his advancement . . ."

QUESTIONS

1. The real claimant in this case was the insurance company. Do you think it right that they should be able to escape from a risk that they had been paid to take?

2. Is the remedy of subrogation based on principles of tort, contract, equity or restitution (unjust enrichment)? Do you think adequate consideration was given to this question in *Lister*? (cf. *Morris v Ford Motor Co* (1973)).

3. "Commentators and judges should think twice before making off-hand comments that insurance should be relevant to the scope of tort liability, that judges should take into account 'the realities of insurance' or that they should address the comparative insurability of parties" (*Stapleton* (1995) 58 M.L.R. pp.820, 843). Why should they think twice?

4. "There is no doubt that insurance profoundly influences the practical operation of the law of tort" (Lewis (2005) 25 L.S. 85, 86). How? (cf. **2.6.**)

NOTE

Another point that must be stressed is that *damages* and *damage* are not the same (see e.g. *Adams v Bracknell Forest BC* (2004)). Not all damage will attract compensation (damages) and thus a second descriptive concept, that of an *interest*, needs to be brought into the model. As the next case illustrates, tort can be seen as a matter of protected and unprotected interests.

Spartan Steel & Alloys Ltd v Martin & Co (Contractors) Ltd **[1973] 1 Q.B. 27, CA**

(For facts and further extract see p.159)

Lord Denning MR: ". . . The second consideration is the nature of the hazard, namely, the cutting of the supply of electricity. This is a hazard which we all run. It may be due to a short circuit, to a flash of lightning, to a tree falling on the wires, to an accidental cutting of the cable, or even to the negligence of someone or other. And when it does happen, it affects a multitude of persons; not as a rule by way of physical damage to them or their property, but by putting them to inconvenience, and sometimes to economic loss. The supply is usually restored in a few hours, so the economic loss is not very large. Such a hazard is regarded by most people as a thing they must put up with—without seeking compensation from anyone. Some there are who install a stand-by system. Others seek refuge by taking out an insurance policy against breakdown in the supply. But most people are content to take the risk on themselves. When the supply is cut off, they do not go running round to their solicitor. They do not try to find out whether it was anyone's fault. They just put up with it. They try to make up the economic loss by doing more work next day. This is a healthy attitude which the law should encourage. . ."

2.3 Deterrence

The deterrence aspect of the law of tort manifests it in two main ways. First, there is the direct deterrence effect of imposing damages as a sanction; paying for the harm one causes through bad behaviour is supposed to deter such behaviour. The problem here is that most tort claims arise out of accidents on the road or in the workplace and both these sources attract compulsory insurance. There is, however, a second and subtler manifestation of the deterrence theory. The law and economics school uses the notion of economic efficiency both as a criterion for analysing case law decisions and as a normative principle for determining the outcome of tort litigation.

2.3.1 **Damages as deterrence**

Fault, damages and deterrence come together in the following extract.

Lister v Romford Ice & Cold Storage Co Ltd **[1957] A.C. 555, HL**

(See p.63)

Viscount Simonds: ". . . It was contended, too, that a term should not be implied by law of which the social consequences would be harmful. The common law demands that the servant should exercise his proper skill and care in the performance of his duty: the graver the consequences of any dereliction, the more important it is that the sanction which the law imposes should be maintained. That sanction is that he should be liable in damages to his master: Other sanctions there may be, dismissal perhaps and loss of character and difficulty of getting fresh employment, but an action for damages, whether for tort or for breach of contract, has, even if rarely used, for centuries been available to the master, and now to grant the servant immunity from such an action would tend to create a feeling of irresponsibility in a class of persons from whom, perhaps more than any other, constant vigilance is owed to the community . . ."

QUESTIONS

1. Does an employee undertake never to make a mistake in the performance of his duties? Ought employees to take out insurance against injuring their master or their master's insurance company?
2. Should car drivers be made personally liable for any tort damages they have to pay to victims of their bad driving? What would be the disadvantages, from aims of the law of tort perspective, of such a rule?
3. A company deliberately commits a tort hoping that the profit it will make from the tortious act will be much greater than any damages it will have to pay to the tort victim. Should the victim be able to sue the tortfeasor in damages only for the amount of his loss?

Broome v Cassell & Co **[1972] A.C. 1027, HL**

This was an appeal by publishers of a book (written by David Irving), known by them to be libellous before publication, against an award of punitive (exemplary) damages made by the jury. A majority of the House of Lords (Lords Hailsham L.C., Reid, Morris and Kilbrandon; Viscount Dilhorne and Lords Wilberforce and Diplock dissenting) upheld the award.

Lord Reid: ". . . It was argued that to allow punitive damages in this case would hamper other publishers or limit their freedom to conduct their business because it can always be inferred that publishers publish any book because they expect to profit from it. But punitive damages could not be given unless it was proved that they knew that passages in the book were libellous and could not be justified or at least deliberately shut their eyes to the truth. I would hope that no publisher would publish in such circumstances. There is no question of curtailing the freedom of a reputable publisher."

Lord Kilbrandon: ". . . If a publisher knows, or has reason to believe, that the act of publication will subject him to compensatory damages, it must be that, since he is actuated by the profit-motive, he is confident that by that publication he will not be the loser. Some deterrent, over and above compensatory damages, may in these circumstances be called for."

Lord Diplock (dissenting): ". . . The award of damages as the remedy for all civil wrongs was in England the creature of the common law. It is a field of law in which there has been but little intervention by Parliament. It is judge-made law par excellence. Its original purpose in cases of trespass was to discourage private revenge in a primitive society inadequately policed, at least as much as it was to compensate the victim for the material harm occasioned to him. . . .

No one would today suggest this as a justification for rewarding the victim of a tort for refraining from unlawful vengeance on the wrong-doer. Conversely, the punishment of wrong-doers today is regarded as the function of the state to be exercised subject to safeguards for the accused assured to him by the procedure of the criminal law and with the appropriate punishment assessed by a dispassionate judge and not by a jury roused to indignation by partisan advocacy. One of the most significant and humane developments in English law over the past century and a half has been the increasing protection accorded to the accused under our system of criminal justice. As my noble and learned friend, Lord Reid has pointed out no similar protection is available to a defendant as a party to a civil action. So the survival into the latter half of the twentieth century of the power of a jury in a civil trial to impose a penalty on a defendant simply to punish him had become an anomaly which it lay within the power of this House in its judicial capacity to restrict or to remove; though it would have been anticipating by two years the recent change in the practice of this House if to have done so would have involved overruling one of its own previous decisions."

NOTE

See **Chapter 11**.

QUESTIONS

1. Should the victim have any remedy additional to, or in the place of, a remedy in damages? (cf. *Att-Gen v Blake* (2001); C&MC, p.552.)

2. Does the fear of having to pay high damages deter publication of certain newspaper stories? If so, is this deterrence a legitimate function of tort? (cf. Monbiot, *The Guardian*, July 15, 2008, at p.27.)

2.3.2 Economic efficiency and deterrence

A subtler version of the deterrence theory is to be found in the work of the law and economics school.

Michael A Jones, *Textbook on Torts*, 8th edn (Oxford: OUP, 2002), pp.20–21

"Economic efficiency as an objective of tort is a variant of deterrence. It has been argued, for example, that to the extent that an activity imposes costs on others for which it does not have to pay, the activity is being subsidised and its price does not reflect its true cost. This distorts the market mechanism, because the activity is underpriced, and this leads to inefficiency. The solution is to require activities to 'internalise' these external costs by imposing strict liability for the damage caused by the specific risks created by a particular activity. This increases the price, thereby reducing the level of the activity and hence the amount of damage associated with it. The object is not to eliminate all damage but to achieve an efficient amount, taking into account the costs of prevention. In other words, tort should aim to minimise the sum of accident costs and the costs of preventing accidents. . . .

This theory is known as general deterrence because it seeks to influence behaviour through the pricing of activities, rather than deterring individuals from specific acts. Other theories rely on the deterrent effect of liability rules on individuals. For example, it has been suggested that the tort of negligence leads to efficient results because the standard of reasonable care encourages people to take only those precautions that are justified on the ground of cost, whereas strict liability might lead people to devote more resources to damage prevention than is warranted by the risk. . . .

Ultimately, all economic theorising about tort rests on assumptions about the deterrent effect of liability rules, which have not been empirically tested. . . ."

NOTE

The influence of the economics can now be detected in the reasoning of some judges.

Wildtree Hotels Ltd v Harrow LBC **[2001] 2 A.C. 1, HL**

Lord Hoffmann: ". . . The construction of the railways, which gave rise to most of the 19th century cases on injurious affection, involved massive changes in the urban and rural landscape of the United Kingdom and the disruption of the lives and businesses of very large numbers of people. It is not surprising that strong views were held about the respective claims of the winners and losers in this revolution and the judicial decisions often reveal the opinions of individual judges on questions of economic and social policy. Some were in favour of full compensation for all whose property had been adversely affected by the railway and others thought that the public interest required that liability should be kept within narrow bounds. . . .

In modern economic terms, Bramwell B thought that the railways should not create externalities; that is, costs involuntarily borne by other people which were not taken into account in assessing the profitability of the enterprise. The contrary view is exemplified by Erle CJ in *Ricket v Metropolitan Railway Co* (1865) 5 B & S 149, 163, 169. . . Judges who took this view tended to rely upon a floodgates argument: unless the right to compensation was rigidly confined, everyone whose economic interests had been damaged by the construction of the railways would be entitled to compensation. Post houses and coaching inns were favourite examples.

My Lords, I mention these ancient controversies not only because they still have some resonance today but also because they are an aid to the understanding of the old cases to which your Lordships were referred in the course of the argument. The 19th century authorities on this subject do not display a steady development of the law but the shifting ascendancies of one view or the other. . . ."

NOTES

1. See also Lord Hoffmann's judgments in *Stovin v Wise* (p.175) and *Transco Plc v Stockport MBC* (2004) (p.88).

2. One conceptual focal point between economics and law is the notion of an 'interest'. It is the key concept in economic science because it allows everything, even morality, to become a matter of economic calculation. Only the behaviour of individuals and not their intentions is of importance. Everything becomes a matter of loss and gain. One can understand the

attraction of this key concept for the law of damages since interest can act—and indeed has acted since Roman times (see D.9.2.23.4)—as the bridge between damage and damages. Damages are awarded only to compensate for invasions of recognised interests. If there is no legal interest there is no damage(s) (for a Roman example of an interest that was too speculative see D.9.2.29.3). Equally if one can turn an economic interest into a legal interest, the easier it becomes to demand compensation for its invasion. This interest aspect of tort law will be investigated further in various parts of this book.

3. An economic analysis is valuable, also, because it seemingly provides an empirical justification for an existing legal rule and (or) solution to a case. This is particularly evident in *Stovin v Wise* (1996) (p.175) where Lord Hoffmann uses the 'externalities' argument to justify the non-liability for a mere omission in the tort of negligence. What must not be forgotten, however, is that economic science is not like physics or zoology. It is not a knowledge discipline capable of validation, in part at least, by reference to external realities. There is a large ideological dimension to economic science. For example, is society to be viewed as a mass of interests attaching to individuals or should one be thinking more in terms of group interests? The point to be made, therefore, is that economic science is similar to law in as much as it is in many ways a normative discipline: it is less about providing a theory that explains and predicts and more about what those in positions of political and commercial power *ought* to do. Viewed in this light, justifying one normative rule (mere omissions as in *Stovin*) with another normative rule (externalities) begins to look like a bootstraps argument.

4. For an economic analysis of contract law see C&MC, pp.78–81.

QUESTIONS

1. The basic methodological paradigm underpinning law is authority. One arrives at decisions based on the authority of a statute or a precedent. Is an appeal to economics simply an attempt to provide lawyers with an alternative authority? Why should economists be more authoritative than philosophers or bishops or, indeed, jurists?

2. Imagine that the case of *Miller v Jackson* (1977) (see p.15) had come before a Court of Appeal consisting entirely of judges devoted to the law and economics school of legal analysis. Do you think the reasoning and the result would be very different from the actual reasoning and result in the case?

3. Should privacy be protected by the law of tort only if it can be shown that privacy is an interest capable of having an economic value? If it can be shown to have such a value, would it then become a property interest to be protected like any other item of value? Or is privacy some kind of special interest?

Douglas v Hello! Ltd (No 3) **[2007] 2 W.L.R. 920, HL**

This was an action for damages by the publisher of one magazine against another. The facts are summarized by Lord Hoffmann (below) and the causes of action relied by the claimant were breach of confidence and unlawful interference with contractual obligations. A majority of House of Lords (Lord Hoffmann, Baroness Hale and Lord Brown; Lords Nicholls and Walker dissenting) held that the defendant publishers were liable for breach of confidence but were not liable for the tort of unlawful interference. (Note that this appeal was heard and decided at the same time as *OBG Ltd v Allan*, p.103.)

Lord Hoffmann: ". . . b) In *Douglas v Hello! Ltd (No 3)* [2006] QB 125 the magazine "OK!" contracted for the exclusive right to publish photographs of a celebrity wedding at which all other photography would be forbidden. The rival magazine 'Hello!' published photographs which it knew to have been surreptitiously taken by an unauthorised photographer pretending to be a waiter or guest. 'OK!' says that this was interference by unlawful means with its contractual or business relations or a breach of its equitable right to confidentiality in photographic images of the wedding. . . .

124 Is there any reason of public policy why the law of confidence should not protect information of this form and subject matter? There is in my opinion no question of creating an 'image right' or any other unorthodox form of intellectual property. The information in this case was capable of being protected, not because it concerned the Douglases' image any more than because it concerned their private life, but simply because it was information of commercial value over which the Douglases had sufficient control to enable them to impose an obligation of confidence. Some may view with distaste a world in which information about the events of a wedding, which Warren and Brandeis in their famous article on privacy "The Right to Privacy" (1890) 4 Harvard LR 193 regarded as a paradigm private occasion, should be sold in the market in the same way as information about how to make a better mousetrap. But being a celebrity or publishing a celebrity magazine are lawful trades and I see no reason why they should be outlawed from such protection as the law of confidence may offer. . . ."

Lord Nicholls (dissenting): ". . . **255** As the law has developed breach of confidence, or misuse of confidential information, now covers two distinct causes of action, protecting two different interests: privacy, and secret ("confidential") information. It is important to keep these two distinct. In some instances information may qualify for protection both on grounds of privacy and confidentiality. In other instances information may be in the public domain, and not qualify for protection as confidential, and yet qualify for protection on the grounds of privacy. Privacy can be invaded by further publication of information or photographs already disclosed to the public. Conversely, and obviously, a trade secret may be protected as confidential information even though no question of personal privacy is involved. This distinction was recognised by the Law Commission in its report on Breach of Confidence (1981) (Cmnd 8388), pp.5–6. . . ."

Baroness Hale: ". . . **307** Commercial confidentiality is a different matter. It is moving forward rather than drawing back. The law took a big leap forward with the *Spycatcher* case (*Attorney General v Guardian Newspapers Ltd (No 2)* [1990] 1 AC 109). It was, incidentally, a leap which would have been impossible had the Law Commission's Report on Breach of Confidence (1981) (Law Com No 110) (Cmnd 8558) been implemented by statute. Rather as *Lumley v Gye* had expanded liability for breach of contract beyond the contract breaker to the person who persuaded him to break his contract, *Spycatcher* expanded liability for failing to keep a secret beyond the person to whom it had originally been confided to the person who knowingly took advantage of the secret. There are some secrets which the law will not protect. They may be so trivial or useless that the law should not concern itself with them. There may be a public interest in disclosure greater than the private interest in secrecy. But we have not been given any principled reason why photographic images of this wedding should not be protected. They were undoubtedly a secret unless and until 'OK!' chose to publish the images authorised by the Douglases. 'Hello!' did its best to break what it knew was a secret. There may not have been an entirely identical case before but it is consistent with existing principles to apply them to this case, as the judge did. I confess to having some difficulty in understanding what this has to do with the law of intellectual property. Parliament has devised ways in which an author, inventor or creator can continue to profit from his creativity long after the product has passed into the public domain. Although in both cases the subject matter can be called information, one set of remedies is about rewarding its creator, the other about keeping it quiet. Parliament has intervened in the former but not the latter. . . ."

Lord Brown: ". . . 325 . . . Having paid £1m for an exclusive right it seems to me that 'OK!' ought to be in a position to protect that right and to look to the law for redress were a third party intentionally to destroy it. Like Lord Hoffmann, I would uphold 'OK!'s' claim, as Lindsay J did at first instance, on the ground of breach of confidence. . . ."

QUESTIONS

1. Is this case really a property rather than an obligations problem?

2. In the French *Code civil* both privacy and dignity are located in the law of persons (non patrimonial rights) rather than the law of things (patrimonial rights) (see **2.4.2**). Does *Douglas v Hello!* turn privacy into a patrimonial (commercial) right? What about dignity: ought this to be something a person can sell?

2.4 Protecting rights

The concept of a 'right' fulfils several functions. First and foremost it is a way of viewing law from the position of the individual subject rather than from an objective system of rules. Often a 'right' is seen as the correlative of 'duty' and when the two are put together each individual is said to have both rights (claims to things or on other people) and duties (obligations to others). Secondly, the word 'right' is used as a means of expressing a strict form of liability; here the term is closely associated with the idea of ownership and so when a claimant asserts that he has a right he is asserting a claim against a thing. 'That is mine please return it'. It should be noted here that behaviour is irrelevant to ownership: a claimant in a proprietary action need assert, in principle, only that the defendant has interfered with his title (see *Moorgate Mercantile v Twitchings* (1977)). In the law of tort there are several causes of action which have this proprietary flavour—trespass, conversion and defamation being good examples—and this is the reason why these torts can be seen as protecting rights as much as remedying wrongs. Thirdly, the term 'right' has acquired a constitutional flavour. In many ways this public law aspect is simply the appropriation of the property relationship between person and thing (ownership) by constitutional lawyers to give expression to the relationship between the individual and the state. Yet it is an effective appropriation in as much as the Latin for ownership is *dominium* and this reflects the political and social power inherent in the term. To say that citizens have rights against the state is a way of counterbalancing the idea that all law (and thus all rights) flow from the state. The Human Rights Act 1998 goes some way, therefore, in recognising the individual as a source of law, as a source of rights.

2.4.1 **Property rights**

In French law ownership is famously defined in the *Code civil* as 'the right to enjoy and to dispose of things in the most absolute manner, provided that one does not use them in a way prohibited by statute or regulations' (art.544). In English law (and Roman law) it is nowhere defined; and, indeed, it is arguable that English law needs neither a definition nor ownership itself since what is protected is the best right to *possession*. Thus tort and contract (see Sale of Goods Act 1979 s.16) may talk about interference with ownership (or 'property') but in terms of remedies tort looks to the immediate right to possess. Nevertheless, as the next extracts indicate, tort remedies do seem to give indirect expression to ownership.

Bradford Corporation v Pickles **[1895] A.C. 587, HL**

This was an action for an injunction brought by a local authority against a landowner who, so it was alleged, was deliberately interfering with the natural supply of water to the corporation's waterworks by digging holes on his land. The landowner, it seemed, was trying to bring pressure on the corporation to purchase his land. The House of Lords (Lords Halsbury L.C., Ashbourne, Macnaghten and Watson) gave judgment for the landowner.

> **Lord Halsbury L.C.:** ". . . The acts done, or sought to be done, by the defendant were all done upon his own land, and the interference whatever it is, with the flow of water is an interference with water, which is underground and not shown to be water flowing in any defined stream, but is percolating water, which, but for such interference, would undoubtedly reach the plaintiff's works, and in that sense does deprive them of the water which they would otherwise get. But although it does deprive them of water which they would otherwise get, it is necessary for the plaintiffs to establish that they have a right to the flow of water, and that the defendant has no right to do what he is doing . . .
>
> The very question was . . . determined by this House, [in *Chasemore v Richards*], and it was held that the landowner had a right to do what he had done whatever his object or purpose might be, and although the purpose might be wholly unconnected with the enjoyment of his own estate . . .
>
> The only remaining point is the question of fact alleged by the plaintiffs, that the acts done by the defendant are done, not with any view which deals with the use of his own land or the percolating water through it, but is done, in the language of the pleader, 'maliciously' . . .
>
> This is not a case in which the state of mind of the person doing the act can affect the right to do it. If it was a lawful act, however ill the motive might be, he had a right to do it. If it was an unlawful act, however good his motive might be, he would have no right to do it . . ."
>
> **Lord Macnaghten:** ". . . But the real answer to the claim of the corporation is that in such a case motives are immaterial. It is the act, not the motive for the act, that must be regarded. If the act, apart from motive, gives rise merely to damage without legal injury, the motive, however reprehensible it may be, will not supply that element . . ."

NOTE

This great case is the subject of a whole book: M Taggart, *Private Property and Abuse of Rights in Victorian England* (London: OUP, 2002). The case is important from a rights point of view for several reasons. First, because it indicates how rights can trump 'obligations' or 'wrongful' (in the social sense) behaviour. The House of Lords was not applauding the behaviour of the defendant; it is just that his behaviour did not amount to a legal wrong (*injuria*) and it did not amount to such a wrong because he had the 'right' to do it (see also *Moorgate Mercantile v Twitchings* (1977)). Secondly, the case is interesting from a comparative law viewpoint. Had these facts arisen in France, the landowner would probably have been held legally liable for his behaviour; this liability would result, not from a failure by the law to recognise that a landowner had rights, but because the land owner was *abusing* his rights. Abuse of rights is, in other words, a tort in civil law thinking (see Taggart, *Private Property and Abuse of Rights*, pp.145–166). Thirdly, the case is important because it establishes that merely to intend certain types of damage is not enough to give rise to liability. This of course can be described as a refusal to recognise a doctrine of abuse of rights, but it is in some ways more subtle as the next extracts indicate.

Bernard Rudden, 'The Battle of Manywells Spring', *London Review of Books*, **June 19, 2003, p.24**

"In a perfect world of rational economic actors a problem of [the *Bradford v Pickles*] kind would be solved by agreement. Transaction costs are low, since there are only two players and they are neighbours. If the water rights are valued more by Bradford than they are by Pickles, the town will buy him out. If less, it will not. But in either case the normal process of bargaining should ensure that the resource ends up with one who values it most. In this way litigation is avoided, but even if it takes place, the end of a lawsuit can restart negotiation. If the court forbids Pickles to cut off the water, he can still buy the right to do so if he values it at more than the town does. If, on the other hand, the town loses the lawsuit, it can always offer more money. And even if this fails, the town can apply for an Act authorising compulsory purchase at a price fixed, if necessary, by a jury. Thus the overall system provides for three possible stages of decentralised dispute settlement, all of which require the public utility to pay monetary compensation for its intrusion into others' private property rights. Unless, of course, the others are so saintly as to cede them for nothing.

In all-too-human West Yorkshire nothing like this happened. . . ."

QUESTIONS

1. Do you think that *Bradford* is a much cited case?

2. Do you think that *Bradford* is a much criticised case?

3. How would an adherent to the law and economics school have decided *Bradford*?

PROBLEM

Nick deliberately lets his garden get overgrown to annoy his neighbour Camilla and to block out some of the light to Camilla's kitchen. Can Camilla sue Nick for damages? What if Nick deliberately grew troublesome weeds to annoy Camilla? (cf. *Hollywood Silver Fox Farm v Emmett* (1936), below p.93.)

NOTE

Bradford involved land. The next case concerns moveable property.

RH Willis & Son v British Car Auctions Ltd [1978] 1 W.L.R. 438, CA

This was an action for damages in the tort of conversion by a finance company against a firm of car auctioneers. The auctioneers had sold a car for a client not knowing that the client had no right to sell the vehicle because the car was on hire purchase from the claimant finance company. The auctioneers had taken reasonable steps to check the client's statement that he was owner of the car, but the Court of Appeal (Lord Denning M.R., Roskill L.J. and Brown L.J.) nevertheless held the auctioneers liable.

Lord Denning M.R.: ". . . The question that arises is the usual one: which of the two innocent persons is to suffer? Is the loss to fall on the owners? They have been deprived of the £275 due to them on the car. Or on the auctioneers? They sold it believing that Mr. Croucher was the true owner. In answering that question in cases such as this, the common law has always acted on the maxim nemo dat quod non habet. It has protected the property rights of the true owner. It has enforced them strictly as against anyone who deals with the goods inconsistently with the dominion of the true owner. Even though the true owner may have been very negligent and the defendant may have acted in complete innocence, nevertheless the common law held him liable in conversion. Both the 'innocent acquirer' and the 'innocent handler' have been hit hard. That state of the law has often been criticised. It has been proposed that the law should protect a person who buys goods or handles them in good faith without notice of any adverse title, at any rate where the claimant by his own negligence or otherwise has largely contributed to the outcome. Such proposals have however been effectively blocked by the decisions of the House of Lords in the last century of *Hollins v Fowler* (1875) LR 7 HL 757, and in this century of *Moorgate Mercantile Co Ltd v Twitchings* [1977] AC 890, to which I may add the decision of this court in *Central Newbury Car Auctions Ltd v Unity Finance Ltd* [1957] 1 QB 371.

In some instances the strictness of the law has been mitigated by statute, as for instance, by the protection given to private purchasers by the Hire-Purchase Acts. But in other cases the only way in which the innocent acquirers or handlers have been able to protect themselves is by insurance. They insure themselves against their potential liability. This is the usual method nowadays. When men of business or professional men find themselves hit by the law with new and increasing liabilities, they take steps to insure themselves, so that the loss may not fall on one alone, but be spread among many. It is a factor of which we must take account: see *Post Office v Norwich Union Fire Insurance Society Ltd* [1967] 2 QB 363, 375 and *Morris v Ford Motor Co Ltd* [1973] 1 QB 792, 801.

Sales under the hammer

The position of auctioneers is typical. It is now, I think, well established that if an auctioneer sells goods by knocking down with his hammer at an auction and thereafter delivers them to the purchaser—then although he is only an agent—then if the vendor has no title to the goods, both the auctioneer and the purchaser are liable in conversion to the true owner, no matter how innocent the auctioneer may have been in handling the goods or the purchaser in acquiring. . . This state of the law has been considered by the Law Reform Committee in its 12th Report, Transfer of Title to Chattels (1966), Cmnd. 2958, as to innocent acquirers (see paragraph 39 as to 'Liability of Auctioneers'); and in its 18th Report (Conversion and Detinue) (1971), Cmnd. 4774 as to innocent handlers: paragraphs 46–50. But Parliament has made no change in it: no doubt it would have done so in the Torts (Interference with Goods) Act 1977 if it had thought fit to do so. . . ."

QUESTIONS

1. Why should it be the auctioneers and not the owner of the car (particularly a finance company) who are charged with the burden of insuring against fraud? (cf. *Shogun Finance v Hudson* (2003); C&MC, p.265.)

2. Who profits from hire purchase? Who is in the best position to guard against fraud? Are these points taken account of in *Willis*?

3. What if the owner had carelessly failed to register with an information service (Hire Purchase Information) that this particular car was on hire purchase and that the claimant was the owner? (cf. *Moorgate Mercantile v Twitchins* (1977).)

4. The torts of trespass to goods and conversion protect movable property rights. What amounts to 'property' for this purpose? Does conversion apply only to tangible property or can it be used to claim damages for the interference with an intangible property right? Can one, for example, convert a contractual right?

OBG Ltd v Allan [2007] 2 W.L.R. 920, HL

This was an action for damages brought "by a company in liquidation for damages in respect of losses sustained by the company through acts done by administrative receivers whose appointment was later held to be invalid" and the "causes of action relied upon [were] conversion and wrongful interference with contractual relations" (Lord Nicholls). A majority of the House of Lords (Lords Hoffmann, Walker and Brown; Lord Nicholls and Baroness Hale dissenting) held that no tort had been committed by the defendants. See also p.103.

Lord Nicholls (dissenting): ". . . 224 The cause of action, formerly known as trover but now known as conversion, was founded on a fiction. The standardised plea was that the plaintiff possessed certain goods, that he casually lost them, that the defendant found them, and that the defendant did not return them but instead 'converted them to his own use'. The defendant was not permitted to deny the losing and finding, and so the only issues were the plaintiff's right to possession and the conversion itself. In due course this became the standard remedy for the unauthorised assumption of the powers of the true owner. Any chattel could be lost and found, and so it could be converted. Originally the rule was that intangibles could not be converted.

225 With the expansion of commerce and the increase in dealings with intangible property this rule, described by Professor Prosser as a 'hoary limitation', had to be relaxed. The law provided, in respect of the misappropriation of intangibles, no remedy equivalent to that provided by conversion for the misappropriation of tangibles. So the courts resorted to another legal fiction. They held that in appropriate cases a document embodying or recording a debt or obligation should be treated as having the same value as the debt or obligation.

226 As would be expected, the reach of this useful tool gradually expanded. Now it is not confined to documents of title and negotiable instruments. It includes insurance policies, guarantees, share certificates and much else. In Clerk & Lindsell the principle is said to extend to 'any document which is specially prepared in the ordinary course of business as evidence of a debt or obligation': *Clerk & Lindsell on Torts*, 19th ed (2006), para 17–35.

227 In the past some unconvincing efforts were made to justify this extension as a particular application of the ordinary principles of damages. Now it is openly recognised that this extension involves a legal fiction: see, for instance, Pill and Potter LJJ in *Smith v Lloyds TSB Group plc* [2001] QB 541, 551, 557, and Mance LJ in the present case [2005] QB 762, 784, para 76.

228 Legal fictions, of their nature, conceal what is going on. They are a pretence. They represent an unacknowledged departure from existing principle. By resorting to the fiction of equating the value of a document as a chattel or piece of paper with the value of the rights embodied or recorded on it the courts concealed the reality. The reality is that English law does sometimes provide a remedy for the misappropriation, or conversion, of intangible rights. To that extent the tort of conversion has already jumped the gap between tangibles and intangibles. It did so a long time ago. . . .

Baroness Hale (dissenting): . . . **311** The facts of the OBG case make the point more clearly than I could ever do. The defendants took control over all the company's assets. They entered the company's premises and changed the locks. They took charge of all its plant and machinery and other chattels. They had no right to do so. No one disputes that they are strictly liable in trespass to land and conversion no matter how bona fide their belief that they were entitled to do this. They also took charge of the company's business and closed it down. The judge found that the company was doomed, so that there was no goodwill to be attached to disposing of it as a going concern. But among the company's assets were the debts and other contractual liabilities it was owed. The judge found that the defendants obtained less for these assets than would have been obtained in an orderly winding up. This is not improbable. The receivers' obligations and priorities were different from those of the company, its other creditors and shareholders. They might well result in lower realisations than the company might have achieved for itself. Accepting, as we must, the judge's findings on this, it makes no sense that the defendants should be strictly liable for what was lost on the tangible assets but not for what was lost on the intangibles. . . ."

NOTE

Baroness Hale's section of judgment devoted to conversion (paras 308–311) is well worth reading in the law report.

2.4.2 Personality rights

Personality rights in civil law thinking are different from patrimonial (property and obligation) rights in that the former belong to the law of persons and the latter to the law of things. This distinction, which goes back to Roman legal classification, is to be found in the modern codes. Thus, for example, invasions of privacy and dignity are rights located not in the 'tort' section of the *Code civil* (Book 3 Title IV) but in the section on Persons (Book I). Personality rights are, accordingly, distinguished from obligation rights simply by their location in the institutional system. English law has no imposed structure and thus has no easy means of distinguishing between different kinds of right; all claims for invasion of non-contractual rights tend to end up as 'tort' or property problems as the next case indicates.

Wainwright v Home Office **[2004] 2 A.C. 406, HL**

(For facts see p.29)

Lord Hoffmann: ". . . **18** The need in the United States to break down the concept of 'invasion of privacy' into a number of loosely-linked torts must cast doubt upon the value of any high-level generalisation which can perform a useful function in enabling one to deduce the rule to be applied in a concrete case. English law has so far been unwilling, perhaps unable, to formulate any such high-level principle. There are a number of common law and statutory remedies of which it may be said that one at least of the underlying values they protect is a right of privacy. Sir Brian Neill's well known article 'Privacy: a challenge for the next century' in *Protecting Privacy* (ed B Markesinis, 1999) contains a survey. Common law torts include trespass, nuisance, defamation and malicious falsehood; there is the equitable action for breach of confidence and statutory remedies under the Protection from Harassment Act 1997 and the Data Protection Act 1998. There are also extra-legal remedies under Codes of Practice applicable to broadcasters and newspapers. But there are gaps; cases in which the courts have considered that an invasion of privacy deserves a remedy which the existing law does not offer. Sometimes the perceived gap can be filled by judicious development of an existing principle. The law of breach of confidence has in recent years undergone such a process: see in particular the judgment of Lord Phillips of Worth Matravers MR in *Campbell v MGN Ltd* [2003] QB 633. On the other hand, an attempt to create a tort of telephone harassment by a radical change in the basis of the action for private nuisance in *Khorasandjian v Bush* [1993] QB 727 was held by the House of Lords in *Hunter v Canary Wharf Ltd* [1997] AC 655 to be a step too far. The gap was filled by the 1997 Act.

19 What the courts have so far refused to do is to formulate a general principle of 'invasion of privacy' (I use the quotation marks to signify doubt about what in such a context the expression would mean) from which the conditions of liability in the particular case can be deduced. The reasons were discussed by Sir Robert Megarry V-C in *Malone v Metropolitan Police Comr* [1979] Ch 344, 372–381. . . .

31 There seems to me a great difference between identifying privacy as a value which underlies the existence of a rule of law (and may point the direction in which the law should develop) and privacy as a principle of law in itself. The English common law is familiar with the notion of underlying values-principles only in the broadest sense-which direct its development. A famous example is *Derbyshire County Council v Times Newspapers Ltd* [1993] AC 534, in which freedom of speech was the underlying value which supported the decision to lay down the specific rule that a local authority could not sue for libel. But no one has suggested that freedom of speech is in itself a legal principle which is capable of sufficient definition to enable one to deduce specific rules to be applied in concrete cases. That is not the way the common law works.

32 Nor is there anything in the jurisprudence of the European Court of Human Rights which suggests that the adoption of some high level principle of privacy is necessary to comply with article 8 of the Convention. The European Court is concerned only with whether English law provides an adequate remedy in a specific case in which it considers that there has been an invasion of privacy contrary to article 8(1) and not justifiable under article 8(2). . . .

41 Commentators and counsel have nevertheless been unwilling to allow *Wilkinson v Downton* to disappear beneath the surface of the law of negligence. Although, in cases of actual psychiatric injury, there is no point in arguing about whether the injury was in some sense intentional if negligence will do just as well, it has been suggested (as the claimants submit in this case) that damages for distress falling short of psychiatric injury can be recovered if there was an intention to cause it. This submission was squarely put to the Court of Appeal in *Wong v Parkside Health NHS Trust* [2003] 3 All ER 932 and rejected. Hale LJ said that before the passing of the Protection from Harassment Act 1997 there was no tort of intentional harassment which gave a remedy for anything less than physical or psychiatric injury. That leaves *Wilkinson v Downton* with no leading role in the modern law. . . .

44 I do not resile from the proposition that the policy considerations which limit the heads of recoverable damage in negligence do not apply equally to torts of intention. If someone actually intends to cause harm by a wrongful act and does so, there is ordinarily no reason why he should not have to pay compensation. But I think that if you adopt such a principle, you have to be very careful about what you mean by intend. In *Wilkinson v Downton* Wright J wanted to water down the concept of intention as much as possible. He clearly thought, as the Court of Appeal did afterwards in *Janvier v Sweeney* [1919] 2 KB 316, that the plaintiff should succeed whether the conduct of the defendant was intentional or negligent. But the *Victorian Railway Comrs* case 13 App Cas 222 prevented him from saying so. So he devised a concept of imputed intention which sailed as close to negligence as he felt he could go.

46 Even on the basis of a genuine intention to cause distress, I would wish, as in *Hunter's* case [1997] AC 655, to reserve my opinion on whether compensation should be recoverable. In institutions and workplaces all over the country, people constantly do and say things with the intention of causing distress and humiliation to others. This shows lack of consideration and appalling manners but I am not sure that the right way to deal with it is always by litigation. The Protection from Harassment Act 1997 defines harassment in section 1(1) as a 'course of conduct' amounting to harassment and provides by section 7(3) that a course of conduct must involve conduct on at least two occasions. If these requirements are satisfied, the claimant may pursue a civil remedy for damages for anxiety: section 3(2). The requirement of a course of conduct shows that Parliament was conscious that it might not be in the public interest to allow the law to be set in motion for one boorish incident. It may be that any development of the common law should show similar caution.

47 In my opinion, therefore, the claimants can build nothing on *Wilkinson v Downton* [1897] 2 QB 57. It does not provide a remedy for distress which does not amount to recognised psychiatric injury and so far as there may a tort of intention under which such damage is recoverable, the necessary intention was not established. I am also in complete agreement with Buxton LJ [2002] QB 1334, 1355–1356, paras 67–72, that *Wilkinson v Downton* has nothing to do with trespass to the person. . . ."

NOTES

1. Privacy and harassment caused difficulties for several reasons. First, because there existed no specific cause of action for either of these complaints. Facts involving one or the other had to be squeezed into one of the existing torts and if this proved impossible there was obviously a presumption of no liability. Statute has now intervened to modify the law. In the case of privacy, the statute in question is the Human Rights Act 1998 which has incorporated art.8 of the European Convention into UK law. One should note, however,

that it is by no means evident that art.8(2) covers invasion by a non-public authority. So this gives rise to a problem about the so-called 'horizontal effect' of the Convention. Is privacy a right to be protected from any invasion or only from an invasion by 'a public authority'? One way around this problem is to use the remedy of an injunction to develop the law. Equity would always grant an injunction to protect an existing right and so a claimant could now go to court and, instead of trying to fit the complaint into an existing cause of action, simply point to article 8. The right exists as part of English law and equity should protect it. The next step is to award equitable damages in lieu of an injunction (see *Jaggard v Sawyer* (1995); C&MC, p.557). Finally equitable and common law thinking could be merged into a new tort of privacy. As for harassment, this now has its own specific legislation which is no doubt one reason why the judges felt able to resist developing the case-law in this area.

2. A second reason why harassment and privacy caused difficulties is to be found in the nature of the damage. Mental distress is less well protected in English tort law than more obvious forms of personal injury. Thus the woman harassed by cricket balls in *Miller v Jackson* (1977) (see p.15) attracted no sympathy from judges whereas had she suffered the same fate as Miss Stone (see p.140) she would probably have recovered damages (although Miss Stone did not). A third reason for the difficulties arising from harassment and privacy is reflected in the questions posed below.

3. In *Douglas v Hello! Ltd (No 3)* (2007) (see p.69) Lord Walker said at § 272: "This House has quite recently reaffirmed that English law knows no common law tort of invasion of privacy: *Wainwright v Home Office* [2004] 2 A.C. 406. But the law of confidentiality has been, and is being developed in such a way as to protect private information."

QUESTIONS

1. Ought English law to develop a law of persons as a separate category from the law of things? Or, if not separate categories, should English law recognise that personality rights are very different from patrimonial rights?

2. If English law were to develop privacy as a tort would this have serious constitutional implications for a free press? Would it lead to a restriction of the constitutional right of free speech? Why is it that in France few newspapers could, and still cannot, expose the full political and moral corruption of one of its former presidents? Would a privacy law provide a useful source of revenue for politicians who like to cheat on their partners?

3. Do you think that the tort of defamation (see **Chapter 8**) should be seen as protecting personality rights or patrimonial rights?

4. Are personality 'rights' in reality only 'values' in the eyes of the common law? (cf. *Douglas v Hello!* (2007), p.69.)

5. Does *Wainwright* in effect mean that public officials have the right to humiliate members of the public provided they commit no actual trespass? (cf. *Wainwright v UK* (2006), p.29.)

6. Where is the line to be drawn between behaviour designed to humiliate and harassment?

2.4.3 Constitutional rights

Distinguishing personality and constitutional rights is not always easy since there is a considerable overlap. Indeed, human rights are as much a constitutional as a personality question. Some torts such as trespass have, as we saw in *R v Governor of Brockhill Prison, Ex p Evans (No 2)* (2001) (p.28), an old and important constitutional role in as much as they act as a restraint on governmental power. In the area of medical law personality and constitutional rights continue to overlap as the next case illustrates.

In Re F. (Mental Patient: Sterilisation) [1990] 2 A.C. 1, HL

This was an action for a declaration by the mother of a 36–year-old mentally incapable woman that it would be lawful for doctors to sterilise the mentally retarded woman. Evidence was submitted that the woman would be unable to cope with pregnancy and that any other form of contraception would be ineffective or dangerous. The House of Lords (Lords Bridge, Brandon, Griffiths, Goff and Jauncey) upheld the decisions of the lower courts granting the declaration.

Lord Brandon: ". . . At common law a doctor cannot lawfully operate on adult patients of sound mind, or give them any other treatment involving the application of physical force however small ('other treatment'), without their consent. If a doctor were to operate on such patients, or give them other treatment, without their consent, he would commit the actionable tort of trespass to the person. There are, however, cases where adult patients cannot give or refuse their consent to an operation or other treatment. One case is where, as a result of an accident or otherwise, an adult patient is unconscious and an operation or other treatment cannot be safely delayed until he or she recovers consciousness. Another case is where a patient, though adult, cannot by reason of mental disability understand the nature or purpose of an operation or other treatment. The common law would be seriously defective if it failed to provide a solution to the problem created by such inability to consent. In my opinion, however, the common law does not so fail. In my opinion, the solution to the problem which the common law provides is that a doctor can lawfully operate on, or give other treatment to, adult patients who are incapable, for one reason or another, of consenting to his doing so, provided that the operation or other treatment concerned is in the best interests of such patients. The operation or other treatment will be in their best interests if, but only if, it is carried out in order either to save their lives, or to ensure improvement or prevent deterioration in their physical or mental health. . . ."

NOTES

1. Although English law thinks more in terms of liberties rather than rights, the starting point for the tort of trespass to the person (and often trespass to land and to goods) is simple enough. The body is inviolable and thus any *intentional* interference with the person (or his or her things) is prima facie a trespass (see **Chapter 3**). This is an important constitutional principle because it means that no person can in principle be arrested, imprisoned or otherwise molested without legal justification (although they can be humiliated) (*R (G) v Chief Constable of West Yorkshire* (2008), at para.29). If jailers or policemen cannot show justification they can be sued for damages in trespass by their victims (but cf. *Wainwright*, pp.29, 77, 95). In the field of public law most of the justifications used by agents of the state are granted by legislation and this means that many trespass actions end up as statutory interpretation cases (see in particular the Police and Criminal Evidence Act 1984, together with the anti-terrorism legislation). Strict liability has a vital function here; and thus the importance of *Brockhill* (see p.28) is that it indicates clearly that justification and reasonableness are quite different notions.

2. Reasonableness suggests the tort of negligence. What, then, if a person's body (or goods) are negligently invaded by a public authority? In this situation a quite different tort comes into play and it may be that the function of protecting constitutional rights gives way to policy considerations that favour the state over the individual (see e.g. *Hill v Chief Constable of West Yorks* (1989), above p.39 and **Chapter 9**). However it was this very conflict between rights and reasonableness that once made the boundary between trespass and negligence a difficult one (see e.g. *Esso v Southport* (1954), above p.5). And this conflict between rights on the one hand and policy and reasonableness on the other has been brought back into play by the Human Rights Act 1998 (see e.g. *Z v UK* (2001)).

3. In the case of medical treatment, consent is what usually negates any liability in trespass; but Lord Goff in *Re F* indicated how necessity is another important defence (see p.372). Note also the important role in *Re F* of the concept of an 'interest'.

QUESTIONS

1. What or whose interests is sterilisation really protecting?

2. Is it ever in a patient's best interest that he or she be allowed to die? (cf. *Airedale NHS Trust v Bland* (1993).)

2.4.4 **Environmental rights**

Environmental rights present particular conceptual difficulties for many European legal systems both because they concern 'right holders' who may not yet exist (future generation) and because they do not attach to the individual. The rights attach to humans as a class whereas tort law thinking tends to start out from the individual with a particular interest to protect. Nevertheless the law of tort is not completely impotent as the next case indicates.

Attorney-General v PYA Quarries Ltd **[1957] 2 Q.B. 169, CA**

This was a relator action brought by a local authority in the name of the Attorney-General for an injunction to stop a quarry owner from causing a nuisance through its activities. Local residents complained of flying stones, dust and vibration. The owner claimed that its activities did not affect a sufficient number of people to amount to a public nuisance, but the Court of Appeal (Denning L.J., Romer L.J. and Parker L.J.) upheld the injunctions.

Romer L.J.: ". . . I do not propose to attempt a more precise definition of a public nuisance than those which emerge from the textbooks and authorities to which I have referred. It is, however, clear, in my opinion, that any nuisance is 'public' which materially affects the reasonable comfort and convenience of life of a class of Her Majesty's subjects. The sphere of the nuisance may be described generally as 'the neighbourhood'; but the question whether the local community within that sphere comprises a sufficient number of persons to constitute a class of the public is a question of fact in every case. It is not necessary, in my judgment, to prove that every member of the class has been injuriously affected; it is sufficient to show that a representative cross-section of the class has been so affected for an injunction to issue."

Denning L.J.: ". . . I decline to answer the question how many people are necessary to make up Her Majesty's subjects generally. I prefer to look to the reason of the thing and to say that a public nuisance is a nuisance which is so widespread in its range or so indiscriminate in its effect that it would not be reasonable to expect one person to take proceedings on his own responsibility to put a stop to it, but that it should be taken on the responsibility of the community at large.

Take the blocking up of a public highway or the non-repair of it. It may be a footpath very little used except by one or two householders. Nevertheless, the obstruction affects everyone indiscriminately who may wish to walk along it. Take next a landowner who collects pestilential rubbish near a village or permits gypsies with filthy habits to encamp on the edge of a residential neighbourhood. The householders nearest to it suffer the most, but everyone in the neighbourhood suffers too. In such cases the Attorney-General can take proceedings form injunction to restrain the nuisance: and when he does so he acts in defence of the public right, not for any sectional interest: see *Attorney-General v Bastow*. But when the nuisance is so concentrated that only two or three property owners are affected by it, such as the three attornies in Clifford's Inn, then they ought to take proceedings on their own account to stop it and not expect the community to do it for them: see *Rex v Lloyd*, and the precedent in Chitty's *Criminal Law* (1826), vol III, pp 664–665.

Applying this test, I am clearly of opinion that the nuisance by stones, vibration and dust in this case was at the date of the writ so widespread in its range and so indiscriminate in its effect that it was a public nuisance. . . ."

NOTES

1. A local authority can now bring such a claim in its own name: Local Government Act 1972 s.222.

2. See also *Esso Petroleum v Southport Corporation* (1953–56) (p.5); *Wheeler v Saunders* (1996) (p.238); *Marcic v Thames Water* (2004) (p.239); *Cambridge Water v Eastern Counties Leather* (1994) (p.244).

3. There is no doubt that one function of tort is to protect property not just from direct interference (trespass) but also from indirect ones. Where such interference is indirect and it affects a neighbouring landowner or occupier the tort of private nuisance is the main cause of action (see **Chapters 5–6**). If the interference is more widespread, then, as Denning L.J. suggested, the tort of public nuisance might be relevant (see **6.2.1**). Difficulties arise when the environmental interest of a group of individuals comes into conflict with the economic interests of commerce. The question then becomes one of where the public interest is said to lie. Here damage is important: if the interference causes physical damage to person or property it may be easier to sue in tort than when the damage is noise or smell pollution. All the same, offensive sights might amount to 'pollution' (see *Thompson-Schwab v Costaki* (1956)).

QUESTIONS

1. To what extent ought English law to give expression to the principle that it is the polluter who should pay for environmental damage? (cf. *Cambridge Water* (1994), p.244.)

2. Does the law of tort go far enough in providing remedies in respect of mental distress caused by noise pollution? Do individuals have a human right not to suffer such distress? (cf. *Hatton v UK* (2003), p.207.)

3. Can the law of contract be used to protect the mental interest arising in respect of noise pollution? (cf. *Farley v Skinner* (2002); C&MC, p.543.)

4. If the community benefits as a whole from an economic activity (public interest), why should the community not pay for the burden this activity may cause to individuals who suffer from the activity? (cf. *Dennis v MOD* (2003), p.205.)

PROBLEM

One northern city in the UK is often plagued by a ghastly smell emanating from an industrial bone-boiling farm on its perimeter. This undoubtedly amounts to a prima facie 'statutory nuisance' under s.79 of the Environmental Protection Act 1990. Read s.80 of this Act and explain why you think it is that the local authority has not been able to use this statute to eliminate the smell? Advise local residents if they could use the torts of public or private nuisance to obtain an injunction (see generally **6.2**).

2.5 Protecting interests

We have already mentioned in passing that tort can be analysed in terms of interests. Thus the notion of an interest can be seen as a starting point for defining the function of a tort remedy.

Revenue and Customs Commissioners v Total Network SL **[2008] 2 W.L.R. 711, HL**

(For facts and further extracts see p.117)

Lord Hope: ". . . **26** . . . The claim that is made in this case is presented as a claim for damages. . . . The function of an action of damages is to provide a remedy for interests that are recognised by the law as entitled to protection. Obvious examples are protection against injury to the person, to reputation and to privacy. Economic interests are entitled to protection too, such as a person's business or his property. As Hazel Carty, *An Analysis of the Economic Torts* (2001), p.3, puts it, the economic torts are to be seen as protecting against the infliction of economic harm. Tony Weir, *A Casebook on Tort* (10th ed, 2004), p.17, makes the same point. Compensation, he says, is the principal function of tort law. The very concept of compensation entails the notion or harm or damage, since only harm or damage can be compensated. . . ."

NOTE

The various interests have also been helpfully set out by the European Group on Tort Law in its draft code.

European Group on Tort Law, *Principles of European Tort Law* **(2003)**

"**Art. 2:102. Protected interests**

(1) The scope of protection of an interest depends on its nature; the higher its value, the precision of its definition and its obviousness, the more extensive is its protection.

(2) Life, bodily or mental integrity and liberty enjoy the most extensive protection.

(3) Extensive protection is granted to property rights, including those in intangible property.

(4) Protection of pure economic interests or contractual relationships may be more limited in scope. In such cases, due regard must be had especially to the proximity between the actor and the endangered interest, or to the fact that the actor is aware of the fact that he will cause damage even though his interests are necessarily valued lower than those of the victim.

(5) The scope of protection may also be affected by the nature of liability, so that an interest may receive more extensive protection against intentional harm than in other cases.

(6) In determining the scope of protection, the interests of the actor, especially in liberty of action and in exercising his rights, as well as public interests also have to be taken into consideration."

NOTE

These principles are offered as a guide to the cases in this book. They should be continually referred to and readers should reflect upon whether they accurately reflect English tort law.

2.6 Tort and insurance

The existence of insurance impacts upon the law of tort in a number of ways, some of which have already been discussed. However one important question is the extent to which insurance should affect the function of the law of tort.

Richard Lewis, 'Insurance and the Tort System', 2005, *Legal Studies,* **Volume 25, 85, pp.86, 89, 116 (footnotes omitted)**

"There is no doubt that insurance profoundly influences the practical operation of the law of tort. Liability insurance is not merely an ancillary device to protect the insured, but is the 'primary medium for the payment of compensation, and tort law [is] a subsidiary part of the process'. Although the majority of defendants in tort are individual people, they are almost all insured. . . . Insurers determine how the defence is to be conducted and, for example, commonly make admissions without the consent of the insured, and settle cases in spite of the policyholder's objection. . . .

Insurers' influence upon settlements is even more pronounced than it is upon decided cases. For the lawyer asked by his client to advise on the merits of a case it is the realities of the litigation system that are of concern rather than the formal rules of law. Practitioners would agree. . . that the textbook rules of tort are often transformed when they come to be used in the system in three ways: first, they are simplified; secondly, they are made more liberal; and thirdly, they are made more inequitable. . . .

. . . Much more difficult to assess is the potential for insurance to affect the outcome of individual claims. Proving that the facts of cases have been moulded to fit the deeper pocket of insurers cannot be done by resort to the law reports alone, but it remains the suspicion of many a practitioner. Although it is easier to assess the influence of insurance upon the rules of tort, rather than the facts found in individual cases, the picture is by no means clear. . . ."

QUESTIONS

1. Why and how is insurance capable of transforming the textbook rules of tort law?

2. As the above extracted article makes clear (and this useful article should be read in full in the journal), the insurance question is given added importance once one remembers that public law requires that both the main factual sources of personal injury litigation, the road and the workplace, be covered by liability insurance. But what if a driver does not have insurance?

Horton v Sadler [2007] 1 A.C. 307, HL

Lord Bingham: ". . . 6 The growth of motor traffic and the increasing number of accidents to which it gave rise prompted enactment of the Third Parties (Rights Against Insurers) Act 1930 and the Road Traffic Acts of 1930 and 1934, which made third party motor insurance compulsory and facilitated recovery against insurers where judgments were obtained against motorists who were in breach of policy conditions or whose policies were voidable. But this legislation did not address the problem which arose from injuries caused by motorists who could not meet a judgment and were not insured at all. This problem was resolved by what Sir Ralph Gibson in *Silverton v Goodall and Motor Insurers' Bureau* [1997] PIQR P451, 453–454, called 'a novel piece of extra statutory machinery': the formation by insurers writing motor business of the MIB as a company limited by guarantee, of which the insurers were members, to administer a fund provided by them (and ultimately by the general body of insured motorists) to compensate victims of accidents caused by uninsured drivers. The administration of the scheme was governed by a series of agreements between the bureau and successive ministers or Secretaries of State for Transport, the first made in June 1946, the most recent (. . .) on 21 December 1988. This last agreement gives effect to the obligations of the United Kingdom under the Second Council Directive on Motor Insurance (84/5/EEC) of 30 December 1983. . . ."

QUESTION

Should insurance now replace fault as the main criterion of liability?

JA Jolowicz, 'Liability for Accidents', [1968] *Cambridge Law Journal* 50, p.50

"It is submitted that a suitable criterion is to be found in the concept of risk and that a satisfactory body of legal rules could quite rapidly be developed by the courts if in every case they were to pose the question, 'Whose risk was it that this damage might occur?' in place of the present 'Whose fault was it that this damage did occur?' It is essential, however, that the traditional refusal of the courts to consider the factor of insurance be reversed. It is perhaps this refusal of the courts to face up to the facts of contemporary life which has led them to overlook loss distribution as it already exists and to insist on fault as the criterion of liability as if every defendant had to find the damages from his own pocket. . . ."

NOTE

The judges remain to be convinced.

Morgans v Launchbury [1973] A.C. 127, HL

This was an action for damages by passengers injured in a car accident against the owner of the car they were using for their pub-crawl. The owner had lent the car to her husband on condition that he got a friend to drive if he got too drunk. The husband did get too drunk, but the friend he got to drive drove carelessly causing a collision. If the friend was acting as an 'agent' of the owner when the collision occurred the owner's insurance would be liable to the injured passengers for the careless driving. In the Court of Appeal, Lord Denning M.R. had 'sought to extend the liability of a car owner for negligent driving of his car by other persons, because the car owner is the person who has or ought to have a motor insurance policy' (Lord Pearson). However, the House of Lords (Lords Wilberforce, Pearson, Cross and Salmon and Viscount Dilhorne), reversing a majority decision of the Court of Appeal, held the owner not liable on this 'agency' ground.

> **Lord Pearson**: ". . . It seems to me that these innovations [of Lord Denning MR], whether or not they may be desirable, are not suitable to be introduced by judicial decision. They raise difficult questions of policy, as well as involving the introduction of new legal principles rather than extension of some principle already recognised and operating. The questions of policy need consideration by the government and Parliament, using the resources at their command for making wide inquiries and gathering evidence and opinions as to the practical effects of the proposed innovations. Apart from the transitional difficulty of current policies of insurance being rendered insufficient by judicial changes in the law, there is the danger of injustice to owners who for one reason or another are not adequately covered by insurance or perhaps not effectively insured at all (for example, if they have forgotten to renew their policies or have taken out policies which are believed by them to be valid but are in fact invalid, or have taken their policies from an insolvent insurance company). Moreover, lack of insurance cover would in some cases defeat the object of the proposed innovation, because uninsured or insufficiently insured owners would often be unable to pay damages awarded against them in favour of injured plaintiffs. Any extension of car owners' liability ought to be accompanied by an extension of effective insurance cover. How would that be brought about? And how would it be paid for? Would the owner of the car be required to take out a policy for the benefit of any person who may drive the car? Would there be an exception for

some kinds of unlawful driving? A substantial increase in premiums for motor insurance would be likely to result and to have an inflationary effect on costs and prices. It seems to me that, if the proposed innovations are desirable, they should be introduced not by judicial decision but by legislation after suitable investigation and full consideration of the questions of policy involved. . . ."

NOTE

Some academics are equally sceptical about insurance as a criterion of liability.

Peter Cane, *Tort Law and Economic Interests*, 2nd edn (Oxford: Clarendon Press, 1996), pp.427–429 (footnotes omitted)

"The insurability argument purports to be an argument about where the law ought to place the loss; but it is quite inconsistent with notions of personal responsibility and corrective justice which underlie the common law of obligations. To take an extreme case, it is not possible to insure against liability for intentional wrongdoing, but this fact provides no good argument for not imposing liability for such wrongdoing; nor, conversely, does the fact that property can easily be protected from theft by loss insurance provide a good reason for not imposing tort liability on thieves. The real weakness of the insurance argument is that insurance is essentially a group or social phenomenon, whereas the common law of obligations is concerned with individuals. Disputes between individuals do not provide a good medium through which to decide what is the best pattern of insurance in a particular area . . . As Weinrib says, the invocation of insurance in tort disputes undermines the conception of tort law as concerned with the immediate personal interaction of the doer and the sufferer of harm. . . ."

QUESTIONS

1. Are Cane's two extreme cases really relevant in any argument attacking Jolowicz's risk and insurability thesis (see above p.86)?

2. Would it be that difficult to discover the insurability position in the following cases: *Read v J Lyons* (1947) (p.209); *Jolley v Sutton LBC* (2000) (p.403); *The Wagon Mound (No 1)* (1961) (p.400)? What about the following contract (but with a tort aspect) cases: *The Moorcock* (1889); *Shogun Finance v Hudson* (2003)?

NOTES

1. This comment by Cane is valuable in the way that it highlights the structural, more than the functional, difficulty of attempting to marry tort and insurance. The model of private law from Roman to modern times is strictly individualist in its design; it is based on relations between individual persons with individual things (property) and between one individual and another individual (obligations). In short, it sees society as consisting strictly of individuals and society itself is little more than the sum of these parts (cf. environmental rights). Of course this model has been distorted by the recognition that certain groups of individuals, if the group has legal personality, are treated as if it (they) were an individual; a large multinational corporation is just an ordinary person according to the legal institutional model. Thus insurance can impact on this model only in terms of

adding a new relational dimension: the defendant, if held liable, can deflect the burden towards a third party. However this third party can in turn demand to 'stand in the shoes' of the assured and take over any legal rights he may have against others (subrogation) and this may have an unfortunate distorting effect on loss-spreading (*Lister v Romford Ice* (1957), p.63).

2. Insurance can be important, according to Jolowicz, for potential claimants as well. If the party suffering damage were the one in the better position to shoulder the risk of this damage, then he, she or it would not be able to demand compensation from the party that caused the harm, even if this latter party had been negligent. One example to be found in the law reports of this kind of approach is *Lamb v Camden LBC* (1981). Jolowicz's approach is not above criticism as Cane indicates. Nevertheless, whatever the weakness of Jolowicz's thesis, it does have one very positive feature: it provides an alternative viewpoint for analysing cases.

3. Recently the role of insurance has been raised by the judiciary in a case involving property damage and the strict liability rule in *Rylands v Fletcher* (1868) (p.243). The difference between the two Law lords indicates that the debate is by no means settled.

Transco Plc v Stockport Metropolitan Borough Council **[2004] 2 A.C. 1, HL**

(For facts see p.246)

Lord Hoffmann: ". . . **46**. Secondly, so far as the rule [in *Rylands v Fletcher*] does have a residuary role to play, it must be borne in mind that it is concerned only with damage to property and that insurance against various forms of damage to property is extremely common. A useful guide in deciding whether the risk has been created by a 'non-natural' user of land is therefore to ask whether the damage which eventuated was something against which the occupier could reasonably be expected to have insured himself. Property insurance is relatively cheap and accessible; in my opinion people should be encouraged to insure their own property rather than seek to transfer the risk to others by means of litigation, with the heavy transactional costs which that involves. The present substantial litigation over £100,000 should be a warning to anyone seeking to rely on an esoteric cause of action to shift a commonplace insured risk. . . ."

Lord Hobhouse: ". . . **60**. Thirdly, it is argued that the risk of property damage is 'insurable', just as is public liability. It is then said that, since insurers are likely to be the real parties behind any litigation, the rule has become unnecessary. This is an unsound argument for a number of reasons. It is historically unsound: in the second half of the 19th century there already existed in England, as the common law judges were well aware, a developed insurance market. The existence of an insurance market does not mean that such insurance is available free of charge: premiums have to be paid. Some risks may only be insurable at prohibitive rates or at rates which for the proposer are not commercially viable and so make the risk, for him, commercially uninsurable. (Indeed, in recent times it has been the experience that some insurers will not cover certain risks at all, *eg* loss or damage caused by flooding.) The rationale, he who creates the risk must bear the risk, is not altered at all by the existence of an insurance market. It is an application of the same concept, an acknowledgement of risk. The economic burden of insuring against the risk must be borne by he who creates it and has the control of it. Further, the magnitude of the burden will depend upon who ultimately has to bear the loss: the rule provides the answer to this. The argument that insurance makes the rule unnecessary is no more valid than saying that, because some people can afford to and sensibly do take out comprehensive car insurance, no driver should be civilly liable for his negligent driving. It is unprincipled to abrogate for all citizens a legal rule merely because it may be unnecessary as between major corporations. . . ."

QUESTIONS

1. Should tort textbooks now have a chapter entitled 'Esoteric Torts'? What would be the criteria for inclusion in this chapter?

2. "Without insurance, it is probable that tort liability itself could not survive" (Richard Lewis). Discuss.

2.7 Compensation culture

Claims that the UK is in the grip of a 'compensation culture' are, it seems, frequently being made (see Williams (2005) 25 LS 499). Such a culture is one in which there is an ever increasing number of unmerited tort actions for damages which, in turn, impacts upon professional attitudes and risk-taking. Doctors, public officials, entrepreneurs and the like become defensive in their attitudes. Much of this is probably myth, based on anecdotal evidence, but it is an argument that undoubtedly suits insurance companies, if only as an excuse for putting up their premiums (Williams, (2005) 25, at 513). Moreover it is an argument that certainly influences some politicians (see Compensation Act 2006 s.1, p.140) and it even seems to be having some effect on the judges as well.

Majrowski v Guy's and St Thomas' NHS Trust **[2007] 1 A.C. 224, HL**

(For facts see p.262)

Baroness Hale: ". . . **69** The promoters might have considered that our law does not generally award damages for anxiety and injury to feelings unless these are so severe as to amount to a recognised psychiatric illness. Discrimination and harassment are statutory exceptions to this rule. But the rule has a sound policy basis in limiting the scope for claiming compensation. There is already concern amongst some of our legislators that the scope for claiming compensation, even for recognised physical injuries, has gone too far. The avowed purpose of the Compensation Bill currently before Parliament is to reign in the so-called 'compensation culture'. The fear is that, instead of learning to cope with the inevitable irritations and misfortunes of life, people will look to others to compensate them for all their woes, and those others will then become unduly defensive or protective. . . ."

QUESTIONS

1. Is there any real evidence that we are in the grip of a 'compensation culture'? (cf. Williams (2005) 25 LS 499.)

2. In whose interest is it (besides insurance companies) to promote the idea of a compensation culture?

3. Does the 'compensation culture' include or exclude politicians and other public figures who sue newspapers for defamation?

4. Does the 'compensation culture' include supermarkets and other large multinationals who sue those that criticise them? (cf. Writers criticise Tesco, *The Guardian* April 30, 2008, p.7.)

3 Liability for individual acts (1): harm intentionally caused

Continental civil lawyers tend to divide delictual (tort) liability into two categories: damage arising from fault (*culpa*) and damage arising from risk. All blameworthy acts—whether they arise from intention, recklessness, gross fault or mere carelessness—amount to fault for this purpose. For example, if D deliberately pushes C into a ditch causing him serious personal injury, C will be able to sue D in France for damages on the basis of article 1382 of the *Code civil* which states that any "human act whatever which causes damage to another obliges him by whose fault it occurred to make reparation". However even if D only carelessly knocked C into the ditch, C would still be able to use article 1382 to claim damages for his injuries. As article 1383 makes clear, fault for this purpose includes negligence and imprudence. The same was true of Roman law: the identical form of action for wrongful damage was available whether the defendant wilfully caused the damage or whether he was guilty of the slightest *culpa* (*culpa levissima*) (D.9.2.44pr).

English law, in contrast, tends to divide tortious liability into three behavioural categories. It has a broad category of strict liability where fault is not normally an essential element; and, with respect to fault liability, it distinguishes between damage arising out of intentional acts and damage arising out of negligent behaviour. Thus, in the ditch example, if D deliberately pushed C, the cause of action would lie in trespass; but if he only carelessly knocked C, the cause of action would be in negligence (see *Letang v Cooper*, above, p.3). This chapter and the next reflect this distinction between intentionally and negligently caused damage. However it has to be said at the outset that English law does not in fact frame liability specifically around the idea of intention to damage; liability depends upon the existence of a cause of action (see **1.7**; and see also e.g. *Esso v Southport*, p.5 and *Douglas v Hello!*, p.69). And so if a claimant, despite being wilfully harmed, cannot establish such a cause of action he cannot in theory succeed. This said, wilful and abusive behaviour can be a powerful ingredient.

3.1 Intention and interests

It would be tempting to think that any wilfully caused damage ought to be actionable. Indeed, such behaviour, if it caused harm, would prima facie appear to fall within CC art.1382. Yet a moment's reflection should soon convince one that matters are not quite so simple. Deliberately causing physical harm is one thing, but intentionally inflicting other kinds of damage can be more problematic. For example, if D wishes to prevent C winning a bicycle race and places a log in the road in order to cause him to crash, there is little problem, not just about liability for any physical injury, but also about liability for the loss of a chance of winning (*Chaplin v Hicks* (1911)). But it would be quite different if D decided, being an excellent cyclist himself, to enter the race with the sole motive of depriving C of the chance of winning. Lawyers tend to analyse this latter situation by saying that there is no injuria; that is to say there is no legal wrong despite the existence of intention and of damage (*Bradford Corp v Pickles*, above, p.72). Yet part of the problem is also the nature of the harm itself. And so it is not possible simply to focus upon behaviour: it is necessary to link it to the interest invaded.

3.1.1 **Health interest**

Where a person deliberately causes physical (as opposed to mental) personal injury this will normally amount to a trespass unless of course the act is covered by consent (e.g. operating surgeon) or justification (often provided by statute). One traditional source for this trespass liability is *Wilkinson v Downton* (1897) (p.8); but the authority of this precedent as a trespass (as opposed to negligence) case has now been put into question by *Wainright v Home Office* (2004) (p.77). Another difficulty, on occasions, is actually defining the health interest, as the next extract shows.

Rothwell v Chemical & Insulating Co Ltd [2007] 3 W.L.R. 876, HL

Lord Hoffmann: "**1** My Lords, the question is whether someone who has been negligently exposed to asbestos in the course of his employment can sue his employer for damages on the ground that he has developed pleural plaques. These are areas of fibrous thickening of the pleural membrane which surrounds the lungs. Save in very exceptional cases, they cause no symptoms. Nor do they cause other asbestos-related diseases. But they signal the presence in the lungs and pleura of asbestos fibres which may independently cause life-threatening or fatal diseases such as asbestosis or mesothelioma. In consequence, a diagnosis of pleural plaques may cause the patient to contemplate his future with anxiety or even suffer clinical depression.

2 Proof of damage is an essential element in a claim in negligence and in my opinion the symptomless plaques are not compensatable damage. Neither do the risk of future illness or anxiety about the possibility of that risk materialising amount to damage for the purpose of creating a cause of action, although the law allows both to be taken into account in computing the loss suffered by someone who has actually suffered some compensatable physical injury and therefore has a cause of action. In the absence of such compensatable injury, however, there is no cause of action under which damages may be claimed and therefore no computation of loss in which the risk and anxiety may be taken into account. It follows that in my opinion the development of pleural plaques, whether or not associated with the risk of future disease and anxiety about the future, is not actionable injury. The same is true even if the anxiety causes a recognised psychiatric illness such as clinical depression. The right to protection against psychiatric illness is limited and does not extend to an illness which would be suffered only by an unusually vulnerable person because of apprehension that he may suffer a tortious injury. The risk of the future disease is not actionable and neither is a psychiatric illness caused by contemplation of that risk. . . ."

[Lords Hope, Scott, Rodger and Mance agreed with Lord Hoffmann that there was no actionable damage.]

QUESTIONS

1. Is dyslexia a form of personal injury? (cf. *Adams v Bracknell Forest BC* (2005).)

2. Are anxiety and (or) clinical depression, as interests, only indirectly protected by the law of tort?

3.1.2 **Property interest**

Deliberate physical damage inflicted *directly* on the property of another will prima facie be a trespass. However deliberately damage inflicted *indirectly* is more problematic as *Bradford Corporation v Pickles* (1895) (p.72) shows. Nevertheless the law of tort is not always impotent.

Hollywood Silver Fox Farm Ltd v Emmett **[1936] 2 K.B. 468, KBD**

This was an action for an injunction and for damages brought by the breeder of silver foxes against his neighbour who had carried out a threat to fire a shotgun, on his own land, but close to where the foxes were kept. Vixens are extremely nervous during the breeding season and a loud noise will deter them from breeding and possibly make them kill their young. The defendant claimed he was shooting rabbits on his own land, but Macnaghten J. granted the remedies.

Macnaghten J.: ". . . In *Christie v Davey* the plaintiffs, Mr and Mrs Christie, and the defendant lived side by side in semi-detached houses in Brixton. Mrs Christie was a teacher of music, and her family were also musical, and throughout the day sounds of music pervaded their house and were heard in the house of their neighbour. The defendant did not like the music that he heard, and by way of retaliation he took to making noises himself, beating trays and rapping on the wall. The action came on for trial before North J, who delivered judgment in favour of the plaintiffs and granted an injunction restraining the defendant from causing or permitting any sounds or noises in his house so as to vex or annoy the plaintiffs or the occupiers of their house. In the course of his judgment, he said at page 326, after dealing with the facts as he found them, 'The result is that I think I am bound to interfere for the protection of the plaintiffs. In my opinion the noises which were made in the defendant's house were not of a legitimate kind. They were what, to use the language of Lord Selborne in *Gaunt v Fynney*, "ought to be regarded as excessive and unreasonable." I am satisfied that they were made deliberately and maliciously for the purpose of annoying the plaintiffs.' Then come the significant words: 'If what has taken place had occurred between two sets of persons both perfectly innocent, I should have taken an entirely different view of the case. But I am persuaded that what was done by the defendant was done only for the purpose of annoyance, and in my opinion it was not a legitimate use of the defendant's house to use it for the purpose of vexing and annoying his neighbours.'. . .

The cases to which I have referred were decided before the decision of the House of Lords in *Bradford Corporation v Pickles*; and the question therefore arises whether those cases must now be considered as overruled. It is to be observed that in *Allen v Flood* Lord Watson discussed fully the case of *Keeble v Hickeringill* and said with reference to that case: 'No proprietor has an absolute right to create noises upon his own land, because any right which the law gives him is qualified by the condition that it must not be exercised to the nuisance of his neighbours or of the public. If he violates that condition he commits a legal wrong, and if he does so intentionally he is guilty of a malicious wrong, in its strict legal sense.'

In my opinion the decision of the House of Lords in *Bradford Corporation v Pickles* has no bearing on such cases as this. I therefore think that the plaintiff is entitled to maintain this action. I think also that in the circumstances an injunction should be granted restraining the defendant from committing a nuisance by the discharge of firearms or the making of other loud noises in the vicinity of the Hollywood Silver Fox Farm during the breeding season—namely, between January 1 and June 15—so as to alarm or disturb the foxes kept by the plaintiffs at the said farm, or otherwise to injure the plaintiff company."

NOTE

One important aspect of this case is that the harm to the claimant's foxes was caused indirectly and that was why the claim was framed in nuisance. Had the defendant directly shot the foxes he would have been liable in trespass and had he negligently caused their damage he might have had to pay damages through liability in the tort of negligence (see **Chapter 4**).

QUESTIONS

1. What if the defendant had no desire to cause damage to his neighbour's silver foxes; he just felt that he had to shoot rabbits on his land to protect his own crops?

2. What if the defendant had held a firework party to mark his wedding anniversary?

3.1.3 **Mental health interest**

The deliberately infliction of mental distress (rather than severe psychological damage) is not of itself actionable. The claimant has to fit such a claim into an existing cause of action, although statute has provided some help here.

Hunter v Canary Wharf Ltd **[1997] A.C. 655, HL**

Lord Hoffmann:. . . "The perceived gap in *Khorasandjian v Bush* was the absence of a tort of intentional harassment causing distress without actual bodily or psychiatric illness. This limitation is thought to arise out of cases like *Wilkinson v Downton* [1897] 2 QB 57 and *Janvier v Sweeney* [1919] 2 KB 316. The law of harassment has now been put on a statutory basis (see the Protection from Harassment Act 1997) and it is unnecessary to consider how the common law might have developed. But as at present advised, I see no reason why a tort of intention should be subject to the rule which excludes compensation for mere distress, inconvenience or discomfort in actions based on negligence: see *Hicks v Chief Constable of the South Yorkshire Police* [1992] 2 All ER 65. The policy considerations are quite different. I do not therefore say that *Khorasandjian v Bush* was wrongly decided. But it must be seen as a case on intentional harassment, not nuisance. . . ."

NOTE

Lord Hoffmann has now added the following qualification.

Wainwright v Home Office **[2004] 2 A.C. 406, HL**

(For facts see p.29)

> **Lord Hoffmann**: ". . . **45** If. . . one is going to draw a principled distinction which justifies abandoning the rule that damages for mere distress are not recoverable, imputed intention will not do. The defendant must actually have acted in a way which he knew to be unjustifiable and intended to cause harm or at least acted without caring whether he caused harm or not. . . ."

NOTE

While it remains true that any deliberate infliction of personal injury will be a trespass, *Wilkinson* has now been re-interpreted as a negligence case: see Lord Hoffmann in *Wainwright* at § 44 (above p.77).

3.1.4 **Reputation interest**

Where the mental distress is caused by an untrue statement which in turn can be seen as invading a person's reputation, then the tort of defamation may be relevant (see **Chapter 8**). A deliberate lie that invades a person's business reputation may also be actionable according to the following precedent.

Ratcliffe v Evans **[1892] 2 Q.B. 524, CA**

This was an action for damages brought by the owner of a business against a person who had published in a local weekly newspaper that the claimant's firm had gone out of business. The plaintiff claimed that his business had suffered general loss as a result of the publication. The jury found that although the words were not defamatory they were not published in good faith and awarded £120 in damages. The Court of Appeal (Lord Esher M.R., Fry L.J. and Bowen L.J.) dismissed an appeal.

> **Bowen L.J.**: ". . . That an action will lie for written or oral falsehoods, not actionable per se nor even defamatory, where they are maliciously published, where they are calculated in the ordinary course of things to produce, and where they do produce, actual damage, is established law. Such an action is not one of libel or of slander, but an action on the case for damage wilfully and intentionally done without just occasion or excuse, analogous to an action for slander of title. To support it, actual damage must be shewn, for it is an action which only lies in respect of such damage as has actually occurred. . . ."

NOTE

See now Defamation Act 1952 s.3.

3.1.5 **Constitutional interest**

The deliberate imprisonment of a person without lawful justification will amount to the tort of false imprisonment, a species of trespass.

R v Governor of Brockhill Prison, Ex p Evans (No 2) **[2001] 2 A.C. 19, HL**

(See also p.29)

Lord Steyn: ". . . It is common ground that the tort of false imprisonment involves the infliction of bodily restraint which is not expressly or impliedly authorised by the law. The plaintiff does not have to prove fault on the part of the defendant. It is a tort of strict liability. These propositions are also common ground. There the agreement ends. The parties invoke competing principles of law. The Solicitor-General argued that the question whether the governor had authority to detain the respondent for an extra 59 days must be determined on the basis law as it then stood. He said that the governor was obliged to obey the law. Consequently, he submitted, that his conduct was authorised by law and he did not commit the tort of false imprisonment. And he said that the principled arguments underpinning his case are reinforced by the injustice of holding the governor liable in tort.

Counsel for the applicant took as his starting point that the tort of false imprisonment is one of strict liability. He submitted that once the applicant's imprisonment for the 59 days was held to be unlawful that is determinative of the issue. Relying on the declaratory theory of judicial decisions—that the law has always been as it is now expounded—he said that legal principle ruled out any defence by the Governor of having relied on the earlier and incorrect view of the law. He said these principles are reinforced by the injustice of leaving the victim of a substantial period of unlawful imprisonment without a remedy.

My Lords, the principles of law invoked by the two sides pull in opposite directions. I am advisedly speaking of principles as opposed to rules. As *Dworkin, Taking Rights Seriously: with a reply to critics* (1977), pp 24–26 observed, rules have an 'all or nothing' quality: they are either determinative or irrelevant. On the other hand, principles are general norms which may be in competition: the dimension and weight of principles need to be considered. In a sense therefore principles have a function not widely different from the role of analogies in the law: *MacCormick, Legal Reasoning and Legal Theory* (1994), pp. 231–232. It is a matter of judgment how the weight of the competing principles in the present case should be assessed. Similarly, both sides assert that the justice of the case—to the wrongly detained woman and to the governor doing his job in accordance with law—favour their particular interpretation. Again, one must consider the comparative potency of these claims to the just solution of the case. . . .

It is also instructive that on remarkably similar facts the New South Wales Court of Appeal in *Colwell v Corrective Services Commission of New South Wales* (1988) 13 NSWLR 714 came to the same conclusion . . . that the Commission could be liable for unlawful imprisonment in spite of the fact that those responsible for the detention acted in good faith in accordance with the law as they understood it: see also Fordham, 'False Imprisonment in Good Faith' (2000) Tort L Rev 53. This decision provides support for the view of the majority in the present case from an important common law jurisdiction.

Finally, article 5 of the European Convention for the Protection of Human Rights and Fundamental Freedoms (1953) (Cmd. 8969) provides as follows:

'1. Everyone has the right to liberty and security of person. No one shall be deprived of his liberty save in the following cases and in accordance with a procedure prescribed by law:

> (a) the lawful detention of a person after conviction by a competent court;... 5. Everyone who has been the victim of arrest or detention in contravention of the provisions of this article shall have an enforceable right to compensation.'

In my view these provisions rule out the defence that the Governor acted in accordance with the law as it was understood at the time. Article 5 reinforces the view which I have accepted. . . .

Finally, the appellant challenged the Court of Appeal's decision to increase the damages to £5,000. The period of unlawful detention was substantial. This decision was well within the power of the Court of Appeal and I have no reason to doubt the appropriateness of the substituted award.

My Lords, I would uphold the decision and reasoning of the majority in the Court of Appeal. I would dismiss the appeal."

[The appeal was dismissed]

NOTE

The defendant in the above case did not act in bad faith. What if a public official deliberately, and in bad faith, injures a citizen?

Three Rivers District Council v Governor and Company of The Bank of England (No 3) **[2003] 2 A.C. 1, HL**

(For facts see p.122)

Lord Hobhouse: ". . . I will start by putting the tort in its legal context. Typically, a tort involves the invasion by the defendant of some legally protected right of the plaintiff, for example, trespass to property or trespass to the person. Conversion is another example. Such conduct on the part of the defendant is actionable as such and the belief of the defendant as to the legality of what he did is irrelevant. It is no defence for the defendant to say that he believed that he had statutory or other legal authority if he did not. The legal justification must actually exist otherwise he is liable in tort. (*Northern Territory v Mengel* 69 AJLR 527, 547)

On the other hand, where the plaintiff is not entitled to complain of the invasion of such a right but bases his claim on some loss which he has suffered consequentially upon some act of the defendant which the defendant mistakenly believed was authorised by the law, the defendant's honest belief provides him with an answer to the plaintiff's claim notwithstanding any actual illegality. Thus the holder of a public office who acts honestly will not be liable to a third party indirectly affected by something which the official has done even if it turns out to have been unlawful. Illegality without more does not give a cause of action. (*Lonrho Ltd v Shell Petroleum Co Ltd (No 2)* [1982] AC 173, 189; *Dunlop v Woollahra Municipal Council* [1982] AC 158, 172; *Mengel* at p 546) There is no principle in English law that an official is the guarantor of the legality of everything he does; but he is liable if he injures another by an act which is itself tortious if not justified and he is unable to justify it, however honestly he may have acted.

> The subject matter of the tort of misfeasance in public office operates in the area left unoccupied by these limits. . . ."

NOTE

The importance of this extract from Lord Hobhouse is that it distinguishes between torts protecting *rights* and torts arising from *wrongs*. From the claimant's viewpoint, the latter are more concerned with protected *interests*.

3.1.6 Trade and business interest

The distinction made by Lord Hobhouse is valuable for understanding legal reasoning. If one wants to grant a legal remedy for the invasion of a particular interest, it can be a useful ploy to turn the 'interest' into a 'right'. Lord Denning does just this in the next extract.

Ex parte Island Records **[1978] Ch. 122, CA**

Lord Denning M.R.: ". . . The question . . . becomes this: has the plaintiff a particular right which he is entitled to have protected? To this the answer which runs through all the cases is: a man who is carrying on a lawful trade or calling has a right to be protected from any unlawful interference with it . . . It is a right which is in the nature of a right of property . . . [The Attorney-General] has, we are told, refused his consent to a relator action—presumably because no public rights are involved. So perforce if the law is to be obeyed—and justice to be done—the courts must allow a private individual himself to bring an action against the offender—in those cases where his private rights and interests are specially affected by the breach [of the criminal law]. This principle is capable of extension so as to apply not only to rights of property or rights in the nature of it, but to other rights or interests . . ."

NOTE

Lord Denning's analysis is perhaps over-optimistic. Not all deliberate invasions of another's lawful trade are actionable.

Mogul Steamship Co v McGregor, Gow & Co **(1889) 23 Q.B.D. 598, *CA*; [1892] A.C. 25, HL**

This was an action for damages brought by one shipping firm against an association of other shipping firms who it was alleged had conspired to keep the claimant out of the tea trade. The association had lowered their own freight rates to below an economic figure; they refused contracts to anyone who booked space on non-combination ships; they gave rebates to those who used only combination vessels; and they shadowed any non-combination ship with the object of 'stealing' its trade. The claimant was soon ruined. The claimant's action was dismissed and appeals to the Court of Appeal and House of Lords (Lords Halsbury L.C., Watson, Bramwell, Macnaghten, Morris, Hannen and Field) were also dismissed.

Bowen L.J. (Court of Appeal): "We are presented in this case with an apparent conflict or antinomy between two rights that are equally regarded by the law—the right of the plaintiffs to be protected in the legitimate exercise of their trade, and the right of the defendants to carry on their business as seems best to them, provided they commit no wrong to others. The plaintiffs complain that the defendants have crossed the line which the common law permits; and inasmuch as, for the purposes of the present case, we are to assume some possible damage to the plaintiffs, the real question to be decided is whether, on such an assumption, the defendants in the conduct of their commercial affairs have done anything that is unjustifiable in law. . . .

What, then, are the limitations which the law imposes on a trader in the conduct of his business as between himself and other traders? There seem to be no burdens or restrictions in law upon a trader which arise merely from the fact that he is a trader, and which are not equally laid on all other subjects of the Crown. His right to trade freely is a right which the law recognises and encourages, but it is one which places him at no special disadvantage as compared with others. No man, whether trader or not, can, however, justify damaging another in his commercial business by fraud or misrepresentation. Intimidation, obstruction, and molestation are forbidden; so is the intentional procurement of a violation of individual rights, contractual or other, assuming always that there is no just cause for it. . . . [The defendants] have done nothing more against the plaintiffs than pursue to the bitter end a war of competition waged in the interest of their own trade. To the argument that a competition so pursued ceases to have a just cause or excuse when there is ill-will or a personal intention to harm, it is sufficient to reply (. . .) that there was here no personal intention to do any other or greater harm to the plaintiffs than such as was necessarily involved in the desire to attract to the defendants' ships the entire tea freights of the ports, a portion of which would otherwise have fallen to the plaintiffs' share. I can find no authority for the doctrine that such a commercial motive deprives of 'just cause or excuse' acts done in the course of trade which would but for such a motive be justifiable. So to hold would be to convert into an illegal motive the instinct of self-advancement and self-protection, which is the very incentive to all trade. To say that a man is to trade freely, but that he is to stop short at any act which is calculated to harm other tradesmen, and which is designed to attract business to his own shop, would be a strange and impossible counsel of perfection. . . . To attempt to limit English competition in this way would probably be as hopeless an endeavour as the experiment of King Canute. But on ordinary principles of law no such fetter on freedom of trade can in my opinion be warranted. . . ."

Lord Bramwell: "My Lords, the plaintiffs in this case do not complain of any trespass, violence, force, fraud, or breach of contract, nor of any direct tort or violation of any right of the plaintiffs, like the case of firing to frighten birds from a decoy; nor of any act, the ultimate object of which was to injure the plaintiffs, having its origin in malice or ill-will to them. . . .

The Master of the Rolls says the lowering of the freight far beyond a lowering for any purpose of trade was not an act done in the exercise of their own free right of trade, but for the purpose of interfering with the plaintiffs' right to a free course of trade; therefore a wrongful act as against the plaintiffs' right; and as injury to the plaintiffs followed, they had a right of action. I cannot agree. If there were two shopkeepers in a village and one sold an article at cost price, not for profit therefore, but to attract customers or cause his rival to leave off selling the article only, it could not be said he was liable to an action. I cannot think that the defendants did more than they had a legal right to do. . . ."

NOTE

This tea-clipper case must be treated with caution since the commercial liberty protected by the House of Lords has long since gone thanks to European competition law and the Competition Act 1998 s.2. Yet it still has an important conceptual relevance in as much as it confirms the principle that the infliction of deliberate economic damage is not in itself actionable. Something more must be shown. If the defendants had been guilty of trespass, nuisance, direct intimidation or some other established wrong (like a conspiracy to commit a crime), then the invasion of the claimant's economic interest would have been actionable (see e.g. *Revenue and Customs Commissioners v Total Network* (2008), below p.177). The point to be stressed of course is that Lord Denning's assertion in *Island Records* is too wide: he was trying to turn a commercial interest into a property interest.

QUESTION

Tea clippers (a sailing technological wonder of their time whose development owed everything to capitalism) often raced and one of the great races, China to London, took place in 1866 between *Taeping* and *Ariel*. The winner would get 10 shillings a ton bonus. The two ships arrived in London docks within ten minutes of each other: what happened with the prize bonus? What if (which was not the case) one of the ships had taken an illegal short cut and as a result had secured the prize money: could the owner of the ship which came in second sue the winner and, if so, for how much?

3.1.7 Employment interest

A person who loses a job is of course losing his or her means of income (if only temporarily). What is the position if one person deliberately engineers the dismissal of another person?

Allen v Flood **[1898] A.C. 1, HL**

This was an action for damages by two woodworkers, who had once done ironwork, against the representative of the ironworkers union. The representative, reflecting the discontent of ironworkers working in a dockyard with the two woodworkers who had once done ironwork, had gone to the employers and informed them that the ironworkers would not turn up for work the next day and thereafter until the two woodworkers were dismissed. The employees were on day-to-day contracts and thus refusing to turn up for work would not have amounted to a breach of any of the employment contracts. The employers dismissed the woodworkers who succeeded in their action against the representative at first instance and in the Court of Appeal. The case was reargued before seven Law lords and opinions were taken from judges summoned to attend (a procedure no longer current). A majority of the House of Lords (Lords Watson, Herschell, Macnaghten, Shand, Davey and James; Lords Halsbury L.C., Ashbourne and Morris dissenting) allowed an appeal. (A majority of the judges who had delivered opinions to the Law lords were in favour of the claimants.)

    Lord Halsbury L.C. (dissenting): ". . . I see it is suggested by one of your Lordships that the action for malicious prosecution is supposed to be an exception. I am not quite certain that I understand what is the proposition to which it is an exception. If it means that there is no other form of procedure known to the law wherein malice may make the distinction between a lawful and an unlawful act, I am unable to agree. Maliciously procuring a person to be made a bankrupt, maliciously and without reasonable or probable cause presenting a petition to wind up a company, or maliciously procuring an arrest, are equally cases wherein the state of mind of the person procuring the arrest may affect the question of the lawfulness or unlawfulness of the act done. . . ."

Lord Watson: ". . . Although the rule may be otherwise with regard to crimes, the law of England does not, according to my apprehension, take into account motive as constituting an element of civil wrong. Any invasion of the civil rights of another person is in itself a legal wrong, carrying with it liability to repair its necessary or natural consequences, in so far as these are injurious to the person whose right is infringed, whether the motive which prompted it be good, bad, or indifferent. But the existence of a bad motive, in the case of an act which is not in itself illegal, will not convert that act into a civil wrong for which reparation is due. A wrongful act, done knowingly and with a view to its injurious consequences, may, in the sense of law, be malicious; but such malice derives its essential character from the circumstance that the act done constitutes a violation of the law. There is a class of cases which have sometimes been referred to as evidencing that a bad motive may be an element in the composition of civil wrong; but in these cases the wrong must have its root in an act which the law generally regards as illegal, but excuses its perpetration in certain exceptional circumstances from considerations of public policy. These are well known as cases of privilege, in which the protection which the law gives to an individual who is within the scope of these considerations consists in this—that he may with immunity commit an act which is a legal wrong and but for his privilege would afford a good cause of action against him, all that is required in order to raise the privilege and entitle him to protection being that he shall act honestly in the discharge of some duty which the law recognises, and shall not be prompted by a desire to injure the person who is affected by his act. Accordingly, in a suit brought by that person, it is usual for him to allege and necessary for him to prove an intent to injure in order to destroy the privilege of the defendant. But none of these cases tend to establish that an act which does not amount to a legal wrong, and therefore needs no protection, can have privilege attached to it; and still less that an act in itself lawful is converted into a legal wrong if it was done from a bad motive. . . ."

Lord Herschell: ". . . I can imagine no greater danger to the community than that a jury should be at liberty to impose the penalty of paying damages for acts which are otherwise lawful, because they choose, without any legal definition of the term, to say that they are malicious. No one would know what his rights were. The result would be to put all our actions at the mercy of a particular tribunal whose view of their propriety might differ from our own. . . ."

NOTES

1. The holding in this case did not survive for very long, for the judges a few years later developed the tort of conspiracy: *Quinn v Leathem* (1901); and see now *Revenue and Customs Commissioners v Total Network SL* (2008) (below p.117). Nevertheless it should be seen as one of a trilogy of cases, all decided at the end of the 19th century, marking the limits of liability for damage intentionally caused. The other two cases are, of course, *Mogul SS* (1892) (p.98) and *Bradford Corporation v Pickles* (1895) (p.72).

2. If the deliberate act which results in another's loss of a job is of itself a wrong, then the actor may be liable to a claim in damages.

Rookes v Barnard [1964] A.C. 1129, HL

This was an action for damages brought by a draughtsman, who had been dismissed from his job at BOAC, against the union officials who had told BOAC that unless the claimant was sacked there would be a strike. If there had been a strike by BOAC skilled draughtsman this would have amounted to a breach of their contracts of employment which incorporated a no-strike clause. Thus the plaintiff claimed that that the strike warning amounted to a threat to do a wrongful act. The trial judge instructed the jury to award exemplary damages, which they did, but his decision was reversed by the Court of Appeal. An appeal to the House of Lords (Lords Reid, Evershed, Hodson, Devlin and Pearce) was allowed.

Lord Reid: ". . . This case. . . raises the question whether it is a tort to conspire to threaten an employer that his men will break their contracts with him unless he dismisses the plaintiff, with the result that he is thereby induced to dismiss the plaintiff and cause him loss. . . .

. . .A person is no more entitled to sue in respect of loss which he suffers by reason of a tort committed against someone else than he is entitled to sue in respect of loss which he suffers by reason of breach of a contract to which he is not a party. What he sues for in each case is loss caused to him by the use of an unlawful weapon against him—intimidation of another person by unlawful means. So long as the defendant only threatens to do what he has a legal right to do he is on safe ground. At least if there is no conspiracy he would not be liable to anyone for doing the act, whatever his motive might be, and it would be absurd to make him liable for threatening to do it but not for doing it. But I agree with Lord Herschell (*Allen v Flood*) that there is a chasm between doing what you have a legal right to do and doing what you have no legal right to do, and there seems to me to be the same chasm between threatening to do what you have a legal right to do and threatening to do what you have no legal right to do. It must follow from *Allen v Flood* that to intimidate by threatening to do what you have a legal right to do is to intimidate by lawful means. But I see no good reason for extending that doctrine. Threatening a breach of contract may be a much more coercive weapon than threatening a tort, particularly when the threat is directed against a company or corporation, and, if there is no technical reason requiring a distinction between different kinds of threats, I can see no other ground for making any such distinction. . . ."

Lord Devlin: ". . . I find. . . nothing to differentiate a threat of a breach of contract from a threat of physical violence or any other illegal threat. The nature of the threat is immaterial, because, as Professor Hamson points out, its nature is irrelevant to the plaintiff's cause of action. All that matters to the plaintiff is that, metaphorically speaking, a club has been used. It does not matter to the plaintiff what the club is made of—whether it is a physical club or an economic club, a tortuous club or an otherwise illegal club. If an intermediate party is improperly coerced, it does not matter to the plaintiff how he is coerced.

I think, therefore, that at common law there is a tort of intimidation and that on the facts of this case each of the respondents has committed it, both individually (since the jury has found that each took an overt and active part) and in combination with others. . . ."

QUESTION

Is there really no difference between a threat to commit violence and a threat to break a contract?

3.1.8 Contract interest

A person's employment is of course a contractual right. Yet it is also a kind of 'property' in that it is an identifiable asset, if only an abstract one. Is the same true of contracts in general?

OBG Ltd v Allan **[2007] 2 W.L.R. 920, HL**

This was an action for damages brought by a company against liquidators. The facts were summed up by Lord Hoffmann as follows: "In *OBG Ltd v Allan* [2005] QB 762 the defendants were receivers purportedly appointed under a floating charge which is admitted to have been invalid. Acting in good faith, they took control of the claimant company's assets and undertaking. The claimant says that this was not only a trespass to its land and a conversion of its chattels but also the tort of unlawful interference with its contractual relations. It claims that the defendants are liable in damages for the value of the assets and undertaking, including the value of the contractual claims, as at the date of their appointment. Alternatively, it says the defendants are liable for the same damages in conversion." A majority of the House of Lords (Lords Hoffmann, Walker and Brown; Lord Nicholls and Baroness Hale dissenting) held that no tort had been committed by the defendants.

> **Lord Nicholls** (dissenting in part): "**137** My Lords, before your Lordships' House are three appeals. They were heard consecutively because the legal issues overlap. The first appeal, *OBG Ltd v Allan* [2005] QB 762, concerns a claim by a company in liquidation for damages in respect of losses sustained by the company through acts done by administrative receivers whose appointment was later held to be invalid. The causes of action relied upon are conversion and wrongful interference with contractual relations. . . .
>
> **139** Counsel's submissions were wide-ranging. In particular the House is called upon to consider the ingredients of the tort of interference with a business by unlawful means and the tort of inducing breach of contract. These are much vexed subjects. Nearly 350 reported decisions and academic writings were placed before the House. There are many areas of uncertainty. Judicial observations are not always consistent, and academic consensus is noticeably absent. In the words of one commentator, the law is in a 'terrible mess'. So the House faces a daunting task. For good measure your Lordships have also to review the scope of the tort of conversion.
>
> **140** I shall consider first the ingredients of the relevant economic torts.
>
> *Interference with the claimant's business by unlawful means*
>
> **141** I start with the tort comprising interference with a trade or business by unlawful means or, more shortly, the tort of unlawful interference. The gist of this tort is intentionally damaging another's business by unlawful means. Intention is an essential ingredient. The tort is not one of strict liability for harm inflicted on another's business, nor is it a tort based on negligence. The defendant must have intended to inflict the harm of which complaint is made. That is the starting point. . . .
>
> **142** But intent to harm is not enough. Intentional harm of another's business is not of itself tortious. Competition between businesses regularly involves each business taking steps to

promote itself at the expense of the other. One retail business may reduce its prices to customers with a view to diverting trade to itself and away from a competitor shop. Far from prohibiting such conduct, the common law seeks to encourage and protect it. The common law recognises the economic advantages of competition. . . .

The tort of inducing a breach of contract

168 The other tort requiring consideration is the tort of inducing a breach of contract. This tort is known by various names, reflecting differing views about its scope. At its inception in 1853 this tort was concerned with a simple tripartite situation of a non-party to a contract inducing a contracting party to break her contract. Did the other party to the contract have a cause of action against the non-party?. . .

187 This extension [in *Torquay Hotel Co Ltd v Cousins* [1969] 2 Ch 106] of the *Lumley v Gye* tort must be going too far. To hold a defendant liable where the intentional harm is inflicted by lawful means runs counter to the limit on liability long established in English law. So long as this general limit is maintained in respect of other forms of interference with a claimant's business, and Lord Denning did not suggest this should be changed, the extension in liability proposed by him and seemingly approved by Lord Diplock is irrational. Despite the high authority of these cases, I have to say that on this occasion these distinguished judges fell into error. They were led astray by the width of Lord Macnaghten's observations made in 1901, long before the unlawful interference tort became shaped. The jurisprudence of the economic torts had not then been thought through.

188 For these reasons this extension of the inducement tort of *Lumley v Gye* cannot stand consistently with the economic torts having a coherent framework. This extension is productive of obscurity and, hence, uncertainty. This, in turn, as Lord Diplock himself once said, is destructive of the rule of law: see *Merkur Island Shipping Corpn v Laughton* [1983] 2 AC 570, 612.

189 I feel bound to say therefore that the ambit of the *Lumley v Gye* tort should properly be confined to inducing a breach of contract. The unlawful interference tort requires intentional harm effected by unlawful means, and there is no in-between hybrid tort of 'interfering with contractual relations'. In so far as authorities suggest or decide otherwise they should not now be followed. I leave open the question of how far the *Lumley v Gye* principle applies equally to inducing a breach of other actionable obligations such as statutory duties or equitable or fiduciary obligations. . . .

A bird's-eye view

194 It may be helpful to pause and take on overall look at where this leaves the law. The effect of the views expressed above is to draw a sharp distinction between two economic torts. One tort imposes primary liability for intentional and unlawful interference with economic interests. The other tort imposes accessory liability for inducing a third party to commit an actionable wrong, notably a breach of contract, but possibly some other actionable civil wrongs as well.

195 This overall framework, it is to be hoped, should assist in the more coherent development of the economic torts. On this I am comforted by noting that this twofold structure substantially accords with the views of at least some commentators, including *Hazel Carty, An Analysis of the Economic Torts*, (2001), pp 271--276, and Ken Oliphant (1999) 62 MLR 320, 322. . . .''

Lord Hoffmann: ''. . . **14** Some writers regret the failure of English law to accept bad motive as a ground for liability, as it is in the United States and Germany: see for example *Heydon, Economic Torts* , 2nd ed (1978), p 28. But I agree with Tony Weir's opinion, forcibly expressed in his Clarendon Law Lectures on *Economic Torts* (1997) that we are better off without it. It seems to have created a good deal of uncertainty in the countries which have adopted such a principle. Furthermore, the rarity of actions for conspiracy (in which a bad motive can, exceptionally, found liability) suggests that it would not have made much practical difference. . .

31 Is there something to be said in principle for a unified theory? Tony Weir, in the Clarendon Law Lectures to which I have referred, makes a bravura case for a one. Not, it is true, the version adopted in *DC Thomson v Deakin*, which he thinks paid too much attention to the contractual nature of the claimant's rights. Weir would prefer *Lumley v Gye* to be swallowed up by the tort of intentionally causing loss by unlawful means, treating the 'seduction' of the contracting party as a species of unlawful means and not distinguishing between interference with contractual rights and damage to economic expectations. The example of what Lord Atkin achieved for negligence in *Donogue v Stevenson* [1932] AC 562 always beckons: see Weir, at p 25. But this too is a form of seduction which may lure writers onto the rocks.

32 . . . I . . . do not think that the two causes of action can be brought within a unified theory and agree with Professor Peter Cane, 'Mens Rea in Tort Law' (2000) 20 Oxford JLS 533, 552, that

> 'The search for 'general principles of liability' based on types of conduct is at best a waste of time, and at worst a potential source of serious confusion; and the broader the principle, the more is this so. Tort law is a complex interaction between protected interests, sanctioned conduct, and sanctions; and although there are what might be called 'principles of tort liability', by and large, they are not very 'general'. More importantly, they cannot be stated solely in terms of the sorts of conduct which will attract tort liability. Each principle must refer, as well, to some interest protected by tort law and some sanction provided by tort law.'

. . .

39 To be liable for inducing breach of contract, you must know that you are inducing a breach of contract. It is not enough that you know that you are procuring an act which, as a matter of law or construction of the contract, is a breach. You must actually realize that it will have this effect. Nor does it matter that you ought reasonably to have done so. . . .

43 On the other hand, if the breach of contract is neither an end in itself nor a means to an end, but merely a foreseeable consequence, then in my opinion it cannot for this purpose be said to have been intended. That, I think, is what judges and writers mean when they say that the claimant must have been "targeted" or "aimed at". . . .

47 The essence of the tort therefore appears to be (a) a wrongful interference with the

> actions of a third party in which the claimant has an economic interest and (b) an intention thereby to cause loss to the claimant. The old cases of interference with potential customers by threats of unlawful acts clearly fell within this description. . . .”

NOTES

1. Much of the area of trade union liability and industrial disputes is governed by statute and falls outside most foundational tort courses: see now Trade Union and Labour Relations (Consolidation) Act 1992. However *OBG v Allan* is an important case in tort in that it has narrowed the liability of inducing breach of contract by holding that the Court of Appeal decision in *Torquay Hotel Co Ltd v Cousins* (1969) was a step too far. There has to be an actual breach of contract in order for a defendant to be liable under this cause of action; merely 'interfering' with contractual relations is not enough. Another reason why the case is important is that the law Lords have refused to create a single 'economic tort'; liability remains attached to individual causes of action.

2. The main difficulty with these economic torts (see **3.1.6–3.1.8**) is to define their limits and *OBG* has gone some way in trying to do this (and see also *Revenue and Customs Commissioners v Total Network SL* (2008), p.117). As far as the common law of tort is concerned, not every intentional injury causing economic loss will be actionable otherwise all industrial action by ill-treated workers would be tortious (although much of it can be thanks now to complex legislation) and all calls to boycott certain products would equally be actionable (although anyone calling for such a boycott now runs the risk of being subject to an Anti-Social Behaviour Order). One notion developed by the courts is that of 'legitimate interest' as related to the behaviour of the defendant. Thus if the defendant is acting to protect a well established interest this may give rise either to the non-existence of any economic tort or to a defence based on justification. For example, a trade association can impose fines on its members and any threat of expulsion for non-payment will not amount to blackmail or an economic tort (*Thorne v Motor Trade Association* (1937)). Even behaviour that is illegal might not be actionable at common law if it was not aimed at the claimant (*Lonrho v Shell Petroleum Co Ltd (No 2)* (1982)). However if a defendant intentionally damages a claimant in circumstances where he has no interest of his own to protect it may be that the damage will be actionable even if the behaviour itself does not actually fit into any civil or criminal wrong category (*Gulf Oil (GB) Ltd v Page* (1987)). It is of course these latter cases that make this area so complex, particularly where the remedy sought is an interlocutory (emergency) injunction rather than damages. Probably no principle is foolproof (and industrial action is governed by statute) but if one is able to add a proprietary dimension—the defendant is interfering with the claimant's 'property *right*'—it sometimes gives further conceptual strength to the granting of a remedy (see *Ex p Island Records*, above).

3.2 Assault and battery

An intentional attack on another amounts to an assault which is both a crime and a tort (trespass). The intentional touching of another without justification amounts in theory to a battery (trespass); in practice of course the law has to tolerate some intentional touching. Trespass normally requires a direct invasion. Just what amounts to 'direct' can sometimes give rise to problems as the next case illustrates.

Fagan v Metropolitan Police Commissioner **[1969] 1 Q.B. 439, QBD**

This was an appeal by way of case stated against a conviction for assaulting a police officer in the execution of his duty. The defendant was directed by a policeman to park his car in a particular spot, but the car, seemingly accidentally, came to rest on the policeman's foot. When the latter asked the defendant to remove the car he received an abusive reply. However, after several more requests, the defendant reluctantly reversed the vehicle off the policeman's foot. The appeal was dismissed by the Divisional Court (Lord Parker C.J. and James J.; Bridge J. dissenting).

James J.: ". . . In our judgment the question arising, which has been argued on general principles, falls to be decided on the facts of the particular case. An assault is any act which intentionally—or possibly recklessly—causes another person to apprehend immediate and unlawful personal violence. Although 'assault' is an independent crime and is to be treated as such, for practical purposes today 'assault' is generally synonymous with the term 'battery' and is a term used to mean the actual intended use of unlawful force to another person without his consent. On the facts of the present case the 'assault' alleged involved a 'battery.' Where an assault involves a battery, it matters not, in our judgment, whether the battery is inflicted directly by the body of the offender or through the medium of some weapon or instrument controlled by the action of the offender. An assault may be committed by the laying of a hand upon another, and the action does not cease to be an assault if it is a stick held in the hand and not the hand itself which is laid on the person of the victim. So for our part we see no difference in principle between the action of stepping on to a person's toe and maintaining that position and the action of driving a car on to a person's foot and sitting in the car whilst its position on the foot is maintained.

To constitute the offence of assault some intentional act must have been performed: a mere omission to act cannot amount to an assault. Without going into the question whether words alone can constitute an assault, it is clear that the words spoken by the appellant could not alone amount to an assault: they can only shed a light on the appellant's action. For our part we think the crucial question is whether in this case the act of the appellant can be said to be complete and spent at the moment of time when the car wheel came to rest on the foot or whether his act is to be regarded as a continuing act operating until the wheel was removed. In our judgment a distinction is to be drawn between acts which are complete—though results may continue to flow—and those acts which are continuing. Once the act is complete it cannot thereafter be said to be a threat to inflict unlawful force upon the victim. If the act, as distinct from the results thereof, is a continuing act there is a continuing threat to inflict unlawful force. If the assault involves a battery and that battery continues there is a continuing act of assault.

For an assault to be committed both the elements of actus reus and mens rea must be present at the same time. The 'actus reus' is the action causing the effect on the victim's mind (see the observations of Park B in *Regina v St George*. The 'mens rea' is the intention to cause that effect. It is not necessary that mens rea should be present at the inception of the actus reus; it can be superimposed upon an existing act. On the other hand the subsequent inception of mens rea cannot convert an act which has been completed without mens rea into an assault.

In our judgment the Willesden magistrates and quarter sessions were right in law. On the facts found the action of the appellant may have been initially unintentional, but the time came when knowing that the wheel was on the officer's foot the appellant (1) remained seated in the car so that his body through the medium of the car was in contact with the officer, (2) switched off the ignition of the car, (3) maintained the wheel of the car on the foot and (4) used words indicating the intention of keeping the wheel in that position. For our part we cannot regard such conduct as mere omission or inactivity.

There was an act constituting a battery which at its inception was not criminal because there was no element of intention but which became criminal from the moment the intention was formed to produce the apprehension which was flowing from the continuing act. The fallacy of the appellant's argument is that it seeks to equate the facts of this case with such a case as where a motorist has accidentally run over a person and, that action having been completed, fails to assist the victim with the intent that the victim should suffer.

We would dismiss this appeal"

Bridge J. (dissenting): "I fully agree with my Lords as to the relevant principles to be applied. No mere omission to act can amount to an assault. Both the elements of actus reus and mens rea must be present at the same time, but the one may be superimposed on the other. It is in the application of these principles to the highly unusual facts of this case that I have, with regret, reached a different conclusion from the majority of the court. I have no sympathy at all for the appellant, who behaved disgracefully. But I have been unable to find any way of regarding the facts which satisfies me that they amounted to the crime of assault. This has not been for want of trying. But at every attempt I have encountered the inescapable question: after the wheel of the appellant's car had accidentally come to rest on the constable's foot, what was it that the appellant did which constituted the act of assault? However the question is approached, the answer I feel obliged to give is: precisely nothing. The car rested on the foot by its own weight and, remained stationary by its own inertia. The appellant's fault was that he omitted to manipulate the controls to set it in motion again.

Neither the fact that the appellant remained in the driver's seat nor that he switched off the ignition seem to me to be of any relevance. The constable's plight would have been no better, but might well have been worse, if the appellant had alighted from the car leaving the ignition switched on. Similarly I can get no help from the suggested analogies. If one man accidentally treads on another's toe or touches him with a stick, but deliberately maintains pressure with foot or stick after the victim protests, there is clearly an assault. But there is no true parallel between such cases and the present case. It is not, to my mind, a legitimate use of language to speak of the appellant 'holding' or 'maintaining' the car wheel on the constable's foot. The expression which corresponds to the reality is that used by the justices in the case stated. They say, quite rightly, that he 'allowed' the wheel to remain.

With a reluctantly dissenting voice I would allow this appeal and quash the appellant's conviction."

NOTES

1. Although a criminal case, the judgments are equally relevant for tort since an assault and a battery are both forms of trespass to the person. One might note how the old adage that 'not doing is no trespass' still has a resonance in the modern law. However the line

between act and omission can be difficult to draw on occasions and depends on how one sees the world. Was the act of coming to rest on the constable's foot and the subsequent reluctance to reverse off it a single act? Or was it two distinct acts? It matters in cases where intention is a constituent of liability since the guilty mind (mens rea) and criminal act (actus reus) must coincide. Thus if D sets out to kill V in stormy weather, but on arriving at V's house finds him trapped under a fallen tree and returns home without aiding him or calling the emergency services, D will probably not, at common law, be guilty of unlawful killing.

2. One of the difficulties in saying that any unlawful touching of another amounts to a trespass is that ordinary horseplay, which results in unintentional injury, appears actionable without proof of fault. Would it not be better if this kind of case was dealt with as a negligence problem?

Wilson v Pringle **[1987] Q.B. 237, CA**

This was an action for damages by one schoolboy against another in respect of an injury arising out of horseplay in a school corridor. The defendant pulled at a bag being carried by the claimant causing the latter to fall and sustain a serious injury. The claimant sought summary judgment on the ground that the defendant's admission that he pulled at the bag amounted in itself to the tort of trespass (battery) and the trial judge agreed. However the Court of Appeal (O'Connor L.J., Croom-Johnson L.J. and Balcombe L.J.) allowed an appeal on this point and gave leave for the defendant to defend the action.

Croom-Johnson L.J.: ". . . The defendant in the present case has sought to add to the list of necessary ingredients. He has submitted that before trespass to the person will lie it is not only the touching that must be deliberate but the infliction of injury. The plaintiff's counsel, on the other hand, contends that it is not the injury to the person which must be intentional, but the act of touching or battery which precedes it: as he put it, what must be intentional is the application of force and not the injury. . . .

. . .[W]hat does entitle an injured plaintiff to sue for the tort of trespass to the person? Reference must be made to one further case: *Williams v Humphrey* (unreported), 12 February 1975, a decision of Talbot J. There the defendant, a boy just under 16, pushed the plaintiff into a swimming pool and caused him physical injury. The judge found the defendant acted negligently and awarded damages. But there was another claim in trespass. Talbot J rejected the submission that the action would not lie unless there was an intent to injure. He held that it was sufficient, if the act was intentional, that there was no justification for it. In the present Order 14 [summary judgement] proceedings the judge relied upon that decision. The reasoning in *Williams v Humphrey* is all right as far as it goes, but it does not go far enough. It did not give effect to the reasoning of the older authorities, such as *Tuberville v Savage*. . . that for there to be either an assault or a battery there must be something in the nature of hostility. It may be evinced by anger, by words or gesture. Sometimes the very act of battery will speak for itself, as where somebody uses a weapon on another. . . ."

QUESTIONS

1. When people push others into swimming pools do they not intend some harm? Is such behaviour not a practical joke? Are not practical jokes that end in serious injury a matter of trespass rather than negligence? (cf. *Wainwright v Home Office* (2004), p.29)

2. D deliberately travels on the underground in London during the rush hour because he likes to find himself in physical contact with others. Is he continually committing a trespass while travelling?

3. A surgeon operates upon a patient without the latter's consent: can the patient sue in trespass or only in negligence? (cf. *Sidaway v Bethlem Royal Hospital* (1985)).

NOTE

In *Blake v Galloway* (2004) a group of teenagers were involved in good-natured and high-spirited horseplay that involved the throwing twigs and pieces of wood at each other. The claimant was hit, and seriously injured, in the eye by a piece of bark thrown by the defendant. The claim for damages in negligence and trespass was rejected by the Court of Appeal. Dyson L.J. stated: "By participating in this game, the claimant must be taken to have impliedly consented to the risk of a blow on any part of his body, provided that the offending missile was thrown more or less in accordance with the tacit understandings or conventions of the game" (§ 24). Indeed, he added that the victims of horseplay "will usually not be able to recover damages unless they can show that the injury has been caused by a failure to take care which amounts to recklessness or a very high degree of carelessness, or that it was caused deliberately (i.e. with intent to cause harm)" (§ 25). See also *Mullin v Richards* (1998) (p.150).

3.3 False imprisonment

False imprisonment also amounts to the tort of trespass and thus is an action of considerable importance in constitutional law since it is often the police that imprison. Nevertheless the tort has a role in private law.

> **Bird v Jones (1845) 115 E.R. 668, QB**
>
> **Patteson J.:.** ". . . Now the facts of this case appear to be as follows. A part of Hammersmith Bridge which is ordinarily used as a public footway was appropriated for seats to view a regatta on the river, and separated for that purpose from the carriage way by a temporary fence. The plaintiff insisted on passing along the part so appropriated, and attempted to climb over the fence. The defendant, being clerk of the Bridge Company, seized his coat, and tried to pull him back: the plaintiff, however, succeeded in climbing over the fence. The defendant then stationed two policemen to prevent and, they did prevent, the plaintiff from proceeding forwards along the footway; but he was told that he might go back into the carriage way, and proceed to the other side of the bridge, if be pleased. The plaintiff would not do so, but remained where he was above half an hour: and then, on the defendant still refusing to suffer him to go forwards along the footway, he endeavoured to force his way, and, in so doing, assaulted the defendant: whereupon he was taken into custody. . . .
>
> I have no doubt that, in general, if one man compels another to stay in any given place against his will, he imprisons that other just as much as if he locked him up in a room: and I agree that it is not necessary, in order to constitute an imprisonment, that a man's person should be touched. I agree, also, that the compelling a man to go in a given direction against his will may amount to imprisonment. But I cannot bring my mind to the conclusion that, if

one man merely obstructs the passage of another in a particular direction, whether by threat of personal violence or otherwise, leaving him at liberty to stay where he is or to go in any other direction if he pleases, he can be said thereby to imprison him. He does him wrong, undoubtedly if there was a right to pass in that direction, and would be liable to an action on the case for obstructing the passage, or of assault, if, on the party persisting in going in that direction, he touched his person, or so threatened him as to amount to an assault. But imprisonment is, as I apprehend, a total restraint of the liberty of the person, for however short a time, and not a partial obstruction of his will, whatever inconvenience it may bring on him. The quality of the act cannot, however, depend on the right of the opposite party. If it be an imprisonment to prevent a man passing along the public highway, it must be equally so to prevent him passing further along a field into which he has broken by a clear act of trespass. . . ."

Coleridge J.: ". . . I am of opinion that there was no imprisonment. To call it so appears to me to confound partial obstruction and disturbance with total obstruction and detention. A prison may have its boundary large or narrow, visible and tangible, or, though real, still in the conception only; it may itself be moveable or fixed: but a boundary it must have; and that boundary the party imprisoned must be prevented from passing; he must be prevented from leaving that place, within the ambit of which the party imprisoning would confine him, except by prison-breach. Some confusion seems to me to arise from confounding imprisonment of the body with mere loss of freedom: it is one part of the definition of freedom to be able to go whithersoever one pleases; but imprisonment is something more than the mere loss of this power; it includes the notion of restraint within some limits defined by a will or power exterior to our own."

[Williams J. was of the opinion that there was no imprisonment; Lord Denman C.J. dissented.]

QUESTION

The imprisonment must be total. But what if the defendant demands money before allowing the claimant to leave an enclosure?

Robinson v Balmain New Ferry Co Ltd [1910] A.C. 295, PC

This was an action for damages for false imprisonment against a ferry company. The Privy Council (Lords Loreburn L.C., Macnaghten, Collins and Sir Arthur Wilson) held the company not liable.

Lord Loreburn L.C.: ". . . The plaintiff paid a penny on entering the wharf to stay there till the boat should start and then be taken by the boat to the other side. The defendants were admittedly always ready and willing to carry out their part of this contract. Then the plaintiff changed his mind and wished to go back. The rules as to the exit from the wharf by the turnstile required a penny for any person who went through. This the plaintiff refused to pay, and he was by force prevented from going through the turnstile. He then claimed damages for assault and false imprisonment.

There was no complaint, at all events there was no question left to the jury by the plaintiff's request, of any excessive violence, and in the circumstances admitted it is clear to their Lordships that there was no false imprisonment at all. The plaintiff was merely called upon to leave the wharf in the way in which he contracted to leave it. There is no law requiring the defendants to make the exit from their premises gratuitous to people who come there upon a definite contract which involves their leaving the wharf by another way; and the defendants were entitled to resist a forcible passage through their turnstile.

The question whether the notice which was affixed to these premises was brought home to the knowledge of the plaintiff is immaterial, because the notice itself is immaterial.

When the plaintiff entered the defendants' premises there was nothing agreed as to the terms on which he might go back, because neither party contemplated his going back. When he desired to do so the defendants were entitled to impose a reasonable condition before allowing him to pass through their turnstile from a place to which he had gone of his own free will. The payment of a penny was a quite fair condition, and if he did not choose to comply with it the defendants were not bound to let him through. He could proceed on the journey he had contracted for. . . ."

QUESTIONS

1. The notice mentioned by Lord Loreburn stated: "Notice. A Fare of One Penny Must Be Paid on Entering or Leaving the Wharf. No Exception Will Be Made to This Rule Whether the Passenger has Travelled by the Ferry or Not". Do you really think the notice was immaterial? What if there had been evidence that the company did on occasions refund money to those who did not use the ferry?

2. Why were the defendants entitled to impose a reasonable condition before allowing a person to pass through their turnstile?

3. What if the plaintiff, having entered the wharf, suddenly got a severe attack of sickness and could not face the crossing?

4. What if a child, without money, had entered and had then been refused exit until he paid? What if the inability of the child to return home for twelve hours had caused his parents to suffer severe psychological damage?

5. A group of miners refuse to continue working underground because they consider conditions to be unsafe. The manager of the mine refuses to take them to the surface until the time stipulated in their contracts of employment which in effect means that they have to remain underground for over two hours. Is this false imprisonment? (cf. *Herd v Weardale Colliery* (1915).)

6. Must the imprisoned person have been aware of his or her imprisonment? And if imprisoned by the authorities, must the imprisoned person be informed of the reasons for the imprisonment? (See next case.)

Murray v Ministry of Defence [1988] 1 W.L.R. 692, HL

This was an action for damages for false imprisonment brought against the MOD by a woman whose house was searched by soldiers in Northern Ireland. The soldiers arrived at 7am and a corporal accompanied the claimant upstairs so that she could get dressed. When they returned downstairs about half an hour later the corporal formerly arrested the claimant. The woman argued that she was falsely imprisoned between 7am and the time she was formerly arrested and one of the legal issues that arose was whether it would still be false imprisonment even if she had been unaware that she was being restrained while getting dressed. The House of Lords (Lords Keith, Templeman, Oliver, Jauncey and Griffiths) held that the arrest was not unlawful as it had been reasonable under the emergency legislation to delay formal arrest until the premises had been searched.

Lord Griffiths: ". . . The question remains, however, whether the failure to tell the plaintiff that she was being arrested until the soldiers were about to leave the house renders the arrest unlawful. It has been well-settled law, at least since *Christie v Leachinsky*, that a person must be informed of the reason for his arrest at or within a reasonable time of the arrest. There can be no doubt that in ordinary circumstances, the police should tell a person the reason for his arrest at the time they make the arrest. If a person's liberty is being restrained, he is entitled to know the reason. If the police fail to inform him, the arrest will be held to be unlawful, with the consequence that if the police are assaulted as the suspect resists arrest, he commits no offence, and if he is taken into custody, he will have an action for wrongful imprisonment. However, it is made plain in the speeches in *Christie v Leachinsky* that there are exceptions to this general rule. . . .

Although on the facts of this case I am sure that the plaintiff was aware of the restraint on her liberty from 7.00 a.m., I cannot agree with the Court of Appeal that it is an essential element of the tort of false imprisonment that the victim should be aware of the fact of denial of liberty. The Court of Appeal relied upon *Herring v Boyle*, for this proposition which they preferred to the view of Atkin LJ to the opposite effect in *Meering v Grahame-White Aviation Co Ltd*,. . .

In the first place it is not difficult to envisage cases in which harm may result from unlawful imprisonment even though the victim is unaware of it. Dean William L Prosser gave two examples in his article in the Columbia Law Review, vol. 55 (June 1955), p 847 ('False Imprisonment: Consciousness of Confinement'), in which he attacked section 42 of the *Restatement of Torts* which at that time stated the rule that "there is no liability for intentionally confining another unless the person physically restrained knows of the confinement." Dean Prosser wrote, at p 849:

> "Let us consider several illustrations. A locks B, a child two days old, in the vault of a bank. B. is, of course, unconscious of the confinement, but the bank vault cannot be opened for two days. In the meantime, B. suffers from hunger and thirst, and his health is seriously impaired; or it may be that he even dies. Is this no tort? Or suppose that A abducts B, a wealthy lunatic, and holds him for ransom for a week. B. is unaware of his confinement, but vaguely understands that he is in unfamiliar surroundings, and that something is wrong. He undergoes mental suffering affecting his health. At the end of the week, he is discovered by the police and released without ever having known that he has been imprisoned. Has he no action against B? . . . If a child of two is kidnapped, confined, and deprived of the care of its mother for a month, is the kidnapping and the confinement in itself so minor a matter as to call for no redress in tort at all?"

The Restatement of Torts has now been changed and requires that the person confined "is conscious of the confinement or is harmed by it" (*Restatement of the Law, Second, Torts 2d* (1965), section 35, p 52).

If a person is unaware that he has been falsely imprisoned and has suffered no harm, he can normally expect to recover no more than nominal damages, and it is tempting to redefine the tort in the terms of the present rule in the American Restatement of Torts. On reflection, however, I would not do so. The law attaches supreme importance to the liberty of the individual and if he suffers a wrongful interference with that liberty it should remain actionable even without proof of special damage. . . ."

NOTES

1. See also *R. v Governor of Brockhill Prison, Ex p Evans (No 2)* (2001) (p.28).

2. Police, security guards, store detectives and the like are only liable if they detain someone whom they suspect of a crime if they have detained unlawfully. Powers to stop and search and to arrest are to be found principally in the Police and Criminal Evidence Act 1984 (PACE) but new legislation is giving the police and other authorities ever more powers (see e.g. the Terrorism Acts). Some of the technicalities of arrest under PACE can be found in *Davidson v Chief Constable of North Wales* (1994). Note also the remedy of self-help: *R. v Self* (1992) (see p.464).

QUESTION

What if a person finds himself lawfully imprisoned but the lawful imprisonment is the result of police and Crown Prosecution Service carelessness with respect to the evidence. If both had done their jobs properly both would have realised that the person imprisoned had nothing to do with the crime for which he was being held. Should the person imprisoned be able to sue for damages? If so, in what tort? (cf. *Elguzouli-Daf v Commissioner of Police for the Metropolis* (1995), p.351; *Brooks v Comr of Police for the Metropolis* (2005).)

3.4 Harassment

We have already seen that there is no tort of harassment at common law: *Wainwright v Home Office* (p.29). However under statute harassment can give rise to a civil remedy.

Protection from Harassment Act 1997 (c.40)

"**1 Prohibition of harassment**

(1) A person must not pursue a course of conduct—

    (a) which amounts to harassment of another, and
    (b) which he knows or ought to know amounts to harassment of the other.

(1A) A person must not pursue a course of conduct—

    (a) which involves harassment of two or more persons, and
    (b) which he knows or ought to know involves harassment of these persons, and
    (c) by which he intends to persuade any person (whether or not one of those mentioned above)—

        (i) not to do something that he is entitled or required to do, or
        (ii) to do something that he is not under any obligation to do.

(2) For the purposes of this section, the person whose course of conduct is in question ought to know that it amounts to or involves harassment of another if a reasonable person in possession of the same information would think the course of conduct amounted to or involved harassment of the other.

(3) Subsection (1) or (1A) does not apply to a course of conduct if the person who pursued it shows—

> (a) that it was pursued for the purpose of preventing or detecting crime,
>
> (b) that it was pursued under any enactment or rule of law or to comply with any condition or requirement imposed by any person under any enactment, or
>
> (c) that in the particular circumstances the pursuit of the course of conduct was reasonable.
>
> **3 Civil remedy**
>
> (1) An actual or apprehended breach of section 1(1) may be the subject of a claim in civil proceedings by the person who is or may be the victim of the course of conduct in question.
>
> (2) On such a claim, damages may be awarded for (among other things) any anxiety caused by the harassment and any financial loss resulting from the harassment. . . .
>
> **3A Injunctions to protect persons from harassment within section 1(1A)**
>
> (2) In such a case—
>
> > (a) any person who is or may be a victim of the course of conduct in question, or
> >
> > (b) any person who is or may be a person falling within section 1(1A)(c),
>
> may apply to the High Court or a county court for an injunction. . .”

QUESTIONS

1. Will an employer be liable for harassment of one of his employees by another employee? (See **Chapter 7** and *Majrowski v Guy's & St Thomas's NHS Trust* (2007), p.262.)

2. A firm of solicitors continually sends letters, on behalf of an aggressive client, to a person threatening her with legal action when the solicitors know full well that their client has no actionable case. Could this amount to statutory harassment? Could *Adams v Bracknell Forest BC* (2005) be of relevance to this question?

3. Is 'anxiety' in s.3(2) the same as mental distress?

3.5 Fraud and lies

Several torts can be relevant where one causes deliberate damage through false statements or other behaviour amounting to fraud. Much depends upon the nature of the statement or other behaviour, the intention of the author, whether the statement was published, and the interest invaded.

3.5.1 Deceit

The elements of the tort of deceit are set out in *Bradford Building Society v Borders* (1941) (p.321). The main obstacle facing a claimant wishing to use the tort of deceit is that fraud must be proved. This is often not easy, but it may be possible for a victim to use the tort of negligence instead: see e.g. *Spring v Guardian Insurance* (1995) (p.287).

3.5.2 **Defamation and malicious falsehood**

If there is no fraud as such but still a deliberate lie that harms another, the torts of defamation and malicious prosecution may be available.

Joyce v Sengupta [1993] 1 W.L.R. 337, CA

This was an action for damages, brought by a woman who had worked as a maid in the royal household, against a newspaper and journalist, in respect of an article published in the paper which made very serious allegations about the claimant. Legal aid was not available for defamation and so the claimant based her action on the tort of malicious falsehood. The trial judge struck out the claim as an abuse of process, but an appeal against this decision was allowed by the Court of Appeal (Sir Donald Nicholls V.C., Butler-Sloss L.J. and Sir Michael Kerr).

Sir Donald Nicholls V.C.: ". . . Before turning to the issues raised by the appeal I should comment briefly on the difference between defamation and malicious falsehood. The remedy provided by the law for words which injure a person's reputation is defamation. Words may also injure a person without damaging his reputation. An example would be a claim that the seller of goods or land is not the true owner. Another example would be a false assertion that a person has closed down his business. Such claims would not necessarily damage the reputation of those concerned. The remedy provided for this is malicious falsehood, sometimes called injurious falsehood or trade libel. This cause of action embraces particular types of malicious falsehood such as slander of title and slander of goods, but it is not confined to those headings.

Falsity is an essential ingredient of this tort. The plaintiff must establish the untruth of the statement of which he complains. Malice is another essential ingredient. A genuine dispute about the ownership of goods or land should not of itself be actionable. So a person who acted in good faith is not liable. Further, since the object of this cause of action is to provide a person with a remedy for a false statement made maliciously which has caused him damage, at common law proof of financial loss was another essential ingredient. The rigour of this requirement was relaxed by statute. I shall have to return to the question of damages at a later stage. For present purposes it is sufficient to note that if a plaintiff establishes that the defendant maliciously made a false statement which has caused him financial damage, or in respect of which he is relieved from proving damage by the Defamation Act 1952, the law gives him a remedy. The false statement may also be defamatory, or it may not. As already mentioned, it need not be defamatory. Conversely, the fact that the statement is defamatory does not exclude a cause of action for malicious falsehood, although the law will ensure that a plaintiff does not recover damages twice over for the same loss. . . .

So far as the statement of claim is concerned I am satisfied that, although open to criticism here and there, it does disclose the essentials of a cause of action for malicious falsehood. . . ."

NOTE

This case is not as such an action for fraud since the motive of the defendants was not criminal profiteering (just unpleasant profiteering). The relevant tort for fraud is deceit. Nevertheless the tort of malicious falsehood might be a valuable alternative on occasions where fraud itself cannot easily be proved but malice and recklessness can. *Joyce* reaffirms the point that the existence of one cause of action within a set of facts will not exclude others. For another case where a claimant uses a tort other than defamation to obtain damages for false statements see *Spring v Guardian Assurance* (1995) (p.287). These cases of deliberate wrongdoing often raise questions of exemplary damages (see **11.2.3**).

QUESTIONS

1. What was the main interest was being protected in *Joyce*?

2. Is it true to say that maliciously causing mental distress is actionable in tort? (cf. *Wainwright v Home Office* (2004), p.29.)

3.5.3 Conspiracy

We have seen from the case of *Mogul Steamship v McGregor* (1892) (above p.98) that a conspiracy to do something lawful with the intention of injuring another may not be actionable. However a conspiracy to do something unlawful will be different.

***Revenue and Customs Commissioners v Total Network SL* [2008] 2 W.L.R. 711, HL**

This was an action for damages brough by the UK tax authorities against a company for the equivalent of amounts of VAT claimed to have been lost through what are known as carousel frauds. The cause of action was the tort of conspiracy to cause damage by unlawful means. A preliminary question of law arose as to whether the claimants were entitled to bring such an action and the House of Lords (Lords Scott, Walker and Mance; Lords Hope and Neuberger dissenting in part) held that they were (see Lord Hope below).

Lord Hope: "**1** The issue in this case is whether the Commissioners can maintain a civil claim for damages under the tort of unlawful means conspiracy against a participant in a missing trader intra-community, or carousel, fraud. Two questions need to be considered. The first is whether it is open to the Commissioners to maintain a cause of action in damages at common law as a means of recovering VAT from a person who has not been made accountable or otherwise liable for that tax by Parliament. The second is whether, if so, it is an essential requirement of the tort of unlawful means conspiracy that the conduct which is said to amount to the unlawful means should give rise to a separate action in tort against at least one of the conspirators. . . .

44 The situation that is contemplated is that of loss caused by an unlawful act directed at the claimants themselves. The conspirators cannot, on the Commissioners' primary contention, be sued as joint tortfeasors because there was no independent tort actionable by the Commissioners. This is a gap which needs to be filled. For reasons that I have already explained, I do not accept that the Commissioners suffered economic harm in this case. But assuming that they did, they suffered that harm as a result of a conspiracy which was entered into with an intention of injuring them by the means that were deliberately selected by the conspirators. If, as Lord Wright said in *Crofter Hand Woven Harris Tweed Co v Veitch* [1942] AC 435, 462, it is in the fact of the conspiracy that the unlawfulness resides, why should that principle not apply here? As a subspecies of the tort of unlawful means conspiracy, the case

---

is virtually indistinguishable from the tort of conspiracy to injure. The fact that the unlawful means were not in themselves actionable does not seem, in this context at least, to be significant. As Professor Joe Thomson put it in *An island legacy—The delict of conspiracy*, Comparative and Historical Essays in Scots Law, ed Carey Miller and Meyers (1992), p 148, the rationale of the tort is conspiracy to injure. These factors indicate that a conspiracy is tortious if an intention of the conspirators was to harm the claimant by using unlawful means to persuade him to act to his own detriment, even if those means were not in themselves tortious. . . ."

Lord Scott: ". . . **56** . . . We were taught at Law School that the action on the case was the means whereby our judicial forbears allowed tortious remedies in damages where harm had been caused in circumstances where the conduct of the authors of the harm had been sufficiently reprehensible to require the conclusion that they ought to be held responsible for the harm. The law whereby harm caused by negligence can be remedied by an action in tort for damages results from a development of the action on the case. The law enabling an action for tortious damages to be brought where two or more persons have joined together with the predominant intention of injuring another person and have successfully carried out their intention is another, and for present purposes highly relevant, example of a judicial development of the action on the case. This is the so-called 'lawful means' conspiracy which is tortious notwithstanding that the means employed to cause the harm are themselves neither criminal nor tortious. The essential ingredient of this type of action is the combination of people all intent on causing harm to the victim, not on the type of means employed for doing so. As it was put by Viscount Simon in *Crofter Hand Woven Harris Tweed Co.Ltd v Veitch* [1942] AC 435 at 445

> 'If that predominant purpose is to damage another person and damage results, that is tortious conspiracy. If the predominant purpose is the lawful protection or promotion of any lawful interest of the combiners (no illegal means being employed), it is not a tortious conspiracy, even though it causes damage to another person.'

Where, however, unlawful means are employed by the conspirators to achieve their object and their object involves causing harm to the victim, the intent to cause that harm does not have to be the predominant purpose of the conspiracy. This difference between the torts of lawful means conspiracy and unlawful means conspiracy is sometimes described as anomalous. In my opinion it is not. The difference reflects and demonstrates the essential flexibility of the action on the case. It is not all conduct foreseeably likely to cause, and that does cause, economic harm to another that is tortious. Nor should it be. The circumstances must be such as to make the conduct sufficiently reprehensible to justify imposing on those who have brought about the harm liability in damages for having done so. Bearing that in mind, the proposition that a combination of two or more people to carry out a scheme that is criminal in its nature and is intended to cause economic harm to some person does not, when carried out with that result, constitute a tort actionable by that person is, in my opinion, unacceptable. Such a proposition is not only inconsistent with the jurisprudence of tortious conspiracy, as Lord Walker has demonstrated and explained, but is inconsistent also with the historic role of the action on the case."

Lord Mance: ". . . **119** Caution is nonetheless necessary about the scope of the tort of conspiracy by unlawful means. Not every criminal act committed in order to injure can or should give rise to tortious liability to the person injured, even where the element of conspiracy is present. The pizza delivery business which obtains more custom, to the detriment of its competitors, because it instructs its drivers to ignore speed limits and jump red lights (Lord Walker in *OBG Ltd. v. Allan* [2007] UKHL 21; [2007] 2 WLR 920, para. 266) should not be liable, even if the claim be put as a claim in conspiracy involving its drivers and directors. And—as in relation to the tort of causing loss by unlawful means inflicted on a third party—there is a legitimate objection to making liability 'depend upon whether the defendant has done something which is wrongful for reasons which have nothing to do with the damage inflicted on the claimant': per Lord Hoffmann in *OBG Ltd. v. Allan* at para. 59. . . ."

QUESTIONS

1. Would *Mogul SS v McGregor Gow* (1892) (p.98) be decided differently today?

2. In what ways, if any, does *Total Network* modify the decision in *OBG Ltd v Allan* (2007) (above p.103)?

3. Does *Total Network* suggest that the action on the case is by no means dead and buried?

4. Camilla, Paula and Elsbeth, three excellent track cyclists all with many medals, decide between them to enter a World Championship pursuit race with the sole and malicious intention of preventing Sue from winning the event. If they succeed in their purpose can Sue sue Camilla, who has won the race, for damages?

3.6 Abuse of public power

We have already seen that the tort of trespass is of central importance to victims of abusive behaviour by public officials that directly interferes with the physical and constitutional well being of the victim. But where the interference and damage from abusive behaviour is more indirect, or where the interference itself might be lawful but the motive malicious, other torts become relevant. Two common law torts in particular apply to public authorities: malicious prosecution and misfeasance in public office. Added to these two there is now a statutory action created by the Human Rights Act 1998. Other torts, such as malicious falsehood and defamation, might equally be available on occasions depending on the facts.

3.6.1 Malicious prosecution

The main elements of the tort of malicious prosecution are set out in the next case.

Martin v Watson **[1996] A.C. 74, HL**

Lord Keith of Kinkel: "My Lords, the background to the proceedings which give rise to this appeal is a long history of mutual antagonism between neighbours. The appellant plaintiff, Mr Martin, and the respondent defendant, Mrs Watson, lived next door to each other in Orpington. The garden of each dwelling abutted on that of the other. Relations between the parties and their respective spouses were acrimonious for many years, for reasons which need not be gone into. Eventually the defendant began to make accusations that the plaintiff had indecently exposed himself to her. . . . [T]he plaintiff was arrested and taken to the police station, where he was interviewed and bailed to attend court the next day upon a charge related to the events of 20 July 1989. He duly did so but the Crown Prosecution Service offered no evidence and he was discharged.

In the circumstances the plaintiff brought this action for malicious prosecution against the defendant in Bromley County Court. On 13 July 1992 Judge Goodman, after trial, gave judgment in favour of the plaintiff and awarded him damages of £3,500. The defendant was granted leave to appeal to the Court of Appeal, which on 21 January 1994 by a majority (Ralph Gibson and Hobhouse LJJ, McCowan LJ dissenting) [1994] QB 425 allowed the appeal and set aside the judgment of Judge Goodman. The plaintiff now appeals, with leave given by the Court of Appeal, to your Lordships' House.

It is common ground that the ingredients of the tort of malicious prosecution are correctly stated in *Clerk & Lindsell on Torts*, 16th ed. (1989), p. 1042, para. 19–05:

> 'In action of malicious prosecution the plaintiff must show first that he was prosecuted by the defendant, that is to say, that the law was set in motion against him on a criminal charge; secondly, that the prosecution was determined in his favour; thirdly, that it was without reasonable and probable cause; fourthly, that it was malicious. The onus of proving every one of these is on the plaintiff.'

Judge Goodman found that all four of these ingredients had been proved. . . .

The question at issue is whether or not the defendant is properly to be regarded, in all the circumstances, as having set the law in motion against the plaintiff. Curiously enough, there appears to be no reported English decision dealing with the situation where the defendant in a malicious prosecution action has falsely and maliciously accused the plaintiff to a police officer of having committed an offence, with the result that a prosecution has been initiated by the police officer. A number of decisions in other Commonwealth countries have, however, considered such a state of affairs. . . .

. . .Where an individual falsely and maliciously gives a police officer information indicating that some person is guilty of a criminal offence and states that he is willing to give evidence in court of the matters in question, it is properly to be inferred that he desires and intends that the person he names should be prosecuted. Where the circumstances are such that the facts relating to the alleged offence can be within the knowledge only of the complainant, as was the position here, then it becomes virtually impossible for the police officer to exercise any independent discretion or judgment, and if a prosecution is instituted by the police officer the proper view of the matter is that the prosecution has been procured by the complainant. . . .

Mr Munby, for the defendant, mounted a powerful argument to the effect that considerations of policy pointed against a decision in favour of the plaintiff in the present case. Such a decision, so it was maintained, would tend to discourage members of the public from bringing criminal activities to the notice of the police, lest they should find themselves harassed by actions of malicious prosecution in the event that the alleged perpetrator of the offence were acquitted. The logical result, if this argument were accepted, would be to stultify completely the tort of malicious prosecution since the rationale would apply not only to those giving information which resulted in a police prosecution but also to those who themselves signed the charge sheet or laid the information. There is no good ground here for making a distinction between persons who procure a police prosecution and those who are technically prosecutors. It is said that victims of sexual assaults would be particularly discouraged from complaining. This, however, could not be so where the alleged perpetrator was a stranger to the complainant, and where the parties are known to each other a prosecution is unlikely to follow unless there is some evidence other than that of the complainant herself. Further, false accusations of sexual offences are by no means unknown, and there are many other types of offences of which a person may be falsely accused. It is to be kept in mind also that in actions for malicious prosecution the onus lies on the plaintiff to prove malice and want of reasonable cause. This would not be possible in the case of genuine complaints. It is suggested that adequate remedies for false accusations are available by way of prosecution for attempting to pervert the course of justice or wasting the time of the police, and also by way of prosecution for perjury if the complainant has actually given false evidence. But none of these remedies affords any compensation to a person who may have been arrested and imprisoned and perhaps subjected to the ordeal of a trial. . . .

. . .To deny any remedy to a person whose liberty has been interfered with as a result of unfounded and malicious accusations in such circumstances would constitute a serious denial of justice.

My Lords, for these reasons I would set aside the order of the Court of Appeal [1994] QB 425 and restore the judgment of Judge Goodman. The defendant must pay the plaintiff's costs in the Court of Appeal. The defendant was legally aided before your Lordships' House but the plaintiff was not. The plaintiff will be entitled to his costs here against the legal aid fund, subject to the usual opportunity for objection."

[Lords Slynn, Lloyd, Nicholls and Steyn agreed with Lord Keith]

NOTE

The actual person guilty of abusing public power was, in this case, not a public official. Normally in malicious prosecution cases it is a police officer that is the defendant, but, as this case shows, the tort is not confined to public officials. Perhaps the defendant in this case should be seen as a kind of temporary public official the moment she brought the public prosecution machinery into play in her dealings with her next-door neighbour.

3.6.2 Misfeasance in public office

The tort of misfeasance in public office has been reviewed and re-stated recently in a major House of Lords decision.

Three Rivers District Council v Governor and Company of The Bank of England (No 3) [2003] 2 A.C. 1, HL

This was an action for damages brought against the Bank of England by a large group of depositors who had lost money when the Bank of Credit and Commerce International (BCCI) collapsed. The cause of action was the tort of misfeasance in public office. The "plaintiffs allege that named senior officials of the Banking Supervision Department of the Bank, but not two successive Governors of the Bank, acted in bad faith (a) in licensing BCCI in 1979, when they knew that it was unlawful to do so; (b) in shutting their eyes to what was happening at BCCI after the licence was granted; and (c) in failing to take steps to close BCCI when the known facts cried out for action at least by the mid 80s" (Lord Steyn). The defendants successfully argued before the trial judge and a majority of the Court of Appeal that the action should be struck out. The House of Lords, having restated the tort of misfeasance in public office, sent the case back to the trial judge for a further hearing.

> **Lord Steyn**: ". . . The present appeal to the House, described as the plaintiffs legal appeal, is brought by the plaintiffs with the leave of the Court of Appeal given on 21 January 1999. The order of the Court of Appeal contemplated that the House would determine 'the legal issues as to the correct test for misfeasance in public office. . . before any consideration of whether the facts alleged or capable of being alleged are capable of meeting that test'. . . .

> *Misfeasance in public office*

> *The early history*

> The history of the development of the tort has been described by Clarke J and in the judgments in the Court of Appeal: see also Arrowsmith, *Civil liability and Public Authorities*, (1992), pp. 226-234. It is traceable to the 17th century: *Turner v Sterling* (1671) 2 Vent 24. But the first solid basis for this new head of tort liability, based on an action on the case, is to be found in *Ashby v White* (1703), best reported in 1 *Smith's Leading Cases* (13th ed) 253. The view ultimately prevailed that an action would lie by an elector who was wilfully denied a right to vote by a returning officer. Despite the recognition of the tort in a number of cases in the 18th and 19th centuries, the Court of Appeal in 1907 denied the existence of the tort in *Davis v. Bromley Corporation* [1908] 1 KB 170. But by 1981 the Privy Council described the tort as 'well established': *Dunlop v. Woollahra Municipal Council* [1982] AC 158, at 172F. An examination of the ingredients of the tort was still required. The first step towards that goal was the judgments in the Court of Appeal in *Bourgoin SA v Ministry of Agriculture, Fisheries and Food* [1986] QB 716. The present case is the first occasion on which the House has been called on to review the requirements of the tort in a comprehensive manner. Your Lordships are however not asked to prepare an essay on the tort of misfeasance in public office but to state the ingredients of the tort so far as it may be material to the concrete disposal of the issues arising on the pleadings in this case.

> *The matrix of the tort*

> The coherent development of the law requires the House to consider the place of the tort of misfeasance in public office against the general scheme of the law of tort. It is well established that individuals in the position of the depositors cannot maintain an action for compensation for losses they suffered as a result of the Bank's breach of statutory duties:

Yuen Kun-Yeu v Attorney-General of Hong Kong [1988] AC 175 (PC); *Davis v. Radcliffe* [1990] 1 WLR 821 (PC). Judicial review is regarded as an adequate remedy. Similarly, persons in the position of the depositors cannot sue the Bank for losses resulting from the negligent licensing, supervision or failure to withdraw a licence: *Yuen Kun-Yeu v Attorney-General of Hong Kong*; *Davis v Radcliffe*. The availability of the tort of misfeasance in public office has been said to be one of the reasons justifying the non-actionability of a claim in negligence where there is an act of maladministration: *Calveley v Chief Constable of the Merseyside Police* [1989] AC 1228, at 1238F. It is also established that an ultra vires act will not per se give rise to liability in tort: *X (Minors) v Bedfordshire County Council* [1995] 2 AC 633. And there is no overarching principle in English law of liability in tort for 'unlawful, intentional and positive acts': see *Lonrho Ltd v Shell Petroleum Co Ltd (No 2)* [1982] AC 173, 187G in which the House refused to follow *Beaudesert Shire Council v Smith* (1966) 120 CLR 145, which was subsequently overruled by the Australian High Court in *Northern Territory v Mengel* (1995) 69 AJLR 527. The tort of misfeasance in public office is an exception to 'the general rule that, if conduct is presumptively unlawful, a good motive will not exonerate the defendant, and that, if conduct is lawful apart from motive, a bad motive will not make him liable': *Winfield and Jolowicz on Tort*, 15th ed, (1998), p. 55; *Bradford Corporation v Pickles* [1895] AC 587; *Allen v Flood* [1898] AC 1. The rationale of the tort is that in a legal system based on the rule of law executive or administrative power 'may be exercised only for the public good' and not for ulterior and improper purposes: *Jones v Swansea City Council* [1990] 1 WLR 54, 85F, per Nourse LJ; a decision reversed on the facts but not on the law by the House of Lords: [1990] 1 WLR 1453, at 1458. The tort bears some resemblance to the crime of misconduct in public office: *Reg v Bowden* [1996] 1 WLR 98.

The ingredients of the tort

It is now possible to consider the ingredients of the tort. That can conveniently be done by stating the requirements of the tort in a logical sequence of numbered paragraphs.

(1) *The defendant must be a public officer*

It is the office in a relatively wide sense on which everything depends. Thus a local authority exercising private-law functions as a landlord is potentially capable of being sued: *Jones v Swansea City Council*. In the present case it is common ground that the Bank satisfies this requirement.

(2) *The second requirement is the exercise of power as a public officer*

This ingredient is also not in issue. The conduct of the named senior officials of the Banking Supervision Department of the Bank was in the exercise of public functions. Moreover, it is not disputed that the principles of vicarious liability apply as much to misfeasance in public office as to other torts involving malice, knowledge or intention: *Racz v. Home Office* [1994] 2 AC 45.

(3) *The third requirement concerns the state of mind of the defendant*

The case law reveals two different forms of liability for misfeasance in public office. First there is the case of targeted malice by a public officer ie conduct specifically intended to injure a person or persons. This type of case involves bad faith in the sense of the exercise of public power for an improper or ulterior motive. The second form is where a public officer acts knowing that he has no power to do the act complained of and that the act will probably injure the plaintiff. It involves bad faith inasmuch as the public officer does not have an honest belief that his act is lawful. . . .

The basis for the action lies in the defendant taking a decision in the knowledge that it is an excess of the powers granted to him and that it is likely to cause damage to an individual or individuals. It is not every act beyond the powers vesting in a public officer which will ground the tort. . .

. . .This is an organic development, which fits into the structure of our law governing intentional torts. The policy underlying it is sound: reckless indifference to consequences is as blameworthy as deliberately seeking such consequences. It can therefore now be regarded as settled law that an act performed in reckless indifference as to the outcome is sufficient to ground the tort in its second form. . . .

Initially, counsel for the plaintiffs argued that in this context recklessness is used in an objective sense. . . . The difficulty with this argument was that it could not be squared with a meaningful requirement of bad faith in the exercise of public powers which is the raison d'etre of the tort. But, understandably, the argument became more refined during the oral hearing and counsel for the plaintiffs accepted that only reckless indifference in a subjective sense will be sufficient. This concession was rightly made. The plaintiff must prove that the public officer acted with a state of mind of reckless indifference to the illegality of his act: *Rawlinson v Rice* [1997] 2 NZLR 651. Later in this judgment I will discuss the requirement of reckless indifference in relation to the consequences of the act.

(4) *Duty to the plaintiff*

The question is who can sue in respect of an abuse of power by a public officer. . . . It would be unwise to make general statements on a subject which may involve many diverse situations. What can be said is that, of course, any plaintiff must have a sufficient interest to found a legal standing to sue. Subject to this qualification, principle does not require the introduction of proximity as a controlling mechanism in this corner of the law. The state of mind required to establish the tort, as already explained, as well as the special rule of remoteness hereafter discussed, keeps the tort within reasonable bounds. There is no reason why such an action cannot be brought by a particular class of persons, such as depositors at a bank, even if their precise identities were not known to the bank. . . .

(5) *Causation*

Causation is an essential element of the plaintiffs cause of action. It is a question of fact. The majority in the Court of Appeal and Auld LJ held that it is unsuitable for summary determination. That is plainly correct. This conclusion disposes of agreed issue 3 so far as it relates to the tort of misfeasance.

(6) *Damage and Remoteness*

The claims by the plaintiffs are in respect of financial losses they suffered. These are, of course, claims for recovery of consequential economic losses. The question is when such losses are recoverable. It would have been possible, as a matter of classification, to discuss this question under paragraph 3 in which the required state of mind for this tort was examined. It is, however, convenient to consider it under the traditional heading of remoteness. . . ."

(See p.97 for further extract)

QUESTIONS

1. Prison officials release a highly dangerous criminal from prison knowing that they have no lawful power to do so. The prisoner, while free, kills a member of the public. Can the victim (or more precisely his estate) sue the Home Office in damages for misfeasance in public office? (cf. *Akenzua v Home Secretary* (2003), p.340)

2. Must physical or economic damage be proved before a claimant can succeed in the tort of misfeasance in public office? Could a victim of an abuse by a public official argue that the tort is designed to protect a 'constitutional' right and that actual damage does not therefore have to be proved?

Watkins v Home Office [2006] 2 A.C. 395, HL

This was an action for damages by a serving prisoner against the Home Office in respect of the opening of his mail in breach of Prison Rules. The cause of action was misfeasance in public office. The prisoner was unable to establish actual loss or damage, but the Court of Appeal held that the wrongful and malicious act of the prison officers amounted to a breach of the prisoner's constitutional right and that, accordingly, proof of special damage was unnecessary. An appeal to the House of Lords (Lords Bingham, Hope, Rodger, Walker and Carswell) was allowed.

Lord Rodger: ". . . **62** The term 'constitutional right' works well enough, alongside equivalent terms, in the field of statutory interpretation. But, even if it were otherwise suitable, it is not sufficiently precise to define a class of rights whose abuse should give rise to a right of action in tort without proof of damage. Moreover, any expansion to cover abuse of rights under 'constitutional statutes', as defined by Laws LJ in *Thoburn v Sunderland City Council* [2003] QB 151, 186E -G, would carry with it similar problems of deciding which statutes fell within the definition. Even supposing that these could be resolved, it is by no means clear that the abuse of 'constitutional rights' or rights under 'constitutional statutes' should necessarily attract a remedy which would be denied for the abuse of other important rights. Is the prisoner who suffers no material harm from abuse of his right to correspond with his solicitor necessarily more deserving of a remedy than the patient who is actually perfectly healthy but whose general practitioner maliciously refuses to see him? Or than the applicant who is not actually entitled to a social security benefit but who is maliciously denied the appropriate hearing by the relevant official? At least within the realm of tort law, questions about the availability of a remedy are best answered by looking at the substance of the supposed wrong rather than by reference to a somewhat imprecise label which lawyers might attach to it in another connection. . . .

64 My Lords, despite the encircling difficulties, it might be worth trying to deploy the concept of constitutional rights in the law of tort if it represented a way forward which best fitted the present state of the law. But it does not. Most of the references to 'constitutional rights' are to be found in cases dealing with situations before the Human Rights Act 1998 brought Convention rights into our law. In using the language of 'constitutional rights', the judges were, more or less explicitly, looking for a means of incorporation avant la lettre, of having the common law supply the benefits of incorporation without incorporation. Now that the Human Rights Act 1998 is in place, such heroic efforts are unnecessary: the Convention rights form part of our law and provide a rough equivalent of a written code of constitutional rights, albeit not one tailor-made for this country. In general, at least, where the matter is not already covered by the common law but falls within the scope of a Convention right, a claimant can be expected to invoke his remedy under the Human Rights Act rather than to seek to fashion a new common law right: *Wainwright v Home Office* [2004] 2 AC 406, 423, para 33, per Lord Hoffmann. It may be-as counsel for the Home Secretary was inclined to concede, even though the point was not fully argued, that someone in the respondent's position could now bring proceedings under section 8 of the Human Rights Act 1998 for damages for breach of certain of the guarantees in articles 6 and 8 of the Convention. But, if so, in considering whether to award damages, the courts would apply the principles developed by the European Court of Human Rights: *R (Greenfield) v Secretary of State for the Home Department* [2005] 1 WLR 673. Exemplary damages form no part of the existing jurisprudence of that court. Therefore, in my view, it would be wrong in principle for the House now to develop the common law so as to create a situation where exemplary damages could be awarded when they would not be available in equivalent proceedings for breach of the relevant Convention right. No award of exemplary damages would be competent, either, it may be noted, in equivalent proceedings under Scots law. . . ."

NOTES

1. Another case where the harm suffered by the claimant was not recognised as 'damage' is *Rothwell v Chemical & Insulating Co Ltd* (2007) (p.92).

2. With respect to exemplary damages, see **11.2.3**.

QUESTION

Does the expression 'constitutional right' have any legal meaning in itself or is it just an expression referring to certain interests that the law will (or might) protect via its system of causes of action and remedies?

3.6.3 Abuse of a human right

There is no tort at common law of invading or abusing a human right. However statute has established the possibility of an action against a 'public authority'.

Human Rights Act 1998 (c.42)

"**6. Acts of public authorities**

(1) It is unlawful for a public authority to act in a way which is incompatible with a Convention right.

(2) Subsection (1) does not apply to an act if—

(a) as the result of one or more provisions of primary legislation, the authority could not have acted differently; or

(b) in the case of one or more provisions of, or made under, primary legislation which cannot be read or given effect in a way which is compatible with the Convention rights, the authority was acting so as to give effect to or enforce those provisions.

(3) In this section "public authority" includes—

(a) a court or tribunal,. . .

7. Proceedings

(1) A person who claims that a public authority has acted (or proposes to act) in a way which is made unlawful by section 6(1) may—

(a) bring proceedings against the authority under this Act in the appropriate court or tribunal, or
(b) rely on the Convention right or rights concerned in any legal proceedings,

but only if he is (or would be) a victim of the unlawful act. . . .

(8) Nothing in this Act creates a criminal offence.

8. Judicial remedies

(1) In relation to any act (or proposed act) of a public authority which the court finds is (or would be) unlawful, it may grant such relief or remedy, or make such order, within its powers as it considers just and appropriate.
(2) But damages may be awarded only by a court which has power to award damages, or to order the payment of compensation, in civil proceedings.
(3) No award of damages is to be made unless, taking account of all the circumstances of the case, including—

(a) any other relief or remedy granted, or order made, in relation to the act in question (by that or any other court), and
(b) the consequences of any decision (of that or any other court) in respect of that act,
the court is satisfied that the award is necessary to afford just satisfaction to the person in whose favour it is made.

(4) In determining—

(a) whether to award damages, or
(b) the amount of an award,

the court must take into account the principles applied by the European Court of Human Rights in relation to the award of compensation under Article 41 of the Convention."

NOTES

1. Note the expression 'take into account' in s.8(4). See also s.2 of the Act.

2. The scope of s.7 may be more limited than it might first appear.

Wainwright v Home Office [2004] 2 A.C. 406, HL

(For facts see p.29)

Lord Hoffmann: ". . . **51** Article 8 is more difficult. Buxton LJ thought [2002] QB 1334, 1352, para 62, that the Wainwrights would have had a strong case for relief under section 7 if the 1998 Act had been in force. Speaking for myself, I am not so sure. Although article 8 guarantees a right of privacy, I do not think that it treats that right as having been invaded and requiring a remedy in damages, irrespective of whether the defendant acted intentionally, negligently or accidentally. It is one thing to wander carelessly into the wrong hotel bedroom and another to hide in the wardrobe to take photographs. Article 8 may justify a monetary remedy for an intentional invasion of privacy by a public authority, even if no damage is suffered other than distress for which damages are not ordinarily recoverable. It does not follow that a merely negligent act should, contrary to general principle, give rise to a claim for damages for distress because it affects privacy rather than some other interest like bodily safety: compare *Hicks v Chief Constable of South Yorkshire Police* [1992] 2 All ER 65."

NOTES

1. This extract illustrates once again how (i) the difference between intentional and unintentional behaviour and (ii) the nature of the interest invaded are vital components in assessing liability. A deliberate invasion of privacy is one thing while a negligent invasion is another.
2. However see now *Wainwright v UK* (2006) (p.31).

3.7 Abuse of the judicial process

The tort of malicious prosecution indicates that the common law has long regarded the deliberate misuse of the judicial process as capable of giving rise to an action for damages. To what extent is the common law prepared to extend the law beyond malicious prosecution? The next case indicates that there may be a more general tort.

Gibbs v Rea [1998] A.C. 786, PC

This was an action for damages brought against a drugs squad police officer for the malicious procurement of a search warrant. The defendant had obtained the warrant to search the claimant's home and workplace, but there was no documented evidence indicating grounds for suspicion. Indeed the claimant was able to show that there was no reasonable grounds for suspecting him of drug-trafficking and the defendant was unable to rebut this evidence. The trial judge dismissed the claim but the Court of Appeal of the Cayman Islands allowed an appeal and awarded the claimant damages. The Privy Council (Lords Steyn and, Hutton and Gault J.; Lords Goff and Hope dissenting) dismissed an appeal.

Gault J. (delivering the judgment of the Privy Council): ". . . On the first issue their Lordships agree with the conclusions reached by the courts below and accepted by counsel.

That it is an actionable wrong to procure the issue of a search warrant without reasonable cause and with malice has long been recognised though seldom successfully prosecuted: *Elsee v Smith* (1822) 2 Chit. 304, *Hope v Evered* (1886) 17 Q.B.D. 338, 340, *Everett v Ribbands* [1952] 2 Q.B. 198, 205, *Reynolds v Commissioner of Police of the Metropolis* [1985] Q.B. 881, 886. Generally any damage will arise from execution rather than issue of a warrant but there may be special circumstances in which it can be shown that the issue of the warrant will itself cause harm. It is the essential element of malice that distinguishes the cause of action from that of trespass where entry is made without authority or on the authority of a warrant invalid on its face. It is akin to malicious prosecution which is a well established tort and to the less common tort of maliciously procuring an arrest: *Roy v Prior* [1971] A.C. 470. The true foundation of each is intentional abuse of the processes of the court. Malice in this context has the special meaning common to other torts and covers not only spite and ill-will but also improper motive. In the present context the requirement of improper motive would be satisfied by proof of intent to use the process of the court for granting a warrant for a purpose other than to search in the permitted circumstances. . . ."

NOTES

1. In *Keegan v Chief Constable of Merseyside* (2003) (below, p.353) Ward L.J. noted that there are four ingredients of the tort. These are "(1) that there was a successful application for the search warrant; (2) that the defendant did not have reasonable and probable cause to make the application; (3) that the defendant acted with malice; and (4) that the damage resulted from the issue or execution of the warrant" (§ 26).

2. It may be that there is a more general tort of abuse of the court process.

Speed Seal Products v Paddington [1985] 1 W.L.R. 1327, CA

This was a counterclaim for damages brought by a defendant against a plaintiff who sought an injunction for breach of confidence. The defendant had worked for the plaintiff on the design of oil-pipe couplings but had left to set up his own business. The defendant alleged that the injunction action was not brought in good faith and thus amounted to the tort of abuse of court process. The Court of Appeal (Fox L.J. and Lloyd L.J. and Sir George Waller) agreed with the trial judge that the defendant's counterclaim should not be struck out as he had an arguable case.

Fox L.J.: ". . . But quite apart from these contentions, the defendants advance a further argument. They say that there is a tort of abuse of process of the court established by *Grainger v Hill*. . . .

It is clear that the court distinguished the case from one of malicious prosecution, and accordingly rejected the arguments based upon non-determination of the original proceedings. They regarded the wrong as abuse of the process. And the abuse, as I understand it, was that the purpose of the original proceeding was not the recovery of the debt (which was not due) but the extortion of the register. . . .

It seems to me that if allegations of fact pleaded in the draft counterclaim are established at the trial, the decision in *Grainger v Hill* provides a basis for an arguable case that there has been an actionable abuse of the process of the court. I express no view as to the strength of the defendants' case. It is enough to say that I think that a sufficiently arguable case has been demonstrated to justify giving leave to amend the defence by adding a counterclaim as asked. It will be open to the defendants to support it by such arguments as may be available, whether based on *Grainger v Hill* or not. . . ."

NOTE

This case is probably as close as English law will get to a general doctrine of abuse of rights since it goes some way in saying that intentionally causing economic loss to another might be actionable where the actor is pursuing no legitimate interest (and see *Gulf Oil Ltd v Page* (1987); cf. *Femis-Bank Ltd v Lazar* (1991)). Thus the case needs to be read alongside the economic torts cases extracted earlier in the chapter (and see Taggart, *Private Property and Abuse of Rights in Victorian England*, (London: Oxford University Press, 2002), pp.145–166) and cases like *White & Carter (Councils) v McGregor* (1962) (C&MC, p.386) where Lord Reid hints at an abuse of process where a person sues in debt with no legitimate interest in play). But *Speed Seal* is not laying down any normative principle in the abstract, for the absence of a legitimate interest is not enough. The abuse still needs to be inserted into an existing specific category: abuse of legal process, nuisance, economic tort, malicious prosecution and so on. There is, in other words, no general duty not intentionally to cause loss (and how could there be?).

4 Liability for individual acts (2): harm negligently caused

In the last chapter, which attempted to bring together all the torts based upon harm intentionally caused, the fragmented nature of that area of law was evident from the outset. It is a matter of bringing together a range of diverse torts (causes of action) (cf. **1.7**). The main reason for this fragmentation is that behaviour is not enough; the nature of the harm—or the interest invaded— is a fundamental constituent of liability because intentionally causing physical loss is not the same as intentionally causing economic harm. Moreover the notion of 'intention' is itself difficult. With respect to damage negligently caused the position at first sight looks very different. The area seems dominated by a single tort, itself, perhaps, governed by a single principle (the 'neighbour principle'). This is the tort of negligence with its principle of liability based upon a common duty of care. In truth the position turns out to be more complex since the nature of the harm (interest) does prove important even if this has to be concealed within the tort of negligence itself (rather than expressed via separate causes of action). This said, harm caused by careless behaviour is not completely confined to the single tort of negligence since unreasonable behaviour can be an ingredient of other torts such as nuisance. In addition, some take the view that the tort of breach of statutory duty is a form of statutory negligence, although it is probably more helpful to say that it is based on *unlawful* behaviour.

4.1 Negligence as a cause of action

Negligence as an independent tort was established by the following decision.

Donoghue v Stevenson **[1932] A.C. 562, HL**

This was an action for damages brought by the consumer of a bottle of ginger-beer against the manufacturer of the drink. The consumer, Mrs Donoghue, alleged that she had gone to a café with a friend who had bought her a bottle of ginger beer, some of which she poured over an ice cream and then consumed. When Mrs Donoghue poured some more of the beer out of the opaque bottle, she claimed that a decomposed snail emerged with the liquid and that she suffered physical and psychological damage as a result. Mrs Donoghue asserted that the manufacturer owed her a legal duty to keep such foreign bodies out of his products, but the latter agued in return that, even if he had been careless, he owed her no legal duty of care. A preliminary question of law was thus raised as to whether, as a matter of law, a legal duty was owed by the manufacturer to Mrs Donoghue. A bare majority of the House of Lords (Lords Atkin, Macmillan and Thankerton; Lords Buckmaster and Tomlin dissenting) held that such a duty did exist.

Lord Atkin: ". . . At present I content myself with pointing out that in English law there must be, and is, some general conception of relations giving rise to a duty of care, of which the particular cases found in the books are but instances. The liability for negligence, whether you style it such or treat it as in other systems as a species of 'culpa', is no doubt based upon a general public sentiment of moral wrongdoing for which the offender must pay. But acts or omissions which any moral code would censure cannot in a practical world be treated so as to give a right to every person injured by them to demand relief. In this way rules of law arise which limit the range of complainants and the extent of their remedy. The rule that you are to love your neighbour becomes in law, you must not injure your neighbour; and the lawyer's question, who is my neighbour? receives a restricted reply. You must take reasonable care to avoid acts or omissions which you can reasonably foresee would be likely to injure your neighbour. Who, then, in law is my neighbour? The answer seems to be— persons who are so closely and directly affected by my act that I ought reasonably to have them in contemplation as being so affected when I am directing my mind to the acts or omissions which are called in question. This appears to me to be the doctrine of *Heaven v Pender*. . . There will no doubt arise cases where it will be difficult to determine whether the contemplated relationship is so close that the duty arises. But in the class of case now before the court I cannot conceive any difficulty to arise. A manufacturer puts up an article of food in a container which he knows will be opened by the actual consumer. There can be no inspection by any purchaser and no reasonable preliminary inspection by the consumer. Negligently, in the course of preparation, he allows the contents to be mixed with poison. It is said that the law of England and Scotland is that the poisoned consumer has no remedy against negligent manufacturer. If this were the result of the authorities, I should consider the result a grave defect in the law, and so contrary to principle that I should hesitate long before following any decision to that effect which had not the authority of this House. I would point out that, in the assumed state of the authorities, not only would the consumer have no remedy against manufacturer, he would have none against any one else, for in the circumstances alleged there would be no evidence of negligence against any one other than the manufacturer; and, except the case of a consumer who was also a purchaser, no contract and no warranty of fitness, and in the case of the purchase of a specific article under its patent or trade name, which might well the case in the purchase of some articles of food or drink, no warranty protecting even the purchaser-consumer . . . I do not think so ill of our jurisprudence as to suppose that its principles are so remote from the ordinary needs of civilised society and the ordinary claims it makes upon its members as to deny a legal remedy where there is so obviously a social wrong . . .

In my opinion several decided cases support the view that in such a case as the present the manufacturer owes a duty to the consumer to be careful . . .'"

NOTES

1. This case is the starting point for the modern UK tort of negligence. Despite being a Scottish case, it is equally an English precedent because the House of Lords stated that they were declaring the law of England as well. Just why the case is so important is to be found in a number of factors. First it extended 'contract' in that the original supplier, if also the manufacturer, could be liable to an ultimate consumer of the product despite the absence of any direct contractual relationship between the two. If Mrs Donoghue had bought the beer herself she could have sued the café owner in contract without having to

prove fault (*Frost v Aylesbury Dairy Co Ltd* (1905); C&MC, p.61). In allowing her to sue the manufacturer she has to prove fault, but this is less of a burden than it might seem thanks to a later case establishing that the defect itself is prima facie evidence of negligence (*Grant v Australian Knitting Mills Ltd* (1936)). Legislation has further improved the position of the third-party consumer (Consumer protection Act 1987, below p.184).

2. Secondly it established a general principle of liability. Normally a case is rarely much of an authority beyond its own material facts, but Lord Atkin famously stated his neighbour principle. This is what lifts negligence liability out of its imprisonment within specific factual categories and establishes the tort as a general cause of action prima facie applicable, seemingly, to any set of facts where damage is caused, by a careless act, to anyone within the 'neighbour' range of 'proximity'. However the neighbour principle was not to be as abstract as it might first have appeared. One material fact was the damage suffered by Mrs Donoghue which was physical illness. Later cases, citing earlier ones, identified the 'interest' forming the object of manufacturer's duty as the threat to health, not the threat to the pocket (see Consumer Protection Act 1987 s.5(2)). Put another way, the physical injury suffered by Mrs Donoghue and her economic loss (loss of a bottle of drinkable beer) are two quite different types of 'damage' (*Birse Construction Ltd v Haiste Ltd*, p.462).

3. Thirdly, it was never proved whether or not there was a snail in the ginger-beer bottle (*Freeman v Home Office (No 2)* (1984), at pp 555–556). This is because the case never went to trial. The appeal that reached the House of Lords was a 'striking out' action; that is to say the defendant asked the court on a preliminary question of law to strike out the case as disclosing no cause of action. Even if, argued the defendant, all the facts, including negligence, were proved by the claimant, these facts would still not make him liable since they disclosed no duty of care. What the House of Lords had to decide, then, was whether they did disclose a duty of care and, in order to decide this question, it was assumed that there was a snail in the bottle. Having lost the preliminary question of law action, Stevenson settled the case (see Rodger (1988) 41 CLP 1). Many subsequent duty of care cases are striking out claims and some have proved problematic from a human rights position (see *Barrett v Enfield LBC* (2001) and *Z v UK* (2001): read both in the law reports).

QUESTIONS

1. Imagine that the friend who purchased the ginger beer in the café for Mrs Donoghue had run out of the premises before paying for the drink but after Mrs Donoghue had drunk some of the contents. Could the café owner demand that Mrs Donoghue pay for the beer? If your answer to this question is 'yes', does this mean that *Donoghue v Stevenson* went to the House of Lords on a false premise?

2. Is every decision in the tort of negligence since 1932 based on the premise that the thing that does the damage to the claimant is analogous (or not) to a bottle of ginger beer?

FURTHER NOTE

The next major development in the tort of negligence was the decision in *Hedley Byrne*. This decision extended liability to damage done by careless words (misrepresentation) and although it looks at first sight a major extension of *Donoghue v Stevenson* it is probably more accurate to see the case as a development in the area of the tort of deceit (see *Peek v Derry* (1887) CA; cf. (1889) HL)), perhaps with the idea of filling gaps in the law of contract rather than in extending *Donoghue* as such (cf. Supply of Goods and Services Act 1982 s.13).

Hedley Byrne & Co v Heller & Partners Ltd [1964] A.C. 465, HL

This was an action for damages brought by a firm of advertising agents against a bank in respect of financial loss incurred by the agents when one of their clients, to whom they had extended credit, went into liquidation. The advertising agents had extended the credit on the basis of a credit reference supplied by the defendant bank. The bank denied liability on the ground either that they owed no duty of care to the agency or that they were protected by an exclusion clause. The House of Lords (Lords Reid, Morris, Hodson, Devlin and Pearce), while giving judgment for the bank on the basis of the clause, nevertheless decided that such facts could give rise to a duty of care.

Lord Reid: ". . . The appellants' first argument was based on *Donoghue v Stevenson*. That is a very important decision, but I do not think that it has any direct bearing on this case. That decision may encourage us to develop existing lines of authority, but it cannot entitle us to disregard them. Apart altogether from authority, I would think that the law must treat negligent words differently from negligent acts. The law ought so far as possible to reflect the standards of the reasonable man, and that is what *Donoghue v Stevenson* sets out to do. The most obvious difference between negligent words and negligent acts is this. Quite careful people often express definite opinions on social or informal occasions even when they see that others are likely to be influenced by them; and they often do that without taking that care which they would take if asked for their opinion professionally or in a business connection. The appellant agrees that there can be no duty of care on such occasions, and we were referred to American and South African authorities where that is recognised, although their law appears to have gone much further than ours has yet done. But it is at least unusual casually to put into circulation negligently made articles which are dangerous. A man might give a friend a negligently-prepared bottle of home-made wine and his friend's guests might drink it with dire results. But it is by no means clear that those guests would have no action against the negligent manufacturer.

Another obvious difference is that a negligently made article will only cause one accident, and so it is not very difficult to find the necessary degree of proximity or neighbourhood between the negligent manufacturer and the person injured. But words can be broadcast with or without the consent or the foresight of the speaker or writer. It would be one thing to say that the speaker owes a duty to a limited class, but it would be going very far to say that he owes a duty to every ultimate 'consumer' who acts on those words to his detriment. It would be no use to say that a speaker or writer owes a duty but can disclaim responsibility if he wants to. He, like the manufacturer, could make it part of a contract that he is not to be liable for his negligence: but that contract would not protect him in a question with a third party, at least if the third party was unaware of it.

So it seems to me that there is good sense behind our present law that in general an innocent but negligent misrepresentation gives no cause of action. There must be something more than the mere misstatement. I therefore turn to the authorities to see what more is required. The most natural requirement would be that expressly or by implication from the circumstances the speaker or writer has undertaken some responsibility, and that appears to me not to conflict with any authority which is binding on this House . . .

A reasonable man, knowing that he was being trusted or that his skill and judgment were being relied on, would, I think have three courses open to him. He could keep silent or decline to give the information or advice sought: or he could give an answer with a clear qualification that he accepted no responsibility for it or that it was given without that reflection or inquiry which a careful answer would require: or he could simply answer without any such qualification. If he chooses to adopt the last course he must, I think, be held to have accepted some responsibility for his answer being given carefully, or to have accepted a relationship with the inquirer which requires him to exercise such care as the circumstances require . . .

The appellants founded on a number of cases in contract where very clear words were required to exclude the duty of care which would otherwise have flowed from the contract. To that argument there are, I think, two answers. In the case of a contract it is necessary to exclude liability for negligence, but in this case the question is whether an undertaking to assume duty to take care can be inferred: and that is a very different matter. And, secondly, even in cases of contract general words may be sufficient if there was no other kind of liability to be excluded except liability for negligence: the general rule is that a party is not exempted from liability for negligence 'unless adequate words are used'—per Scrutton LJ in *Rutter v Palmer*. It being admitted that there was here a duty to give an honest reply, I do not see what further liability there could be to exclude except liability for negligence: there being no contract there was no question of warranty.

I am therefore of opinion that it is clear that the respondents never undertook any duty to exercise care in giving their replies. The appellants cannot succeed unless there was such a duty and therefore in my judgment this appeal must be dismissed."

Lord Morris: ". . . My Lords, I consider that it follows and that it should now be regarded as settled that if someone possessed of a special skill undertakes, quite irrespective of contract, to apply that skill for the assistance of another person who relies upon such skill, a duty of care will arise. The fact that the service is to be given by means of or by the instrumentality of words can make no difference. Furthermore, if in a sphere in which a person is so placed that others could reasonably rely upon his judgment or his skill or upon his ability to make careful inquiry, a person takes it upon himself to give information or advice to, or allows his information or advice to be passed on to, another person who, as he knows or should know, will place reliance upon it, then a duty of care will arise . . ."

Lord Devlin: ". . . [T]he distinction is now said to depend on whether financial loss is caused through physical injury or whether it is caused directly. The interposition of the physical injury is said to make a difference of principle. I can find neither logic nor common sense in this. If irrespective of contract, a doctor negligently advises a patient that he can safely pursue his occupation and he cannot and the patient's health suffers and he loses his livelihood, the patient has a remedy. But if the doctor negligently advises him that he cannot safely pursue his occupation when in fact he can and he loses his livelihood, there is said to be no remedy. Unless, of course, the patient was a private patient and the doctor accepted half a guinea for his trouble: then the patient can recover all. I am bound to say my Lords, that I think this to be nonsense. It is not the sort of nonsense that can arise even in the best system of law out of the need to draw nice distinctions between borderline cases. It arises, if it is the law, simply out of a refusal to make sense. The line is not drawn on any intelligible principle. It just happens to be the line which those who have been driven from the extreme assertion that negligent statements in the absence of contractual or fiduciary duty give no cause of action have in the course of their retreat so far reached . . .

I think . . . that there is ample authority to justify your Lordships in saying now that the categories of special relationships which may give rise to a duty to take care in word as well as in deed are not limited to contractual relationships or to relationships of fiduciary duty, but include also relationships which in the words of Lord Shaw in *Nocton v Lord Ashburton* are 'equivalent to contract', that is, where there is an assumption of responsibility in circumstances in which, but for the absence of consideration, there would be a contract. Where there is an express undertaking, an express warranty as distinct from mere representation, there can be little difficulty. The difficulty arises in discerning those cases in which the undertaking is to be implied. In this respect the absence of consideration is not irrelevant. Payment for information or advice is very good evidence that it is being relied upon and that the informer or adviser knows that it is. Where there is no consideration, it will be necessary to exercise greater care in distinguishing between social and professional relationships and between those which are of a contractual character and those which are not. It may often be material to consider whether the adviser is acting purely out of good nature or whether he is getting his reward in some indirect form. The service that a bank performs in giving a reference is not done simply out of a desire to assist commerce. It would discourage the customers of the bank if their deals fell through because the bank had refused to testify to their credit when it was good . . ."

Lord Pearce: ". . . To import such a duty the representation must normally, I think, concern a business or professional transaction whose nature makes clear the gravity of the inquiry and the importance and influence attached to the answer . . ."

NOTE

Those suffering loss as a result of a misstatement need no longer prove fraud provided they can establish a *special relationship*. Thus, in the words of Lord Steyn, "the rule was established that irrespective of contract, if someone possessed of a special skill undertakes to apply that skill for the assistance of another person who relies upon such skill, a duty of care will arise" (*Arthur JS Hall & Co v Simons* (2002) at p.676). The case extends the tort of negligence into the realm of protecting a pure economic interest. However there must normally be (i) a misstatement and (ii) a *voluntary assumption* of responsibility by the defendant together with (iii) *reliance* by the claimant. Yet it may be that 'reliance' will be interpreted quite generously when the duty problem is closely associated, directly or indirectly, with a contractual relationship. Thus liability can attach to a reference from an ex-employer (*Spring v Guardian Assurance* (1995), below p.287) and to a breach of contract by a solicitor where only a third party (and not the contracting party) suffers loss as a result of the breach (*White v Jones*, below p.289). What is particularly important about *Hedley Byrne* is its central place in the law of obligations in as much as it straddles the divide between contract and tort.

PROBLEM

Tony asks Geoffrey, a solicitor, at a cocktail party if it is OK for him, Tony, to be a witness to his friend's will under which the friend has bequeathed to him his house. Geoffrey, who has had a few drinks, replies that it "is perfectly legal". After the friend's death Tony learns that he cannot inherit because he is a witness to the will. Can Tony sue Geoffrey for damages for a lost house?

QUESTIONS

1. Could a person who negligently withdraws a contractual offer before it has been accepted by the offeree ever be liable for any financial loss caused to the offeree by the withdrawal?

2. Can the principle of *Hedley Byrne* cover a failure to take action?

Customs and Excise Commissioners v Barclays Bank Plc **[2007] 1 A.C. 181, HL**

This was an action for damages in negligence by the Customs and Excise Commissioners against a bank in respect of tax money that the Commissioners had been unable to recover from two companies who banked with the defendant. They had been unable to recover the tax because the bank had, allegedly, negligently failed to prevent payments from the companies' accounts in breach of injunctions. A preliminary question of law arose as to whether the bank owed the claimants a duty of care. The House of Lords (Lords Bingham, Hoffmann, Rodger, Walker and Mance) held that there was no such duty.

Lord Hoffmann: "25 My Lords, the question in this case is whether a bank served with a freezing order (ci-devant *Mareva* injunction) upon a customer's account owes a duty to the claimant to take reasonable care to ensure that no payments are made out of the account. The Court of Appeal held that it did but in my opinion it does not. . . .

31 How does one determine whether a duty of care is owed? In cases of pure economic loss such as this, it is not sufficient that the bank ought reasonably to have foreseen that unless they had proper systems in place and their employees took reasonable care to give effect to any freezing orders which came along, the beneficiaries of those orders might suffer loss. In the case of personal or physical injury, reasonable foreseeability of harm is usually enough, in accordance with the principle in *Donoghue v Stevenson* [1932] AC 562, to generate a duty of care. In the case of economic loss, something more is needed. . . .

35 There is a tendency, which has been remarked upon by many judges, for phrases like 'proximate', 'fair, just and reasonable' and 'assumption of responsibility' to be used as slogans rather than practical guides to whether a duty should exist or not. These phrases are often illuminating but discrimination is needed to identify the factual situations in which they provide useful guidance. For example, in a case in which A provides information to C which he knows will be relied upon by D, it is useful to ask whether A assumed responsibility to D: *Hedley Byrne & Co Ltd v Heller & Partners Ltd* [1964] AC 465: *Smith v Eric S Bush* [1990] 1 AC 831. Likewise, in a case in which A provides information on behalf of B to C for the purpose of being relied upon by C, it is useful to ask whether A assumed responsibility to C for the information or was only discharging his duty to B: *Williams v Natural Life Health Foods Ltd* [1998] 1 WLR 830. Or in a case in which A provided information to B for the purpose of enabling him to make one kind of decision, it may be useful to ask whether he assumed responsibility for its use for a different kind of decision: *Caparo Industries plc v Dickman* [1990] 2 AC 605. In these cases in which the loss has been caused by the claimant's reliance on information provided by the defendant, it is critical to decide whether the

defendant (rather than someone else) assumed responsibility for the accuracy of the information to the claimant (rather than to someone else) or for its use by the claimant for one purpose (rather than another). The answer does not depend upon what the defendant intended but, as in the case of contractual liability, upon what would reasonably be inferred from his conduct against the background of all the circumstances of the case. The purpose of the inquiry is to establish whether there was, in relation to the loss in question, the necessary relationship (or 'proximity') between the parties and, as Lord Goff of Chieveley pointed out in *Henderson v Merrett Syndicates Ltd* [1995] 2 AC 145, 181, the existence of that relationship and the foreseeability of economic loss will make it unnecessary to undertake any further inquiry into whether it would be fair, just and reasonable to impose liability. In truth, the case is one in which, but for the alleged absence of the necessary relationship, there would be no dispute that a duty to take care existed and the relationship is what makes it fair, just and reasonable to impose the duty.

36 It is equally true to say that a sufficient relationship will be held to exist when it is fair, just and reasonable to do so. Because the question of whether a defendant has assumed responsibility is a legal inference to be drawn from his conduct against the background of all the circumstances of the case, it is by no means a simple question of fact. Questions of fairness and policy will enter into the decision and it may be more useful to try to identify these questions than simply to bandy terms like 'assumption of responsibility' and 'fair, just and reasonable'. In *Morgan Crucible Co plc v Hill Samuel & Co Ltd* [1991] Ch 295, 300–303 I tried to identify some of these considerations in order to encourage the evolution of lower-level principles which could be more useful than the high abstractions commonly used in such debates. . . .

39 There is, in my opinion, a compelling analogy with the general principle that, for the reasons which I discussed in *Stovin v Wise* [1996] AC 923, 943–944, the law of negligence does not impose liability for mere omissions. It is true that the complaint is that the bank did something: it paid away the money. But the payment is alleged to be the breach of the duty and not the conduct which generated the duty. The duty was generated ab extra, by service of the order. The question of whether the order can have generated a duty of care is comparable with the question of whether a statutory duty can generate a common law duty of care. The answer is that it cannot: see *Gorringe v Calderdale Metropolitan Borough Council* [2004] 1 WLR 1057. The statute either creates a statutory duty or it does not. (That is not to say, as I have already mentioned, that conduct undertaken pursuant to a statutory duty cannot generate a duty of care in the same way as the same conduct undertaken voluntarily.) But you cannot derive a common law duty of care directly from a statutory duty. Likewise, as it seems to me, you cannot derive one from an order of court. The order carries its own remedies and its reach does not extend any further. . . ."

QUESTIONS

1. Did the claimant fail in this case because of the type of damage (economic loss) or because the loss was caused by a mere omission? (cf. below **4.3.2** and **4.3.4**.)

2. Did the claimant fail: (i) because there was not sufficient 'proximity'; (ii) because it was not 'fair and reasonable' to impose a duty of care; (iii) for 'policy' reasons; or (iv) because there was no 'assumption of responsibility'?

3. What if the Customs and Excise had carelessly lost CDs containing the personal and financial details of 25 million taxpayers: could the banks, which had to spend millions changing their customers pass codes, etc. sue the Customs and Excise for damages?

4.2 Breach of duty

The tort of negligence traditionally requires three questions to be answered in the positive. Did the defendant owe the claimant a duty of care? Was the defendant in breach of this duty? Did the breach cause the claimant's damage? It may seem odd to put the breach of duty question before the question about the actual existence of a duty. However, there is good reason for doing this in as much as the breach of duty question is the major question of fact. Was the defendant, on the facts of the case as presented to the court, actually careless? If there was no negligence then there cannot even be the beginnings of any liability under the neighbour principle.

The reason why the breach and the duty questions are separate is to be found in the history of the common law. All questions of fact in the courts of common law were, until the end of the 19th century (and sometimes beyond), decided by a jury. Questions of law were decided by the judge. The breach question, being a question of fact, was for the jury. Whether or not a duty existed was for the judge. The result was that if a jury found for the plaintiff on the negligence question, the judge could still deny liability on the basis of no duty. In other words, the existence or non-existence of a duty of care is in reality a 'control device'. Juries have disappeared from negligence cases thanks to statute and an important case (*Ward v James* (1966)) and so it is the trial judge who now renders a verdict on the facts. Yet this change has had an important consequence. Juries did not give reasons for their verdicts and thus their decisions could never form part of the precedent system. Judges, in contrast, have to give reasons; and even if answers to questions of fact do not in theory form precedents, in practice breach of duty cases easily appear as authoritative. Great care must be taken not to intermix breach, duty and causal questions, although judges often do allow concepts from one question to carry over into the other questions.

4.2.1 Defining negligence

The classic definition of negligence was given by Alderson B. in *Blyth v Proprietors of the Birmingham Waterworks* (1856). "Negligence", he said, "is the omission to do something which a reasonable man, guided upon those considerations which ordinarily regulate the conduct of human affairs, would do, or doing something which a prudent and reasonable man would not do" (cf. Roman law: D.9.2.31). The point must be made again that this is a definition of negligence and not the tort of negligence. The distinction is crucial because the mere causing of harm by a negligent act was, and is, never capable of giving rise to liability in itself; there has to be a pre-existing duty to take care and it is the breach of this duty—the negligent act or omission—which legally creates the liability. The European Group on Tort Law have also proposed a definition.

European Group on Tort Law, *Principles of European Tort Law* (2003)

"**Art. 4:102. Required standard of conduct**

(1) The required standard of conduct is that of the reasonable person in the circumstances, and depends, in particular, on the nature and value of the protected interest involved, the dangerousness of the activity, the expertise to be expected of a person carrying it on, the foreseeability of the damage, the relationship of proximity or special reliance between those involved, as well as the availability and the costs of precautionary or alternative methods.

(2) The above standard may be adjusted when due to age, mental or physical disability or due to extraordinary circumstances the person cannot be expected to conform to it.

(3) Rules which prescribe or forbid certain conduct have to be considered when establishing the required standard of conduct."

NOTE

The UK Parliament has also attempted to provide, if not a definition of breach of duty, then a legislative guide.

Compensation Act 2006 (c.29)

"**1 Deterrent effect of potential liability**

A court considering a claim in negligence or breach of statutory duty may, in determining whether the defendant should have taken particular steps to meet a standard of care (whether by taking precautions against a risk or otherwise), have regard to whether a requirement to take those steps might—

(a) prevent a desirable activity from being undertaken at all, to a particular extent or in a particular way, or

(b) discourage persons from undertaking functions in connection with a desirable activity.

2 Apologies, offers of treatment or other redress

An apology, an offer of treatment or other redress, shall not of itself amount to an admission of negligence or breach of statutory duty."

QUESTION

Can a court conclude that some activities, although perfectly legal, are nevertheless 'undesirable'?

4.2.2 Ordinary standard of care

The general test of negligence is founded on a single expression, that of 'reasonableness'.

Bolton v Stone [1951] A.C. 850, HL

This was an action for damages by a person who had been standing on a public highway against a cricket club for an injury sustained after being struck by a cricket ball. The ball had been hit out of the cricket ground by a visiting batsman and the claimant argued that the club had been negligent in failing to build a fence that was sufficiently high so as to prevent such escapes. An appeal by the cricket club was allowed by the House of Lords (Lords Reid, Radcliffe, Porter, Normand and Oaksey).

Lord Oaksey: ". . . Cricket has been played for about ninety years on the ground in question and no ball has been proved to have struck anyone on the highways near the ground until the respondent was struck, nor has there been any complaint to the appellants. In such circumstances was it the duty of the appellants, who are the committee of the club, to take some special precautions other than those they did take to prevent such an accident as happened? The standard of care in the law of negligence is the standard of an ordinarily careful man, but in my opinion an ordinarily careful man does not take precautions against every foreseeable risk. He can, of course, foresee the possibility of many risks, but life would be almost impossible if he were to attempt to take precautions against every risk which he can foresee. He takes precautions against risks which are reasonably likely to happen. Many foreseeable risks are extremely unlikely to happen and cannot be guarded against except by almost complete isolation. The ordinarily prudent owner of a dog does not keep his dog always on a lead on a country highway for fear it may cause injury to a passing motor cyclist, nor does the ordinarily prudent pedestrian avoid the use of the highway for fear of skidding motor cars. It may very well be that after this accident the ordinarily prudent committee man of a similar cricket ground would take some further precaution, but that is not to say that he would have taken a similar precaution before the accident. . . ."

Lord Reid: "My Lords, it was readily foreseeable that an accident such as befell the respondent might possibly occur during one of the appellants' cricket matches. Balls had been driven into the public road from time to time and it was obvious that, if a person happened to be where a ball fell, that person would receive injuries which might or might not be serious. On the other hand it was plain that the chance of that happening was small. . . .

This. . . raises sharply the question what is the nature and extent of the duty of a person who promotes on his land operations which may cause damage to persons on an adjoining highway. Is it that he must not carry out or permit an operation which he knows or ought to know clearly can cause such damage, however improbable that result may be, or is it that he is only bound to take into account the possibility of such damage if such damage is a likely or probable consequence of what he does or permits, or if the risk of damage is such that a reasonable man, careful of the safety of his neighbour, would regard that risk as material?

I do not know of any case where this question has had to be decided or even where it has been fully discussed. Of course there are many cases in which somewhat similar questions have arisen. but generally speaking if injury to another person from the defendants' acts is reasonably foreseeable the chance that injury will result is substantial and it does not matter in which way the duty is stated. In such cases I do not think that much assistance is to be got from analysing the language which a judge has used. More assistance is to be got from cases where judges have clearly chosen their language with care in setting out a principle, but even so, statements of the law must be read in light of the facts of the particular case. Nevertheless, making all allowances for this, I do find at least a tendency to base duty rather on the likelihood of damage to others than on its foreseeability alone. . . .

It would take a good deal to make me believe that the law has departed so far from the standards which guide ordinary careful people in ordinary life. In the crowded conditions of modern life even the most careful person cannot avoid creating some risks and accepting others. What a man must not do, and what I think a careful man tries not to do, is to create a risk which is substantial. Of course there are numerous cases where special circumstances require that a higher standard shall be observed and where that is recognized by the law. But I do not think that this case comes within any such special category. It was argued that this case comes within the principle in *Rylands v. Fletcher*, but I agree with your Lordships that there is no substance in this argument. In my judgment the test to be applied here is whether the risk of damage to a person on the road was so small that a reasonable man in the position of the appellants, considering the matter from the point of view of safety, would have thought it right to refrain from taking steps to prevent the danger. . . .

. . .But I think that this case is not far from the borderline. If this appeal is allowed, that does not in my judgment mean that in every case where cricket has been played on a ground for a number of years without accident or complaint those who organize matches there are safe to go on in reliance on past immunity. I would have reached a different conclusion if I had thought that the risk here had been other than extremely small, because I do not think that a reasonable man considering the matter from the point of view of safety would or should disregard any risk unless it is extremely small. . . ."

Lord Radcliffe: "My Lords, I agree that this appeal must be allowed. I agree with regret, because I have much sympathy with the decision that commended itself to the majority of the members of the Court of Appeal. I can see nothing unfair in the appellants being required to compensate the respondent for the serious injury that she has received as a result of the sport that they have organized on their cricket ground at Cheetham Hill. But the law of negligence is concerned less with what is fair than with what is culpable, and I cannot persuade myself that the appellants have been guilty of any culpable act or omission in this case. . . ."

NOTE

This case is foundational for several reasons. First it keeps separate the two concepts of reasonable (question of fact) and foreseeable (often a question of law, or at least one for the judge). Thus just because an accident is foreseeable this does not necessarily make failing to guard against it unreasonable (note the opening words in the extract from Lord Reid's judgment). The breach of duty question is, therefore, always this: did the defendant behave *unreasonably*? In answering this question the court will of course look at the likelihood of a particular accident occurring, but it is utterly wrong to say that Miss Stone failed in her claim because her injury was *unforeseeable*. Secondly, as a result of this emphasis on reasonableness, economic considerations can come into play. The risk of injury can be measured against the costs of guarding against it: see e.g. *Latimer v AEC Ltd* (1952); Compensation Act 2006 s.1 (p.140). See also Lord Reid's judgment in *The Wagon Mound (No 2)* (1967).

QUESTIONS

1. Does *Bolton v Stone* effectively mean that it is the victims of risky activities who must bear the burden of the risk rather than those undertaking the activity? Can employers base safety considerations simply on the equation between cost and risk or could profitability of the firm's activity be a consideration? (cf. *Latimer v AEC* (1952); Compensation Act 2006 s.1, p.140.)

2. Imagine that a local authority was the owner of the cricket ground at Cheetham Hill and the authority was worried about the safety of the road users. Could the local authority have ordered the club to vacate the premises? (cf. *Wheeler v Leicester CC* (1985).) If the local authority was not the owner of the ground, could it have nevertheless sought an injunction to prevent the playing of cricket? (cf. *Miller v Jackson*, above p.15.)

3. Would it not have been reasonable for the cricket club to insure against injury to any person outside of the ground and the law to reflect this fact by making the club strictly liable for any such injury?

4. In the unlikely event that these events had taken place in France, would the club have been strictly liable? (cf. CC art 1384.)

FURTHER NOTE

The reasonable man test is one that applies to the population in general. Given that many people undertake weekend DIY jobs, what standard is expected of their work?

> **Wells v Cooper [1958] 2 Q.B. 265, CA**
>
> This was an action for damages by a visitor to the defendant's house injured when a door handle came away from the back door. The defendant had fixed the handle to the door himself, but the trial judge held he had not been negligent in his work. The claimant's appeal to the Court of Appeal (Jenkins L.J., Parker L.J. and Pearce L.J.) failed.
>
> **Jenkins L.J.:** ". . . [W]e think the standard of care and skill to be demanded of the defendant in order to discharge his duty of care to the plaintiff in the fixing of the new handle in the present case must be the degree of care and skill to be expected of a reasonably competent carpenter doing the work in question. This does not mean that the degree of care and skill required is to be measured by reference to the contractual obligations as to the quality of his work assumed by a professional carpenter working for reward, which would, in our view, set the standard too high. The question is simply what steps would a reasonably competent carpenter wishing to fix a handle such as this securely to a door such as this have taken with a view to achieving that object. . . .
>
> . . .There is no doubt that he was doing his best to make the handle secure and believed that he had done so. Accordingly, he must be taken to have discharged his duty of reasonable care, unless the belief that three-quarter inch screws would be adequate was one which no reasonably competent carpenter could reasonably entertain, or, in other words, an obvious blunder which should at once have been apparent to him as a reasonably competent carpenter. The evidence adduced on the plaintiff's side failed, in the judge's view, to make that out. . . ."

QUESTIONS

1. Was such an accident foreseeable? Does it matter if it was?

2. If the handle had been fixed by a professional carpenter employed by the defendant could the claimant have successfully sued the carpenter?

3. Can you think of any reason why a court *might* today hold such a householder liable (although this is not to suggest that it actually would)?

NOTE

In *Wells* the occupier was an ordinary human householder undertaking the activity (DIY job) himself. What if an occupier invites another person to carry out an activity or a job on the occupier's land?

Gwilliam v West Hertfordshire Hospital NHS Trust **[2003] Q.B. 443, CA**

This was an action for damages by a visitor to a hospital injured on a fund-raising day as a result of the negligence of an independent contractor hired by the hospital to run a "splat-wall". The claimant had been injured while using this entertainment described by Waller L.J. as an "inherently risky" activity (para.42). The claimant sought to recover damages from the independent contractor but it transpired that his insurance had lapsed and so she settled for a low figure fearing that he would not be able to meet any higher award. The claimant then sued the hospital for the outstanding amount of damages. The Court of Appeal (Lord Woolf C.J. and Waller L.J.; Sedley L.J. dissenting) held by majority that although the hospital owed her a duty to check that the contractor had insurance, it had done enough to discharge this duty and so was not in breach.

> **Lord Woolf C.J.:** ". . . **15**. . . . In these circumstances, on the facts of this case (and these issues are fact specific), in the absence of any other credentials, it seems to me that, in order to discharge the common duty of care, Mr Wynne was under an obligation to enquire into the insurance position of Club Entertainments so as to confirm the firm's suitability to be entrusted with the supply and operation of the 'splat-wall'. . . .
>
> **16**. Mr Wynne did enquire as to the insurance position although it is true that he did not ask to see the policy. However, as the judge found, 'Mr Wynne had no reason to believe that insurance was not in force'. This last conclusion is one which I am prepared to accept on the limited evidence called. If the position was to be otherwise, it would involve finding that the hospital would not only be required to inquire into the insurance position, they would be required to check the terms of the insurance policy. This I would regard as being an unreasonable requirement. . . .
>
> **17**. In the result, therefore, I consider that the judge came to the right decision, not because there was no duty but because the duty had been fulfilled."

> **Waller L.J.:** ". . . **45**. This is an aspect which the judge did not consider. However, it is at this stage where it seems to me that the claimant has serious difficulties. If there was a duty to inspect the insurance certificate of Club Entertainments then the hospital would obviously be in breach of it. But as it seems to me the only duty is to act reasonably. In the context of this case Mr Wynne checked whether there was insurance and indeed made a contract for that insurance to be in place. To impose a duty that goes further than that would, as it seems to me, be unreasonable. Thus it is that, in my view, the appeal of the appellant must fail."

> **Sedley L.J.** (dissenting) ". . . **58**. Even accepting that this case affects only the liability of an occupier, occupiers are a large and heterogeneous class, and the duty owed by them to their visitors is not a special duty but the common duty of care. What is there, in a legal system which offers equality before the law by seeking to treat like cases alike, to contain this case in a category peculiar to its own facts? If the ambit of a public institution's duty to its visitors embraces an obligation to check on contractors' insurance, why will a private person whose garden is used for a local fete not equally be liable to pay a sum representing full personal injury damages to a visitor injured, perhaps badly, by the negligent supervision of a coconut shy or a greasy pole by an uninsured stallholder? Or why will a householder who fails to check that his or her builder is insured not have to pay heavy damages to a neighbour who has been unable to make a worthwhile claim against the builder when a nail through a water

pipe brings the neighbour's ceiling down or a carelessly handled blowtorch burns their house down. None of these scenarios, as the courts well know, is in the least fanciful; and we cannot say in advance whether—and if so, why—it will be a differentiating factor that the host of local fete is not raising money for herself, or that the stallholder is a volunteer rather than a contractor, or that the victim of fire or flood is a neighbour rather than a visitor. The scenarios are made worse, not better, if the difference between a potentially ruinous tort liability and no liability at all can lie in a perfunctory enquiry met by a casual and verifiably negligent answer. . . .''

QUESTIONS

1. What if the defendant had not been a hospital but a commercial enterprise holding an open day for local families to promote the benefits of genetically modified crops? Would the court have found the enterprise liable?

2. If the defendant in *Wells v Cooper* (above) had decided to have all his door handles renewed by a professional carpenter, would he have been under a duty to check that the carpenter had liability insurance? What if it was a hospital which decided to employ a professional to renew its door handles?

3. Is it right that an occupier might be able to disclaim responsibility for some dangerous activity on his land, and from which he profits, simply by saying that the activity is being carried out by an independent contractor?

4.2.3 Vulnerable victims

One term that recurs in this breach of duty question is that of guarding against a 'risk'. Is this to be measured simply in terms of the activity in question or must one take into account the needs of specific individuals, or classes of individuals, likely to affected by the activity?

Hayley v London Electricity Board **[1965] A.C. 778, HL**

This was an action for damages by a blind pedestrian against the LEB which had excavated a trench in the street and erected a two-foot high barrier consisting of a long-handled hammer to protect the public. The claimant, being blind, had not seen the barrier, had tripped over it, and had fallen into the hole sustaining injury. The trial judge and the Court of Appeal held that the defendants had not been negligent, but an appeal to the House of Lords (Lords Reid, Morton, Evershed, Hodson and Guest) was allowed.

Lord Reid: ''. . . In deciding what is reasonably foreseeable one must have regard to common knowledge. We are all accustomed to meeting blind people walking alone with their white sticks on city pavements. No doubt there are many places open to the public where for one reason or another one would be surprised to see a blind person walking alone, but a city pavement is not one of them. And a residential street cannot be different from any other. The blind people we meet must live somewhere and most of them probably left their homes unaccompanied. It may seem surprising that blind people can avoid ordinary obstacles so well as they do, but we must take account of the facts. There is evidence in this case about the number of blind people in London and it appears from Government publications that the proportion in the whole country is near one in 500. By no means all are sufficiently skilled or confident to venture out alone but the number who habitually do so must be very large. I find it quite impossible to say that it is not reasonably foreseeable that a blind person may pass along a particular pavement on a particular day.

No question can arise in this case of any great difficulty in affording adequate protection for the blind. In considering what is adequate protection again one must have regard to common knowledge. One is entitled to expect of a blind person a high degree of skill and care because none but the most foolhardy would venture to go out alone without having that skill and exercising that care. We know that in fact blind people do safely avoid all ordinary obstacles on pavements; there can be no question of padding lamp posts as was suggested in one case. But a moment's reflection shows that a low obstacle in an unusual place is a grave danger: on the other hand, it is clear from the evidence in this case and also, I think, from common knowledge that quite a light fence some two feet high is an adequate warning. There would have been no difficulty in providing such a fence here. The evidence is that the Post Office always provide one, and that the respondents have similar fences which are often used. Indeed the evidence suggests that the only reason there was no fence here was that the accident occurred before the necessary fences had arrived. . . .

I can see no justification for laying down any hard-and-fast rule limiting the classes of persons for whom those interfering with a pavement must make provision. It is said that it is impossible to tell what precautions will be adequate to protect all kinds of infirm pedestrians or that taking such precautions would be unreasonably difficult or expensive. I think that such fears are exaggerated, and it is worth recollecting that when the courts sought to lay down specific rules as to the duties of occupiers the law became so unsatisfactory that Parliament had to step in and pass the Occupiers' Liability Act, 1957. It appears to me that the ordinary principles of the common law must apply in streets as well as elsewhere, and that fundamentally they depend on what a reasonable man, careful of his neighbour's safety, would do having the knowledge which a reasonable man in the position of the defendant must be deemed to have. . . ."

QUESTIONS

1. Were the defendants in effect arguing that from an economic perspective the risk of injury to blind people, with respect to street works, should be born by the blind people themselves?

2. Those carrying out work on the public highways are expected to be aware of disabled members of the public, especially if precautions are inexpensive when measured against the risk. Does an employer have to be similarly aware of employees with special disabilities?

Paris v Stepney BC [1951] A.C. 367, HL

This was an action for damages by an employee against his employer. The employee, who had been blind in one eye, worked as a fitter in the defendant's garage; while using a hammer to remove a bolt on a vehicle a chip of metal flew into the employee's one good eye and he was rendered totally blind. The employer had not supplied goggles to employees and there was evidence to the effect that it was not usual to supply them in trades of this nature. The employee claimed that the defendant had been negligent in not supplying goggles and a majority of the House of Lords (Lords Normand, Oaksey and MacDermott; Lords Simonds and Morton dissenting), reversing the Court of Appeal, accepted his argument.

Lord Normand: ". . . It may be said that, if it is obvious that goggles should have been supplied to a one-eyed workman, it is scarcely less obvious that they should have been supplied to all the workmen, and therefore that the judgment rests on an unreal or insufficient distinction between the gravity of the risk run by a one-eyed man and the gravity of the risk run by a two-eyed man. I recognize that the argument has some force but I do not assent to it. Blindness is so great a calamity that even the loss of one of two good eyes is not comparable; and the risk of blindness from sparks of metal is greater for a one-eyed man than for a two-eyed man, for it is less likely that both eyes should be damaged than that one eye should, and the loss of one eye is not necessarily or even usually followed by blindness in the other. . . ."

Lord Oaksey: ". . . The duty of an employer towards his servant is to take reasonable care for the servant's safety in all the circumstances of the case. The fact that the servant has only one eye if that fact is known to the employer, and that if he loses it he will be blind, is one of the circumstances which must be considered by the employer in determining what precautions if any shall be taken for the servant's safety. The standard of care which the law demands is the care which an ordinarily prudent employer would take in all the circumstances. As the circumstances may vary infinitely it is often impossible to adduce evidence of what care an ordinarily prudent employer would take. In some cases, of course, it is possible to prove that it is the ordinary practice for employers to take or not to take a certain precaution, but in such a case as the present, where a one-eyed man has been injured, it is unlikely that such evidence can be adduced. The court has, therefore, to form its own opinion of what precautions the notional ordinarily prudent employer would take. . . ."

QUESTION

Assuming that an employer must act reasonably towards a vulnerable employee, are there limits as to what the employer is expected to do?

Coxall v Goodyear Great Britain Ltd [2003] 1 W.L.R. 536, HL

This was an action for damages by an employee against his employer in respect of asthma contracted while he was working as a paint operator in the defendants' factory. Although the system of work was reasonable, it was discovered that the claimant had a mild predisposition to contracting asthma and the works doctor wrote a memo to the employer saying that the claimant should not continue as a paint operator. The memo did not reach the relevant team manager and the claimant, although he knew of the memo and its content, continued as a paint operator only subsequently to be taken seriously ill. The trial judge held that the defendants were in breach of their duty of care and this decision was upheld by the Court of Appeal (Simon Brown L.J. and Brooke L.J.).

Simon Brown L.J.: ". . . **25** For my part, I readily acknowledge that conflicting principles, perhaps even philosophies, are here in play. On the one hand is the principle expressed by Sellers LJ in *Withers* [1961] 1 WLR 1314, 1317 that 'imposing a restriction on the freedom of the individual . . . is foreign to the whole spirit of the common law of our country' (or, as Devlin LJ put it, at p 1320, 'The relationship between employer and employee is not that of a schoolmaster and pupil'). On the other hand employers clearly must bear some overall responsibility for the health and safety of their workforce.

26 How, then, is the undoubted tension between these principles to be resolved? To my mind this can only be achieved by reference to the individual facts of each case. Powerfully though Mr Beard's [counsel for the defendants] arguments were advanced, I think in the end they go too far and prove too much. I simply cannot accept the *Withers* principle in quite the absolute terms he suggests, namely as a principle in no way dependent upon the magnitude of the risk in question. If the defendants' argument here were sound, it would follow that employers would be immune from liability even, say, if they retained as spidermen employees whom they knew to suffer intermittently from vertigo or epileptic fits. That cannot, I think, be right.

27 Rather it seems to me that the principal consideration in determining whether or not any particular case falls within the *Withers* principle must be the actual nature and extent of the known risk. The risk in *Withers* itself, be it noted, was variously described in the judgments as 'some risk' (Sellers LJ: 'there may be some risk'), 'a slight risk' and 'a small risk'. *Kossinski* 15 KIR 225 concerned only a tennis elbow. The plaintiff in *Henderson* [1997] PIQR P413 had not even been advised by her own doctor to stop work.

28 How then do matters stand in the present case? I confess I have not found it an altogether easy one. For my part I regard the *Withers* principle as no less effective today than when it was first adumbrated. True it is that employers' responsibilities towards their workforce have grown down the years. But society's increasing respect for an employee's autonomy to my mind represents a countervailing consideration. And the risk of precipitating claims for unfair dismissal is by no means to be discounted.

29 All that said, however, cases will undoubtedly arise when, despite the employee's desire to remain at work notwithstanding his recognition of the risk he runs, the employer will nevertheless be under a duty in law to dismiss him for his own good so as to protect him against physical danger. The spiderman example I have given above is an obvious one. The present case, of course, is very much less obvious. I conclude, however, that in this instance too the duty arose. It is a striking feature of this case that all three of the defendants' staff most directly concerned with the claimant's welfare (the works doctor, the line manager and the health and safety manager) all thought that he should cease work. . .

30 It follows that, in my judgment, whilst the judge was wrong to decide (if, indeed, he did) that the *Withers* principle was not binding upon him, he was nevertheless correct in concluding that the defendants were negligent in having failed to follow their own doctor's advice (because, of course, they had not received it) and failed 'either to move or in the final analysis to dismiss' the claimant. . . . ."

NOTE AND QUESTIONS

1. Compare this decision with *Withers v Perry Chain Co* (1961) (read it in the law report). In *Barber v Somerset CC* (2004) Lord Rodger, on the basis of *Withers*, said: "where the risk is small, the common law has taken the view that the employee can decide whether to run it. . . . I draw particular attention to Devlin L.J.'s view that the employer is under no

common law obligation to offer alternative safe employment" (§ 30). *Barber's* case involved an action for damages by a schoolteacher against his local authority employer for stress caused by overwork: do you think the claim was successful?

2. What if the employer had sound evidence to believe that dismissing the employee would cause him greater physical harm than continuing to employ him in the paint plant?

3. To what extent has the *Withers* principle been modified by *Coxall*? Is it really helpful to talk here of a 'principle' if the facts of each case are crucial?

4. Does *Coxall* indicate a changing philosophy with respect to the duties of employers towards their workforce?

4.2.4 Inexperienced defendants

Where an inexperienced person undertakes an activity such as learning to drive, what standard is expected: that of a reasonably experienced person (i.e. normal driver) or that of the reasonably inexperienced driver (reasonable learner driver)?

Nettleship v Weston [1971] 2 Q.B. 691, CA

This was an action for damages for personal injury by a (non-professional) driving instructor against an inexperienced learner driver. The trial judge dismissed the claim, but an appeal to the Court of Appeal (Lord Denning M.R., Megaw L.J. and Salmon L.J.) was allowed, although damages were reduced by 50 per cent for contributory negligence.

Lord Denning M.R.: ". . . The driver owes a duty of care to every passenger in the car, just as he does to every pedestrian on the road: and he must attain the same standard of care in respect of each. If the driver were to be excused according to the knowledge of the passenger, it would result in endless confusion and injustice. . . . The knowledge of the passenger may go to show that he was guilty of contributory negligence in ever accepting the lift—and thus reduce his damages—but it does not take away the duty of care, nor does it diminish the standard of care which the law requires of the driver: see *Dann v Hamilton* [1939] 1 KB 509 and *Slater v Clay Cross Co Ltd* [1956] 2 QB 264, 270. . . .

The special factor in this case is that Mr. Nettleship was not a mere passenger in the car. He was an instructor teaching Mrs. Weston to drive. Seeing that the law lays down, for all drivers of motor cars, a standard of care to which all must conform, I think that even a learner driver, so long as he is the sole driver, must attain the same standard towards all passengers in the car, including an instructor. . . . He may, of course, be guilty of contributory negligence and have his damages reduced on that account. He may, for instance, have let the learner take control too soon, he may not have been quick enough to correct his errors, or he may have participated in the negligent act himself: see *Stapley v Gypsum Mines Ltd* [1953] AC 663. But, apart from contributory negligence, he is not excluded unless it be that he has voluntarily agreed to incur the risk. . . ."

Megaw L.J.: ". . . In my judgment, in cases such as the present it is preferable that there should be a reasonably certain and reasonably ascertainable standard of care, even if on occasion that may appear to work hardly against an inexperienced driver, or his insurers. The standard of care required by the law is the standard of the competent and experienced driver: and this is so, as defining the driver's duty towards a passenger who knows of his inexperience, as much as towards a member of the public outside the car; and as much in civil as in criminal proceedings. . . ."

NOTES

1. The idea that an inexperienced road user should be liable for negligence even if he was doing his best is not new. A Roman law text states that people have no business undertaking tasks in which they know or ought to know that their inexperience will be a danger to others (D.9.2.8.1).

2. Children are almost by definition inexperienced. Moreover they intend to indulge in child-like activities such as horseplay (see e.g. *Wilson v Pringle* (1987), p.109). What if it goes wrong? What standard is expected of (i) the children involved and/or (ii) any adult supervisor?

Mullin v Richards [1998] 1 W.L.R. 1304, CA

This was an action for damages for personal injuries brought by one 15-year-old schoolgirl against another and against the local education authority. Both had been having a mock sword fight with plastic rulers in the classroom when one of the rulers broke and a piece went into the claimant's eye. The trial judge dismissed the claim against the education authority but awarded damages against the schoolgirl subject to a reduction for contributory negligence. The Court of Appeal (Hutchison L.J., Sir John Vinelott and Butler-Sloss L.J.) held the schoolgirl not liable.

Hutchison L.J.: ". . . The argument centres on foreseeability. The test of foreseeability is an objective one; but the fact that the first defendant was at the time a 15-year-old schoolgirl is not irrelevant. The question for the judge is not whether the actions of the defendant were such as an ordinarily prudent and reasonable adult in the defendant's situation would have realised gave rise to a risk of injury, it is whether an ordinarily prudent and reasonable 15-year-old schoolgirl in the defendant's situation would have realised as much. . . .

. . .This was in truth nothing more than a schoolgirls' game such as on the evidence was commonplace in this school and there was, I would hold, no justification for attributing to the participants the foresight of any significant risk of the likelihood of injury. They had seen it done elsewhere with some frequency. They had not heard it prohibited or received any warning about it. They had not been told of any injuries occasioned by it. They were not in any sense behaving culpably. So far as foresight goes, had they paused to think they might, I suppose, have said: 'It is conceivable that some unlucky injury might happen,' but if asked if there was any likelihood of it or any real possibility of it, they would, I am sure, have said that they did not foresee any such possibility. . . .

. . . I have to say that I appreciate that this result will be disappointing to the plaintiff for whom one can have nothing but sympathy, because she has suffered a grave injury through no fault of her own. But unfortunately she has failed to establish in my view that anyone was legally responsible for that injury and, accordingly, her claim should have failed."

QUESTIONS

1. Does the argument centre on foreseeability in breach of duty questions? Did Hutchison L.J. actually base his decision on foreseeability?

2. Are there special standards for different age groups?

3. What if the 15-year-old had been learning to drive a sit-on lawnmower and had run over the gardener?

4. If the claimant had been poked in the eye during the swordfight by the other girl could she have sued in trespass?

5. Did the schoolgirl not consent to the injury? (cf. *Blake v Galloway* (2004), noted above p.110.)

6. If a teacher comes across the two pupils having a mock sword fight with rulers, can the teacher confiscate the rulers or will this amount to trespass to goods? (cf. Education and Inspections Act 2006 s.94.)

4.2.5 **Professional skills**

Where the defendant is a professional person alleged to have been negligent in the exercise of his or her professional skill the reasonable man test is inappropriate. The test for professional negligence is set out in the next case which, although a first instance decision (and note the jury), is nevertheless regarded as the *locus classicus* (see e.g. *A v Essex CC* (2004) at § 57).

Bolam v Friern Hospital Management Committee **[1957] 1 W.L.R. 582, QBD**

This was an action for damages by a patient against a hospital in respect of injuries received while undergoing electro-convulsive therapy. The claimant alleged that the doctor had been negligent in the way he carried out the treatment. The trial took place before McNair J. and a jury and a verdict was given for the defendant.

McNair J.: "Members of the jury, it is now my task to try to help you to reach a true verdict, bearing in mind that you take the law from me and that the facts are entirely a matter for your consideration. You will only give damages if you are satisfied that the defendants have been proved to be guilty of negligence. . . .

. . . I must tell you what in law we mean by 'negligence'. In the ordinary case which does not involve any special skill, negligence in law means a failure to do some act which a reasonable man in the circumstances would do, or the doing of some act which a reasonable man in the circumstances would not do; and if that failure or the doing of that act results in injury, then there is a cause of action. How do you test whether this act or failure is negligent? In an ordinary case it is generally said you judge it by the action of the man in the street. He is the ordinary man. In one case it has been said you judge it by the conduct of the man on the top of a Clapham omnibus. He is the ordinary man. But where you get a situation which involves the use of some special skill or competence, then the test as to whether there has been negligence or not is not the test of the man on the top of a Clapham omnibus, because he has not got this special skill. The test is the standard of the ordinary skilled man exercising and professing to have that special skill. A man need not possess the highest expert skill; it is well established law that it is sufficient if he exercises the ordinary skill of an ordinary competent man exercising that particular art. . . ."

NOTE

McNair J. also said that a doctor would not be guilty of negligence "if he had acted in accordance with a practice accepted as proper by a responsible body of medical men skilled in that particular art". Thus if a defendant could show that there was a section of medical opinion that would have done or omitted to do what the doctor had done, he would seemingly not have been negligent. Although the *Bolam* test was approved by the House of Lords in *Sidaway v Bethlem Royal Hospital* (1985), the 'responsible body of medical men' aspect arose for consideration in the next case.

Bolitho v City and Hackney Health Authority **[1998] A.C. 232, HL**

This was an action for damages by a parent, suing in her own right and as administratrix of her dead child's estate, against a health authority. The claimant alleged that her child's death was the result of the negligence of a doctor who had failed to attend the child when he had a breathing crisis while in hospital. A competent doctor, it was argued, would have arranged for an intubation. The judge held that the doctor had been negligent in failing to attend but that even if she had attended she would not have organised an intubation. Thus the mere failure to attend was not necessarily the cause of the child's death. The question then became one of whether it would have been negligent for the doctor not to have arranged for an intubation. On this question the judge, having heard from an expert witness that intubation would have been inappropriate, decided that any decision not to have organised an intubation would not have been negligent. The hospital was thus held not liable. This decision was upheld by the House of Lords (Lords Browne-Wilkinson, Slynn, Nolan, Hoffmann and Clyde).

> **Lord Browne-Wilkinson**: ". . . The locus classicus of the test for the standard of care required of a doctor or any other person professing some skill or competence is the direction to the jury given by McNair J in *Bolam v Friern Hospital Management Committee*. . .
>
> My Lords, I agree. . . the court is not bound to hold that a defendant doctor escapes liability for negligent treatment or diagnosis just because he leads evidence from a number of medical experts who are genuinely of opinion that the defendant's treatment or diagnosis accorded with sound medical practice. In the *Bolam* case itself, McNair J [1957] 1 WLR 583, 587 stated that the defendant had to have acted in accordance with the practice accepted as proper by a 'responsible body of medical men.' Later, at p 588, he referred to 'a standard of practice recognised as proper by a competent reasonable body of opinion.' Again, in the passage which I have cited from *Maynard's* case [1984] 1 WLR 634, 639, Lord Scarman refers to a 'respectable' body of professional opinion. The use of these adjectives—responsible, reasonable and respectable—all show that the court has to be satisfied that the exponents of the body of opinion relied upon can demonstrate that such opinion has a logical basis. In particular in cases involving, as they so often do, the weighing of risks against benefits, the judge before accepting a body of opinion as being responsible, reasonable or respectable, will need to be satisfied that, in forming their views, the experts have directed their minds to the question of comparative risks and benefits and have reached a defensible conclusion on the matter. . . .
>
> . . . In my judgment that is because, in some cases, it cannot be demonstrated to the judge's satisfaction that the body of opinion relied upon is reasonable or responsible. In the vast majority of cases the fact that distinguished experts in the field are of a particular opinion

will demonstrate the reasonableness of that opinion. In particular, where there are questions of assessment of the relative risks and benefits of adopting a particular medical practice, a reasonable view necessarily presupposes that the relative risks and benefits have been weighed by the experts in forming their opinions. But if, in a rare case, it can be demonstrated that the professional opinion is not capable of withstanding logical analysis, the judge is entitled to hold that the body of opinion is not reasonable or responsible. . . .

Even if this is to put too favourable a meaning on the judge's judgment, when the evidence is looked at it is plainly not a case in which Dr Dinwiddie's views can be dismissed as illogical. According to the accounts of Sister Sallabank and Nurse Newbold, although Patrick had had two severe respiratory crises, he had recovered quickly from both and for the rest presented as a child who was active and running about. Dr Dinwiddie's view was that these symptoms did not show a progressive respiratory collapse and that there was only a small risk of total respiratory failure. Intubation is not a routine, risk-free process. Dr Roberton, a consultant paediatrician at Addenbrooke's Hospital, Cambridge, described it as 'a major undertaking—an invasive procedure with mortality and morbidity attached—it was an assault.' It involves anaesthetising and ventilating the child. A young child does not tolerate a tube easily 'at any rate for a day or two' and the child unless sedated tends to remove it. In those circumstances it cannot be suggested that it was illogical for Dr Dinwiddie, a most distinguished expert, to favour running what, in his view, was a small risk of total respiratory collapse rather than to submit Patrick to the invasive procedure of intubation. . . ."

NOTES

1. This case is seen as important in as much as Lord Browne-Wilkinson seems to be qualifying the *Bolam* test. Not only must there be a respectable body of opinion supporting a particular medical practice in order to escape an accusation of negligence but this opinion must have a 'logical basis'. In other words the mere existence of the body of medical opinion is no longer enough.

2. See also *Roe v MOH* (1954) (p.356) for another classic medical case on breach of duty.

QUESTIONS

1. How can judges know if a body of medical opinion has a logical basis? If the opinion is held by a respectable number of medical experts does this not in itself suggest that there is a basis in logic? And, anyway, what is actually meant by 'logic' in this situation? Is there a difference in this context between 'logical basis' and 'reasonable'?

2. Is it 'logical' to believe (a) in witchcraft (b) in God (c) in aliens from outer space and/or (d) astrology?

3. Is it negligent for a doctor to make an error of judgment? (cf. *Whitehouse v Jordan* (1981).)

4. Is it negligent for a driver to make an error of judgment?

PROBLEM

Elspeth enters hospital for an operation but the surgeon, acting in what he believed Elsbeth's best interests, decides not to inform Elsbeth that there is a one per cent risk of a serious spinal injury associated with the operation. The risk materialises. Can Elsbeth sue the hospital for (a) trespass or (b) negligence? (cf. *Sidaway v Bethlem Royal Hospital* (1985)). What if evidence could be produced that Elsbeth would have had the operation even if she had been informed of the risk? (cf. *Chester v Afshar* (2005), below p.393.)

4.2.6 **Breach of duty and precedent**

It is tempting to treat the cases extracted under this breach of duty question as binding precedents. They are not, and nor can they be, as the Law lord in the next case explains.

Qualcast (Wolverhampton) Ltd v Haynes [1959] A.C. 743, HL

This was an action for damages by an employee against an employer for an injury suffered in the latter's iron foundry when molten metal spilt onto his boots. The employee was not wearing protective spats or boots, although they were available from the employer. The trial judge thought that he was bound as a question of law to hold the defendants liable since precedent appeared to indicate that an employer is under a duty to urge its employees to wear safety equipment. However the House of Lords (Lords Radcliffe, Keith, Somerville and Denning; Lord Cohen dissenting in part) held the employers not liable.

> **Lord Somervell**: ". . . I hope it may be worth while to make one or two general observations on the effect on the precedent system of the virtual abolition of juries in negligence actions. Whether a duty of reasonable care is owed by A to B is a question of law. . . When negligence cases were tried with juries the judge would direct them as to the law . . . The question whether on the facts in that particular case there was or was not a failure to take reasonable care was a question for the jury. There was not, and could not be, complete uniformity of standard. One jury would attribute to the reasonable man a greater degree of prescience than would another. The jury's decision did not become part of our law citable as a precedent. In those days it would only be in very exceptional circumstances that a judge's direction would be reported or be citable. So far as the law is concerned they would all be the same. Now that negligence cases are mostly tried without juries, the distinction between the functions of judge and jury is blurred. A judge naturally gives reasons for the conclusion formerly arrived at by a jury without reasons. It may sometimes be difficult to draw the line, but if the reasons given by a judge for arriving at the conclusion previously reached by a jury are to be treated as 'law' and citable, the precedent system will die from a surfeit of authorities . . ."

NOTE

Lord Denning's judgment is also worth reading (in the law report).

QUESTION

If these facts arose again today and came before the two judges in *Coxall v Goodyear* (above), do you think that they would have found the employer negligent?

4.2.7 **Proof of breach**

The doctrine of res ipsa loquitur (the thing speaks for itself) may give rise to a situation where the defendant will need to provide an explanation as to how the accident happened: see *Cassidy v*

MOH (1951) (p.263); *Roe v MOH* (1954) (p.356). If no such explanation is forthcoming the court may presume negligence: *Ward v Tesco* (1976) (C&MC, p.183); *Henderson v HE Jenkings* (1970) (p.195).

4.3 Duty of care

In French law culpable behaviour, provided it causes damage, is of itself enough to generate liability (CC art.1382). In English law, in contrast, it is not a negligent act that generates a liability to pay damages in tort; it is a breach of a duty of care and so if there was no duty there can be no damages action (*Gautret v Egerton* (1867)). The importance of this duty requirement is that it was a question of law to be decided by judges and not juries. Until 1932 the main duty underpinning damages claims was either contractual or one arising out of some particular set of circumstances where the law imposed an obligation (and that is why there are negligence cases before 1932). The importance of the great case of *Donoghue v Stevenson* (1932) (p.131) was that it elevated the non-contractual 'duty of care' to a new level of abstraction; duty was no longer confined to specific categories of fact. However, this can mask as much as it can reveal since the old specific liabilities approach has not been completely abandoned; it has, to an extent, been incorporated into the tort of negligence under the heading of 'duty of care'. Thus duty can be broken down into a number of categories: economic loss, psychological harm, pure omissions, and public bodies. This last category is not equivalent to the other three since it cuts across them in as much as many of the public body duty cases can equally be categorised as pure economic loss, psychological harm or omission problems. Yet public bodies do raise special policy problems as we have seen (*Hill v Chief Constable of West Yorks* (1989), above p.39; and see *Jain v Trent Strategic Health Authority* (2008), p.348); and they will be considered in a separate chapter (**Chapter 9**). Equally, negligent words as opposed to acts. can be problematic (see **Chapter 8**). Accordingly, duty of care will be considered in this chapter only in its basic outline; other duty cases will appear in other chapters.

4.3.1 Methodological approach

Duty of care is not just a matter of applying a rule; it is as much a question of method and approach. This has been described by Lord Diplock in *Home Office v Dorset Yacht Co* (1970) (see above p.34) as an "analytical and inductive process" recalling the methodology set out by Lord Simon in *Lupton* (1972) (see above p.35). But care must be taken here as the next case indicates.

Caparo Plc v Dickman **[1990] 2 A.C. 605, HL**

(For facts see below p.162)

Lord Bridge: ". . . The most comprehensive attempt to articulate a single general principle is reached in the well known passage from the speech of Lord Wilberforce in *Anns v Merton London Borough Council* [1978] AC 728, 751–752:

'Through the trilogy of cases in this House—*Donoghue v Stevenson* [1932] AC 562, *Hedley Byrne & Co Ltd v Heller & Partners Ltd* [1964] AC 465, and *Dorset Yacht Co Ltd v Home*

Office [1970] AC 1004, the position has now been reached that in order to establish that a duty of care arises in a particular situation, it is not necessary to bring the facts of that situation within those of previous situations in which a duty of care has been held to exist. Rather the question has to be approached in two stages. First one has to ask whether, as between the alleged wrongdoer and the person who has suffered damage there is a sufficient relationship of proximity or neighbourhood such that, in the reasonable contemplation of the former, carelessness on his part may be likely to cause damage to the latter—in which case a prima facie duty of care arises. Secondly, if the first question is answered affirmatively, it is necessary to consider whether there are any considerations which ought to negative, or to reduce or limit the scope of the duty or the class of person to whom it is owed or the damages to which a breach of it may give rise: see *Dorset Yacht* case [1970] AC 1004 per Lord Reid at p 1027.'

But since the *Anns* case a series of decisions of the Privy Council and of your Lordships' House, notably in judgments and speeches delivered by Lord Keith of Kinkel, have emphasised the inability of any single general principle to provide a practical test which can be applied to every situation to determine whether a duty of care is owed and, if so, what is its scope: see *Governors of Peabody Donation Fund v Sir Lindsay Parkinson & Co Ltd* [1985] AC 210, 239f-241c; *Yuen Kun Yeu v Attorney-General of Hong Kong* [1988] AC 175, 190e-194f; *Rowling v Takaro Properties Ltd* [1988] AC 473, 501d-g; *Hill v Chief Constable of West Yorkshire* [1989] AC 53, 60b-d. What emerges is that, in addition to the foreseeability of damage, necessary ingredients in any situation giving rise to a duty of care are that there should exist between the party owing the duty and the party to whom it is owed a relationship characterised by the law as one of 'proximity' or 'neighbourhood' and that the situation should be one in which the court considers it fair, just and reasonable that the law should impose a duty of a given scope upon the one party for the benefit of the other. But it is implicit in the passages referred to that the concepts of proximity and fairness embodied in these additional ingredients are not susceptible of any such precise definition as would be necessary to give them utility as practical tests, but amount in effect to little more than convenient labels to attach to the features of different specific situations which, on a detailed examination of all the circumstances, the law recognises pragmatically as giving rise to a duty of care of a given scope. Whilst recognising, of course, the importance of the underlying general principles common to the whole field of negligence, I think the law has now moved in the direction of attaching greater significance to the more traditional categorisation of distinct and recognisable situations as guides to the existence, the scope and the limits of the varied duties of care which the law imposes. . . ."

Lord Oliver: ". . . . . .Perhaps, therefore, the most that can be attempted is a broad categorisation of the decided cases according to the type of situation in which liability has been established in the past in order to found an argument by analogy. . . ."

NOTE

The difference of approach between Lord Wilberforce in *Anns* and the judges in *Caparo* is of historical and conceptual importance. Lord Wilberforce (who knew something of French law) was trying to steer English law towards a more civilian approach to liability. That is to say, he was trying to see the ratio decidendi of *Donoghue*, as (re)interpreted by *Hedley Byrne* and *Dorset Yacht*, as a general principle of liability abstracted from any particular factual situation. *Caparo* has put a stop to this and returned to the categories of liability approach. Of course these categories are not as rigid as those of the old forms of action; but the material facts of negligence cases retain their precedent force and thus reasoning is by analogy rather than deduction. See also *Goodwill v British Pregnancy Advisory Service* (1996) (p.36).

QUESTIONS

1. Compare and contrast the method of Lord Diplock in *Home Office v Dorset Yacht* (1970) (p.34) with the method advocated in *Caparo*. Are they very different? Will each method lead to a different result?

2. What is the difference between 'proximity', 'foreseeability' and 'duty'?

3. Does it all come down, in the end, to policy? (cf. Lord Denning in *Spartan Steel* (1973) below, p.159.) or to 'fairness' and 'reasonableness'? Or do the terms 'proximity' and 'relationship' still have a certain normative force?

Stovin v Wise **[1996] A.C. 923, HL**

(For facts see p.175)

Lord Nicholls (dissenting): ". . . The *Caparo* tripartite test elevates proximity to the dignity of a separate heading. This formulation tends to suggest that proximity is a separate ingredient, distinct from fairness and reasonableness, and capable of being identified by some other criteria. This is not so. Proximity is a slippery word. Proximity is not legal shorthand for a concept with its own, objectively identifiable characteristics. Proximity is convenient shorthand for a relationship between two parties which makes it fair and reasonable one should owe the other a duty of care. This is only another way of saying that when assessing the requirements of fairness and reasonableness regard must be had to the relationship of the parties. . . ."

NOTE

One must not forget reasoning by analogy (see also above p.36).

Marc Rich & Co v Bishop Rock Marine Co Ltd **[1996] 1 A.C. 211, HL**

(For facts see p.324)

Lord Steyn: ". . . In the course of their submissions counsel took your Lordships on a tour of many of the landmark cases on negligence from *Donoghue v Stevenson* [1932] AC 562 to *White v Jones* [1995] 2 WLR 187. In this area the common law develops incrementally on the basis of a consideration of analogous cases where a duty has been recognised or desired. But none of the cases cited provided any realistic analogy to be used as a springboard for a decision one way or the other in this case. The present case can only be decided on the basis of an intense and particular focus on all its distinctive features, and then applying established legal principles to it. No doubt those principles are capable of further development but, for present purposes, the applicable principles can readily be identified and require no re-examination."

QUESTION

What do you think these "distinctive features" might be?

NOTE

Above all it is probably very dangerous to think that beneath all the duty of care cases there is some single rule or general principle which, if correctly identified and applied, will produce the correct result. As the next extracts show this is not the common law way.

***Customs and Excise Commissioners v Barclays Bank Plc* [2007] 1 A.C. 181, HL**

(For facts and further extracts see p.137)

Lord Rodger: ". . . **51** Part of the function of appeal courts is to try to assist judges and practitioners by boiling down a mass of case law and distilling some shorter statement of the applicable law. The temptation to try to identify some compact underlying rule which can then be applied to solve all future cases is obvious. Mr Brindle submitted that in this area the House had identified such a rule in the need to find that the defendant had voluntarily assumed responsibility. But the unhappy experience with the rule so elegantly formulated by Lord Wilberforce in *Anns v Merton London Borough Council* [1978] AC 728, 751–752, suggests that appellate judges should follow the philosopher's advice to 'Seek simplicity, and distrust it'.

52 Therefore it is not surprising that there are cases in the books-notably *Ministry of Housing and Local Government v Sharp* [1970] 2 QB 223, approved by Lord Slynn of Hadley in *Spring v Guardian Assurance plc* [1995] 2 AC 296, 332F-G-which do not readily yield to analysis in terms of a voluntary assumption of responsibility, but where liability has none the less been held to exist. I see no reason to treat these cases as exceptions to some over-arching rule that there must be a voluntary assumption of responsibility before the law recognises a duty of care. Such a rule would inevitably lead to the concept of voluntary assumption of responsibility being stretched beyond its natural limits-which would in the long run undermine the very real value of the concept as a criterion of liability in the many cases where it is an appropriate guide. In any event, as. . . Lord Goff himself recognised that, although it may be decisive in many situations, the presence or absence of a voluntary assumption of responsibility does not necessarily provide the answer in all cases. Indeed in *Hedley Byrne* Lord Reid saw it as only one possible basis, the other being where the defendant has 'accepted a relationship with the inquirer which requires him to exercise such care as the circumstances require': [1964] AC 465, 486. So I would reject Mr Brindle's submission on this point. . . ."

Lord Walker: ". . . **69** Your Lordships are, I think, largely at one as to what I might call the basic approach to the problem. The development of the tort of negligence since the seminal case of *Donoghue v Stevenson* [1932] AC 562 has not been one of steady advance along a broad front. It has been a much more confused series of engagements with salients and beachheads, and retreats as well as advances. It has sometimes been only long after the event that it has been possible to assess the true significance of some clash of arms. That may be the case with the decision of this House in *Hedley Byrne & Co Ltd v Heller & Partners Ltd* [1964] AC 465, as has been suggested in an important article, criticising what she calls the 'pockets of case law' approach, by Professor Jane Stapleton, 'Duty of Care and Economic Loss: A Wider Agenda' (1991) 107 LQR 249, especially at pp 259–263. The whole article, although published 15 years ago (that is, soon after the revision or displacement of *Anns v Merton London Borough Council* [1978] AC 728) contains much that is still very relevant.

70 The complicating factors are not limited to the distinction between pure economic loss and personal injury or physical damage to property. Other factors are the interface with breach of statutory duty and the position of public authorities, especially local authorities in discharging their statutory functions in relation to social services, education and highways; special rules relating to defective premises, product liability and marine transport; the distinction (elusive though it sometimes is) between acts and omissions; and the recognition of the need for particular caution in imposing duties of care in tort (other than lawyers' duties to their own clients) in the context of hostile litigation. . . ."

NOTE

Duty of care problems are, in short, no longer solvable simply by reference to the type of damage. The status of the parties (public or private entities) is another element that must be considered, as is the nature of the behaviour that has caused the damage (act or omission). The different categories of damage remain, of course, important since it is undoubtedly true that physical damage is an interest better protected in the tort of negligence than pure economic loss and psychological injury (see e.g. *Rothwell v Chemical & Insulating Co Ltd* (2007), below p.168).

4.3.2 **Pure economic loss**

Establishing new duty situations may be a matter of method, but there are some types of damage which in the past have defined the limits of duty. Pure economic loss is one such form of damage.

Spartan Steel & Alloys Ltd v Martin & Co (Contractors) Ltd **[1973] 1 Q.B. 27, CA**

This was an action for damages by the owners of a factory against a firm of contractors for damage and loss suffered when the supply of electricity was cut off as a result of the contractors, while excavating with a mechanical shovel on the highway, carelessly cutting through an electric cable. The factory owners claimed damages under three heads: (i) damage to metal in a furnace when the power failed; (ii) loss of profit on the ruined metal in the furnace; and (iii) loss of profit on four other metal melting operations that could have been carried out if the electricity had not been off. A majority of the Court of Appeal (Lord Denning M.R. and Lawton L.J.; Edmund Davies L.J. dissenting) held that the plaintiffs could recover under heads (i) and (ii), but not under head (iii).

Lord Denning M.R.: ". . . At bottom I think the question of recovering economic loss is one of policy. Whenever the courts draw a line to mark out the bounds of duty, they do it as matter of policy so as to limit the responsibility of the defendant. Whenever the courts set bounds to the damages recoverable—saying that they are, or are not, too remote—they do it as matter of policy so as to limit the liability of the defendant.

In many of the cases where economic loss has been held not to be recoverable, it has been put on the ground that the defendant was under no duty to the plaintiff. Thus where a person is injured in a road accident by the negligence of another, the negligent driver owes a duty to the injured man himself, but he owes no duty to the servant of the injured man—see *Best v Samuel Fox & Co Ltd*: nor to the master of the injured man—*Inland Revenue Commissioners v Hambrook*: nor to anyone else who suffers loss because he had a contract with the injured man—see *Simpson & Co v Thomson*: nor indeed to anyone who only suffers economic loss on account of the accident: see *Kirkham v Boughey*. Likewise, when property is damaged by the negligence of another, the negligent tortfeasor owes a duty to the owner or possessor of the chattel, but not to one who suffers loss only because he had a contract entitling him to use the chattel or giving him a right to receive it at some later date: see *Elliott Steam Tug Co Ltd v Shipping Controller* and *Margarine Union GmbH v Cambay Prince Steamship*.

In other cases, however, the defendant seems clearly to have been under a duty to the plaintiff, but the economic loss has not been recovered because it is too remote. Take the illustration given by Blackburn J in *Cattle v Stockton Waterworks Co*, when water escapes from a reservoir and floods a coal mine where many men are working. Those who had their tools or clothes destroyed could recover: but those who only lost their wages could not. Similarly, when the defendants' ship negligently sank a ship which was being towed by a tug, the owner of the tug lost his remuneration, but he could not recover it from the negligent ship: though the same duty (of navigation with reasonable care) was owed to both tug and tow: see *Société Anonyme de Remorquage à Hélice v Bennetts*. In such cases if the plaintiff or his property had been physically injured, he would have recovered: but, as he only suffered economic loss, he is held not entitled to recover. This is, I should think, because the loss is regarded by the law as too remote: see *King v Phillips*.

On the other hand, in the cases where economic loss by itself has been held to be recoverable, it is plain that there was a duty to the plaintiff and the loss was not too remote. Such as when one ship negligently runs down another ship, and damages it, with the result that the cargo has to be discharged and reloaded. The negligent ship was already under a duty to the cargo owners: and they can recover the cost of discharging and reloading it, as it is not too remote: see *Morrison Steamship Co Ltd v Greystoke Castle (Cargo Owners)*. Likewise, when a banker negligently gives a reference to one who acts on it, the duty is plain and the damage is not too remote: see *Hedley Byrne & Co Ltd v Heller & Partners Ltd*.

The more I think about these cases, the more difficult I find it to put each into its proper pigeon-hole. Sometimes I say: 'There was no duty'. In others I say: 'The damage was too remote'. So much so that I think the time has come to discard those tests which have proved so elusive. It seems to me better to consider the particular relationship in hand, and see whether or not, as a matter of policy, economic loss should be recoverable, or not. Thus in *Weller & Co v Foot and Mouth Disease Research Institute* it was plain that the loss suffered by the auctioneers was not recoverable, no matter whether it is put on the ground that there was no duty or that the damage was too remote. Again in *Electrochrome Ltd. v Welsh Plastics Ltd*, it is plain that the economic loss suffered by the plaintiffs' factory (due to the damage to the fire hydrant) was not recoverable, whether because there was no duty or that it was too remote . . ."

Edmund Davies L.J. (dissenting): ". . . For my part, I cannot see why the £400 loss of profit here sustained should be recoverable and not the £1,767. It is common ground that both types of loss were equally foreseeable and equally direct consequences of the defendants' admitted negligence, and the only distinction drawn is that the former figure represents the profit lost as a result of the physical damage done to the material in the furnace at the time when power was cut off. But what has that purely fortuitous fact to do with legal principle? In my judgment, nothing . . ."

(For a further extract see p.65)

NOTES

1. This rather dated decision from the Court of Appeal is hardly the latest word on duty of care and economic loss. Nevertheless it retains a certain vitality for several reasons. First, because Lord Denning's judgment gives us a flavour of the historical background to what might be described as the economic loss rule. His judgment refers to several of the old authorities which first established the rule. Secondly, because his judgment also is frank—perhaps too frank—about the policy aspect to the rule (see above p.65). One cannot imagine a House of Lords judge (although Lord Denning was once there) talking about running around to one's solicitor, but one knows what he meant. Thirdly, because the case neatly emphasises the boundary between physical damage and pure economic loss and to this extent it remains an important authority. Many of the later economic loss cases fall more (although not always completely) within the sphere of *Hedley Byrne* whose facts were rather different since there was no physical damage whatsoever (save perhaps some sleepless nights for some sensitive media types).

2. *Spartan* also indicates that the economic loss rule in negligence can be applied even to claimants who had suffered physical injury. If the court can make a clear distinction between *damnum emergens* (consequential loss) and *lucrum cessans* (failure to make a gain) the latter could be excluded as a head of damages. However care must be taken here. Economic loss could and can always be recovered in the tort of negligence as part of the loss consequential to the physical harm; thus in *Spartan* damages were recoverable in respect of the loss of profits on the ruined 'melt' because this was an economic 'interest' that attached to damaged tangible property. It was only the 'pure' economic loss that attached to no item of damaged property that could not be recovered (loss of a 'pure' economic expectation). Equally, economic interests attaching to the claimant as a person can be recovered if the claimant has suffered personal injuries and this economic loss will include loss of earnings past, present and future; indeed damages are sub-divided into non-pecuniary and pecuniary (see **11.3**).

3. The so-called economic loss rule—which, it must be noted, applies for the main part only to the tort of negligence plus, on occasions, to breach of statutory duty (see e.g. *Merlin v British Nuclear Fuels Plc* (1990))—has been justified in a number of ways. Lord Denning has said it is a matter of policy (*Spartan Steel*) while Tony Weir argues that people and tangible things are more important interests than money (*A Casebook on Tort*, 10th edn (London: Sweet & Maxwell, 2004), pp.6–7). Whatever the justification the rule is breaking down, and at one point nearly disappeared (*Junior Books Ltd v Veitchi Co Ltd* (1983)). The approach is now this. The causing of *physical damage* has universally to be justified whereas the infliction of *pure economic loss* does not (*Customs & Excise v Barclays Bank* (2007), pp.137, 158). Yet even although the logic of the rule suggests that where a defendant does carelessly cause physical damage to property there must, almost

by definition, be a duty of care, it may be that a duty will be denied if policy and (or) fairness demand such a denial, say because of the insurance position (*Marc Rich & Co v Bishop Rock Marine Co Ltd* (1996), below p.324). One can still talk of an economic loss rule in negligence, but one is forced back, these days, to the circumstances of each case (*Customs & Excise v Barclays Bank* (2007), p.137). The rule is subject to exceptions, if only, sometimes, because the distinction between the physical and economic is not always an easy one (*Murphy v Brentwood DC* (1991); and see *McFarlane v Tayside HB* (2000), above p.56).

4. The first important major exception to the economic loss rule was the decision in *Hedley Byrne* (1964) (above p.134). Yet, as the next case shows, it is not always easy for a claimant to recover (and see also *Mutual Life Citizens Assurance Co v Evatt* (1971)).

Caparo Plc v Dickman **[1990] 2 A.C. 605, HL**

The claimant company brought an action for damages against a firm of accountants which had audited the accounts of another company which the claimant had taken over. The successful take-over bid was based upon published accounts that showed a healthy profit when, according to the claimants, it should have showed a loss. The claimants thus argued that they suffered financial loss in paying much more for the shares than they would have had to pay if the accounts had been accurate. The House of Lords (Lords Bridge, Lord Roskill, Ackner, Oliver and Jauncey) dismissed the claim: the accountants owed no duty of care to the claimant company either as a potential investor or as a shareholder.

Lord Oliver: ". . . For my part, however, I can see nothing in the statutory duties of a company's auditor to suggest that they were intended by Parliament to protect the interests of investors in the market and I see no reason in policy or in principle why it should be either desirable or appropriate that the ambit of the special relationship required to give rise to liability in cases such as the present should be extended beyond those limits which are deducible from the cases of *Hedley Byrne* and *Smith v Eric S Bush*. Those limits appear to me to be correctly and admirably stated in the passages from the judgment of Richmond P in the *Scott Group* case to which I have already referred. In particular, I see no reason why any special relationship should be held to arise simply from the circumstance that the affairs of the company are such as to render it susceptible to the attention of predators in the market who may be interested in acquiring all or the majority of the shares rather than merely a parcel of shares by way of addition to portfolio. It follows that I would dismiss the respondents' cross-appeal. . . .

In seeking to ascertain whether there should be imposed on the adviser a duty to avoid the occurrence of the kind of damage which the advisee claims to have suffered it is not, I think, sufficient to ask simply whether there existed a 'closeness' between them in the sense that the advisee had a legal entitlement to receive the information upon the basis of which he has acted or in the sense that the information was intended to serve his interest or to protect him. One must, I think, go further and ask, in what capacity was his interest to be served and from what was he intended to be protected? A company's annual accounts are capable of being utilised for a number of purposes and if one thinks about it it is entirely foreseeable that they may be so employed. But many of such purposes have absolutely no connection with the recipient's status or capacity, whether as a shareholder, voting or non-voting, or as a debenture-holder. Before it can be concluded that the duty is imposed to protect the recipient against harm which he suffers by reason of the particular use that he chooses to make of the information which he receives, one must, I think, first ascertain the purpose for which the information is required to be given. Indeed the paradigmatic *Donoghue v Stevenson* case of a manufactured article requires, as an essential ingredient of liability, that the article has been used by the consumer in the manner in which it was intended to be used: see *Grant v Australian Knitting Mills Ltd* [1936] AC 85, 104 and *Junior Books Ltd v Veitchi Co Ltd* [1983] 1 AC 520, 549, 552. . .

In my judgment, accordingly, the purpose for which the auditors' certificate is made and published is that of providing those entitled to receive the report with information to enable them to exercise in conjunction those powers which their respective proprietary interests confer upon them and not for the purposes of individual speculation with a view to profit. The same considerations as limit the existence of a duty of care also, in my judgment, limit the scope of the duty and I agree. . . that the duty of care is one owed to the shareholders as a body and not to individual shareholders.

To widen the scope of the duty to include loss caused to an individual by reliance upon the accounts for a purpose for which they were not supplied and were not intended would be to extend it beyond the limits which are so far deducible from the decisions of this House. It is not, as I think, an extension which either logic requires or policy dictates and I, for my part, am not prepared to follow the majority of the Court of Appeal in making it. In relation to the purchase of shares of other shareholders in a company, whether in the open market or as a result of an offer made to all or a majority of the existing shareholders, I can see no sensible distinction, so far as a duty of care is concerned, between a potential purchaser who is, vis-à-vis the company, a total outsider and one who is already the holder of one or more shares. . ."

NOTE

This case is *not* authority for the proposition that accountants can never be liable to those who rely upon their accounts: see *Morgan Crucible v Hill Samuel* (1991); *Galoo Ltd v Bright Grahame Murray* (1995); *Law Society v KPMG* (2000). The key concept is 'interest': ought the accountants to have had the claimant's particular interest in mind when the accounts (or whatever) were published? 'Interest' here does not of course stand alone; it attaches to the status and capacity of the claimant and so at a descriptive level 'proximity' will depend upon all three notions. In addition, in order to be able to jump from 'proximity' (descriptive) to 'duty' (normative), it must be "fair, just and reasonable that the law should impose a duty" (Lord Bridge). When analysing a set of facts these descriptive tools are vital.

QUESTIONS

1. Traditionally there were three requirements before liability could be established in the tort of negligence: duty, breach and causation. Is there now a fourth requirement of fair and reasonable? Or is this fourth requirement applicable only in certain types of duty case? Could it ever be applicable in cases of physical damage?

2. A claimant seeking a large sum of money from the defendant successfully applies for a freezing injunction to freeze the bank account of the defendant. However the bank, which

had been notified of the injunction, carelessly fails to take action and the defendant is able to move all his money in the account out of the UK jurisdiction. Can the claimant sue the bank for an amount equivalent to the sum he hoped to get from the defendant?

Customs and Excise Commissioners v Barclays Bank Plc [2007] 1 A.C. 181, HL

(For facts see p.137)

> **Lord Bingham**: ". . . 23 Lastly, it seems to me in the final analysis unjust and unreasonable that the bank should, on being notified of an order which it had no opportunity to resist, become exposed to a liability which was in this case for a few million pounds only, but might in another case be for very much more. For this exposure it had not been in any way rewarded, its only protection being the commissioners' undertaking to make good (if ordered to do so) any loss which the order might cause it, protection scarcely consistent with a duty of care owed to the commissioners but in any event valueless in a situation such as this. . ."

QUESTION

Is the law of contract an influence on Lord Bingham's decision?

4.3.3 Psychological harm

In addition to pure economic loss, psychological harm is another type of damage that gives rise to duty problems.

Best v Samuel Fox & Co Ltd [1952] A.C. 716, HL

This was an action for damages by the wife of an employee against her husband's employer. The husband had been injured as a result of the negligence of his employers and he had recovered damages from his employers; his injuries, however, rendered him incapable of sexual intercourse and so his wife sued on her own behalf for her mental distress at the loss of both sexual relations and the chance of having children. The House of Lords (Lords Porter, Goddard, Oaksey, Morton and Reid) rejected her claim.

> **Lord Porter**: ". . . The salient fact, as I see it, is that the wife had herself suffered no physical injury and could only base her claim on the circumstance that she had lost the consortium of her husband by reason of the injury to him. Such a claim was put forward on the analogy of the enticement cases . . . In that class of case, however, the wrong is a deliberate action taken with the object of inducing the wife to leave her husband or the husband to leave his wife—malicious because it is their mutual duty to give consortium to one another, and the defendant has persuaded the errant spouse not to fulfil that duty. . .
>
> On behalf of the appellant it is urged that a husband can bring an action for the loss of the consortium of his wife by reason of any tort which deprives him of that consortium and that in the circumstances prevailing today a wife must have a similar right. Even, however, if it be assumed that in enticement cases the husband and wife have equal rights it does not follow that today they have equal rights and liabilities one towards the other in all respects. I do not think it possible to say that a change in the outlook of the public, however great, must

inevitably be followed by a change in the law of this country. The common law is a historical development rather than a logical whole, and the fact that a particular doctrine does not logically accord with another or others is no ground for its rejection . . ."

Lord Goddard: ". . . Negligence, if it is to give rise to legal liability must result from a breach of duty owed to a person who thereby suffers damage. But what duty was owed here by the employers of the husband to the wife? If she has an action in this case so must the wife of any man run over in the street by a careless driver. The duty there which gives rise to the husband's cause of action arises out of what may for convenience be called proximity; the driver owes a duty not to injure other persons who are using the road on which he is driving. He owes no duty to persons not present except to those whose property may be on or adjoining the road which it is his duty to avoid injuring. It may often happen that an injury to one person may affect another; a servant whose master is killed or permanently injured may lose his employment, it may be of long standing, and the misfortune may come when he is of an age when it would be very difficult for him to obtain other work, but no one would suggest that he thereby acquires a right of action against the wrongdoer. Damages for personal injury can seldom be a perfect compensation, but where injury has been caused to a husband or father it has never been the case that his wife or children whose style of living or education may have radically to be curtailed have on that account a right of action other than that which, in the case of death, the Fatal Accidents Act, 1846, has given . . ."

QUESTIONS

1. Why did Mrs Best's claim fail? Was it because of the type of damage she suffered or was it because her damage was not foreseeable? What if the injury to her husband had been the result of a deliberate assault by (i) a policeman attempting to arrest the husband or (ii) a car driver motivated by road-rage?

2. What if Mrs Best had suffered a similar level of mental agony on seeing the family home go up in flames as a result of the negligence of heating engineers working in the house under a contract made with her husband? (cf. *Attia v British Gas* (1988).

NOTES

1. *Best* is not authority for the proposition that mental distress is an unprotected interest in the law of obligations (see e.g. *Farely v Skinner* (2001)). Nor does it mean that members of a victim's family can never sue in their own right (as Lord Goddard indicates at the end of the extract). As Lord Porter observes, the common law is not a logical whole.

2. It is not just the nature of the damage that is the cause of the duty problem. It is the structure of the various relationships, for psychological damage usually arises in three party situations (tortfeasor, victim and third party claimant suffering shock). In standard two-party situations psychological damage, seemingly, gives rise to no conceptual difficulty.

Page v Smith [1996] 1 A.C. 155, HL

This was an action for damages by a car driver in respect of chronic fatigue syndrome (or ME) triggered by an accident in which the claimant suffered no other personal injury. His claim was allowed by a majority of the House of Lords (Lords Ackner, Browne-Wilkinson and Lloyd; Lords Keith and Jauncey dissenting).

Lord Keith: (dissenting):. "...The defendant can be liable only if the hypothetical reasonable man in his position should have foreseen that the plaintiff, regarded as a person of normal fortitude, might suffer nervous shock leading to an identifiable illness. For this purpose the nature of the accident is to be taken into account. The collision which occurred between the two cars is described by the trial judge as one of 'moderate severity.' No one involved sustained any bodily injury whatever. The plaintiff was able to drive his car home after the accident, though the damage to the car was such that owing to its age it was not economic to repair it, so that it was written off. ... Whether this recrudescence was attributable to the accident is debatable. ... In my opinion a reasonable man in the position of the defendant would not have foreseen that an accident of the nature that he actually brought about might inflict on a person of normal susceptibility such mental trauma as to result in illness. There is no question of the plaintiff having been terrified by his experience, as the plaintiff foreseeably was in *Dulieu v White & Sons* [1901] 2 KB 669, or having suffered an 'acute emotional trauma,' to use the expression of Lord Bridge of Harwich in *McLoughlin v O'Brian* [1983] 1 AC 410, 433. ...."

Lord Lloyd: "This is the fourth occasion on which the House has been called on to consider 'nervous shock.' On the three previous occasions, *Bourhill v Young* [1943] AC 92, *McLoughlin v O'Brian* [1983] 1 AC 410 and *Alcock v. Chief Constable of South Yorkshire Police* [1992] 1 AC 310, the plaintiffs were, in each case, outside the range of foreseeable physical injury. Thus, in *Bourhill v Young* [1943] AC 92 the plaintiff was 'not in any way physically involved in the collision:' see per Lord Russell of Killowen, at p 101. The defendant's motor cycle was already some 45 feet past the plaintiff when he collided with a motor car, and was killed. The plaintiff was on the far side of a tramcar, and so shielded from the physical consequences of the accident. If, therefore, liability was to be established, it could only be on the basis that the defendant should have foreseen injury by nervous shock. The plaintiff did, in fact, suffer injury to her health as a result of the shock which she sustained. But as the defendant could not reasonably foresee that she would suffer injury by shock, it was held that she could not recover.

Likewise, in *McLoughlin v O'Brian* [1983] 1 AC 410, the plaintiff was at home two miles away when her husband and three children were involved in a road accident. When she reached the hospital about two hours later, she heard that her daughter had been killed and saw the extent of her son's injuries. The shock which she suffered resulted in psychiatric illness. It was held by this House, reversing the Court of Appeal and the trial judge, that the plaintiff could recover damages, since it was reasonably foreseeable that, unlike Mrs Bourhill, she would suffer nervous shock as a result of injuries to her family.

Alcock v Chief Constable of South Yorkshire Police [1992] 1 AC 310 was the case arising out of the disaster at the Hillsborough football stadium. A number of plaintiffs brought actions for damages for nervous shock. Two of the plaintiffs were present at the stadium. Others saw the disaster on television. They all failed either because the relationship between the plaintiffs and the victims was not sufficiently close, or because watching the scene on television did not create the necessary degree of proximity.

In all these cases the plaintiff was the secondary victim of the defendant's negligence. He or she was in the position of a spectator or bystander. In the present case, by contrast, the plaintiff was a participant. He was himself directly involved in the accident, and well within the range of foreseeable physical injury. He was the primary victim. This is thus the first occasion on which your Lordships have had to decide whether, in such a case, the foreseeability of physical injury is enough to enable the plaintiff to recover damages for nervous shock.

The factual distinction between primary and secondary victims of an accident is obvious and of long-standing. . . .

Suppose, in the present case, the plaintiff had been accompanied by his wife, just recovering from a depressive illness, and that she had suffered a cracked rib, followed by an onset of psychiatric illness. Clearly, she would have recovered damages, including damages for her illness, since it is conceded that the defendant owed the occupants of the car a duty not to cause physical harm. Why should it be necessary to ask a different question, or apply a different test, in the case of the plaintiff? Why should it make any difference that the physical illness that the plaintiff undoubtedly suffered as a result of the accident operated through the medium of the mind, or of the nervous system, without physical injury? If he had suffered a heart attack, it cannot be doubted that he would have recovered damages for pain and suffering, even though he suffered no broken bones. It would have been no answer that he had a weak heart. . . .

Nor in the case of a primary victim is it appropriate to ask whether he is a person of "ordinary phlegm." In the case of physical injury there is no such requirement. The negligent defendant, or more usually his insurer, takes his victim as he finds him. The same should apply in the case of psychiatric injury. There is no difference in principle,. . . . Since the number of potential claimants is limited by the nature of the case, there is no need to impose any further limit by reference to a person of ordinary phlegm. Nor can I see any justification for doing so. . . .

In conclusion, the following propositions can be supported. 1. In cases involving nervous shock, it is essential to distinguish between the primary victim and secondary victims. 2. In claims by secondary victims the law insists on certain control mechanisms, in order as a matter of policy to limit the number of potential claimants. Thus, the defendant will not be liable unless psychiatric injury is foreseeable in a person of normal fortitude. These control mechanisms have no place where the plaintiff is the primary victim. 3. In claims by secondary victims, it may be legitimate to use hindsight in order to be able to apply the test of reasonable foreseeability at all. Hindsight, however, has no part to play where the plaintiff is the primary victim. 4. Subject to the above qualifications, the approach in all cases should be the same, namely, whether the defendant can reasonably foresee that his conduct will expose the plaintiff to the risk of personal injury, whether physical or psychiatric. If the answer is yes, then the duty of care is established, even though physical injury does not, in fact, occur. There is no justification for regarding physical and psychiatric injury as different 'kinds of damage.' 5. A defendant who is under a duty of care to the plaintiff, whether as primary or secondary victim, is not liable for damages for nervous shock unless the shock results in some recognised psychiatric illness. It is no answer that the plaintiff was predisposed to psychiatric illness. Nor is it relevant that the illness takes a rare form or is of unusual severity. The defendant must take his victim as he finds him. . . ."

NOTE

Even in some two party situations psychological damage can give rise, if not to duty problems, then to 'damage' issues.

Rothwell v Chemical & Insulating Co Ltd [2007] 3 W.L.R. 876, HL

(See also p.92)

Lord Hoffmann: ". . . **32** Counsel for the defendant invited the House to depart from the decision in *Page v Smith* on the ground that it was wrongly decided. It has certainly had no shortage of critics, chief of whom was Lord Goff of Chieveley in *Frost v Chief Constable of South Yorkshire Police* [1999] 2 AC 455, supported by a host of academic writers. But I do not think that it would be right to depart from *Page v Smith*. It does not appear to have caused any practical difficulties and is not, I think, likely to do so if confined to the kind of situation which the majority in that case had in mind. That was a foreseeable event (a collision) which, viewed in prospect, was such as might cause physical injury or psychiatric injury or both. Where such an event has in fact happened and caused psychiatric injury, the House decided that it is unnecessary to ask whether it was foreseeable that what actually happened would have that consequence. Either form of injury is recoverable. . . ."

Lord Scott: ". . . **74** In my opinion . . . a cause of action in tort cannot be based on the presence of asymptomatic pleural plaques, the attendant anxiety about the risk of future illness and the risk itself. It cannot be so based because the gist of the tort of negligence is damage and none of these things, individually or collectively, constitutes the requisite damage.

99 Mr Allan argued that, leaving aside *Page v Smith*, the defendants owed Mr Grieves a duty of care not to cause him foreseeable psychiatric harm. I have no doubt that the defendants owed him a duty of care not to cause him psychiatric harm as a result of developing asbestosis or mesothelioma. In practice, a claim for such harm would simply be an element in his overall claim for damages for the illness. But what he asserts is the very different duty to take reasonable care not to cause him psychiatric harm as a result of learning of the risk that he would develop these illnesses. Again, in my view, it would be anomalous to recognise such a duty when the law considers that the risk itself is not actionable. That can only be because the law proceeds on the view that ordinarily people in such a position can be expected to handle that information, very unpleasant though it is, without suffering any morbid effects. Moreover, as already pointed out, the mechanism which caused Mr Grieves's illness was not the defendants' act in exposing him to the asbestos dust, but the doctor's telling him of the heightened risk that he would develop asbestosis or mesothelioma in the future. . . ."

QUESTION

If the pleural plaques had triggered in Mr Gieves chronic fatigue syndrome (or ME) would be have been able to recover?

NOTES

1. It is in three-party situations that duty problems are normally encountered. The starting point is that a third party (C) who witnesses an accident in which a victim (V) is injured or killed by the careless act of the defendant (D) will not have an action in negligence for nervous shock (*Bourhill v Young* (1943)). C is said to be too remote and owed no duty of care (the unforeseeable plaintiff). There were, however, exceptions to this rule based upon a relationship between V and C. The most important of these relationships was, and remains, a family one, now described as "a close tie of love and affection" (Law

Comm Report No 249, Draft Negligence (Psychiatric Illness) Bill cl.1(3)(b)). Thus if V is injured or killed by D's negligent act and the accident is witnessed by C, his mother (or probably any family member in the Law Comm Bill category cl.3(4)), then D will be liable to C for C's nervous shock. And this will be true even if C does not witness the actual accident but sees the victim in a bad state in the hospital shortly (but how long?) after the accident (*McLoughlin v O'Brien* (1983)). Two other relationships were once of importance. If V and C were co-employees and C witnessed an accident at the workplace attributable to the employer's negligence there was some authority that this might allow C to sue for nervous shock (*Dooley v Cammell Laird* (1951); cf. *Hunter v British Coal* (1998)). Equally if C was a rescuer who intervened to help after an accident caused by D's negligence it seemed that C would have an action against D for nervous shock (*Chadwick v British Railways Board* (1967)). The symmetry once seemed fairly clear: a nervous shock plaintiff would no longer be 'unforeseeable' if there existed some relationship between the victim and plaintiff (claimant) that brought him of her into the range of proximity and thus duty. However this is no longer the legal position.

2. The symmetry was fundamentally modified in two important cases arising out of the dreadful Hillsborough stadium tragedy in which the police were negligent. In the first case relatives or friends of those killed who witnessed the events, either directly or indirectly on television or radio, claimed damages for nervous shock; their claims were dismissed on the ground that they were outside the scope of proximity (*Alcock* (1992)). Either there was not a sufficient close tie of love and affection or, if there was, the claimants were too far removed from the accident. Basically secondary claimants (three-party situations) must (i) have a close tie of love and affection with victims; (ii) be close to the incident; and (iii) witness the accident *directly* (sight and sound), although there might be some *very limited* exceptions. In the second case police officers who had been present at the stadium brought claims for psychiatric injury on the basis that they were both rescuers and employees of the police force; the Court of Appeal allowed their claims. The case then went to the House of Lords.

White (Frost) v Chief Constable of South Yorkshire [1999] 2 A.C. 455, HL

This was an action for damages by a group of police officers against their employer for psychiatric damage suffered while tending the victims of the Hillsborough tragedy. The police authority admitted negligence but contested liability in respect of the psychiatric harm suffered by these particular employees. The House of Lords held that liability in respect of this psychiatric damage on the basis either of an employer's duty of care relationship (Lords Browne-Wilkinson, Griffiths, Steyn and Hoffmann; Lord Goff dissenting) or a rescuer relationship (Lord Griffiths dissenting) could not be established.

Lord Steyn: ". . . The contours of tort law are profoundly affected by distinctions between different kinds of damage or harm: see *Caparo Industries Plc v Dickman* [1990] 2 AC 605 at 618E per Lord Bridge of Harwich. . . .

Policy considerations and psychiatric harm

Policy considerations have undoubtedly played a role in shaping the law governing recovery for pure psychiatric harm. The common law imposes different rules for the recovery of compensation for physical injury and psychiatric harm. Thus it is settled law that bystanders at tragic events, even if they suffer foreseeable psychiatric harm, are not entitled to recover damages: *Alcock v Chief Constable of South Yorkshire Police* [1992] 1 AC 310. The courts have regarded the policy reasons against admitting such claims as compelling. . . .

I do not doubt that public perception has played a substantial role in the development of this branch of the law. But nowadays we must accept the medical reality that psychiatric harm may be more serious than physical harm. It is therefore necessary to consider whether there are other objective policy considerations which may justify different rules for the recovery of compensation for physical injury and psychiatric harm. And in my view it would be insufficient to proceed on the basis that there are unspecified policy considerations at stake. If, as I believe, there are such policy considerations it is necessary to explain what the policy considerations are so that the validity of my assumptions can be critically examined by others.

My impression is that there are at least four distinctive features of claims for psychiatric harm which in combination may account for the differential treatment. Firstly, there is the complexity of drawing the line between acute grief and psychiatric harm: see Hedley, Nervous Shock: Wider Still and Wider, 1997 CLJ 254. . . . Secondly, there is the effect of the expansion of the availability of compensation on potential claimants who have witnessed gruesome events. I do not have in mind fraudulent or bogus claims. In general it ought to be possible for the administration of justice to expose such claims. But I do have in mind the unconscious effect of the prospect of compensation on potential claimants. Where there is generally no prospect of recovery, such as in the case of injuries sustained in sport, psychiatric harm appears not to obtrude often. . . . The litigation is sometimes an unconscious disincentive to rehabilitation. . . .

The third factor tis important. The abolition or a relaxation of the special rules governing the recovery of damages for psychiatric harm would greatly increase the class of persons who can recover damages in tort. . . . Fourthly, the imposition of liability for pure psychiatric harm in a wide range of situations may result in a burden of liability on defendants which may be disproportionate to tortious conduct involving perhaps momentary lapses of concentration, e.g. in a motor car accident. . . .

The police officers' claims

In the present case, the police officers were more than mere bystanders. They were all on duty at the stadium. They were all involved in assisting in the course of their duties in the aftermath of the terrible events. And they have suffered debilitating psychiatric harm. The police officers therefore argue, and are entitled to argue, that the law ought to provide compensation for the wrong which caused them harm. This argument cannot be lightly dismissed. But I am persuaded that a recognition of their claims would substantially expand the existing categories in which compensation can be recovered for pure psychiatric harm. Moreover, as the majority in the Court of Appeal was uncomfortably aware, the awarding of damages to these police officers sits uneasily with the denial of the claims of bereaved relatives by the decision of the House of Lords in *Alcock*. The decision of the Court of Appeal has introduced an imbalance in the law of tort which might perplex the man on the Underground. . . .

Thus far and no further

My Lords, the law on the recovery of compensation for pure psychiatric harm is a patchwork quilt of distinctions which are difficult to justify. There are two theoretical solutions. The first is to wipe out recovery in tort for pure psychiatric injury. The case for such a course has been argued by Professor Stapleton. But that would be contrary to precedent and, in any event, highly controversial. Only Parliament could take such a step. The second solution is to abolish all the special limiting rules applicable to psychiatric harm. That appears to be the course advocated by *Mullany and Handford, Tort Liability for Psychiatric Damage*. They would allow claims for pure psychiatric damage by mere bystanders: see (1997) 113 LQR 410, at 415. Precedent rules out this course and, in any event, there are cogent policy considerations against such a bold innovation. In my view the only sensible general strategy for the courts is to say thus far and no further. The only prudent course is to treat the pragmatic categories as reflected in authoritative decisions such as the *Alcock* case [1992] 1 AC 310 and *Page v Smith* [1996] AC 155 as settled for the time being but by and large to leave any expansion or development in this corner of the law to Parliament. In reality there are no refined analytical tools which will enable the courts to draw lines by way of compromise solution in a way which is coherent and morally defensible. It must be left to Parliament to undertake the task of radical law reform. . . ."

Lord Griffiths (dissenting on the rescuer point) ". . . If the rescuer is in no physical danger it will only be in exceptional cases that personal injury in the form of psychiatric injury will be foreseeable for the law must take us to be sufficiently robust to give help at accidents that are a daily occurrence without suffering a psychiatric breakdown. But where the accident is of a particularly horrifying kind and the rescuer is involved with the victims in the immediate aftermath it may be reasonably foreseeable that the rescuer will suffer psychiatric injury as Mr Chadwick did when trying to bring relief and comfort to the victims of the Lewisham train disaster. Mr Chadwick suffered his injury because of the terrible impact on his mind of the suffering he witnessed in his rescue attempt, and not because of any fear for his own safety: see *Chadwick v British Railways Board* [1967] 1 WLR 912. What rescuer ever thinks of his own safety? It seems to me that it would be a very artificial and unnecessary control, to say a rescuer can only recover if he was in fact in physical danger. A danger to which he probably never gave thought, and which in the event might not cause physical injury. . . ."

NOTE

If psychiatric injury were to be treated as physical injury, all claimants would be primary victims and all could bring actions for their damage in the normal way against the tortfeasor. The law does not do this except (i) when the shock claimant was present at the scene of the accident and (ii) either suffered some physical injury or was immediately threatened with such injury (see *Page v Smith* (1996), above p.165). Rescuers are on the whole secondary victims and thus must prove the three *Alcock* conditions before they can recover; however, if their lives were immediately threatened by say falling masonry or whatever, they will be treated as primary victims (*Chadwick* (1967)). In *Frost* the police were not so threatened and thus had to prove the *Alcock* conditions, which they could not. Note, with regard to this complexity, that bereavement has its own rule (Fatal Accidents Act 1976 s.1A).

QUESTION

Can 'lesser' forms of psychological damage ever be recovered in the tort of negligence?

D v East Berkshire NHS Trust [2005] 2 A.C. 373, HL

This was an action for damages in negligence by parents against a local authority. The House of Lords (Lords Nicholls, Steyn, Rodger and Brown; Lord Bingham dissenting) held, on a preliminary question of law, that the parents were owed no duty of care. The general question for consideration in the House of Lords is set out by Lord Bingham.

Lord Bingham (dissenting): "**1** My Lords, the question in this appeal is whether the parent of a minor child falsely and negligently said to have abused or harmed the child may recover common law damages for negligence against a doctor or social worker who, discharging professional functions, has made the false and negligent statement, if the suffering of psychiatric injury by the parent was a foreseeable result of making it and such injury has in fact been suffered by the parent. . . ."

Lord Nicholls: ". . . **85** In my view the Court of Appeal reached the right conclusion on the issue arising in the present cases. Ultimately the factor which persuades me that, at common law, interference with family life does not justify according a suspected parent a higher level of protection than other suspected perpetrators is the factor conveniently labelled 'conflict of interest'. A doctor is obliged to act in the best interests of his patient. In these cases the child is his patient. The doctor is charged with the protection of the child, not with the protection of the parent. The best interests of a child and his parent normally march hand-in-hand. But when considering whether something does not feel 'quite right', a doctor must be able to act single-mindedly in the interests of the child. He ought not to have at the back of his mind an awareness that if his doubts about intentional injury or sexual abuse prove unfounded he may be exposed to claims by a distressed parent. . . ."

Lord Rodger: ". . . **100** In the field of negligence the common law 'develops incrementally on the basis of a consideration of analogous cases where a duty has been recognised or desired': *Marc Rich & Co AG v Bishop Rock Marine Co Ltd* [1996] AC 211, 236B-C, per Lord Steyn. The test to be applied is whether the situation is one 'in which the court considers it fair, just and reasonable that the law should impose a duty of a given scope upon the one party for the benefit of the other': *Caparo Industries plc v Dickman* [1990] 2 AC 605, 618A, per Lord Bridge of Harwich. In applying that test, the court has regard to analogous cases where a duty of care has, or has not, been held to exist. On the other hand, when applying the test, I do not actually find it helpful to bear in mind-what is in any event obvious—that the public policy consideration which has first claim on the loyalty of the law is that wrongs should be remedied. Harm which constitutes a 'wrong' in the contemplation of the law must, of course, be remedied. But the world is full of harm for which the law furnishes no remedy. For instance, a trader owes no duty of care to avoid injuring his rivals by destroying their long-established businesses. If he does so and, as a result, one of his competitors descends into a clinical depression and his family are reduced to penury, in the eyes of the law they suffer no wrong and the law will provide no redress-because competition is regarded as operating to the overall good of the economy and society. A young man whose fiancée deserts him for his best friend may become clinically depressed as a result, but in the circumstances the fiancée owes him no duty of care to avoid causing this suffering. So he too will have no right to damages for his illness. The same goes for a middle-aged woman whose husband runs off with a younger woman. Experience suggests that such intimate matters are best left to the individuals themselves. However badly one of them may have treated the other, the law does not get involved in awarding damages.

101 Other relationships are also important. We may have children, parents, grandparents, brothers, sisters, uncles and aunts-not to mention friends, colleagues, employees and employers-who play an essential part in our lives and contribute to our happiness and prosperity. We share in their successes, but are also affected by anything bad which happens to them. So it is—and always has been—readily foreseeable that if a defendant injures or kills someone, his act is likely to affect not only the victim but many others besides. To varying degrees, these others can plausibly claim to have suffered real harm as a result of the defendant's act. For the most part, however, the policy of the law is to concentrate on compensating the victim for the effects of his injuries while doing little or nothing for the others. In technical language, the defendants owe a duty of care to the victim but not to the third parties, who therefore suffer no legal wrong.

102 So, when someone negligently kills another, at common law his relatives have no right to recover damages for the distress and loss which this causes them. Of course, sections 1(1) and 1A of the Fatal Accidents Act 1976 modify the common law by providing that the wrongdoer is liable to certain dependants for the loss they suffer due to the death of the victim, and to certain relatives for their bereavement. But the defendant is liable only if he would have been liable to the victim if he had lived. The statute thus remains true to the common law position that the tortfeasor owed a duty of care to the victim but not to the dependants. So, for instance, a surgeon operating on a child will readily foresee that, if he is careless and the child dies, her parents will suffer extreme distress which may well make them ill. Nevertheless, her parents will have no common law right to damages for that distress or illness. They may have a claim for bereavement damages under section 1A of the 1976 Act—but only because the surgeon owed a duty of care to their daughter, as his patient.

104 . . . In the present case it is apposite to recall that, a fortiori, the common law does not give damages 'for the mental anguish and even illness which may flow from having lost a wife, parent or child or from being compelled to look after an invalid': [1992] 1 AC 310, 409G-H, per Lord Oliver. So, for instance, if a doctor carelessly fails to diagnose a child's illness and, as a result, her distraught parents, who have to nurse her over many months, suffer psychiatric harm, they recover nothing by way of damages-because, in the contemplation of the law of tort, the doctor and the patient's parents are not in a relationship of sufficient proximity or directness as to give rise to a duty of care to them on the part of the doctor.

105 For the most part, then, the settled policy of the law is opposed to granting remedies to third parties for the effects of injuries to other people. The appellants are seeking to introduce an exception to that approach.

106 The defendants now accept that the doctors owed a duty of care to the children whom they examined and assessed. As the precedents show, it by no means follows that they owed any similar duty of care to the parents. Here the appellants formulate the alleged duty in this way: the doctors were under a duty not to cause harm to a parent foreseeably at risk of suffering harm by failing to exercise reasonable and proper care in making a diagnosis of child abuse. Despite the terms of the alleged duty, counsel for the appellants was at pains to argue that in substance it was the same as the duty which the doctors already owed to the child: if they performed their duty to the child, they would ipso facto perform their duty to the parents. As I shall suggest in a moment, assimilating the two duties in this way tends to conceal the real nature of the appellants' complaint. But, even on counsel's formulation, the similarity in the content of the two duties is no reason for holding that the supposed duty was owed to the parents. The content of a duty of care and the range of persons to whom it is owed are quite separate matters, the latter raising issues of proximity. For instance, when riding his motorbike, John Young owed certain other road users a duty of care to avoid injuring them, but he did not owe that duty to Mrs Bourhill alighting on the other side of the tram—even though, in substance, any duty of care to her in the way he drove his motorbike would have been the same as the one he already owed to the other road users: *Bourhill v Young* [1943] AC 92. In *Alcock v Chief Constable of South Yorkshire Police* the House dismissed the plaintiffs' claims, even although, again, as a practical matter the content of the duty which they said was owed to them was no different from the content of the duty which the chief constable admittedly owed to the people killed or injured in the crush. The plaintiffs were simply not persons to whom he owed that duty. . . .

108 That being so, on the assumption that the appellants are claiming the same duty of care as was owed to their children, it seems to me that there would have to be some factor, over and above the foreseeable harm which the parents suffered, before the law would hold that the doctors and parents were in sufficient proximity to give rise to a duty of care. Mr Langstaff suggested that the necessary degree of proximity could be found in the fact that the parents themselves had taken the children to see the doctor. That is indeed what happened in these cases. But in itself this can hardly be a criterion for attaching liability to the defendants. For example, there is nothing in the nervous shock cases to suggest that taking the child to the hospital would, in itself, create the necessary proximity for a successful claim by her parents. Something more, by way of actually experiencing the critical event, is required. More generally, it would in my view be unacceptable for a doctor to be liable in damages to a father who took his daughter to the surgery, but not to a father whose daughter happened to be taken by someone else who was looking after her for the day when her symptoms developed. If that supposed distinction is rejected, I am unable to see why it would be fair, just and reasonable for the doctors to owe the parents a duty of care of this kind when, for instance, a defendant who negligently injures a child travelling in his car owes no duty of care to the parents who may foreseeably develop a psychiatric illness as a result of the strain of caring for her. I would therefore reject the appellants' submission that the defendants owed substantially the same duty of care to the parents as to the children. . . ."

Lord Brown: ". . . **136** . . . The point to be made . . . is that the public interest in law enforcement and the administration of justice does sometimes require potential liabilities to be excluded notwithstanding that those 'wronged' are left uncompensated. . . .

138 I . . . readily [acknowledge] the legitimate grievances of these particular appellants, against whom no suspicions whatever remain, sufferers from a presumed want of profes-sional skill and care on the part of the doctors treating their children. It is they, I acknowledge, who are paying the price of the law's denial of a duty of care. But it is a price they pay in the interests of children generally. The well-being of innumerable children up and down the land depends crucially upon doctors and social workers concerned with their safety being subjected by the law to but a single duty: that of safeguarding the child's own welfare. It is that imperative which in my judgment must determine the outcome of these appeals. For these reasons, together with those given by my noble and learned friends, Lord Nicholls of Birkenhead and Lord Rodger of Earlsferry, I would dismiss them."

(For further extracts see p.344)

QUESTIONS

1. Did the parents fail because of the type of damage they suffered?

2. Is it in the best interests of the child to have clinically depressed parents?

3. Why should it be the non-professional individual and not the professionals who have to bear the price of professional failure?

4.3.4 Omissions

Another complex area of duty of care is where a defendant's negligence consists, not in a positive act which causes damage, but in a failure to act. Here the direct cause is either an event of nature (e.g. flood or landslide) or the act of a person other than the defendant (e.g. thief or a builder whose incompetence is not noticed by local authority inspector). In principle there is no liability for such a mere omission on the basis of an absence of duty.

Stovin v Wise [1996] A.C. 923, HL

This was an action for damages for personal injury brought by a motorist against another driver and a local authority. It was alleged that the local authority had been in breach of statutory duty and negligent in failing to take steps to make a particular road junction, known to be dangerous, safe. The judge held both the defendant driver and the local authority liable, but on appeal to the House of Lords (Lords Goff, Jauncey and Hoffmann; Lords Nicholls and Slynn dissenting) a majority held that the local authority was not liable.

> **Lord Hoffmann**: ". . . The judge made no express mention of the fact that the complaint against the council was not about anything which it had done to make the highway dangerous but about its omission to make it safer. Omissions, like economic loss, are notoriously a category of conduct in which Lord Atkin's generalisation in *Donoghue v Stevenson* [1932] AC 562 offers limited help. In the High Court of Australia in *Hargrave v Goldman* (1963) 110 CLR 40, 66, Windeyer J drew attention to the irony in Lord Atkin's allusion, in formulating his 'neighbour' test, to the parable of the Good Samaritan [1932] AC 562, 580:
>
> > 'The priest and the Levite, when they saw the wounded man by the road, passed by on the other side. He obviously was a person whom they had in contemplation and who was closely and directly affected by their action. Yet the common law does not require a man to act as the Samaritan did.'

A similar point was made by Lord Diplock in *Dorset Yacht Co Ltd v Home Office* [1970] AC 1004, 1060. There are sound reasons why omissions require different treatment from positive conduct. It is one thing for the law to say that a person who undertakes some activity shall take reasonable care not to cause damage to others. It is another thing for the law to require that a person who is doing nothing in particular shall take steps to prevent another from suffering harm from the acts of third parties (like Mrs Wise) or natural causes. One can put the matter in political, moral or economic terms. In political terms it is less of an invasion of an individual's freedom for the law to require him to consider the safety of others in his actions than to impose upon him a duty to rescue or protect. A moral version of this point may be called the 'why pick on me?' argument. A duty to prevent harm to others or to render assistance to a person in danger or distress may apply to a large and indeterminate class of people who happen to be able to do something. Why should one be held liable rather than another? In economic terms, the efficient allocation of resources usually requires an activity should bear its own costs. If it benefits from being able to impose some of its costs on other people (what economists call 'externalities,') the market is distorted because the activity appears cheaper than it really is. So liability to pay compensation for loss caused by negligent conduct acts as a deterrent against increasing the cost of the activity to the community and reduces externalities. But there is no similar justification for requiring a person who is not doing anything to spend money on behalf of someone else. Except in special cases (such as marine salvage) English law does not reward someone who voluntarily confers a benefit on another. So there must be some special reason why he should have to put his hand in his pocket. . . .

In terms of public finance, . . . [i]t is one thing to provide a service at the public expense. It is another to require the public to pay compensation when a failure to provide the service has resulted in loss. Apart from cases of reliance, which I shall consider later, the same loss would have been suffered if the service had not been provided in the first place. To require payment of compensation increases the burden on public funds. Before imposing such an additional burden, the courts should be satisfied that this is what Parliament intended. . . .

In my view the creation of a duty of care upon a highway authority, even on grounds of irrationality in failing to exercise a power, would inevitably expose the authority's budgetary decisions to judicial inquiry. This would distort the priorities of local authorities, which would be bound to try to play safe by increasing their spending on road improvements rather than risk enormous liabilities for personal injury accidents. They will spend less on education or social services. I think that it is important, before extending the duty of care owed by public authorities, to consider the cost to the community of the defensive measures which they are likely to take in order to avoid liability. It would not be surprising if one of the consequences of the *Anns* case and the spate of cases which followed was that local council inspectors tended to insist upon stronger foundations than were necessary. In a case like this, I do not think that the duty of care can be used as a deterrent against low standards in improving the road layout. Given the fact that the British road network largely antedates the highway authorities themselves, the court is not in a position to say what an appropriate standard of improvement would be. This must be a matter for the discretion of the authority. On the other hand, denial of liability does not leave the road user unprotected. Drivers of vehicles must take the highway network as they find it. Everyone knows that there are hazardous bends, intersections and junctions. It is primarily the duty of drivers of vehicles to take due care. And if, as in the case of Mrs Wise, they do not, there is compulsory insurance to provide compensation to the victims. There is no reason of policy or justice which requires the highway authority to be an additional defendant. I would therefore allow the appeal."

(For further extract see p.331)

Lord Nicholls (dissenting): ". . . [T]he recognised legal position is that the bystander does not owe the drowning child or the heedless pedestrian a duty to take steps to save him. Something more is required than being a bystander. There must be some additional reason why it is fair and reasonable that one person should be regarded as his brother's keeper and have legal obligations in that regard. When this additional reason exists, there is said to be sufficient proximity. That is the customary label. In cases involving the use of land, proximity is found in the fact of occupation. The right to occupy can reasonably be regarded as carrying obligations as well as rights.

The council was more than a bystander. The council had a statutory power to remove this source of danger, although it was not under a statutory duty to do so. . . .

. . .[I]t may be debatable whether there is anything to be gained, any social utility, in shifting the financial loss from road users to a highway authority. But there can be no room for doubt when the injured road user has no such claim. This may well happen. Then it does seem eminently fair and reasonable that the loss should fall on the highway authority and not the hapless road user. And if the existence of a duty of care in all cases, in the shape of a duty to act as a reasonable authority, has a salutary effect on tightening administrative procedures and avoiding another needless road tragedy, this must be in the public interest. . . ."

(For a further extract see p.157)

QUESTIONS

1. What if economists were to declare that Lord Hoffmann had completely misunderstood economic theory: would this undermine his analysis and his conclusion?

2. Read *East Suffolk Rivers Catchment Board v Kent* (1941) in the law report. If the facts of the case arose again today would it be decided in the same way?

3. Ought a person to be under a duty to save a drowning child in situations presenting no danger to a rescuer? If a child trespasser falls into your garden pond, and is in danger of drowning, are you under a duty to try to rescue him? If so, why?

4. What if it could be shown that positive action by local authorities to make their roads safer has a measurable effect on the accidents statistics. Would this be an argument in favour of imposing a duty of care in *Stovin* type cases?

5. If the real plaintiff in *Stovin* were an insurance company taking over the rights of the accident victim by subrogation (see pp.87–88), would (or should) this be a reason in itself for denying a duty of care?

NOTE

As with shock, there are exceptions to the no duty principle for mere omissions, usually based upon some pre-existing relationship between claimant (C) and the person failing to act (D). Thus if D owed a pre-existing duty to C, then there might be liability (*Reeves v Commissioner of Police for the Metropolis* (2000), below p.377); equally once D has intervened he may be liable if he makes matters worse (*Barrett v Ministry of Defence* (1995)). On the whole such defendants are usually public bodies and much may depend upon the nature of the statutory duty that D has failed to perform (see **Chapter 9**). Sometimes a range of factors may point one way or the other: the nature of the damage, the status of the defendant, the insurance position, any contractual relations and so on (see *Marc Rich* (1996), below p.324; but cf. *Capital & Counties Plc v Hampshire CC* (1997)).

4.4 Causation and remoteness

The third fundamental requirement of the tort of negligence is that there is sufficient causal connection between the defendant's careless act and the claimant's damage. If there is an insufficient causal link the claim will fail. This causal aspect will be dealt with in a separate chapter (**Chapter 10**), but it might be helpful to note here that this causal requirement broadly divides into three categories: (i) cause in fact (which used to be a question for the jury); (ii) cause in law or remoteness of damage (a question of law for the judge); and (iii) defences based on causation such as contributory negligence and mitigation. The causal issue can attach to the damage as a whole or it can, on occasions, attach to just certain categories of damage (see e.g. *Spartan Steel* (1973), above p.159).

4.5 Negligence and unlawfulness

English tort law distinguishes between careless and unlawful acts which cause damage. The first falls within the realm of the tort of negligence and the second within the tort of breach of statutory duty (and also public nuisance).

> *X (Minors) v Bedfordshire County Council* **[1995] 2 A.C. 633, HL**
>
> **Lord Browne-Wilkinson**: ". . . The principles applicable in determining whether such statutory cause of action exists are now well established, although the application of those principles in any particular case remains difficult. The basic proposition is that in the ordinary case a breach of statutory duty does not, by itself, give rise to any private law cause of action. However a private law cause of action will arise if it can be shown, as a matter of construction of the statute, that the statutory duty was imposed for the protection of a limited class of the public and that Parliament intended to confer on members of that class a private right of action for breach of the duty. There is no general rule by reference to which it can be decided whether a statute does create such a right of action but there are a number of indicators. If the statute provides no other remedy for its breach and the Parliamentary intention to protect a limited class is shown, that indicates that there may be a private right of action since otherwise there is no method of securing the protection the statute was intended to confer. If the statute does provide some other means of enforcing the duty that

will normally indicate that the statutory right was intended to be enforceable by those means and not by private right of action: *Cutler v Wandsworth Stadium Ltd* [1949] AC 398; *Lonrho Ltd v Shell Petroleum Co Ltd (No 2)* [1982] AC 173. However, the mere existence of some other statutory remedy is not necessarily decisive. It is still possible to show that on the true construction of the statute the protected class was intended by Parliament to have a private remedy. Thus the specific duties imposed on employers in relation to factory premises are enforceable by an action for damages, notwithstanding the imposition by the statutes of criminal penalties for any breach: see *Groves v Wimborne (Lord)* [1898] 2 QB 402. . . ."

NOTES

1. See also *Groves v Wimborne* (1898) (p.188); *Phillips v Britannia Hygienic Laundry* (1923) (p.196); *R v Transport Secretary, Ex p Factortame Ltd (No 7)* (2001) (p.44).

2. At one time negligence and breach of statutory duty were seen as quite separate causes of action (*London Passenger Transport Board v Upson* (1949)) and this is probably still true today at the formal level. In substance, however, breach of statutory duty has become more closely associated with negligence in a number of ways. It is seen by some as a form of statutory negligence; it is often a concurrent claim in employment liability cases (but not of course in the other great source of tort claims, car accidents: *Phillips v Britannia Hygienic Laundry* (1923), p.196); and in actions against public bodies the two torts can become intertwined in as much as a body such as a local authority can act only pursuant to statutory authority (see *X (Minors)*). Breach of statutory duty is important when it comes to an employer's liability for dangerous plant and equipment (see **5.3**)

5 Liability for things (1): moveable things

The idea of a liability for things, where liability attaches more to a physical object than to a person, finds its fullest expression in art 1384 of the French Civil Code. A person is liable for damage done by things under his control. This is, it must be said, quite a unique provision in civil law systems since strict liability—that is to say liability without fault—is normally based upon risk arising from dangerous activities rather than upon a general liability attaching to a thing, although the two ideas tend to overlap (for example with respect to dangerous animals, buildings and products).

English law recognises such a strict (no fault) liability attaching to things only in a few specific instances such as dangerous products (Consumer Protection Act 1987), dangerous animals (Animals Act 1971 s.2(1)) and things falling off aeroplanes (Civil Aviation Act 1982 s.76(2)). In certain circumstances the owner and (or) the occupier of land might also be strictly liable for damage caused by things on or attaching to the land (and see e.g. Nuclear Installations Act 1965). However it is also possible to talk about a liability for things where the duty is at the same level as that of the ordinary tort of negligence or, in certain circumstances, actually lower. It is still a liability for a thing since this is what actually causes the damage. Thus an employer is now deemed liable for the fault of the manufacturer where injury is caused by a defective tool supplied by the employer (Employers' Liability (Defective equipment) Act 1969); and of course *Donoghue v Stevenson* (1932) (p.131) itself was a liability attaching to a defective product. Where damage has been caused by things on land the position becomes complex because the sources of such liability are complex. Statute plays a fundamental role; however not only are several different statutes to be considered, but the common law continues to have a background role as well (*Gwilliam v West Herts NHS Trust* (2002), §§ 35-44).

5.1 Historical and conceptual considerations

The idea of a law of things, although not a formal category of liability in common law thinking, is nevertheless a useful analytical framework for problem solving. It directs analysis towards 'active' (in the causal sense) things that cause damage and sometimes these active things in themselves bring into play specific statutory rules or common law causes of action. For example, as we have indicated, damage caused by a product, animal or workplace tool will be governed (although not necessarily exclusively) by a specific statutory regime. More generally, damage arising from the unreasonable use of land ought to direct thinking towards private nuisance and where a dangerous thing escapes from land this will bring into play a particular rule arising either from common law

(*Rylands v Fletcher* (1866–68) (p.243)) or from statute (see e.g. Nuclear Installations Act 1965). In fact the notion of a liability for things bring into play a whole spectrum of ideas as the following extract indicates.

> **Ferdinand Stone, 'Liability For Damage Caused By Things', Torts,** *International Encyclopedia of Comparative Law*, **Volume XI, Chapter 5 (footnotes omitted)**
>
> "1. In tracing the history of liability for damage caused by things, one sees the whole spectrum of ideas concerning legal responsibility. One begins with primitive law's concept of thing responsibility, whereby vengeance was wrought upon the thing itself which caused the damage, as if it were possessed of demons. Later, we find the shift to personal responsibility for the damage, based either on the notion of personal fault or negligence with regard to the thing, e.g. in controlling or guarding it, or on the notion of vicarious liability for the thing's 'fault'. Later still, there emerged the modern doctrine which imposes strict liability on persons and enterprises for such damage, either as a 'price' for carrying on the activity or possessing the thing, or on the theory that the activity, being ultra-hazardous, is carried on at one's peril, or on the ground that public policy favors the imposition of strict liability upon the one conducting the activity or having the thing, in view of the general availability of insurance against such risk of damage. This modern doctrine goes by various names: 'liability without fault', 'negligence without fault', 'presumed responsibility', 'fault *per se*', 'objective liability' or 'risk liability'. . . ."

NOTE

Of course, as this extract implies, this idea of a liability for things should not be the only regime that comes into play since tort liability is based upon specific causes of action and these tend to be arranged as a list (breach of statutory duty, negligence, nuisance, trespass and so on: see **1.7**). The nature of the interest invaded (personal injury, physical damage to property and pure economic loss) can be equally important. But a liability for things does help focus the mind on risk as well as fault and thus is a most useful template. Indeed, land (including buildings and structures) is an important formal 'thing' in English tort law in that nearly all textbooks have a chapter on occupiers' liability and so it is certainly not unreasonable to talk in terms of a law of things when it comes to persons suffering damage on property under the occupation of another. When occupiers' liability (see **Chapter 6**) is combined with the specific regimes dealing with moveable property, the French idea of a liability based upon the relationship between person and thing is perhaps not so alien after all.

5.2 Dangerous products

Dangerous products that cause personal injury are now the subject of a specific statutory regime itself the result of a European Directive (Council Directive of July 25, 1985 No 85/374/EEC). One might recall, also, that the whole of the tort of negligence is based on a case about a dangerous product (*Donoghue v Stevenson*, p.131) and this decision remains important in that it indicates that where a defective product does cause damage there is a presumption that the defect is the result of carelessness in its manufacture.

Grant v Australian Knitting Mills Ltd [1936] A.C. 85, PC

This was an action for damages brought by a consumer against both the retailer and the manufacturer of underpants for injury caused to a purchaser by underpants which had not been properly decontaminated of chemicals before leaving the factory. The Privy Council (Viscount Hailsham, Sir Lancelot Sanderson and Lords Wright, Macmillan and Blanesburgh) upheld the claims against both defendants.

Lord Wright: ". . . The principle of *Donoghue's* case can only be applied where the defect is hidden and unknown to the consumer, otherwise the directness of cause and effect is absent: the man who consumes or uses a thing which he knows to be noxious cannot complain in respect of whatever mischief follows, because it follows from his own conscious volition in choosing to incur the risk or certainty of mischance.

If the foregoing are the essential features of *Donoghue's* case they are also to be found, in their Lordships' judgment, in the present case. The presence of the deleterious chemical in the pants, due to negligence in manufacture, was a hidden and latent defect, just as much as were the remains of the snail in the opaque bottle: it could not be detected by any examination that could reasonably be made. Nothing happened between the making of the garments and their being worn to change their condition. The garments were made by the manufacturers for the purpose of being worn exactly as they were worn in fact by the appellant: it was not contemplated that they should be first washed. It is immaterial that the appellant has a claim in contract against the retailers, because that it a quite independent cause of action, based on different considerations, even though the damage may be the same. Equally irrelevant is any question of liability between the retailers and the manufacturers on the contract of sale between them. The tort liability is independent of any question of contract.

It was argued, but not perhaps very strongly, that *Donoghue's* case was a case of food or drink to be consumed internally, whereas the pants here were to be worn externally. No distinction, however, can be logically drawn for this purpose between a noxious thing taken internally and a noxious thing applied externally: the garments were made to be worn next to the skin: indeed Lord Atkin specifically puts as examples of what is covered by the principle he is enunciating things operating externally, such as 'an ointment, a soap, a cleaning fluid or cleaning powder' . . .

The decision in *Donoghue's* case did not depend on the bottle being stoppered and sealed: the essential point in this regard was that the article should reach the consumer or user subject to the same defect as it had when it left the manufacturer. That this was true of the garment is in their Lordships' opinion beyond question. At most there might in other cases be a greater difficulty of proof of the fact . . ."

NOTES

1. Liability for defective products is an area where contract and tort meet and overlap. In *Grant* the plaintiff not only succeeded against the manufacturer but also against the seller of the product. This latter liability was not, however, in negligence but in contract where a term as to quality is implied by statute (Sale of Goods Act 1979 s.14). The tort and contract duties differ in as much as the former is dependant upon the existence of negligence while the latter is strict; if the goods, objectively, are not reasonable fit for

their purpose and (or) of satisfactory (formerly merchantable) quality, the seller will be strictly liable. If a consumer wishes, then, to sue the manufacturer at common law (rather than under statute) carelessness must be proved. However, dangerous goods 'speak for themselves' (res ipsa loquitur) and thus the chemically infected underpants were in themselves evidence of negligence and the manufacturers' evidence that only one pair in a million was contaminated did not save them from liability.

2. Another distinction between tortious and contractual liability is that the former is limited to physical damage. A product that turns out to be defective, but which does no physical damage to anything other than to itself, will not result in liability in the tort of negligence. Poor quality goods, in other words, are regarded as a bad bargain resulting in pure economic loss (cf. **4.3.2**). The purchaser of such a poor product can of course sue the seller in contract for his pure economic loss, but a third party in receipt of the goods (e.g. as a birthday present) will have no direct contractual action, unless the sale contract specifically confers a right to enforce the implied term (Contract (Rights of Third Parties) Act 1999).

3. The contract (strict liability) and tort (negligence) dichotomy has now been eclipsed, where goods cause physical injury, by statute.

Consumer Protection Act 1987 (c.43)

"**1. Purpose and construction of Part I**

(1) This Part shall have effect for the purpose of making such provision as is necessary in order to comply with the product liability Directive and shall be construed accordingly.

(2) In this Part, except in so far as the context otherwise requires—
[. . .]
"dependant" and "relative" have the same meanings as they have in, respectively, the Fatal Accidents Act 1976 and the Damages (Scotland) Act 1976;
"producer", in relation to a product, means—
(a) the person who manufactured it;
(b) in the case of a substance which has not been manufactured but has been won or abstracted, the person who won or abstracted it;
(c) in the case of a product which has not been manufactured, won or abstracted but essential characteristics of which are attributable to an industrial or other process having been carried out (for example, in relation to agricultural produce), the person who carried out that process;
"product" means any goods or electricity and (subject to subsection (3) below) includes a product which is comprised in another product, whether by virtue of being a component part or raw material or otherwise; and

2. Liability for defective products

(1) Subject to the following provisions of this Part, where any damage is caused wholly or partly by a defect in a product, every person to whom subsection (2) below applies shall be liable for the damage.

(2) This subsection applies to—

(a) the producer of the product;

(b) any person who, by putting his name on the product or using a trade mark or other distinguishing mark in relation to the product, has held himself out to be the producer of the product;

(c) any person who has imported the product into a member State from a place outside the member States in order, in the course of any business of his, to supply it to another. . . .

3. Meaning of "defect"

(1) Subject to the following provisions of this section, there is a defect in a product for the purposes of this Part if the safety of the product is not such as persons generally are entitled to expect; and for those purposes "safety", in relation to a product, shall include safety with respect to products comprised in that product and safety in the context of risks of damage to property, as well as in the context of risks of death or personal injury.

(2) In determining for the purposes of subsection (1) above what persons generally are entitled to expect in relation to a product all the circumstances shall be taken into account, including—

(a) the manner in which, and purposes for which, the product has been marketed, its get-up, the use of any mark in relation to the product and any instructions for, or warnings with respect to, doing or refraining from doing anything with or in relation to the product;

(b) what might reasonably be expected to be done with or in relation to the product; and

(c) the time when the product was supplied by its producer to another;

and nothing in this section shall require a defect to be inferred from the fact alone that the safety of a product which is supplied after that time is greater than the safety of the product in question.

4. Defences

(1) In any civil proceedings by virtue of this Part against any person ('the person proceeded against') in respect of a defect in a product it shall be a defence for him to show—

(a) that the defect is attributable to compliance with any requirement imposed by or under any enactment or with any Community obligation; or

(b) that the person proceeded against did not at any time supply the product to another; or

(c) that the following conditions are satisfied, that is to say—

(i) that the only supply of the product to another by the person proceeded against was otherwise than in the course of a business of that person's; and

(ii) that section 2(2) above does not apply to that person or applies to him by virtue only of things done otherwise than with a view to profit; or

(d) that the defect did not exist in the product at the relevant time; or

(e) that the state of scientific and technical knowledge at the relevant time was not such that a producer of products of the same description as the product in question might be expected to have discovered the defect if it had existed in his products while they were under his control; or

(f) that the defect—

(i) constituted a defect in a product ("the subsequent product") in which the product in question had been comprised; and

(ii) was wholly attributable to the design of the subsequent product or to compliance by the producer of the product in question with instructions given by the producer of the subsequent product.

5. Damage giving rise to liability

(1) Subject to the following provisions of this section, in this Part "damage" means death or personal injury or any loss of or damage to any property (including land).

(2) A person shall not be liable under section 2 above in respect of any defect in a product for the loss of or any damage to the product itself or for the loss of or any damage to the whole or any part of any product which has been supplied with the product in question comprised in it.

(3) A person shall not be liable under section 2 above for any loss of or damage to any property which, at the time it is lost or damaged, is not—

(a) of a description of property ordinarily intended for private use, occupation or consumption; and

(b) intended by the person suffering the loss or damage mainly for his own private use, occupation or consumption.

(4) No damages shall be awarded to any person by virtue of this Part in respect of any loss of or damage to any property if the amount which would fall to be so awarded to that person, apart from this subsection and any liability for interest, does not exceed £275.

(5) In determining for the purposes of this Part who has suffered any loss of or damage to property and when any such loss or damage occurred, the loss or damage shall be regarded as having occurred at the earliest time at which a person with an interest in the property had knowledge of the material facts about the loss or damage. . . . . .

6. Application of certain enactments

(7) It is hereby declared that liability by virtue of this Part is to be treated as liability in tort for the purposes of any enactment conferring jurisdiction on any court with respect to any matter. . . . .

7. Prohibition on exclusions from liability

The liability of a person by virtue of this Part to a person who has suffered damage caused wholly or partly by a defect in a product, or to a dependant or relative of such a person, shall not be limited or excluded by any contract term, by any notice or by any other provision."

NOTES AND QUESTIONS

1. The key words in this legislation are: "where any damage is caused wholly or partly by a defect in a product" the producer "shall be liable for the damage" (s 2). And: "there is a defect in a product. . . if the safety of the product is not such as persons generally are entitled to expect" (s.3). The central question is thus likely to focus upon what consumers are "entitled to expect". What are consumers entitled to expect with regard to products such as medicines, tobacco, alcohol, microwave ovens, tins of peas containing a caterpillar (cf. *Smedleys Ltd v Breed* (1974)) and the like? What will be the basis of "entitled"? Will it reflect the consumer or the producer economic interest?

2. Another ambiguous point that arises from this legislation is the extent to which it takes consumer protection beyond the position at common law (negligence and contract). One point of contention is s.4(1)(e) whose words can be compared with those in the Directive which states that the "producer shall not be liable. . . if he proves:. . . that the state of scientific and technical knowledge at the time when he put the product into circulation was not such as to enable the existence of the defect to be discovered" (art.7(e)). The European Commission took the view that s.4(1)(e) was not compatible with art.7(e), but the European Court of Justice held that the two were not necessarily incompatible (*European Commission v UK* (1997)). The European Court stated that it is not just a matter of the wording in the text but how national courts actually interpret the legislation and on this point the Court noted s.1(1) of the 1987 Act.

3. What is the position if someone receives infected blood in a transfusion? Is blood a 'product'? What if there was no medical test in existence capable of detecting the infection in the blood? (cf. *A v National Blood Authority* (2001))

LIBRARY RESEARCH PROBLEM

Research the following cases in the law reports or in C&MC: (i) *Wyngrove's Curator Bonis v Scottish Omnibuses Ltd* (1966); (ii) *Ingham v Emes* (1955) (C&MC, p.457); (iii) *Reed v Dean* (1949) (C&MC, p.471); (iv) *Square v Model Farm Dairies* (1939); (v) *Read v Croydon Corporation* (1938). If the facts of these cases occurred again today could each of the claimants succeed against the producer under the 1987 Act?

5.3 Dangerous industrial equipment

Injury caused to an employee by a dangerous product supplied by an employer might well give rise to a liability on the part the manufacturer of the defective item of equipment. But it was held at common law that there is no liability of the employer unless the employer himself was negligent or in breach of a statute with respect to the dangerous tool or equipment (*Davie v New Merton Board Mills* (1959) below, p.192). This non-liability was criticised (see e.g. *Hamson* [1959] C.L.J. 157) and statute stepped in to remedy the situation. Before looking at this specific statutory extension of liability, it is necessary first to consider the position at common law.

5.3.1 General considerations

The industrial revolution created a new social problem that was to impact upon the law of tort throughout Europe. Accidents in the workplace became increasingly frequent with devastating results not just for the victim but often his family (cf. Fatal Accidents Act 1976, p.416). Many of these accidents resulted from dangerous things such as unfenced factory machinery and gradually Parliament intervened with factory legislation. Equally (and interestingly) the courts responded by creating a strict liability action in tort where such safety legislation was breached by an employer. The 'liability for things' perspective is well expressed in the extract below.

Ferdinand Stone, 'Liability For Damage Caused By Things', Torts, International Encyclopedia of Comparative Law, Volume XI, Chapter 5 (footnotes omitted)

"**17.** Professor *Lawson* has pointed out that in the pre-Industrial Revolution society the dominant precept was that people should not act dangerously and if they did and damage resulted therefrom compensation or restitution should be made. But the Industrial Revolution illustrated dramatically that using dangerous things such as machinery might be meritorious even though some damage resulted. Thus in this period jurists sought ways by which the meritorious use of dangerous things might be encouraged at the same time that deleterious effects might in proper cases be avoided or repaired. . . .

18. In response to the needs of this changed society, jurists turned to and developed the concept of negligence,. . . However, as the risk-producing capacity of an industrialized society increased and as it became more and more difficult for either party to an accident to prove specific facts indicating negligence, machines and factory processes having become exceedingly complex, courts and jurists began to search for a theory or theories of liability which would on the one hand permit the compensation of worthy claims without on the other hand opening the floodgates of liability and litigation to fictitious and fraudulent demands. Out of this search was developed the concept of strict liability. . . ."

5.3.2 Tort of breach of statutory duty

These observations by Stone ought to be born in mind when reading the next case. This is one of the key cases of strict liability in English law and is the foundational precedent for the tort of breach of statutory duty in the context of employer's liability.

Groves v Lord Wimborne [1898] 2 Q.B. 402, CA

AL Smith L.J.: In this case the plaintiff sues the defendant, who is the occupier of the Dowlais Iron Works, for breach of a duty to fence certain machinery imposed upon him as such occupier by the Factory and Workshop Act, 1878, by reason of which breach of duty the plaintiff sustained personal injuries. The learned judge at the trial gave judgment for the defendant, being of opinion that no action lay for the breach of duty alleged by the plaintiff. The Act in question, which followed numerous other Acts in pari materiâ, is not in the nature of a private legislative bargain between employers and workmen, as the learned judge seemed to think, but is a public Act passed in favour of the workers in factories and workshops to compel their employers to do certain things for their protection and benefit. . . . In the present case it is admitted that machinery on the defendant's premises which came within these provisions was not fenced as required by the Act, and that injury was thereby occasioned to the plaintiff, a boy employed on the works. On proof of a breach of this statutory duty imposed on the defendant, and injury resulting to the plaintiff therefrom, primâ facie the plaintiff has a good cause of action. . . .[U]nless it appears from the whole 'purview' of the Act, to use the language of Lord Cairns in the case of *Atkinson v Newcastle Waterworks Co.*, that it was the intention of the Legislature that the only remedy for breach of the statutory duty should be by proceeding for the fine imposed by s 82, it follows that, upon proof of a breach of that duty by the employer and injury thereby occasioned to the workman, a cause of action is established. The question therefore is whether the cause of action which primâ facie is given by s 5 is taken away by any provisions to be found in the remainder of the Act. . . . In dealing with the question whether this was the intention of the Legislature, it is material, as Kelly CB pointed out in giving judgment in the case of *Gorris v Scott*, to consider for whose benefit the Act was passed, whether it was passed in the interests of the public at large or in those of a particular class of persons. The Act now in question, as I have said, was clearly passed in favour of workers employed in factories and workshops, and to compel their employers to perform certain statutory duties for their protection and benefit. It is to be observed in the first place that under the provisions of s 82 not a penny of the fine necessarily goes to the person injured or his family. The provision is only that the whole or any part of it may be applied for the benefit of the injured person or his family, or otherwise, as a secretary of state determines. . . . [I]t cannot have been the intention of the Legislature that the provision which imposes upon the employer a fine as a punishment for neglect of his statutory duty should take away the primâ facie right of the workman to be fully compensated for injury occasioned to him by that neglect. . . . I cannot read this statute in the manner in which it is sought to be read by the defendant. I think that s 5 does give to the workman a right of action upon the statute for injury caused by a breach of the statutory duty thereby imposed, and that he is not relegated to the provisions for the imposition of a fine on the employer, or it may be a workman, as his sole remedy. . . .

[Rigby L.J. and Vaughan Williams L.J. delivered judgments agreeing with AL Smith L.J. .]

NOTE

The Factories Act 1961, which provided that dangerous machinery had to be fenced, gave rise to a considerable body of case law. Once it had been determined that a machine was 'dangerous' within the meaning of the Act, it was no defence that fencing would render the machine unusable (*John Summers v Frost* (1955)). The fact that the accident happened in an unforeseeable way was, equally, no defence (*Millard v Serck Tubes* (1969)). However the courts would look at the purpose of the legislation and so, for example, the object of the fencing provision was to keep the worker out and not bits of the machine in (*Close v Steel Co of Wales* (1962)). Other workplace statutes such as the Mines and Quarries Act 1954 and the Offices, Shops and Railway Premises Act 1963 were also important sources of litigation. All of these Acts have now been replaced by Regulations made under the Health and Safety at Work Act 1974. This piece of primary legislation specifically states that breach "of a duty imposed by health and safety regulations [. . .] shall, so far as it causes damage, be actionable except in so far as the regulations provide otherwise" (s.47(2)).

QUESTION

One problem that can arise in these workplace breach of statutory duty cases is when a piece of required safety equipment or clothing turns out to be defective but this causes an 'unforeseeable' injury. A lorry driver is supplied with a pair of safety boots designed to protect feet from injury by heavy objects. While digging his lorry out of the snow in freezing conditions a boot lets in some water because of a defect in the boot; as a result the driver suffers frostbite and loses his toe. Assuming the boots were perfectly adequate to protect the feet against falling objects, should this permit the employer to escape from having to pay damages?

Fytche v Wincanton Logistics Plc [2004] UKHL 31, HL

Lord Nicholls: 1. "I have had the advantage of reading in draft the speech of my noble and learned friends Lord Hoffmann and Lord Walker of Gestingthorpe. I agree with them. I add a brief word of my own solely because your Lordships are divided on this point of statutory interpretation. To my mind the crucial point in this case is that the existence of a very small and inconspicuous hole in one of Mr. Fytche's steel-capped boots did not constitute a breach of his employer's regulation 4 obligation to ensure he was provided with suitable personal protective equipment. The judge found that the boots were ordinarily satisfactory for Mr. Fytche's work. In other words, the boots were adequate for Mr. Fytche's ordinary conditions of work, tiny hole notwithstanding. That being so, the continuing existence of this hole was not a breach of the employer's regulation 7 obligation to maintain the boot in good repair. Regulation 7 should not be read as imposing, in this respect, a wider obligation than regulation 4. I would dismiss this appeal."

Baroness Hale (dissenting): "... **70.** The issue in this case, as identified by my noble and learned friend Lord Nicholls of Birkenhead in the course of the argument, is who should bear the risk that the boots supplied for a particular reason turn out to have an incidental defect which causes the employee injury while he is at work. I have no difficulty with the conclusion that the employer rather than the employee should bear that risk. There are good policy reasons for imposing strict liability on employers for many of the injuries which their employees suffer at work. The overall object of the legislation is to protect the health and safety of workers: if this fails and they suffer injury, strict liability means that they are compensated for that injury without the need for slow and costly litigation such as this. I appreciate that we have not yet reached the point where there is strict liability for every injury suffered by a worker in the course of his employment, but I see no need to bring in limitations which are not in the statutory language and could, as illustrated above, lead to some very surprising conclusions. I venture to suggest that a non-lawyer would find it odd indeed that Mr Fytche would have recovered damages if his employer had also thought the boots should protect against a weather risk but does not do so because his employer had a different risk in mind. ...."

QUESTIONS

1. Is this really a causation problem? (cf. *Gorris v Scott* (1874), p.366.)

2. Could the driver have sought damages from (a) the seller of the boots and/or (b) the manufacturer of the boots?

5.3.3 Negligence liability

An employee injured in the workplace is not restricted to suing in the tort of breach of statutory duty. He or she can equally claim that the employer was in breach of his common law duty to take care.

Wilsons and Clyde Coal Co Ltd v English **[1938] A.C. 57, HL**

This was an action for damages by an employee at a coalmine, against his employer, for injury suffered when some haulage plant was put into motion while he was making his way along one of the underground roads. The claimant argued that the employers had been negligent in allowing the haulage plant to be in motion at a time when the day shift men were being raised to the surface. The defendants responded in saying that they had delegated their duty to maintain a safe system of work by appointing a qualified manager to deal with the technical management of the mine in accordance with the Coal Mines Act 1911. The House of Lords (Lords Atkin, Thankerton, Macmillan, Wright and Maugham) rejected this defence.

Lord Macmillan: ". . . Now I take it to be settled law that the provision of a safe system of working in a colliery is an obligation of the owner of the colliery. He cannot divest himself of this duty, though he may—and, if it involves technical management and he is not himself technically qualified, must—perform it through the agency of an employee. It remains the owner's obligation, and the agent whom the owner appoints to perform it performs it on the owner's behalf. The owner remains vicariously responsible for the negligence of the person whom he has appointed to perform his obligation for him, and cannot escape liability by merely proving that he has appointed a competent agent. If the owner's duty has not been performed, no matter how competent the agent selected by the owner to perform it for him, the owner is responsible. . . ."

Lord Wright: ". . . This House held that. . . the statutory duty was personal to the employer, in this sense that he was bound to perform it by himself or by his servants. The same principle, in my opinion, applies to those fundamental obligations of a contract of employment. . . and for the performance of which employers are absolutely responsible. When I use the word absolutely, I do not mean that employers warrant the adequacy of plant, or the competence of fellow-employees, or the propriety of the system of work. The obligation is fulfilled by the exercise of due care and skill. But it is not fulfilled by entrusting its fulfilment to employees, even though selected with due care and skill. The obligation is threefold—'the provision of a competent staff of men, adequate material, and a proper system and effective supervision';. . .

There is perhaps a risk of confusion if we speak of the duty as one which can, or cannot, be delegated. The true question is, What is the extent of the duty attaching to the employer? Such a duty is the employer's personal duty, whether he performs or can perform it himself, or whether he does not perform it or cannot perform it save by servants or agents. A failure to perform such a duty is the employer's personal negligence. This was held to be the case where the duty was statutory, and it is equally so when the duty is one attaching at common law. A statutory duty differs from a common law duty in certain respects, but in this respect it stands on the same footing. . . ."

NOTE

This case is important in that it translates Lord Atkin's neighbour principle (see **4.1**) into an employer's duty towards its employees. The duty is usually regarded as tortious, but in theory it can equally be seen as an implied term of the contract of employment (see *Rothwell v Chemical & Insulating Co Ltd* (2007), p.20). The case is important, also, because it shows that this duty is a direct and non-delegable duty. An employer cannot escape liability by saying that it had fulfilled its duty of care in appointing say a safety officer.

5.3.4 **Liability for defective equipment**

However the position is not quite the same when it comes to supplying a tool. At common law the duty is summed up in the short extract below.

Davie v New Merton Board Mills Ltd **[1959] A.C. 604, HL**

Lord Reid: "My Lords, the facts of this case are very simple. The appellant was a maintenance fitter employed by the respondents. In the course of his work he was using in a proper manner a wedged-shaped tool called a drift which was supplied to him by the respondents: he was hammering it for the purpose of separating two pieces of metal. A chip flew off it and struck his eye so that he lost the sight of that eye. The drift was not safe for use because it was much too hard and brittle, and the cause of this was negligence of the manufacturers of the drift, or their servants. The respondents had bought the tool from a reputable merchant, who had in turn bought it from the manufacturers. . . .

. . . The appellant's contention is that the respondents are liable to him in damages because of the negligence of the manufacturers or their servants. . . . .

The conclusion to which I have come is that an employer, besides being liable to his servant for injury caused by the negligence of his own servants, is in some cases liable in respect of the negligence of others. Where, then, is the line to be drawn? On the one hand it appears that an employer is liable for the negligence of an independent contractor whom he has engaged to carry out one of what have been described as his personal duties on his own premises and whose work might normally be done by the employer's own servant—at least if the negligent workmanship is discoverable by reasonable inspection. On the other hand for the reasons which I have given, I am of opinion that he is not liable for the negligence of the manufacturer of an article which he has bought, provided that he has been careful to deal with a seller of repute and has made any inspection which a reasonable employer would make. . . ."

[Viscount Simonds and Lords Morton, Tucker and Keith delivered judgment in favour of the defendants.]

QUESTION

Should the employer not have supplied goggles?

NOTE

The House of Lords could have held that an employer contractually warrants via an implied term that the equipment supplied would not be defective. It failed to do this and so Parliament stepped in.

Employer's Liability (Defective Equipment) Act 1969 (c.37)

"**1. Extension of employer's liability for defective equipment.**

    (1) Where after the commencement of this Act—

        (a) an employee suffers personal injury in the course of his employment in consequence of a defect in equipment provided by his employer for the purposes of the employer's business; and

---

> (b) the defect is attributable wholly or partly to the fault of a third party (whether identified or not),
>
> the injury shall be deemed to be also attributable to negligence on the part of the employer (whether or not he is liable in respect of the injury apart from this subsection), but without prejudice to the law relating to contributory negligence and to any remedy by way of contribution or in contract or otherwise which is available to the employer in respect of the injury.
>
> (2) In so far as any agreement purports to exclude or limit any liability of an employer arising under subsection (1) of this section, the agreement shall be void.
>
> (3) In this section—
>
> 'business' includes the activities carried on by any public body;
>
> 'employee' means a person who is employed by another person under a contract of service or apprenticeship and is so employed for the purposes of a business carried on by that other person, and
>
> 'employer' shall be construed accordingly;
>
> 'equipment' includes any plant and machinery, vehicle, aircraft and clothing;
>
> 'fault' means negligence, breach of statutory duty or other act or omission which gives rise to liability in tort in England and Wales or which is wrongful and gives rise to liability in damages in Scotland; and
>
> 'personal injury' includes loss of life, any impairment of a person's physical or mental condition and any disease. . . .''

NOTE

This statute is very much a liability attaching to a 'thing' (equipment) since the thing itself acts as the means of extending liability from the manufacturer to the employer. The key words in this statute are 'fault' (s.1(1)(b)) and its definition (s.1(3)). This definition is wider than carelessness and includes 'or other act or omission which gives rise to liability in tort'. Thus an employer will presumably be deemed liable if the producer of a defective product is liable under the Consumer Protection Act 1987.

QUESTIONS

1. Is a ship 'equipment' within the meaning of the 1969 Act? (cf. *Coltman v Bibby Tankers* (1988).)

2. Is a flagstone 'equipment'? What about a brick? (cf. *Knowles v Liverpool CC* (1993).)

5.4 Motor vehicles

One social reason for imposing liability on employers for defective equipment is, as we have seen, that the workplace is one of two major factual sources of tort claims. The other major source is road accidents. Damage caused by motor vehicles has, however, not given rise to any special liabilities, except in one rather limited way where an owner lends his or her car to another (see *Morgans v Launchbury* (1973), p.86). The position can be contrasted with France which, since 1985, has a special statutory regime covering road accidents; and even before 1985, motor vehicles fell within the strict liability provision of CC art.1384 thanks to a famous decision in 1930.

5.4.1 Tort of negligence

In England, as the case below re-affirms, a road accident victim must normally prove fault in order to recover damages.

Mansfield v Weetabix Ltd **[1998] 1 W.L.R. 1263, CA**

This was an action for damages by the owners of a shop against the employer and personal representative of a lorry driver whose lorry crashed into their shop. The trial judge held the defendants liable on the ground that the lorry driver had been negligent, but an appeal against this judgment was allowed by the Court of Appeal (Leggatt L.J., Aldous L.J. and Sir Patrick Russell L.J.).

Leggatt L.J.: ". . . In my judgment, the standard of care that Mr Tarleton was obliged to show in these circumstances was that which is to be expected of a reasonably competent driver unaware that he is or may be suffering from a condition that impairs his ability to drive. To apply an objective standard in a way that did not take account of Mr Tarleton's condition would be to impose strict liability. But that is not the law. As Lord Wilberforce said in *Snelling v Whitehead*, The Times, 31 July 1975, a transcript of the speeches in which is before the court:

'The case is one which is severely distressing to all who have been concerned with it and one which should attract automatic compensation regardless of any question of fault. But no such system has yet been introduced in this country and the courts, including this House, have no power to depart from the law as it stands. This requires that compensation may only be obtained in an action for damages and further requires, as a condition of the award of damages against the [driver], a finding of fault, or negligence, on his part. . . it is. . . not disputed that any degree of fault on the part of the [driver], if established, is sufficient for the [plaintiff] to recover. On the other hand, if no blame can be imputed to the [driver], the action, based on negligence, must inevitably fail.'

In the present case the plaintiffs may well have been insured. Others in their position may be less fortunate. A change in the law is, however, a matter for Parliament. Meanwhile, since in my judgment Mr Tarleton was in no way to blame, he was not negligent. I would therefore allow the appeal."

QUESTION

Leggatt L.J. observes that the claimant in this case may well have been insured. Is this the reason why he was prepared to give judgment for the defendants? Which insurance policy should carry the risk of accidental damage to a building: the one attaching to a car or the one attaching to the building?

NOTE

Insurance has proved to be a factor in a number of cases involving damage done by motor vehicles. Note how it is also a factor in the road accident cases extracted elsewhere in the book: *Reid v Rush & Tompkins* (1990) (p.60); *Stovin v Wise* (1996) (p.175); *Morgan v Launchbury* (1973) (p.86); and *Nettleship v Weston* (1971) (p.149). See also *Gorringe v Calderdale MBC* (2004) (p.334) and Lewis (2005) 25 L.S. 85. In the next case insurance may also have been a factor: those who put lorries on the road for profit ought to take the risk of damage they cause even in respect of virtually latent defects. The case remains a negligence case, but it shows how by manipulating the burden (or at least standard) of proof (cf. **4.2.7**) the courts can sometimes get close to a strict liability for things (motor vehicles).

Henderson v HE Jenkins & Sons Ltd **[1970] A.C. 282, HL**

This was an action in damages under the Fatal Accidents Act by a widow against the owners of a runaway lorry that had killed her husband. The owners claimed that the lorry's brakes had failed because of a latent defect undiscoverable by the use of reasonable care and this defence was upheld by the trial judge and Court of Appeal. However a bare majority of the House of Lords (Lords Reid, Donovan and Pearson; Lord Guest and Viscount Dilhorne dissenting) allowed an appeal.

Lord Donovan: ". . . [The defendants] proved that the pipe in question was visually inspected *in situ* once a week; that the brake pedal was on these occasions depressed to check for leaks from the pipe and none seen; that nothing more than such visual inspection of the pipe was required by Ministry of Transport rules or the maker's advice . . .

Yet the kind of load this lorry had been carrying in the past was something which had to be known in order to assess the measure of the duty of reasonable care resting on the [defendants]. For the corrosion of the pipe was caused by some chemical agent. Had the lorry, therefore, been carrying chemicals of any kind? Or had it operated under conditions where salt (also a corrosive agent) might come in contact with the pipe? Or had it at some time been adapted for carrying cattle and done so? If any of these things were the case then clearly visual inspection of the pipe *in situ* would not have been enough. It should have been removed at intervals so that the whole of it, and not merely part of it, could be examined . . .

It was, therefore, incumbent on the [defendants], if they were to sustain their plea of latent defect undiscoverable by the exercise of ordinary care, to prove where the vehicle had been and what it had been carrying whilst in their service and in what conditions it had operated. Only then could the standard of reasonable care be ascertained, and their conduct measured against it . . ."

QUESTION

Is this case an example of what Stone (see p.182) has called "negligence without fault"?

5.4.2 Tort of breach of statutory duty

One reason why the courts have had to manipulate the rules of evidence within the tort of negligence to achieve a stricter liability is because the judges failed to develop the tort of breach of statutory duty beyond industrial accidents. They had their opportunity as the next case shows.

Phillips v Britannia Hygienic Laundry Co Ltd **[1923] 2 K.B. 832, CA**

Bankes L.J.: "This is an appeal from the Divisional Court reversing the county court judge in an action brought by the plaintiff for damage done to his motor van. The axle of the defendants' motor lorry broke and caused the damage. The action in the county court was founded on an alleged breach of a statutory provision contained in the Motor Cars (Use and Construction) Order 1904 and alternatively on the alleged negligence of the defendant. The county court judge absolved the defendant from negligence in relation either to the management of the motor lorry or to the state of its axle, but he found negligence on the part of the repairers to whom the motor lorry had been sent, in not having executed the repairs efficiently, and gave judgment for the plaintiff on the ground that the lorry was not in the condition required by cl 6 of art. II of the Order. On an appeal by the defendants the Divisional Court reversed this judgment. The plaintiff appeals to this court.

I agree with the conclusion of the Divisional Court. If the judgment of the county court judge were to stand it would have very far-reaching consequences . . .

We have not to consider the case of a person injured on the highway. The injury here was done to the appellant's van; and the appellant, a member of the public, claims a right of action as one of a class for whose benefit cl 6 was introduced. He contends that the public using the highway is the class so favoured. I do not agree. In my view the public using the highway is not a class; it is itself the public and not a class of the public. The clause therefore was not passed for the benefit of a class or section of the public. It applies to the public generally, and it is one among many regulations for breach of which it cannot have been intended that a person aggrieved should have a civil remedy . . ."

Atkin L.J.: ". . . This is an important question, and I have felt some doubt upon it, because it is clear that these regulations are in part designed to promote the safety of the public using highways. The question is whether they were intended to be enforced only by the special penalty attached to them in the Act. In my opinion, when an Act imposes a duty of commission or omission, the question whether a person aggrieved by a breach of the duty has a right of action depends on the intention of the Act. Was it intended to make the duty one which was owed to the party aggrieved as well as to the State, or was it a public duty only? . . . I have come to the conclusion that the duty they were intended to impose was not a duty enforceable by individuals injured, but a public duty only, the sole remedy for which is the remedy provided by way of a fine. . . . In particular it is not likely that the legislature intended by these means to impose on the owners of vehicles an absolute obligation to have them roadworthy in all events even in the absence of negligence . . ."

[Younger L.J. agreed]

NOTE

The principles of the tort of breach of statutory duty have been set out in the extract of the judgment of Lord Browne-Wilkinson in *X (Minors) v Bedfordshire CC* at the end of Chapter 4 (p.178). Suffice it to say here that *Phillips* is very much a missed opportunity to introduce a form of strict liability into the second main source of personal injury claims, namely road accidents. Had the result of *Phillips* been different, there would have been a symmetry between industrial and road accidents.

QUESTIONS

1. *Phillips* was not of course a personal injury claim, a point made by Bankes L.J. If it had been, do you think Bankes L.J. would have given judgment for the claimant?

2. Why has the UK not adopted a statutory no-fault regime, like the one in France, to cover victims of road accidents? Is it because the government has (a) no interest in the welfare of traffic accident victims; (b) no wish to upset insurance companies; (c) a belief that the tort of negligence has a moral value vis-à-vis the activity of driving; (d) a belief that the NHS is an adequate social service provision in respect of traffic accident victims; or (e) felt that it is not a vote-winning issue?

5.4.3 Tort of public nuisance

Another attempt to introduce strict liability into highway accidents was made through the tort of public nuisance whose principles are set out in *Esso* (p.5) and *Att-Gen v PYA Quarries* (p.81).

Dymond v Pearce and Others [1972] 1 Q.B. 496, CA

This was an action for damages by a motor cycle passenger against the employers of a lorry driver (second defendant) in respect of personal injuries suffered by the passenger when the motor cycle ran into the back of the parked lorry. The lorry driver had parked his vehicle with the tail lights on, beneath a street lamp on a dual carriageway, and there was a clear view of the lorry for at least 200 yards. The crash occurred when the driver of the motor cycle (first defendant) was looking behind him at girls on the pavement. The Court of Appeal (Sachs L.J., Edmund Davies L.J. and Stephenson L.J.) upheld a judgment that the accident was wholly the fault of the motor cyclist.

Sachs L.J.: "... The leaving of a large vehicle on a highway for any other purpose for a considerable period (it is always a matter of degree) otherwise than in a lay-by *prima facie* results in a nuisance being created, for it narrows the highway. With all respect to the views expressed by the learned trial judge as to the ways of life today, I am unable to accept his conclusion that the parking for many hours for the driver's own convenience of a large lorry on a highway of sufficient importance to have a dual carriageway did not result in the creation of a nuisance ...

But the mere fact that a lorry was a nuisance does not render its driver or owner liable to the plaintiff in damages unless its being in that position was a cause of the accident ...

[The trial judge found] that the sole cause of the accident was the first defendant's negligence ... It entails a parallel conclusion that the nuisance was not a cause of the plaintiff's injuries; that, indeed, in the vast majority of cases is an inevitable conclusion once negligence on the part of a driver of a stationary vehicle is negatived, for only rarely will that which was found not to be a foreseeable cause of an accident also be found to have been in law the actual cause of it ...

It is thus not necessary to decide a further point inherent in much that was canvassed before us as to the ingredients of nuisance of the category under consideration. What would be the position if, even though the third defendant had not been negligent in leaving the lorry as it was in fact left, yet there had occurred some unexpected supervening happening—such as an onset of heavy weather, sea mist or fog, or, for instance, a sudden rear light failure (potent cause of fatalities)—which had so affected the situation that the lorry became the cause of an accident? Should the risk fall entirely on those using the highway properly? Or should some liability attach to the person at fault in creating a nuisance? It may well be that, as I am inclined to think, he who created the nuisance would be under a liability . . . If he was thus liable this might be the only class of case in which an action in nuisance by obstruction of the highway could succeed where one in negligence would fail . . ."

Edmund Davies L.J.: ". . . Where a vehicle has been left parked on the highway for such a length of time or in such other circumstances as constitute it an obstruction amounting to a public nuisance, I remain of the view I expressed in *Parish v Judd* that, in order that a plaintiff who in such proceedings as the present may recover compensation for personal injuries caused by a collision with that obstruction, he must establish that the obstruction constituted a danger . . .

[He then cited Denning L.J. in *Morton v Wheeler*, as to what constitutes a danger—'whether injury may reasonably be anticipated'.] It goes without saying, however, that the person creating a highway obstruction must be alert to such sudden and unpredicted weather changes as those to which we are subject in this country at most seasons, to the possibility that the vehicular or highway lighting may fail or be interfered with in these days of rampant vandalism, and to other circumstances which may convert what was originally a danger-free obstruction into a grave traffic hazard. If he fails to exercise ordinary intelligence in those and similar respects, he can make no proper claim reasonably to have anticipated the probable shape of things to come, and he must expect his conduct to be subjected to the most critical scrutiny in the event of an accident occurring . . .

It is true that in the result, as Denning L.J. said in *Morton v Wheeler*, 'Inasmuch as the test of danger is what may reasonably be foreseen, it is apparent that cases of public nuisance . . . have an affinity with negligence.' Nevertheless, as he went on to point out: 'There is a real distinction between negligence and nuisance. In an action for private damage arising out of a public nuisance, the court does not look at the conduct of the defendant and ask whether he was negligent. It looks at the actual state of affairs as it exists in or adjoining the highway without regard to the merits or demerits of the defendant. If the state of affairs is such as to be a danger . . . the person who created it is liable unless he can show sufficient justification or excuse.'"

NOTES AND QUESTIONS

1. Compare Denning L.J.'s observation (in Edmund Davies L.J.'s judgment) with his analysis of public nuisance and negligence in *Esso v Southport* (p.5). From a factual position, it would seem that public nuisance will be relevant mainly (only?) in situations where motor vehicles obstruct the highway. Could a moving vehicle ever constitute a nuisance? Could *Henderson v Jenkins* (above, p.159) be re-analysed as a public nuisance case?

2. What public nuisance shares with breach of statutory duty is that they are both torts arising out of unlawful (criminal) behaviour.

3. Is 'public nuisance' being used in the same way as res ipsa loquitur (cf. **4.2.7**)?

5.5 Animals

With regard to motor vehicles, it is in some ways difficult to talk about a specific liability for things since claims are in theory founded upon the careless behaviour of the road user. It is a personal liability of the individual based upon his or her individual act. With respect to animals, however, one can certainly talk in terms of a liability for things since the statutory regime that now governs liability is founded on the relationship between defendant (keeper) and animal (thing). Of course liability is still personal to the defendant; the keeper cannot escape liability (as one could in Roman law) by handing over the offending animal to the victim. The relevant statutory scheme is set out in this section, but sandwiched between extracts of speeches from a recent House of Lords decision. These extracts provide a useful introduction to, and commentary on, the Act.

Mirvahedy v Henley [2003] 2 A.C. 491, HL

(For facts and main extracts see p.38)

Lord Walker: ". . . **134** It is not necessary to go far into the old common law rules which imposed strict liability for wild animals (animals ferae naturae) or for tame or domesticated animals with a known vicious propensity (the scienter basis of liability). The old rules were both questionable in their foundations and uncertain in their limits. That appears from two cases decided not very long before the Act, *Behrens v Bertram Mills Circus Ltd* [1957] 2 QB 1 (the case of the trained Burmese elephant which was more docile than many horses until harassed by a small dog) and *Fitzgerald v E D and A D Cooke Bourne (Farms) Ltd* [1964] 1 QB 249 (the case of an unbroken filly in a field crossed by a public footpath). The Goddard Committee (which reported in 1953) (Report of the Committee on the Law of Civil Liability for Damage done by Animals (Cmd 8746)) proposed to abolish strict liability for damage caused by animals, but the Law Commission in its Report on Civil Liability for Animals (published in 1967 (Law Com No 13) as one of the Law Commission's earliest reports) took a different view. The Law Commission recommended that the principle of strict liability should not be abolished, but should be modified and simplified. It is clear that in enacting the Act, Parliament was (in the most general terms) following the Law Commission's recommendations to retain the principle in a modified form. It is unfortunately far from clear that Parliament achieved the objective of simplification. . . .

135 Part of the problem is that section 2 of the Act is expressed in very general terms. It is notable that the Law Commission inquired into the prevalence of particular types of damage caused by animals. Its report contains some detailed statistics about road accidents in which animals were involved. But in section 2 Parliament has not chosen to identify or make specific provision for the varying circumstances in which animals do most commonly cause damage. In practice section 2(1) has a very narrow scope, being almost entirely limited to incidents in (or following escapes from) zoos or circuses. Section 2(2) has to cover the whole range of incidents involving animals of species classified as non-dangerous (which I will call domesticated animals, although that is not an entirely accurate term). That range includes (i) physical injury to humans by biting (especially by dogs) or kicking or knocking down (especially by horses); (ii) injuries caused to livestock (such as a dog worrying a neighbour's sheep, or a cat killing a neighbour's chickens); (iii) road traffic accidents, especially those caused by animals straying on the highway; (iv) damage caused by livestock getting out on to neighbouring land and destroying crops or gardens; and (v) injury or damage caused by the spread of animal infection or by the smell or noise of animals (a class which shades off into cases normally classified as nuisance). So section 2(2) has a lot of work to do. It is expressed in general, abstract terms and it has to be applied to a wide range of disparate incidents.

136 Other sections of the Act do contain more specific provisions. The case of livestock trespassing on private land is covered by section 4, and there is a special provision as to guard dogs injuring trespassers (section 5(3)). But the only special provision made for animals straying on the highway is the abolition by section 8 (subject to qualifications in section 8(2)) of the old common law rule which gave immunity: see *Searle v Wallbank* [1947] AC 341. . . ."

Animals Act 1971 (c.22)

"**2. Liability for damage done by dangerous animals**.

   (1) Where any damage is caused by an animal which belongs to a dangerous species, any person who is a keeper of the animal is liable for the damage, except as otherwise provided by this Act.

   (2) Where damage is caused by an animal which does not belong to a dangerous species, a keeper of the animal is liable for the damage, except as otherwise provided by this Act, if—

      (a) the damage is of a kind which the animal, unless restrained, was likely to cause or which, if caused by the animal, was likely to be severe; and

      (b) the likelihood of the damage or of its being severe was due to characteristics of the animal which are not normally found in animals of the same species or are not normally so found except at particular times or in particular circumstances; and

      (c) those characteristics were known to that keeper or were at any time known to a person who at that time had charge of the animal as that keeper's servant or, where that keeper is the head of a household, were known to another keeper of the animal who is a member of that household and under the age of sixteen.

3. Liability for injury done by dogs to livestock.

Where a dog causes damage by killing or injuring livestock, any person who is a keeper of the dog is liable for the damage, except as otherwise provided by this Act.

4. Liability for damage and expenses due to trespassing livestock

   (1) Where livestock belonging to any person strays on to land in the ownership or occupation of another and—

      (a) damage is done by the livestock to the land or to any property on it which is in the ownership or possession of the other person; or

      (b) any expenses are reasonably incurred by that other person in keeping the livestock while it cannot be restored to the person to whom it belongs or while it is detained in pursuance of section 7 of this Act, or in ascertaining to whom it belongs;

the person to whom the livestock belongs is liable for the damage or expenses, except as otherwise provided by this Act.

(2) For the purposes of this section any livestock belongs to the person in whose possession it is.

5. Exceptions from liability under sections 2 to 4.

(1) A person is not liable under sections 2 to 4 of this Act for any damage which is due wholly to the fault of the person suffering it.

(2) A person is not liable under section 2 of this Act for any damage suffered by a person who has voluntarily accepted the risk thereof.

(3) A person is not liable under section 2 of this Act for any damage caused by an animal kept on any premises or structure to a person trespassing there, if it is proved either—

    (a) that the animal was not kept there for the protection of persons or property; or

    (b) (if the animal was kept there for the protection of persons or property) that keeping it there for that purpose was not unreasonable.

(4) A person is not liable under section 3 of this Act if the livestock was killed or injured on land on to which it had strayed and either the dog belonged to the occupier or its presence on the land was authorised by the occupier.

(5) A person is not liable under section 4 of this Act where the livestock strayed from a highway and its presence there was a lawful use of the highway.

(6) In determining whether any liability for damage under section 4 of this Act is excluded by subsection (1) of this section the damage shall not be treated as due to the fault of the person suffering it by reason only that he could have prevented it by fencing; but a person is not liable under that section where it is proved that the straying of the livestock on to the land would not have occurred but for a breach by any other person, being a person having an interest in the land, of a duty to fence.

6. Interpretation of certain expressions used in sections 2 to 5.

(1) The following provisions apply to the interpretation of sections 2 to 5 of this Act.

(2) A dangerous species is a species—

    (a) which is not commonly domesticated in the British Islands; and

    (b) whose fully grown animals normally have such characteristics that they are likely, unless restrained, to cause severe damage or that any damage they may cause is likely to be severe.

(3) Subject to subsection (4) of this section, a person is a keeper of an animal if—

    (a) he owns the animal or has it in his possession; or

    (b) he is the head of a household of which a member under the age of sixteen owns the animal or has it in his possession;

and if at any time an animal ceases to be owned by or to be in the possession of a person, any person who immediately before that time was a keeper thereof by virtue of the preceding provisions of this subsection continues to be a keeper of the animal until another person becomes a keeper thereof by virtue of those provisions.

(4) Where an animal is taken into and kept in possession for the purpose of preventing it from causing damage or of restoring it to its owner, a person is not a keeper of it by virtue only of that possession.

(5) Where a person employed as a servant by a keeper of an animal incurs a risk incidental to his employment he shall not be treated as accepting it voluntarily.
. . .

8. Duty to take care to prevent damage from animals straying on to the highway.

(1) So much of the rules of the common law relating to liability for negligence as excludes or restricts the duty which a person might owe to others to take such care as is reasonable to see that damage is not caused by animals straying on to a highway is hereby abolished.

(2) Where damage is caused by animals straying from unfenced land to a highway a person who placed them on the land shall not be regarded as having committed a breach of the duty to take care by reason only of placing them there if—

(a) the land is common land, or is land situated in an area where fencing is not customary, or is a town or village green; and

(b) he had a right to place the animals on that land. . . .

11. General interpretation.

In this Act—

'common land', and 'town or village green' have the same meanings as in the Commons Registration Act 1965;

'damage' includes the death of, or injury to, any person (including any disease and any impairment of physical or mental condition);

'fault' has the same meaning as in the Law Reform (Contributory Negligence) Act 1945;

'fencing' includes the construction of any obstacle designed to prevent animals from straying;

'livestock' means cattle, horses, asses, mules, hinnies, sheep, pigs, goats and poultry, and also deer not in the wild state and, in sections 3 and 9, also, while in captivity, pheasants, partridges and grouse;

'poultry' means the domestic varieties of the following, that is to say, fowls, turkeys, geese, ducks, guinea-fowls, pigeons, peacocks and quails; and

'species' includes sub-species and variety.''

QUESTIONS

1. What if the courts decided to interpret the word 'animal' very widely? Can you think of a range of scenarios to which the Act might apply that were not perhaps foreseen by Parliament?

2. What if C's pet rat escapes into D's neighbouring garden and D (who has a fear of rats) deliberately traps it, resulting in its death. Could C successfully sue D?

3. Is liability under section 4 always for damages or can it be for a debt?

NOTE

Extracts below provide some useful judicial commentary on the Act.

Mirvahedy v Henley **[2003] 2 A.C. 491, HL**

(For facts and main extracts see p.38)

Lord Nicholls: ". . . **9** The purpose of the 1971 Act was to simplify the law. Sections 1 to 6 of the Act made new provision regarding strict liability for damage done by animals. They replace the old rules of the common law. Section 2 contains provisions relating to liability for damage done by dangerous animals. Unfortunately the language of section 2(2) is itself opaque. In this instance the parliamentary draftsman's zeal for brevity has led to obscurity. Over the years section 2(2) has attracted much judicial obloquy.

10 Section 2 places all animals into one or other of two categories, according to their species. Animals either belong to a dangerous species, or they do not. The circumstances in which the keeper of an animal is liable for damage caused by his animal depend upon the category to which the animal belongs.

11 A dangerous species of animal is a species which meets two requirements, set out in section 6(2). A species can include a sub-species or a variety: see section 11. The first requirement (a) is that the species is not commonly domesticated in the British Islands. The second requirement (b) is that fully grown animals of the species 'normally have such characteristics that they are likely, unless restrained, to cause severe damage or that any damage they may cause is likely to be severe'. In short, they are dangerous animals.

12 A tiger satisfies both requirements. It is not commonly domesticated in this country, and it is dangerous. A horse does not satisfy the first requirement. Unlike tigers, horses are commonly domesticated here. So tigers, satisfying both requirements, are a dangerous species of animals. Horses, which do not satisfy the two requirements, are not. . . ."

Lord Hobhouse: ". . . **66** The Act was a reforming act and followed from Report No 13 of the Law Commission on Civil Liability for Animals. Without adopting all the recommendations of the Law Commission, the Act completely recasts the previous law but has retained a recognisable structure derived from the previous law. Thus it retains a distinct category for wild animals 'not commonly domesticated in the British Islands', sections 6(2)(a) and 2(1); and has a residual category which makes use of the former scienter rule based on the keeper's knowledge of the particular animal's actual characteristics: section 2(2)(c).

67 Another feature of the Act is that it uses a double-barrelled concept of dangerousness with alternative criteria either of which suffices. The first is the familiar characteristic that the animal or its species is, unless restrained, likely to cause severe damage; this corresponds to what has sometimes been called a vicious propensity. The second is directed not to the animal's propensities, be they vicious or benign, but to the consequences of anything it may do. Thus the alternative criterion is that it is an animal of which it can be said that 'any damage [it] may cause is likely to be severe': section 6(2)(b). These two alternative criteria are used in conjunction with the criterion of non-domestication to define what is a dangerous species of animal in section 6(2). Using the first alternative, a tiger is a dangerous animal. It is likely, unless restrained, to cause severe injuries to humans: that is its nature. Using the second alternative, an Indian elephant is a dangerous animal, not because it is likely to injure any one, but because, if it does, the injury is likely, as a result of its weight and bulk, to be severe: cf *Behrens v Bertram Mills Circus Ltd* [1957] 2 QB 1. This is a statement about its physical capacity to injure and its inability to limit the consequences of that capacity not about its inclination to injure. In section 2(1) there is a strict liability for damage caused by dangerous animals as defined in section 6(2). In section 2(2) there is a scienter liability for any damage caused by any other animal which is, inter alia, damage of a kind which the animal in question was, unless restrained, likely to cause or which, if caused by that animal, was likely to be severe: section 2(2)(a). . . ."

Lord Walker: ". . . 136. . . . It has not been contended in your Lordships' House (although it was contended at first instance) that section 8 has the effect of excluding possible liability under section 2(2). . . ."

QUESTIONS

1. If D's cat eats his neighbour's pet canary will D be liable under the 1971 Act?
2. Do the facts of *Mirvahedy* fall under s.8 rather than s.2? Or do they fall under s.8 in addition to s.2? Does it matter?
3. What is meant by "normally" in s.2(2)(b) of the 1971 Act? (cf. *Welsh v Stokes* (2008) ([2008] 1 WLR 1224)).

5.6 Aircraft

Aircraft attract their own regime for several reasons. First, legislation excludes any right of action in trespass in respect of aircraft over-flying private property. Secondly, material loss or damage caused by aircraft to person or property is governed by a statutory strict liability provision. And thirdly, aircraft can give rise to a specific conflict of interest: the mental distress to individuals resulting from aircraft noise conflicts with the general public benefit arising from air transport and air defence.

5.6.1 Statute

The starting point of liability for damage caused by aircraft is statute. The 1982 Act, set out below, suppresses certain actions at common law, but establishes a kind of statutory trespass claim.

Civil Aviation Act 1982 (c.16)

"**76. Liability of aircraft in respect of trespass, nuisance and surface damage**.

(1) No action shall lie in respect of trespass or in respect of nuisance, by reason only of the flight of an aircraft over any property at a height above the ground which,

having regard to wind, weather and all the circumstances of the case is reasonable, or the ordinary incidents of such flight, so long as the provisions of any Air Navigation Order and of any orders under section 62 above have been duly complied with and there has been no breach of section 81 below.

(2) Subject to subsection (3) below, where material loss or damage is caused to any person or property on land or water by, or by a person in, or an article, animal or person falling from, an aircraft while in flight, taking off or landing, then unless the loss or damage was caused or contributed to by the negligence of the person by whom it was suffered, damages in respect of the loss or damage shall be recoverable without proof of negligence or intention or other cause of action, as if the loss or damage had been caused by the wilful act, neglect, or default of the owner of the aircraft.

(3) Where material loss or damage is caused as aforesaid in circumstances in which—

(a) damages are recoverable in respect of the said loss or damage by virtue only of subsection (2) above, and

(b) a legal liability is created in some person other than the owner to pay damages in respect of the said loss or damage,

the owner shall be entitled to be indemnified by that other person against any claim in respect of the said loss or damage.

77. Nuisance caused by aircraft on aerodromes.

(1) An Air Navigation Order may provide for regulating the conditions under which noise and vibration may be caused by aircraft on aerodromes and may provide that subsection (2) below shall apply to any aerodrome as respects which provision as to noise and vibration caused by aircraft is so made.

(2) No action shall lie in respect of nuisance by reason only of the noise and vibration caused by aircraft on an aerodrome to which this subsection applies by virtue of an Air Navigation Order, as long as the provisions of any such Order are duly complied with."

PROBLEM

A number of inhabitants of a village suffer severe psychiatric injury when they witness a plane crashing nearby. Are they entitled to damages under s.76(2) of the 1982 Act? And, if so, ought an analogy to be made with *Wilkinson v Downton* (p.8) or with *Frost v Chief Constable of S Yorks* (p.169)? (cf. *Glen v Korean Airlines* (2003).)

5.6.2 Common law (tort of private nuisance)

Despite the statutory defence in ss.76–77 of the 1982 Act, the tort of private nuisance still has an important role to play in respect of mental distress damage caused by aircraft.

Dennis v Ministry of Defence [2003] EWHC 793, QBD

Buckley J.: "1. This case concerns the effect of noise from Harrier jet fighters on the 1st Claimant's neighbouring estate. It is alleged to constitute a nuisance at common law and/or to infringe his human rights, and also to infringe the human rights of his wife, the 2nd Claimant. A declaration and damages are sought, alternatively damages of some £10,000, 000. . . .

Nuisance at Common Law

30. This case raises an important and problematic point of principle in the law of nuisance. Namely, whether and in what circumstances a sufficient public interest can amount to a defence to a claim in nuisance. In several cases the point has arisen in a less dramatic form than here. For example, the local cricket club case: *Miller v Jackson* [1977] QB 966 and *Kennaway v Thompson* [1981] QB 88 in which the Court of Appeal affirmed the principle in *Shelfer v City of London Electric Lighting Company* [1894] 1 Ch. 287, namely, the fact that the wrong doer is in some sense a public benefactor has never been considered a sufficient reason to refuse an injunction. (See Lindley LJ. At 315/6). *Clerk and Lindsell* concludes that public interest is 'not in itself a defence, but a factor in assessing reasonableness of user'. 18th Edition paragraph 19.72. *Fleming The Law of Torts* 9th Edition at 471 points out that some weight is accorded to the utility of the defendant's conduct, but suggests that the argument 'must not be pushed too far.' He cites Bohlen Studies 429:

> 'If the public be interested let the public as such bear the costs.'

He points out this can be achieved by holding the defendant liable and leaving him to include the cost in charges to the public, or by statutory authority with provision for compensation. The former suggestion, of course, would only apply to a service provider capable of raising charges. . . .

45. Where there is a real public interest in a particular use of land, I can see no objection in principle to taking that public interest into account, in one way or another, in deciding what is best to be done. . . .

46. The problem with putting the public interest into the scales when deciding whether a nuisance exists, is simply that if the answer is no, not because the claimant is being over sensitive, but because his private rights must be subjugated to the public interest, it might well be unjust that he should suffer the damage for the benefit of all. If it is to be held that there is no nuisance, there can be no remedy at common law. As this case illustrates, the greater the public interest, the greater may be the interference. If public interest is considered at the remedy stage and since the court has a discretion, the nuisance may continue but the public, in one way or another, pays for its own benefit. . . . Allowing a human rights claim but denying a remedy in nuisance would, of course, be another solution, but it would be one that reflected adversely on the flexibility of the common law. . . .

47. The principles or policy underlying these considerations are that public interest should be considered and that selected individuals should not bear the cost of the public benefit. I am in favour of giving effect to those principles. I believe it is necessary to do so if the common law in this area is to be consistent with the developing jurisprudence on human rights.

48. I therefore hold that a nuisance is established but that the public interest clearly demands that RAF Wittering should continue to train pilots. . . .

49. I do not believe that the conclusion at which I have arrived is prohibited by authority. The facts of this case are extreme and not analogous to others to which I was referred. I am conscious that there is no authority directly in point which supports my solution. However, save where it may be considered more appropriate to leave the matter to legislation, the common law should develop in line with European decisions on human rights, which I consider later. . . ."

QUESTIONS

1. Is the nuisance liability for the aircraft noise attaching to the use of aircraft or to the use of the land?

2. Has *Dennis* been put into question by the House of Lords' decision in *Marcic v Thames Water* (p.239)?

5.6.3 **Human rights**

As Buckley J. suggests, an alternative head of claim by the victims of aircraft noise might now be available thanks to Human Rights Act 1998.

***Dennis v Ministry of Defence* [2003] EWHC 793, QBD**

(See above p.205)

Buckley J.: ". . . **55**. The claims here are on behalf of both Claimants (Mr and Mrs Dennis). It is alleged that the aircraft noise constitutes an interference with their human rights under the Human Rights Act 1998. . . .

61. In view of my findings on the extent of noise interference and the agreed fact that it significantly reduces the market value of the Estate, I am satisfied there is an interference both with Article 1 and Article 8 rights. . . .

63. . . . In my view, common fairness demands that where the interests of a minority, let alone an individual, are seriously interfered with because of an overriding public interest, the minority should be compensated. To its credit the MOD appears to accept that principle since it operates the voluntary schemes to which I have referred. . . ."

QUESTION

What are the rights and remedies of those living near a commercial airport?

***Hatton v UK* (2003) 37 EHRR 611, ECHR (Grand Chamber)**

THE COURT: ". . . **3**. The applicants alleged that Government policy on night flights at Heathrow airport gave rise to a violation of their rights under Article 8 of the Convention and that they were denied an effective domestic remedy for this complaint, contrary to Article 13 of the Convention. . . .

6. On 7 November 2000 the Chamber delivered its judgment in which it held, by five votes to two, that there had been a violation of Article 8 of the Convention and by, six votes to one, that there had been a violation of Article 13. The Chamber also decided, by six votes to one, to award compensation for non-pecuniary damage of 4,000 pounds sterling ('GBP') to each applicant, and a global sum of GBP 70,000 in respect of legal costs and expenses. . . .

7. On 19 December 2001 the Government requested, pursuant to Article 43 of the Convention and Rule 73, that the case be referred to the Grand Chamber. The Panel of the Grand Chamber accepted this request on 27 March 2002. . . .

84. The applicants complained that the Government policy on night flights at Heathrow introduced in 1993 violated their rights under Article 8 of the Convention,. . .

96. Article 8 protects the individual's right to respect for his or her private and family life, home and correspondence. There is no explicit right in the Convention to a clean and quiet environment, but where an individual is directly and seriously affected by noise or other pollution, an issue may arise under Article 8. . . .

98. Article 8 may apply in environmental cases whether the pollution is directly caused by the State or whether State responsibility arises from the failure properly to regulate private industry. Whether the case is analysed in terms of a positive duty on the State to take reasonable and appropriate measures to secure the applicants' rights under paragraph 1 of Article 8 or in terms of an interference by a public authority to be justified in accordance with paragraph 2, the applicable principles are broadly similar. In both contexts regard must be had to the fair balance that has to be struck between the competing interests of the individual and of the community as a whole; and in both contexts the State enjoys a certain margin of appreciation in determining the steps to be taken to ensure compliance with the Convention. Furthermore, even in relation to the positive obligations flowing from the first paragraph of Article 8, in striking the required balance the aims mentioned in the second paragraph may be of a certain relevance. . .

125. Whether in the implementation of that regime the right balance has been struck in substance between the Article 8 rights affected by the regime and other conflicting community interests depends on the relative weight given to each of them. The Court accepts that in this context the authorities were entitled, having regard to the general nature of the measures taken, to rely on statistical data based on average perception of noise disturbance. . . .

126. As to the economic interests which conflict with the desirability of limiting or halting night flights in pursuance of the above aims, the Court considers it reasonable to assume that those flights contribute at least to a certain extent to the general economy. . . .

130. There has accordingly been no violation of Article 8 of the Convention. . . .

139. As the Chamber found, Section 76 of the [Civil Aviation] 1982 Act prevents actions in nuisance in respect of excessive noise caused by aircraft at night. The applicants complain about the flights which were permitted by the 1993 Scheme, and which were in accordance with the relevant regulations. No action therefore lay in trespass or nuisance in respect of lawful night flights. . . .

140. The question which the Court must address is whether the applicants had a remedy at national level to 'enforce the substance of the Convention rights . . . in whatever form they may happen to be secured in the domestic legal order' (*Vilvarajah and Others v United Kingdom*) . . . In. . . its judgment in the case of *Smith and Grady v United Kingdom*, the Court concluded that judicial review was not an effective remedy on the grounds that the domestic courts defined policy issues so broadly that it was not possible for the applicants to make their Convention points regarding their rights under Article 8 of the Convention in the domestic courts.

141. The Court recalls that judicial review proceedings were capable of establishing that the 1993 Scheme was unlawful because the gap between Government policy and practice was too wide (see *R v Secretary of State for Transport, ex parte Richmond LBC (No. 2)* [1995] Environmental Law Reports p. 390). However, it is clear, as noted by the Chamber, that the scope of review by the domestic courts was limited to the classic English public law concepts, such as irrationality, unlawfulness and patent unreasonableness, and did not at the time (that is, prior to the entry into force of the Human Rights Act 1998) allow consideration of whether the claimed increase in night flights under the 1993 Scheme represented a justifiable limitation on the right to respect for the private and family lives or the homes of those who live in the vicinity of Heathrow airport.

142. In these circumstances, the Court considers that the scope of review by the domestic courts in the present case was not sufficient to comply with Article 13. There has therefore been a violation of Article 13 of the Convention. . . .”

QUESTIONS

1. If s.76 of the Civil Aviation Act 1982 prevents actions in nuisance (see para.139 in *Hatton*), why were the claimants in *Dennis* able to succeed in nuisance?

2. Is it fair and just that a burden (or price) associated with a public good that benefits everyone in a particular society should fall on the shoulders of just a few individuals in that society?

3. Should the court have addressed the issue of aircraft and climate change?

5.7 Liability for dangerous things in general

In this final section on damage caused by moveable things a general question can be posed. Does English law recognise a strict form of liability, perhaps based on risk (and perhaps analogous to dangerous animals), for damage done by a dangerous thing under the control of another? A definitive answer to this question has been given by the House of Lords.

Read v J Lyons & Co [1947] A.C. 156, HL

This was an action for damages for personal injury brought by a Ministry of Supply factory inspector (the appellant) against the operators of a munitions factory (the respondents) where she had been directed to work. The appellant was injured by an unexplained explosion in the shell shop and in her action she did not plead or prove negligence; the trial judge accordingly treated her action as based on the rule in *Rylands v Fletcher* (on which see p.243 below). He held the respondents liable. However his decision was overturned by the Court of Appeal whose judgment was upheld by the House of Lords (Viscount Simon and Lords Macmillan, Porter, Simonds and Uthwatt).

Viscount Simon: ". . . Now, the strict liability recognised by this House to exist in *Rylands v Fletcher* is conditioned by two elements which I may call the condition of 'escape' from the land of something likely to do mischief if it escapes, and the condition of 'non-natural use' of the land. . . . It is not necessary to analyse this second condition on the present occasion, for in the case now before us the first essential condition of 'escape' does not seem to me to be present at all. . . ."

Lord Macmillan: ". . . In my opinion the appellant's statement of claim discloses no ground of action against the respondents. The action is one of damages for personal injuries. Whatever may have been the law of England in early times I am of opinion that as the law now stands an allegation of negligence is in general essential to the relevancy of an action of reparation for personal injuries. . . . The emphasis formerly was on the injury sustained and the question was whether the case fell within one of the accepted classes of common law actions; the emphasis now is on the conduct of the person whose act has occasioned the injury and the question is whether it can be characterised as negligent. I do not overlook the fact that there is at least one instance in the present law in which the primitive rule survives, namely, in the case of animals *ferae naturae* or animals *mensuetae naturae* which have shown dangerous proclivities. The owner or keeper of such an animal has an absolute duty to confine or control it so that it shall not do injury to others and no proof of care on his part will absolve him from responsibility. But this is probably not so much a vestigial relic of otherwise discarded doctrine as a special rule of practical good sense. At any rate, it is too well established to be challenged. But such an exceptional case as this affords no justification for its extension by analogy. . . .

In an address characterised by much painstaking research Mr Paull for the appellant sought to convince your Lordships that there is a category of things and operations dangerous in themselves and that those who harbour such things or carry on such operations in their premises are liable apart from negligence for any personal injuries occasioned by these dangerous things or operations. I think that he succeeded in showing that in the case of dangerous things and operations the law has recognised that a special responsibility exists to take care. But I do not think that it has ever been laid down that there is absolute liability apart from negligence where persons are injured in consequence of the use of such things or the conduct of such operations. . . . Should it be thought that this is a reasonable liability to impose in the public interest it is for Parliament so to enact. . . .

Your Lordships' task in this House is to decide particular cases between litigants and your Lordships are not called upon to rationalise the law of England. That attractive if perilous field may well be left to other hands to cultivate. It has been necessary in the present instance to examine certain general principles advanced on behalf of the appellant because it was said that consistency required that these principles should be applied to the case in hand. Arguments based on legal consistency are apt to mislead for the common law is a practical code adapted to deal with the manifold diversities of human life, and as a great American judge has reminded us, 'the life of the law has not been logic; it has been experience.' For myself, I am content to say that in my opinion no authority has been quoted from case or textbook which would justify your Lordships, logically or otherwise, in giving effect to the appellant's plea. I would accordingly dismiss the appeal."

Lord Porter: ". . . Normally at the present time in an action of tort for personal injuries if there is no negligence there is no liability. . . .

It was urged upon your Lordships that it would be a strange result to hold the respondents liable if the injured person was just outside their premises but not liable if she was just within them. There is force in the objection, but the liability is itself an extension of the general rule and, in my view, it is undesirable to extend it further. . . ."

Lord Uthwatt: ". . . In substance the appellant was on the respondents' premises in performance of a statutory duty incumbent on her as a citizen, but it is, I think, obvious that this circumstance did not alter the nature of the duty which the respondents owed to her as a person who with their consent was present on their premises on business bent. . . .

Is there any good reason consistent with respect for the rights of dominion and user incident to the occupation of land, and with an appreciation of the position of an invitee, for subjecting the occupier carrying on a dangerous but lawful business to an absolute duty to safeguard the invitee from harm?. . ."

QUESTIONS

1. How would you answer Lord Uthwatt's question?

2. How would a case such as this have been decided in France? (cf. p.336.)

3. Is the whole result of this case premised on the categorisation of the appellant as a 'visitor' or 'invitee' and the respondents as an 'occupier'? Are such status categories realistic given the actual occupations of each party?

6 Liability for things (2): immovable things

In this second chapter on liability for things the emphasis will be on land. This emphasis will embrace not just damage caused by the land itself (landslips, lakes and the like) together with buildings and other structures that give rise to liability, but harm resulting from activities on the land to people on and off the premises. Again it must be stressed that English law does not really start off from the idea of a liability for things; liability depends upon establishing particular causes of action such as public nuisance, private nuisance, trespass and (or) negligence. However a number of dichotomies can be mentioned at the outset. As we shall see, English law distinguishes between damage to persons on the premises and damage to persons off the premises. It also distinguishes between harm directly caused by the occupier of land (for example knocking down a neighbour's fence or cutting down his trees) (see **Chapter 3**) and harm indirectly caused (for example smoke or fumes resulting from activities on the land). In addition the dichotomy between fault and strict liability is ever present in problems arising out of acts and omissions on land and it tends to express itself in conceptual arguments about the distinction between negligence and nuisance. Yet another dichotomy is the one between statutory and common law liability. The duty of care owed by an occupier of land to persons on his premises may seem to have its roots in Lord Atkin's neighbour principle (above p.131), but the duty is statute based. This is why occupiers' liability attracts its own chapters in many tort textbooks.

Emphasising land as the foundation of liability means that the various actors involved can get lost behind the props so to speak. This must be rectified in that the problem-solver must move from the land to the various persons who are associated with the property. In terms of potential defendants one tends to think of the owners, yet absentee landlords will indicate immediately that the possessor or occupier of the land or building might be just as relevant. As for potential claimants, these can embrace people lawfully on the property of another (visitors) or indeed people unlawfully on the land (trespassers). Passers-by and neighbours are other groups of potential claimants. In short the class, or 'status', of the various persons associated with land are important focal points when it comes to analysing factual situations.

Finally, one should note by way of introduction that one particular cause of action, liability for the escape of a dangerous thing brought onto land, is based upon a single 19th century precedent. Yet the case of *Rylands v Fletcher* can be seen as something more than a mere extension of the tort of nuisance. Like CC art.1384 it had the potential for a wide-ranging liability for dangerous things based upon the notion of risk or hazardous activity. The case, therefore, could have been one that transcended this chapter on immovable property to act as a rallying point for a liability for things in general. It is now clear, however, that it has lost this potential (*Transco Plc v Stockport MBC*, p.246).

6.1 Liability for land and structures (1): on the land

Liability for damage caused by land and things on or attached to land is complex for a variety of reasons. First, it is governed primarily by four statutes: the Occupiers' Liability Act 1957; the

Occupiers' Liability Act 1984; the Defective Premises Act 1972; and the Unfair Contract terms Act 1977. The first two statutes apply only in relation to damage to victims incurred on the premises and this is the justification for distinguishing between 'on the land' and 'off the land' (see **6.2**). Secondly, the statutes differentiate between various classes of person and so for example 'occupiers' must be distinguished from non-occupiers and perhaps from 'landlords'. Equally 'visitors' must be differentiated from 'trespassers'. Thirdly, as in other areas of tort law, the nature of the damage can be vital; the distinction between personal injury, physical damage to property and pure economic loss must be kept in mind when analysing problems. Finally, it may be important on occasions to distinguish between damage occurring as a result of the state of the land, buildings or other natural and man-made structures and damage resulting from activities on the land.

6.1.1 Occupier's duty to visitors

The duty of an occupier of land to persons on the premises was once very complex because the occupier owed differing duties depending upon the status of the person entering the property. All this changed in 1957.

Occupiers' Liability Act 1957 (5 & 6 Eliz. II, c.31)

1. Preliminary.

"(1) The rules enacted by the two next following sections shall have effect, in place of the rules of the common law, to regulate the duty which an occupier of premises owes to his visitors in respect of dangers due to the state of the premises or to things done or omitted to be done on them.

(2) The rules so enacted shall regulate the nature of the duty imposed by law in consequence of a person's occupation or control of premises and of any invitation or permission he gives (or is to be treated as giving) to another to enter or use the premises, but they shall not alter the rules of the common law as to the persons on whom a duty is so imposed or to whom it is owed; and accordingly for the purpose of the rules so enacted the persons who are to be treated as an occupier and as his visitors are the same (subject to subsection (4) of this section) as the persons who would at common law be treated as an occupier and as his invitees or licensees.

(3) The rules so enacted in relation to an occupier of premises and his visitors shall also apply, in like manner and to the like extent as the principles applicable at common law to an occupier of premises and his invitees or licensees would apply, to regulate—

(a) the obligations of a person occupying or having control over any fixed or moveable structure, including any vessel, vehicle or aircraft; and

(b) the obligations of a person occupying or having control over any premises or structure in respect of damage to property, including the property of persons who are not themselves his visitors.

(4) A person entering any premises in exercise of rights conferred by virtue of:—

(a) section 2(1) of the Countryside and Rights of Way Act 2000, or

    (b) an access agreement or order under the National Parks and Access to the Countryside Act, 1949,

is not, for the purposes of this Act, a visitor of the occupier of those premises.

2. Extent of occupier's ordinary duty.

(1) An occupier of premises owes the same duty, the "common duty of care", to all his visitors, except in so far as he is free to and does extend, restrict, modify or exclude his duty to any visitor or visitors by agreement or otherwise.

(2) The common duty of care is a duty to take such care as in all the circumstances of the case is reasonable to see that the visitor will be reasonably safe in using the premises for the purposes for which he is invited or permitted by the occupier to be there.

(3) The circumstances relevant for the present purpose include the degree of care, and of want of care, which would ordinarily be looked for in such a visitor, so that (for example) in proper cases—

    (a) an occupier must be prepared for children to be less careful than adults; and

    (b) an occupier may expect that a person, in the exercise of his calling, will appreciate and guard against any special risks ordinarily incident to it, so far as the occupier leaves him free to do so.

(4) In determining whether the occupier of premises has discharged the common duty of care to a visitor, regard is to be had to all the circumstances, so that (for example)—

    (a) where damage is caused to a visitor by a danger of which he had been warned by the occupier, the warning is not to be treated without more as absolving the occupier from liability, unless in all the circumstances it was enough to enable the visitor to be reasonably safe; and

    (b) where damage is caused to a visitor by a danger due to the faulty execution of any work of construction, maintenance or repair by an independent contractor employed by the occupier, the occupier is not to be treated without more as answerable for the danger if in all the circumstances he had acted reasonably in entrusting the work to an independent contractor and had taken such steps (if any) as he reasonably ought in order to satisfy himself that the contractor was competent and that the work had been properly done.

(5) The common duty of care does not impose on an occupier any obligation to a visitor in respect of risks willingly accepted as his by the visitor (the question whether a risk was so accepted to be decided on the same principles as in other cases in which one person owes a duty of care to another).

(6) For the purposes of this section, persons who enter premises for any purpose in the exercise of a right conferred by law are to be treated as permitted by the occupier to be there for that purpose, whether they in fact have his permission or not."

6.1.2 Occupier

One of the first questions to arise out of this statute is this. Who is an 'occupier'?

Wheat v E Lacon & Co Ltd [1966] A.C. 552, HL

This was an action for damages by a paying guest against an owner of a public house. The House of Lords (Viscount Dilhorne and Lords Denning, Morris, Pearce and Pearson) dismissed the claim but held that the owners were an occupier of the premises.

Lord Denning: "My Lords, The 'Golfers' Arms' at Great Yarmouth is owned by the brewery company, E Lacon & Co Ltd. The ground floor was run as a public-house by Mr Richardson as manager for the brewery company. The first floor was used by Mr and Mrs Richardson as their private dwelling. In the summer Mrs Richardson took in guests for her private profit. Mr and Mrs Wheat and their family were summer guests of Mrs Richardson. About 9 pm one evening, when it was getting dark, Mr Wheat fell down the back staircase in the private portion and was killed. Winn J held that there were two causes: (i) the handrail was too short because it did not stretch to the foot of the stairs; (ii) someone had taken the bulb out of the light at the top of the stairs.

The case raises this point of law: did the brewery company owe any duty to Mr Wheat to see that the handrail was safe to use or to see that the stairs were properly lighted? That depends on whether the brewery company was 'an occupier' of the private portion of the 'Golfers' Arms,' and Mr Wheat its 'visitor' within the Occupiers' Liability Act, 1957: for, if so, the brewery company owed him the 'common duty of care.'. . .

In the occupiers' Liability Act, 1957, the word 'occupier' is used in the same sense as it was used in the common law cases on occupiers' liability for dangerous premises. It was simply a convenient word to denote a person who had a sufficient degree of control over premises to put him under a duty of care towards those who came lawfully on to the premises. Those persons were divided into two categories, invitees and licensees: and a higher duty was owed to invitees than to licensees. But by the year 1956 the distinction between invitees and licensees had been reduced to vanishing point. The duty of the occupier had become simply a duty to take reasonable care to see that the premises were reason ably safe for people coming lawfully on to them: and it made no difference whether they were invitees or licensees: see *Slater v Clay Cross Co Ltd*. The Act of 1957 confirmed the process. It did away, once and for all, with invitees and licensees and classed them all as 'visitors'; and it put upon the occupier the same duty to all of them, namely, the common duty of care. This duty is simply a particular instance of the general duty of care which each man owes to his 'neighbour.'. . . Translating this general principle into its particular application to dangerous premises, it becomes simply this: wherever a person has a sufficient degree of control over to a person coming lawfully there, then he is an 'occupier' and the person coming lawfully there is his 'visitor': and the 'occupier' is under a duty to his "visitor" to use reasonable care. In order to be an 'occupier' it is not necessary for a person to have entire control over the premises. He need not have exclusive occupation. Suffice it that he has some degree of control. He may share the control with others. Two or more may be 'occupiers.' And whenever this happens, each is under a duty to use care towards persons coming lawfully on to the premises, dependent on his degree of control. If each fails in his duty, each is liable to a visitor who is injured in consequence of his failure, but each may have a claim to contribution from the other.

In *Salmond on Torts*, 14th ed (1965), p. 372, it is said that an 'occupier' is 'he who has the immediate supervision and control and the power of permitting or prohibiting the entry of other persons.' This definition was adopted by Roxburgh J in *Hartwell v Grayson, Rollo and Clover Docks Ltd* and by Diplock LJ in the present case. There is no doubt that a person who fulfils that test is an 'occupier.' He is the person who says 'come in.' But I think that test is too narrow by far. There are other people who are 'occupiers,' even though they do not say 'come in.' If a person has any degree of control over the state of the premises it is enough. . . .

What did the common duty of care demand of each of these occupiers towards their visitors? Each was under a duty to take such care as "in all the circumstances of the case" is reasonable to see that the visitor will be reasonably safe. So far as the brewery company are concerned, the circumstances demanded that on the ground floor they should, by their servants, take care not only of the structure of the building, but also the furniture, the state of the floors and lighting, and so forth, at all hours of day or night when the premises were open. But in regard to the private portion, the circumstances did not demand so much of the brewery company. They ought to see that the structure was reasonably safe, including the handrail, and that the system of lighting was efficient. But I doubt whether they were bound to see that the lights were properly switched on or the rugs laid safely on the floor. The brewery company were entitled to leave those day-to-day matters to Mr and Mrs Richardson. They, too, were occupiers. The circumstances of the case demanded that Mr and Mrs Richardson should take care of those matters in the private portion of the house. And of other matters, too. If they had realised the handrail was dangerous, they should have reported it to the brewery company.

We are not concerned here with Mr and Mrs Richardson. The judge has absolved them from any negligence and there is no appeal. We are only concerned with the brewery company. They were, in my opinion, occupiers and under a duty of care. In this respect I agree with Sellers LJ and Winn J, but I come to a different conclusion on the facts. I can see no evidence of any breach of duty by the brewery company. . . ."

NOTE

The occupiers were held not liable because there was no breach of the s.2 common duty of care. In other words, they had on the facts not been careless.

6.1.3 **Visitor**

Having defined an occupier, the next question is to determine who is a 'visitor'.

Phipps v Rochester Corporation **[1955] 1 Q.B. 450, QBD**

This was an action for damages by a young boy, five years old at the time of the accident, who was injured on the defendants' land when he fell into a trench dug on the land to lay a pipe. The defendants knew that people crossed the land and seemingly did not object; the child was accordingly an invitee (visitor) and not a trespasser. However the judge held the corporation not liable.

Devlin J.: "... A licensor who tacitly permits the public to use his land without discriminating between its members must assume that the public may include little children. But as a general rule he will have discharged his duty towards them if the dangers which they may encounter are only those which are obvious to a guardian or of which he has given a warning comprehensible by a guardian. To every general rule there are, of course, exceptions. A licensor cannot divest himself of the obligation of finding out something about the sort of people who are availing themselves of his permission and the sort of use they are making, of it. He may have to take into account the social habits of the neighbourhood. No doubt there are places where little children go to play unaccompanied. If the licensor knows or ought to anticipate that, he may have to take steps accordingly. But the responsibility for the safety of little children must rest primarily upon the parents; it is their duty to see that such children are not allowed to wander about by themselves, or at the least to satisfy themselves that the places to which they do allow their children to go unaccompanied are safe for them to go to. It would not be socially desirable if parents were, as a matter of course, able to shift the burden of looking after their children from their own shoulders to those of persons who happen to have accessible bits of land. Different considerations may well apply to public parks or to recognized playing grounds where parents allow their children to go unaccompanied in the reasonable belief that they are safe. . . ."

NOTE

This case was decided before the 1957 Act and thus the issue to be determined was whether the child was a 'licensee'. However it remains relevant because a 'licensee' is a 'visitor' and thus the occupier of the land, had this case occurred after 1957, would owe a s.2 common duty of care to the child. The occupier was not liable because he had 'discharged his duty', that is to say he had not been negligent. Where Devlin J. is confusing is that he justifies this discharge on the basis of a parental 'duty'. This is fair enough in one sense, but care must be taken to keep the existence of a duty and its breach quite separate.

QUESTION

Given that Devlin J.'s decision remains of relevance in relation to the 1957 Act, are different types of duty being reintroduced under the guise of breach?

6.1.4 **Independent contractor**

The 1957 Act specifically states in s.2(3)(b) that an occupier is entitled to expect that a person who enters in the exercise of a calling will appreciate any risks with respect to this calling. This section was considered in the next case.

Roles v Nathan **[1963] 1 W.L.R. 1117, CA**

Lord Denning M.R.: "This case arises out of a tragic accident which took place on Friday, December 12, 1958, when two chimney sweeps were overcome by fumes, and died in the basement of the Manchester Assembly Rooms. Their widows bring the action against the occupier, Mr Nathan, claiming that he was at fault and in breach of the duty of care which is now laid down by the Occupiers' Liability Act, 1957. . . .

The occupier now appeals and says that it is not a case of negligence and contributory negligence, but that, on the true application of the Occupiers' Liability Act, 1957, the occupier was not liable at all. . . .

. . .[T]he Act goes on to give examples of the circumstances that are relevant. The particular one in question here is in subsection (3) of section 2. . .

. . .The risk of a defective window is a special risk, but it is ordinarily incident to the calling of a window cleaner, and so he must take care for himself, and not expect the householder to do so. Likewise in the case of a chimney sweep who comes to sweep the chimneys or to seal up a sweep-hole. The householder can reasonably expect the sweep to take care of himself so far as any dangers from the flues are concerned. These chimney sweeps ought to have known that there might be dangerous fumes about and ought to have taken steps to guard against them. They ought to have known that they should not attempt to seal up a sweep-hole whilst the fire was still alight. They ought to have had the fire withdrawn before they attempted to seal it up, or at any rate they ought not to have stayed in the alcove too long when there might be dangerous fumes about. All this was known to these two sweeps; they were repeatedly warned about it, and it was for them to guard against the danger. It was not for the occupier to do it, even though he was present and heard the warnings. When a householder calls in a specialist to deal with a defective installation on his premises, he can reasonably expect the specialist to appreciate and guard against the dangers arising from the defect. The householder is not bound to watch over him to see that he comes to no harm. I would hold, therefore, that the occupier here was under no duty of care to these sweeps, at any rate in regard to the dangers which caused their deaths. If it had been a different danger, as for instance if the stairs leading to the cellar gave way, the occupier might no doubt be responsible, but not for these dangers which were special risks ordinarily incidental to their calling.

Even if I am wrong about this point, and the occupier was under a duty of care to these chimney sweeps, the question arises whether the duty was discharged by the warning that was given to them. . . .

. . .I am quite clear that the warnings which were given to the sweeps were enough to enable them to be reasonably safe. The sweeps would have been quite safe if they had heeded these warnings. They should not have come back that evening and attempted to seal up the sweep-hole while the fire was still alight. They ought to have waited till next morning, and then they should have seen that the fire was out before they attempted to seal up the sweep-hole. In any case they should not have stayed too long in the sweep-hole. In short, it was entirely their own fault. The judge held that it was contributory negligence. I would go further and say that under the Act the occupier has, by the warnings, discharged his duty.

I would therefore be in favour of allowing this appeal and entering judgment for the defendants."

[Harman L.J. agreed that the appeal should be allowed; Pearson L.J. dissented.]

QUESTIONS

1. Could this case be explained in terms of causation? (cf. **Chapter 10**.)

2. What if an independent contractor, while working on the occupier's land, injures another visitor on the same property? If the independent contractor turns out to have no insurance, might the occupier be liable under the 1957 Act?

***Gwilliam v West Hertfordshire Hospital NHS Trust* [2003] Q.B. 443, CA**

(For facts and other extracts see p.144)

> **Waller L.J.:** ". . . **40.** If one goes back to the wording of section 2(4)(b) of the 1957 Act it will be seen that there are two obligations on the employer of an independent contractor, one is 'to act reasonably in entrusting the work to an independent contractor' and the other is to take steps to satisfy himself about the competence etc. If a hospital reasonably wishes to have a somewhat hazardous activity on its land in order to raise money, but wishes to entrust the operation of that activity to an independent contractor, has the hospital acted 'reasonably' in the selection of that independent contractor if it has not checked the viability and/or insurance position so far as that independent contractor is concerned? In my view, the language of that section of the 1957 Act allows for consideration of the viability of the independent contractor. It might be said that the section only related to work of 'construction, maintenance or repair' but I would suggest that the concepts identified by the section also reflect the position at common law and that, thus, if someone like the hospital seeks to use an independent contractor for carrying out the sort of activities that are the subject of this case, it may be held not to act reasonably if it does not check the viability of that independent contractor. . . .
>
> **43.** I would emphasise that I am not saying that, in relation to every independent contractor employed, there is a duty to check the insurance or viability. It is the nature of the activities which, if not extra-hazardous, were hazardous, in which people were being invited by the hospital to take part, which to my mind distinguishes this case from other cases involving independent contractors. . . ."

6.1.5 **Occupier's duty to trespassers**

The 1957 Act established a common duty of care between occupier and visitor; it said nothing about the person who entered land as a trespasser. Logically, therefore, one could conclude that, up until 1984, no duty was owed to the trespasser. But, as the extract below indicates, the legal situation was not quite so simple. In 1984 the position was amended by statute and this Act immediately follows the judicial extract below.

***Tomlinson v Congleton BC* [2004] 1 A.C. 46, HL**

(For facts see below p.223)

> **Lord Hoffmann:** ". . . **6** The 1957 Act was passed to amend and codify the common law duties of occupiers to certain persons who came upon their land. The common law had distinguished between invitees, in whose visit the occupier had some material interest, and licensees, who came simply by express or implied permission. Different duties were owed to each class. The Act, on the recommendation of the Law Reform Committee (Third Report: Occupiers' Liability to Invitees, Licensees and Trespassers (1954) (Cmd 9305)), amalgamated (without redefining) the two common law categories, designated the combined class 'visitors' (section 1(2)) and provided that (subject to contrary agreement) all visitors should be owed a 'common duty of care'. . . .

8 . . . At common law the only duty to trespassers was not to cause them deliberate or reckless injury, but after an inconclusive attempt by the House of Lords to modify this rule in *Herrington v British Railways Board* [1972] AC 877, the Law Commission recommended the creation of a statutory duty to trespassers: see its Report on Liability for Damage or Injury to Trespassers and Related Questions of Occupiers' Liability (1976) (Law Com No 75) (Cmnd 6428). The recommendation was given effect by the 1984 Act. . . ."

Occupiers' Liability Act 1984 (c.3)

1. Duty of occupier to persons other than his visitors.

(1) The rules enacted by this section shall have effect, in place of the rules of the common law, to determine—

    (a) whether any duty is owed by a person as occupier of premises to persons other than his visitors in respect of any risk of their suffering injury on the premises by reason of any danger due to the state of the premises or to things done or omitted to be done on them; and

    (b) if so, what that duty is.

(2) For the purposes of this section, the persons who are to be treated respectively as an occupier of any premises (which, for those purposes, include any fixed or movable structure) and as his visitors are—

    (a) any person who owes in relation to the premises the duty referred to in section 2 of the Occupiers' Liability Act 1957 (the common duty of care), and

    (b) those who are his visitors for the purposes of that duty.

(3) An occupier of premises owes a duty to another (not being his visitor) in respect of any such risk as is referred to in subsection (1) above if—

    (a) he is aware of the danger or has reasonable grounds to believe that it exists;

    (b) he knows or has reasonable grounds to believe that the other is in the vicinity of the danger concerned or that he may come into the vicinity of the danger (in either case, whether the other has lawful authority for being in that vicinity or not); and

    (c) the risk is one against which, in all the circumstances of the case, he may reasonably be expected to offer the other some protection.

(4) Where, by virtue of this section, an occupier of premises owes a duty to another in respect of such a risk, the duty is to take such care as is reasonable in all the circumstances of the case to see that he does not suffer injury on the premises by reason of the danger concerned.

(5) Any duty owed by virtue of this section in respect of a risk may, in an appropriate case, be discharged by taking such steps as are reasonable in all the circumstances of the case to give warning of the danger concerned or to discourage persons from incurring the risk.

(6) No duty is owed by virtue of this section to any person in respect of risks willingly accepted as his by that person (the question whether a risk was so accepted to be decided on the same principles as in other cases in which one person owes a duty of care to another).

(6A) At any time when the right conferred by section 2(1) of the Countryside and Rights of Way Act 2000 is exercisable in relation to land which is access land for the purposes of Part I of that Act, an occupier of the land owes (. . .) no duty by virtue of this section to any person in respect of—

    (a) a risk resulting from the existence of any natural feature of the landscape, or any river, stream, ditch or pond whether or not a natural feature, or

    (b) a risk of that person suffering injury when passing over, under or through any wall, fence or gate, except by proper use of the gate or of a stile. . . .

(7) No duty is owed by virtue of this section to persons using the highway, and this section does not affect any duty owed to such persons.

(8) Where a person owes a duty by virtue of this section, he does not, by reason of any breach of the duty, incur any liability in respect of any loss of or damage to property.

(9) In this section—

'highway' means any part of a highway other than a ferry or waterway;
'injury' means anything resulting in death or personal injury, including any disease and any impairment of physical or mental condition; and
'movable structure' includes any vessel, vehicle or aircraft.

NOTE

The relationship between the Act of 1957 and that of 1984 is dealt with in the following extracts.

Tomlinson v Congleton BC **[2004] 1 A.C. 46, HL**

(For facts see below p.223)

Lord Hoffmann: ". . . **38** . . . Parliament has made it clear that in the case of a lawful visitor, one starts from the assumption that there is a duty whereas in the case of a trespasser one starts from the assumption that there is none."

Lord Hobhouse: ". . . **68** The two Acts apply the same general policy and the 1984 Act is a supplement to the 1957 Act. . . . The 1984 Act made provision for when a duty of care should be owed to persons who were not visitors (I will for the sake of convenience call such persons 'trespassers') and what the duty should then be, that is, a duty of care in the terms of section 1(3), more narrow than that imposed by the 1957 Act. Thus the duty owed to visitors and the lesser duty which may be owed to trespassers was defined in appropriate terms. But, in each Act, there are further provisions which define the content of the duty and, depending upon the particular circumstances, its scope and extent. . . ."

NOTE

Many of the cases that have arisen since 1984 have involved trespassers entering property and diving into pools, lakes or sea with tragic results (for one of the latest see *Evans v Kosmar Villa Holidays Ltd* (2008)). Two cases that came before the Court of Appeal seemed to go in different directions, but the matter now appears to have been settled on appeal from one of these cases to the House of Lords.

Tomlinson v Congleton BC **[2004] 1 A.C. 46, HL**

This was an action for damages by a teenager who had entered land owned by the local authority and dived into a lake on the property suffering severe injury when his head struck the bottom. The defendant local authority was aware that people were attracted by the lake and prominent notices declared that swimming was prohibited. The defendants were equally aware that these notices were often ignored and they intended, when finances permitted, to plant vegetation around the lake that would physically prevent people from entering the water. However at the time of the accident the vegetation plan had not been executed. A majority of the Court of Appeal gave judgment for the teenager, but this was reversed by the House of Lords (Lords Nicholls, Hoffmann, Hobhouse and Scott; Lord Hutton dubitante).

Lord Hoffmann: ". . . **4** It is a terrible tragedy to suffer such dreadful injury in consequence of a relatively minor act of carelessness. It came nowhere near the stupidity of Luke Ratcliff, a student who climbed a fence at 2.30 a m on a December morning to take a running dive into the shallow end of a swimming pool (see *Ratcliff v McConnell* [1999] 1 WLR 670) or John Donoghue, who dived into Folkestone Harbour from a slipway at midnight on 27 December after an evening in the pub: *Donoghue v Folkestone Properties Ltd* [2003] QB 1008. John Tomlinson's mind must often recur to that hot day which irretrievably changed his life. He may feel, not unreasonably, that fate has dealt with him unfairly. And so in these proceedings he seeks financial compensation: for the loss of his earning capacity, for the expense of the care he will need, for the loss of the ability to lead an ordinary life. But the law does not provide such compensation simply on the basis that the injury was dispropor- tionately severe in relation to one's own fault or even not one's own fault at all. Perhaps it should, but society might not be able to afford to compensate everyone on that principle, certainly at the level at which such compensation is now paid. The law provides compensa- tion only when the injury was someone else's fault. In order to succeed in his claim, that is what Mr Tomlinson has to prove. . . .

The scope of the duty under the 1984 Act

25 The conditions in section 1(3) of the 1984 Act determine whether or not a duty is owed to 'another' in respect of 'any such risk as is referred to in subsection (1)'. Two conclusions follow from this language. First, the risks in respect of which the Act imposes a duty are limited to those mentioned in subsection (1)(a)—risks of injury 'by reason of any danger due to the state of the premises or to things done or omitted to be done on them'. The Act is not concerned with risks due to anything else. Secondly, the conditions have to be satisfied in respect of the claimant as 'another'; that is to say, in respect of a class of persons which includes him and a description of risk which includes that which caused his injury. . . .

28 Mr Braithwaite was inclined to accept the difficulty of establishing that the risk was due to the state of the premises. . . . Ward LJ said that the water was 'a siren call strong enough to turn stout men's minds'. In my opinion this is gross hyperbole. The trouble with the island of the Sirens was not the state of the premises. It was that the Sirens held mariners spellbound until they died of hunger. The beach, give or take a fringe of human bones, was an ordinary Mediterranean beach. If Odysseus had gone ashore and accidentally drowned himself having a swim, Penelope would have had no action against the Sirens for luring him there with their songs. Likewise in this case, the water was perfectly safe for all normal activities. In my opinion 'things done or omitted to be done' means activities or the lack of precautions which cause risk, like allowing speedboats among the swimmers. It is a mere circularity to say that a failure to stop people getting into the water was an omission which gave rise to a duty to take steps to stop people from getting into the water.

29 It follows that in my opinion, there was no risk to Mr Tomlinson due to the state of the premises or anything done or omitted upon the premises. That means that there was no risk of a kind which gave rise to a duty under the 1957 or 1984 Acts. I shall nevertheless go on to consider the matter on the assumption that there was. . . .

Free will

44 The second consideration, namely the question of whether people should accept responsibility for the risks they choose to run, is the point made by Lord Phillips of Worth Matravers MR in *Donoghue v Folkestone Properties Ltd* [2003] QB 1008, 1024, para 53 and which I said was central to this appeal. Mr Tomlinson was freely and voluntarily undertaking an activity which inherently involved some risk. By contrast, Miss Bessie Stone (*Bolton v Stone* [1951] AC 850), to whom the House of Lords held that no duty was owed, was innocently standing on the pavement outside her garden gate at 10 Beckenham Road, Cheetham when she was struck by a ball hit for six out of the Cheetham Cricket Club ground. She was certainly not engaging in any activity which involved an inherent risk of such injury. So compared with *Bolton v Stone*, this is an a fortiori case.

45 I think it will be extremely rare for an occupier of land to be under a duty to prevent people from taking risks which are inherent in the activities they freely choose to undertake upon the land. If people want to climb mountains, go hang-gliding or swim or dive in ponds or lakes, that is their affair. Of course the landowner may for his own reasons wish to prohibit such activities. He may be think that they are a danger or inconvenience to himself or others. Or he may take a paternalist view and prefer people not to undertake risky activities on his land. He is entitled to impose such conditions, as the Council did by prohibiting swimming. But the law does not require him to do so.

46 My Lords, as will be clear from what I have just said, I think that there is an important question of freedom at stake. It is unjust that the harmless recreation of responsible parents and children with buckets and spades on the beaches should be prohibited in order to comply with what is thought to be a legal duty to safeguard irresponsible visitors against dangers which are perfectly obvious. The fact that such people take no notice of warnings cannot create a duty to take other steps to protect them. I find it difficult to express with appropriate moderation my disagreement with the proposition of Sedley LJ [2003] 2 WLR 1120, 1135, para 45, that it is "only where the risk is so obvious that the occupier can safely assume that nobody will take it that there will be no liability". A duty to protect against obvious risks or self-inflicted harm exists only in cases in which there is no genuine and informed choice, as in the case of employees, or some lack of capacity, such as the inability of children to recognise danger (*Herrington v British Railways Board* [1972] AC 877) or the despair of prisoners which may lead them to inflict injury on themselves: *Reeves v Comr of Police of the Metropolis* [2000] 1 AC 360. . . ."

Lord Scott: ". . . **91** In the present case it seems to me unreal to regard Mr Tomlinson's injury as having been caused while he was a trespasser. His complaint, rejected by the trial judge but accepted by the majority in the Court of Appeal, was that the council ought to have taken effective steps to discourage entry by visitors into the waters of the lake. The notices were held to be inadequate discouragement. But, if there was this duty, it was a duty owed to visitors. The people who read the notices, or who could have read them but failed to do so, would have been visitors. These were the people to be discouraged. The alleged duty was a 1957 Act duty. . . .

94 . . . [The claimant] was a high-spirited young man enjoying himself with his friends in a pleasant park with a pleasant water facility. If he had set out to swim across the lake, it might have been relevant to speak of his taking an obvious risk. If he had climbed a tree with branches overhanging the lake and had dived from a branch into the water he would have been courting an obvious danger. But he was not doing any such thing. He was simply sporting about in the water with his friends, giving free rein to his exuberance. And why not? And why should the council be discouraged by the law of tort from providing facilities for young men and young women to enjoy themselves in this way? Of course there is some risk of accidents arising out of the joie-de-vivre of the young. But that is no reason for imposing a grey and dull safety regime on everyone. This appeal must be allowed."

QUESTIONS

1. Did the House of Lords hold in *Bolton v Stone* (see p.140) that the cricket club owed no duty of care to Miss Stone?
2. Which of the following reasons best explains the decision in *Congleton*: (i) the claimant was the cause of his own misfortune; (ii) the local authority was not in breach of its duty; (iii) a holding for the claimant would result, ultimately, in fewer recreational facilities for the rest of the population; (iv) the local authority owed no duty to the claimant in respect of the damage that actually occurred?
3. Can the Congleton BC now abandon its plan to plant vegetation around the lake?
4. What if the claimant had been a boy of 11 years of age?

Keown v Coventry Healthcare NHS Trust **[2006] 1 W.L.R. 953, CA**

This was an action for damages for personal injury brought by a boy, who was eleven at the time of the accident, against a hospital. The boy had climbed on to an external fire escape on a hospital building and had fallen about thirty feet suffering serious injury. The trial judge had found the hospital liable, subject to contributory negligence on behalf of the claimant. However an appeal against liability was allowed by the Court of Appeal (Mummery L.J., Longmore L.J. and Lewison J.).

Longmore L.J.: ". . . 3 The parties accepted that Mr Keown must be treated as a trespasser while climbing the fire escape. This was apparently on the basis that children playing in the grounds were not lawful visitors but it could also have been because this case must be the closest one will come to in real life to the example of a trespasser given by Scrutton LJ in *The Carlgarth* [1927] P 93, 110: 'When you invite a person into your house to use the staircase, you do not invite him to slide down the banisters, you invite him to use the staircase in the ordinary way in which it is used.'. . .

6. The relevant law governing the liability of occupiers to trespassers is contained in the Occupiers' Liability Act 1984. The recorder's findings were of course prompted by the relevant provisions of the Act which are section 1(1)(3)(4):. . .

11 These authorities would conclude the question in Mr Porter's favour if the claimant was an adult. Does it make any difference that the claimant was a child when the accident occurred?

12 The answer is that premises which are not dangerous from the point of view of an adult can be dangerous for a child but it must be a question of fact and degree. In para 46 of the *Tomlinson* case Lord Hoffmann said that a duty to protect against obvious risks exists only in cases where there was no genuine and informed choice as in the case of some lack of capacity such as the inability of children to recognise danger. Thus injury suffered by a toddler crawling into an empty and derelict house could be injury suffered by reason of a danger due to the state of the premises where injury suffered by an adult in the same circumstances might not be. But it would not be right to ignore a child's choice to indulge in a dangerous activity in every case merely because he was a child. Mr Keown was 11 at the time he decided to climb the fire escape; the judge's finding was, at paras 15 and 42, that he appreciated not only that there was a risk of falling but also that what he was doing was dangerous and that he should not have been climbing the exterior of the fire escape. In these circumstances it cannot be said that Mr Keown did not recognise the danger and it does not seem to me to be seriously arguable that the risk arose out of the state of the premises which were as one would expect them to be. Rather it arose out of what Mr Keown chose to do. . . .

16 Whether the claimant could bring himself within section 1(3)(c) is more doubtful. Was the risk of suffering an injury from falling from the unguarded or unfenced fire escape a risk against which the trust 'may reasonably be expected to offer [the claimant] some protection'?

17 My tentative (obiter) view is that it would not be reasonable to expect a National Health Service trust to offer protection from such a risk. If it had to offer protection from the risk of falling from a normal fire escape, it would presumably have to offer the same protection from falling from drain pipes, balconies, roofs (on one view of Morison J's decision in the *Young* case [2005] EWHC 1342 (QB)), windows and even trees in the grounds. This seems to me to be going too far. I say this for two reasons. First, the resources of a National Health Service trust are much more sensibly utilised in the treatment and care of patients together with the proper remuneration of nurses and doctors rather than catering for the contingency (one hopes infrequent) that children will climb where they know they should not go. Secondly, if the courts say that such protection should be afforded, it will not just be a matter of putting a fence round a fire-escape or hiring an extra security guard. It is more likely that what will happen will be what in due course the judge found, at para 25, happened in this case. The trust has now built a perimeter fence round the entire site; there is only one entrance; anyone coming in is asked their business; children are turned away. It is right to say that this has occurred not just because of Mr Keown's accident but also because of break-ins which happened subsequently. It is not unfair to say, however, that the hospital ground is becoming a bit like a fortress. The amenity which local people had of passing through the grounds to the neighbouring streets and which children had of harmlessly playing in the grounds has now been lost. It is not reasonable to expect that this should happen to avoid the occasional injury, however sad it is when such injury occurs. Windows and trees have already attracted the attention of the courts in the context of the Occupiers' Liability Act 1957, see *Lewis v Six Continents* The Times, 20 January 2006 and *Tomlinson v Congleton Borough Council* [2004] 1 AC 46, para 90 per Lord Scott of Foscote. The duty under the 1984 Act cannot be higher. . . ."

QUESTION

1. If the NHS Trust did not have to pay the damages itself, that is to say if it were covered by liability insurance, would the court have been more ready to impose liability?

2. Could it be said that the responsibility for this 11-year-old rested primarily on the parents? (cf. *Phipps v Rochester Corporation*, p.217.)

3. Could the NHS Trust have made the extra security guard redundant after reading the judgments in this case?

6.2 Liability for land and structures (2): off the land

The distinction between duties owed by an occupier and (or) owner to persons on the land and off the land is alluded to in s.1(7) of the Occupiers' Liability Act 1984. As one might expect, the main reason for such a difference of duty is to be found in different causes of action. The duty owed by an occupier to his visitor is, of course, one that arises out of the tort of negligence ('common duty of care'). However, liability for the state of the premises to persons on the highway predates the establishment of a general tort of negligence and sounded in the tort of public nuisance. This tort is often regarded as one of strict liability. Where the victim is on neighbouring private land, rather than the highway, the tort of private nuisance is relevant provided that there is some degree of continuity with respect to the nuisance. A single escape from land of a dangerous thing could give rise to a claim under the rule in *Rylands v Fletcher* (p.243). Again these last two torts are often regarded as strict liability, although negligence is gradually invading their territory. Statute has also created some extra duties.

6.2.1 Liability to persons on the highway (public nuisance)

Liability in public nuisance to persons off the premises can arise, as the next three extracts show, either from activities being carried out on the land or from the state of the premises or other man-made (?) structures on the land.

Wandsworth LBC v Railtrack Plc [2002] Q.B. 756, CA

Chadwick L.J.: "29 I agree that this appeal should be dismissed.

30 Wandsworth London Borough Council is the highway authority in respect of that part of Balham High Road which adjoins Balham station. The street is crossed by a railway bridge which is now vested in Railtrack plc as part of its undertaking. The construction of the railway bridge is such that it provides a convenient roost to the numerous feral pigeons attracted to the area by the ready availability of food in the vicinity. The obvious consequences of pigeon infestation ensue, to the annoyance and inconvenience of pedestrians using the highway beneath the bridge. The judge found, 'as a matter of fact and degree' that the pigeon infestation and the fouling caused by it amounted to a nuisance; that is to say that there was a substantial interference with the comfort and convenience of the public or a significant class of the public who use the footpaths or pavements. There is no challenge to that finding. Nor could there be; the evidence was overwhelming.

31 It is the duty of the council, as local highway authority, to assert and protect the rights of the public to the use and enjoyment of Balham High Road, including the pavements provided for pedestrian use: see section 130(1) of the Highways Act 1980. In furtherance of that duty the council has brought these proceedings against Railtrack plc as the owners of the bridge. The issue on this appeal is whether the judge was right to find, as he did, that Railtrack were liable for the public nuisance arising from the pigeon infestation.

32 The liability of a landowner for a public nuisance on or emanating from his land was recognised by this court over one hundred years ago in *Attorney General v Tod Heatley* [1897] 1 Ch 560. . . . Liability in public nuisance arises where the landowner has knowledge of the existence of a nuisance on or emanating from his land, where there are means reasonably open to him for preventing or abating it, and where he fails to take those means within a reasonable time. . . .

33 The three elements of knowledge, means to abate and failure to take those means are all present in the present case. In my view, the judge was plainly correct to find that liability in public nuisance had been established. I agree, also, that he was entitled to make an order for the payment of damages in addition to the declaration which he granted."

[Kennedy L.J. delivered a judgment dismissing the appeal and Rougier L.J. agreed with the judgments.]

QUESTION

An old tree on D's land collapses onto the highway and destroys C's parked car. Assuming the collapse was caused by a latent disease in the roots, will D be liable to C? (cf. *Caminer v Northern and London Investment Trust* (1951).)

NOTES

1. See also *Att-Gen v PYA Quarries* (p.81).

2. *Wandsworth* dealt with a nuisance to those on the highway. The next case concerns a dangerous state of affairs that injures a neighbouring property.

Wringe v Cohen [1940] 1 K.B. 229, CA

This was an action for damages by the owner of a shop against the landlord of a neighbouring property for damage caused to the shop when the gable end of the defendant's house collapsed during a storm. The Court of Appeal (Slesser LJ, Luxmoore LJ and Atkinson J) dismissed an appeal from a County Court judgment holding the defendant liable.

Atkinson J.: ". . . In our judgment if, owing to want of repair, premises on a highway become dangerous and, therefore, a nuisance, and a passer-by or an adjoining owner suffers damage by their collapse, the occupier, or the owner if he has undertaken the duty of repair, is answerable whether he knew or ought to have known of the danger or not. The undertaking to repair gives the owner control of the premises, and a right of access thereto for the purpose of maintaining them in a safe condition. On the other hand, if the nuisance is created, not by want of repair, but, for example, by the act of a trespasser, or by a secret and unobservable operation of nature, such as a subsidence under or near the foundations of the premises, neither an occupier nor an owner responsible for repair is answerable, unless with knowledge or means of knowledge he allows the danger to continue. In such a case he has in no sense caused the nuisance by any act or breach of duty. I think that every case decided in the English Courts is consistent with this view.

By common law it is an indictable offence for an occupier of premises on a highway to permit them to get into a dangerous condition owing to non-repair. It was not and is not necessary in an indictment to aver knowledge or means of knowledge . . ."

QUESTIONS

1. Was the defendant held liable in public or private nuisance?

2. What is the level of duty owed by an occupier to a passer-by? Does the next case give a clear answer?

Mint v Good [1951] 1 K.B. 517, CA

This was an action for damages by a boy against the owner of premises for injury sustained by the boy on a public highway when a wall on the premises collapsed onto him. The trial judge dismissed the action against the owner on the ground that the owner, who had let the premises to tenants, had not reserved the right of entry to make repairs. An appeal to the Court of Appeal (Somervell L.J., Denning L.J. and Birkett, L.J.) was allowed.

Denning L.J.: ". . . The law of England has always taken particular care to protect those who use a highway. It puts on the occupier of adjoining premises a special responsibility for the structures which he keeps beside the highway. So long as those structures are safe, all well and good; but if they fall into disrepair, so as to be a potential danger to passers-by, then they are a nuisance, and, what is more, a public nuisance; and the occupier is liable to anyone using the highway who is injured by reason of the disrepair. It is no answer for him to say that he and his servants took reasonable care; for, even if he has employed a competent independent contractor to repair the structure, and has every reason for supposing it to be safe, the occupier is still liable if the independent contractor did the work badly: see *Tarry v Ashton*.

The occupier's duty to passers-by is to see that the structure is as safe as reasonable care can make it; a duty which is as high as the duty which an occupier owes to people who pay to come on to his premises. He is not liable for latent defects, which could not be discovered by reasonable care on the part of anyone, nor for acts of trespassers of which he neither knew, nor ought to have known: see *Barker v Herbert*; but he is liable when structures fall into dangerous disrepair, because there must be some fault on the part of someone or other for that to happen; and he is responsible for it to persons using the highway, even though he was not actually at fault himself. That principle was laid down in this court in *Wring v Cohen*, where it is to be noted that the principle is confined to 'premises on a highway' . . .

The question in this case is whether the owner, as well as the occupier, is under a like duty to passers-by? I think he is. The law has shown a remarkable development on this point during the last sixteen years. The three cases of *Wilchick v Marks and Silverstone*, *Wringe v Cohen* and *Heap v Ind Coope and Allsopp Ltd* show that the courts are now taking a realistic view of these matters. They recognise that the occupying tenant of a small dwelling-house does not in practice do the structural repairs, but the owner does; and that if a passer-by is injured by the structure being in dangerous disrepair, the occupier has not the means to pay damages, but the owner has, or, at any rate, he can insure against it. If a passer-by is injured by the structure falling on him, he should be entitled to damages from someone, and the person who ought to pay is the owner, because he is in practice responsible for the repairs . . .

That is sufficient for the decision of this case, but I venture to doubt in these days whether a landlord can exempt himself from liability to passers-by by taking a covenant from a tenant to repay the structure adjoining the highway . . . The liability of the owner is ta liability in tort and cannot be affected by the terms of the agreement between himself and his tenant. Just as a manufacturer who is liable under the principle in *Donoghue v Stevenson* cannot exempt himself from liability to the public by the terms of his contract with the wholesaler, so also I should doubt whether a property owner could exempt himself by the terms of his contract with the tenant . . .″

QUESTION

Is Denning L.J. holding the landlord liable in negligence or public nuisance? Does it matter? (cf. Denning L.J.'s judgment in *Esso v Southport Corpn*, p.5.)

NOTE

A landlord's duty in respect of demised premises is now subject to a statutory duty.

Defective Premises Act 1972 (c.35)

"**3. Duty of care with respect to work done on premises not abated by disposal of premises**.

(1) Where work of construction, repair, maintenance or demolition or any other work is done on or in relation to premises, any duty of care owed, because of the doing of the work, to persons who might reasonably be expected to be affected by defects in the state of the premises created by the doing of the work shall not be abated by the subsequent disposal of the premises by the person who owed the duty. . . .

4. Landlord's duty of care in virtue of obligation or right to repair premises demised.

(1) Where premises are let under a tenancy which puts on the landlord an obligation to the tenant for the maintenance or repair of the premises the landlord owes to all persons who might reasonably be expected to be affected by defects in the state of the premises a duty to take such care as is reasonable in all the circumstances to see that they are reasonably safe from personal injury or from damage to their property caused by a relevant defect.

(2) The said duty is owed if the landlord knows (whether as the result of being notified by the tenant or otherwise) or if he ought in all the circumstances to have known of the relevant defect. . . .″

QUESTION

Is this statutory duty of care in section 4 a lower duty than the one in (i) *Wringe v Cohen* and (ii) *Mint v Good*?

6.2.2 Liability to neighbours (private nuisance)

Where an activity on land, or the state of the property, causes injury to a neighbouring occupier or landowner a different cause of action comes into play. It is a matter of private rather than public nuisance. The distinction between public nuisance, private nuisance and negligence is explained in the first short extract. And this is followed by decisions setting out the main elements of private nuisance.

Wandsworth LBC v Railtrack Plc **[2002] Q.B. 756, CA**

(For facts and decision see p.227)

> **Kennedy L.J.:** "... **6** Public nuisance is also a crime, and a person is said to be guilty if he does an act not warranted by law or omits to discharge a legal duty if the effect of the act is to endanger the life, health, property, morals or comfort of the public, or to obstruct the public in the exercise or enjoyment of rights common to all: see *Archbold, Criminal Pleading, Evidence and Practice*, 2001 ed, para 31–40. Private nuisance is different. It is the wrongful interference with another's use or enjoyment of land, or of some right over or in connection therewith, and negligence arises where the relationship between the parties is such as to give rise to a duty of care. ...."

NOTE

The overlap of public and private nuisance is to be found in the next case as well. However, before turning to this case, it may be useful to examine, once again, the basic elements of public and private nuisance in Denning L.J.'s judgment in *Esso v Southport* (p.5). More detailed principles with respect to private nuisance are contained in the case extracted below.

Halsey v Esso Petroleum Co Ltd **[1961] 1 W.L.R. 683, QBD**

This was an action for damages and an injunction against an oil company in respect of a nuisance associated with one of the company's oil distribution depots in London. The claimant complained of acid smuts from the depot's chimneys which caused damage to his washing in his garden and car parked on the highway; of a pungent and nauseating smell; of noise from the boilers; and of noise at night from road tankers coming and going from the depot. The judge held there was a public nuisance in respect of the damage to the car and of the noise at night; and a private nuisance with regard to the washing and the boiler noise. The acid smuts also gave rise to a liability under *Rylands v Fletcher* (see p.243).

> **Veale J.:** "... So far as the present case is concerned, liability for nuisance by harmful deposits could be established by proving damage by the deposits to the property in question, provided of course that the injury was not merely trivial. Negligence is not an ingredient of

the cause of action, and the character of the neighbourhood is not a matter to be taken into consideration. On the other hand, nuisance by smell or noise is something to which no absolute standard can be applied. It is always a question of degree whether the interference with comfort or convenience is sufficiently serious to constitute a nuisance. The character of the neighbourhood is very relevant and all the relevant circumstances have to be taken into account. What might be a nuisance in one area is by no means necessarily so in another. In an urban area, everyone must put up with a certain amount of discomfort and annoyance from the activities of neighbours, and the law must strike a fair and reasonable balance between the right of the plaintiff on the one hand to the undisturbed enjoyment of his property, and the right of the defendant on the other hand to use his property for his own lawful enjoyment. That is how I approach this case. . . .

It is said by the defendants that since the public highway is for the use of everyone, the plaintiff cannot complain if all the defendants do is to make use of their right to use the public highway. I agree, if that is all that the defendants have done. If a person makes an unreasonable use of the public highway, for instance, by parking stationary vehicles on it, a member of the public who suffers special damage has a cause of action against him for public nuisance. Similarly, in my view, if a person makes an unreasonable use of the public highway by concentrating in one small area of the highway vehicles in motion and a member of the public suffers special damage, he is equally entitled to complain, although in most cases concentration of moving as opposed to stationary vehicles will be more likely to be reasonable. This is a question of reasonable user. . .”

NOTES

1. This case brings out two important points. First, the difference between public (damage to car on the highway) and private (damage to washing) nuisance, but there may be an overlap where the nuisance can be associated with both private land (depot) and public highway (road tankers). Secondly, the role of the character of the locality: this is only relevant in respect of intangible damage (noise and smell).

2. Private nuisance is a tort arising out of the use of land. It is, in other words, a liability that attaches to real property. This real property dimension affects claimants as well, as the next case confirms.

Hunter v Canary Wharf Ltd **[1997] A.C. 655, HL**

This case concerned two damages actions for nuisance, brought by two groups of plaintiffs, in respect of a large building known as Canary Wharf. The first group complained of interference with their television reception caused by the building, while the second group complained of excessive amounts of dust caused by construction work associated with the building. The House of Lords (Lords Goff, Hoffmann, Lloyd and Hope; Lord Cooke dissented in part) dismissed the actions.

Lord Goff: “. . . In both actions, Judge Fox-Andrews QC made orders for the trial of a number of preliminary issues of law. Of the issues of law in the first action, two have survived to reach your Lordships’ House, viz. (1) whether interference with television reception is capable of constituting an actionable nuisance, and (2) whether it is necessary to have an interest in property to claim in private nuisance and, if so, what interest in property will satisfy this requirement. In the second action, the only issue to reach your Lordships' House is the latter of these two issues. . . .

Interference with television signals

I turn first to consider the question whether interference with television signals may give rise to an action in private nuisance. This question was first considered over 30 years ago by Buckley J in *Bridlington Relay Ltd. v Yorkshire Electricity Board* [1965] Ch 436. . . . Certainly it can be asserted with force that for many people television transcends the function of mere entertainment, and in particular that for the aged, the lonely and the bedridden it must provide a great distraction and relief from the circumscribed nature of their lives. That interference with such an amenity might in appropriate circumstances be protected by the law of nuisance has been recognised in Canada, in *Nor-Video Services Ltd. v Ontario Hydro* (1978) 84 DLR (3d) 221, 231.

However, as I see the present case, there is a more formidable obstacle to this claim. This is that the complaint rests simply upon the presence of the defendants' building on land in the neighbourhood as causing the relevant interference. . . .

As a general rule, a man is entitled to build on his own land, though nowadays this right is inevitably subject to our system of planning controls. Moreover, as a general rule, a man's right to build on his land is not restricted by the fact that the presence of the building may of itself interfere with his neighbour's enjoyment of his land. The building may spoil his neighbour's view (. . .); in the absence of an easement, it may restrict the flow of air on to his neighbour's land (. . .); and, again in the absence of an easement, it may take away light from his neighbour's windows (. . .): nevertheless his neighbour generally cannot complain of the presence of the building, though this may seriously detract from the enjoyment of his land. . . . From this it follows that, in the absence of an easement, more is required than the mere presence of a neighbouring building to give rise to an actionable private nuisance. Indeed, for an action in private nuisance to lie in respect of interference with the plaintiff's enjoyment of his land, it will generally arise from something emanating from the defendant's land. Such an emanation may take many forms—noise, dirt, fumes, a noxious smell, vibrations, and suchlike. Occasionally activities on the defendant's land are in themselves so offensive to neighbours as to constitute an actionable nuisance, as in *Thompson-Schwab v Costaki* [1956] 1 WLR 335, where the sight of prostitutes and their clients entering and leaving neighbouring premises were held to fall into that category. Such cases must however be relatively rare. . . .

For these reasons I would dismiss the appeal of the plaintiffs in the first action on this issue.

Right to sue in private nuisance

I turn next to the question of the right to sue in private nuisance. In the two cases now under appeal before your Lordships' House, one of which relates to interference with television signals and the other to the generation of dust from the construction of a road, the plaintiffs consist in each case of a substantial group of local people. Moreover they are not restricted to householders who have the exclusive right to possess the places where they live, whether as freeholders or tenants, or even as licensees. They include people with whom householders share their homes, for example as wives or husbands or partners, or as children or other relatives. All of these people are claiming damages in private nuisance, by reason of interference with their television viewing or by reason of excessive dust. . . .

It follows that, on the authorities as they stand, an action in private nuisance will only lie at the suit of a person who has a right to the land affected. Ordinarily, such a person can only sue if he has the right to exclusive possession of the land, such as a freeholder or tenant in possession, or even a licensee with exclusive possession. . . . But a mere licensee on the land has no right to sue.

The question therefore arises whether your Lordships should be persuaded to depart from established principle, and recognise such a right in others who are no more than mere licensees on the land. At the heart of this question lies a more fundamental question, which relates to the scope of the law of private nuisance. Here I wish to draw attention to the fact that although, in the past, damages for personal injury have been recovered at least in actions of public nuisance, there is now developing a school of thought that the appropriate remedy for such claims as these should lie in our now fully developed law of negligence, and that personal injury claims should be altogether excluded from the domain of nuisance. The most forthright proponent of this approach has been Professor Newark, in his article 'The Boundaries of Nuisance,' 65 LQR 480 from which I have already quoted. Furthermore, it is now being suggested that claims in respect of physical damage to the land should also be excluded from private nuisance: see, eg, the article by Mr Conor Gearty on 'The Place of Private Nuisance in a Modern Law of Torts' [1989] CLJ 214. In any event, it is right for present purposes to regard the typical cases of private nuisance as being those concerned with interference with the enjoyment of land and, as such, generally actionable only by a person with a right in the land. Characteristic examples of cases of this kind are those concerned with noise, vibrations, noxious smells and the like. The two appeals with which your Lordships are here concerned arise from actions of this character.

For private nuisances of this kind, the primary remedy is in most cases an injunction, which is sought to bring the nuisance to an end, and in most cases should swiftly achieve that objective. The right to bring such proceedings is, as the law stands, ordinarily vested in the person who has exclusive possession of the land. He or she is the person who will sue, if it is necessary to do so. Moreover he or she can, if thought appropriate, reach an agreement with the person creating the nuisance, either that it may continue for a certain period of time, possibly on the payment of a sum of money, or that it shall cease, again perhaps on certain terms including the time within which the cessation will take place. The. . . . efficacy of arrangements such as these depends upon the existence of an identifiable person with whom the creator of the nuisance can deal for this purpose. If anybody who lived in the relevant property as a home had the right to sue, sensible arrangements such as these might in some cases no longer be practicable. . . ."

Lord Hoffmann: ". . . Nuisance is a tort against land, including interests in land such as easements and profits. A plaintiff must therefore have an interest in the land affected by the nuisance. . . .

Once it is understood that nuisances 'productive of sensible personal discomfort' (*St Helen's Smelting Co v Tipping*, 11 HL Cas 642, 650) do not constitute a separate tort of causing discomfort to people but are merely part of a single tort of causing injury to land, the rule that the plaintiff must have an interest in the land falls into place as logical and, indeed, inevitable. . . ."

Lord Cooke (dissenting in part): ". . . Inhabitants of the Isle of Dogs and many another concentrated urban area might react with incredulity, and justifiably so, to the suggestion that the amenity of television and radio reception is fairly comparable to a view of the surroundings of their homes. Neither in nature nor in value is that so. It may be suspected that only a lawyer would think of such a suggestion. . . ."

NOTE

The television aspect of this case is obviously an important point. But *Hunter* is a key case because it re-emphasises the difference between the torts of negligence and private nuisance. The latter attaches to land and both the claimant and the defendant must have legal connections (interest) in real property; nuisance is, in this respect, a true liability for things (land), although it extends to activities (unreasonable) on such property. Negligence in contrast attaches to a careless act of an individual. Fault, of course, may be relevant in assessing whether an activity on land amounts to an unreasonable use. Thus deliberately to annoy a neighbour will give rise to liability in private nuisance: *Hollywood Silver Fox Farm v Emmett* (see p.93).

6.2.3 Nuisance by omission (nuisance and negligence)

Liability in nuisance is not restricted to unreasonable activities on land. It can arise out of the state of the land itself or something on it. Even if the defendant did not cause the nuisance, he may become liable if he adopts it or fails to remedy a continuing nuisance.

Delaware Mansions Ltd v Westminster CC [2002] 1 A.C. 321, HL

This was an action for damages by the owner of a building adjoining the highway against a highway authority for the latter's failure to remove a tree whose roots were causing damage to the claimant's land and buildings. The House of Lords (Lords Steyn, Browne-Wilkinson, Cooke, Clyde and Hutton) held the authority liable for continuing a nuisance.

Lord Cooke: "3 My Lords, this case raises an issue, on which there is surprisingly little authority in English law, about the recoverability of remedial expenditure incurred after encroachment by tree roots. . . .

29 . . . I think that the answer to the issue falls to be found by applying the concepts of reasonableness between neighbours (real or figurative) and reasonable foreseeability which underlie much modern tort law and, more particularly, the law of nuisance. . . .

31 In both the second *Wagon Mound* case and *Goldman v Hargrave* the judgments, which repay full rereading, are directed to what a reasonable person in the shoes of the defendant would have done. The label nuisance or negligence is treated as of no real significance. In this field, I think, the concern of the common law lies in working out the fair and just content and incidents of a neighbour's duty rather than affixing a label and inferring the extent of the duty from it.

33 Approaching the present case in the light of those governing concepts and the judge's findings, I think that there was a continuing nuisance. . . . Having regard to the proximity of the plane tree to Delaware Mansions, a real risk of damage. . . ."

NOTE AND QUESTIONS

In *Holbeck Hall Hotel Ltd v Scarborough BC* (2000) Stuart-Smith L.J. said the "duty arises when the defect is known and the hazard or danger to the claimants' land is reasonably foreseeable, that is to say it is a danger which a reasonable man with knowledge of the defect should have foreseen as likely to eventuate in the reasonably near future. It is the existence of the defect coupled with the danger that constitutes the nuisance; it is knowledge or presumed knowledge of the nuisance that involves liability for continuing it when it could reasonably be abated" (§ 42). Does this test suggest that the key to liability for nuisance by omission (unreasonable use of land) is actually similar to the test for liability in negligence (unreasonable behaviour)? Perhaps the key is in the nature of the damage as the next extract suggests.

Cambridge Water Co v Eastern Counties Leather Plc [1994] 2 A.C. 264, HL

(For facts see p.244)

Lord Goff: ". . . Of course, although liability for nuisance has generally been regarded as strict, at least in the case of a defendant who has been responsible for the creation of a nuisance, even so that liability has been kept under control by the principle of reasonable user—the principle of give and take as between neighbouring occupiers of land, under which 'those acts necessary for the common and ordinary use and occupation of land and houses may be done, if conveniently done, without subjecting those who do them to an action': see *Bamford v Turnley* (1862) 3 B & S 62, 83, per Bramwell B. The effect is that, if the user is reasonable, the defendant will not be liable for consequent harm to his neighbour's enjoyment of his land; but if the user is not reasonable, the defendant will be liable, even though he may have exercised reasonable care and skill to avoid it. Strikingly, a comparable principle has developed which limits liability under the rule in *Rylands v Fletcher*. This is the principle of natural use of the land. . . .

It is, of course, axiomatic that in this field we must be on our guard, when considering liability for damages in nuisance, not to draw inapposite conclusions from cases concerned only with a claim for an injunction. This is because, where an injunction is claimed, its purpose is to restrain further action by the defendant which may interfere with the plaintiff's enjoyment of his land, and *ex hypothesi* the defendant must be aware, if and when an injunction is granted, that such interference may be caused by the act which he is restrained from committing. It follows that these cases provide no guidance on the question whether foreseeability of harm of the relevant type is a prerequisite of the recovery of damages for causing such harm to the plaintiff. . . . Here, as I have said, it is still the law that the fact that the defendant has taken all reasonable care will not of itself exonerate him from liability, the relevant control mechanism being found within the principle of reasonable user. But it by no means follows that the defendant should be held liable for damage of a type which he could not reasonably foresee; and the development of the law of negligence in the past 60 years points strongly towards a requirement that such foreseeability should be a prerequisite of liability in damages for nuisance, as it is of liability in negligence. For if a plaintiff is in ordinary circumstances only able to claim damages in respect of personal injuries where he can prove such foreseeability on the part of the defendant, it is difficult to see why, in common justice, he should be in a stronger position to claim damages for interference with the enjoyment of his land where the defendant was unable to foresee such damage. . . ."

NOTE

In *Morris v Network Rail* (2004) Buxton L.J. said that "it is difficult to see any further life in some particular rules of the law of nuisance, such as for instance the concept of 'abnormal sensitiveness' drawn from *Robinson v Kilvert* (1889). . . . It is very difficult not to think that such particular rules are now subsumed under the general view of the law of nuisance expressed in *Delaware Mansions*: not dissimilarly to the way in which the generalisation of the law of negligence initiated by *Donoghue v Stevenson* has rendered obsolete the previous categories of dangerous chattels; duties of occupiers of land; duties attaching to specific trades; and the like" (§ 35).

PROBLEM

Paula, the owner of a sound studio, suffers severe financial harm resulting from loss of trade caused by electronic interference, emanating from the signalling system used by the nearby railway, with the sound recording process. When the signalling system was introduced the railway company was unaware that it would cause such problems. Can Paula sue the railway company in nuisance for (i) damages for the financial loss and/or (ii) an injunction to stop the interference? (cf. *Morris v Nework Rail* (2004).)

6.3 Public and private interests

One particular problem associated with nuisance, hinted at by Lord Hoffmann in *Hunter*, is the clash of interests that can arise when it comes to socially useful activities that nevertheless cause harm or annoyance to neighbours. Should the public interest be allowed to override the private interest? This problem was at the heart of *Miller v Jackson* (see p.15) and *Dennis v MOD* (p.205) and it also brings into play an economic analysis of tort (see **2.3.2**).

6.3.1 Private nuisance and public benefit

Two nuisance points should be noted with respect to *Miller v Jackson*. The first is that undue sensitivity used be a defence to a nuisance claim and thus if a defendant's activity caused damage to the plaintiff's stock of paper only because the plaintiff had particularly sensitive paper on his land there was no liability (*Robinson v Kilvert* (1889)). One can understand why the cricket loving judges ('manly sport') were keen to brand the wife as ultra-sensitive. However, as we have seen above, it has recently been asserted that this sensitivity defence is no longer relevant now that foreseeability has become a central test in nuisance (*Delaware*, above p.235). An unduly sensitive activity interfered with by the defendant land user will probable be 'unforeseeable' (see Buxton L.J. in *Morris v Network Rail* above.

Secondly, coming to the nuisance is no defence (*Sturges v Bridgman* (1879)). This precedent seems to have been treated in rather a cavalier way Lord Denning M.R. in *Miller*, although the dissenting judge thought he was bound by it. In *Dennis* the principle that the judge applied is more profound than it might first seem. The costs of a public benefit should not be allowed to fall on a few individual shoulders but should be borne by the community as a whole (through the payment of damages by the state). What if such a principle were to be applied more widely? (cf. *Dunne v NW Gas Board*, p.337.)

6.3.2 Cost of activities

The idea that a defendant should pay for his activity is not new as the next extract indicates.

Bamford v Turnley (1862) 122 E.R. 27, Ex CH

This was an action for damages by a householder against a neighbour whose brickworks caused unpleasant smoke and smells. The jury gave a verdict for the defendant and this was upheld by the Court of Queen's Bench. A further appeal by the claimant to Exchequer Chamber was allowed (Pollock C.B. dissenting).

Bramwell B.: ". . . I am of opinion that this judgement should be reversed. The defendant has done that which, if done wantonly or maliciously, would be actionable as being a nuisance to the plaintiff's habitation by causing a sensible diminution of the comfortable enjoyment of it. This, therefore, calls on the defendant to justify or excuse what he has done. And his justification is this: He says that the nuisance is not to the health of the inhabitants of the plaintiffs house, that it is of a temporary character, and is necessary for the beneficial use of his, the defendant's land, and that the public good requires he should be entitled to do what he claims to do. . . .

But it is said that, temporary or permanent, it is lawful because it is for the public benefit. Now, in the first place, that law to my mind is a bad one which, for the public benefit, inflicts loss on an individual without compensation. . . .It is for the public benefit there should be railways, but it would not be unless the gain of having the railway was sufficient to compensate the loss occasioned by the use of the land required for its site; and accordingly no one thinks it would be right to take an individual's land without compensation to make a railway. It is for the public benefit that trains should run, but not unless they pay their expenses. . . ."

NOTE

See also Lord Hoffmann in *Wildtree Hotels v Harrow LBC* (2001) (p.68).

6.3.3 Statutory authority

One way of allowing the public interest to override the private interest is for Parliament to provide a statutory defence to any claims in trespass and (or) nuisance (see e.g. Civil Aviation Act 1982 (p.204)). But what if Parliament provides a statutory planning regime: will the grant of planning permission act in itself as a defence to a nuisance claim?

Wheeler v JJ Saunders Ltd [1996] Ch. 19, CA

This was an action for an injunction and for damages by a veterinary surgeon and his wife against a farm in respect of a number of acts and activities including the smell from pigs said to constitute a nuisance. The judge having awarded damages and an injunction, the defendants appealed arguing that since they had obtained planning permission for the pig farm they should not have been held liable in nuisance. The Court of Appeal (Staughton L.J., Peter Gibson L.J. and Sir John May L.J.) upheld the judge's decision on the nuisance aspect of the case.

Staughton L.J.: ". . . I do not consider that planning permission necessarily has the same effect as statutory authority. Parliament is sovereign and can abolish or limit the civil rights of individuals. . . . The planning authority. . . has only the powers delegated to it by Parliament. It is not in my view self-evident that they include the power to abolish or limit civil rights in any or all circumstances. The process by which planning permission is obtained allows for objections by those who might be adversely affected, but they have no right of appeal if their objections are overruled. It is not for us to say whether the private bill procedure in Parliament is better or worse. It is enough that it is different. . . .

It would in my opinion be a misuse of language to describe what has happened in the present case as a change in the character of a neighbourhood. It is a change and abuse of a very small piece of land, a little over 350 square metres according to the dimensions on the plan, for the benefit of the applicant and to the detriment of the objectors in the quiet enjoyment of their house. It is not a strategic planning decision affected by considerations of public interest. Unless one is prepared to accept that any planning decision authorises any nuisance which must inevitably come from it, the argument that the nuisance was authorised by planning permission in this case must fail. I am not prepared to accept that premise. It may be—I express no concluded opinion—that some planning decisions will authorise some nuisances. But that is as far as I am prepared to go. There is no immunity from liability for nuisance in the present case. I would dismiss the second part of this appeal."

Peter Gibson L.J.: ". . . I am not prepared to accept that the principle applied in the *Gillingham* case must be taken to apply to every planning decision. The court should be slow to acquiesce in the extinction of private rights without compensation as a result of administrative decisions which cannot be appealed and are difficult to challenge. . . ."

Sir John May: ". . . Further, if a planning permission could authorise a nuisance, then so also could it in an appropriate case license a trespass. But in planning cases where, in addition to permission, a way-leave is for instance required for electric cables, or a highway has to be stopped up or opened, then the permission alone is never enough and the procedures to obtain a way-leave or to interfere with the highway have to be followed. . . ."

QUESTION

What if, in *Halsey v Esso* (above p.231), the oil company's depot had been specifically authorised by the grant of local authority planning permission: would the claimant have been debarred from suing for all his various heads of damage?

NOTE

Planning regimes are not the only form of possible statutory authority, as the next case indicates.

Marcic v Thames Water Utilities Ltd [2004] 2 A.C. 42, HL

This was an action for damages by a householder against a water company in respect of damage caused to the claimant's premises by flooding. This flooding resulted from inadequate sewers. The Court of Appeal held that the householder had a claim in private nuisance and under the Human Rights Act 1998. However an appeal to the House of Lords (Lords Nicholls, Steyn, Hoffmann, Hope and Scott) was allowed.

Lord Nicholls: "**1** My Lords, this appeal concerns flooding of a particularly unpleasant kind: from foul water sewers as well as surface water sewers. Sewer flooding is a nationwide environmental problem, arising largely from the building of ever more houses to meet the housing demand. Sewers and drains, sufficient when laid in the 19th century or later, are no longer adequate to cope with the volume of surface water entering the public drainage system in times of heavy rainfall. Overloaded surface water sewers spill into the foul water sewers. As a result, all too often water and untreated sewage overflow at the lower levels of the drainage system, causing misery for the people living there. . . .

34 In my view the cause of action in nuisance asserted by Mr Marcic is inconsistent with the statutory scheme. Mr Marcic's claim is expressed in various ways but in practical terms it always comes down to this: Thames Water ought to build more sewers. This is the only way Thames Water can prevent sewer flooding of Mr Marcic's property. . . .

35 The difficulty I have with this line of argument is that it ignores the statutory limitations on the enforcement of sewerage undertakers' drainage obligations. . . .

42 In the present case the interests Parliament had to balance included, on the one hand, the interests of customers of a company whose properties are prone to sewer flooding and, on the other hand, all the other customers of the company whose properties are drained through the company's sewers. The interests of the first group conflict with the interests of the company's customers as a whole in that only a minority of customers suffer sewer flooding but the company's customers as a whole meet the cost of building more sewers. As already noted, the balance struck by the statutory scheme is to impose a general drainage obligation on a sewerage undertaker but to entrust enforcement of this obligation to an independent regulator who has regard to all the different interests involved. Decisions of the director are of course subject to an appropriately penetrating degree of judicial review by the courts. . . ."

Lord Hoffmann: ". . . **61** Why should sewers be different? If the *Sedleigh-Denfield* case [1940] AC 880 lays down a general principle that an owner of land has a duty to take reasonable steps to prevent a nuisance arising from a known source of hazard, even though he did not himself create it, why should that not require him to construct new sewers if the court thinks it would have been reasonable to do so?

62 The difference in my opinion is that the *Sedleigh-Denfield*, *Goldman* and *Leakey* cases were dealing with disputes between neighbouring land owners simply in their capacity as individual land owners. In such cases it is fair and efficient to impose reciprocal duties upon each landowner to take whatever steps are reasonable to prevent his land becoming a source of injury to his neighbour. Even then, the question of what measures should reasonably have been taken may not be uncomplicated. As Lord Wilberforce said in *Goldman's* case [1967] 1 AC 645, 663, the court must (unusually) have regard to the individual circumstances of the defendant. In *Leakey's* case [1980] QB 485, 526 Megaw LJ recoiled from the prospect of a detailed examination of the defendant's financial resources and said it should be done on a broad basis.

63 Nevertheless, whatever the difficulties, the court in such cases is performing its usual function of deciding what is reasonable as between the two parties to the action. But the exercise becomes very different when one is dealing with the capital expenditure of a statutory undertaking providing public utilities on a large scale. The matter is no longer confined to the parties to the action. If one customer is given a certain level of services, everyone in the same circumstances should receive the same level of services. So the effect of a decision about what it would be reasonable to expect a sewerage undertaker to do for the plaintiff is extrapolated across the country. This in turn raises questions of public interest. Capital expenditure on new sewers has to be financed; interest must be paid on borrowings and privatised undertakers must earn a reasonable return. This expenditure can be met only be charges paid by consumers. Is it in the public interest that they should have to pay more? And does expenditure on the particular improvements with which the plaintiff is concerned represent the best order of priorities?

64 These are decisions which courts are not equipped to make in ordinary litigation. It is therefore not surprising that for more than a century the question of whether more or better sewers should be constructed has been entrusted by Parliament to administrators rather than judges. . . ."

QUESTIONS

1. The Law Lords seem to be treating the water company as a public utility balancing the public interest against the private. But, being a private company, would not their profit interest be a major consideration? What if they thought that the building of extra sewers would not go down well with the shareholders?

2. On being privatised, a water company makes its team of rat killers redundant. Several years later an area served by the water company suffers a plague of rats emerging from the sewers. Can householders who have suffered from the rats sue the water company for damages? Might the householders have an action based on a breach of a human right?

6.3.4 **Nuisance and human rights**

The Human Rights Act 1998 has introduced a whole new dimension into nuisance cases, that is to say into cases where home life is invaded by an activity of a neighbour. For the European Convention of Human Rights and Fundamental Freedoms guarantees in art.8 "the right to respect for his private and family life, his home and his correspondence". This article is considered in the following nuisance case.

Marcic v Thames Water Utilities Ltd **[2004] 2 A.C. 42, HL**

(For facts see p.239)

Lord Nicholls: ". . . **37** I turn to Mr Marcic's claim under the Human Rights Act 1998. His claim is that as a public authority within the meaning of section 6 of the Human Rights Act 1998 Thames Water has acted unlawfully. Thames Water has conducted itself in a way which is incompatible with Mr Marcic's Convention rights under article 8 of the Convention and article 1 of the First Protocol to the Convention. His submission was to the following effect. The flooding of Mr Marcic's property falls within the first paragraph of article 8 and also within article 1 of the First Protocol. That was common ground between the parties. Direct and serious interference of this nature with a person's home is prima facie a violation of a person's right to respect for his private and family life (article 8) and of his entitlement to the peaceful enjoyment of his possessions (article 1 of the First Protocol). The burden of justifying this interference rests on Thames Water. At the trial of the preliminary issues Thames Water failed to discharge this burden. The trial judge found that the system of priorities used by Thames Water in deciding whether to carry out flood alleviation works might be entirely fair. The judge also said that on the limited evidence before him it was not possible to decide this issue, or to decide whether for all its apparent faults the system fell within the wide margin of discretion open to Thames Water and the director: [2002] QB 929, 964, para 102.

38 To my mind the fatal weakness in this submission is the same as that afflicting Mr Marcic's claim in nuisance: it does not take sufficient account of the statutory scheme under which Thames Water is operating the offending sewers. The need to adopt some system of priorities for building more sewers is self-evident. So is the need for the system to be fair. A fair system of priorities necessarily involves balancing many intangible factors. Whether the system adopted by a sewerage undertaker is fair is a matter inherently more suited for decision by the industry regulator than by a court. And the statutory scheme so provides. Moreover, the statutory scheme provides a remedy where a system of priorities is not fair. An unfair system of priorities means that a sewerage undertaker is not properly discharging its statutory drainage obligation so far as those who are being treated unfairly are concerned. The statute provides what should happen in these circumstances. The director is charged with deciding whether to make an enforcement order in respect of a sewerage undertaker's failure to drain property properly. Parliament entrusted this decision to the director, not the courts."

Lord Hoffmann: ". . . **71** That leaves only the question of whether the remedies provided under the 1991 Act do not adequately safeguard Mr Marcic's Convention rights to the privacy of his home and the protection of his property. The judge, who found for Mr Marcic on this ground, did not have the benefit of the decision of the Grand Chamber of the European Court of Human Rights in *Hatton v United Kingdom* (Application No 36022/97) The Times, 10 July 2003. That decision makes it clear that the Convention does not accord absolute protection to property or even to residential premises. It requires a fair balance to be struck between the interests of persons whose homes and property are affected and the interests of other people, such as customers and the general public. National institutions, and particularly the national legislature, are accorded a broad discretion in choosing the solution appropriate to their own society or creating the machinery for doing so. There is no reason why Parliament should not entrust such decisions to an independent regulator such as the director. He is a public authority within the meaning of the 1998 Act and has a duty to act in accordance with Convention rights. If (which there is no reason to suppose) he has exceeded the broad margin of discretion allowed by the Convention, Mr Marcic will have a remedy under section 6 of the 1998 Act. But that question is not before your Lordships. His case is that he has a Convention right to have the decision as to whether new sewers should be constructed made by a court in a private action for nuisance rather than by the director in the exercise of his powers under the 1991 Act. In my opinion there is no such right. . . ."

NOTE AND QUESTION

Two other important cases, already extracted, are *Dennis v MOD* (p.207) and *Hatton v UK* (p.207). What will be the effect, if any, of *Hatton* and (or) *Marcic* on *Dennis*?

6.4 Liability for dangerous things brought onto land

Nuisance normally involves some kind of continuing state of affairs arising out of an activity or the state of the property. A single isolated noise or smell will not in principle ground liability in nuisance however annoying. Sometimes, however, a single escape of a thing can cause serious damage to a neighbour and while there is some authority that such an incident might amount to a nuisance (see e.g. *British Celanese v AH Hunt Ltd* (1969)), the escape can give rise to an independent cause of action in tort.

6.4.1 **Dangerous things**

The precedent for this independent cause of action is set out next.

Rylands v Fletcher (1866) L.R. 1 Ex. 265, Ex Ch., (1868) L.R. 3 HL 330, HL

This was an action for damages by a landowner against his neighbour in respect of damage done by water escaping from a reservoir on the defendant's land. The escape occurred as a result of negligent work carried out by the contractors who constructed the reservoir. The Court of Exchequer Chamber gave judgment for the plaintiff and an appeal to the House of Lords (Lords Cairns and Cranworth) was dismissed.

> **Blackburn J.** (Court of Exchequer Chamber): ". . . We think that the true rule of law is, that the person who for his own purposes brings on his lands and collects and keeps there anything likely to do mischief if it escapes, must keep it in at his peril, and, if he does not do so, is *prima facie* answerable for all the damage which is the natural consequence of its escape. He can excuse himself by showing that the escape was owing to the plaintiff's default; or perhaps that the escape was the consequences of *vis major*, or the act of God; but as nothing of this sort exists here, it is unnecessary to inquire what excuse would be sufficient. . . ."

> **Lord Cairns L.C.** (House of Lords): ". . . [I]f, in what I may term the natural user of that land, there had been any accumulation of water, either on the surface or underground, and if, by the operation of the laws of nature, that accumulation of water had passed off into the close occupied by the plaintiff, the plaintiff could not have complained that the result had taken place. . . .

> On the other hand if the defendants, not stopping at the natural use of their close, had desired to use it for any purpose which I may term a non-natural use,. . . then it appears to me that that which the defendants were doing they were doing at their own peril; and, if in the course of their doing it, the evil arose to which I have referred, the evil, namely, of the escape of the water and its passing away to the close of the plaintiff and injuring the plaintiff, then for the consequence of that, in my opinion, the defendants would be liable . . ."

QUESTIONS

1. Is the rule set out in the House of Lords identical to the rule set out by Blackburn J.?

2. Why were there seemingly only two Law Lords in this House of Lords decision? (cf. *Heuston* (1970) 86 L.Q.R. 160.)

NOTE

This great case has become less important than it deserves thanks to the failure of English judges to develop its potential. Just as *Donoghue v Stevenson* (p.131) became the basis for negligence liability, so *Rylands* could have become the fundamental starting point for a strict liability for things. Blackburn J.'s rule was, admittedly, not as abstract as CC art.1384, yet it could have acted as the foundation for a liability for dangerous things analogous to the strict liability for dangerous animals. This opportunity was lost when the House of Lords rendered its judgments in *Read v Lyons* (p.209). Matters were not helped by Lord Cairns, whose rewording of Blackburn J.'s 'not naturally there' (see Blackburn J.'s judgment in the law report) with 'non-natural use' meant that later judges could restrict the precedent within narrow limits. Another opportunity was lost more recently, as the next case indicates.

Cambridge Water Co v Eastern Counties Leather Plc **[1994] 2 A.C. 264, HL**

This was an action for damages by a water utilities company against a tanning factory in respect of contamination caused by a solvent known as perchloroethene (PCE) used by the defendants in the process of degreasing pelts at its tanning works. The PCE had seeped into the ground beneath the defendants' works and was conveyed in percolating water in the direction of the claimant's borehole. The damages action was based on three causes of action: negligence, nuisance and the rule in *Rylands v Fletcher* (1868). The judge dismissed the claims but the Court of Appeal allowed an appeal. An appeal to the House of Lords (Lords Templeman, Goff, Jauncy, Lowry and Woolf) was allowed.

Lord Goff: ". . . It can be argued that the rule in *Rylands v Fletcher* should not be regarded simply as an extension of the law of nuisance, but should rather be treated as a developing principle of strict liability from which can be derived a general rule of strict liability for damage caused by ultra-hazardous operations on the basis of which persons conducting such operations may properly be held strictly liable for the extraordinary risk to others involved in such operations. As is pointed out in Fleming on *The Law of Torts*, pp 327–328, this would lead to the practical result that the cost of damage resulting from such operations would have to be absorbed as part of the overheads of the relevant business rather than be borne (where there is no negligence) by the injured person or his insurers, or even by the community at large. Such a development appears to have been taking place in the United States, as can be seen from paragraph 519 of the *Restatement of Torts* (2d) vol 3 (1977). The extent to which it has done so is not altogether clear; and I infer from paragraph 519, and the Comment on that paragraph, that the abnormally dangerous activities there referred to are such that their ability to cause harm would be obvious to any reasonable person who carried them on.

I have to say, however, that there are serious obstacles in the way of the development of the rule in *Rylands v Fletcher* in this way. First of all, if it was so to develop, it should logically apply to liability to all persons suffering injury by reason of the ultra-hazardous operations; but the decision of this House in *Read v J Lyons & Co Ltd* [1947] AC 156, which establishes that there can be no liability under the rule except in circumstances where the injury has been caused by an escape from land under the control of the defendant, has effectively precluded any such development. Professor Fleming has observed that 'the most damaging effect of the decision in *Read v J Lyons & Co Ltd* is that it prematurely stunted the development of a general theory of strict liability for ultra-hazardous activities' (see Fleming on *Torts*, p 341). Even so, there is much to be said for the view that the courts should not be proceeding down the path of developing such a general theory. In this connection, I refer in particular to the *Report of the Law Commission on Civil Liability for Dangerous Things and Activities* (1970) (Law Com No 32). In paragraphs 14–16 of the Report, the Law Commission expressed serious misgivings about the adoption of any test for the application of strict liability involving a general concept of 'especially dangerous' or 'ultra-hazardous' activity, having regard to the uncertainties and practical difficulties of its application. If the Law Commission is unwilling to consider statutory reform on this basis, it must follow that judges should if anything be even more reluctant to proceed down that path.

Like the judge in the present case, I incline to the opinion that, as a general rule, it is more appropriate for strict liability in respect of operations of high risk to be imposed by Parliament, than by the courts. If such liability is imposed by statute, the relevant activities can be identified, and those concerned can know where they stand. Furthermore, statute can where appropriate lay down precise criteria establishing the incidence and scope of such liability.

It is of particular relevance that the present case is concerned with environmental pollution. The protection and preservation of the environment is now perceived as being of crucial importance to the future of mankind; and public bodies, both national and international, are taking significant steps towards the establishment of legislation which will promote the protection of the environment, and make the polluter pay for damage to the environment for which he is responsible—as can be seen from the WHO, EEC and national regulations to which I have previously referred. But it does not follow from these developments that a common law principle, such as the rule in *Rylands v Fletcher*, should be developed or rendered more strict to provide for liability in respect of such pollution. On the contrary, given that so much well-informed and carefully structured legislation is now being put in place for this purpose, there is less need for the courts to develop a common law principle to achieve the same end, and indeed it may well be undesirable that they should do so.

Having regard to these considerations, and in particular to the step which this House has already taken in *Read v J Lyons & Co Ltd* [1947] AC 156 to contain the scope of liability under the rule in *Rylands v Fletcher*, it appears to me to be appropriate now to take the view that foreseeability of damage of the relevant type should be regarded as a prerequisite of liability in damages under the rule. . . .

The facts of the present case

Turning to the facts of the present case, it is plain that, at the time when the PCE was brought onto [the defendants'] land, and indeed when it was used in the tanning process there, nobody at [the defendants works] could reasonably have foreseen the resultant damage which occurred at CWC's borehole at Sawston . . .

In the result, since those responsible at [the defendant company] could not at the relevant time reasonably have foreseen that the damage in question might occur, the claim of [the claimant] for damages under the rule in *Rylands v Fletcher* must fail. . . .”

NOTE

The introduction of foreseeability does not, of course, mean that the rule in *Rylands v Fletcher* is no longer in the category of a liability for things since the foresight attaches as much to the thing as to the act of bringing it onto land. There must be an awareness of the risk and it is possible that foreseeability in this context is analogous to the state of scientific knowledge in s.4(1)(e) of the Consumer Protection Act 1987 (p.184). However, as *Cambridge* itself indicates, the requirement weakens the idea both that it is the polluter who should pay and that liability for a dangerous thing should be fully strict. The latest decision on *Rylands* has possibly weakened the cause of action even further. However this latest decision subjects the cause of action to a wide-ranging review.

Transco Plc v Stockport Metropolitan Borough Council **[2004] 2 A.C. 1, HL**

This was an action for damages by a gas-pipe owner against a local authority in respect of damage done to a gas pipe by the escape of water from premises owned by the local authority. The escape of water was caused by the failure of a water supply pipe on the local authority's land, but both the failure and the escape were not due to any negligence on the part of the defendants. The claimant based his action on the rule in *Rylands v Fletcher*, but the House of Lords (Lords Bingham, Hoffmann, Hobhouse, Scott and Walker) held that the local authority was not liable.

Lord Hoffmann: ". . . 29. It is tempting to see, beneath the surface of the rule [in *Rylands v Fletcher*], a policy of requiring the costs of a commercial enterprise to be internalised; to require the entrepreneur to provide, by insurance or otherwise, for the risks to others which his enterprise creates. That was certainly the opinion of Bramwell B, who was in favour of liability when the case was before the Court of Exchequer: (1865) 3 H & C 774. He had a clear and consistent view on the matter: see *Bamford v Turnley* (1862) 3 B & S 62, 84-85 and *Hammersmith and City Railway Co v Brand* (1867) LR 2 QB 223, 230-231. But others thought differently. They considered that the public interest in promoting economic development made it unreasonable to hold an entrepreneur liable when he had not been negligent: see *Wildtree Hotels Ltd v Harrow London Borough Council* [2001] 2 AC 1, 8–9 for a discussion of this debate in the context of compensation for disturbance caused by the construction and operation of works authorised by statutory powers. On the whole, it was the latter view—no liability without fault—which gained the ascendancy. With hindsight, *Rylands v Fletcher* can be seen as an isolated victory for the internalisers. The following century saw a steady refusal to treat it as laying down any broad principle of liability. . . .

Where stands the rule today?

39. I pause at this point to summarise the very limited circumstances to which the rule has been confined. First, it is a remedy for damage to land or interests in land. As there can be few properties in the country, commercial or domestic, which are not insured against damage by flood and the like, this means that disputes over the application of the rule will tend to be between property insurers and liability insurers. Secondly, it does not apply to works or enterprises authorised by statute. That means that it will usually have no application to really high risk activities. As Professor Simpson points out ([1984] 13 J Leg Stud 225) the Bradfield Reservoir was built under statutory powers. In the absence of negligence, the occupiers whose lands had been inundated would have had no remedy. Thirdly, it is not particularly strict because it excludes liability when the escape is for the most common reasons, namely vandalism or unusual natural events. Fourthly, the cases in which there is an escape which is not attributable to an unusual natural event or the act of a third party will, by the same token, usually give rise to an inference of negligence. Fifthly, there is a broad and ill-defined exception for 'natural' uses of land. It is perhaps not surprising that counsel could not find a reported case since the second world war in which anyone had succeeded in a claim under the rule. It is hard to escape the conclusion that the intellectual effort devoted to the rule by judges and writers over many years has brought forth a mouse.

Is it worth keeping?

40. In *Burnie Port Authority v General Jones Pty Ltd* (1994) 179 CLR 520 a majority of the High Court of Australia lost patience with the pretensions and uncertainties of the rule and decided that it had been "absorbed" into the law of negligence. Your Lordships have been invited by the respondents to kill off the rule in England in similar fashion. It is said, first, that in its present attenuated form it serves little practical purpose; secondly, that its application is unacceptably vague ('an essentially unprincipled and ad hoc subjective determination' said the High Court (at p 540) in the *Burnie* case) and thirdly, that strict liability on social grounds is better left to statutory intervention.

41. There is considerable force in each of these points. . . .

43. But despite the strength of these arguments, I do not think it would be consistent with the judicial function of your Lordships' House to abolish the rule. It has been part of English law for nearly 150 years and despite a searching examination by Lord Goff of Chieveley in the *Cambridge Water* case [1994] 2 AC 264, 308, there was no suggestion in his speech that it could or should be abolished. I think that would be too radical a step to take. . . .

49. In my opinion the Court of Appeal was right to say that it was not a 'non-natural' user of land. I am influenced by two matters. First, there is no evidence that it created a greater risk than is normally associated with domestic or commercial plumbing. True, the pipe was larger. But whether that involved greater risk depends upon its specification. One cannot simply assume that the larger the pipe, the greater the risk of fracture or the greater the quantity of water likely to be discharged. I agree with my noble and learned friend Lord Bingham of Cornhill that the criterion of exceptional risk must be taken seriously and creates a high threshold for a claimant to surmount. Secondly, I think that the risk of damage to property caused by leaking water is one against which most people can and do commonly insure. This is, as I have said, particularly true of Transco, which can be expected to have insured against any form of damage to its pipe. It would be a very strange result if Transco were entitled to recover against the council when it would not have been entitled to recover against the Water Authority for similar damage emanating from its high pressure main.

50. I would therefore dismiss the appeal."

Lord Hobhouse: ". . . **56**. This approach was entirely in keeping with the economic and political culture of the 19th Century, *laissez faire* and an understanding of the concept of risk. During the 20th Century and particularly during the second half, the culture has changed. Government has increasingly intervened to limit the freedom of a landowner to use his land as he chooses, *eg* through the planning laws, and has regulated or forbidden certain dangerous or antisocial uses of land such as the manufacture or storage of explosives or the emission of noxious effluents. Thus the present state of the law is that some of the situations where the rule in *Rylands v Fletcher* applies are now also addressed by the first type of solution. But this does not deprive the rule of its utility. The area of regulation is not exhaustive; it does not necessarily give the third party affected an adequate or, even, any say; the Government decision may give priority to some national or military need which it considers must over-ride legitimate individual interests; it will not normally deal with civil liability for damage to property; it does not provide the third party with adequate knowledge and control to evaluate and protect himself from the consequent risk and insurance cost. As Lord Goff pointed out in *Cambridge Water* (*inf*), the occasions where *Rylands v Fletcher* may have to be invoked by a claimant may be reducing but that is not to say that it has ceased to be a valid part of English law. The only way it could be rendered obsolete is by a compulsory strict public liability insurance scheme for all persons using their land for dangerous purposes. However this would simply be to re-enact *Rylands v Fletcher* in another guise.

57. *Rylands v Fletcher* was unremarkable in the mid 19th century since there was then nothing peculiar about strict liability. There were many other fields in which strict liability existed, for example conversion. For those following a 'common' calling, such as common carriers or common inn-keepers, liability was also strict. Although the origins were already present in the 19th century in the defence of 'inevitable accident' in trespass cases, it was only later that the generalised criterion of negligence was developed, culminating in *Donoghue v Stevenson* [1932] AC 562. That is a fault—*ie*, breach of a duty of care—not a risk concept. But, where the situation arises as between landowners and arises from the dangerous use of his land by one of them, the risk concept remains relevant. He who creates the relevant risk and has, to the exclusion of the other, the control of how he uses his land, should bear the risk. It would be unjust to deny the other a risk based remedy and introduce a requirement of proving fault. . . .”

(For further extracts see p.88)

QUESTION

Do you think that Blackburn J. thought that he was conceiving a mouse?

6.4.2 **Dangerous activities**

Rylands v Fletcher was a genuine liability for things in that liability attached to the escape of a thing rather than from a dangerous activity. However some US jurisdictions have used this English precedent to develop a rule of strict liability arising from ultra-hazardous activities. One might note European tort thinking as well.

European Group on Tort Law, *Principles of European Tort Law* (2003)

“**Art. 5:101. Abnormally dangerous activities**

(1) A person who carries on an abnormally dangerous activity is strictly liable for damage characteristic to the risk presented by the activity and resulting from it.

(2) An activity is abnormally dangerous if

    a) it creates a foreseeable and highly significant risk of damage even when all due care is exercised in its management and

b) it is not a matter of common usage.

(3) A risk of damage may be significant having regard to the seriousness or the likelihood of the damage.

(4) This Article does not apply to an activity which is specifically subjected to strict liability by any other provision of these Principles or any other national law or international convention."

NOTE

The decision in *Read v Lyons* (1947) (p.209) would suggest that this European code principle does not represent English law. Nevertheless a reversal of the burden of proof within negligence (*res ipsa loquitur*: see **4.2.7**) might go far in achieving a measure of strict liability in practice (and see *Henderson v Jenkins* (1970), p.195).

6.4.3 Liability for the escape of fire

One 'thing' around which a liability for things and a liability for dangerous activities can coalesce is fire. Liability for the spread of fire is complex, first because it can bring into play a range of heads of liability such as *Rylands v Fletcher*, negligence and nuisance. And, secondly, because there is a statutory defence "against any person in whose house, chamber, stable, barn or other building, or in whose estate any fire shall *accidentally* begin" (Fires Prevention (Metropolis) Act 1774 s.86 emphasis added). The word "accidentally" has been construed narrowly with the result that defendants have been held liable in the heads mentioned above. Moreover risk can also have its role as the next judicial extract indicates.

Smith v Littlewoods Organisation Ltd [1987] A.C. 241, HL (Scotland)

This was an action for damages by the owner of a café against a neighbouring owner of a derelict cinema in respect of damage done by a fire deliberately started in the empty cinema by vandals who had broken into the premises. The action failed in the House of Lords (Lords Keith, Brandon, Griffiths, Mackay and Goff).

Lord Goff: ". . . It is, in my opinion, consistent with the existence of such liability that an occupier who negligently causes or permits a source of danger to be created on his land, and can reasonably foresee that third parties may trespass on his land and, interfering with the source of danger, may spark it off, thereby causing damage to the person or property of those in the vicinity, should be held liable to such a person for damage so caused to him. It is useful to take the example of a fire hazard, not only because that is the relevant hazard which is alleged to have existed in the present case, but also because of the intrinsically dangerous nature of fire hazards as regards neighbouring property. Let me give an example of circumstances in which an occupier of land might be held liable for damage so caused. Suppose that a person is deputed to buy a substantial quantity of fireworks for a village fireworks display on Guy Fawkes night. He stores them, as usual, in an unlocked garden shed abutting onto a neighbouring house. It is well known that he does this. Mischievous boys from the village enter as trespassers and, playing with the fireworks, cause a serious fire which spreads to and burns down the neighbouring house. Liability might well be imposed in such a case; for, having regard to the dangerous and tempting nature of fireworks, interference by naughty children was the very thing which, in the circumstances, the purchaser of the fireworks ought to have guarded against.

But liability should only be imposed under this principle in cases where the defender has negligently caused or permitted the creation of a source of danger on his land, and where it is foreseeable that third parties may trespass on his land and spark it off, thereby damaging the pursuer or his property. Moreover, it is not to be forgotten that, in ordinary households in this country, there are nowadays many things which might be described as possible sources of fire if interfered with by third parties, ranging from matches and firelighters to electric irons and gas cookers and even oil-fired central heating systems. These are commonplaces of modern life; and it would be quite wrong if householders were to be held liable in negligence for acting in a socially acceptable manner. No doubt the question whether liability should be imposed on defenders in a case where a source of danger on his land has been sparked off by the deliberate wrongdoing of a third party is a question to be decided on the facts of each case, and it would, I think, be wrong for your Lordships' House to anticipate the manner in which the law may develop: but I cannot help thinking that cases where liability will be so imposed are likely to be very rare.

There is another basis upon which a defender may be held liable for damage to neighbouring property caused by a fire started on his (the defender's) property by the deliberate wrongdoing of a third party. This arises where he has knowledge or means of knowledge that a third party has created or is creating a risk of fire, or indeed has started a fire, on his premises, and then fails to take such steps as are reasonably open to him (in the limited sense explained by Lord Wilberforce in *Goldman v Hargrave* [1967] 1 AC 645, 663–664) to prevent any such fire from damaging neighbouring property. If, for example, an occupier of property has knowledge, or means of knowledge, that intruders are in the habit of trespassing upon his property and starting fires there, thereby creating a risk that fire may spread to and damage neighbouring property, a duty to take reasonable steps to prevent such damage may be held to fall upon him. He could, for example, take reasonable steps to keep the intruders out. He could also inform the police; or he could warn his neighbours and invite their assistance. If the defender is a person of substantial means, for example, a large public company, he might even be expected to employ some agency to keep a watch on the premises. What is reasonably required would, of course, depend on the particular facts of the case. I observe that, in *Goldman v Hargrave*, such liability was held to sound in nuisance; but it is difficult to believe that, in this respect, there can be any material distinction between liability in nuisance and liability in negligence . . ."

NOTE

In the firework example given by Lord Goff, liability under the rule in *Rylands v Fletcher* would probably be avoided thanks to the decision in *Perry v Kendricks Transport* (1956). This case is authority for the rule that an act of a third party facilitating the escape is a defence for the occupier of the land.

6.4.4 Liability for the escape of nuclear radiation

A range of pollution situations arising from the escape of noxious material is now governed by statute. With respect to nuclear radiation the relevant legislation is the Nuclear Installations Act

1965 whose provision about causing "injury to any person or damage to any property" (s.7(1)(a)) has given rise to difficulty. Where is the line to be drawn between damage (to property) and pure financial loss? See now *Blue Circle Industries v Ministry of Defence* (1999).

7 Liability for people

We have already seen how, in addition to fault liability given expression in CC art.1382, French law also has a field of strict liability based on the relationship between persons and things. Yet CC art.1384 is even wider: it states that one "is liable not only for the damage that one causes by one's own act, but also for that which is caused by the act of persons for whom one is responsible". In other words, there is, besides the liability for things, also a liability for persons. More generally in European law—and indeed in English law—the idea of a liability for people is based upon two separate ideas. These are given expression in the articles from the *Principles of European Tort Law* extracted in the first section below. In terms of structure, whereas a liability for things is based on a person-thing-person pattern, liability for persons is founded on three party situations. These are claimant-actor-defendant, and one obvious focal point is the relationship between actor (the person who actually causes the damage to the claimant) and the defendant. Yet again, however, this structure can become hidden in English law behind the forms of liability (nuisance, negligence, vicarious liability, etc.) and other conceptual focal points such as 'duty' and 'causation'.

7.1 Three party situations: general considerations

The starting point for understanding liability for people is to look at the various principles upon which such liability is based. These are, evidently, the normal principles of liability (cf. 1.7); yet one needs to go beyond these principles because institutional structures such as the legal person (corporation) and contract have an important role to play in understanding why liability is imposed in certain situations.

7.1.1 Foundational tort principles

The foundational principles set out below do not necessarily fully represent English law but they certainly come quite close to capturing its structure.

European Group on Tort Law, *Principles of European Tort Law* (2003)

"**Art. 4:103. Duty to protect others from damage**

A duty to act positively to protect others from damage may exist if law so provides, or if the actor creates or controls a dangerous situation, or when there is a special relationship between parties or when the seriousness of the harm on the one side and the ease of avoiding the damage on the other side point towards such a duty.

Art. 6:102. Liability for auxiliaries

(1) A person is liable for damage caused by his auxiliaries acting within the scope of their functions provided that they violated the required standard of conduct (Art. 4:102).

(2) An independent contractor is not regarded as an auxiliary for the purposes of this Article."

NOTE

Two quite different principles can give rise to a liability for a tortious act committed by another. The first is based on a direct duty of care and is illustrated by the next extract.

Home Office v Dorset Yacht Co Ltd [1970] A.C. 1004, HL

This was an action for damages by the owners of a yacht (in truth their insurance company subrogated to their rights) against the Home Office in respect of damage done to the yacht by escaping borstal boys. It was claimed that the three officers supervising the boys had been negligent and that the Home Office was to be vicariously liable for the officers' behaviour. The Home Office, on a preliminary question of law, claimed that the facts disclosed no duty of care. A majority of the House of Lords (Lords Reid, Morris, Pearson and Diplock; Viscount Dilhorne dissenting) disagreed with them.

Lord Reid: ". . . *Donoghue v Stevenson* may be regarded as a milestone, and the well-known passage in Lord Atkin's speech should I think be regarded as a statement of principle. It is not to be treated as if it were a statutory definition. It will require qualification in new circumstances. But I think that the time has come when we can and should say that it ought to apply unless there is some justification or valid explanation for its exclusion . . .

It is argued that it would be contrary to public policy to hold the Home Office or its officers liable to a member of the public for this carelessness—or, indeed, any failure of duty on their part. The basic question is: who shall bear the loss caused by that carelessness—the innocent [plaintiff] or the Home Office, who are vicariously liable for the conduct of their careless officers? . . . [His Lordship then discussed the American case of *Williams v State of New York* where the state was held not liable for the negligence of prison warders on the ground of public policy] . . . It may be that public servants of the State of New York are so apprehensive, easily dissuaded from doing their duty and intent on preserving public funds from costly claims that they could be influenced in this way. But my experience leads me to believe that Her Majesty's servants are made of sterner stuff. So I have no hesitation in rejecting this argument. I can see no good ground in public policy for giving this immunity to a government department . . ."

Lord Pearson: ". . . The borstal boys were under the control of the Home Office's officers, and control imports responsibility . . ."

Lord Diplock: "My Lords, this appeal is about the law of negligence. Regrettably, as I think, it comes before your Lordships' House upon a preliminary question of law which is said to arise upon the facts pleaded in the statement of claim. This makes it necessary to identify the precise question of law raised by those facts which are very summarily pleaded. Some of them relate to the acts of seven youths undergoing sentences of Borstal training; others relate to the acts and omissions of persons concerned in the management of Borstals and, in particular, to the acts and omissions of three officers of the Portland Borstal.

It is alleged and conceded that the defendant, the Home Office, is vicariously responsible for the tortuous acts of the three Borstal officers and any other persons concerned in the management of Borstals. It is not contended that the Home Office is vicariously liable for any tortuous acts of the youths undergoing sentences of Borstal training. . . ."

Viscount Dilhorne (dissenting): ". . . I think that it is clear that the *Donoghue v Stevenson* principle cannot be regarded as an infallible test of the existence of a duty of care, nor do I think that, if that test is satisfied, there arises any presumption of the existence of such a duty . . .

I, of course, recognise that the common law develops by the application of well established principles to new circumstances but I cannot accept that the application of Lord Atkin's words, which, though they applied in *Deyong v Shenburn*, and might have applied in *Commissioner for Railways v Quinlan*, were not held to impose a new duty on a master to his servant or on an occupier to a trespasser, suffices to impose a new duty on the Home Office and on others in charge of persons in lawful custody of the kind suggested . . .

The absence of authority shows that no such duty now exists. If there should be one, that is, in my view, a matter for the legislature and not for the courts . . ."

QUESTION

Ought an insurance company (the real claimant in *Dorset*) be able to recoup its money from the public purse? Who was paid to take the risk of damage to, or theft of, property?

NOTES

1. The two ideas set out in the extract from the *Principles of European Tort Law* (PETL) can both be found in the facts of this case. The first idea, given expression in PETL art.6.102, is called vicarious liability in English law. An employer will be automatically liable for a tort committed by its employee acting in the course of his employment (see **7.2**). Thus if one of the prison officers was in breach of a duty of care towards the claimant, then the Home Office would be liable under the principle of vicarious liability (see Lord Diplock).

2. There is, however, a second idea that *could* arise out of these facts. This is whether the Home Office, as a legal person, owed a direct duty of care to the claimant. If so, and the Home Office itself was in breach of this duty, then the Home Office would be *directly* liable to the claimant under the *Donoghue v Stevenson* neighbour principle (see **4.1**). This idea is given expression in PETL art.4.103 and see *Mattis v Pollock* (2003) (p.275).

3. Note also a third idea mentioned by Lord Diplock. Could one argue that the Home office is vicariously liable for the acts of the borstal boys? This is unlikely because the boys were not employees (see **7.2.3**). But it is an interesting question all the same and probably one that would be dealt with as part of the second idea mentioned above.

4. This idea of two duties of care (one owed by the employee and the other owed by the employer) towards the claimant is specifically discussed in the next extract.

Phelps v Hillingdon LBC [2001] 2 A.C. 619, HL

This was a claim by a local authority to strike out various actions for damages brought against it. The House of Lords (Lords Slynn, Jauncey, Lloyd, Nicholls, Clyde, Hutton and Millett) refused to allow the striking out of the claims.

Lord Slynn: "My Lords, the appeals in these four cases were heard together. They all raise questions as to the liability of a local education authority for what is said to have been a failure, either by the local authority or by employees for whom the local authority was vicariously liable, in the provision of appropriate educational services for children at school. . . .

I do not, rule out the possibility of a direct claim in all situations where the local authority is exercising its powers. . . .

Since the authority can only act through its employees or agents, and if they are negligent vicarious liability will arise, it may rarely be necessary to invoke a claim for direct liability. After the argument in these cases, I do not, however, accept the absolute statement that an education authority 'owes no common law duty of care . . . in the exercise of the powers . . . relating to children with special educational needs' under the Act of 1981. . . .'"

Lord Nicholls: ". . . So far I have been considering the duties owed to a child by individual educational psychologists and teachers, and the resultant vicarious liability of local education authorities. This leaves unresolved the question whether the education authority itself owes a duty of care to the children in its schools. It was common ground, and rightly so, that the educational obligations imposed on local education authorities by statute cannot give rise to a (private law) action for damages for breach of statutory duty at the suit of pupils in their schools. But does an education authority owe to school pupils a duty at common law to take reasonable care in discharging its educational functions, either as regards children with special educational needs or generally?

This is an exceedingly difficult question. One of the difficulties lies in identifying satisfactorily what are the types of case which would be left without remedy if direct liability, as distinct from vicarious liability, were excluded. This, in turn, makes it difficult to evaluate the validity of drawing a distinction between direct liability and vicarious liability of local education authorities in this context. . . .'"

QUESTION

A child in a state school is injured as a result of a defective door. Which person or body is likely to be liable and will such liability be direct or vicarious?

7.1.2 Liability based on property interests

Liability for the acts of others—or apparent acts of others—can arise from legal ideas other than those outlined above. One fundamental idea is the property relationship. This can manifest itself in a number of ways, but a relationship of bailment is of particular importance. In *Morris v Martin* (1966) (p.24) the defendant was liable, at least according to Diplock L.J., because it was a bailee and this relationship in itself can give rise to liability. Although enforced through a tort remedy (once detinue but now conversion), bailment is a proprietary rather than a personal relationship; and so the claimant in *Morris* was in essence demanding the return of her property and it was no answer for the defendant to say that it was not he who stole the stole. But, this said, the case is also seen as a vicarious liability precedent, the court deciding that the employee who stole the stole was not acting outside the course of his employment (or the scope of his function to use the PETL expression). Bailment involves only moveable property, yet real property can also create liabilities on the part of occupiers and (or) landlords for acts done by third parties: see *Smith v Littlewoods* (p.249).

7.1.3 Local authorities

Nuisance and negligence are two torts that can arise in three party situations and as the previous extract indicates local authorities are particularly vulnerable to such actions (see e.g. *Phelps v Hillingdon LBC* (2001), above p.255). The position of such public bodies will be examined in detail in **Chapter 9**. Suffice it to note for the present that the three party negligence cases involving local authorities or other governmental agencies often raise the duty questions of a mere omission (see e.g. *Stovin v Wise* (1996), p.175) and (or) pure economic loss (*Murphy v Brentwood DC* (1991)).

7.1.4 Contract

Liability of one person for the acts of another can also arise in situations where there is a contractual relationship between the claimant and the defendant. Here the relevant principle is summed up in Article 8.107 of the *Principles of European Contract Law*: "A party who entrusts performance of the contract to another person remains responsible for performance". One Privy Council decision giving expression to this principle is *Wong Mee Wan v Kwan Kin Travel Services* (1996) (C&MC, p.460); another important case is *Photo Production Ltd v Securicor* (1980) which should be read in C&MC at p.70 and p.406. See also *Evans v Kosmar Villa Holidays Ltd* (2008).

7.2 Liability for employees

English law, like French law (see CC art.1384), has a very clear rule with regard to damage caused by employees. An employer (master) will be vicariously liable for torts committed by an employee (servant) acting in the course of his employment. Such liability is strict in the sense that once the employee would be personally liable to the claimant the employer will be *automatically* liable as well. The claimant, when suing the employer, has in other words to prove only (i) that there was a *tort* (ii) committed by a *servant* (employee) (iii) acting in the *course of his employment*. Each of these requirements will be examined below after an introductory sub-section looking at the background and theory basis to vicarious liability.

7.2.1 Vicarious liability: general considerations

The rule, as we have seen, is easily stated as the following statutory extract indicates.

Police Act 1996 (c.16)

"**88. Liability for wrongful acts of constables**.

(1) The chief officer of police for a police area shall be liable in respect of any unlawful conduct of constables under his direction and control in the performance or purported

performance of their functions in like manner as a master is liable in respect of any unlawful conduct of his servants in the course of their employment, and accordingly shall, in the case of a tort, be treated for all purposes as a joint tortfeasor."

QUESTION

What if a police officer maliciously abuses his power: can the victim of such an abuse of power sue under s.88? (cf. *Racz v Home Office* (1994).)

NOTE

A more detailed description of vicarious liability is given in the next extract.

Majrowski v Guy's and St Thomas' NHS Trust **[2007] 1 A.C. 224, HL**

(For facts see p.262)

Lord Nicholls: ". . . 7 Vicarious liability is a common law principle of strict, no-fault liability. Under this principle a blameless employer is liable for a wrong committed by his employee while the latter is about his employer's business. The time-honoured phrase is 'while acting in the course of his employment'. It is thus a form of secondary liability. The primary liability is that of the employee who committed the wrong. (To a limited extent vicarious liability may also exist outside the employment relationship, for instance, in some cases of agency. For present purposes these other instances can be put aside.)

8 This principle of vicarious liability is at odds with the general approach of the common law. Normally common law wrongs, or torts, comprise particular types of conduct regarded by the common law as blameworthy. In respect of these wrongs the common law imposes liability on the wrongdoer himself. The general approach is that a person is liable only for his own acts.

9 Whatever its historical origin, this common law principle of strict liability for another person's wrongs finds its rationale today in a combination of policy factors. They are summarised in Professor Fleming's *Law of Torts*, 9th ed (1998), pp 409–410. Stated shortly, these factors are that all forms of economic activity carry a risk of harm to others, and fairness requires that those responsible for such activities should be liable to persons suffering loss from wrongs committed in the conduct of the enterprise. This is 'fair', because it means injured persons can look for recompense to a source better placed financially than individual wrongdoing employees. It means also that the financial loss arising from the wrongs can be spread more widely, by liability insurance and higher prices. In addition, and importantly, imposing strict liability on employers encourages them to maintain standards of 'good practice' by their employees. For these reasons employers are to be held liable for wrongs committed by their employees in the course of their employment.

10 With these policy considerations in mind, it is difficult to see a coherent basis for confining the common law principle of vicarious liability to common law wrongs. The rationale underlying the principle holds good for equitable wrongs. The rationale also holds

good for a wrong comprising a breach of a statutory duty or prohibition which gives rise to civil liability, provided always the statute does not expressly or impliedly indicate otherwise. A precondition of vicarious liability is that the wrong must be committed by an employee in the course of his employment. A wrong is committed in the course of employment only if the conduct is so closely connected with acts the employee is authorised to do that, for the purposes of the liability of the employer to third parties, the wrongful conduct may fairly and properly be regarded as done by the employee while acting in the course of his employment: see *Lister v Hesley Hall Ltd* [2002] 1 AC 215, 245, para 69, per Lord Millett, and *Dubai Aluminium Co Ltd v Salaam* [2003] 2 AC 366, 377, para 23. If this prerequisite is satisfied the policy reasons underlying the common law principle are as much applicable to equitable wrongs and breaches of statutory obligations as they are to common law torts. . . ."

QUESTIONS

1. We have seen that it has been authoritatively stated that that 'our law of torts is concerned not with activities but with acts' (see above p.15). Is vicarious liability an exception to this assertion? If so, why, in the name of 'fairness', is an activities approach to liability not more widely adopted in the law of tort?

2. Should parents be vicariously liable for the torts committed by their children? Would such a rule be fair?

NOTE

Although the rule of vicarious liability is well established and uncontroversial as a principle of liability, its theoretical basis is by no means clear. Various explanations have been proposed (including the one by Lord Nicholls above), but none completely explains all the cases. The following extract examines this basis.

Lister v Hesley Hall Ltd **[2002] 1 A.C. 215, HL**

(For facts and further extracts see p.272)

Lord Millett: ". . . 65. Vicarious liability is a species of strict liability. It is not premised on any culpable act or omission on the part of the employer; an employer who is not personally at fault is made legally answerable for the fault of his employee. It is best understood as a loss-distribution device: (see Cane's edition of *Atiyah's Accidents, Compensation and the Law* 6th ed (1999), p 85 and the articles cited by Atiyah in his monograph on *Vicarious Liability in the Law of Torts*, at p 24. The theoretical underpinning of the doctrine is unclear. Glanville Williams wrote ('Vicarious Liability and the Master's of Indemnity' (1957) 20 MLR 220, 231):

'Vicarious liability is the creation of many judges who have had different ideas of its justification or social policy, or no idea at all. Some judges may have extended the rule more widely or confined it more narrowly than its true rationale would allow; yet the rationale, if we can discover it, will remain valid so far as it extends'.

Fleming observed (*The Law of Torts*, 9th ed (1998), p 410) that the doctrine cannot parade as a deduction from legalistic premises. He indicated that it should be frankly recognised as having its basis in a combination of policy considerations, and continued: 'Most important of these is the belief that a person who employs others to advance his own economic interest should in fairness be placed under a corresponding liability for losses incurred in the course of the enterprise. . .' *Atiyah, Vicarious Liability in the Law of Torts* wrote to the same effect. He suggested, at p 171: 'The master ought to be liable for all those torts which can fairly be regarded as reasonably incidental risks to the type of business he carries on'. These passages are not to be read as confining the doctrine to cases where the employer is carrying on business for profit. They are based on the more general idea that a person who employs another for his own ends inevitably creates a risk that the employee will commit a legal wrong. If the employer's objectives cannot be achieved without a serious risk of the employee committing the kind of wrong which he has in fact committed, the employer ought to be liable. The fact that his employment gave the employee the opportunity to commit the wrong is not enough to make the employer liable. He is liable only if the risk is one which experience shows is inherent in the nature of the business. . . ."

NOTE

A company can only act through its human 'agents' and rules of vicarious liability should be viewed within this context (cf. *Photo Production v Securicor* (1980); C&MC, pp 70 and 406). The principle of vicarious liability is not just a tort rule; it is equally part of company law in that it deems some acts as company acts (see further Lord Hoffmann in *Meridian Global Funds Management v Securities Commission* (1995); and Lord Reid in *Tesco Supermarkets v Nattrass* (1972), C&MC, p.70)). Nevertheless the whole notion of a company as a fictional person (*persona ficta*) gives rise to structural oddities. In one sense company employees remain 'persons' separate from the 'person' of the company and thus a company may have a defence in criminal law when one of its employees, in carrying out his employment duties, commits a crime: see *Tesco v Nattrass* (1972). Equally the company, held liable under the vicarious liability rule, can sue the employee who actually committed the tort either in debt for contribution (see **11.6**) or in damages for breach of his contract of employment: *Lister v Romford Ice & Cold Storage Co* (1957) (p.63).

7.2.2 Tort

Three requirements have to be fulfilled before an employer can be held vicariously responsible for the act of another. The first requirement is that there was an actual tort.

Staveley Iron & Chemical Co v Jones **[1956] A.C. 627, HL**

This was an action for damages by an employee against his employer for an injury sustained due, so it was alleged, to the negligence of a fellow employee crane driver. Denning L.J. in the Court of Appeal appeared to have suggested that the employer would be vicariously liable to the employee even if the latter could not actually prove negligence on the part of the crane-driver. The House of Lords (Lords Morton, Porter, Reid, Tucker and Cohen) disagreed with Denning L.J. on this point but held that the crane-driver had been negligent.

Lord Morton: ". . . My Lords, what the court has to decide in the present case is: Was the crane driver negligent? If the answer is 'Yes,' the employer is liable vicariously for the negligence of his servant. If the answer is 'No,' the employer is surely under no liability at all. Cases such as this, where an employer's liability is vicarious, are wholly distinct from cases where an employer is under a personal liability to carry out a duty imposed upon him as an employer by common law or statute. In the latter type of case the employer cannot discharge himself by saying: 'I delegated the carrying out of this duty to a servant, and he failed to carry it out by a mistake or error of judgment not amounting to negligence.' To such a case one may well apply the words of Denning LJ: '[The employer] remains responsible even though the servant may, for some reason, be immune.' These words, however, are, in my view, incorrect as applied to a case where the liability of the employer is not personal but vicarious. In such a case if the servant is 'immune,' so is the employer. See, for instance, *Esso Petroleum Co Ltd v Southport Corporation*. . .

Although I have felt bound to express my dissent from this passage in the judgment of Denning LJ I am glad to find myself in agreement with the views expressed by him and by his colleagues that the crane driver was negligent,. . .".

Lord Reid: ". . . The Court of Appeal reversed the decision of Sellers J, but different views were expressed on the law. Denning LJ, as I read his judgment, did not find it necessary to hold that the crane driver was herself negligent. He said: 'The employer is made liable, not so much for the crane driver's fault, but rather for his own fault committed through her. . . . He acts by his servant; and his servant's acts are, for this purpose, to be considered as his acts. Qui facit per alium facit per se. He cannot escape by the plea that his servant was thoughtless or inadvertent or made an error of judgment. If he takes the benefit of a machine like this, he must accept the burden of seeing that it is properly handled. It is for this reason that the employer's responsibility for injury may be ranked greater than that of the servant who actually made the mistake.'

My Lords, if this means that the appellants could be held liable even if it were held that the crane driver was not herself guilty of negligence, then I cannot accept that view. Of course, an employer may be himself in fault by engaging an incompetent servant or not having a proper system of work or in some other way. But there is nothing of that kind in this case. Denning LJ appears to base his reasoning on a literal application of the maxim qui facit per alium facit per se, but, in my view, it is rarely profitable and often misleading to use Latin maxims in that way. It is a rule of law that an employer, though guilty of no fault himself, is liable for damage done by the fault or negligence of his servant acting in the course of his employment. The maxims respondeat superior and qui facit per alium facit per se are often used, but I do not think that they add anything or that they lead to any different results. The former merely states the rule baldly in two words, and the latter merely gives a fictional explanation of it. . . .

. . .Hodson and Romer LJJ do not follow Denning LJ on this point and they appear to me to base their judgments on the crane driver having been negligent. I think she was negligent. The system was that there were two safety checks. Jones was supposed to see to the first, centring, and the crane driver was responsible for the second, pausing after taking the weight of the load. The first was not done but, as I have said, there is insufficient evidence to find that Jones was guilty of contributory negligence. But the fact that the first check was omitted is no excuse for failure to carry out the second, and the crane driver gave no reason to explain her failure. I am therefore of opinion that this appeal should be dismissed."

QUESTIONS

1. Is this case an example of the House of Lords deciding a question of pure fact?

2. Is the use of Latin phrases useful? (cf. *Kidner* (1995) 15 LS 47, 56ff.)

3. Could not negligence have been presumed, the employer only escaping liability if it could prove an absence of fault?

4. Can an employer be liable for a breach of duty which is of a type that is imposed on the employee rather than upon the employer?

Majrowski v Guy's and St Thomas' NHS Trust **[2007] 1 A.C. 224, HL**

This was an action for damages for breach of statutory duty by an employee against his employer. The employee claimed that he had been unlawfully harassed by another employee in breach of section 1 of the Protection of Harassment Act 1997 and that the employer was vicariously liable for this harassment. The judge had struck out the action but a majority of the Court of Appeal held that the employer could be vicariously liable for such a breach of the 1997 Act. An appeal to the House of Lords (Lords Nicholls, Hope, Carswell and Brown and Baroness Hale) was dismissed.

Lord Nicholls: "**1** My Lords, the Protection from Harassment Act 1997 prohibits harassment. A person must not pursue a course of conduct which amounts to harassment of another. A breach of this prohibition may be the subject, amongst other matters, of a claim for damages. The question raised by this appeal is whether an employer is vicariously liable for harassment committed by an employee in the course of his employment. . . .

27 I turn to the practical effect of the legislation. Vicarious liability for an employee's harassment of another person, whether a fellow employee or not, will to some extent increase employers' burdens. That is clear. But, here again, this does not suffice to show Parliament intended to exclude the ordinary common law principle of vicarious liability. Parliament added harassment to the list of civil wrongs. Parliament did so because it considered the existing law provided insufficient protection for victims of harassment. The inevitable consequence of Parliament creating this new wrong of universal application is that at times an employee will commit this wrong in the course of his employment. This prompts the question: why should an employer have a special dispensation in respect of the newly-created wrong and not be liable if an employee commits this wrong in the course of his employment? The contemporary rationale of employers' vicarious liability is as applicable to this new wrong as it is to common law torts.

28 Take a case where an employee, in the course of his employment, harasses a non-employee, such as a customer of the employer. In such a case the employer would be liable if his employee had assaulted the customer. Why should this not equally be so in respect of harassment? In principle, harassment arising from a dispute between two employees stands on the same footing. If, acting in the course of his employment, one employee assaults another, the employer is liable. Why should harassment be treated differently?. . ."

NOTE

See also Equality Act 2006 s.74 (research in the library).

QUESTIONS

1. Might the kind of defence set out in s.74(4) of the Equality Act 2006 apply by way of analogy to a situation like the one in *Majrowski*?

2. Will an employer always be liable if an employee assaults a customer? (cf. *Keppel Bus Co Ltd v Sa'ad bin Ahmad* (1974), p.272.)

3. One prisoner assaults another prisoner in the prison workshop. Might the Home office be liable for this assault?

7.2.3 **Employee**

The second requirement is that the tort must have been committed by an employee. However distinguishing an employee from an independent contractor is sometimes by no means easy.

Cassidy v Ministry of Health **[1951] 2 K.B. 343, CA**

This was an action for damages in respect of the negligent performance of an operation in one of the defendant's NHS hospitals. The claimant had entered the hospital for an operation on his left hand because he could not use it very well; however when he left he could not use it at all. The claimant alleged that someone must have been careless—the doctor, surgeon or a nurse—but he could not point to whom it was. The trial judge dismissed the action because the claimant had failed to prove that anyone had been negligent, but an appeal to the Court of Appeal (Somervell L.J., Singleton L.J. and Denning L.J.) was allowed.

Denning L.J.: ". . . The truth is that, in cases of negligence, the distinction between a contract of service and a contract for services only becomes of importance when it is sought to make the employer liable, not for a breach of his own duty of care, but for some collateral act of negligence of those whom he employs. He cannot escape the consequences of a breach of his own duty, but he can escape responsibility for collateral or casual acts of negligence if he can show that the negligent person was employed, not under a contract of service but only under a contract for services. Take first an instance when an employer is under no duty himself: he is riding passively in a car along a road; he is not under any duty of care himself to road-users, but the driver is. If the driver is a chauffeur employed under a contract of service, the employer is liable for his negligence: but if the driver is a taximan employed under a contract for services, the employer is not liable.

Take now an instance where an employer is under a duty himself:- Suppose an employer has a lamp which overhangs his shop door; he is himself under a duty to his customers to use reasonable care to see that it is safe, and he cannot escape that duty by employing an independent contractor to do it. He is liable, therefore, if the independent contractor fails to discover a patent defect which any careful man should have discovered, and in consequence the lamp falls on a customer; but he is not liable if the independent contractor drops a hammer on the head of the customer, because that is not negligence in the employer's department of duty. It is collateral or casual negligence by one employed under a contract for services. The employer would, however, have been liable if he had got his servant to mend the lamp and his servant dropped the hammer; because that would be negligence by one employed under a contract of service. . . .

Turning now to the facts in this case, this is the position: the hospital authorities accepted the plaintiff as a patient for treatment, and it was their duty to treat him with reasonable care. They selected, employed, and paid all the surgeons and nurses who looked after him. He had no say in their selection at all. If those surgeons and nurses did not treat him with proper care and skill, then the hospital authorities must answer for it, for it means that they themselves did not perform their duty to him. I decline to enter into the question whether any of the surgeons were employed only under a contract for services, as distinct from a contract of service. The evidence is meagre enough in all conscience on that point. But the liability of the hospital authorities should not, and does not, depend on nice considerations of that sort. The plaintiff knew nothing of the terms on which they employed their staff: all he knew was that he was treated in the hospital by people whom the hospital authorities appointed; and the hospital authorities must be answerable for the way in which he was treated.

This conclusion has an important bearing on the question of evidence. If the plaintiff had to prove that some particular doctor or nurse was negligent, he would not be able to do it. But he was not put to that impossible task: he says, 'I went into the hospital to be cured of two stiff fingers. I have come out with four stiff fingers, and my hand is useless. That should not have happened if due care had been used. Explain it, if you can'. I am quite clearly of opinion that that raises a prima facie case against the hospital authorities: see per Goddard, LJ, in *Mahon v Osborne*. They have nowhere explained how it could happen without negligence. They have busied themselves in saying that this or that member of their staff was not negligent. But they have called not a single person to say that the injuries were consistent with due care on the part of all the members of their staff. They called some of the people who actually treated the man, namely Dr Fahrni, Dr Ronaldson, and Sister Hall, each of whom protested that he was careful in his part; but they did not call any expert at all, to say that this might happen despite all care. They have not therefore displaced the prima facie case against them and are liable to damages to the plaintiff. . . ."

NOTE

See also *Roe v Minister of Health* (1954) (p.356).

QUESTION

How should one approach this employee issue in terms of method?

Hall v Lorimer **[1992] 1 W.L.R. 939, QBD**

Mummery J.: ". . . In order to decide whether a person carries on business on his own account it is necessary to consider many different aspects of that person's work activity. This is not a mechanical exercise of running through items on a check list to see whether they are present in, or absent from, a given situation. The object of the exercise is to paint a picture from the accumulation of detail. The overall effect can only be appreciated by standing back from the detailed picture which has been painted, by viewing it from a distance and by making an informed, considered, qualitative appreciation of the whole. It is a matter of evaluation of the overall effect of the detail, which is not necessarily the same as the sum total of the individual details. Not all details are of equal weight or importance in any given situation. The details may also vary in importance from one situation to another.

[Mummery J.'s decision was upheld by the Court of Appeal.]

NOTE

The question of who is an employee has arisen in cases that are not actually vicarious liability problems, for the term is used in national insurance and tax legislation. These cases have, however, a precedent value for tort (but cf. *Kidner* (1995) 15 LS 47).

Market Investigations Ltd v Ministry of Social Security [1969] 2 Q.B. 173, QBD

Cooke J.: "The appellant company in this case, Market Investigations Ltd, are engaged in the field of market research. In addition to their permanent staff at the headquarters office, they employ interviewers for about eight to ten thousand interviews annually to provide information for the company's customers about the habits and opinions of members of the general public, retailers or other people in commerce, industry and the professions. . . .

. . . The sole issue for determination in the appeal is whether, as the company say, Mrs Irving was employed during the relevant period under a series of contracts for services or, as the Minister says, she was employed during that period under a series of contracts of service. . . .

I think it is fair to say that there was at one time a school of thought according to which the extent and degree of the control which B was entitled to exercise over A in the performance of the work would be a decisive factor. However, it has for long been apparent that an analysis of the extent and degree of such control is not in itself decisive. . . .

The observations of Lord Wright, of Denning LJ and of the judges of the Supreme Court suggest that the fundamental test to be applied is this: 'Is the person who has engaged himself to perform these services performing them as a person in business on his own account?' If the answer to that question is 'yes,' then the contract is a contract for services. If the answer is 'no,' then the contract is a contract of service. No exhaustive list has been compiled and perhaps no exhaustive list can be compiled of the considerations which are relevant in determining that question, nor can strict rules be laid down as to the relative weight which the various considerations should carry in particular cases. The most that can be said is that control will no doubt always have to be considered, although it can no longer be regarded as the sole determining factor; and that factors which may be of importance are such matters as whether the man performing the services provides his own equipment, whether he hires his own helpers, what degree of financial risk he takes, what degree of responsibility for investment and management he has, and whether and how far he has an opportunity of profiting from sound management in the performance of his task. . . .

In the present case it is clear that on each occasion on which Mrs Irving engaged herself to act as an interviewer for a particular survey she agreed with the company, in consideration of a fixed remuneration, to provide her own work and skill in the performance of a service for the company. I therefore proceed to ask myself two questions: First, whether the extent and degree of the control exercised by the company, if no other factors were taken into account, be consistent with her being employed under a contract of service. Second, whether when the contract is looked at as a whole, its nature and provisions are consistent or inconsistent with its being a contract of service, bearing in mind the general test I have adumbrated. . . .

It is apparent that the control which the company had the right to exercise in this case was very extensive indeed. It was in my view so extensive as to be entirely consistent with Mrs Irving's being employed under a contract of service. The fact that Mrs Irving had a limited discretion as to when she should do the work was not in my view inconsistent with the existence of a contract of service. . . . Nor is there anything inconsistent with the existence of a contract of service in the fact that Mrs Irving was free to work for others during the relevant period. It is by no means a necessary incident of a contract of service that the servant is prohibited from serving any other employer. Again, there is nothing inconsistent with the existence of a contract of service in the master having no right to alter the place or area within which the servant has agreed to work. So far as concerns practical limitations on a master's power to give instructions to his servant, there must be many cases when such practical limitations exist. For example, a chauffeur in the service of a car hire company may, in the absence of radio communication, be out of reach of instructions for long periods. . . .

. . .The opportunity to deploy individual skill and personality is frequently present in what is undoubtedly a contract of service. I have already said that the right to work for others is not inconsistent with the existence of a contract of service. Mrs Irving did not provide her own tools or risk her own capital, nor did her opportunity of profit depend in any significant degree on the way she managed her work.

Taking all the factors into account. . . I am clearly of opinion that on the facts of this case the Minister was right in concluding that Mrs Irving was employed by the company under a series of contracts of service, and the appeal accordingly must fail."

QUESTION

Are the following 'employees' for the purposes of vicarious liability: (i) casual workers fruit picking on a farm; (ii) taxi drivers who own their own cars and who work when they want directed to clients by a radio call centre; (iii) borstal boys doing prison work; (iv) a young person helping his local milkman do the milk rounds; (v) a young person doing a paper round every morning; (vi) a lorry driver working in company uniform but whose contract with the company specifically states that he is an independent contractor who must purchase his own uniform and lorry (out of an interest free loan provided by the company)? (cf. *Kidner* (1995) 15 LS 47.)

7.2.4 Transferred employee

One particular problem that can arise in vicarious liability is that of the transferred employee. For example, a crane-hire firm hires out one of its cranes, together with a driver, to a construction company for a longish period during which the crane driver carelessly injures someone on the site. The issue here is not one of whether or not the driver is an employee; it is a matter of which 'employer'—the crane-hire firm or the construction company—is to be liable to the victim. The approach adopted by the House of Lords over half a century ago is set out in the next extract.

Mersey Docks and Harbour Board v Coggins and Griffith (Liverpool) Ltd [1947] A.C. 1, HL

This was an action for damages by a dockyard employee against a harbour authority in respect of personal injuries suffered when he was run over by a crane carelessly driven by a man called Newall. The harbour authority had hired out the crane and its driver Newall to a firm of stevedores and it was stipulated that drivers would be servants of anyone hiring such a crane. Newall himself, when asked in court from whom he took is orders, replied "I take no orders from anybody". The trial judge held that the crane driver was the employee of the harbour board when the accident occurred and appeals to the Court of Appeal and House of Lords (Lords Porter, Uthwatt, Simon, Macmillan and Simonds) were dismissed.

> **Lord Macmillan**: ". . . [I]t is always open to an employer to show, if he can, that he has for a particular purpose or on a particular occasion temporarily transferred the services of one of his general servants to another party so as to constitute him pro hac vice the servant of that other party with consequent liability for his negligent acts. The burden is on the general employer to establish that such a transference has been effected. Agreeing as I do with the trial judge and the Court of Appeal, I am of opinion that, on the facts of the present case, Newall was never so transferred from the service and control of the appellant board to the service and control of the stevedores as to render the stevedores answerable for the manner in which he carried on his work of driving the crane. The stevedores were entitled to tell him where to go, what parcels to lift and where to take them, that is to say, they could direct him as to what they wanted him to do; but they had no authority to tell him how he was to handle the crane in doing his work. In driving the crane, which was the appellant board's property confided to his charge, he was acting as the servant of the appellant board, not as the servant of the stevedores. It was not in consequence of any order of the stevedores that he negligently ran down the plaintiff; it was in consequence of his negligence in driving the crane, that is to say, in performing the work which he was employed by the appellant board to do. . ."

QUESTION

Why could both employers not be vicariously liable?

Viasystems (Tynside) Ltd v Thermal Transfer (Northern) Ltd [2006] Q.B. 510, CA

This was an action for damages brought against three defendants in respect of severe water damage to the claimant's factory caused by the negligence of a fitter's mate. The trial judge gave judgement for the claimant against the first defendant (breach of contract) and the third defendant (vicarious liability), but dismissed the claim against the second defendant. The Court of Appeal (May and Rix L.JJ.) allowed an appeal and held that the second defendant was also vicariously liable for the damage. The facts are stated in more detail below.

May L.J.: "... **3** In July 1998, the claimants engaged the first defendants to install air conditioning in their factory. The first defendants sub-contracted ducting work to the second defendants. The second defendants contracted with the third defendants to provide fitters and fitters' mates on a labour-only basis. One such fitter was Mr Megson. His mate was Darren Strang. They were installing the ductwork under the instruction or supervision of Mr Horsley, a self-employed fitter contracted to the second defendants. Both Mr Megson and Darren Strang were thus employed by the third defendants.

4 At the time of the accident, the men were working in a roof space. Access was by crawling boards using the roof purlins. Mr Megson needed some fittings and sent Darren Strang to get them. Darren was away for a few minutes, during which Mr Horsley was helping Mr Megson with the ducting. Mr Horsley naturally expected Darren to return by a sensible route, but he did not so return. On the contrary, he attempted to return by crawling through some sections of ducting that were in place. These moved and came into contact with part of a fire protection sprinkler system. The relevant part of this system fractured, hence the flood. The judge had no difficulty in finding that Darren was negligent, as he obviously was. . . .

12 The parties' cases and the judge's decision were predicated on an assumption that only one of the second or third defendants could in law be vicariously liable for Darren Strang's negligence, not both. Before we began hearing the appeal, counsel drew our attention to the discussion in *Atiyah, Vicarious Liability in the Law of Torts* (1967) in a chapter entitled 'The Borrowed Servant', p 152, at p 156, where it is suggested that it is strange that the courts have never countenanced what might be an obvious solution in some cases, namely holding both the general and the temporary employer vicariously liable for an employee's negligence. We considered that this interesting possibility should be examined in this appeal. If it were permissible in law to hold both the second and third defendants vicariously liable, the facts of this appeal might be a paradigm example of a case in which the court should do so. So we adjourned the hearing of the appeal to enable counsel to research and make further submissions. They have done so, and we are most grateful. . . .

20 As Professor Atiyah pointed out, it has been assumed since the early 19th century to be the law that, where an employee, who is lent by one employer to work for another, is negligent, liability must rest on one employer or the other, but not both. But the foundation on which this rests is a slender one and the contrary has never been properly argued. I agree that the House of Lords implicitly proceeded on this assumption in the *Mersey Docks* case [1947] AC 1; but the point was not argued, and I do not consider that the facts would have sustained a finding that both employers were vicariously liable. . . .

46 In summary. . . there has been a long-standing assumption, technically unsupported by authority binding this court, that a finding of dual vicarious liability is not legally permissible. An assumption of such antiquity should not lightly be brushed aside, but the contrary has scarcely been argued and never considered in depth. This is not surprising, because in many, perhaps most, factual situations, a proper application of the *Mersey Docks* principles would not yield dual control, as it so plainly does in the present case. I am sceptical whether any of the cases from this jurisdiction which I have considered would, if they were re-examined, yield dual vicarious liability. . . .

48 Academic commentary tends to favour the possibility of dual vicarious liability, but feels that authority constrains it. Other jurisdictions have reacted variously, giving no clear lead. Their decisions range from articulating the assumption to favouring or adopting dual liability.

49 In my judgment, there is, in a modern context, little intrinsic sense in, or justification for, the assumption. Multiplicity of claims is not a modern impediment. A contest between two defendants, where only one could be liable, is just as likely as a claim against the same two defendants, if both could be liable. The underlying basis for the assumption appears to be the notion, exposed as a device by Denning LJ in *Denham's* case [1955] 2 QB 437, that, to find a temporary employer vicariously liable, you have to look for a transfer of employment. Although the nature and incidence of the employee's employment is plainly material, I do not read the *Mersey Docks* case [1947] AC 1 as saying that these are the determinative matters in all cases. If, on the facts of a particular case, the core question is who was entitled, and in theory obliged, to control the employee's relevant negligent act so as to prevent it, there will be some cases in which the sensible answer would be each of two 'employers'. The present is such a case. In my judgment, dual vicarious liability should be a legal possibility, and I would hold that it is. It follows that I would allow this appeal to the extent of holding each of the second and third defendants vicariously liable for Darren Strang's negligence. . . ."

Rix L.J.: ". . . **77** In my judgment, if consideration is given to the function and purposes of the doctrine of vicarious liability, then the possibility of dual responsibility provides a coherent solution to the problem of the borrowed employee. Both employers are using the employee for the purposes of their business. Both have a general responsibility to select their personnel with care and to encourage and control the careful execution of their employees' duties, and both fall within the practical policy of the law which looks in general to the employer to organise his affairs in such a way as to make it fair, just and convenient for him to bear the risk of his employees' negligence. I am here using the expression "employee" in the extended sense used in the authorities relating to the borrowed employee. The functional basis of the doctrine of vicarious liability has become increasingly clear over the years. The Civil Liability (Contribution) Act 1978 now provides a clear and fair statutory basis for the assessment of contribution between the two employers. In my judgment, the existence of the possibility of dual responsibility will be fairer and will also enable cases to be settled more easily. . . ."

QUESTIONS

1. Is the theory of vicarious liability now based on functionalism (what vicarious liability does) rather than upon formalism (conceptual basis of vicarious liability)?

2. If functionalism is the right theoretical basis, does this mean that some tort principles are now to be founded on functionalism and activity? If so, might this test be useful to apply to every tort case? Could an activity-functional approach to tort liability transform the whole subject?

3. A solicitor employed by a medium sized firm does some part-time teaching (paid by the hour) at a local university. If this solicitor harasses a student, whom might the student sue (besides the solicitor himself)?

7.2.5 **Course of employment**

The third requirement of vicarious liability is that the employee must have been acting in the course of his employment when the tort was committed. Thus a van driver supplied with a company van might well be acting on 'a frolic of his own' if he carelessly injures another road user while using the van one Sunday for a family picnic.

Smith v Stages **[1989] A.C. 928, HL**

This was an action for damages for personal injuries by a car passenger named Machin against a co-employee, who was driving the car, called Stages. The employer of the two men was joined as second defendant. The personal injuries resulted from a car accident which occurred when the men were returning from a job to which they had been sent by their employer. The car accident had been caused by Stages' negligence, but it turned out that he was uninsured and thus Machin argued that the employer was vicariously liable for Stages negligence. The employer claimed that Stages was not acting in the course of his employment when the accident occurred. The House of Lords (Lords Goff, Lowry, Keith, Brandon and Griffiths) held the employer liable.

Lord Goff: ". . . We can begin with the simple proposition that, in ordinary circumstances, when a man is travelling to or from his place of work, he is not acting in the course of his employment. So a bank clerk who commutes to the City of London every day from Sevenoaks, is not acting in the course of his employment when he walks across London Bridge from the station to his bank in the City. This is because he is not employed to travel from his home to the bank; he is employed to work at the bank, his place of work, and so his duty is to arrive there in time for his working day. Nice points can arise about the precise time, or place, at which he may be held to have arrived at work; but these do not trouble us in the present case. Likewise, of course, he is not acting in the course of his employment when he is travelling home after his day's work is over. If however a man is obliged by his employer to travel to work by means of transport provided by his employer, he may be held to be acting in the course of his employment when so doing. . . .

I approach the matter as follows. I do not regard this case as an ordinary case of travelling to work. It would be more accurate to describe it as a case where an employee, who has for a short time to work for his employers at a different place of work some distance away from his usual place of work, has to move from his ordinary base to a temporary base (here lodgings in Pembroke) from which he will travel to work at the temporary place of work each day. For the purpose of moving base, a normal working day was set aside for Stages' journey, for which he was paid as for an eight hour day. In addition to his day's pay he was given a travel allowance for his journey, and an allowance for his lodgings at his temporary base in Pembroke. In my opinion, in all the circumstances of the case, Stages was required by the employers to make this journey, so as to make himself available to do his work at the Pembroke Power Station, and it would be proper to describe him as having been employed to do so. . . .

I turn to Stages' journey back. Another ordinary working day, Tuesday, 30 August, was made available for the journey, with the same pay, to enable him to return to his base in the Midlands to be ready to travel to work on the Wednesday morning. In my opinion, he was employed to make the journey back, just as he was employed to make the journey out to Pembroke. If he had chosen to go to sleep on the Monday morning and afternoon for eight hours or so, and then to drive home on the Monday evening so that he could have Tuesday free (as indeed Mr Pye expected him to do), that would not have detracted from the proposition that his journey was in the course of his employment. For this purpose, it was irrelevant that Monday was a bank holiday. Of course, it was wrong for him to succumb to the temptation of driving home on the Monday morning, just after he had completed so long a spell of work; but once again that cannot alter the fact that his journey was made in the course of his employment. . . .”

QUESTIONS

1. Did Stages' lack of insurance put him in breach of his contract of employment? Did it put him in breach of any duty towards Machin?

2. What if the employers had specifically instructed both men not to travel by car: if they had disobeyed this instruction would this mean that, while in the car, they were automatically outside of the course of their employment?

3. What if they had given a lift to a hitchhiker: if he had been injured in the accident would he have been able to sue the employer?

4. What if Stages and Machin carelessly left the car with the keys in the ignition while they went for a cup of tea and a thief knocked down and injured a passer-by while driving off in the car: could the passer-by sue the employer?

NOTE

In considering the above questions, read *Rose v Plenty* (1976) in the law report.

7.2.6 Criminal act

One of the most difficult problems in the course of employment requirement is where the employee's tortious act is also a criminal act. Does this automatically take the act outside the course of employment?

Morris v CW Martin & Sons Ltd **[1966] 1 Q.B. 716, CA**

(For facts and further extract see p.24)

Salmon L.J.: “. . . A bailee for reward is not answerable for a theft by any of his servants but only for a theft by such of them as are deputed by him to discharge some part of his duty of taking reasonable care. A theft by any servant who is not employed to do anything in relation to the goods bailed is entirely outside the scope of his employment and cannot make the master liable. So in this case, if someone employed by the defendants in another depot had broken in and stolen the fur, the defendants would not have been liable. Similarly in my view if a clerk employed in the same depot had seized the opportunity of entering the room where the fur was kept and had stolen it, the defendants would not have been liable. The mere fact that the master, by employing a rogue, gives him the opportunity to steal or defraud does not make the master liable for his depredations: *Ruben v Great Fingall Consolidated*. It might be otherwise if the master knew or ought to have known that his servant was dishonest, because then the master could be liable in negligence for employing him. . . ."

NOTE

This case is important for vicarious liability because it established that a criminal act of an employee would not necessarily take him outside the course of his employment (and see *Photo Production v Securicor* (1980), C&MC, pp.70 and 406). The test was whether the employee was doing what he was employed to do (a test that has now been modified as will be seen). In *Morris* he was employed to handle the stole, which no doubt he did rather too well, and this *authorised contact* with the thing in issue was enough to keep his criminal act within the scope of his employment. Nevertheless this test had its limits: see e.g. *Keppel Bus Co Ltd v Sa'ad bin Ahmad* (1974) (read it in the law report). In *Keppel* the Privy Council held that the employer of a bus conductor who deliberately injured a passenger was not liable for this damage. But the problem with cases like *Keppel* was that it seemed an affront to common sense that because the conductor's behaviour was worse than careless, the company could escape liability (for if the conductor had negligently injured the passenger with his ticket machine the bus company would of course have been liable). The next case, perhaps now the major leading precedent on course of employment, has gone some way in recognising this latter criticism.

Lister v Hesley Hall Ltd [2002] 1 A.C. 215, HL

This was an action for damages against the employer of a warden of a boarding house in which the claimants had been resident when young teenagers. The claimants had been sexually abused by the warden while in residence and they claimed damages from the employer on the basis both of a breach of a direct duty of care and of vicarious liability. The judge dismissed the direct claims against the employer and held that the employer could not be vicariously liable for the warden's torts against the boys. However he held that the employers were vicariously liable for the warden's failure to report the abuses. An appeal by the employers was allowed by the Court of Appeal, but this was overturned on further appeal to the House of Lords (Lords Steyn, Clyde, Hutton, Hobhouse and Millett).

Lord Steyn: "My Lords, . . . **1.** The central question before the House is whether as a matter of legal principle the employers of the warden of a school boarding house, who sexually abused boys in his care, may depending on the particular circumstances be vicariously liable for the torts of their employee. . . .

14. Vicarious liability is legal responsibility imposed on an employer, although he is himself free from blame, for a tort committed by his employee in the course of his employment. Fleming observed that this formula represented 'a compromise between two conflicting policies: on the one end, the social interest in furnishing an innocent tort victim with recourse against a financially responsible defendant; on the other, a hesitation to foist any undue burden on business enterprise': *The Law of Torts*, 9th ed (1998), pp 409–410.

15. For nearly a century English judges have adopted Salmond's statement of the applicable test as correct. Salmond said that a wrongful act is deemed to be done by a 'servant' in the course of his employment if 'it is either (a) a wrongful act authorised by the master, or (b) a wrongful and unauthorised mode of doing some act authorised by the master': *Salmond on Torts*, 1st ed (1907), p 83; and *Salmond and Heuston on Torts*, 21st ed (1996), p 443. . . .

16. It is not necessary to embark on a detailed examination of the development of the modern principle of vicarious liability. But it is necessary to face up to the way in which the law of vicarious liability sometimes may embrace intentional wrongdoing by an employee. If one mechanically applies *Salmond's* test, the result might at first glance be thought to be that a bank is not liable to a customer where a bank employee defrauds a customer by giving him only half the foreign exchange which he paid for, the employee pocketing the difference. A preoccupation with conceptualistic reasoning may lead to the absurd conclusion that there can only be vicarious liability if the bank carries on business in defrauding its customers. Ideas divorced from reality have never held much attraction for judges steeped in the tradition that their task is to deliver principled but practical justice. How the courts set the law on a sensible course is a matter to which I now turn. . . .

19. The classic example of vicarious liability for intentional wrong doing is *Morris v C W Martin & Sons Ltd* [1966] 1 QB 716. . . .

22. The Court of Appeal treated the *Morris v C W Martin & Sons Ltd* [1966] 1 QB 716 line of authority as applicable only in bailment cases. That was the Court of Appeal's answer to the argument that, in the context of vicarious liability, the law ought not to incur the reproach of showing greater zeal in protecting jewellery than in protecting children. My Lords, I trust that I have already shown that *Morris's* case cannot be so easily dismissed. It is only necessary to add that in *Photo Production Ltd v Securicor Transport Ltd* [1980] AC 827 the House of Lords took the view that the principles enunciated in *Morris's* case by Diplock and Salmon LJ are of general application. . . .

24. It is useful to consider an employer's potential liability for non-sexual assaults. If such assaults arise directly out of circumstances connected with the employment, vicarious liability may arise: see Rose, 'Liability for an employee's assaults' (1977), 40 MLR 420, 432-433. Butler-Sloss LJ considered this analogy. . . . If I correctly understand [her] passage, it appears to be indicating that there could not be vicarious liability by an employer for a brutal assault, or serious sexual misconduct, whatever the circumstances. That appears to be a case of saying 'The greater the fault of the servant, the less the liability of the master': *Morris v C W Martin & Sons Ltd* [1966] 1 QB 716, 733, per Diplock LJ. A better approach is to concentrate on the relative closeness of the connection between the nature of the employment and the particular tort.

25. In my view the approach of the Court of Appeal in *Trotman v North Yorkshire County Council* [1999] LGR 584 was wrong. It resulted in the case being treated as one of the employment furnishing a mere opportunity to commit the sexual abuse. The reality was that the county council were responsible for the care of the vulnerable children and employed the deputy headmaster to carry out that duty on its behalf. And the sexual abuse took place while the employee was engaged in duties at the very time and place demanded by his employment. The connection between the employment and the torts was very close. I would overrule *Trotman v North Yorkshire County Council*. . . ."

Lord Millett: ". . . **79**. . . . [I]t is no answer to say that the employee was guilty of intentional wrongdoing, or that his act was not merely tortious but criminal, or that he was acting exclusively for his own benefit, or that he was acting contrary to express instructions, or that his conduct was the very negation of his employer's duty. The cases show that where an employer undertakes the care of a client's property and entrusts the task to an employee who steals the property, the employer is vicariously liable. This is not only in accordance with principle but with the underlying rationale if Atiyah has correctly identified it. Experience shows that the risk of theft by an employee is inherent in a business which involves entrusting the custody of a customer's property to employees. But the theft must be committed by the very employee to whom the custody of the property is entrusted. He does more than make the most of an opportunity presented by the fact of his employment. He takes advantage of the position in which the employer has placed him to enable the purposes of the employer's business to be achieved. If the boys in the present case had been sacks of potatoes and the defendant, having been engaged to take care of them, had entrusted their care to one of its employees, it would have been vicariously liable for any criminal damage done to them by the employee in question, though not by any other employee. Given that the employer's liability does not arise from the law of bailment, it is not immediately apparent that it should make any difference that the victims were boys, that the wrongdoing took the form of sexual abuse, and that it was committed for the personal gratification of the employee. . . .

82. In the present case the warden's duties provided him with the opportunity to commit indecent assaults on the boys for his own sexual gratification, but that in itself is not enough to make the school liable. The same would be true of the groundsman or the school porter. But there was far more to it than that. The school was responsible for the care and welfare of the boys. It entrusted that responsibility to the warden. He was employed to discharge the school's responsibility to the boys. For this purpose the school entrusted them to his care. He did not merely take advantage of the opportunity which employment at a residential school gave him. He abused the special position in which the school had placed him to enable it to discharge its own responsibilities, with the result that the assaults were committed by the very employee to whom the school had entrusted the care of the boys. . . . I would hold the school liable. . . .

84. I would hold the school vicariously liable for the warden's intentional assaults, not (as was suggested in argument) for his failure to perform his duty to take care of the boys. That is an artificial approach based on a misreading of *Morris v Martin*. The cleaners were vicariously liable for their employee's conversion of the fur, not for his negligence in failing to look after it. Similarly in *Photo Production v Securicor Transport Ltd* the security firm was vicariously liable for the patrolman's arson, not for his negligence. The law is mature enough to hold an employer vicariously liable for deliberate, criminal wrongdoing on the part of an employee without indulging in sophistry of this kind. I would also not base liability on the warden's failure to report his own wrongdoing to his employer, an approach which I regard as both artificial and unrealistic. Even if such a duty did exist, on which I prefer to express no opinion, I am inclined to think that it would be a duty owed exclusively to the employer and not a duty for breach of which the employer could be vicariously liable. The same reasoning would not, of course, necessarily apply to the duty to report the wrongdoing of fellow employees, but it is not necessary to decide this. . . ."

NOTE

This case is an important precedent because it has gone some way in developing, if not expanding, the course of employment test in situations where the employee's wrongful act was criminal. The test is now this: there will be liability 'where the unauthorised acts of the employee are so *connected with* acts which the employer has authorised that they may properly be regarded as being within the scope of his employment'. Or, to quote a more recent observation: "What matters is the closeness of the connection between the offending conduct of the employee with the nature and circumstances of that employment. . . . It is the breach of the duty, as much as the duty itself, which is caught by the new test" (Auld L.J. in *Majrowski v Guy's and St Thomas's NHS Trust* (2005) at § 38; and see the decision of the House of Lords, above p.262). In short, the key word is 'connection'. The effect of *Lister* can be felt in the next case.

Mattis v Pollock [2003] 1 W.L.R. 2158, CA

This was an action for damages, by the victim of a serious assault, against the owner of a nightclub which had employed the doorman who had carried out the attack. The doorman, while on duty, had become involved in a dispute in which he instigated a violent confrontation with a group wishing to enter the club. The group fought back and the doorman escaped to his flat. Later the doorman reappeared with a knife and attacked the claimant, for which he was later was convicted and imprisoned. The claimant based his action on the breach of a direct duty of care with respect to the hiring of the doorman and on the vicarious liability of the owner for the tort of the doorman. The trial judge dismissed the claim but the Court of Appeal (Judge L.J., Dyson L.J. and Pumfrey J.) allowed an appeal.

Judge L.J. (delivering judgment of the court): ". . . **19** The essential principle we derive from the reasoning in the *Lister* and *Dubai Aluminium* cases is that Mr Pollock's vicarious liability to Mr Mattis for Cranston's attack requires a deceptively simple question to be answered. Approaching the matter broadly, was the assault 'so closely connected' with what Mr Pollock authorised or expected of Cranston in the performance of his employment as doorman at his nightclub, that it would be fair and just to conclude that Mr Pollock is vicariously liable for the damage Mr Mattis sustained when Crantson stabbed him. . . .

30 Cranston was indeed employed by Mr Pollock to keep order and discipline at the nightclub. That is what bouncers are employed to do. Moreover, however, he was encouraged and expected to perform his duties in an aggressive and intimidatory manner, which included physical man-handling of customers. In our judgment, this aspect of the evidence was not sufficiently addressed by Judge Seymour QC. He suggested that the evidence went no further than a single incident of inappropriate violence (on 18 July) which would not have justified immediate dismissal. Whether, taking Cranston's behaviour as a whole, it would have been appropriate to dismiss him, is a moot point. The reality was that Mr Pollock should not have been employing Cranston at all, and certainly should not have been encouraging him to perform his duties as he did. It was not perhaps anticipated that

Cranston's behaviour would be counter-productive, and that by way of self-defence, and indeed revenge, his behaviour would provoke a violent response. That is because the customers with whom he tangled were supposed to be intimidated, and to go quietly. The whole point of any physical confrontation with Mr Pollock's customers in the nightclub, whether engineered by Cranston or not, was that he should win it.

31 Judge Seymour QC accurately noted that the incident might have ended at a number of different stages before Mr Mattis was stabbed. Nevertheless, that did not of itself provide the definitive answer to the question whether Mr Pollock should be held vicariously liable for the stabbing. . . . Cranston was still in his working hours, and if he had not found an immediate target on whom to vent his anger outside the club, it seems probable that he would have returned inside the club to ascertain whether any of his attackers were still there. If so, on the facts found here, we have little doubt that he would have been violent within the premises, as he was outside them. In any event his return to the immediate vicinity was motivated by a need to revenge the physical injuries and public humiliation he had sustained inside the club. The incident had wholly undermined his reputation and status as the doorman Mr Pollock expected him to be. And the words he used as he stabbed Mr Mattis demonstrated that he had Mr Mattis's intervention in defence of Mr Cook in the forefront of his mind, and that his actions were directly linked to the incident which had taken place earlier in the club.

33 The issue of Mr Pollock's personal, as opposed to vicarious liability, was not closely canvassed in argument. Judge Seymour QC's robust approach to this aspect of his decision derived from his conclusion that personal liability would not survive the reasoning which had led him to conclude that the claim based on vicarious liability must fail. In the circumstances of this case we accept the validity of this approach adding, however, that personal liability would not necessarily and always follow the establishment of vicarious liability. In the present case, however, it does. Mr Pollock chose to employ Cranston, knowing and approving of his aggressive tendencies, which he encouraged rather than curbed, and the assault on Mr Mattis represented the culmination of an incident which began in Mr Pollock's premises and involved his customers, in which his employee behaved in the violent and aggressive manner which Mr Pollock expected of him.

34 Given the particular circumstances in which we have found that vicarious liability is established, if we had to decide the point, Mr Pollock's personal liability would also follow.''

QUESTION

Can you modify these facts as to time and place so as to produce a factual situation in which the nightclub owner would *not* be liable for the revenge attack by the doorman?

7.3 Liability for non-employees

Vicarious liability normally comes into play only when the actor who commits the tort is an employee of the defendant. What is the position if the actor is not actually an employee?

7.3.1 Unauthorised user

For example, what is the position if a stranger (or other unauthorised user) injures someone while using the defendant's property?

Topp v London Country Bus (South West) Ltd **[1993] 1 W.L.R. 976, CA**

Dillon L.J.: ". . . The claim is a claim for damages arising out of the death of the plaintiff's wife, Mrs Jacqueline Topp, on 25 April 1988. . . . The defendants run a bus service in the region of Epsom, and one of their buses was hijacked by a third party, who has never been identified, at about 11 pm on 25 April. Very shortly afterwards the bus, driven by the hijacker, knocked down and killed Mrs Topp as she was cycling home from work in Dorking Road, Epsom. . . .

In accordance with usual practice, the driver, Mr Green, left the bus in that lay-by at the bus stop at about 2.35 p.m. on 24 April 1988. He left it unlocked, with the ignition key in it. He had then a 40-minute rest period before resuming his duties driving a different bus. . . . It was taken by somebody who has never been traced just before 11.15 at night, driven for a relatively short distance until the point where Mrs Topp was knocked down and killed, and it was abandoned round the corner from there.

In these circumstances, the plaintiff's claim is founded in negligence on the basis that the bus company, knowing that there must be a threat that a bus left ready to be driven away might be stolen and that whoever stole it, a joyrider, might drive dangerously and kill or injure someone else or damage property, was in breach of duty in failing to collect the bus or see that it was locked, without an ignition key and not capable of being driven away.

. . .[I]t seems to me, as it did to May J, that there is no valid distinction between the present case and a decision of another division of this court (Stephen Brown, Nourse and Balcombe LJJ) in *Denton v United Counties Omnibus Co*. In that case, an omnibus owned by the defendants was unlawfully taken, by some person whose identity was never discovered, in the early hours of the morning from the defendants' bus station in the centre of Northampton. It was driven about a mile from the bus station and it collided with the plaintiff's motor car, which he had parked in a road near to his dwelling house, causing substantial damage to the car. Fortunately for the plaintiff in that case, the consequences of the unlawful taking of the bus were not so grave as in the present case.

. . .It was held by this court that the bus company owed no duty of care to the plaintiff and that the plaintiff's claim for damages must therefore be dismissed. All these cases in a certain sense depend on their own facts, but it is inevitable that there should be careful consideration of what, if any, valid distinctions there may be between cases which it is said should be decided differently.

I cannot see any valid distinction between the present case and *Denton's* case. . . ."

Rose L.J.: "I agree. I doubt whether, for my part, I would have found, as the judge did, that there was in the circumstances of this case a relationship of proximity between the defendants and Mrs Topp. But I entirely agree with the judge that no duty of care is shown either in principle or having regard to the authority of this court in *Denton v United Counties Omnibus Co*, which seems to me, for the reasons given by Dillon LJ, to be indistinguishable from the present case."

Peter Gibson J.: "I also agree and I share with Rose LJ the doubt as to whether the judge was right in finding that the label of proximity could be attached to the relationship between Mrs Topp and the defendants."

NOTE AND QUESTION

This is a typical example of the reluctance of English law to hold one person liable for torts committed by another person (a point often made by Tony Weir). Moreover, English law takes the view that owners of vehicles are entitled to be careless with their property if they wish (*Moorgate Mercantile v Twitchings* (1977)). Yet such a rule is probably fine where the damage is financial or at least of a type amenable to insurance protection. But is it right that the Topp family should have to bear the burden of a devastating accident arising from a train of events that is perfectly foreseeable? Do sensible vehicle owners leave their vehicles on a public highway unlocked and with the keys in the ignition? One might argue that the driver left the keys in the ignition so that a relief driver could use the bus without having to search out the first driver. Yet is this a safe system of operation? The decision in *Topp* is, with respect, a scandal (see **7.3.4** below).

7.3.2 Authorised car driver

However, where a car owner lends his or her car to another, the common law will hold the car owner liable provided that he or she has an interest in the journey: see *Morgans v Launchbury* (p.86). Normally, of course, many insurance policies cover drivers named by the owner. This form of liability is sometimes said to vicarious and thus an example of the doctrine extending beyond the employment relationship.

7.3.3 Independent contractors

The logic of vicarious liability is inescapable. If the doctrine normally applies only in cases where the tortious act is committed by an employee, then a tort committed by an independent contractor (by definition not an employee) cannot implicate the employer in liability. This logic was reconfirmed in the next extracted case.

Salsbury v Woodland [1970] 1 Q.B. 324, CA

This was an action for damages by a bystander in the street who had been watching a tree-felling operation on the defendant's land. The defendant occupier had employed an independent contractor to cut down the tree, but owing to a "near miracle of incompetence" (Sachs L.J.) the contractor allowed the tree to fall into the road taking with it some telephone wires. A car approached this scene too fast and the claimant, sensing the inevitable collision, dived out of the way and, in doing so, injured himself. The Court of Appeal (Widgery L.J., Harman L.J. and Sachs L.J.) held that the occupier was not liable.

> **Widgery L.J.:** ". . . It is trite law that an employer who employs an independent contractor is not vicariously responsible for the negligence of that contractor. He is not able to control the way in which the independent contractor does the work, and the vicarious obligation of a master for the negligence of his servant does not arise under the relationship of employer and independent contractor. I think that it is entirely accepted that those cases—and there are some—in which an employer has been held liable for injury done by the negligence of an independent contractor are in truth cases where the employer owes a direct duty to the person injured, a duty which he cannot delegate to the contractor on his behalf. The whole

question here is whether the occupier is to be judged by the general rule, which would result in no liability, or whether he comes within one of the somewhat special exceptions—cases in which a direct duty to see that care is taken rests upon the employer throughout the operation. . . .

In truth, according to the authorities there are a number of well-determined classes of case in which this direct and primary duty upon an employer to see that care is taken exists. Two such classes are directly relevant for consideration in the present case. The first class concerns what have sometimes been described as 'extra-hazardous acts'—acts commissioned by an employer which are so hazardous in their character that the law has thought it proper to impose this direct obligation on the employer to see that care is taken. An example of such a case is *Honeywill & Stein Ltd v Larkin Bros (London's Commercial Photographers) Ltd* [1934] 1 KB 191. Other cases which one finds in the books are cases where the activity commissioned by the employer is the keeping of dangerous things within the rule in *Rylands v Fletcher* (1868) LR 3 HL 330 and where liability is not dependent on negligence at all.

I do not propose to add to the wealth of authority on this topic by attempting further to define the meaning of 'extra-hazardous acts'; but I am confident that the act commissioned in the present case cannot come within that category. The act commissioned in the present case, if done with ordinary elementary caution by skilled men, presented no hazard to anyone at all.

The second class of case, which is relevant for consideration, concerns dangers created in a highway. There are a number of cases on this branch of the law, a good example of which is *Holliday v National Telephone Co* [1899] 2 QB 392. These, on analysis, will all be found to be cases where work was being done in a highway and was work of a character which would have been a nuisance unless authorised by statute. It will be found in all these cases that the statutory powers under which the employer commissioned the work were statutory powers which left upon the employer a duty to see that due care was taken in the carrying out of the work, for the protection of those who passed on the highway. In accordance with principle, an employer subject to such a direct and personal duty cannot excuse himself, if things go wrong, merely because the direct cause of the injury was the act of the independent contractor.

This again is not a case in that class. It is not a case in that class because in the instant case no question of doing work in the highway, which might amount to a nuisance if due care was not taken, arises. In my judgment, the present case is clearly outside the well defined limit of the second class to which I have referred. . . ."

QUESTIONS

1. What if the tree-felling independent contractor did not have liability insurance? Could the bystander sue the employer of the contractor?

2. A military hospital is closed down in order to save the army money and its activities are handed over to the private sector. A soldier injured on active service is negligently treated in the private hospital and suffers further harm. Can he sue the MOD for damages for this further harm? (cf. *A (A Child) v Minister of Defence* (2004).)

7.3.4 Non-delegable duty

There do appear to be some cases where an employer is held liable for torts committed by an independent contractor. However, as the next extracts will indicate, a close examination of these cases will reveal that they are not actually vicarious liability decisions. The defendant is in breach of a *direct* duty to the claimant and such a duty cannot be delegated to an independent contractor.

McDermid v Nash Dredging and Reclamation Co [1987] A.C. 906, HL

This was an action for damages by a deckhand on a tug against his employer for an injury received from mooring ropes which entrapped him when the tug moved off without warning. The accident was caused by the negligence of the captain of the tug, but as the captain was not actually employed by the defendants it was argued that he was not a servant and thus could not involve the defendants in liability. The House of Lords (Lords Bridge, Hailsham, Brandon, Mackay and Ackner) dismissed an appeal against a decision holding the defendants liable.

Lord Brandon: ". . . My Lords, the Court of Appeal regarded the case as raising difficult questions of law on which clear authority was not easy to find. With great respect to the elaborate judgment of that court, I think that they have treated the case as more difficult than it really is. A statement of the relevant principle of law can be divided into three parts. First, an employer owes to his employee a duty to exercise reasonable care to ensure that the system of work provided for him is a safe one. Secondly, the provision of a safe system of work has two aspects: (a) the devising of such a system and (b) the operation of it. Thirdly, the duty concerned has been described alternatively as either personal or non-delegable. The meaning of these expressions is not self-evident and needs explaining. The essential characteristic of the duty is that, if it is not performed, it is no defence for the employer to show that he delegated its performance to a person, whether his servant or not his servant, whom he reasonably believed to be competent to perform it. Despite such delegation the employer is liable for the non-performance of the duty.

In the present case the relevant system of work in relation to the plaintiff was the system for unmooring the tug *Ina*. In the events which occurred the defendants delegated both the devising and the operating of such system to Captain Sas, who was not their servant. An essential feature of such system, if it was to be a safe one, was that Captain Sas would not work the tug's engines ahead or astern until he knew that the plaintiff had completed his work of unmooring the tug. The system which Captain Sas devised was one under which the plaintiff would let him know that he had completed that work by giving two knocks on the outside of the wheelhouse. I have already said that I agree with the Court of Appeal that there was scope, on the evidence, for a finding that that system was not a safe one. I shall assume, however, in the absence of any contrary finding by Staughton J, that that system, as devised by Captain Sas, was safe. The crucial point, however, is that, on the occasion of the plaintiff's accident, Captain Sas did not operate that system. He negligently failed to operate it in that he put the tug's engines astern at a time when the plaintiff had not given, and he, Captain Sas, could not therefore have heard, the prescribed signal of two knocks by the plaintiff on the outside of the wheelhouse. For this failure by Captain Sas to operate the system which he had devised, the defendants, as the plaintiff's employers, are personally, not vicariously, liable to him.

It was contended for the defendants that the negligence of Captain Sas was not negligence in failing to operate the safe system which he had devised. It was rather casual negligence in the course of operating such system, for which the defendants, since Captain Sas was not their servant, were not liable. I cannot accept that contention. The negligence of Captain Sas was not casual but central. It involved abandoning the safe system of work which he had devised and operating in its place a manifestly unsafe system. In the result there was a failure by the defendants, not in devising a safe system of work for the plaintiff, but in operating one.

On these grounds, which while not differing in substance from those relied on by the Court of Appeal are perhaps more simply and directly expressed, I agree with that court that the defendants are liable to the plaintiff. . . ."

NOTE

The defendant employer was held liable because he was in breach of a direct duty to the employee to provide a safe system of work. This duty is non-delegable. Equally, a carrier of goods by sea is under a direct non-delegable duty (as bailee) to the owner of the goods to provide a seaworthy ship.

Riverstone Meat Co Pty Ltd v Lancashire Shipping Co Ltd [1961] A.C. 807, HL

This was an action for damages by the owner of a cargo in respect of its damage while being transported in the defendants' unseaworthy ship. The ship was unseaworthy because it had been negligently repaired by a firm of independent contractors employed by the defendant. The defendants argued that they were not to be liable for the cargo damage because they had fulfilled their obligations towards the owner by hiring a firm of competent contractors. The trial judge and Court of Appeal dismissed the owner's action, but an appeal to the House of Lords (Lords Radcliffe, Merriman, Hodson and Keith and Viscount Simonds) was allowed.

Lord Radcliffe: ". . . I see no ground,. . . for saying that the carriers themselves were negligent in anything that they did. . . .

But there is, on the other hand, a way of looking at the intrinsic nature of the obligation that is materially different from this. It is to ask the question, when there has been damage to cargo and that damage is traceable to unseaworthiness of the vessel, whether that unseaworthiness is due to any lack of diligence in those who have been implicated by the carriers in the work of keeping or making the vessel seaworthy. . . .

Such general considerations as occur to me appear to favour the cargo owner's claim. He is not in any sense behind the scenes with regard to what is done to the vessel or how or when it is done. His concern with it begins and ends with the loading and discharge of his goods. The carrier, on the other hand, must have some form of ownership of the vessel and some measure of responsibility for seeing that it is fit and in proper condition for the carriage undertaken. He may qualify that responsibility by stipulation, if the law allows him to; or the law may write out the terms of his responsibility for him; but within those limits the responsibility is there. I should regard it as unsatisfactory, where a cargo owner has found his goods damaged through a defect in the seaworthiness of the vessel, that his rights of recovering from the carrier should depend on particular circumstances in the carrier's situation and arrangements with which the cargo owner has nothing to do; as, for instance, that liability should depend upon the measure of control that the carrier had exercised over persons engaged on surveying or repairing the ship or upon such questions as whether the carrier had, or could have done, whatever was needed by the hands of his own servants or had been sensible or prudent in getting it done by other hands. Carriers would find themselves liable or not liable, according to circumstances quite extraneous to the sea carriage itself. . . ."

Lord Keith: ". . . We are not faced with a question in the realm of tort, or negligence. The obligation is a statutory contractual obligation. The novelty, if there is one, is that the statutory obligation is expressed in terms of an obligation to exercise due diligence, etc. There is nothing, in my opinion, extravagant in saying that this is an inescapable personal obligation. The carrier cannot claim to have shed his obligation to exercise due diligence to make his ship seaworthy by selecting a firm of competent ship repairers to make his ship seaworthy. Their failure to use due diligence to do so is his failure. The question, as I see it, is not one of vicarious responsibility at all. . . ."

QUESTION

If a carrier has to warrant the seaworthiness of his ship, why did the House of Lords decide in *Davie v New Merton Board Mills* (1959) (p.192) that an employer does not warrant the safety of equipment supplied to an employee? Are things more important than people in the eyes of the law?

NOTES

1. The carrier was of course a bailee of the cargo and thus the case could well be seen as falling, today, within Diplock L.J.'s analysis in *Morris v Martin* (1966) (p.24).

2. By way of analogy to the carrier, an occupier and a landlord can be under a non-delegable duty to users of the highway in respect to the state of the property: see e.g. *Wringe v Cohen* (1940) (p.228). This duty is given expression through the tort of public nuisance. Nevertheless there are occasions when the owner or occupier can escape liability under the independent contractor principle: see e.g. *Rowe v Herman* (1997).

7.4 Liability for children

Vicarious liability in French law extends beyond employees and includes children (CC art.1384). Parents have, accordingly, been held strictly liable for a traffic accident caused by their teenage son riding his moped. In English law there is no such vicarious liability; victims injured by the act of a child will prima facie have to sue the child, who will probably have neither assets nor insurance. However the victim may be able to sue the parents or guardian if they owed him or her a direct duty of care in respect of the child.

Carmarthenshire CC v Lewis [1955] A.C. 549, HL

This was an action for damages by the widow of a lorry driver against a local authority in respect of an accident caused by the escape of a child from a nursery school. A majority of the House of Lords (Lords Goddard, Reid, Tucker and Keith; Lord Oaksey dissenting) held the authority liable.

Lord Reid: ". . . In these circumstances, two questions arise for decision. In the first place, was the escape of the child David into the street attributable to negligence of the appellants or of those for whom they are responsible? If it was, then it appears to me to be obvious that his being there alone might easily lead to an accident, and if the child had been killed or injured the appellants would have been liable in damages, for they certainly owed a duty to the child to protect him from injury. But then a second question is raised by the appellants. They say that, although they owed a duty to the child, they owed no duty to other users of the highway, and that even if they were negligent in letting the child escape onto the street they cannot be held responsible for damage to others caused by the action of the child when there.

On the first question I am of opinion that the appellants were negligent. . . . The actions of a child of this age are unpredictable, and I think that it ought to have been anticipated by the appellants or their responsible officers that in such a case a child might well try to get out onto the street and that if it did a traffic accident was far from improbable. . . .

I turn now to the second question, which is one of novelty and general importance. If the appellants are right it means that no matter how careless the person in charge of a young child may be, and no matter how obvious it may be that the child may stray into a busy street and cause an accident, yet that person is under no liability for damage to others caused solely by the action of the child because his only duty is towards the child under his care. . . .

. . .There is no absolute duty; there is only a duty not to be negligent, and a mother is not negligent unless she fails to do something which a prudent or reasonable mother in her position would have been able to do and would have done. Even a housewife who has young children cannot be in two places at once and no one would suggest that she must neglect her other duties, or that a young child must always be kept cooped up. But I think that all but the most careless mothers do take many precautions for their children's safety and the same precautions serve to protect others. I cannot see how any person in charge of a child could be held to have been negligent in a question with a third party injured in a road accident unless he or she had failed to take reasonable and practicable precaution for the safety of the child. . . .

. . .Moreover, a person who brings his animal onto a road or street and then negligently fails to look after it there is not free from liability. Counsel for the appellants did not argue that this rather illogical distinction should be applied to children, and it would be strange if a person in charge of a child were under a different duty according to whether he let the child stray from his house or garden or took the child onto the road and then let it stray there. Counsel took the only logical course and argued that even if a person takes a child into the street and then takes no care of it he cannot be held liable for damage suffered by a third party as a result of its actions, and that argument gains no support from the rules which apply to animals. . . ."

QUESTIONS

1. If a master is to be liable for torts committed by his servant, why should a parent not be strictly liable for torts committed by their child? Would such a liability materially increase household insurance premiums? Should car accidents be excluded (or at least subject to a separate insurance regime)?

2. A child of ten cycles to his local shop in order to buy a packet of turkey twizzlers for his parents; on the way back the child carelessly knocks down a pedestrian. Ought the pedestrian to be able to sue the parents for his injuries?

8 Liability for words

The idea of a liability for persons and for things is well established in civilian thinking if not in the common law mind. The category of a liability for words is rather different since this is something that probably does make more sense in English law than it does in continental thinking. Outside contract (which started life as a form of trespass liability for words), harm arising from words has not only attracted its own tort, that of defamation, but has also given rise to its own sub-category within the law of negligence. Negligent misrepresentation is both an offshoot from the neighbour principle and something of an independent area within tort thanks to the requirement of a particular type of duty of care based upon a special relationship (*Hedley Byrne v Heller* (1964), p.134). Defamation and negligence are not the only torts of relevance in this area. The tort of deceit (fraudulent misrepresentation) is of course important and so are some of the economic torts since they can often involve verbal threats. Indeed, where the words form part of an illicit agreement there may be liability in conspiracy (*Revenue & Customs v Total Network* (2008), p.117). Even trespass can be relevant (see e.g. *Wilkinson v Downton* (1897), p.8; but cf. *Wainwright v Home office* (2004), p.77) and this tort is now supplemented by a statutory tort of harassment (see Protection from Harassment Act 1997, p.114; *Majrowski v Guy's and St Thomas' NHS Trust* (2007), p.262). In short, words are an important vehicle for causing damage and in English law they can act as a focal point for a number of torts.

8.1 General considerations: words and interests

To talk in terms of a coherent law of liability arising from words is impossible, just as it is to talk of a fully comprehensive liability for things or liability for persons. These broad terms are, in English law at least, organising ideas and no more (although useful ones). Other categories and concepts need to be bought into play. This is true even for a well-defined category like the tort of negligence; notions such as duty and interest (personal injury, economic etc.) are equally important when it comes to analysing a litigation problem arising out of carelessly caused harm. The first extract in this chapter will thus raise the issue of the relationship between words and protected interests as well as introducing the two main torts associated with harm arising from words.

> **Peter Birks, 'Equity in the Modern Law: An Exercise in Taxonomy', (1996) 26** *The University of Western Australia Law Review* **1, pp.5–6 (footnotes omitted)**
>
> "The House of Lords recently decided *Spring v Guardian Assurance* [see below p.287]. An employer wrote a reference which made incorrect assertions of fact about a former employee and thus caused that employee pure economic loss. Was the employer liable in negligence?

The answer was yes. This is somewhat surprising. The reference was a communication which was subject to qualified privilege having been written as a matter of duty to a person with an interest to receive it. In defamation the employer could not therefore have been liable without proof of malice. One commentator asks whether, if the case had been argued in defamation, the House of Lords would have changed the law applicable to that tort. Since the law seemingly was that such a defendant could not be liable except for malice, and since the law is that he can be liable for negligence, one might equally put the question differently. Has not the decision in negligence changed the law of defamation?

This is a conundrum of disorderly categories. It is a species of problem which disfigures the law. It is discreditably elementary. Two categories intersect. Defamation is a wrong, like inducing breach of contract or interference with chattels, which is manifestly named by reference to the interest infringed. Defamation is an infringement of the interest in reputation. Negligence is a wrong named by reference to a kind of fault. It follows that the two categories must intersect. In other words infringement of the interest in reputation will often be negligent. Is there then one wrong or two? My canary is yellow and eats seeds. If all birds are seed-eaters, yellow, or others, my canary counts twice. Are there two birds or one? If there come to be two birds, the double-vision is due to bent classification. There is only one bird.

. . . The whole law of tort is bedevilled by the same essentially trivial problem. The law cannot tolerate, or should not be able to tolerate, torts named so as to intersect. . . ."

NOTES

1. Professor Birks sadly died in 2004. An obituary recording his enormous contribution to academic law can be found in *The Guardian*, July 16, 2004, p.31.

2. This extract from Birks is important in a number of ways. First, it shows how particular torts can be linked to particular interests: defamation is a tort protecting the reputation interest. Secondly it emphasises in outline the difference, in the area of liability for words, between the torts of defamation and negligence. Thirdly, it suggests that law and legal method should be one of deduction; solutions to legal problems are not to be found by searching amongst the facts to see if they can be fitted within some tort or other (cf. e.g. *Esso v Southport* (1954) per Denning L.J., above p.5). It is a matter of logical inference from a carefully constructed reasoning model of non-intersecting categories. Nevertheless the assumptions that Professor Birks makes are open to challenge. One might start by asking what interests negligence protects. If one reasonable response is to say that, where there has been a misrepresentation, it will protect economic interests, one could argue that the House of Lords was thus justified in applying *Hedley Byrne* (1964) (p.134) to the facts of *Spring v Guardian Assurance* (1995) (see below p.287). After all Mr Spring suffered severe economic loss as a result of the incorrect reference letter (as various newspapers reported at the time). But a further challenge can also be mounted, as the next extract will indicate.

Stephen Waddams, *Dimensions of Private Law*, Cambridge University Press, 2003, pp.12–13, 14 (footnotes omitted)

"A related problem is the absence of uniformity in the reasoning and conclusions of judges, both within particular jurisdictions and from one jurisdiction to another. Thus in *White v*

Jones [see below p.289] . . . where loss was caused to an intended beneficiary by a lawyer's failure to prepare a will in due time, the three majority judges and the two dissenting judges all took different approaches. A differently constituted panel of English judges could very well have reached the opposite conclusion, as has indeed occurred on this question in other common law jurisdictions. This diversity also tends to impede a close analogy between judicial reasoning and the mapping of geographical territory. . . .

Another obstacle to conceptual organization has been the complexity of the relation between facts and law. The facts of a case are defined in relation to legal principles, but the principles themselves are formulated in relation to facts, real or hypothetical. Facts may be stated at countless levels of particularity, and legal issues and legal rules may be formulated at countless levels of generality. No map or scheme could possibly classify all imaginable facts, for there is no limit whatever to the number of facts that may be postulated of a sequence of human events. The selection of legally relevant facts is a matter not of empirical investigation but of judgment, and not wholly separable from the formulation of the applicable legal rule. Facts are selected and marshalled to fit perceived rules of law, but the rules themselves change in response to facts, often by deploying concepts and categories that had not formerly been supposed to be applicable. . . ."

NOTES

1. These important and insightful paragraphs from Professor Waddams could well have been located at the very beginning of this book. But they are particularly apt here because, as we have seen from the Professor Birks extract, the law has been developing quite rapidly for half a century. Moreover, situations where harm is said to arise from words are particularly complex, not just because the meaning of language is complex, but equally because of "the cumulative weight of a number of legal concepts operating concurrently" (Waddams, above). Duty, right, interest, fault, damage and so on are often competing within the judgments in complex misrepresentation and defamation cases.

2. It might be useful to turn by way of introduction to the law itself to short extracts from the two cases that have stimulated the above debate between academic writers.

Spring v Guardian Assurance Plc **[1995] 2 A.C. 296, HL**

In this action for damages by an employee against an ex-employer, in respect of economic loss arising out of an inaccurate reference, a majority of the House of Lords (Lords Goff, Lowry, Slynn and Woolf; Lord Keith dissenting) gave judgment for the employee.

Lord Goff: ". . . The central issue in this appeal is whether a person who provides a reference in respect of another who was formerly engaged by him as a member of his staff (at this point I use a deliberately neutral term) may be liable in damages to that other in respect of economic loss suffered by him by reason of negligence in the preparation of the reference. . . .

Prima facie (ie, subject to the point on defamation, which I will have to consider later), it is my opinion that an employer who provides a reference in respect of one of his employees to a prospective future employer will ordinarily owe a duty of care to his employee in respect of the preparation of the reference. The employer is possessed of special knowledge, derived from his experience of the employee's character, skill and diligence in the performance of his duties while working for the employer. . . . The provision of such references is a service regularly provided by employers to their employees; indeed, references are part of the currency of the modern employment market. Furthermore, when such a reference is provided by an employer, it is plain that the employee relies upon him to exercise due skill and care in the preparation of the reference before making it available to the third party. In these circumstances, it seems to me that all the elements requisite for the application of the *Hedley Byrne* principle are present. I need only add that, in the context under consideration, there is no question of the circumstances in which the reference is provided being, for example, so informal as to negative an assumption of responsibility by the employer. . . .

. . . Since, for the reasons I have given, it is my opinion that in cases such as the present the duty of care arises by reason of an assumption of responsibility by the employer to the employee in respect of the relevant reference, I can see no good reason why the duty to exercise due skill and care which rests upon the employer should be negatived because, if the plaintiff were instead to bring an action for damage to his reputation, he would be met by the defence of qualified privilege which could only be defeated by proof of malice. It is not to be forgotten that the *Hedley Byrne* duty arises where there is a relationship which is, broadly speaking, either contractual or equivalent to contract. In these circumstances, I cannot see that principles of the law of defamation are of any relevance. . . ."

Lord Keith (dissenting): ". . . In my opinion the same grounds of public policy are applicable where the claim is based not on defamation as such but on negligence associated with the making or publication of an untrue statement, where the occasion on which that was done was a privileged one in the sense in which that expression is used in the context of defamation law. If liability in negligence were to follow from a reference prepared without reasonable care, the same adverse consequences would flow as those sought to be guarded against by the defence of qualified privilege. Those asked to give a reference would be inhibited from speaking frankly lest it should be found that they were liable in damages through not taking sufficient care in its preparation. They might well prefer, if under no legal duty to give a reference, to refrain from doing so at all. Any reference given might be bland and unhelpful and information which it would be in the interest of those seeking the reference to receive might be withheld. . . ."

Lord Slynn: ". . . [T]he starting-point in my view is that the suggested claim in negligence and the torts of defamation and injurious and malicious falsehood do not cover the same ground, as Mr Tony Weir shows in his note in [1993] CLJ 376. They are separate torts, defamation not requiring a proof by the plaintiff that the statement was untrue (though justification may be a defence) or that he suffered economic damage, but being subject to defences quite different from those in negligence, such as the defence of qualified privilege which makes it necessary to prove malice. Malicious falsehood requires proof that the statement is false, that harm has resulted and that there was express malice. Neither of these involves the concept of a duty of care. The essence of a claim in defamation is that a person's reputation has been damaged; it may or not involve the loss of a job or economic loss. A claim that a reference has been given negligently is essentially based on the fact, not so much that reputation has been damaged, as that a job, or an opportunity, has been lost. A statement carelessly made may not be defamatory—a statement that a labourer is 'lame,' a secretary 'very arthritic,' when neither statement is true, though they were true of some other employee mistakenly confused with the person named.

I do not for my part consider that to recognise the existence of a duty of care in some situations when a reference is given necessarily means that the law of defamation has to be changed or that a substantial section of the law relating to defamation and malicious falsehood is 'emasculated' (Court of Appeal, at p. 437). They remain distinct torts. It may be that there will be less resort to these torts because a more realistic approach on the basis of a duty of care is adopted. If to recognise that such a duty of care exists means that there have to be such changes—either by excluding the defence of qualified privilege from the master-servant situation or by withdrawing the privilege where negligence as opposed to express malice is shown—then I would in the interests of recognising a fair, just and reasonable result in the master-servant situation accept such change. . . ."

NOTES

1. This case is ideal for anyone who wishes to approach liability from the position of damage done by words. First, Lord Goff sets out the requirements of liability under the *Hedley Byrne* principle (cf. p.134). These are special relationship, reliance and professional (rather than informal) context. Secondly, the majority take a step towards a more general idea of a liability for words in refusing to erect liability barriers between those various independent torts—defamation, malicious falsehood and negligence—which can apply in factual situations involving reference letters (see **3.5.2** for the tort of malicious falsehood).

2. The case is also important for some points made in observations that have *not* been extracted above (for want of space). For example, Lord Woolf specifically said the case was about the balancing of *interests* between employers and employees (for an analogous type of interest analysis see *D v East Berks NHS Trust* (2005), p.172). In other words, the nature and severity of the damage vis-à-vis the behaviour of the writer of the reference are vital focal points. Furthermore, Lord Woolf also made the point that the claim was for pure economic loss; this is the typical damage that arises from misstatements. In addition, two judges stressed the importance and role of the particular facts in arriving at the decision as to whether principle (*Hedley Byrne*) and policy dictate liability. In short, the decision confirms Professor Waddams' analysis of the common law mentality.

3. But Professor Waddams specifically mentions another case. This decision, set out below, can be seen as extending the *Hedley Byrne* principle (either directly or by way of analogy) and thus it could be relevant in establishing the idea of a 'misstatement' by silence or inaction.

White v Jones **[1995] 2 A.C. 207, HL**

This was an action for damages in negligence brought against a firm of solicitors by two disappointed daughters who expected to benefit under their late father's will. They did not benefit as a result of the solicitor's negligence. The House of Lords (Lords Goff, Browne-Wilkinson and Nolan; Lords Keith and Mustill dissenting) allowed their claim.

Lord Goff: "My Lords, in this appeal, your Lordships' House has to consider for the first time the much discussed question whether an intended beneficiary under a will is entitled to recover damages from the testator's solicitors by reason of whose negligence the testator's intention to benefit him under the will has failed to be carried into effect . . . In the present case, the testator's solicitors negligently delayed the preparation of a fresh will in place of a previous will which the testator had decided to revoke, and the testator died before the new will was prepared. The plaintiffs were the two daughters of the testator who would have benefited under the fresh will but received nothing under the previous will which, by reason of the solicitors' delay, remained unrevoked. . . .

. . . [T]he question is one which has been much discussed, not only in this country and other common law countries, but also in some civil law countries, notably Germany. . . . In Germany a disappointed beneficiary may be entitled to claim damages from the testator's negligent solicitor under the principle known as contract with protective effect for third parties (*Vertrag mit Schutzwirkung für Dritte*). . . . It also appears that a similar conclusion would be reached in France: . . ., which appears to be based on the broad principle that a notary is responsible, even as against third parties, for all fault causing damage committed by him in the exercise of his functions. On facts very similar to those of the present case, the Court of Appeal of Amsterdam has held a notary liable in negligence to the intended beneficiary . . .

The conceptual difficulties

Even so, it has been recognised on all hands that *Ross v Caunters* raises difficulties of a conceptual nature, and that as a result it is not altogether easy to accommodate the decision within the ordinary principles of our law of obligations . . .

It is right however that I should immediately summarise these conceptual difficulties. They are as follows.

(1) First, the general rule is well established that a solicitor acting on behalf of a client owes a duty of care only to his client. . . .
(2) A further reason is given which is said to reinforce the conclusion that no duty of care is owed by the solicitor to the beneficiary in tort. Here, it is suggested, is one of those situations in which a plaintiff is entitled to damages if, and only if, he can establish a breach of contract by the defendant. . . . Such a claim falls within the exclusive zone of contractual liability; and it is contrary to principle that the law of tort should be allowed to invade that zone . . .
(3) A third, and distinct, objection is that, if liability in tort was recognised in cases such as *Ross v Caunters*, it would be impossible to place any sensible bounds to cases in which such recovery was allowed . . .
(4) Other miscellaneous objections were taken, though in my opinion they were without substance . . .
(5) There is however another objection of a conceptual nature, which was not adumbrated in argument before the Appellate Committee. In the present case, unlike *Ross v Caunters* itself, there was no act of the defendant solicitor which could be characterised as negligent. All that happened was that the solicitor did nothing at all for a period of

time . . . As a general rule, however, there is no liability in tortious negligence for an omission, unless the defendant is under some pre-existing duty. Once again, therefore, the question arises how liability can arise in the present case in the absence of a contract . . .

The impulse to do practical justice

Before addressing the legal questions which lie at the heart of the present case, it is, I consider, desirable to identify the reasons of justice which prompt judges and academic writers to conclude . . . that a duty should be owed . . . to a disappointed beneficiary. The principal reasons are, I believe, as follows.

(1) In the forefront stands the extraordinary fact that, if such a duty is not recognised, the only persons who might have a valid claim (ie the testator and his estate) have suffered no loss, and the only person who has suffered a loss (ie the disappointed beneficiary) has no claim . . . It can therefore be said that, if the solicitor owes no duty to the intended beneficiaries, there is a lacuna in the law which needs to be filled. This I regard as being a point of cardinal importance in the present case.

(2) The injustice of denying such a remedy is reinforced if one considers the importance of legacies in a society which recognises (. . .) the right of citizens to leave their assets to whom they please, and in which, as a result, legacies can be of great importance to individual citizens, providing very often the only opportunity for a citizen to acquire a significant capital sum; or to inherit a house, so providing a secure roof over the heads of himself and his family; or to make special provision for his or her old age . . .

(3) There is a sense in which the solicitors' profession cannot complain if such a liability may be imposed upon their members. If one of them has been negligent in such a way as to defeat his client's testamentary intentions, he must regard himself as very lucky indeed if the effect of the law is that he is not liable to pay damages in the ordinary way. . . .

(4) That such a conclusion is required as a matter of justice is reinforced by consideration of the role played by solicitors in society . . .

A contractual approach

It may be suggested that, in cases such as the present, the simplest course would be to solve the problem by making available to the disappointed beneficiary, by some means or another, the benefit of the contractual rights (such as they are) of the testator or his estate against the negligent solicitor, as is for example done under the German principle of *Vertrag mit Schutzwirkung für Dritte*. Indeed that course has been urged upon us by Professor Markesinis in 'An Expanding Tort Law' (1987) 103 LQR 354 at 396–397, echoing a view expressed by Professor Fleming in 'Comparative Law of Torts' (1986) 4 OJLS 235 at 241. Attractive though this solution is, there is unfortunately a serious difficulty in its way. The doctrine of consideration still forms part of our law of contract, as does the doctrine of privity of contract which is considered to exclude the recognition of a *jus quaesitum tertio*. To proceed as Professor Markesinis has suggested may be acceptable in German law, but in this country could be open to criticism as an illegitimate circumvention of these long-established doctrines; and this criticism could be reinforced by reference to the fact that, in the case of carriage of goods by sea, a contractual solution to a particular of transferred loss, and to other cognate problems, was provided only by recourse to Parliament. Furthermore, I myself do not consider that the present case provides a suitable occasion for reconsideration of doctrines so fundamental as these . . .

The tortious solution

I therefore return to the law of tort for a solution to the problem. For the reasons I have already given, an ordinary action in tortious negligence on the lines proposed by Megarry V-C in *Ross v Caunters* [1980] Ch 297 must, with the greatest respect, be regarded as inappropriate, because it does not meet any of the conceptual problems which have been raised. Furthermore, for the reasons I have previously given, the *Hedley Byrne* principle cannot, in the absence of special circumstances, give rise on ordinary principles to an assumption of responsibility by the testator's solicitor towards an intended beneficiary. Even so, it seems to me that it is open to your Lordships' House, as in *Linden Gardens Trust Ltd v Lenesta Sludge Disposals Ltd* [1994] 1 AC 85, to fashion a remedy to fill a lacuna in the law and so prevent the injustice which would otherwise occur on the facts of cases such as the present. In the *Lenesta Sludge* case, as I have said, the House made available a remedy as a matter of law to solve the problem of transferred loss in the case before them. The present case is, if anything, *a fortiori*, since the nature of the transaction was such that, if the solicitors were negligent and their negligence did not come to light until after the death of the testator, there would be no remedy for the ensuing loss unless the intended beneficiary could claim. In my opinion, therefore, your Lordships' House should in cases such as these extend to the intended beneficiary a remedy under the *Hedley Byrne* principle by holding that the assumption of responsibility by the solicitors towards his client should be held in law to extend to the intended beneficiary who (as the solicitor can reasonably foresee) may, as a result of the solicitor's negligence, be deprived of his intended legacy in circumstances in which neither the testator nor his estate will have a remedy against the solicitor . . . I only wish to add that, with the benefit of experience during the 15 years in which *Ross v Caunters* has been regularly applied, we can say with some confidence that a direct remedy by the intended beneficiary against the solicitor appears to create no problems in practice. That is therefore the solution which I would recommend to your Lordships. . . ."

Lord Keith of Kinkel (dissenting): ". . . To admit the plaintiffs' claim in the present case would in substance, in my opinion, be to give them the benefit of a contract to which they were not parties.

Further, there is, in my opinion, no decided case the grounds of decision in which are capable of being extended incrementally and by way of analogy so as to admit of a remedy in tort being made available to the plaintiffs . . .

Upon the whole matter I have found the conceptual difficulties involved in the plaintiffs' claim, which are fully recognised by all your Lordships, to be too formidable to be resolved by any process of reasoning compatible with existing principles of law . . .

I would therefore allow the appeal."

Lord Mustill (dissenting): ". . . Here,. . . to enable the estate, in title of the deceased testator, to recover a sum equivalent to the disappointed expectations of the beneficiaries would be to compensate it for a loss which it not only had not, but could not have, suffered. The plaintiffs' complaint and the consequent damage are quite different from the complaint and the damage to which the estate succeeded on the death of the testator. To allow them to be treated as if they were the same would extend the boundaries of a contractual obligation far further than has ever been previously contemplated; and, I suspect further than has been contemplated even in the majority of those jurisdictions where concepts of privity are less rigorous than in our own.

Furthermore, even if the doctrine [of transferred loss] were to be fully received into English law I am unable to visualise how it could help the plaintiffs here. As its name denotes it is concerned with the transfer of loss to the claimant from someone else. In the present case the intended beneficiaries do not need such a transfer, for they already have a loss. Their problem is to find a cause of action, and to achieve this a quite different kind of transfer would be required . . .”

NOTES

1. This case is obviously an important precedent, but it is not that easy to decide exactly what the precedent is. The view seems to be that the courts fashioned a remedy for a particular set of circumstances on the ground of practical justice (see e.g. Lord Steyn in *Att-Gen v Blake* (2001), above p.58). And so one can seemingly predict that the case is an important professional liability authority (see **8.5** below), at least where the professional defendant is a solicitor. But what are the wider implications? It may be that the principle of liability for negligent misstatement as established by *Hedley Byrne* (p.134) is capable of extension not just directly but also by analogy. However in *White* all the ingredients of *Hedley Byrne* seemed to be weak or missing: there was, it seems, no misstatement as such, no reliance, and no special relationship. Yet, as Professor Waddams indicates (see above p.286), much depends on how one views the facts. If one talks of a ‘family’ solicitor it becomes possible to argue that such a solicitor owes a duty not just to individuals but to the family as a whole. One relies upon the family solicitor and it is a professional relationship that could be said to be special vis-à-vis each of the testator’s immediate family. Perhaps, then, the facts do have something compelling in them, just as in the family case of *Jackson v Horizon Holidays* (1975) (C&MC, p.396) where the Court of Appeal also achieved a kind of ‘practical justice’. One might note, equally, how the House of Lords ‘fashioned’ a remedy to aid a family member in *Beswick v Beswick* (1968) (C&MC, p.564). But cf. *D v East Berks NHS Trust* (2005) (pp.72, 344).

2. For a case where the claimant argued that a local authority was negligent in failing to put up warning words see: *Gorringe v Calderdale MBC* (2002) (p.344).

3. Can a person be liable for economic loss for a failure to issue instructions? (cf. *Customs & Excise Commissioners v Barclays Bank* (2007), p.137.)

8.2 Defamation (1): general liability

One of the key torts giving rise to a liability for words is the tort of defamation. This, at a very abstract level, is an easy tort to comprehend once one appreciates how it neatly falls into two parts, namely elements of liability (this section) and defences (next section: **8.3**). Perhaps one should add a third part, that of damages, since they have given rise to their own rules and legislative intervention (see **11.4.5**). At a more detailed level it is exceptionally complex. This complexity results from a number of factors: the meaning of language, the ever-more detailed procedural refinements (including jury trial), the plethora of case law and, now, the human rights dimension. This latter point helps emphasise that defamation extends beyond the category of tort and into the realm of constitutional law. It is a central topic in freedom of expression.

8.2.1 Introduction to defamation

The following extracts are intended to provide a number of general observations on the tort of defamation.

Horrocks v Lowe [1975] A.C. 135, HL

Lord Diplock: ". . . My Lords, as a general rule English law gives effect to the ninth commandment that a man shall not speak evil falsely of his neighbour. It supplies a temporal sanction: if he cannot prove that defamatory matter which he published was true, he is liable in damages to whomever he has defamed, except where the publication is oral only, causes no damage and falls outside the categories of slander actionable per se. The public interest that the law should provide an effective means whereby a man can vindicate his reputation against calumny has nevertheless to be accommodated to the competing public interest in permitting men to communicate frankly and freely with one another about matters in respect of which the law recognises that they have a duty to perform or an interest to protect in doing so. What is published in good faith on matters of these kinds is published on a privileged occasion. It is not actionable even though it be defamatory and turns out to be untrue. With some exceptions. . . the privilege is not absolute but qualified. It is lost if the occasion which gives rise to it is misused. For in all cases of qualified privilege there is some special reason of public policy why the law accords immunity from suit—the existence of some public or private duty, whether legal or moral, on the part of the maker of the defamatory statement which justifies his communicating it or of some interest of his own which he is entitled to protect by doing so. If he uses the occasion for some other reason he loses the protection of the privilege . . ."

NOTES

1. Defamation divides into two sub-torts, slander and libel. The distinction was once easy enough to comprehend: slander was concerned with verbal defamation while libel dealt with written defamation. However new forms of communication have created ambiguous areas: see e.g. *Youssoupoff v MGM Pictures* (1934); Defamation Act 1952 s.16; Theatres Act 1968 s.4.

2. Defamation is not only a tort of strict liability—reputation being treated as equivalent to a property right (Ibbetson, *A Historical Introduction to the Law of Obligations*, OUP, 1999, p.186)—but libel (words in permanent form) does not require proof of any actual damage. It is actionable *per se*. This latter point is not true of slander (spoken words) save in certain situations.

3. The strict nature of defamation has given rise to much criticism, some of which is reflected in Lord Steyn's observation in the next extract. However Lord Nicholls defends the need to protect the reputation interest.

***Reynolds v Times Newspapers Ltd* [2001] 2 A.C. 127, HL.**

(For facts and further extracts see p.312)

Lord Steyn (dissenting): ". . . *Weir, A Casebook on Tort*, 8th ed., (1996) describes defamation as 'the oddest' of the torts. He explains (at p. 525):

'he (the plaintiff) can get damages (swingeing damages!) for a statement made to others without showing that the statement was untrue, without showing that the statement did him the slightest harm, and without showing that the defendant was in any way wrong to make it (much less that the defendant owed him any duty of any kind)'

Weir, at p. 530, observes that 'the courts could arguably have done more to prevent the law becoming as absurd, complex and unfair as it is, without resigning themselves to saying, as Diplock LJ did, that the law of defamation 'has passed beyond redemption by the courts' (*Slim v. Daily Telegraph Ltd*. [1968] 2 QB 157, 179). Weir states that 'the law of England is certainly stricter than that of any free country. . .' at p. 528. The argument for addressing the chilling effect of our defamation law on political speech and for striking a better balance between freedom of speech and defamation is strong: see Eric Barendt and others, *Libel and the Media: The Chilling Effect*, (1997), Clarendon Press, Oxford, pp. 191–192. . . ."

Lord Nicholls: ". . . Reputation is an integral and important part of the dignity of the individual. It also forms the basis of many decisions in a democratic society which are fundamental to its well-being: whom to employ or work for, whom to promote, whom to do business with or to vote for. Once besmirched by an unfounded allegation in a national newspaper, a reputation can be damaged for ever, especially if there is no opportunity to vindicate one's reputation. When this happens, society as well as the individual is the loser. For it should not be supposed that protection of reputation is a matter of importance only to the affected individual and his family. Protection of reputation is conducive to the public good. It is in the public interest that the reputation of public figures should not be debased falsely. In the political field, in order to make an informed choice, the electorate needs to be able to identify the good as well as the bad. Consistently with these considerations, human rights conventions recognise that freedom of expression is not an absolute right. Its exercise may be subject to such restrictions as are prescribed by law and are necessary in a democratic society for the protection of the reputations of others. . . ."

QUESTION

Is dignity the interest protected by defamation?

8.2.2 Defamatory statements

The first substantive question in defamation concerns its definition. As we shall see, the standard definition—the publication of a statement which tends to lower a person in the estimation of right-thinking members of society—turns out to be meaningless and thus a more practical question is this. What amounts to a defamatory statement?

Berkoff v Burchill [1996] 4 All E.R. 1008, CA

Neill L.J.: "This appeal raises questions as to the meaning of the word 'defamatory' and as to the nature of an action for defamation. The facts can be stated quite shortly. The plaintiff, Mr Steven Berkoff is an actor, director and writer who is well known for his work on stage, screen and television. The first defendant, Miss Julie Burchill, is a journalist and writer who at the material times was retained to write articles about the cinema for the Sunday Times. The second defendants, Times Newspapers Limited, are the publishers of the Sunday Times.

In the issue of the Sunday Times dated 30 January 1994 Miss Burchill wrote a review of the film 'The Age of Innocence'. In the course of the review, in a general reference to film directors, Miss Burchill wrote:

'. . . film directors, from Hitchcock to Berkoff are notoriously hideous-looking people.'

Nine months later Miss Burchill returned to the same theme in a review of the film 'Frankenstein'. In this review, which was published in the issue of the Sunday Times dated 6 November 1994, Miss Burchill described a character in the film called 'the Creature'. She wrote:

'The Creature is made as a vessel for Waldman's brain, and rejected in disgust when it comes out scarred and primeval. It's a very new look for the Creature—no bolts in the neck or flat-top hairdo—and I think it works; its a lot like Stephen Berkoff, only marginally better-looking.'. . .

It will be seen from this collection of definitions that words may be defamatory, even though they neither impute disgraceful conduct to the plaintiff nor any lack of skill or efficiency in the conduct of his trade or business or professional activity, if they hold him up to contempt scorn or ridicule or tend to exclude him from society. On the other hand insults which do not diminish a man's standing among other people do not found an action for libel or slander. The exact borderline may often be difficult to define. . . .

It is trite law that the meaning of words in a libel action is determined by the reaction of the ordinary reader and not by the intention of the publisher, but the perceived intention of the publisher may colour the meaning. In the present case it would in my view be open to a jury to conclude that in the context the remarks about Mr Berkoff gave the impression that he was not merely physically unattractive in appearance but actually repulsive. It seems to me that to say this of someone in the public eye who makes his living, in part at least, as an actor, is capable of lowering his standing in the estimation of the public and of making him an object of ridicule

I confess that I have found this to be a far from easy case, but in the end I am satisfied that it would be wrong to decide this preliminary issue in a way which would withdraw the matter completely from the consideration of a jury."

Millett L.J. (dissenting): "Many a true word is spoken in jest. Many a false one too. But chaff and banter are not defamatory, and even serious imputations are not actionable if no one would take them to be meant seriously. The question, however, is how the words would be understood, not how they were meant, and that issue is pre-eminently one for the jury. So, however difficult it may be, we must assume that Miss Julie Burchill might be taken seriously. The question then is: is it defamatory to say of a man that he is 'hideously ugly'?. . .

The submission illustrates the danger of trusting to verbal formulae. Defamation has never been satisfactorily defined. All attempted definitions are illustrative. None of them is exhaustive. All can be misleading if they cause one to forget that defamation is an attack on reputation, that is on a man's standing in the world. . . .

The line between mockery and defamation may sometimes be difficult to draw. When it is it should be left to the jury to draw it. Despite the respect which is due to the opinion of Neill LJ, whose experience in this field is unrivalled, I am not persuaded that the present case could properly be put on the wrong side of the line. A decision that it is an actionable wrong to describe a man as "hideously ugly" would be an unwarranted restriction on free speech. And if a bald statement to this effect would not be capable of being defamatory, I do not see how a humorously exaggerated observation to the like effect could be. People must be allowed to poke fun at one another without fear of litigation. It is one thing to ridicule a man; it is another to expose him to ridicule. Miss Burchill made a cheap joke at Mr Berkoff's expense; she may thereby have demeaned herself, but I do not believe that she defamed Mr Berkoff.

If I have appeared to treat Mr Berkoff's claim with unjudicial levity it is because I find it impossible to take it seriously. Despite the views of my brethren, who are both far more experienced than I am, I remain of the opinion that the proceedings are as frivolous as Miss Burchill's article. The time of the Court ought not to be taken up with either of them. I would allow the appeal and dismiss the Action."

Phillips L.J.: ". . . Where the issue is whether words have damaged a Plaintiff's reputation by exposing him to ridicule, that question cannot be answered simply by considering whether the natural and ordinary meaning of the words used is defamatory per se. The question has to be considered in the light of the actual words used and the circumstance in which they are used. There are many ways of indicating that a person is hideously ugly, ranging from a simple statement of opinion to that effect, which I feel could never be defamatory, to words plainly intended to convey that message by way of ridicule.

The words used in this case fall into the latter category. Whether they have exposed the Plaintiff to ridicule to the extent that his reputation has been damaged must be answered by the Jury. The preliminary point raised by the Defendant cannot be answered in the affirmative and this appeal should be dismissed."

NOTE

This case is 'important' in that it indicates that almost any statement critical of another, however frivolous, can be defamatory. Furthermore it perhaps gives some support to the following editorial comment: "Libel is often played as farce. Vain pop stars, self-important actresses and—yes—even editors can cut comic figures as they seek to protect their precious reputations in the mock Gothic majesty of the High Court. But the dishonest use of libel laws to suppress legitimate reporting activities of people in public life is no joke" (Editorial, *The Guardian*, June 9, 1999, p.21). This editorial was written after yet another politician had been exposed as a liar, cheat and perjurer in defamation proceedings initiated by the politician (hoping to get a tax-free windfall).

QUESTIONS

1. It so happened that in 1994 there were two academics at Lancaster University with the name 'Geoffrey Samuel'. What would have been the position if a newspaper had printed a defamatory article about Geoffrey Samuel of Lancaster University believing, wrongly, that the defamatory allegation was true of one of the academics (and not knowing of the existence of the second academic)? Could both academics sue? (cf. *Newstead v London Express Newspapers* (1940).)

2. What is the position if a magazine prints a serious story about a named woman raped by a named man. The story is based on a true experience but the names of the woman and the man are changed to fictional names. However it so happens that there are real people with these names. Can they both sue the magazine for defamation? (cf. *Hulton & Co v Jones* (1910).)

3. An Internet pornography site advertises itself using the photograph of a model. However the model has a very similar face to a respectable vicar and there is some gossip among the parishioners. Can the vicar sue the Internet site publisher for defamation? (cf. *O'Shea v MGN* (2001).)

4. Millett L.J. talks of a 'man's standing in the world'. What about a woman's?

8.2.3 Innuendo

What if a journalist had written of an actor that he made Frankenstein Creature look handsome? In other words, what if the journalist had made disparaging marks by innuendo? As the next case shows, innuendo can amount to defamation but there are some limits.

> *Lewis v Daily Telegraph* **[1964] A.C. 234HL**
>
> This was an action for damages in defamation brought by a company and its chairman against two newspapers. The newspapers had published columns headed 'Fraud Squad Probe Firm' and 'Inquiry on Firm by City Police' and went on to state that the police were inquiring into the affairs of claimant company. The claimants alleged that the words were defamatory in that they suggested that the two claimants were guilty of fraud. The trial judge directed the jury that the words were capable of bearing the alleged defamatory innuendo and the jury returned verdicts in favour of the claimants. They awarded damages of £25,000 to the chairman and £75,000 to the company against one newspaper and £17,000 and £100,000 against the other newspaper (very large sums indeed in 1964). On appeal the House of Lords (Lords Reid, Jenkins, Hodson and Devlin; Lord Morris dissenting) held that the words were not capable of bearing the alleged defamatory meaning and ordered new trials. The majority also indicated that they would have ordered a new trial on the ground that the damages awarded were excessive.
>
> **Lord Reid**: ". . . The gist of the two paragraphs is that the police, the City Fraud Squad, were inquiring into the appellants' affairs. There is no doubt that in actions for libel the question is what the words would convey to the ordinary man: it is not one of construction in the legal sense. The ordinary man does not live in an ivory tower and he is not inhibited by a

knowledge of the rules of construction. So he can and does read between the lines in the light of his general knowledge and experience of worldly affairs. I leave aside questions of innuendo where the reader has some special knowledge which might lead him to attribute a meaning to the words not apparent to those who do not have that knowledge. That only arises indirectly in this case. . . .

What the ordinary man would infer without special knowledge has generally been called the natural and ordinary meaning of the words. But that expression is rather misleading in that it conceals the fact that there are two elements in it. Sometimes it is not necessary to go beyond the words themselves, as where the plaintiff has been called a thief or a murderer. But more often the sting is not so much in the words themselves as in what the ordinary man will infer from them, and that is also regarded as part of their natural and ordinary meaning. Here there would be nothing libellous in saying that an inquiry into the appellants' affairs was proceeding: the inquiry might be by a statistician or other expert. The sting is in inferences drawn from the fact that it is the fraud squad which is making the inquiry. What those inferences should be is ultimately a question for the jury, but the trial judge has an important duty to perform.

Generally the controversy is whether the words are capable of having a libellous meaning at all, and undoubtedly it is the judge's duty to rule on that. . . .

What the ordinary man, not avid for scandal, would read into the words complained of must be a matter of impression. I can only say that I do not think that he would infer guilt of fraud merely because an inquiry is on foot. And, if that is so, then it is the duty of the trial judge to direct the jury that it is for them to determine the meaning of the paragraph but that they must not hold it to impute guilt of fraud because as a matter of law the paragraph is not capable of having that meaning. So there was here, in my opinion, misdirection of the two juries sufficiently serious to require that there must be new trials.

. . . Then it is said that if that is so there can be no difference between an allegation of suspicious conduct and an allegation of guilt. To my mind, there is a great difference between saying that a man has behaved in a suspicious manner and saying that he is guilty of an offence, and I am not convinced that you can only justify the former statement by proving guilt. I can well understand that if you say there is a rumour that X is guilty you can only justify it by proving that he is guilty, because repeating someone else's libellous statement is just as bad as making the statement directly. . . ."

Lord Devlin: ". . . Just as a bare statement of suspicion may convey the impression that there are grounds for belief in guilt, so a bare statement of the fact of an inquiry may convey the impression that there are grounds for suspicion. I do not say that in this case it does; but I think that the words in their context and in the circumstances of publication are capable of conveying that impression. But can they convey an impression of guilt? Let it be supposed, first, that a statement that there is an inquiry conveys an impression of suspicion; and, secondly, that a statement of suspicion conveys an impression of guilt. It does not follow from these two suppositions that a statement that there is an inquiry conveys an impression of guilt. For that, two fences have to be taken instead of one. While, as I have said, I am prepared to accept that the jury could take the first, I do not think that in a case like the present, where there is only the bare statement that a police inquiry is being made, it could take the second in the same stride. If the ordinary sensible man was capable of thinking that where ever there was a police inquiry there was guilt, it would be almost impossible to give accurate information about anything: but in my opinion he is not. I agree with the view of the Court of Appeal. . . ."

NOTES

1. This leading case is important not just for the innuendo point. It indicates that companies, as well as humans, have reputations that the tort will protect. (Do companies also have human rights?) It was once held that even local authorities could sue in defamation but this has been overruled by the House of Lords in *Derbyshire CC v Times Newspapers* (1993) and this decision probably extends to all government institutions (see e.g. *Goldsmith v Bhoyrul* (1998)). Furthermore the case is important in helping one to understand why defamation is a complex tort: procedural niceties are vital not just because of juries but equally because of the various preliminary striking out defences that are often raised. In addition the *Lewis* case is important in as much as it illustrates the daft level of damages that juries can award (cf. **Chapter 11**).

2. Although a company can, it seems, sue for defamation (being a legal person: see *Jameel (Mohammed) v Wall Street Journal* (2007), below p.302), a loose group of persons cannot if the group is defamed. Thus to say that 'all politicians are sleazebags' is not defamatory of every politician who is not.

QUESTION

Should large corporations have the legal right to pursue those who criticise their products, even if the factual basis of the criticisms turns out to be inaccurate?

Steel and Morris v United Kingdom (2005) 41 EHRR 403, ECtHR

This case arose out of a successful claim for damages in defamation by a large multi-national corporation (McDonalds) against two individual environmental campaigners who had distributed leaflets containing many allegations about the corporation's products, some of which were found by the English courts to be defamatory. The two campaigners were ordered by the English court to pay large damages to the corporation, but they successfully argued that there had been an infringement of their human rights.

"**88.** The Court must weigh a number of factors in the balance when reviewing the proportionality of the measure complained of. First, it notes that the leaflet in question contained very serious allegations on topics of general concern, such as abusive and immoral farming and employment practices, deforestation, the exploitation of children and their parents through aggressive advertising and the sale of unhealthy food. The Court has long held that 'political expression', including expression on matters of public interest and concern, requires a high level of protection under Article 10 (see, for example, *Thorgeir*

Thorgeirson v. Iceland, judgment of 25 June 1992, Series A no. 239, and also *Hertel v. Switzerland*, judgment of 25 August 1998, *Reports* 1998-VI, § 47). . . .

94. The Court. . . does not consider that the fact that the plaintiff in the present case was a large multinational company should in principle deprive it of a right to defend itself against defamatory allegations or entail that the applicants should not have been required to prove the truth of the statements made. It is true that large public companies inevitably and knowingly lay themselves open to close scrutiny of their acts and, as in the case of the businessmen and women who manage them, the limits of acceptable criticism are wider in the case of such companies (see *Fayed v. the United Kingdom*, judgment of 21 September 1994, Series A no. 294-B, § 75). However, in addition to the public interest in open debate about business practices, there is a competing interest in protecting the commercial success and viability of companies, for the benefit of shareholders and employees, but also for the wider economic good. The State therefore enjoys a margin of appreciation as to the means it provides under domestic law to enable a company to challenge the truth, and limit the damage, of allegations which risk harming its reputation (see *Markt Intern Verlag GmbH and Beerman v. Germany*, judgment of 20 November 1989, Series A no. 165, §§ 33-38).

95. If, however, a State decides to provide such a remedy to a corporate body, it is essential, in order to safeguard the countervailing interests in free expression and open debate, that a measure of procedural fairness and equality of arms is provided for. The Court has already found that the lack of legal aid rendered the defamation proceedings unfair, in breach of Article 6 § 1. The inequality of arms and the difficulties under which the applicants laboured are also significant in assessing the proportionality of the interference under Article 10. As a result of the law as it stood in England and Wales, the applicants had the choice either to withdraw the leaflet and apologise to McDonald's, or bear the burden of proving, without legal aid, the truth of the allegations contained in it. Given the enormity and complexity of that undertaking, the Court does not consider that the correct balance was struck between the need to protect the applicants' rights to freedom of expression and the need to protect McDonald's rights and reputation. The more general interest in promoting the free circulation of information and ideas about the activities of powerful commercial entities, and the possible 'chilling' effect on others are also important factors to be considered in this context, bearing in mind the legitimate and important role that campaign groups can play in stimulating public discussion (see, for example, *Lingens v. Austria*, judgment of 8 July 1986, Series A no. 103, § 44, *Bladet Tromsø* § 64, *Thorgeir Thorgeirson* § 68). The lack of procedural fairness and equality therefore gave rise to a breach of Article 10 in the present case.

96. Moreover, the Court considers that the size of the award of damages made against the two applicants may also have failed to strike the right balance. Under the Convention, an award of damages for defamation must bear a reasonable relationship of proportionality to the injury to reputation suffered (see *Tolstoy Miloslavsky v. the United Kingdom*, judgment of 13 July 1995, Series A, No. 316-B, § 49). The Court notes on the one hand that the sums eventually awarded in the present case (GBP 36,000 in the case of the first applicant and GBP 40,000 in the case of the second applicant) although relatively moderate by contemporary standards in defamation cases in England and Wales, were very substantial when compared to the modest incomes and resources of the two applicants. While accepting, on the other hand, that the statements in the leaflet which were found to be untrue contained serious allegations, the Court observes that not only were the plaintiffs large and powerful corporate entities but that, in accordance with the principles of English law, they were not required to, and did not, establish that they had in fact suffered any financial loss as a result of the publication of the 'several thousand' copies of the leaflets found to have been distributed by the trial judge (see paragraph 45 above and compare, for example, *Hertel v. Switzerland*, cited above, § 49).

97. While it is true that no steps have to date been taken to enforce the damages award against either applicant, the fact remains that the substantial sums awarded against them have remained enforceable since the decision of the Court of Appeal. In these circumstances, the Court finds that the award of damages in the present case was disproportionate to the legitimate aim served.

98. In conclusion, given the lack of procedural fairness and the disproportionate award of damages, the Court finds that there has been a violation of Article 10. . . .

109. The Court has found violations of Articles 6 § 1 and 10 based, principally, on the fact that the applicants had themselves to carry out the bulk of the legal work in these exceptionally long and difficult proceedings to defend their rights to freedom of expression. In these circumstances the applicants must have suffered anxiety and disruption to their lives far in excess of that experienced by a represented litigant, and the Court also notes in this connection the medical evidence submitted by Ms Steel. It awards compensation for non-pecuniary damage of EUR 20,000 to the first applicant and EUR 15,000 to the second applicant."

QUESTION

Should a corporate person be able to obtain substantial damages in defamation without having to prove damage?

Jameel (Mohammed) v Wall Street Journal **[2007] 1 A.C. 359, HL**

(For facts see p.316)

Lord Bingham: ". . . **24** The tort of defamation exists to afford redress for unjustified injury to reputation. By a successful action the injured reputation is vindicated. The ordinary means of vindication is by the verdict of a judge or jury and an award of damages. Most plaintiffs are individuals, who are not required to prove that they have suffered financial loss or even that any particular person has thought the worse of them as a result of the publication complained of. I do not understand this rule to be criticised. Thus the question arises whether a corporation with a commercial reputation within the jurisdiction should be subject to a different rule.

25 There are of course many defamatory things which can be said about individuals (for example, about their sexual proclivities) which could not be said about corporations. But it is not at all hard to think of statements seriously injurious to the general commercial reputation of trading and charitable corporations: that an arms company has routinely bribed officials of foreign governments to secure contracts; that an oil company has wilfully and unnecessarily damaged the environment; that an international humanitarian agency has wrongfully succumbed to government pressure; that a retailer has knowingly exploited child labour; and so on. The leading figures in such corporations may be understood to be personally implicated, but not, in my opinion, necessarily so. Should the corporation be entitled to sue in its own right only if it can prove financial loss? I do not think so, for two main reasons.

26 First, the good name of a company, as that of an individual, is a thing of value. A damaging libel may lower its standing in the eyes of the public and even its own staff, make people less ready to deal with it, less willing or less proud to work for it. If this were not so, corporations would not go to the lengths they do to protect and burnish their corporate images. I find nothing repugnant in the notion that this is a value which the law should protect. Nor do I think it an adequate answer that the corporation can itself seek to answer the defamatory statement by press release or public statement, since protestations of innocence by the impugned party necessarily carry less weight with the public than the prompt issue of proceedings which culminate in a favourable verdict by judge or jury. Secondly, I do not accept that a publication, if truly damaging to a corporation's commercial reputation, will result in provable financial loss, since the more prompt and public a company's issue of proceedings, and the more diligent its pursuit of a claim, the less the chance that financial loss will actually accrue.

27 I do not on balance consider that the existing rule should be changed, provided always that where a trading corporation has suffered no actual financial loss any damages awarded should be kept strictly within modest bounds."

Lord Hoffmann (dissenting on the proof of damage issue): ". . . **90** . . . Mr Robertson submitted that a commercial company like the second claimant should not be able to sue for libel unless it can prove special damage. That would involve overruling the contrary decision of the Court of Appeal in *South Hetton Coal Co Ltd v North-Eastern News Association Ltd* [1894] 1 QB 133 and the statement of the law by Lord Keith of Kinkel in *Derbyshire County Council v Times Newspapers Ltd* [1993] AC 534, 547. For my part, I would accept Mr Robertson's submission but as I understand that a majority of your Lordships would reject it and I agree on this point with the opinion of my noble and learned friend, Baroness Hale of Richmond, I shall not detain your Lordships long with my own reasons.

91 In the case of an individual, his reputation is a part of his personality, the 'immortal part' of himself and it is right that he should be entitled to vindicate his reputation and receive compensation for a slur upon it without proof of financial loss. But a commercial company has no soul and its reputation is no more than a commercial asset, something attached to its trading name which brings in customers. I see no reason why the rule which requires proof of damage to commercial assets in other torts, such as malicious falsehood, should not also apply to defamation."

Lord Scott: ". . . **120** . . . The reputation of a corporate body is capable of being, and will usually be, not simply something in which its directors and shareholders may take pride, but an asset of positive value to it. Why else do trading companies pay very substantial sums of money in advertising their names in TV commercials which usually say next to nothing of value about the services or products on offer from the company in question but endeavour to present an image of the company that is attractive and likely to cement the name of the corporation in the public memory? Why do commercial companies sponsor sporting competitions, so that one has the XLtd Grand National or the YLtd Open Golf Championship or the ZLtd Premiership? It is surely because reputation matters to trading companies and because these sponsorship activities, associating the name of the company with popular sporting events, are believed to enhance the sponsor's reputation to its commercial advantage. The organisers of a variety of activities some sporting, some cultural, some charitable, are constantly on the look-out for sponsorship of the activity in question by some commercial company. The choice of sponsor and the reputation of the sponsor matter to these organisers. Who would these days choose a cigarette manufacturing company to sponsor an athletic event or a concert in aid of charity? If reputation suffers, sponsorship invitations may be reduced, advertising opportunities may become difficult, customers may take their custom elsewhere. If trade suffers, profits suffer.

121 It seems to me plain beyond argument that reputation is of importance to corporations. Proof of actual damage caused by the publication of defamatory material would, in most cases, need to await the next month's financial figures, but the figures would likely to be inconclusive. Causation problems would usually be insuperable. Who is to say why receipts are down or why advertising has become more difficult or less effective? Everyone knows that fluctuations happen. Who is to say, if the figures are not down, whether they would have been higher if the libel had not been published? How can a company about which some libel, damaging to its reputation, has been published ever obtain an interlocutory injunction if proof of actual damage is to become the gist of the action?. . .

125 My Lords, I can see no good reason why your Lordships should now disqualify corporations from bringing libel actions unless able to allege and prove actual damage caused by the libel. . . .

126 And, in particular, I can see nothing in article 10 of the European Convention on Human Rights that requires a different conclusion. The right to freedom of expression was never intended, in my opinion, to allow defamatory statements, whether of individuals or companies, to be published with impunity. If a defamer can neither justify the statement nor claim the protection afforded by the law to fair comment on matters of public interest or to statements that qualify for privilege, he must, in my opinion, be prepared to answer for the libel. . . ."

QUESTIONS

1. Are the reasons set out by Lord Scott in para.121 really convincing? Could they not be used just as easily to deny granting damages without proof of damage?

2. Why should profits be protected by the law of defamation (a strict liability tort) when they are not so well protected by the law of negligence?

3. Do companies have dignity? Did Steel and Morris invade the dignity of McDonalds?

4. Do companies have human rights? If so, should they have the right to vote?

5. Local authorities and other state bodies cannot sue in defamation (*Derbyshire CC v Times Newspapers* (1993)). When these bodies all become privatised, will this restriction disappear?

8.2.4 **Publication**

Defamation is strictly a three party tort: there has to be publication of the statement defamatory of the claimant to a third party. If there is no publication there can be no action. In other words, defamation is not a tort of insult (unlike the Roman law injuria); and so if Miss Burchill (above p.296) had simply sent her comments to Mr Berkoff in a private letter, or had insulted him out of the hearing of anyone else, the latter would have no claim (but cf. *Bryanston Finance v de Vries* (1975)). Indeed, even if the letter had been opened by one of Mr Berkoff's employees there would probably be no publication, unless perhaps Miss Burchill should have known that a secretary or the like would open the letter (see *Huth v Huth* (1915)). No doubt if Miss Burchill had written her comments on a postcard things would not be so simple. New forms of communication are, however, creating challenges for the law of defamation as the next extract indicates.

Loutchansky v Times Newspapers Ltd (Nos 2–5) **[2002] 2 Q.B. 783, CA**

This was an action in damages by a claimant whom a newspaper had alleged to be a member of the Russian mafia. Various issues arose, one of which was limitation in relation to publication of the article as archive material on the Internet. The Court of Appeal's view (Lord Phillips M.R., Simon Brown L.J. and Tuckey L.J.) is set out in Lord Phillips' judgment of the court.

Lord Phillips M.R.: ". . . **57** It is a well established principle of the English law of defamation that each individual publication of a libel gives rise to a separate cause of action, subject to its own limitation period. *Duke of Brunswick v Harmer* 14 QB 185 provides a striking illustration of this principle. On 19 September 1830 an article was published in the 'Weekly Dispatch'. The limitation period for libel was then six years. The article defamed the Duke of Brunswick. Seventeen years after its publication an agent of the Duke purchased a back number containing the article from the 'Weekly Dispatch''s office. Another copy was obtained from the British Museum. The Duke sued on those two publications. The defendant contended that the cause of action was time-barred, relying on the original publication date. The Court of Queen's Bench held that the delivery of a copy of the newspaper to the plaintiff's agent constituted a separate publication in respect of which suit could be brought.

58 In *Godfrey v Demon Internet Ltd* [2001] QB 201 the plaintiff brought an action in defamation against the defendants, who were Internet service providers. They had received and stored on their news server an article, defamatory of the plaintiff, which had been posted by an unknown person using another service provider. The issue was whether the defendants had a defence under section 1(1) of the Defamation Act 1996. The judge held that they did not. He observed, at pp 208–209:

'In my judgment the defendants, whenever they transmit and whenever there is transmitted from the storage of their news server a defamatory posting, publish that posting to any subscriber to their ISP who accesses the newsgroup containing that posting. Thus every time one of the defendants' customers accesses soc.culture.thai and sees that posting defamatory of the plaintiff there is a publication to that customer.'

59 This decision was consistent with the *Duke of Brunswick* case 14 QB 185 and Lord Lester did not suggest to the contrary. . . .

74 We do not accept that the rule in the *Duke of Brunswick* case imposes a restriction on the readiness to maintain and provide access to archives that amounts to a disproportionate restriction on freedom of expression. We accept that the maintenance of archives, whether in hard copy or on the Internet, has a social utility, but consider that the maintenance of archives is a comparatively insignificant aspect of freedom of expression. Archive material is stale news and its publication cannot rank in importance with the dissemination of contemporary material. Nor do we believe that the law of defamation need inhibit the responsible maintenance of archives. Where it is known that archive material is or may be defamatory, the attachment of an appropriate notice warning against treating it as the truth will normally remove any sting from the material.

75 Turning to the defendants' wider argument, it is true that to permit an action to be based on a fresh dissemination of an article published long ago is at odds with some of the reasons for the introduction of a 12-month limitation period for defamation. But the scale of such publication and any resulting damage is likely to be modest compared with that of the original publication. In the present case, as the judge observed, the action based on the Internet publication is subsidiary to the main action.

76 The change in the law of defamation for which the defendants contend is a radical one. In our judgment they have failed to make out their case that such a change is required. The Internet single publication appeal is therefore dismissed."

QUESTIONS

1. Is Lord Phillips' proposition in para.74 really practical or does it show a lack of understanding both of the workings of the Internet and of the role of archives?

2. A celebrity person slanders the claimant's business in the hearing of several other people and these people report the slander to the press. The press widely publishes the slander and the claimant's business suffers as a result. Can the claimant claim damages for this business loss from (i) the celebrity and (ii) the press?

8.2.5 Liability for publication

The position at common law is that it is not only the author of the defamatory material who can be held liable in defamation. Printers, publishers and distributors can also be sued. The position has now been modified by statute.

Defamation Act 1996 (c.31)

"**1 Responsibility for publication.**

(1) In defamation proceedings a person has a defence if he shows that—

(a) he was not the author, editor or publisher of the statement complained of,
(b) he took reasonable care in relation to its publication, and

   (c) he did not know, and had no reason to believe, that what he did caused or contributed to the publication of a defamatory statement. . . .

(3) A person shall not be considered the author, editor or publisher of a statement if he is only involved—

   (a) in printing, producing, distributing or selling printed material containing the statement

   (b) in processing, making copies of, distributing, exhibiting or selling a film or sound recording (as defined in Part I of the Copyright, Designs and Patents Act 1988) containing the statement

   (c) in processing, making copies of, distributing or selling any electronic medium in or on which the statement is recorded, or in operating or providing any equipment, system or service by means of which the statement is retrieved, copied, distributed or made available in electronic form

   (d) as the broadcaster of a live programme containing the statement in circumstances in which he has no effective control over the maker of the statement

   (e) as the operator of or provider of access to a communications system by means of which the statement is transmitted, or made available, by a person over whom he has no effective control.

   In a case not within paragraphs (a) to (e) the court may have regard to those provisions by way of analogy in deciding whether a person is to be considered the author, editor or publisher of a statement. . . .

(5) In determining for the purposes of this section whether a person took reasonable care, or had reason to believe that what he did caused or contributed to the publication of a defamatory statement, regard shall be had to—

   (a) the extent of his responsibility for the content of the statement or the decision to publish it,

   (b) the nature or circumstances of the publication, and

   (c) the previous conduct or character of the author, editor or publisher. . . ."

QUESTION

Why did the law not extend this reasonable care defence to the author, editor and publisher? Might it be because the law treats reputation as akin to a property right? Ought reputation to be part of the law of property?

8.3 Defamation (2): defences

Given that almost any critical statement made of another can be defamatory, the defences are of major constitutional importance since they are the only effective means of protecting freedom of speech. There are three traditional defences (if one excludes death as a 'defence', for a defamation claim dies with the defamed person: Law Reform (Miscellaneous Provisions) Act 1934 s.1(1)). These three defences are justification or truth, fair comment and privilege. In addition to these three defences there is now a statutory offer of amends defence.

8.3.1 **Justification**

Truth is a complete defence to an action in defamation, as the next extracts indicate.

Reynolds v Times Newspapers Limited **[2001] 2 A.C. 127, HL**

(For facts see p.312)

> **Lord Nicholls:** ". . . Historically the common law has set much store by protection of reputation. Publication of a statement adversely affecting a person's reputation is actionable. The plaintiff is not required to prove that the words are false. Nor, in the case of publication in a written or permanent form, is he required to prove he has been damaged. But, as Littledale J said in *McPherson v. Daniels* (1829) 10 B & C 263, 272, 'the law will not permit a man to recover damages in respect of an injury to a character which he does not or ought not to possess'. Truth is a complete defence. If the defendant proves the substantial truth of the words complained of, he thereby establishes the defence of justification. With the minor exception of proceedings to which the Rehabilitation of Offenders Act 1974 applies, this defence is of universal application in civil proceedings. It avails a defendant even if he was acting spitefully. . . ."

Defamation Act 1952 (15 & 16 Geo. VI & 1 Eliz. III, c.66)

"**5 Justification.**

In an action for libel or slander in respect of words containing two or more distinct charges against the plaintiff, a defence of justification shall not fail by reason only that the truth of every charge is not proved if the words not proved to be true do not materially injure the plaintiff's reputation having regard to the truth of the remaining charges."

NOTE

The onus is on the defendant to prove truth and thus a reasonable belief that the allegation is true is not enough for this particular defence. However proof of conviction of a crime is enough to establish justification even if the defamed convicted person believes that the conviction was a miscarriage of justice (Civil Evidence Act 1968 s.13).

8.3.2 **Fair (honest) comment**

Fair comment honestly held on a matter of fact is also a defence.

Defamation Act 1952 (15 & 16 Geo. VI & 1 Eliz. III, c.66)

"**6 Fair comment.**

In an action for libel or slander in respect of words consisting partly of allegations of fact and partly of expression of opinion, a defence of fair comment shall not fail by reason only that the truth of every allegation of fact is not proved if the expression of opinion is fair comment having regard to such of the facts alleged or referred to in the words complained of as are proved."

NOTE

The Act uses the expression 'fair'. However, as the next extract shows, this term is no longer accurate.

Reynolds v Times Newspapers Limited **[2001] 2 A.C. 127, HL**

(For facts see p.312)

Lord Nicholls: ". . . One established exception is the defence of comment on a matter of public interest. This defence is available to everyone, and is of particular importance to the media. The freedom of expression protected by this defence has long been regarded by the common law as a basic right, long before the emergence of human rights conventions. In 1863 Crompton J observed in *Campbell v. Spottiswoode* (1863) 3 B & S 769, 779, that 'it is the right of all the Queen's subjects to discuss public matters'. The defence is wide in its scope. Public interest has never been defined, but in *London Artists Ltd. v. Littler* [1969] 2 QB 375, 391, Lord Denning MR rightly said that it is not to be confined within narrow limits. He continued:

'Whenever a matter is such as to affect people at large, so that they may be legitimately interested in, or concerned at, what is going on; or what may happen to them or others; then it is a matter of public interest on which everyone is entitled to make fair comment.'

Traditionally one of the ingredients of this defence is that the comment must be fair, fairness being judged by the objective standard of whether any fair-minded person could honestly express the opinion in question. Judges have emphasised the latitude to be applied in interpreting this standard. So much so, that the time has come to recognise that in this context the epithet 'fair' is now meaningless and misleading. Comment must be relevant to the facts to which it is addressed. It cannot be used as a cloak for mere invective. But the basis of our public life is that the crank, the enthusiast, may say what he honestly thinks as much as the reasonable person who sits on a jury. The true test is whether the opinion, however exaggerated, obstinate or prejudiced, was honestly held by the person expressing it: see Diplock J in *Silkin v. Beaverbrook Newspapers Ltd.* [1958] 1 WLR 743, 747.

It is important to keep in mind that this defence is concerned with the protection of comment, not imputations of fact. If the imputation is one of fact, a ground of defence must be sought elsewhere. Further, to be within this defence the comment must be recognisable as comment, as distinct from an imputation of fact. The comment must explicitly or implicitly indicate, at least in general terms, what are the facts on which the comment is being made: see the discussion in *Duncan and Neill on Defamation*, 2nd ed. (1983), pp. 58–62.

One constraint does exist upon this defence. The comment must represent the honest belief of its author. If the plaintiff proves he was actuated by malice, this ground of defence will fail. . . ."

NOTES

1. The comment must be 'fair' and the facts upon which it is based must be accurate. Thus if Miss Burchill (above p.296) had described a character in a film or play acted by Mr Berkoff as being hideously ugly or less good looking than the Creature Frankenstein, it

may be that Burchill would have had the defence of fair comment. She is entitled to comment on a public fact such as a film or public performance. She equally could have described his acting in derogatory terms, just as he would be entitled to criticise, say, the literary quality of her newspaper columns. However the defence of·fair comment will fail if actuated by malice, proof of which rests on the claimant.

2. The distinction between fact and comment is, of course, more complex than Lord Nicholls would seem to admit and this is yet another reason why defamation as a tort is so complex. Could Miss Burchill (p.296) have claimed that she was simply stating a fact when she described Mr Berkoff in the way she did? If ugliness is a question of opinion, what if a weather forecaster describes a day as 'dull'? Or what if she talks of an 'ugly storm'? A doctor states that a patient is displaying the symptoms of a particular disease: is this a statement of fact or opinion? What if the patient demands a 'second opinion'?

QUESTIONS

1. Is a restaurant critic safe from defamation if, without malice, he or she gives a particular restaurant a very bad review?

2. If a journalist describes, without malice, the commercial policy of a large supermarket as being aggressive and bullying is the journalist leaving himself open to a defamation action?

3. Is a book reviewer, who describes without malice a law book as contributing to legal knowledge what the film *Carry On Up the Kyber* contributes to political science, leaving himself open to a defamation action?

8.3.3 Privilege (1): absolute privilege

The law recognises, as the next extract indicates, that there are some situations where the public interest and (or) the interests of justice require that statements, even if defamatory, should be published to persons having an interest in receiving the statement. There are two forms of privilege, absolute and qualified.

Reynolds v Times Newspapers Limited **[2001] 2 A.C. 127, HL**

(For facts see p.312)

Lord Nicholls: ". . . The defence of honest comment on a matter of public interest, then, does not cover defamatory statements of fact. But there are circumstances, in the famous words of Parke B. in *Toogood v. Spyring* (1834) 1 CM & R 181, 193, when the 'common convenience and welfare of society' call for frank communication on questions of fact. In *Davies v. Snead* (1870) LR 5 QB 608, 611, Blackburn J spoke of circumstances where a person is so situated that it 'becomes right in the interests of society' that he should tell certain facts to another. There are occasions when the person to whom a statement is made has a special interest in learning the honestly held views of another person, even if those views are defamatory of someone else and cannot be proved to be true. When the interest is of sufficient importance to outweigh the need to protect reputation, the occasion is regarded as privileged.

> Sometimes the need for uninhibited expression is of such a high order that the occasion attracts absolute privilege, as with statements made by judges or advocates or witnesses in the course of judicial proceedings. . . ."

NOTE

Some forms of absolute privilege are based in statute.

Defamation Act 1996 (c.31)

> "**14 Reports of court proceedings absolutely privileged**.
> (1) A fair and accurate report of proceedings in public before a court to which this section applies, if published contemporaneously with the proceedings, is absolutely privileged. . . ."

NOTE

See also (for example) the Competition Act 1998 s.57 and the Local Government Act 2000 s.74.

8.3.4 Privilege (2): qualified privilege

One of the classic statements of privilege is to be found in the next case.

Watt v Longsdon [1930] 1 K.B. 130, CA

This was an action for damages in defamation brought by a director of a company against another director of the same company in respect of a letter written by a foreign manager of the company. The letter accused the claimant of gross immorality. The defendant director, before obtaining further evidence against the claimant, showed the letter to the chairman and to the claimant's wife, the latter commencing divorce proceedings as a result. The allegations in the letter were unfounded but the defendant believed them to be true. The Court of Appeal (Scrutton L.J., Greer L.J. and Russell L.J.) held that the publication of the letter to the chairman of the board was privileged but the publication to the wife was not. The court also held that in the publication to the wife there was evidence of malice which ought to be left to the jury.

> **Scrutton L.J.:** ". . . By the law of England there are occasions on which a person may make defamatory statements about another which are untrue without incurring any legal liability for his statements. These occasions are called privileged occasions. A reason frequently given for this privilege is that the allegation that the speaker has 'unlawfully and maliciously published,' is displaced by proof that the speaker had either a duty or an interest to publish, and that this duty or interest confers the privilege. But communications made on these occasions may lose their privilege: (1.) they may exceed the privilege of the occasion by going beyond the limits of the duty or interest, or (2.) they may be published with express malice, so that the occasion is not being legitimately used, but abused. . . . The question whether the occasion was privileged is for the judge, and so far as 'duty' is concerned, the question is: Was there a duty, legal, moral, or social, to communicate? As to legal duty, the judge should

have no difficulty; the judge should know the law; but as to moral or social duties of imperfect obligation, the task is far more troublesome. The judge has no evidence as to the view the community takes of moral or social duties. All the help the Court of Appeal can give him is contained in the judgment of Lindley LJ in *Stuart v Bell*: 'The question of moral or social duty being for the judge, each judge must decide it as best he can for himself . . .' . . . It is not surprising that with such a standard both judges and text-writers treat the matter as one of great difficulty in which no definite line can be drawn. . . .''

NOTES AND QUESTIONS

1. The key concept is 'interest'. Does the recipient of the statement have an 'interest' in hearing it? Could this concept of an interest be extended to the public in general? Could, in other words, qualified privilege attach to a defamatory statement made in a newspaper but which the public have an 'interest' in reading?

2. Qualified privilege differs from absolute in that it can be rebutted by proof of malice as Lord Nicholls goes on to explain in the next extract.

Reynolds v Times Newspapers Ltd **[2001] 2 A.C. 127, HL**

This was an action for damages for defamation by a former Irish Prime Minster against a newspaper which had implied that he had lied to the Irish Parliament. At the trial the jury ruled that the words were not true, but the newspaper also argued that the article should be covered by qualified privilege. This latter argument was rejected by the trial judge. On appeal the Court of Appeal set aside the jury verdict and the judgment and ordered a new trial; it also decided that the defendant could not rely upon qualified privilege. The House of Lords (Lords Nicholls, Cooke and Hobhouse; Lords Steyn and Hope dissenting), by a majority, dismissed an appeal, although they reassessed the scope of qualified in the light of the coming into force of the Human Rights Act 1998.

Lord Nicholls: ". . . Sometimes the need for uninhibited expression is of such a high order that the occasion attracts absolute privilege, as with statements made by judges or advocates or witnesses in the course of judicial proceedings. More usually, the privilege is qualified in that it can be defeated if the plaintiff proves the defendant was actuated by malice.

The classic exposition of malice in this context is that of Lord Diplock in *Horrocks v. Lowe* [1975] AC 135, 149. If the defendant used the occasion for some reason other than the reason for which the occasion was privileged he loses the privilege. Thus, the motive with which the statement was made is crucial. If desire to injure was the dominant motive the privilege is lost. Similarly, if the maker of the statement did not believe the statement to be true, or if he made the statement recklessly, without considering or caring whether it was true or not. . . .

Over the years the courts have held that many common form situations are privileged. Classic instances are employment references, and complaints made or information given to the police or appropriate authorities regarding suspected crimes. The courts have always emphasised that the categories established by the authorities are not exhaustive. The list is not closed. The established categories are no more than applications, in particular circumstances, of the underlying principle of public policy. . . .

The requirement that both the maker of the statement and the recipient must have an interest or duty draws attention to the need to have regard to the position of both parties when deciding whether an occasion is privileged. But this should not be allowed to obscure the rationale of the underlying public interest on which privilege is founded. The essence of this defence lies in the law's recognition of the need, in the public interest, for a particular recipient to receive frank and uninhibited communication of particular information from a particular source. That is the end the law is concerned to attain. The protection afforded to the maker of the statement is the means by which the law seeks to achieve that end. Thus the court has to assess whether, in the public interest, the publication should be protected in the absence of malice.

In determining whether an occasion is regarded as privileged the court has regard to all the circumstances. . .

Statutory privilege

Many, if not all, of the common law categories of case where reports of proceedings attract privilege are now the subject of statutory privilege. Successive statutes have extended the categories. The Law of Libel Amendment Act 1888 granted qualified privilege to fair and accurate reports published in newspapers of a limited range of public meetings. In 1948 the Report of the Committee on the Law of Defamation (Cmd 7536), chaired by Lord Porter, recommended that the classes of reports subject to qualified privilege should be extended, and that they should be re-classified into two categories: those where statements were privileged without explanation or contradiction, and those where privilege was conditional on publication on request of a letter or statement by way of explanation or contradiction. The Defamation Act 1952 gave effect to these recommendations. Among the publications having qualified privilege without explanation or contradiction was a fair and accurate report of proceedings in public of the Irish legislature. Until abandoned, this was one of the defendants' pleaded defences in the present proceedings.

In 1975 the committee on defamation chaired by Faulks J considered a proposal that a statutory qualified privilege should be created to protect statements made, whether in a newspaper or elsewhere, if the matter was of public interest and the publisher believed the statement of facts was true and he had taken reasonable care in relation to such facts. In its report (Cmnd. 5909) the committee did not accept this proposal. The committee considered this would seriously alter the balance of the law of defamation against a defamed plaintiff. The committee noted that the common law defence of qualified privilege was available to the media as much as anyone else, and referred to the *Cox v. Feeney* line of cases.

In 1991 the Supreme Court Procedure Committee, chaired by Neill LJ, in its Report on Practice and Procedure in Defamation considered that fair and accurate coverage by the British media of statements and proceedings abroad ought to be protected by qualified privilege in circumstances which would attract privilege if comparable statements or proceedings occurred in this country. The committee recommended this result should be achieved by statute. The committee regarded the 'duty' test as too stringent in modern conditions and productive of too much uncertainty. The committee was opposed to the introduction of a defence similar to the 'public figure' defence enunciated by the United States Supreme Court in *New York Times Co. v. Sullivan* (1964) 376 US 254.

The Defamation Act 1996 broadly gave effect to the Neill committee recommendations. The Act contained an extended list of categories of statutory qualified privilege. In the Act of 1996 and the Act of 1952 statutory privilege was additional to any common law privilege, but did not protect publication of any matter which was not of public concern and the publication of which was not for the public benefit: see section 15 of the Act of 1996 and section 7 of the Act of 1952. . . .

A new category of privileged subject-matter?

I turn to the appellants' submissions. The newspaper seeks the incremental development of the common law by the creation of a new category of occasion when privilege derives from the subject-matter alone: political information. . . .

These are powerful arguments, but I do not accept the conclusion for which the newspaper contended. My reasons appear from what is set out below.

My starting point is freedom of expression. The high importance of freedom to impart and receive information and ideas has been stated so often and so eloquently that this point calls for no elaboration in this case. At a pragmatic level, freedom to disseminate and receive information on political matters is essential to the proper functioning of the system of parliamentary democracy cherished in this country. This freedom enables those who elect representatives to Parliament to make an informed choice, regarding individuals as well as policies, and those elected to make informed decisions. Freedom of expression will shortly be buttressed by statutory requirements. Under section 12 of the Human Rights Act 1998, expected to come into force in October 2000, the court is required, in relevant cases, to have particular regard to the importance of the right to freedom of expression. The common law is to be developed and applied in a manner consistent with article 10 of the European Convention for the Protection of Human Rights and Fundamental Freedoms (Cmd. 8969), and the court must take into account relevant decisions of the European Court of Human Rights (sections 6 and 2). To be justified, any curtailment of freedom of expression must be convincingly established by a compelling countervailing consideration, and the means employed must be proportionate to the end sought to be achieved.

Likewise, there is no need to elaborate on the importance of the role discharged by the media in the expression and communication of information and comment on political matters. It is through the mass media that most people today obtain their information on political matters. Without freedom of expression by the media, freedom of expression would be a hollow concept. The interest of a democratic society in ensuring a free press weighs heavily in the balance in deciding whether any curtailment of this freedom bears a reasonable relationship to the purpose of the curtailment. In this regard it should be kept in mind that one of the contemporary functions of the media is investigative journalism. This activity, as much as the traditional activities of reporting and commenting, is part of the vital role of the press and the media generally. . . .

The crux of this appeal . . . lies in identifying the restrictions which are fairly and reasonably necessary for the protection of reputation. Leaving aside the exceptional cases which attract absolute privilege, the common law denies protection to defamatory statements, whether of comment or fact, proved to be actuated by malice, in the *Horrocks v. Lowe* [1975] AC 135 sense. This common law limitation on freedom of speech passes the 'necessary' test with flying colours. This is an acceptable limitation. Freedom of speech does not embrace freedom to make defamatory statements out of personal spite or without having a positive belief in their truth. . . .

Conclusion

My conclusion is that the established common law approach to misstatements of fact remains essentially sound. The common law should not develop 'political information' as a new 'subject-matter' category of qualified privilege, whereby the publication of all such information would attract qualified privilege, whatever the circumstances. That would not provide adequate protection for reputation. Moreover, it would be unsound in principle to distinguish political discussion from discussion of other matters of serious public concern. The elasticity of the common law principle enables interference with freedom of speech to be confined to what is necessary in the circumstances of the case. This elasticity enables the court to give appropriate weight, in today's conditions, to the importance of freedom of expression by the media on all matters of public concern.

Depending on the circumstances, the matters to be taken into account include the following. The comments are illustrative only.

1. The seriousness of the allegation. The more serious the charge, the more the public is misinformed and the individual harmed, if the allegation is not true.
2. The nature of the information, and the extent to which the subject-matter is a matter of public concern.
3. The source of the information. Some informants have no direct knowledge of the events. Some have their own axes to grind, or are being paid for their stories.
4. The steps taken to verify the information.
5. The status of the information. The allegation may have already been the subject of an investigation which commands respect.
6. The urgency of the matter. News is often a perishable commodity.
7. Whether comment was sought from the defendant. He may have information others do not possess or have not disclosed. An approach to the defendant will not always be necessary.
8. Whether the article contained the gist of the plaintiff's side of the story.
9. The tone of the article. A newspaper can raise queries or call for an investigation. It need not adopt allegations as statements of fact.
10. The circumstances of the publication, including the timing.

This list is not exhaustive. The weight to be given to these and any other relevant factors will vary from case to case. Any disputes of primary fact will be a matter for the jury, if there is one. The decision on whether, having regard to the admitted or proved facts, the publication was subject to qualified privilege is a matter for the judge. This is the established practice and seems sound. A balancing operation is better carried out by a judge in a reasoned judgment than by a jury. Over time, a valuable corpus of case law will be built up.

In general, a newspaper's unwillingness to disclose the identity of its sources should not weigh against it. Further, it should always be remembered that journalists act without the benefit of the clear light of hindsight. Matters which are obvious in retrospect may have been far from clear in the heat of the moment. Above all, the court should have particular regard to the importance of freedom of expression. The press discharges vital functions as a bloodhound as well as a watchdog. The court should be slow to conclude that a publication was not in the public interest and, therefore, the public had no right to know, especially when the information is in the field of political discussion. Any lingering doubts should be resolved in favour of publication.

Privilege and the facts of this case

The appellant newspaper's primary submission was that they never had the opportunity of pleading and proving a case that the 'circumstantial test' was satisfied, because this test had not been formulated until the Court of Appeal gave judgment. I am not persuaded by this line of argument. . . .

Was the information in the 'Sunday Times' article information the public was entitled to know? The subject matter was undoubtedly of public concern in this country. However, these serious allegations by the newspaper, presented as statements of fact but shorn of all mention of Mr Reynolds' considered explanation, were not information the public had a right to know. I agree with the Court of Appeal this was not a publication which should in the public interest be protected by privilege in the absence of proof of malice. The further facts the defendants wish to assert and prove at the retrial would make no difference, either on this point or overall. I would dismiss this appeal."

NOTE

There is no doubt that this case is one of the most important decisions on defamation in recent years. It has clearly expanded the defence of qualified privilege in the light of the Human Rights Act 1998. It seemed at first not such a radical decision, but more recently the House of Lords has reasserted the importance *Reynolds*.

Jameel (Mohammed) v Wall Street Journal [2007] 1 A.C. 359, HL

This was an action for damages for defamation by a Saudi Arabian businessman and his trading company against the publisher of an article that suggested that the company might be involved in the channelling of terrorist funds. The defendant sought to rely on the defence of qualified privilege but the judge rejected this defence and the jury awarded damages to both claimants. The Court of Appeal dismissed an appeal but the House of Lords (Lords Bingham, Hoffmann, Hope, Scott and Baroness Hale) allowed an appeal on the qualified privilege defence.

Lord Hoffmann: ". . . 43 The newspaper's principal defence was based on *Reynolds v Times Newspapers Ltd* [2001] 2 AC 127. It is called in the trade '*Reynolds* privilege' but the use of the term privilege, although historically accurate, may be misleading. A defence of privilege in the usual sense is available when the defamatory statement was published on a privileged occasion and can be defeated only by showing that the privilege was abused. . . .

46 Although Lord Nicholls uses the word 'privilege', it is clearly not being used in the old sense. It is the material which is privileged, not the occasion on which it is published. There is no question of the privilege being defeated by proof of malice because the propriety of the conduct of the defendant is built into the conditions under which the material is privileged.

The burden is upon the defendant to prove that those conditions are satisfied. I therefore agree with the opinion of the Court of Appeal in *Loutchansky v Times Newspapers Ltd (Nos 2–5)* [2002] QB 783, 806 that '*Reynolds* privilege' is 'a different jurisprudential creature from the traditional form of privilege from which it sprang'. It might more appropriately be called the *Reynolds* public interest defence rather than privilege. . . .

Applying Reynolds

(a) The public interest of the material

48 The first question is whether the subject matter of the article was a matter of public interest. In answering this question, I think that one should consider the article as a whole and not isolate the defamatory statement. It is true that Lord Nicholls said, in the passage which I have quoted above, that the question is whether the publication of 'particular material' was privileged because of its value to the public. But the term 'particular material' was in my opinion being used by contrast with the generic privilege advocated by the newspaper. It was saying that one must consider the contents of each publication and not decide the matter simply by reference to whether it fell within a general category like political information. But that did not mean that it was necessary to find a separate public interest justification for each item of information within the publication. Whether it was justifiable to include the defamatory statement is a separate question, to which I shall return in a moment. . . .

50 In answering the question of public interest, I do not think it helpful to apply the classic test for the existence of a privileged occasion and ask whether there was a duty to communicate the information and an interest in receiving it. The *Reynolds* defence was developed from the traditional form of privilege by a generalisation that in matters of public interest, there can be said to be a professional duty on the part of journalists to impart the information and an interest in the public in receiving it. The House having made this generalisation, it should in my opinion be regarded as a proposition of law and not decided each time as a question of fact. If the publication is in the public interest, the duty and interest are taken to exist. The *Reynolds* defence is very different from the privilege discussed by the Court of Appeal in *Blackshaw v Lord* [1984] QB 1, where it was contemplated that in exceptional circumstances there could be a privileged occasion in the classic sense, arising out of a duty to communicate information to the public generally and a corresponding interest in receiving it. The Court of Appeal there contemplated a traditional privilege, liable to be defeated only by proof of malice. But the *Reynolds* defence does not employ this two-stage process. It is not as narrow as traditional privilege nor is there a burden upon the claimant to show malice to defeat it. So far as Lord Cooke of Thorndon said in *Reynolds*, at p 224, and in *McCartan Turkington Breen v Times Newspapers Ltd* [2001] 2 AC 277, 301 that the principle in *Reynolds* was essentially the same, I respectfully think that he did not fully analyse the differences: see the comment in *Loutchansky v Times Newspapers Ltd (Nos 2–5)* [2002] QB 783, 806.

(b) Inclusion of the defamatory statement

51 If the article as a whole concerned a matter of public interest, the next question is whether the inclusion of the defamatory statement was justifiable. The fact that the material was of public interest does not allow the newspaper to drag in damaging allegations which serve no public purpose. They must be part of the story. And the more serious the allegation, the more important it is that it should make a real contribution to the public interest element in the article. But whereas the question of whether the story as a whole was a matter of public interest must be decided by the judge without regard to what the editor's view may have been, the question of whether the defamatory statement should have been included is often a matter of how the story should have been presented. And on that question, allowance must be made for editorial judgment. If the article as a whole is in the public interest, opinions may reasonably differ over which details are needed to convey the general message. The fact that the judge, with the advantage of leisure and hindsight, might have made a different editorial decision should not destroy the defence. That would make the publication of articles which are, ex hypothesi, in the public interest, too risky and would discourage investigative reporting.

52 In the present case, the inclusion of the names of large and respectable Saudi businesses was an important part of the story. It showed that co-operation with the United States Treasury's requests was not confined to a few companies on the fringe of Saudi society but extended to companies which were by any test within the heartland of the Saudi business world. To convey this message, inclusion of the names was necessary. Generalisations such as 'prominent Saudi companies', which can mean anything or nothing, would not have served the same purpose. . . .

55 In this case, Eady J said that the concept of 'responsible journalism' was too vague. It was, he said, 'subjective'. I am not certain what this means, except that it is obviously a term of disapproval. (In the jargon of the old Soviet Union, 'objective' meant correct and in accordance with the Party line, while 'subjective' meant deviationist and wrong.) But the standard of responsible journalism is as objective and no more vague than standards such as 'reasonable care' which are regularly used in other branches of law. Greater certainty in its application is attained in two ways. First, as Lord Nicholls said, a body of illustrative case law builds up. Secondly, just as the standard of reasonable care in particular areas, such as driving a vehicle, is made more concrete by extra-statutory codes of behaviour like the Highway Code, so the standard of responsible journalism is made more specific by the Code of Practice which has been adopted by the newspapers and ratified by the Press Complaints Commission. This too, while not binding upon the courts, can provide valuable guidance.

56 In *Reynolds*, Lord Nicholls gave his well-known non-exhaustive list of ten matters which should in suitable cases be taken into account. They are not tests which the publication has to pass. In the hands of a judge hostile to the spirit of *Reynolds*, they can become ten hurdles at any of which the defence may fail. That is how Eady J treated them. The defence, he said, can be sustained only after 'the closest and most rigorous scrutiny' by the application of what he called 'Lord Nicholls's ten tests'. But that, in my opinion, is not what Lord Nicholls meant. As he said in *Bonnick*, at p 309, the standard of conduct required of the newspaper must be applied in a practical and flexible manner. It must have regard to practical realities.

57 . . . In my opinion it is unnecessary and positively misleading to go back to the old law on classic privilege. It is the principle stated in *Reynolds* and encapsulated by Lord Nicholls in *Bonnick* which should be applied. On this question I have had the advantage of reading in draft the opinion of my noble and learned friend, Baroness Hale of Richmond, and wholeheartedly concur in her remarks. . . .

> **62** . . . The fact that the defamatory statement is not established at the trial to have been true is not relevant to the *Reynolds* defence. It is a neutral circumstance. The elements of that defence are the public interest of the material and the conduct of the journalists at the time. In most cases the *Reynolds* defence will not get off the ground unless the journalist honestly and reasonably believed that the statement was true but there are cases ('reportage') in which the public interest lies simply in the fact that the statement was made, when it may be clear that the publisher does not subscribe to any belief in its truth. In either case, the defence is not affected by the newspaper's inability to prove the truth of the statement at the trial. . . ."

NOTES

1. The effect of *Reynolds* is to introduce into defamation via the defence of qualified privilege an element of fault focused on the 'reasonable journalist' (see *Roberts v Gable* (2008), especially para.32). This has been necessary because, as Lord Nicholls indicated in *Reynolds*, the European Convention of Human Rights and Fundamental Freedoms guarantees freedom of expression in Article 10. The problem was that the judges had allocated to themselves the job of reviewing editorial decisions founded on criteria (Lord Nicholls' ten points) that were interpreted in a way that was possibly more intrusive than the criteria the courts apply when it comes to judicial review of administrative decisions. The effect, then, of the *Reynolds* decision is to introduce into English law a power to review media decisions; but the effect of *Jameel* is to assert that the ten points are not to be treated as obstacles to press freedom but a code seemingly in support of it.

2. A full review of the present scope and extent of the qualified privilege defence as it relates to journalism can be found in Ward L.J.'s judgment in *Roberts v Gable* (2008), especially at paras 32 and 61 (read in the law report).

QUESTIONS

1. Sedley L.J. has stated that it is not for judges to determine the editorial policy of the press (see above p.41). Does not the notion of the reasonable journalist in fact allow the judges to do just this?

2. Does the *Reynolds* defence apply only to journalists and reporters?

PROBLEM

In *Roberts v Gable* (2008) an action for damages for defamation was brought by members of a right-wing political party against the author of an article published in a magazine that specialised in exposing fascist and racist groups. The article said this: "(i) the first claimant stole money collected at a British National Party ('BNP') rally, (ii) he did not return it until threatened with being reported to the police, (iii) both claimants threatened to kneecap, torture and kill Dave Hill and Robert Jeffries alias Bob James, and the families of Dave Hill and Robert Jeffries alias Bob James and (iv) both claimants might be subject to police investigation." The defendant raised the defences of justification and qualified privilege. Study the judgments (above) in *Reynolds* and *Jameel* and, assuming that the journalist cannot actually prove the truth of the allegations, decide whether or not the defence of qualified privilege might be successful.

8.3.5 Offer of amends

Legislation now offers a new, if somewhat limited, defence.

Defamation Act 1996 (c.31)

"**2 Offer to make amends**.

(1) A person who has published a statement alleged to be defamatory of another may offer to make amends under this section.

(2) The offer may be in relation to the statement generally or in relation to a specific defamatory meaning which the person making the offer accepts that the statement conveys ("a qualified offer"). . . .

(4) An offer to make amends under this section is an offer—

   (a) to make a suitable correction of the statement complained of and a sufficient apology to the aggrieved party,

   (b) to publish the correction and apology in a manner that is reasonable and practicable in the circumstances, and

   (c) to pay to the aggrieved party such compensation (if any), and such costs, as may be agreed or determined to be payable. . . . .

3 Accepting an offer to make amends.

(1) If an offer to make amends under section 2 is accepted by the aggrieved party, the following provisions apply.

(2) The party accepting the offer may not bring or continue defamation proceedings in respect of the publication concerned against the person making the offer, but he is entitled to enforce the offer to make amends,. . .

4 Failure to accept offer to make amends.

(1) If an offer to make amends under section 2, duly made and not withdrawn, is not accepted by the aggrieved party, the following provisions apply.

(2) The fact that the offer was made is a defence (subject to subsection (3)) to defamation proceedings in respect of the publication in question by that party against the person making the offer.

   A qualified offer is only a defence in respect of the meaning to which the offer related.

(3) There is no such defence if the person by whom the offer was made knew or had reason to believe that the statement complained of—

   (a) referred to the aggrieved party or was likely to be understood as referring to him, and

   (b) was both false and defamatory of that party

but it shall be presumed until the contrary is shown that he did not know and had no reason to believe that was the case.

(4) The person who made the offer need not rely on it by way of defence, but if he does he may not rely on any other defence.

   If the offer was a qualified offer, this applies only in respect of the meaning to which the offer related.

(5) The offer may be relied on in mitigation of damages whether or not it was relied on as a defence."

NOTE

Careful reading of these provisions will soon indicate they do not offer much protection for the press.

8.4 Misrepresentation and misstatement

The case of *Spring v Guardian Assurance* (1995) (above p.287) has already indicated how defamation and the tort of negligent misstatement (*Hedley Byrne v Heller* (1964), p.134) can overlap. Yet misstatement and misrepresentation are governed by rules that are very different from defamation: the basis of liability is the defendant's fault and even proof of carelessness will not be enough in itself to establish liability. The claimant must also prove a special relationship. Defamation, in contrast, arises simply out of the invasion of the claimant's reputation interest, and fault, if it has any role at all, is restricted to certain defences. Liability, in other words, is strict. Negligence and defamation are not, however, the only torts relevant to damage done by words. Where there has been an intentional misrepresentation—a deliberate lie—the tort of deceit will come into play and even a completely innocent misrepresentation, where it has led to a contract, may attract the equitable remedy of rescission (*Redgrave v Hurd* (1881); C&MC, p.240). This latter remedy takes one outside tort and into contract, but misrepresentation in general is a field of liability that often operates at the frontier between tort and contract.

8.4.1 Deceit

The first distinction that needs to be made is between fraudulent and negligent misstatement. Where the defendant has told a deliberate lie, and this results in loss to another, the tort of deceit may be available. Its elements of liability are neatly summarised in the next extract.

Bradford Building Society v Borders **[1941] 2 All E.R. 205, HL**

Viscount Maugham: "... My Lords, we are dealing here with a common law action of deceit, which requires four things to be established. First, there must be a representation of fact made by words, or, it may be, by conduct. The phrase will include a case where the defendant has manifestly approved and adopted a representation made by some third person. On the other hand, mere silence, however morally wrong, will not support an action of deceit: *Peek v Gurney* per Lord Chelmsford, and per Lord Cairns, and *Arkwright v Newbold*. Secondly, the representation must be made with a knowledge that it is false. It must be wilfully false, or at least made in the absence of any genuine belief that it is true: *Derry v Peek* and *Nocton v Ashburton (Lord)*. Thirdly, it must be made with the intention that it should be acted upon by the plaintiff, or by a class of persons which will include the plaintiff, in the manner which resulted in damage to him: *Peek v Gurney* and *Smith v Chadwick*. If, however, fraud be established, it is immaterial that there was no intention to cheat or injure the person to whom the false statement was made: *Derry v Peek*, and *Peek v Gurney*. Fourthly, it must be proved that the plaintiff has acted upon the false statement and has sustained damage by so doing: *Clarke v Dickson*. I am not, of course, attempting to make a complete statement of the law of deceit, but only to state the main facts which a plaintiff must establish ..."

NOTES

1. See also the Fraud Act 2006.

2. The main difficulty facing any claimant wishing to sue in deceit is that fraud must be proved. And this is by no means easy. Nevertheless, if the claimant succeeds he can expect the courts to be more generous when it comes to assessing compensation.

Smith New Court Securities Ltd v Scrimgeour Vickers Ltd **[1997] A.C. 254, HL**

This was an action for damages in the tort of deceit against a defendant who had induced, by fraudulent misrepresentation, the claimants to buy shares at a price which, soon after the purchase, dropped considerably. The trial judge awarded damages of over £10 million, but this was reduced to just over £1 million by the Court of Appeal. The House of Lords (Lords Browne-Wilkinson, Keith, Mustill, Slynn and Steyn) reinstated the trial judge's award.

Lord Browne-Wilkinson: ". . . In sum, in my judgment the following principles apply in assessing the damages payable where the plaintiff has been induced by a fraudulent misrepresentation to buy property: (1) the defendant is bound to make reparation for all the damage directly flowing from the transaction; (2) although such damage need not have been foreseeable, it must have been directly caused by the transaction; (3) is assessing such damage, the plaintiff is entitled to recover by way of damages the full price paid by him, but he must give credit for any benefits which he has received as a result of the transaction; (4) as a general rule, the benefits received by him include the market value of the property acquired as at the date of acquisition; but such general rule is not to be inflexibly applied where to do so would prevent him obtaining full compensation for the wrong suffered; (5) although the circumstances in which the general rule should not apply cannot be comprehensively stated, it will normally not apply where either (a) the misrepresentation has continued to operate after the date of the acquisition of the asset so as to induce the plaintiff to retain the asset or (b) the circumstances of the case are such that the plaintiff is, by reason of the fraud, locked into the property. (6) In addition, the plaintiff is entitled to recover consequential losses caused by the transaction; (7) the plaintiff must take all reasonable steps to mitigate his loss once he has discovered the fraud.

In the circumstances, it would not in my judgment compensate Smith for the actual loss they have suffered (ie the difference between the contract price and the resale price eventually realised) if Smith were required to give credit for the shares having a value of 78p on 21 July 1989. Having acquired the shares at 82p for stock Smith could not commercially have sold on that date at 78p. It is not realistic to treat Smith as having received shares worth 78p each when in fact, in real life, they could not commercially have sold or realised the shares at that price on that date. In my judgment, this is one of those cases where to give full reparation to Smith, the benefit which Smith ought to bring into account to be set against its loss for the total purchase price paid should be the actual resale price achieved by Smith when eventually the shares were sold. . . ."

Lord Steyn: ". . . That brings me to the question of policy whether there is a justification for differentiating between the extent of liability for civil wrongs depending on where in the sliding scale from strict liability to intentional wrongdoing the particular civil wrong fits in. It may be said that logical symmetry and a policy of not punishing intentional wrongdoers by civil remedies favour a uniform rule. On the other hand, it is a rational and defensible strategy to impose wider liability on an intentional wrongdoer. As *Hart and Honoré, Causation in the Law*, 2nd ed. (1985), p 304 observed, an innocent plaintiff may, not without reason, call on a morally reprehensible defendant to pay the whole of the loss he caused. The exclusion of heads of loss in the law of negligence, which reflects considerations of legal policy, does not necessarily avail the intentional wrongdoer. Such a policy of imposing more stringent remedies on an intentional wrongdoer serves two purposes. First it serves a deterrent purpose in discouraging fraud. Counsel for Citibank argued that the sole purpose of the law of tort generally, and the tort of deceit in particular, should be to compensate the victims of civil wrongs. That is far too narrow a view. Professor Glanville Williams identified four possible purposes of an action for damages in tort: appeasement, justice, deterrence and compensation: see 'The Aims of the Law of Tort' (1951) 4 CLP 137. He concluded, at p 172:

'Where possible the law seems to like to ride two or three horses at once; but occasionally a situation occurs where one must be selected. The tendency is then to choose the deterrent purpose for tort of intention, the compensatory purpose for other torts.'

And in the battle against fraud civil remedies can play a useful and beneficial role. Secondly, as between the fraudster and the innocent party, moral considerations militate in favour of requiring the fraudster to bear the risk of misfortunes directly caused by his fraud. I make no apology for referring to moral considerations. The law and morality are inextricably interwoven. To a large extent the law is simply formulated and declared morality. And, as *Oliver Wendell Holmes, The Common Law* (ed. M De W Howe), p 106, observed, the very notion of deceit with its overtones of wickedness is drawn from the moral world. . . .''

QUESTIONS

1. Is this case authority for the proposition that "bad people pay more" (Weir)?

2. Is this case authority for the proposition that morality is formally part of the law of tort?

8.4.2 **Negligence**

Before 1964 damages actions at common law for damage done by words had to be based either on a breach of contract or on the torts of defamation, deceit or one of the economic torts. The position was changed by the *Hedley Byrne* case (1964) (see p.134). Other cases of importance are: *Caparo Industries v Dickman* (1990) (p.162); *Spring v Guardian Assurance* (1995) (p.287); *White v Jones* (1995) (p.289). For a case of misstatement causing personal injury see *Wilkinson v Downton* (1897) (p.8).

8.4.3 **Statute**

Where a person suffers loss as a result of entering a contract induced by a misrepresentation, damages used to be recoverable only if the claimant could prove, before 1964, fraud and, after 1964, negligence. This position has now been amended by statute: see Misrepresentation Act 1967 s.2 (C&MC, p.237). One interesting question with respect to s.2(1) is whether damages are to be awarded according to the principles of the tort of negligence or the tort of deceit. For a judicial analysis of s.2 see *Witter Ltd v TBP Industries* (1996) (C&MC, p.238).

8.5 Professional liability

Many of the negligent misstatement cases can be classified not only under the tort of negligence or under liability for words. They can equally be seen as professional liability cases since a great many of them involve professional defendants such as bankers, solicitors surveyors and the like. A category of 'professional liability' is valuable because the breach of duty test is not one dependent upon the reasonable man test (see **4.2.4**). It is dependent upon the reasonable man exercising the particular professional skill in question. Another reason why professional liability is a useful category is because it acts as a meeting point of contractual and non-contractual obligations which, as the next case shows, can directly influence the outcome of a litigation problem. Often the damage in these professional liability questions (except of course in the case of medical negligence) is pure economic loss and this is another factor that makes them problematic (cf. **4.3.2**). However, another interesting aspect of the next extracted case is that the damage was physical.

Marc Rich & Co v Bishop Rock Ltd **[1996] 1 A.C. 211, HL**

This was an action for damages by owners of a cargo lost at sea against a firm of ship surveyors. The action was dismissed by the House of Lords (Lords Steyn, Keith, Jauncey and Browne-Wilkinson; Lord Lloyd dissenting).

Lord Steyn: ". . . In this case the question is whether a classification society owed a duty of care to a third party, the owners of cargo laden on a vessel, arising from the careless performance of a survey of a damaged vessel by the surveyor of the classification society which resulted in the vessel being allowed to sail and subsequently sinking. It is a novel question. In England no classification society, engaged by owners to perform a survey, has ever been held liable to cargo owners on the ground of a careless conduct of any survey. Your Lordships have also been informed that there is apparently no reported case in which such a duty has been recognised in any foreign court. Given the fact that surveyors of classification societies have regularly performed occasional surveys of laden vessels for over a century and a half the novel nature of the problem may not be entirely without significance. Ultimately, however, the problem must be considered in accordance with our tort law as it now stands without any a priori disposition for or against the legal sustainability of such a claim. . . .

(a) Direct physical loss?

Counsel for the cargo owners argued that the present case involved the infliction of *direct* physical loss. At first glance the issue of directness may seem a matter of terminology rather than substance. In truth it is a material factor. The law more readily attaches the consequences of actionable negligence to directly inflicted physical loss than to indirectly inflicted physical loss. For example, if the NKK surveyor had carelessly dropped a lighted cigarette into a cargo hold known to contain a combustible cargo, thereby causing an explosion and the loss of the vessel and cargo, the assertion that the classification society was in breach of a duty of care might have been a strong one. That would be a paradigm case of directly inflicted physical loss. . . . In the present case the shipowner was primarily responsible for the vessel sailing in a seaworthy condition. The role of the NKK was a subsidiary one. In my view the carelessness of the NKK surveyor did not involve the direct infliction of physical damage in the relevant sense. That by no means concludes the answer to the general question. But it does introduce the right perspective on one aspect of this case. . . .

(f) Policy factors

Counsel for the cargo owners argued that a decision that a duty of care existed in this case would not involve wide ranging exposure for NKK and other classification societies to claims in tort. That is an unrealistic position. . . .

At present the system of settling cargo claims against shipowners is a relatively simple one. The claims are settled between the two sets of insurers. If the claims are not settled, they are resolved in arbitration or court proceedings. If a duty is held to exist in this case as between the classification society and cargo owners, classification societies would become potential defendants in many cases. An extra layer of insurance would become involved. The settlement process would inevitably become more complicated and expensive. Arbitration proceedings and court proceedings would often involve an additional party. And often similar issues would have to be canvassed in separate proceedings since the classification societies would not be bound by arbitration clauses in the contracts of carriage. If such a duty is recognised, there is a risk that classification societies might be unwilling from time to time to survey the very vessels which most urgently require independent examination. It will also divert men and resources from the prime function of classification societies, namely to save life and ships at sea. These factors are, by themselves, far from decisive. But in an overall assessment of the case they merit consideration.

Is the imposition of a duty of care fair, just and reasonable?

Like Mann LJ in the Court of Appeal [1994] 1 WLR 1071, 1085H, I am willing to assume (without deciding) that there was a sufficient degree of proximity in this case to fulfil that requirement for the existence of a duty of care. The critical question is therefore whether it would be fair, just and reasonable to impose such a duty. For my part I am satisfied that the factors and arguments advanced on behalf of cargo owners are decisively outweighed by the cumulative effect, if a duty is recognised, of the matters discussed [earlier]. . . . and the other considerations of policy. By way of summary, I look at the matter from the point of view of the three parties concerned. I conclude that the recognition of a duty would be unfair, unjust and unreasonable as against the shipowners who would ultimately have to bear the cost of holding classification societies liable, such consequence being at variance with the bargain between shipowners and cargo owners based on an internationally agreed contractual structure. It would also be unfair, unjust and unreasonable towards classification societies, notably because they act for the collective welfare and unlike shipowners they would not have the benefit of any limitation provisions. Looking at the matter from the point of view of cargo owners, the existing system provides them with the protection of the Hague Rules or Hague-Visby Rules. But that protection is limited under such Rules and by tonnage limitation provisions. Under the existing system any shortfall is readily insurable. In my judgment the lesser injustice is done by not recognising a duty of care. It follows that I would reject the primary way in which counsel for the cargo owners put his case. . . ."

Lord Lloyd (dissenting): ". . . How. . . does the position of a surveyor, called in by shipowners because the vessel is leaking, differ from that of the shiprepairer? The answer is that it differs not at all. If it is fair, just and reasonable to hold a shiprepairer liable to an unlimited extent for damage to cargo on board caused by his negligence, even though the damage does not occur until after the vessel has sailed, why should it not be fair, just and reasonable in the case of a surveyor? Suppose in the case of the inspection cover, the surveyor negligently tells the fitter that four bolts are sufficient to secure the cover, instead of the usual six, how could it be fair, just and reasonable that the surveyor should not be liable? On what principle would the fitter be liable in such circumstances, when he acts unadvised, but not the surveyor who advises him? No 'coherent system of law' to use the language of Sir Donald Nicholls V-C in *White v Jones* [1993] 3 WLR 730, 740, should permit such a result. . . .

Conclusion

The overriding consideration in the present case is that the cargo owners, as we are asked to assume, have suffered physical damage to their cargo, and such damage was caused by Mr Ducat's negligence, for which NKK are responsible on ordinary principles of respondeat superior. . . . We are not here asked to extend the law of negligence into a new field. We are not even asked to make an incremental advance. All that is required is a straightforward application of *Donoghue v Stevenson*. The ground is already marked out by cases such as *Haseldine v CA Daw & Son Ltd* [1941] 2 KB 343, *Clay v AJ Crump & Sons Ltd* [1964] 1 QB 533, *Voli v Inglewood Shire Council* (1963) 110 CLR 74 and *Muirhead v Industrial Tank Specialities Ltd* [1986] QB 507, 532. In physical damage cases proximity very often goes without saying. Where the facts cry out for the imposition of a duty of care between the parties, as they do here, it would require an exceptional case to refuse to impose a duty on the ground that it would not be fair, just and reasonable. Otherwise there is a risk that the law of negligence will disintegrate into a series of isolated decisions without any coherent principles at all, and the retreat from *Anns* will turn into a rout. . . ."

QUESTIONS

1. Is this a case where policy defeated the logical application of a rule?
2. Do you think that the claimants regarded the cargo as anything more than an economic asset?

PROBLEM

A large property company owns many commercial buildings which form the major part of its investment assets. A potential tenant of one of these buildings hires a reputable firm of surveyors to carry out a survey of the building, but an employee of the surveyors negligently causes a fire in the building and it is totally destroyed. The property company's building insurance pays an indemnity to the property company for this loss and then seeks to reclaim the money in an action for negligence against the surveyors. Will the action in negligence succeed?

8.6 Threats

Threats are a means of causing damage by words and threats of violence aimed directly at a victim can amount in themselves to trespass (*Read v Cocker* (1853); and see Protection from Harassment

Act 1997 s.4). But many threats are of an economic kind and this takes one into the realm of the economic torts (or trade, business and labour relations torts). This is a complex area often outside many foundational tort courses, but some of the basic cases are to be found in **Chapter 3**. One leading economic tort case involving damage arising out of a threatening statement is *Rookes v Barnard* (1964) (p.102). Note also that harassment is now actionable (see p.114)

Protection from Harassment Act 1997 (c.40)

"**7 Interpretation of this group of sections**

(2) References to harassing a person include alarming the person or causing the person distress.

(3) A 'course of conduct' must involve—

(a) in the case of conduct in relation to a single person (see section 1(1)), conduct on at least two occasions in relation to that person, or

(b) in the case of conduct in relation to two or more persons (see section 1(1A)), conduct on at least one occasion in relation to each of those persons. . .

(4) 'Conduct' includes speech."

NOTE

See also p.114 for further extracts from the 1997 Act.

9 Liability of public bodies

In continental systems the distinction between public and private law is fundamental and this reflects itself in tort law in the difference between civil and administrative liability. In other words the tortious liability of state bodies or officials is part of administrative rather than private law. Now, according to traditional English constitutional theory, a separate chapter on the liability of public bodies in tort ought to be superfluous since the common law recognises no formal distinction between public and private law. Everybody, public or private, is subject to the same liability rules. The position, however, proves in substance to be a little more complex.

9.1 Public and private law

The distinction between public and private law has generated much literature both on the continent (as one might expect given that it is a division that goes back to Roman law) and in the United Kingdom. Something thus needs to be said about the nature of the distinction and its relevance to the common law.

9.1.1 Nature of the distinction

The first, and still the most influential, definition was given by the Roman jurist Ulpian who was assassinated in 223 (or 228) AD.

> **Justinian, *Digest*, Book 1, Title 1**
>
> "**1**. ULPIAN . .. **2**. There are two branches of this subject: public law and private law. Public law is that which pertains to the position of the Roman state (*status rei Romanae*), private that which pertains to individual interests (*utilitates*): for certain matters are of public interest others of private. Public law consists of religious rites, the priesthood and public offices. Private law is tripartite, for it derived from the rules of natural law, the *ius gentium* and civil law."

NOTE

Public law is concerned with the interests of the state—with the public interest—private law, with the interests of individuals. However this does not give the whole picture even with respect to Roman law itself. Another basis for the distinction is to be found in the difference between two types of power relations upon which much of Roman law might be said to be based. This is the difference between *dominium* (ownership) and *imperium* (sovereignty). Private law might be said to be about ownership (and its satellite institutions) while public law is about sovereignty (and associated concepts). However in medieval feudal Europe the distinction had little meaning since political power (*imperium*) was based upon the grant of land (*dominium*). With the decline of feudalism and the rise of the nation state the Roman model once again became the basis of legal and political thinking.

9.1.2 Theoretical and practical considerations

One recurring problem with the public/private distinction is the isolation of a definitional and practical theory upon which the distinction can be based.

André Demichel & Pierre Lalumière, *Le droit public*, 7th edn (Presses Universitaires de France, 1996), pp.6–11 (translation Geoffrey Samuel)

"The distinction [between public and private law] is made up of several elements which are superimposed on each other without always overlapping.

1. **The factual distinction.**—The factual distinction between public and private law rests on a simple idea: public law being the law applicable to the state and to administrative officials, the distinction criterion between public and private law will be the intervention of the state in legal relations. As soon as this intervention takes place, the law applicable will have the character of public law. Thus public law will be the law dealing with the organisation of the state and its relation with individuals; private law will be just the law dealing with relations between private individuals.

2. **The formal distinction.**—Public and private law can be distinguished from a formal viewpoint, through technique. In this sense, as soon as concepts and legal techniques foreign to the ordinary law of private relationships are used, there is public law. . . .

3. **The functional distinction.**—The functional distinction refers to the respective objectives of public and private law rules. The latter would protect only private interests while public law rules would be destined to safeguarding the public interest (*l'intérêt général*). . . .

At the end of the day, none of the possible criteria of distinction has in itself an absolute value. Can then the three criteria taken together permit the putting of a given fact into public or private law? In fact, even this cumulative use cannot give a definitive character to a distinction which has, in essence, a relative character. . . ."

QUESTIONS

1. How might privatisation of public utilities fit within the above schemes?

2. Is human rights law part of public or private law?

3. Should a private corporate body ever be treated as a 'public authority'? If so, upon what test? (cf. *R. (Beer) v Hampshire Farmers' Markets Ltd* (2004))

9.1.3 Traditional common law position

The common law, perhaps because of its feudal past, does not in form distinguish between civil and administrative liability as the following extracts clearly indicate.

Hill v Chief Constable of West Yorkshire **[1989] A.C. 53, HL**

(For facts and other extract see p.39)

Lord Keith: ". . . There is no question that a police officer, like anyone else, may be liable in tort to a person who is injured as a direct result of his acts or omissions. So he may be liable in damages for assault, unlawful arrest, wrongful imprisonment and malicious prosecution, and also for negligence. Instances where liability for negligence has been established are *Knightley v Johns* [1982] 1 WLR 349 and *Rigby v Chief Constable of Northamptonshire* [1985] 1 WLR 1242. Further, a police officer may be guilty of a criminal offence if he wilfully fails to perform a duty which he is bound to perform by common law or by statute: see *Reg v Dytham* [1979] QB 722, where a constable was convicted of wilful neglect of duty because, being present at the scene of a violent assault resulting in the death of the victim, he had taken no steps to intervene. . . ."

Stovin v Wise **[1996] A.C. 923, HL**

(For facts and other extract see p.175)

Lord Hoffmann: ". . . Since *Mersey Docks and Harbour Board Trustees v Gibbs* (1866) LR 1 HL 93 it has been clear law that in the absence of express statutory authority, a public body is in principle liable for torts in the same way as a private person. But its statutory powers or duties may restrict its liability. For example, it may be authorised to do something which necessarily involves committing what would otherwise be a tort. In such a case it will not be liable: *Allen v Gulf Oil Refining Ltd* [1981] AC 1001. Or it may have discretionary powers which enable it to do things to achieve a statutory purpose notwithstanding that they involve a foreseeable risk of damage to others. In such a case, a bona fide exercise of the discretion will not attract liability: *X (Minors) v Bedfordshire County Council* [1995] 2 AC 633 and *Dorset Yacht Co Ltd v Home Office* [1970] AC 1004. . . ."

Tony Weir, Governmental Liability, [1989] *Public Law* **40, pp.47–48**

"From the point of view of the tort lawyer, local government is much more important than central government. Local government may decide less, but it does more, and tort liability attaches to people who do rather than to people who decide . .. The liability of central government may admittedly be in impressive in amount . .. But generally, apart from the prisons and to a smaller extent the military, central government does not seem to be very vulnerable to tort suits. They do not occupy schools, though they seek increasingly to control them; and they do not mend the sidewalks, they only deny the ha'porth of tar required to mend them. Quite different is local government. Everyone sues them, even the Minister for Local Government himself . .."

NOTE

Another reason why English law does not easily distinguish between public and private law is to be found in the next extract.

Davey v Spelthorne Borough Council **[1984] A.C. 262, HL**

Lord Wilberforce: ". . . The expressions 'private law' and 'public law' have recently been imported into the law of England from countries which, unlike our own, have separate systems concerning public law and private law. No doubt they are convenient expressions for descriptive purposes. In this country they must be used with caution, for, typically, English law fastens not on principles but on remedies. The principle remains intact that public authorities and public servants are, unless clearly exempted, answerable in the ordinary courts for wrongs done to individuals. . ."

NOTE

As mentioned at the outset, there is much academic writing on this topic. However Carlow Harlow's article, which set off the whole (later 20th century) debate, remains by far the most intellectually original piece: (1980) 43 *Modern Law Review* 241. A good (and original) tribute to this article is: M Taggart, "The Peculiarities of the English: Resisting the Public/Private Distinction", in P. Craig & R. Rawlings (eds), *Law and Administration in Europe: Essays in Honour of Carol Harlow* (Oxford: OUP, 2003), p.107.

9.1.4 **Changing attitudes**

As Lord Wilberforce hinted, the public/private division was beginning to find its way into common law thinking in the 1980s. Indeed in *O'Reilly v Mackman* (1983) Lord Diplock appeared formally to accept the distinction. The use of 'private' law remedies to enforce 'public' law rights could, said Lord Diplock, amount to an abuse of process. However, as the next extract shows, the importation was to cause as many problems as it solved.

Mercury Communications Ltd v Director General of Telecommunications **[1996] 1 W.L.R. 48, HL**

Lord Slynn: ". .. The recognition by Lord Diplock [in *O'Reilly v Mackman* [1983] 2 AC 237] that exceptions exist to the general rule may introduce some uncertainty but it is a small price to pay to avoid the over-rigid demarcation between procedures reminiscent of earlier disputes as to the forms of action and of disputes as to the competence of jurisdictions apparently encountered in civil law countries where a distinction between public and private law has been recognised. It is of particular importance, as I see it, to retain some flexibility as the precise limits of what is called 'public law' and what is called 'private law' are by no means worked out. The experience of other countries seems to show that the working out of this distinction is not always an easy matter. In the absence of a single procedure allowing all remedies—quashing, injunctive and declaratory relief, damages—some flexibility as to the use of different procedures is necessary. It has to be borne in mind that the overriding question is whether the proceedings constitute an abuse of the process of the court. . . ."

NOTE

Despite these reservations, the distinction can prove useful when it comes to constitutionally sensitive matters.

R. v Somerset CC, Ex p. Fewings [1995] 1 W.L.R. 1037, CA

This was an action for judicial review to quash a local authority decision to ban hunting on land owned by the authority. A majority of the Court of Appeal (Sir Thomas Bingham M.R. and Swinton Thomas L.J.; Simon Brown L.J. dissenting) upheld the judge's decision to quash the decision.

> **Sir Thomas Bingham M.R.:** ". . . The point is often made that unelected unrepresentative judges have no business to be deciding questions of potentially far-reaching social concern which are more properly the preserve of elected representatives at national or local level. In some cases the making of such decisions may be inescapable, but in general the point is well made. In the present case it certainly is. The court has no role whatever as an arbiter between those who condemn hunting as barbaric and cruel and those who support it as a traditional country sport more humane in its treatment of deer or foxes (as the case may be) than other methods of destruction such as shooting, snaring, poisoning or trapping. This is of course a question on which most people hold views one way or the other. But our personal views are wholly irrelevant to the drier and more technical question which the court is obliged to answer. That is whether the county council acted lawfully in making the decision it did on the grounds it did. In other words, were members entitled in reaching their decision to give effect to their acceptance of the cruelty argument?
>
> In seeking to answer that question it is, as the judge very clearly explained, at pp 523–525, critical to distinguish between the legal position of the private landowner and that of a land-owning local authority. To the famous question asked by the owner of the vineyard ('Is it not lawful for me to do what I will with mine own?' St. Matthew, chapter 20, verse 15) the modern answer would be clear: 'Yes, subject to such regulatory and other constraints as the law imposes.' But if the same question were posed by a local authority the answer would be different. It would be: 'No, it is not lawful for you to do anything save what the law expressly or impliedly authorises. You enjoy no unfettered discretions. There are legal limits to every power you have.' As Laws J put it, at p 524, the rule for local authorities is that any action to be taken must be justified by positive law. . . ."

NOTE

This case emphasises the distinction between *dominium* and *imperium*. The local authority was indeed the owner of the land and an ordinary private owner has the right do as he wishes with, or on, his own property (see *Bradford Corporation v Pickles* (1895), p.72). However a local authority is not an ordinary owner since it must exercise the rights of ownership, not in its own 'private' interests, but in the 'public' interests of the community. What the public/private distinction is doing here is to subject the power of *dominium* to principles that apply to *imperium*, for the authority was in substance exercising public rather than private power. *Fewings* indicates why the result of *Bradford Corporation* would have been different if the parties had been reversed; if the corporation had been digging holes on its land deliberately to harm a private citizen the latter could probably have had the decision to dig holes quashed through a judicial review action in administrative law.

9.1.5 Public and private remedies

Lord Wilberforce indicated above that English law tends to fasten onto remedies rather than rights. In actions against public bodies the form of the remedy is of particular importance: if the claimant wants damages a cause of action in tort must be established: see *X (Minors) v Bedfordshire County Council* (1995) (p.32); *Three Rivers District Council v Governor and Company of The Bank of England (No 3)* (1996) (p.122); and the next case.

Gorringe v Calderdale MBC [2004] 1 W.L.R. 1057, HL

This was an action for damages by a car driver against a local authority in respect of personal injuries suffered in a serious car accident. The claimant's "case is, first, that the absence of suitable road signage constituted a failure 'to maintain' the road in such a condition as to be safe for use; and, secondly, that the council's common law duty of care required it to put into effect safety measures that included the positioning of the road signs in order to discharge its section 39 [of the Road Traffic Act 1988] duty" (Lord Scott). The House of Lords (Lords Steyn, Hoffmann, Scott, Rodger and Brown) dismissed the claim.

Lord Steyn: ". . . **2** There are . . . a few remarks that I would wish to make about negligence and statutory duties and powers. This is a subject of great complexity and very much an evolving area of the law. No single decision is capable of providing a comprehensive analysis. It is a subject on which an intense focus on the particular facts and on the particular statutory background, seen in the context of the contours of our social welfare state, is necessary. On the one hand the courts must not contribute to the creation of a society bent on litigation, which is premised on the illusion that for every misfortune there is a remedy. On the other hand, there are cases where the courts must recognise on principled grounds the compelling demands of corrective justice or what has been called 'the rule of public policy which has first claim on the loyalty of the law: that wrongs should be remedied': *M (A Minor) v Newham London Borough Council* and *X (Minors) v Bedfordshire County Council* [1995] 2 AC 633, 663, per Sir Thomas Bingham MR. Sometimes cases may not obviously fall in one category or the other. Truly difficult cases arise. . . ."

Lord Hoffmann: ". . . **17** The alternative claim is for common law negligence. . . . If the highway authority at common law owed no duty other than to keep the road in repair and even that duty was not actionable in private law, it is impossible to contend that it owes a common law duty to erect warning signs on the road. It is not sufficient that it might reasonably have foreseen that in the absence of such warnings, some road users might injure themselves or others. Reasonable foreseeability of physical injury is the standard criterion for determining the duty of care owed by people who undertake an activity which carries a risk of injury to others. But it is insufficient to justify the imposition of liability upon someone who simply does nothing: who neither creates the risk nor undertakes to do anything to avert it. The law does recognise such duties in special circumstances: see, for example, *Goldman v Hargrave* [1967] 1 AC 645 on the positive duties of adjoining landowners to prevent fire or harmful matter from crossing the boundary. But the imposition of such a liability upon a highway authority through the law of negligence would be inconsistent with the well established rules which have always limited its liability at common law. . . .

38 My Lords, I must make it clear that this appeal is concerned only with an attempt to impose upon a local authority a common law duty to act based solely on the existence of a broad public law duty. We are not concerned with cases in which public authorities have actually done acts or entered into relationships or undertaken responsibilities which give rise to a common law duty of care. In such cases the fact that the public authority acted pursuant to a statutory power or public duty does not necessarily negative the existence of a duty. A hospital trust provides medical treatment pursuant to the public law duty in the 1977 Act, but the existence of its common law duty is based simply upon its acceptance of a professional relationship with the patient no different from that which would be accepted by a doctor in private practice. The duty rests upon a solid, orthodox common law foundation and the question is not whether it is created by the statute but whether the terms of the statute (for example, in requiring a particular thing to be done or conferring a discretion) are sufficient to exclude it. The law in this respect has been well established since *Geddis v Proprietors of Bann Reservoir* (1878) 3 App Cas 430. . . ."

Lord Scott: ". . . **70** . . . The reason why damages in a private action for breach of the statutory duty imposed by section 39 [of the Road Traffic Act 1988] cannot be recovered is because section 39, correctly construed, does not impose a duty owed to any individual. It imposes a duty owed to the public as a whole. It forms part of the corpus of public law, not private law, and can only be enforced by the procedures and remedies available for enforcing public law duties. . . ."

Lord Rodger: . . . **93** If traffic authorities carry out their duties under section 39, this should help to make the roads safer by informing their decisions as to the repairs and modifications, including the placing of warning signs, that should be carried out. In the exercise of their public law powers and duties, highway authorities do often, or even usually, warn of prospective dangers at junctions or crests in the road, but drivers cannot rely on them always having done so. Drivers must take care for themselves and drive at an appropriate speed, irrespective of whether or not there is a warning sign. By insisting that drivers always look out for dangers themselves and not rely on others, the common law supports the overall policy of promoting road safety. If drivers fail to drive carefully and others are injured, the others can recover compensation from the drivers' insurers or from the Motor Insurers' Bureau. Neither the drivers nor their passengers, nor indeed their insurers, can recover damages from the highway authorities for not having placed a warning sign. If that settled pattern is to be changed, it is for Parliament to make the change and to approve the additional funding needed by the authorities to handle and meet the claims. . . ."

Lord Brown: ". . . **100** I agree with the reasons given in the speech of my noble and learned friend, Lord Hoffmann, for distinguishing that line of authority-essentially because the common law duty of care in those cases was found or suggested to have arisen not by reference to the existence of the respective authorities' statutory powers and duties but rather from the relationships in fact created between those authorities and the children for whom in differing ways they had assumed responsibility. I would add, moreover, this further distinction. Unless in those cases the court were to find the authority's various responsibilities capable of giving rise to a common law duty of care, those wronged children, themselves wholly blameless, would go uncompensated, however inadequately their interests had been safeguarded. In the highway context, by contrast, the claimant (or some other road user involved in the accident) will almost inevitably himself have been at fault. In these circumstances it seems to me entirely reasonable that the policy of the law should be to leave the liability for the accident on the road user who negligently caused it rather than look to the highway authority to protect him against his own wrong. . . ."

NOTE

A sort of distinction between public and private law has always existed in common law at the level of remedies (cf. Lord Scott above). The old prerogative writs, now amalgamated into the action for judicial review, were for the most part available only against public bodies (although habeas corpus was one exception and was used in family law). Today judicial review lies only against public and quasi-public bodies. Of course the distinction was not watertight because the 'private' law forms of action such as trespass were available against public bodies (see e.g. *Cooper v Wandsworth Board of Works* (1863)). Today this remains true of the causes of action in tort. However some of these causes of action, like abuse of public office, are available only against public officials. Note also that liability under the Human Rights Act 1998 ss 6–8 applies only to a 'public authority' (see *R (Beer) v Hampshire Farmers' Markets Ltd* (2004)).

9.1.6 Individual and the community

One theme to be found at the heart of French public law is the dichotomy between the individual and the community.

Jacques Moreau, *La responsabilité administrative*, Presses Universitaires de France, 1986, pp.108–110 (translation Geoffrey Samuel)

"Indeed, at first sight the choice made by the Conseil d'État to apply the system of liability without fault seems to be explicable by the idea of risk. It is because the administration has created certain exceptional risks, in exposing its officials for service reasons, that in the case of accident the latter are compensated without having to prove fault by the service; it is because of the special risks for third parties caused by 'dangerous things' or 'dangerous methods' that the victims can obtain compensation as soon as they show abnormal and special damage together with a causal link. Interpreting this case law certain writers. .. have seen in it the ratification of what they call the 'socialisation of risk'.

This idea is not wrong, but it has only a limited explanatory value. For a start, many public works (roads, bridges, canals, walls. ..) do not in themselves harbour particular dangers, and the basis of liability which might be valuable for a hydroelectric or nuclear power station loses all *raison d'être* in the majority of public works damages cases. Furthermore, the application of strict liability to those who voluntarily or occasionally assist in public service tallies only imperfectly with the idea of danger. .. Finally, except by distorting the sense of language, the case law of *Couitéas*, on the refusal of intervention of the police force and *Sté La Fleurette*, with its recent developments concerning the application of administrative regulations, are difficult to reconcile with any notion of 'social risk' or 'legislative risk', even if certain specialists have constructed elaborate structures here!

In the. .. cases just cited, the justification of liability without fault is rather that a certain equilibrium has been broken—and must be re-established by the award of damages—between, on the one hand, a behaviour of the administration that is taken to be inspired by the general interest aim (it is, among other things a part of the definition of the notion of public works) and which 'benefits everyone' and, on the other hand, a 'burden', a relatively serious injury which falls only upon certain persons (adjoining owners, those who assist the administration, public officials exposed to risk, those destined to be affected by certain administrative regulations). The sought after basis of liability is, then, *the equality of citizens before public burdens*, as the frequent conclusions of the *commissaires de gouvernement* and the judgments of certain cases indicate more and more clearly. . . .”

QUESTION

How would the *Conseil d'État* have decided *Read v J Lyons & Co* (1947) (p.209)?

NOTE

In English law this community (equality) principle mentioned by Professor Moreau seems to have been used to arrive at exactly the opposite result.

Dunne v North Western Gas Board [1964] 2 Q.B. 806, CA

This was an action for damages in respect of personal injuries suffered by the claimant as a result of a gas explosion in the street. The claimant based his claim in nuisance and on the strict liability rule in *Rylands v Fletcher* (see p.243). The Court of Appeal (Sellers L.J., Danckwerts L.J. and Davies L.J.) dismissed the claim.

Sellers L.J.: “. . . Gas, water and also electricity services are well-nigh a necessity of modern life, or at least are generally demanded as a requirement for the common good, and one or more are being taken with considerable despatch to every village and hamlet in the country with either statutory compulsion or sanction. It would seem odd that facilities so much sought after by the community and approved by their legislators should be actionable at common law because they have been brought to places where they are required and have escaped without negligence by an unforeseen sequence of mishaps. A sequence of events may be just as unforeseeable and unavoidable and as extraneous to an individual or a supplier of services as an act of God is recognised to be. . . .”

QUESTIONS

1. How might this case have been decided under French law?

2. Does the judge in *Dennis v MOD* (2003) (p.205) start out from a different premise or does he simply draw a different conclusion?

9.2 Central government

Continental systems often view the state as a corporate legal person but this is not the case in English common law. There is no developed legal notion of the state as a juridical entity capable of suing and being sued. Instead there is the notion of the 'Crown' (a concept that of course precedes that of the 'state') which had the great disadvantage, from a tort victim's point of view, of protecting the central government from liability since 'the King could do no wrong'. However the position was altered by statue.

Crown Proceedings Act 1947 (10 & 11 Geo VI, c.44)

"1 Right to sue the Crown

Where any person has a claim against the Crown after the commencement of this Act, and, if this Act had not been passed, the claim might have been enforced, subject to the grant of His Majesty's fiat, by petition of right, or might have been enforced by a proceeding provided by any statutory provision repealed by this Act, then, subject to the provisions of this Act, the claim may be enforced as of right, and without the fiat of His Majesty, by proceedings taken against the Crown for that purpose in accordance with the provisions of this Act.

2 Liability of the Crown in tort

(1) Subject to the provisions of this Act, the Crown shall be subject to all those liabilities in tort to which, if it were a private person of full age and capacity, it would be subject:—

    (*a*) in respect of torts committed by its servants or agents;

    (*b*) in respect of any breach of those duties which a person owes to his servants or agents at common law by reason of being their employer; and

    (*c*) in respect of any breach of the duties attaching at common law to the ownership, occupation, possession or control of property:

Provided that no proceedings shall lie against the Crown by virtue of paragraph (*a*) of this subsection in respect of any act or omission of a servant or agent of the Crown unless the act or omission would apart from the provisions of this Act have given rise to a cause of action in tort against that servant or agent or his estate. . . ."

NOTES

Because there is no concept of the state, central government consists, instead, of various government departments and agencies and when things go wrong, resulting in injury, damage or loss to another, the department may well have to answer either for the act of their employee (vicarious liability) or breach of a non-delegable duty: see *Home Office v Dorset Yacht Co* (1970) (p.254). In claims of negligence the main issue is often one of duty: did the government department owe a duty of care to the claimant?

Rowley v Secretary of State for Work and Pensions **[2007] 1 W.L.R. 2861, CA**

A mother and her children brought actions for damages against the Secretary of State for Work and Pensions in respect of damage caused by the negligence of the Child Support Agency (CPS). They alleged that the CPS had made errors in assessing the liability and amounts payable and that they were guilty of delay; this negligent behaviour had, they claimed, caused economic loss and, in the case of one child, psychological harm. The claims were struck out on the ground that the Secretary of State owed them no duty of care and an appeal to the Court of Appeal was dismissed (Waller, Keene and Dyson L.JJ.).

Dyson L.J.: ". . . **47** The first claimant seeks damages for psychological injury. But in the overwhelming majority of cases, the loss suffered by a person as a result of incompetence on the part of the CSA will be pure economic loss. It is convenient, therefore, to start by considering whether a common law duty of care is owed not to cause pure economic loss.

The general approach to the question whether a duty of care not to cause such loss exists has been considered by the courts on a number of occasions in recent years. . . .

49 Where the question is whether a public authority owes a common law duty of care, it is also necessary to consider (i) whether to impose a duty of care would be inconsistent with the statutory scheme under which it is acting, and (ii) the relevance of the fact (if it be the case) that the statute confers no private law right of action for breach of statutory duty. . . .

51 The principal reason advanced by Mr ter Haar to support the argument that the Secretary of State owes a duty of care on the grounds of an assumption of responsibility is that the person with care is not obliged to have recourse to the 1991 Act. A person with care may obtain maintenance from the absent parent by other means, e.g. by agreement. But that, in my view, is not a sufficient reason for holding that there is an assumption of responsibility by the Secretary of State whenever he performs his functions under the statutory scheme. The critical question is whether the Secretary of State *voluntarily* assumes responsibility and that does not depend on whether the parent chooses or is obliged to make an application for a maintenance assessment. . . .

54 When a person with care applies to the Secretary of State for a maintenance assessment to be made, he is obliged to make it. In making the assessment, he is not a volunteer in any sense. It is true that the 1991 Act also gives the Secretary of State certain discretionary powers, for example, the power to make an interim maintenance assessment, to collect maintenance and to seek liability orders for the purpose of enforcement. But in my judgment, if he decides not to exercise one of these statutory powers, he is not, in making that decision, assuming a voluntary responsibility towards those who are foreseeably affected by it. Likewise if he decides that he will exercise one of the powers, it is not apt to describe what he does when he exercises the power as a voluntary assumption of responsibility. He is not doing anything that is 'akin to contract'. In determining whether or not (and if so how) to exercise his statutory powers, the Secretary of State often has difficult and sensitive decisions to make: see further, at para 82 below. These decisions are amenable to judicial review. They are far removed from a voluntary assumption of responsibility. . . .

72 In my view, the existence of the right of appeal given by section 20 and the right to receive interest on arrears in prescribed circumstances given by section 41, when taken in conjunction with the right to seek judicial review of failures to collect or enforce arrears of maintenance, means that the 1991 Act provides the person with care with substantial protection against incompetence on the part of the CSA. . . .

73 I accept, of course, that the mere fact that there is an alternative remedy is not necessarily a reason for denying the existence of a common law duty of care. It is important to see how comprehensive a remedy is provided and to consider it in the context of the statutory scheme as a whole. Ultimately, what has to be decided is whether, having regard to the purpose of the legislation, Parliament is to be taken as having intended that there should be a right to damages for negligence. The more comprehensive the remedy provided by Parliament, the less likely it is that Parliament is to be taken as having had that intention.

74 In my view, the 1991 Act (taken in conjunction with the right to seek judicial review where the CSA fails to collect or enforce arrears of maintenance) provides a sufficiently comprehensive remedy to lead me to conclude that a duty of care would be inconsistent with the statutory scheme. That is not to say that there will not be cases where the CSA has acted incompetently and loss will be suffered as a result of its incompetence which might be recoverable as damages for negligence (if a duty of care were owed) and cannot be compensated under the statutory scheme. . . .

85 Should there be a duty of care to avoid personal injury? Mr ter Haar submits that different considerations apply in relation to personal injury claims. In many contexts, that is undoubtedly true. But in my view all the reasons that I have given for concluding that it is not fair, just and reasonable to impose a duty of care apply with equal force regardless of the damage that is alleged to have been caused by the CSA's incompetence. In particular, the fact that a common law duty of care would be inconsistent with the statutory scheme is as fatal to a claim in negligence for damages for personal injury as it is to such a claim for pure economic loss. . . ."

QUESTIONS

1. What if the psychological harm had been so severe that it drove the claimant to suicide?

2. Could it be said that the existence of a public law relationship between the Agency and the claimants excluded any private law relationship?

3. Was there no duty of care (i) because of the nature of the damage suffered; (ii) because of the status of the defendant; or (iii) because the defendant's act was a mere omission?

NOTE

Negligence is not, of course, the only tort of relevance to central government liability.

Akenzua v Home Secretary [2003] 1 W.L.R. 741, CA

The estate of a victim of a murder brought an action for damages for abuse of public office against Home Department and Commissioner of Police in respect of the act of one of their officials who had deliberately set free from custody a man known to be a murderer. While free the man murdered the victim. The defendants sought to have the action struck out and were successful at first instance; but an appeal against the striking out by the claimant was allowed by the Court of Appeal (Simon Brown L.J., Sedley L.J. and Scott Baker L.J.)

Sedley L.J.: ". . . 9. The tort of misfeasance in public office originates, at least so far as the law reports take us, in electoral corruption cases beginning in the late 17th century. The right to vote was then a property right, and subsequent cases have likewise typically concerned deprivation of property. There is no reported case where the consequence of the misfeasance has been personal injury or death. But while this may, as Mr Freeland for the Commissioner suggests, be indicative of the historical nature of the tort it cannot be definitive of it. Moreover, no reported decision deals frontally with the question of law which we have to decide. The nature of the tort, however, is now authoritatively described in the decision of the House of Lords in the *Three Rivers* case and it is from this source that the answer to the present appeal has to be derived. . . .

16. Before turning to the arguments, let me put two paradigm cases which were put by the court in argument in varying forms to counsel

(A) A public official corruptly arranges the liberation of a man serving a sentence for attempting to murder his wife, knowing that he will make a further attempt to kill her if allowed to do so. On his release the man finds his wife and kills her.

(B) A public official corruptly arranges the liberation of a man serving a sentence of imprisonment for terrorist bombings, knowing that he will resume his activities if allowed to do so. On his release the man places a bomb in a public place and kills several people.

17. All parties accept that no principle of law excludes the action for misfeasance in public office purely because the consequence is personal injury or death rather than loss of or damage to property. Any other doctrine would give life to the old reproach that the law of England and Wales was more concerned with property than with people. The question is then whether the decision of their Lordships' House in the *Three Rivers* case excludes the action where the predictable victim is neither an identifiable individual nor an identifiable group of individuals.

18. Neither defendant's counsel has been able to explain either the logic or justice of making case A actionable and case B not; yet both counsel submit, in the light of the *Three Rivers* decision, that it is so. Mr Blake, for the claimants, submits that if, as is conceded, case A is actionable as misfeasance in public office at the suit of the victim, so must case B be; and in my judgment he is right. The purpose of the 'class' category of liability is to enlarge case A, not to exclude case B. . . .

21. It follows that the averment that the deceased was a member of a class-any class-is an immaterial averment. Denton killed a single person in the period of his arranged liberty. If he had predictably murdered or maimed more than one person they would form a class for present purposes. What matters is not the predictability of his killing the deceased but the predictability of his killing someone. That is my understanding of the effect of the reasoning in the *Three Rivers* case. It is also case B of my examples. Put another way, but again using the *Three Rivers* taxonomy, Denton's single known victim stands in the same situation as each of those claimants who at the time of the alleged misfeasance in the *Three Rivers* case were only potential depositors; that is to say, she too was a potential victim. The alternative analysis, that the material class was all Denton's potential victims, among whom it is sufficient to be able now to identify the deceased, is feasible but seems to me artificial to the point of torture. On none of these views is the claimants' pleading demurrable. . . ."

QUESTION

Could the Home Department also be liable in the tort of negligence?

NOTES

1. The *Three Rivers* case can be found on p.122.

2. The highway authorities have attracted litigation in respect of the maintenance of public roads: see *Sandhar v Department of Transport* (2005) and *Gorringe v Calderdale MBC* (2004) (p.334).

3. Sometimes state bodies can be claimants in a tort case against a private person or entity: see e.g. *Customs & Excise v Barclays Bank* (2007) (p.137).

9.3 Local authorities

As Tony Weir points out in an extract above (p.331), local authorities find themselves as regular targets for tort claims (see e.g. *Gorringe v Calderdale MBC* (2004), above p.334). The most important of these claims may appear to be those founded on the tort of negligence, but local authorities can equally find themselves facing actions in nuisance and even trespass.

9.3.1 Negligence

Leaving aside the ordinary type of accident claim (where for example a local authority employee drops a hammer on the head of a passer-by), the difficult negligence cases often give rise to two broad types of duty problems. The first is technical; many of the factual situations can display problems of pure economic loss (*Murphy v Brentwood DC* (1991); *Jain v Trent Strategic Health Authority* (2008), p.348) and/or mere omissions (*Stovin v Wise* (1996), p.175). The second type of duty problem is perhaps rooted in the public/private division: the courts have held that there are policy reasons for refusing to hold that the authority owes a duty of care (*X (Minors) v Bedfordshire CC* (1995); *Jain v Trent Strategic Health Authority* (2008), p.348). Of course, in the majority of the cases the technical and the policy become intermixed. The duty of care aspect tends to endow these local authority cases with another characteristic: many are striking out claims in which the authority seeks to put an end to the legal claim at a preliminary stage. This procedure has of itself created problems and as a result the House of Lords seems to have changed direction, as the next case illustrates.

Barrett v Enfield LBC [2001] 2 A.C. 550, HL

This was an action for damages in negligence against a local authority brought by a person who had been in the local authority's care for most of his pre-adult life. He claimed that the local authority had been in breach of its duty to exercise the standard of care of a reasonable parent; and as a result of this breach of duty he suffered physical and psychological injury. The local authority sought to have the action struck out for disclosing no reasonable cause of action. The House of Lords (Lords Browne-Wilkinson, Slynn, Nolan, Steyn and Hutton), reversing the Court of Appeal, refused to strike out the claim.

Lord Slynn: ". . . It is obvious from previous cases and indeed is self-evident that there is a real conflict between on the one hand the need to allow social welfare services exercising statutory powers to do their work in what they as experts consider is the best way in the interests first of the child, but also of the parents and of society, without an unduly inhibiting fear of litigation if something goes wrong, and on the other hand the desirability of providing a remedy in appropriate cases for harm done to a child through the acts or failure to act of such services. . . .

[The] distinction which is sometimes drawn between decisions as to 'policy' and as to 'operational acts' sounds more promising. A pure policy decision where Parliament has entrusted the decision to a public authority is not something which a court would normally be expected to review in a claim in negligence. But again this is not an absolute test. Policy and operational acts are closely linked and the decision to do an operational act may easily

---

involve and flow from a policy decision. Conversely, the policy is affected by the result of the operational act: see *Reg v Chief Constable of Sussex, Ex parte International Trader's Ferry Ltd* [1998] 3 WLR 1260).

Where a statutory power is given to a local authority and damage is caused by what it does pursuant to that power, the ultimate question is whether the particular issue is justiciable or whether the court should accept that it has no role to play. The two tests (discretion and policy/operational) to which I have referred are guides in deciding that question. The greater the element of policy involved, the wider the area of discretion accorded, the more likely it is that the matter is not justiciable so that no action in negligence can be brought. . . . Moreover, I share Lord Browne-Wilkinson's reluctance to introduce the concepts of administrative law into the law of negligence, as Lord Diplock appears to have done [in *Dorset Yacht*]. But in any case I do not read what either Lord Reid or Lord Wilberforce in the *Anns* case (and in particular Lord Reid) said as to the need to show that there has been an abuse of power before a claim can be brought in negligence in the exercise of a statutory discretion as meaning that an action can never be brought in negligence where an act has been done pursuant to the exercise of the discretion. A claim of negligence in the taking of a decision to exercise a statutory discretion is likely to be barred, unless it is wholly unreasonable so as not to be a real exercise of the discretion, or if it involves the making of a policy decision involving the balancing of different public interests; acts done pursuant to the lawful exercise of the discretion can, however, in my view be subject to a duty of care, even if some element of discretion is involved. Thus accepting that a decision to take a child into care pursuant to a statutory power is not justiciable, it does not in my view follow that, having taken a child into care, an authority cannot be liable for what it or its employees do in relation to the child without it being shown that they have acted in excess of power. It may amount to an excess of power, but that is not in my opinion the test to be adopted: the test is whether the conditions in the *Caparo* case have been satisfied. . . .

. . .I consider also that the question whether it is just and reasonable to impose a liability of negligence is not to be decided in the abstract for all acts or omissions of a statutory authority, but is to be decided on the basis of what is proved. The comment of Andenas and Fairgrieve that one of the problems about the uncertainty of the law in this area is that many cases are decided on an application to strike out or on a preliminary issue on assumed facts as stated in the Statement of Claim—'Dealing with such hypothetical facts deprives the courts of the opportunity to apply the operational-policy distinction to concrete facts. It is likely to exacerbate the formulation of clear statements of principle.'—is to be borne in mind. See, also the discussion of the facts in *Phelps v Hillingdon London Borough Council* [1997] 1 WLR 500 where the importance of investigating the precise nature of the service provided was made clear. . . .

Accordingly, I consider that this claim should not be struck out. This does not mean that I think that the appellant must or will win. He faces considerable difficulties, but with great respect to the experience and judgment of the members of the Court of Appeal, I consider that he is entitled to have these matters investigated and not to have them summarily dismissed. I would accordingly allow the appeal."

NOTES

1. Subsequent to this decision the European Court of Human Rights delivered its judgment

on the *X (Minors)* (1995) case: *Z v United Kingdom* (2001). The court held that there had been no violation of art.6 but there was a violation of art.13 (as well as art.3).

2. The question of striking out actions of negligence against local authorities arose again before the House of Lords in *Phelps v Hillingdon LBC* (2001) (read in law report). The position of local authorities in these child abuse cases has now been summed up by Lord Bingham.

D v East Berkshire NHS Trust [2005] 2 A.C. 373, HL

(For facts and other extracts see p.172)

Lord Bingham (dissenting): ". . . **3** The courts below have concluded that in such a situation no duty of care can be owed by the doctor or the social worker to the parent, that accordingly no claim may lie and that these claims brought by the parents must be dismissed with no evidence called and no detailed examination of the facts. In the second appeal there is also a claim by the child, but that has been treated differently. I understand that a majority of my noble and learned friends agree with this conclusion, for which there is considerable authority in the United Kingdom and abroad. But the law in this area has evolved very markedly over the last decade. What appeared to be hard-edged rules precluding the possibility of any claim by parent or child have been eroded or restricted. And a series of decisions of the European Court of Human Rights has shown that application of an exclusionary rule in this sensitive area may lead to serious breaches of Convention rights for which domestic law affords no remedy and for which, at any rate arguably, the law of tort should afford a remedy if facts of sufficient gravity are shown.

4 I would not, for my part, strike out these claims but would allow them to go to trial. A judgment can then be made on the liability of the respective defendants on facts which have been fully explored. At present, we have only an agreed statement of what is, at this stage and for the purpose of legal argument, to be assumed. I take no account of additional factual allegations made by the appellants in their written case which, if true, may well be significant, but which have not been agreed. The facts which have been agreed are important and must be summarised. . . .

22 In *X v Bedfordshire County Council* itself, five child plaintiffs complained that they had been the victims of maltreatment and neglect which had been brought to the notice of the defendant council but on which, for a long time, the council had failed to act. The facts, only assumed when the strike-out application was heard in this country but established or accepted when the claimants took their complaint to Strasbourg, were very strong. An experienced and highly respected child psychiatrist described the children's experiences as 'to put it bluntly, 'horrific'' and added that it was the worst case of neglect and emotional abuse that she had seen in her professional career: *Z v United Kingdom* (2001) 34 EHRR 97, para 40. It was accepted in Strasbourg that the neglect and abuse suffered by the four child applicants reached the threshold of inhuman and degrading treatment (para 74) and a violation of article 3 of the European Convention was found, arising from the failure of the system to protect the child applicants from serious, long-term neglect and abuse (paras 74–75). The court awarded compensation amounting to £320,000, a substantial figure by Strasbourg standards. Yet the local authority's failure to intervene, which had permitted the abuse and neglect to continue, was held by the Court of Appeal and the House of Lords to afford the children no tortious remedy in negligence against the local authority in English law.

23 The facts of *M v Newham London Borough Council* [1995] 2 AC 633 were less stark than in *X v Bedfordshire County Council*, but they were disturbing enough. There was reason to believe that M, aged about four, had been sexually abused. In the course of interview by healthcare professionals the child was thought to identify her mother's current partner as the abuser. In fact, it seems, the child identified a cousin who had earlier lived in the house and who had the same first name. The child was removed from the mother's care for a period of almost a year, during which time the mother was refused sight of the video and transcript made of the child's earlier interview. It was only when the video and transcript were seen by the mother's solicitors that it became clear that the healthcare professional had mistaken the identity of the alleged abuser. Both the mother and the child claimed damages for negligence against the employers of the healthcare professionals involved, but in the domestic proceedings the mother's claim was unanimously dismissed by the Court of Appeal and the House of Lords and the child's claim by a majority of the Court of Appeal and a unanimous House. At Strasbourg, both succeeded in establishing a violation of article 8, a finding based not on the decision to remove the child from the mother's care but on a failure to disclose to the mother immediately thereafter the matters relied on as showing that the child could not be returned safely to her care: if this had been done, it would have avoided the period of separation which followed and was said to have caused psychiatric disorder to both mother and child: *TP and KM v United Kingdom* (2001) 34 EHRR 42, paras 30, 80–83, 115–117. This was, again, a violation for which the English law of tort afforded no remedy. . . .

25 But mention should first be made of the European court decision in *Osman v United Kingdom* (1998) 29 EHRR 245. That case concerned the liability in negligence of the police towards a person claiming to have suffered as the result of a failure to apprehend a suspected criminal. To that extent its factual subject matter resembled that of *Hill v Chief Constable of West Yorkshire* [1989] AC 53, a decision which the domestic court had applied. The court found a violation of article 6 of the Convention because, as it held in para 151 of its judgment, the domestic court's application of the law had served to confer a blanket immunity on the police for their acts and omissions during the investigation and suppression of crime and therefore unjustifiably restricted a claimant's right to have his claim determined on the merits. See also the concurring judgment of Sir John Freeland, at pp 321–322. This decision was the subject of compelling criticism by Lord Browne-Wilkinson in *Barrett v Enfield London Borough Council* [2001] 2 AC 550, 558–560. In that case, the claimant, who had spent his childhood in foster care, claimed damages against a local authority for decisions made and not made during that period. The judge's decision to strike out the claim had been upheld by the Court of Appeal but was unanimously reversed by the House. There are four points worthy of note for present purposes. First, it was accepted that a claim may lie against a local authority arising from childcare decisions in certain circumstances: see pp 557, 573, 575, 587–590. Secondly, the general undesirability of striking out claims arising in uncertain and developing areas of the law without full exploration of the facts was emphasised: pp 557–558, 575. This was a point made in the *Bedfordshire* case, at pp 740–741, and is a point strongly echoed in later cases such as *Waters v Comr of Police of the Metropolis* [2000] 1 WLR 1607, 1613; *W v Essex County Council* [2001] 2 AC 592, 598; *Phelps v*

Hillingdon London Borough Council [2001] 2 AC 619, 659–660; and *L (A Child) v Reading Borough Council* [2001] 1 WLR 1575, 1587. Thirdly, the notion of an exclusionary rule conferring immunity on particular classes of defendant was rejected: pp 559, 570, 575. This rejection has been echoed with approval in later cases such as *Kent v Griffiths* [2001] 1 QB 36, para 38; *S v Gloucestershire County Council* [2001] Fam 313, 338; and *E v United Kingdom* (2002) 36 EHRR 519. Fourthly, it was not considered that the policy factors which had weighed with the House in *X v Bedfordshire County Council* and *M v Newham London Borough Council* had the same weight where complaints related to acts and omissions after a child had been taken into care: [2001] 2 AC 550, 568, 575. The argument that imposition of a duty might lead to defensiveness and excessive caution was discounted, the remedies available to the claimant were not thought to be as efficacious as recognition of a common law duty of care and it was not accepted that imposition of a duty made no contribution to the maintenance of high standards: pp 568, 575. There was nothing to displace the general rule, recognised in the *Bedfordshire* and *Newham* case, at pp 663 and 749, that the public policy consideration which had first claim on the loyalty of the law was that wrongs should be remedied: p 588. . . .

30 In the light of all this authority, coupled with *Z v United Kingdom* 34 EHRR 97 and *TP and KM v United Kingdom* 34 EHRR 42 it could not now be plausibly argued that a common law duty of care may not be owed by a publicly-employed healthcare professional to a child with whom the professional is dealing. . . .”

Lord Nicholls: “. . .**70** There are two cardinal features in these cases. One feature is that a parent was suspected of having deliberately harmed his or her own child or having fabricated the child's medical condition. The other feature, which is to be assumed, is that the ensuing investigation by the doctors was conducted negligently. In consequence, the suspected parent's family life was disrupted, to greater or lesser extent, and the suspected parent suffered psychiatric injury.

71 It is the combination of these features which creates the difficult problem now before the House. In the ordinary course the interests of parent and child are congruent. This is not so where a parent wilfully harms his child. Then the parent is knowingly acting directly contrary to his parental responsibilities and to the best interests of his child. So the liability of doctors and social workers in these cases calls into consideration two countervailing interests, each of high social importance: the need to safeguard children from abuse by their own parents, and the need to protect parents from unnecessary interference with their family life.

72 The first of these interests involves protection of children as the victims of crime. Child abuse is criminal conduct of a particularly reprehensible character: children are highly vulnerable members of society. Child abuse is also a form of criminal conduct peculiarly hard to combat, because its existence is difficult to discover. Babies and young children are unable to complain, older children too frightened. If the source of the abuse is a parent, the child is at risk from his primary and natural protector within the privacy of his home. This both increases the risk of abuse and means that investigation necessitates intrusion into highly sensitive areas of family life, with the added complication that the parent who is responsible for the abuse will give a false account of the child's history.

73 The other, countervailing interest is the deep interest of the parent in his or her family life. Society sets much store by family life. Family life is to be guarded jealously. This is reflected in article 8 of the European Convention on Human Rights. Interference with family life requires cogent justification, for the sake of children and parents alike. So public authorities should, so far as possible, cooperate with the parents when making decisions about their children. Public authorities should disclose matters relied upon by them as justifying interference with family life. Parents should be involved in the decision-making process to whatever extent is appropriate to protect their interests adequately.

74 The question raised by these appeals is how these countervailing interests are best balanced when a parent is wrongly suspected of having abused his child. Public confidence in the child protection system can only be maintained if a proper balance is struck, avoiding unnecessary intrusion in families while protecting children at risk of significant harm: see the Preface to 'Working Together' (1991). Clearly, health professionals must act in good faith. They must not act recklessly, that is, without caring whether an allegation of abuse is well founded or not. Acting recklessly is not acting in good faith. But are health professionals liable to the suspected parents if they fall short of the standards of skill and care expected of any reasonable professional in the circumstances? Are they exposed to claims by the parents for professional negligence? Put differently and more widely, what is the appropriate level of protection for a person erroneously suspected of child abuse? Should he be protected against professional negligence by those charged with protecting the child? Or only against lack of good faith? . . .

77 Stated in this broad form, this is a surprising proposition. In this area of the law, concerned with the reporting and investigation of suspected crime, the balancing point between the public interest and the interest of a suspected individual has long been the presence or absence of good faith. Good faith is required but not more. A report, made to the appropriate authorities, that a person has or may have committed a crime attracts qualified privilege. A false statement ('malicious falsehood') attracts a remedy if made maliciously. Misfeasance in public office calls for an element of bad faith or recklessness. Malice is an essential ingredient of causes of action for the misuse of criminal or civil proceedings. In *Calveley v Chief Constable of the Merseyside Police* [1989] AC 1228, 1238, Lord Bridge of Harwich observed that 'where no action for malicious prosecution would lie, it would be strange indeed if an acquitted defendant could recover damages for negligent investigation'. This must be equally true of a person who has been suspected but not prosecuted.

78 This background accords ill with the submission that those responsible for the protection of a child against criminal conduct owe suspected perpetrators the duty suggested. The existence of such a duty would fundamentally alter the balance in this area of the law. It would mean that if a parent suspected that a babysitter or a teacher at a nursery or school might have been responsible for abusing her child, and the parent took the child to a general practitioner or consultant, the doctor would owe a duty of care to the suspect. The law of negligence has of course developed much in recent years, reflecting the higher standards increasingly expected in many areas of life. But there seems no warrant for such a fundamental shift in the long established balance in this area of the law. . . ."

NOTES AND QUESTIONS

1. Lord Bingham's dissenting speech is extracted here because he gives a concise history of

the duty of care litigation, in the domestic courts and in the human rights court, involving public bodies.

2. Lord Nicholl's speech is extracted at some length because of its conceptual importance. He bases his reasoning on the conflict of two interests, those of the children with those of the parents. But are these the only interests to be considered? Is there not a separate family interest which has been invaded by the state? In § 78 Lord Nicholls clearly thinks that no duty should be owed by the doctor to the suspect; but why should such a duty not be owed given the devastating effect that a child-abuse allegation can have on such a person? Why should there not be some regime of administrative responsibility? Why must it always be the individual who has to pay the cost of administrative incompetence? Is this really in the 'public interest'?

3. Lord Nicholls distinguishes between negligence and good faith. Are the two notions always so different? Could it not be said that the negligence of the officials in *Elguzouli-Daf v Commissioner of Police* (1995) (see below p.351) amounted to bad faith given that they should have known that any carelessness on their part would result in imprisonment? Do you think that *Elguzouli-Daf* still good law? (cf. *Brooks v Comr of Police for the Metropolis* (2005).)

4. Do you think that *D v East Berkshire NHS Trust* has become a basic precedent with respect to whether or not the parents in child abuse accusation cases are owed a duty of care? (cf. *Lawrence v Pembrokeshire CC* (2007).)

5. The liability of public bodies (primarily local authorities) has again been reviewed recently in the Court of Appeal. After examining many of the cases over the past years, Arden L.J. has come up with a number of concluding observations.

Jain v Trent Strategic Health Authority **[2008] 2 W.L.R. 456, CA**

Arden L.J.: ". .. **60** This brief survey [of the cases] demonstrates the difficulty in establishing a duty of care against a public body. Five particular points seem to me to come out of the authorities summarised above which are relevant to this case. First, the cases demonstrate the importance of the incremental approach to the duty of care. The courts develop the law very cautiously where the allocation of public resources is involved. Secondly, it is evident that the courts are reluctant to impose a duty of care if this would result in the defendant public body having a duty to a person at common law that is liable to be in conflict with the duty of care owed to the primary beneficiary of the statutory scheme. Thirdly, at least where loss to the claimant is not only foreseeable but the claimant is in a close relationship with the public authority and has suffered as a result of the incompetence of the public authority, it is the public authority which has to satisfy the court that a duty of care should not lie. More cogent reasons are needed than simply showing little more than that the defendant is a public authority.

61 Fourthly, in the *X* case [1995] 2 AC 633 justiciability was a major consideration if the acts complained of were committed when the authority was exercising a statutory power. However, it is now clear from the *Barret* case [2001] 2 AC 550 that that fact does not exclude the imposition of a common law duty of care. In the present case the parties cited to the judge the helpful statement of the law by Hale L.J. in the *Essex* case [2004] 1 WLR 1881: see above, para 9. That sets out three potential areas of inquiry that arise whenever the question of a common law duty of care arises in the context of statutory functions. The first is whether the matter is justiciable at all and the second is whether, even if it is justiciable, a duty of care would only arise if the public body acted in a way that was so unreasonable as not to amount to an exercise of the discretion at all. The third is whether it is fair, just and reasonable to impose a duty of care.

62 The first at least of those lines of inquiry has assumed less importance as the law has evolved in recent years. As the judgment of the Court of Appeal in *D's* case [2005] 2 AC 373 demonstrates, following the 1998 Act courts have now to consider questions of social policy with which they were not previously concerned. From this, in my judgment, it is possible to conclude that courts will hold that fewer matters are now non-justiciable on the grounds that they involve policy issues. The second line of inquiry also, as it seems to me, reflects a concern about justiciability. Moreover, we have also seen from the *Barret* case [2001] 2 AC 550 that the courts are now reluctant to introduce administrative law concepts into the law of negligence, and that would seem to me to be the result if in any case the court were to conclude that there should be liability only if the act was actually outside the statutory discretion. In the circumstances I conclude that the first two lines of inquiry in the statement by Hale L.J. in the *Essex* case [2004] 1 WLR 1881 are not likely in future to be as important, or to have the same weight, as the third line of inquiry.

63 In the present case no argument has been addressed to this court on justiciability. In the circumstances it is not necessary for me to consider it further in this judgment.

64 The fifth point which I draw from the authorities summarised above is that the 1998 Act has also had a perceptible impact in this field. As a result of that Act giving further protection in domestic law to Convention rights the courts are now more conscious that the denial of a duty of care may result in a violation of Convention rights. The effect has been to encourage courts to identify more specific policy factors and to consider the interests of the individual affected by the decision-making by the public authority. This led the House of Lords in *D's* case [2005] 2 AC 373 to consider whether to shift the emphasis from duty to breach but the majority largely rejected this. In the result the duty of care remains a major control mechanism for the purpose of controlling the potential opening of the floodgates in this field. . . .''

QUESTIONS

1. In the above case of *Jain*, the claimants were proprietors of a nursing home who had suffered serious financial loss after the home had been summarily deregistered by the defendants acting under statutory powers. It was held by the trial judge that the defendants had been negligent in their investigation of the nursing home and he awarded damages on the basis of a breach of duty owed by the defendants to the claimants. The defendants appealed on this duty question: do you think they were successful?

2. One of the judges in the Court of Appeal said this: "The Jains claim recompense from Trent, suing in the tort of negligence. Free from any authority, I take the view that any civilised state which had acted so unjustifiably and so damagingly ought to recompense the injured party" (Jacob L.J.). Does this comment affect your answer as to whether or

not an appeal might be successful? If the Jains do not receive compensation from the state does this mean that the state is 'uncivilised'?

9.3.2 Nuisance

Local authorities are important landowners and thus they can find themselves facing claims arising out of the use and occupation of land. These claims can of course be in common law negligence or founded upon the Occupiers' Liability Act 1957 or 1984 (see in particular *Tomlinson v Congleton BC* (2004), p.223). But nuisance (public and private) can also be an important cause of action.

Lippiatt v South Gloucestershire Council [2000] 1 Q.B. 51, CA

This was an action for an injunction and damages brought by farmers against a local authority for damage done by travellers who had occupied land belonging to the council. The judge struck out the claim, but an appeal was allowed by the Court of Appeal (Evans L.J., Mummery L.J. and Sir Christopher Staughton).

Mummery L.J.: ". . . It is reasonably arguable that the continuing presence of the travellers on the council's land constituted a nuisance to the plaintiffs' use and enjoyment of their rights in their land, even though the travellers' activities involved using the council's land as a launching pad for repeated acts of trespass on the plaintiffs' land.

It is not, contrary to the submission of Mr Spens for the council, a case of the plaintiffs seeking to make the council vicariously liable for individual acts of trespass committed by uncontrolled third parties (ie the travellers) on the plaintiffs' land. It is rather a complaint of a continuing and potentially injurious state of affairs on the council's land, ie the presence of the travellers who, as the council were made aware, repeatedly behaved in the way complained of by the plaintiffs. The council let that state of affairs continue to exist on its land notwithstanding the complaints of the plaintiffs; and that state of affairs was capable of constituting a nuisance for which the council was liable, even if individual acts of the travellers of which the plaintiffs complained occurred on the plaintiffs' land. . . ."

NOTES AND QUESTIONS

1. In *Hussain v Lancaster CC* (1999) the resident owner of a shop on a housing estate brought an action for damages in negligence and nuisance against a local authority. The owner claimed that the authority had failed to prevent him from being seriously harassed by other tenants on the estate. The Court of Appeal held that the master was right to strike out the action and a petition to appeal to the House of Lords was subsequently refused. Might Mr Hussain be more successful today given the coming into force of the Human Rights Act 1998?

2. In *Gorringe v Calderdale MBC* (2004) (see p.334) Lord Scott said: "a highway authority may be liable at common law for damage attributable to dangers that it has introduced, or, in the case of dangers introduced by some third party, that it has unreasonably failed to abate. Members of the public who drive cars on the highways of this country are entitled to expect that the highways will be kept properly in repair. They are entitled to complain if damage is caused by some obstruction or condition of the road or its

surroundings that constitutes a public nuisance. And they are, of course, entitled to complain if they suffer damage by the negligence of some other user of the highway. But an overriding imperative is that those who drive on public highways do so in a manner and at a speed that is safe having regard to such matters as the nature of the road, the weather conditions and the traffic conditions. Drivers are first and foremost themselves responsible for their own safety" (§ 76).

3. *Lippiatt* did not decide that the local authority *was* liable in nuisance—only that it *could be* liable.

9.4 Police and prosecution service

Like local authorities, the police find themselves in a position where they can attract claims in tort. Here the torts tend to fall into two distinct categories. There is what might be called the constitutional torts, that is to say claims arising out of the invasion of constitutional rights (see **2.4.1** and **3.6.1**). And there are those arising out of negligence. However the two cases extracted below might be said to fall within both categories.

Elguzouli-Daf v Commissioner of Police of the Metropolis **[1995] Q.B. 335, CA**

This was a claim for damages brought against the Crown Prosecution Service (CPS) by two men who had been arrested for two quite different serious crimes. The CPS discontinued proceedings against them, but not before the two men had been held in prison for 22 and 85 days respectively. The men claimed that had the CPS not been negligent in respect of investigating the evidence against them, they would not have been detained for such long periods. The Court of Appeal (Steyn L.J., Rose L.J. and Morritt L.J.) confirmed the trial judge's decision to strike out the claims.

Steyn L.J.: ". . . That brings me to the policy factors which, in my view, argue against the recognition of a duty of care owed by the CPS to those it prosecutes. While it is always tempting to yield to an argument based on the protection of civil liberties, I have come to the conclusion that the interests of the whole community are better served by not imposing a duty of care on the CPS. In my view, such a duty of care would tend to have an inhibiting effect on the discharge by the CPS of its central function of prosecuting crime. It would in some cases lead to a defensive approach by prosecutors to their multifarious duties. It would introduce a risk that prosecutors would act so as to protect themselves from claims of negligence. The CPS would have to spend valuable time and use scarce resources in order to prevent law suits in negligence against the CPS It would generate a great deal of paper to guard against the risks of law suits. The time and energy of CPS lawyers would be diverted from concentrating on their prime function of prosecuting offenders. That would be likely to happen not only during the prosecution process but also when the CPS is sued in negligence by aggrieved defendants. The CPS would be constantly enmeshed in an avalanche of interlocutory civil proceedings and civil trials. That is a spectre that would bode ill for the efficiency of the CPS and the quality of our criminal justice system. . . ."

NOTE

This kind of reasoning has been applied to the police as well as to the CPS (see *Hill*, p.39; *Brooks v Comr of Police of the Metropolis* (2005)). But there may be occasions where the proximity is close enough to give rise to a duty.

Swinney v Chief Constable of Northumbria [1997] Q.B. 464, CA

This was an action for damages for personal injury and loss brought against the police by two plaintiffs who had been severely threatened and intimidated by an alleged criminal. The plaintiffs had given confidential information about the alleged criminal to the police, but their names and address had, so they alleged, been carelessly left in a police car which had then been broken into, allowing their names and address to end up in the hands of the alleged criminal. The police applied to have the action struck out but were unsuccessful in the Court of Appeal (Hirst L.J., Peter Gibson L.J. and Ward L.J.).

Ward L.J.: ". . . The greater public good rightly outweighs any individual hardship. On the other hand, it is incontrovertible that the fight against crime is daily dependent upon information fed to the police by members of the public, often at real risk of villainous retribution from the criminals and their associates. The public interest will not accept that good citizens should be expected to entrust information to the police, without also expecting that they are entrusting their safety to the police. The public interest would be affronted were it to be the law that members of the public should be expected, in the execution of public service, to undertake the risk of harm to themselves without the police, in return, being expected to take no more than reasonable care to ensure that the confidential information imparted to them is protected. The welfare of the community at large demands the encouragement of the free flow of information without inhibition. Accordingly, it is arguable that there is a duty of care, and that no consideration of public policy precludes the prosecution of the plaintiffs' claim, which will be judged on its merits later. . . ."

Hirst L.J.: ". . . I wish to end this judgment by stressing a point with which I began, namely that I am upholding no more than the arguability of the plaintiffs' case on these two grounds. It by no means follows that they will succeed on either of them at the trial. Nor, for that matter, does it follow that the plaintiffs will establish, when all the evidence is considered, the necessary substratum of fact as pleaded in the statement of claim on which their whole case depends. . . ."

NOTES

1. Hirst L.J.'s reservation proved a valuable warning: the plaintiffs ultimately lost their case at the trial. For another case where the police were held liable for the breach of a specific duty of care see *Reeves v Commissioner of Police for the Metropolis* (2000) (p.377). But see *Vellino v Chief Constable of Greater Manchester Police* (2002) (p.41).

2. When the police or prison authorities act maliciously they may find themselves having to answer a claim in trespass, malicious prosecution, abuse of the legal process or abuse of public office. Nevertheless it would appear that merely being offensive is not necessarily enough to give rise to a tort: *Wainwright v Home Office* (2004) (p.229). Also the private

interest needs to be weighed against the public interest as the next extract clearly suggests.

Gibbs v Rea [1998] A.C. 786, PC

(For facts and further extract see p.128)

> **Lord Goff and Lord Hope** (dissenting): ". . . In our opinion the greatest care must always be taken to strike the right balance between the public interest in the investigation of crime and the rights of the individual who is seeking to pursue a private law remedy. On the one hand there are the evils of drug trafficking. The offences which lie within this field vary greatly in their character and gravity throughout the complex and clandestine network which links the consumer to the source of the supply. The gathering of evidence against those who are involved in it is often difficult, and it may also be dangerous both for the informant and for the investigator. The court has a responsibility to ensure that the rights of the individual are respected at all times, but it must be careful also not to hamper the police in their legitimate endeavours to seek out and to identify the criminal. The risk that if things go wrong the police will be exposed to a claim of damages for having acted maliciously is just one of the many hazards which they must face. But we should not like to see too easy a resort to this remedy. . . ."

NOTE

These comments come from a dissenting opinion, but they still represent a policy view that underpins the law of tort when it is dealing with constitutional interests as the next case implicitly indicates.

Keegan v Chief Constable of Merseyside [2003] 1 W.L.R. 2187, CA

This was an action for damages by the occupants of a house against the police in respect of a search of the house carried out by the police in the early hours of the morning. The police had obtained a search warrant to search this particular council house on the basis of information given by a suspect who had once lived there. The police did not check with the utility companies or with the local authority as to whether the house was still occupied by the suspect or members of his family. The damages claim was based upon (i) malicious procurement of a search warrant and (ii) trespass; but the trial judge rejected the first claim on the ground that the police did have reasonable cause to obtain a search warrant and did not act with targeted malice or in bad faith. The trespass claim was also dismissed because the entry was lawful. An appeal to the Court of Appeal (Lord Phillips M.R., Kennedy L.J. and Ward L.J.) was dismissed.

> **Ward L.J.:** ". . . **33** That causes me concern. Here a law-abiding family have had their front door smashed by battering ram in the early hours of the morning whilst they were still asleep. It seems to have caused terror and some distress and perhaps even the psychiatric harm upon which a substantial part of the claim is based. Given the inefficiency of the police investigation, the family gain my sympathy. If malice can be inferred from the lack of reasonable and probable cause to believe that stolen cash was on the premises, why should the case not be remitted to the county court to determine whether or not malice can be

established in the light of the finding in the claimant's favour on ingredient number 2? I have given that question anxious consideration.

34 Not without a measure of reluctance, I conclude that the prospects of eventual success are so slender that it is better that this case ends here. The police may have been negligent but it is practically impossible to say that any officer acted without a bona fide belief that he was placing, or allowing another officer of the squad to place before the justices material sufficient to meet the conditions for the issue of the search warrant. It is difficult to see any improper motive for the police action.

35 That an Englishman's home is said to be his castle reveals an important public interest, but there is another important public interest in the detection of crime and the bringing to justice of those who commit it. These interests are in conflict in a case like this and on the law as it stood when these events occurred, which is before the coming into force of the Human Rights Act 1998, which may be said to have elevated the right to respect for one's home, a finding of malice on the part of police is the proper balancing safeguard.

36 Upon careful reflection, I agree with Lord Phillips of Worth Matravers MR and Kennedy LJ that it is inevitable that malice will not be proved in this case.

Trespass

37 I agree that as the warrant on the face of it was lawful, entry pursuant to it was lawful and thus not a trespass upon the property.

Conclusion

38 Sympathy for the claimants is not enough. I agree that the appeal must be dismissed."

QUESTION

Could the occupiers have sued the police in negligence? If not, why not?

9.5 Emergency services

A number of cases have arisen involving allegations of damage caused by carelessness on the part of an emergency service. In some of the cases the courts have refused to impose liability, but in others the public service (police, fire or ambulance) have been held liable in tort.

Kent v Griffiths **[2001] Q.B. 36, CA**

This was an action for damages for negligence by a patient against an ambulance service in respect of the late arrival of an ambulance. The patient had suffered an asthma attack and her doctor called an ambulance at 4.25pm; however the ambulance did not arrive until 5.05pm. Before arrival at the hospital the claimant suffered a respiratory arrest which caused brain damage. The judge found that had the ambulance arrived on time there was a high probability that the arrest would have been averted. He also found that there was no satisfactory explanation for the late arrival of the ambulance and that the crew had falsified the record with respect to the time of arrival. The judge held the ambulance service liable and an appeal to the Court of Appeal (Lord Woolf M.R., Aldous L.J. and Laws L.J.) was dismissed.

Lord Woolf M.R.: "**1**. The issue on this appeal is whether an ambulance service can owe any duty of care to a member of the public on whose behalf a 999 telephone call is made if, due to carelessness, it fails to arrive within a reasonable time. . . .

45. Here what was being provided was a health service. In the case of health services under the 1977 Act the conventional situation is that there is a duty of care. Why should the position of the ambulance staff be different from that of doctors or nurses? In addition the arguments based on public policy are much weaker in the case of the ambulance service than they are in the case of the police or the fire service. The police and fire services' primary obligation is to the public at large. In protecting a particular victim of crime, the police are performing their more general role of maintaining public order and reducing crime. In the case of fire the fire service will normally be concerned not only to protect a particular property where a fire breaks out but also to prevent fire spreading. In the case of both services, there is therefore a concern to protect the public generally. The emergency services that can be summoned by a 999 call do, in the majority of situations, broadly carry out a similar function. But in reality they can be very different. The ambulance service is part of the health service. Its care function includes transporting patients to and from hospital when the use of an ambulance for this purpose is desirable. It is therefore appropriate to regard the LAS as providing services of the category provided by hospitals and not as providing services equivalent to those rendered by the police or the fire service. Situations could arise where there is a conflict between the interests of a particular individual and the public at large. But, in the case of the ambulance service in this particular case, the only member of the public who could be adversely affected was the claimant. It was the claimant alone for whom the ambulance had been called. . . .

47. An important feature of this case is that there is no question of an ambulance not being available or of a conflict in priorities. Again I recognise that where what is being attacked is the allocation of resources, whether in the provision of sufficient ambulances or sufficient drivers or attendants, different considerations could apply. There then could be issues which are not suited for resolution by the courts. However, once there are available, both in the form of an ambulance and in the form of manpower, the resources to provide an ambulance on which there are no alternative demands, the ambulance service would be acting perversely "in circumstances such as the present", if it did not make those resources available. Having decided to provide an ambulance an explanation is required to justify a failure to attend within reasonable time. . . .

49. . . . On the findings of the judge it was delay which caused the further injuries. If wrong information had not been given about the arrival of the ambulance, other means of transport could have been used. . . ."

NOTES AND QUESTION

1. The importance of this case is that it illustrates that the question of liability in negligence will depend upon the circumstances of each case. Why exactly was Lord Woolf prepared

to impose liability on the facts of this case? Is there one single fact that is important or are there several?

2. With respect to the liability of the fire services see *Capital & Counties Plc v Hampshire CC* (1997); and for the lifeboat service see *OLL Ltd v Secretary of State for Transport* (1997).

9.6 National health service

Actions for damages in negligence against the NHS are now a specialist area of tort liability. Such claims have an important public interest dimension since money paid out in damages cannot be used to provide or improve medical services.

Roe v Minister of Health [1954] 2 Q.B. 66, CA

Denning L.J.: "No one can be unmoved by the disaster which has befallen these two unfortunate men. They were both working men before they went into the Chesterfield Hospital in October 1947. Both were insured contributors to the hospital, paying a small sum each week, in return for which they were entitled to be admitted for treatment when they were ill. Each of them was operated on in the hospital for a minor trouble, one for something wrong with a cartilage in his knee, the other for a hydrocele. The operations were both on the same day, 13th October 1947. Each of them was given a spinal anaesthetic by a visiting anaesthetist, Dr Graham. Each of them has in consequence been paralysed from the waist down.

The judge has said that those facts do not speak for themselves, but I think that they do. They certainly call for an explanation. Each of these men is entitled to say to the hospital: "While I was in your hands something has been done to me which has wrecked my life. Please explain how it has come to pass". The reason why the judge took a different view was because he thought that the hospital authorities could disclaim responsibility for the anaesthetist, Dr Graham: and, as it might be his fault and not theirs, the hospital authorities were not called upon to give an explanation. I think that that reasoning is wrong. In the first place, I think that the hospital authorities are responsible for the whole of their staff, not only for the nurses and doctors, but also for the anaesthetists and the surgeons. It does not matter whether they are permanent or temporary, resident or visiting, whole-time or part-time. The hospital authorities are responsible for all of them. The reason is because, even if they are not servants, they are the agents of the hospital to give the treatment. The only exception is the case of consultants or anaesthetists selected and employed by the patient himself. I went into the matter with some care in *Cassidy v Ministry of Health* and I adhere to all I there said. In the second place, I do not think that the hospital authorities and Dr Graham can both avoid giving an explanation by the simple expedient of each throwing responsibility on to the other. If an injured person shows that one or other or both of two persons injured him, but cannot say which of them it was, then he is not defeated altogether. He can call on each of them for an explanation: see *Baker v Market Harborough Industrial Co-operative Society.*

I approach this case, therefore, on the footing that the hospital authorities and Dr Graham were called on to give an explanation of what has happened. But I think that they have done so. They have spared no trouble or expense to seek out the cause of the disaster. The greatest specialists in the land were called to give evidence. In the result, the judge has found that what happened was this. [His lordship discussed how the accident had occurred: disinfectant had seeped into the anaesthetic by means of invisible cracks in the ampoules; the anaesthetic was thus contaminated when used.] . .. That is the explanation of the disaster, and the question is: were any of the staff negligent? I pause to say that once the accident is explained, no question of *res ipsa loquitur* arises. The only question is whether on the facts as now ascertained anyone was negligent . .. If the anaesthetists had foreseen that the ampoules might get cracked with cracks that could not be detected on inspection they would no doubt have dyed the phenol a deep blue; and this would have exposed the contamination. But I do not think that their failure to foresee this was negligence. It is so easy to be wise after the event and to condemn as negligence that which was only a misadventure. We ought always to be on our guard against it, especially in cases against hospitals and doctors. Medical science has conferred great benefits on mankind, but these benefits are attended by considerable risks. Every surgical operation is attended by risks. We cannot take the benefits without taking the risks. Every advance in technique is also attended by risks. Doctors, like the rest of us, have to learn by experience; and experience often teaches in a hard way. Something goes wrong and shows up a weakness, and then it is put right. That is just what happened here. Dr Graham sought to escape the danger of infection by disinfecting the ampoule. In escaping that known danger he unfortunately ran into another danger. He did not know that there could be undetectable cracks, but it was not negligent for him not to know it at that time. We must not look at the 1947 accident with 1954 spectacles. The judge acquitted Dr Graham of negligence and we should uphold his decision . ..

One final word. These two men have suffered such terrible consequences that there is a natural feeling that they should be compensated. But we should be doing a disservice to the community at large if we were to impose liability on hospitals and doctors for everything that happens to go wrong. Doctors would be led to think more of their own safety than of the good of their patients. Initiative would be stifled and confidence shaken. A proper sense of proportion requires us to have regard to the conditions in which hospitals and doctors have to work. We must insist on due care for the patient at every point, but we must not condemn as negligence that which is only a misadventure. I agree with my Lord that these appeals should be dismissed."

[Somervell L.J. and Morris L.J. also delivered judgments dismissing the appeal.]

QUESTIONS

1. "We cannot take the benefits without taking the risks. Every advance in technique is also attended by risks. Doctors, like the rest of us, have to learn by experience; and experience often teaches in a hard way". Was it actually the doctors that had to learn the hard way? Why should it be the two individuals who are left to carry the risks?

2. "Forget the stiff upper lip, this groundswell of litigation is turning us into grasping whingers and self-pitying milksops. . . . Citizens should be discouraged from exploiting public services: suing should become shameful" (Polly Toynbee, *The Guardian*, April 21,

357

1999, p.18.) Were the plaintiffs in *Roe* whingers and self-pitying milksops who ought to be ashamed of themselves?

NOTES

1. See also *Goodwill v British Pregnancy Advisory Service* (1996) (p.36); *McFarlane v Tayside HA* (2000) (p.56); *Gwilliam v West Herts Hospital NHS Trust* (2003) (p.144); *Bolam v Friern Hospital Management Committee* (1957) (p.151); *Bolitho v City and Hackney HA* (1998) (p.152); *Cassidy v MOH* (1951) (p.263); *Rees v Darlington Memorial Hospital NHS Trust* (2004) (pp.423, 426); *Chester v Afshar* (2005) (p.393); *Gregg v Scott* (2005) (p.396).

2. Where a victim suffers personal injury as a result of a medical mishap negligence is now virtually the exclusive tort (*Sidaway v Bethlem Royal Hospital* (1985)). However in mental care cases other torts may be relevant as the next extract indicates.

R. (Munjaz) v Mersey Care NHS Trust [2003] 3 W.L.R. 1505, CA

This was an action for judicial review brought by two detained psychiatric patients who claimed that they had been unlawfully placed in secluded confinement. The Court of Appeal (Lord Phillips M.R., Hale L.J. and Latham L.J.) in its judgment discussed what private law remedies might be available to patients in such a situation and the manner in which these remedies might be restricted by legislation.

Hale L.J.: ". . . **49** As the authorities currently stand, merely confining a detained patient to a particular room or part of the hospital will not amount to the tort of false imprisonment. False imprisonment is the deprivation of liberty without lawful justification. A person who has been deprived of his liberty in pursuance of a lawful power to detain cannot through the medium of the tort of false imprisonment complain about the conditions in which he is detained, at least by those who are lawfully detaining him. This was decided by the House of Lords in *R v Deputy Governor of Parkhurst Prison, Ex p Hague* [1992] 1 AC 58, although their Lordships accepted that unauthorised persons, such as other prisoners, might indeed be guilty of false imprisonment if they confined another prisoner within the prison. We shall return to whether this decision requires to be revisited in the light of the Convention.

50 However, that does not mean that the patient is without a remedy if other torts have been committed against him. If the breach of a duty of care towards the patient causes him physical or psychiatric harm, he has a remedy in the tort of negligence. The use of physical restraint upon a patient, or the administration of physical treatment, without lawful justification will amount to the tort of assault and/or battery which is actionable without proof of harm. This will include the use of excessive force or the use of force to enforce a decision which was unlawful in public law terms: see *Mohammed Holgate v Duke* [1984] AC 437. Evidentially, however, neither will be easy to prove. Where physical restraint is employed in an emergency to prevent an escape or to protect others from harm, the court will not find it easy to criticise the decisions made by those who were there at the time. It was acknowledged by the experts in *S's* case that they were not as well placed as the doctors and nurses on the ward at the time to judge the degree of danger which S presented to staff and patients and those outside the hospital.

51 A further qualification is that individuals acting in pursuance of the 1983 Act cannot be sued, even in respect of acts without lawful justification, unless they are shown to have acted in bad faith or without reasonable care: section 139(1) of the 1983 Act. The leave of a High Court judge must first be obtained: section 139(2). This section does not apply to actions against health authorities and NHS trusts: section 139(4). Nor does it apply to judicial review, which in any event requires the permission of a High Court judge: scc *Ex p Waldron* [1986] QB 824.

52 It follows that there are circumstances in which the use of seclusion will involve the commission of a tort against the patient for which the ordinary tortious remedies will be available. But these will not cover the use of seclusion in itself, or even every use of seclusion of which legitimate complaint might be made, and certainly not every use of seclusion which does not comply with the Code of Practice. . . ."

9.7 Financial institutions

See Financial Services and Markets Act 2000 s.102 and *Three Rivers District Council v Governor and Company of The Bank of England (No 3)* (2000) (p.122). Note also *Yuen Kun Yeu v Att-Gen of Hong Kong* (1988).

10 Causation and general defences

It would perhaps be cynical to describe this chapter as dealing with the question of how to escape from liability. Yet there is a certain truth in such an assertion. Even when carelessness and duty can be shown it is still possible to avoid liability on the basis that it "is axiomatic that the law will not impose liability to pay compensation for damage unless there is a relevant causal connection between the damage and the defendant's tort, breach of contract or statutory duty" (Lord Hoffmann in *Fairchild v Glenhaven Funeral Services* (2002), § 48). The problem, however, is "what amounts to a relevant causal connection?" As Lord Hoffmann has observed, everyone "agrees that there is no scientific or philosophical touchstone for determining the relevant causal connection in any particular case" and so the "relevance of a causal connection depends upon the purpose of the inquiry" (ibid., § 49).

10.1 Approaches and theories

Causation is intrinsically a complex subject and as a result has attracted the attention of theorists both from within and from without the law and, as the extract from Professor Honoré will suggest, no single theory is satisfactory.

10.1.1 Theories of causation

Causation is a means of analysing physical and social facts and is based on the idea that any event or phenomenon is caused by an earlier event or phenomenon. The regression is of course endless and science fiction writers have long developed themes about time travel and the problems that might be created for the contemporary world if a time-traveller, while venturing into the past, kills a life form. When applied to legal events causation is about linking the phenomenon of harm with anterior events and theory is important in two main ways. First, theory is required to distinguish between what one might call potent and non-potent causal events; in other words a theoretical model is needed to distinguish those events that will be regarded as a cause and those that will not. However, given that many judges (at least in England) faced with difficult causation cases will tend to rely upon 'common sense', a second role for theory is to explain the precedents. In short, theory is necessary to explain the past cases and to predict how future cases will be decided. However the next extract suggests that the isolation of a single theory is elusive.

> **AM Honoré, 'Causation and Remoteness of Damage,' Torts,** *International Encyclopedia of Comparative Law*, **Volume XI, Chapter 7**
>
> "1. . . . [I]t is very difficult to construct a theory of causation and remoteness of damage which will at the same time explain the meaning of the terms involved and constitute a useful guide

to decision. The theories tend to induce a feeling of frustration, because they either have little empirical content and so fail to point the way, or are clear-cut but apply to only a segment of the circle of problems which present themselves.

It is not surprising, then, that in many legal systems there are competing theories, that often a theory is officially adopted but not consistently applied, and that in one and the same system different theories are applied to different types of case. This is a wholesome phenomenon, but it makes the standard method of comparison, in which each solution is represented by a single system, unworkable. . . .

105. . . . But in any case the problems to be answered are so various that they cannot be solved by a single formula which remains at all meaningful. . . . It would be unsound to adopt any theory of causation if by it a court was committed to the view that there is only one ground on which the tortfeasor's responsibility can properly be limited. The real function of the theories is rather to emphasize a particular technique of limitation while not rigidly excluding the use of others. . . But though forensically the vaguest formula may often be the best, from the standpoint of legal science it is important to recognize that just as there are several different grounds for imposing a duty to compensate, so there are several different grounds for limiting compensation. . . ."

10.1.2 **European approaches**

The idea that there are various competing theories of causation is specifically confirmed in the next text which, although not having the force of positive law, at least reflects the main models employed in European legal systems. It thus provides an excellent reference point for tort lawyers.

European Group on Tort Law, *Principles of European Tort Law* **(2003)**

Chapter 3. Causation

Section 1. Conditio sine qua non and qualifications

Art. 3:101. Conditio sine qua non

An act or omission (hereafter: activity) is a cause of the victim's damage if, in the absence of the activity, the damage would not have occurred.

Art. 3:102. Concurrent causes

In case of multiple activities, where each of them alone would have caused the damage at the same time, each activity is regarded as a cause of the victim's damage.

Art. 3:103. Alternative causes

(1) In case of multiple activities, where each of them alone would have been sufficient to cause the damage, but it remains uncertain which one in fact caused it, each activity is regarded as a cause to the extent corresponding to the likelihood that it may have caused the victim's damage.

(2) If, in case of multiple victims, it remains uncertain whether a particular victim's damage has been caused by an activity, while it is likely that it did not cause the damage of all victims, the activity is regarded as a cause of the damage suffered by all victims in proportion to the likelihood that it may have caused the damage of a particular victim. Regard is to be had to the background risk and the specific circumstances of each victim.

Art. 3:104. Potential causes

(1) If an activity has definitely and irreversibly led the victim to suffer damage, a subsequent activity which alone would have caused the same damage is to be disregarded.
(2) A subsequent activity is nevertheless taken into consideration

    a) if it has led to additional or aggravated damage, or
    b) if it has led to continuous damage, but only starting from the time that it also would have caused it.

Art. 3:105. Minimal causation

In the case of multiple activities, when it is certain that none of them has caused the entire damage or any determinable part thereof, those that are likely to have minimally contributed to the damage are presumed to have caused equal shares thereof.

Art. 3:106. Alternative and potential causes within the victim's sphere

If an activity, occurrence or other circumstance, including natural events, within the sphere of the victim may have caused the damage, the victim has to bear his loss to the extent that the cause may lie within his own sphere.

Section 2. Scope of Liability

Art. 3:201. Scope of Liability

Where causation has been established under Section 1 of this Chapter, whether and to what extent damage may be attributed to a person depends on factors such as

    a) the foreseeability of the damage to a reasonable person at the time of its occurrence, taking into account in particular the closeness in time or space between the damaging activity and its consequence, or the magnitude of the damage in relation to the normal consequences of such an activity;
    b) the nature and the value of the protected interest (Art. 2:102);
    c) the basis of liability (Art. 1:101);
    d) the extent of the ordinary risks of life; and
    e) the protective purpose of the rule that has been violated.

QUESTIONS

1. An absent-minded professor continues his 9am tort lecture until 10.15am. Several students are injured when a defectively maintained bus, running on time, careers into the main door of the lecture hall. If the lecture should have finished at 9.55am at the latest, could it be said that the professor is the cause of the injured students' damage according

to art.3:101 of the PETL? Will the professor be liable for the damage under any article in Chapter 3 of the PETL?

2. Study Lord Hoffmann's doctor and mountaineer example in the *Banque Bruxelles* case (below p.372). Is the doctor the cause of the mountaineer's injury under art.3:101 of the PETC? Will the doctor be liable under Chapter 3 of the PETL? If not, why not?

3. A barber sets up his chair near to a place where people often play ball games. One day a person kicks a ball which hits the arm of the barber, the result being that a person whom the barber is shaving has his throat cut (D.9.2.11pr). Which person is the cause of this damage? Which person will be liable for this damage? Can causation be used as a means of escaping liability?

10.1.2 Common law approaches to causation

Perhaps because of the complexity the common law has tended to diffuse the topic of causation behind a range of different concepts and levels of approach. For example, in addition to the requirement of cause and connection between tortuous behaviour and damage, causation is to be found behind concepts as wide-ranging as duty of care, contributory negligence, remoteness of damage, mitigation and so on. The approach that will therefore be adopted in this chapter is to distribute the problem of causation between various levels of operation; these are actionability (where causation forms part of the definition of the cause of action), factual causation (where the jury once decided if cause and connection existed in fact), legal causation (alternatively known as remoteness of damage and is a question of law for the judge) and finally damages (which includes the defences of contributory negligence and mitigation).

10.2 Actionability

The first level at which causation operates is actionability. This is to say there are some causes of action specifically requiring a particular type of cause and connection before an action can get off the ground so to speak.

10.2.1 Trespass

Perhaps the leading tort here is trespass. The reason why a causal requirement came to determine actionability is explained in the extract below.

David Ibbetson, *A Historical Introduction to the law of Obligations*, Oxford University Press, 1999, p.159 (footnotes omitted)

"The upshot of this was that by 1700 it was established as a rule, almost certainly introduced by analogy with Roman law, that where the plaintiff had been directly injured by the defendant's act the correct action was trespass, and where the injury was merely consequential case was appropriate. . . An alternative way of putting the same point was that, if the defendant's act was an invasive interference—a trespass, a wrong—the plaintiff should bring trespass, any consequential loss being recovered in damages; if the act was not in itself a trespass, then the correct form was case. . . ."

NOTE

The directness rule still has a role in the modern tort of trespass.

Harnett v Bond [1925] A.C. 669, HL

This was an action for damages in trespass brought against one of the Commissioners at the offices of the Commissioner of Lunacy. The claimant had been confined in a mental asylum but when granted leave went to the offices of the Commissioner to try to prove his sanity. The defendant (Dr Bond), however, came to the conclusion that the claimant was not sane and locked him in a room until the doctor in charge of the asylum (Dr Adam) could come to take him back into custody. The claimant was detained for another nine years before escaping and being found to be perfectly sane. The question arose as to whether the defendant (Dr Bond) should be liable in trespass for the nine years detention which followed the imprisonment in the locked room. The House of Lords (Viscount Cave L.C. and Lords Dunedin, Atkinson, Sumner and Buckmaster) held that the defendant was not to be so liable.

> **Viscount Cave L.C.:** ". . . The defendants having applied to the Court of Appeal for a new trial or judgment, that Court (. . .) unanimously set aside the judgment of Lush J and ordered a new trial as against Dr Bond and that judgment should be entered for Dr Adam. As to Dr Bond, the learned Lords Justices held that the chain of causation had been broken, not only when Dr Adam decided to retain the appellant after his return to Malling Place, but at 'innumerable points' after that date, and that it was plainly not permissible for the jury in assessing damages to treat the whole period of the appellant's captivity as directly caused by the events of December 14, 1912. . . .
>
> My Lords, as regards Dr Bond, I feel no doubt whatever that the Court of Appeal was right in ordering a new trial. . . ."

NOTE

Before an action is trespass will be available the damage must have been directly caused. Indirect damage might give rise to another tort such as nuisance or negligence, but it cannot give rise to trespass: see *Esso v Southport* (p.5). The case of *Wilkinson v Downton* (p.8) might appear to be an exception; however this decision has recently been held not to be a trespass case (*Wainwright*, p.77). Some duty of care cases can be seen in terms of actionability; thus a mere omission could be said to give rise to no duty of care because there is not a sufficient cause and connection: see *Stovin v Wise* (p.175). Duty of care is thus a question of actionability.

QUESTION

What if the defendant in *Harnett* had locked the claimant in the room knowing that he was perfectly sane?

10.2.2 Breach of statutory duty

In another strict liability tort, breach of statutory duty, there is also an important causal requirement which must be fulfilled before there can be an action for damages. Cause and connection between the actual damage suffered and the breach of the statute has to be shown and thus if the damage is independent of the breach there can be no claim.

Gorris v Scott (1874) 9 L.R. Exch. 125, Exch

Kelly C.B.: "This is an action to recover damages for the loss of a number of sheep which the defendant, a shipowner, had contracted to carry, and which were washed overboard and lost by reason (as we must take it to be truly alleged) of the neglect to comply with a certain order made by the Privy Council, in pursuance of the Contagious Diseases (Animals) Act, 1869. The Act was passed merely for sanitary purposes, in order to prevent animals in a state of infectious disease from communicating it to other animals with which they might come in contact. Under the authority of that Act, certain orders were made; amongst others, an order by which any ship bringing sheep or cattle from any foreign port to ports in Great Britain is to have the place occupied by such animals divided into pens of certain dimensions, and the floor of such pens furnished with battens or foot holds. The object of this order is to prevent animals from being overcrowded, and so brought into a condition in which the disease guarded against would be likely to be developed. This regulation has been neglected, and the question is, whether the loss, which we must assume to have been caused by that neglect, entitles the plaintiffs to maintain an action. . . .

But, looking at the Act, it is perfectly clear that its provisions were all enacted with a totally different view; there was no purpose, direct or indirect, to protect against such damage; but, as is recited in the preamble, the Act is directed against the possibility of sheep or cattle being exposed to disease on their way to this country. . . . That being so, if by reason of the default in question the plaintiffs' sheep had been overcrowded, or had been caused unnecessary suffering, and so had arrived in this country in a state of disease, I do not say that they might not have maintained this action. But the damage complained of here is something totally apart from the object of the Act of Parliament, and it is in accordance with all the authorities to say that the action is not maintainable. . .."

[Barons Pigott, Pollock and Amphlett were of the same opinion.]

NOTE

This is a causation case in that the breach of duty could be said not to have caused the loss of the sheep. See also *Bailey v Ayr Engineering Co Ltd* (1958) and *Fytche v Wincanton Logistics Plc* (p.190).

10.2.3 **Negligence**

Causation and actionability can often found in the duty of care question as the next extract indicates.

Rees v Darlington Memorial Hospital NHS Trust [2004] 1 A.C. 309, HL

(For facts see p.423)

Lord Millett ". . . **107** Each of those cases raised an issue of causation. In neither case was it a factual issue, for there was no doubt that the loss was sustained as a direct result of the negligent information which the defendant had supplied. But the law does not hold a person liable for all the foreseeable consequences of his actions. So the question in each case was one of responsibility: was the defendant legally responsible for the loss which his negligence had caused? There was nothing unusual, however, in the nature of the loss; indeed it was commonplace-financial loss arising from a bad investment. The difficulty arose from the causal relationship between the defendant's negligence and the loss sustained by the plaintiff. The solution lay in recognising that a person is only liable for loss which falls within the scope of his duty of care.

108 The problem in a case of wrongful pregnancy is not the same. There is no difficulty about causation, whether as a matter of fact or of legal responsibility. The pregnancy and birth of a child are the very things which the defendants are employed to prevent. It is impossible to say that consequential loss falls outside the scope of their duty of care. They are accordingly liable for the normal and foreseeable heads of loss, such as the mother's pain and suffering (and where appropriate loss of earnings) due to the confinement and delivery. The novelty of the claim in *McFarlane* lay in one particular head of damage-the cost of bringing up a healthy child. The House considered it to be morally repugnant to award damages for the birth of a healthy child. It makes for easier exposition to identify the issue by reference to the head of damage rather than the duty of care. It also has the added advantage that identifying the ratio of *McFarlane* in this way may make it simpler to find the answer to the question raised by the present case. . . ."

NOTE AND QUESTION

In the end, then, the Law Lord thought that this was not a causal problem that functioned at the level of actionability. It was a matter of damages. But what if a child had been born severely disabled and the hospital had carelessly failed to inform the mother of this possibility soon after conception: could the child sue for damages claiming that it would have been better to have been aborted? Would this be a causal problem?

10.2.4 Consent to injury

A person may be prevented from bringing an action for damages on the basis that he consented to the risk of incurring damage. Or, put another way, his injury is not caused by the defendant but by his own willingness to accept the risk of incurring the damage: volenti non fit injuria. However the defence is rarely successful since the courts have long made a distinction between mere knowledge of a risk and actual consent to the injury. Moreover, being a complete defence to an action, the courts have often preferred to apply the damages defence of contributory negligence (see below **10.5.1**)

Morris v Murray **[1991] 2 Q.B. 6, CA**

This was an action for damages brought by a passenger in a light aeroplane against the estate of the pilot of the aircraft. The pilot and the passenger had spent the afternoon drinking alcohol after which the pilot suggested that they go for a flight. The aircraft crashed owing to the negligence of the pilot and as a result the pilot was killed and the passenger injured. The Court of Appeal (Fox L.J., Stocker L.J. and Sir George Waller) held that the passenger had consented to the risk of injury and thus that he had no action.

> **Fox L.J.:** ". . . I think that in embarking upon the flight the plaintiff had implicitly waived his rights in the event of injury consequent on Mr. Murray's failure to fly with reasonable care. The facts go far beyond *Dann v Hamilton* [1939] 1 K.B. 509; *Nettleship v Weston* [1971] 2 Q.B. 691 and *Slater v Clay Cross Co Ltd* [1956] 2 Q.B. 264. It is much nearer to the dangerous experimenting with the detonators in *Imperial Chemical Industries Ltd v Shatwell* [1965] A.C. 656. I would conclude, therefore, that the plaintiff accepted the risks and implicitly discharged Mr. Murray from liability for injury in relation to the flying of the plane. The result, in my view, is that the maxim volenti non fit injuria does apply in this case. The judge appears to have been influenced by the fact that Mr. Murray managed to get the plane airborne. He did, but the take off downwind was irregular and the bizarre movements of the plane in flight must raise the greatest doubts whether he was in proper control of it. The judge thought that the case was analogous to *Owens v Brimmell* [1977] Q.B. 859. But the volenti defence was not in issue in that case.

> Considerations of policy do not lead me to any different conclusion. Volenti as a defence has, perhaps, been in retreat during this century—certainly in relation to master and servant cases. It might be said that the merits could be adequately dealt with by the application of the contributory negligence rules. The judge held that the plaintiff was only 20 per cent to blame (which seems to me to be too low) but if that were increased to 50 per cent so that the plaintiff's damages were reduced by half, both sides would be substantially penalised for their conduct. It seems to me, however, that the wild irresponsibility of the venture is such that the law should not intervene to award damages and should leave the loss where it falls. Flying is intrinsically dangerous and flying with a drunken pilot is great folly. The situation is very different from what has arisen in motoring cases.

> I should mention that the defence of volenti has been abrogated in relation to passengers in motor vehicles covered by comprehensive insurance: section [149(3) the Road Traffic Act 1988]. It is not suggested, however, that there is any similar enactment relating to aircraft and applicable to this case. . . ."

QUESTION

Might this decision be based upon a concern about who should end up the defendant's assets? (Study the case in full in the law report.)

NOTES

1. *ICI v Shatwell* (1965) should be read in the law reports.

2. The defence of volenti is to be found in a range of statutes: see e.g. Occupier's Liability Act 1957 s.2(5); Animals Act 1971 s.5(2); Occupiers' Liability Act 1984 s.1(6).

3. A person can also be deemed to consent to damage via a contractual exclusion clause or a notice. However statute lays down certain restrictions.

Unfair Contract Terms Act 1977 (c.50)

"1 Scope of Part I

(1) For the purposes of this Part of this Act, "negligence" means the breach—

(a) of any obligation, arising from the express or implied terms of a contract, to take reasonable care to exercise reasonable skill in the performance of the contract;

(b) of any common law duty to take reasonable care or exercise reasonable skill (but not any stricter duty);

(c) of the common duty of care imposed by the Occupiers' Liability Act 1957 or the Occupiers' Liability Act (Northern Ireland) 1957.

(2) This Part of this Act is subject to Part III; and in relation to contracts, the operation of sections 2 to 4 and 7 is subject to the exceptions made by Schedule 1.

(3) In the case of both contract and tort, sections 2 to 7 apply (except where the contrary is stated in section 6(4)) only to business liability, that is liability for breach of obligations or duties arising—

(a) from things done or to be done by a person in the course of a business (whether his own business or another's); or

(b) from the occupation of premises used for business purposes of the occupier;

and references to liability are to be read accordingly but liability of an occupier of premises for breach of an obligation or duty towards a person obtaining access to the premises for recreational or educational purposes, being liability for loss or damage suffered by reason of the dangerous state of the premises, is not a business liability of the occupier unless granting that person such access for the purposes concerned falls within the business purposes of the occupier.

(4) In relation to any breach of duty or obligation, it is immaterial for any purpose of this Part of this Act whether the breach was inadvertent or intentional, or whether liability for it arises directly or vicariously.

2 Negligence liability

(1) A person cannot by reference to any contract term or to a notice given to persons generally or to particular persons exclude or restrict his liability for death or personal injury resulting from negligence.

(2) In the case of other loss or damage, a person cannot so exclude or restrict his liability for negligence except in so far as the term or notice satisfies the requirement of reasonableness.

(3) Where a contract term or notice purports to exclude or restrict liability for negligence a person's agreement to or awareness of it is not of itself to be taken as indicating his voluntary acceptance of any risk."

QUESTIONS

1. What would be the effect of this statute on *Ashdown v Samuel Williams* (1957) and *White v Blackmore* (1972)?

2. How does this 1977 Act relate to the Occupiers' Liability Act 1984 s.1(5)?

PROBLEM

A commercial company owns and occupies a piece of land on which is a dilapidated building that sometimes attracts trespassers. The company erects notices stating: 'Danger: Do Not Enter. Dilapidated and Dangerous Building. Trespassers enter entirely at their own risk and are deemed to have consented to, and to be the cause of, any injury'. A homeless teenager enters the land and is injured while sleeping in the building when part of the roof collapses. Can the teenager sue the commercial company for damages?

10.2.5 **Ex turpi causa non oritur actio**

This maxim states that no action can arise out of an illegal cause. Accordingly if the claimant is injured while participating in a criminal activity he may be denied a claim for damages.

Pitts v Hunt **[1991] 1 Q.B. 24, CA**

This was an action for damages by a pillion passenger on a motorcycle driven by the defendant in respect of personal injuries suffered when the motor-cycle was involved in a collision with another vehicle. The claimant and the defendant had been drinking before the journey and the former knew that the latter had no licence or insurance. In addition the claimant had encouraged the defendant to drive in a reckless and dangerous manner. The Court of Appeal (Dillon L.J., Balcombe L.J. and Beldam L.J.) held that the claimant was precluded from bring an action on the ground of illegality.

> **Beldam L.J.:** ". . . On the facts found by the judge in this case the plaintiff was playing a full and active part in encouraging the young rider to commit offences which, if a death other than that of the young rider himself had occurred, would have amounted to manslaughter. And not just manslaughter by gross negligence, on the judge's findings. It would have been manslaughter by the commission of a dangerous act either done with the intention of frightening other road users or when both the plaintiff and the young rider were aware, or but for self-induced intoxication would have been aware, that it was likely to do so, and nevertheless they went on and did the act regardless of the consequences. Thus on the findings made by the judge in this case I would hold that the plaintiff is precluded on grounds of public policy from recovering compensation for the injuries which he sustained in the course of the very serious offences in which he was participating. On a question on which, as Bingham L.J. said in *Saunders v Edwards* [1987] 1 WLR 1116, 1134, the courts have tended to adopt a pragmatic approach, I do not believe that it is desirable to go further in an attempt to categorise the degree of seriousness involved in offences which will preclude recovery of compensation. I would, however, add that the public attitude to driving a motor vehicle on a road when under the influence of drink has, I believe, changed markedly with the increasing number of serious accidents and the dreadful injuries which are the consequence of such driving. The public conscience is ever increasingly being focused not only on those who commit the offence but, in the words of recent publicity, those who ask the driver to drink and drive. . . ."

NOTE

See also *Vellino v Chief Constable of Greater Manchester Police* (2002) (p.41).

QUESTIONS

Is this case much different in its factual structure from *Morris v Murray* (1991) (above p.367)? If not, is there really a need for a separate doctrine of illegality? Could not the cases be solved using the notions of factual causation, volenti and/or contributory negligence?

10.2.6 **Necessity**

An action may prove unsuccessful in situations where the defendant's act was prompted by necessity. In medical liability problems the value of necessity is apparent given that the medical profession is under a duty to save lives (cf. *Re F*, p.80). But what if the police have to destroy a private person's house or shop in order to subdue a dangerous criminal?

Rigby v Chief Constable of Northamptonshire **[1985]** **1 W.L.R. 1242, QBD**

Taylor J.: "On 17 December 1977, the Sportsman's Lodge, a gunsmiths shop in North-ampton owned by the first plaintiff, Michael Rigby, was burned out. The cause of the fire was most unusual. A young psychopath had broken into the premises and armed himself. The police laid siege to the shop. Eventually they fired in a canister of CS gas to smoke out the intruder. The canister set the shop ablaze. The first plaintiff now sues the Chief Constable of Northamptonshire for damages for loss and damage to the premises and contents. The second plaintiff makes a small claim for damage to his guns which were in the first plaintiff's custody in the shop. . . .

There is a surprising dearth of authority as to the nature and limits of necessity as a defence in tort. Mr Machin referred me to three cases. *Cope v Sharpe (No 2)* [1912] 1 KB 496 was a case of alleged trespass where the defendant had sought to prevent a heather fire from spreading. *Creswell v Sirl* [1948] 1 KB 241 was a case of alleged trespass to a dog which the defendant had shot to prevent it worrying sheep. In each case the defence prevailed. . . .

I therefore hold that a defence of necessity is available in the absence of negligence on the part of the defendant creating or contributing to the necessity. In this case there was a dangerous armed psychopath whom it was urgently necessary to arrest. I have already found that it was not negligent of the defendant to be without Ferret. It is conceded that the only alternative was to fire in a CS gas canister, which was done. I therefore find that the defence of necessity prevails and that the cause of action in trespass fails. . . .

Mr O'Brien, whilst accepting that necessity can apply to *Rylands v Fletcher* liability, sought to argue that it has a more limited scope there than in answer to alleged trespass. He based this on the decision in *West v Bristol Tramways Co* [1908] 2 KB 14, the creosote case. However, there the defence was statutory authority and I do not think Mr O'Brien made his submission good. In the result, I conclude that if, which I doubt, this case falls to be considered at all under *Rylands v Fletcher*, necessity would provide a good defence as it does in trespass. . . .

This leads me to consider the remaining allegation of negligence. . . .

> ... Mr O'Brien argues the probability is that a fire appliance (for example the Wellingborough Green Goddess which in fact came later) could have been brought to the scene and would have arrived before 9.20. Bearing all these matters in mind, I conclude that the defendant by his officers was negligent in failing to react to the departure of the Green Goddess by seeking other help, and in using the canister without any fire-fighting equipment. . . .
>
> I am not asked to consider the issue of damages. Suffice it to say, therefore, that in the upshot I find the defendant liable in negligence to both plaintiffs. The damages issue must be tried by another tribunal unless agreed."

QUESTIONS

1. How might these facts have been decided in France? (See *Moreau*, p.336.)

2. If the real plaintiff in *Rigby* were the shop owner's building insurance company, would you still consider it right that the police should have to pay the company damages?

NOTE

In the case of *In Re F* (above p.80) Lord Goff said (at p.74) 'That there exists in the common law a principle of necessity which may justify action which would otherwise be unlawful is not in doubt".

10.3 Factual causation

Factual causation is perhaps the most complex level. In the past this question would have been decided by a jury who would not have given reasons. These days it is a matter for the judge who is expected to motivate his or her conclusions.

Banque Bruxelles Lambert SA v Eagle Star Insurance Co Ltd [1997] A.C. 191, HL

Lord Hoffmann: ". . . There is no reason in principle why the law should not penalise wrongful conduct by shifting on to the wrongdoer the whole risk of consequences which would not have happened but for the wrongful act. Hart and Honoré, in *Causation in the Law*, 2nd ed (1985), p 120, say that it would, for example, be perfectly intelligible to have a rule by which an unlicensed driver was responsible for all the consequences of his having driven, even if they were unconnected with his not having a licence. One might adopt such a rule in the interests of deterring unlicensed driving. But that is not the normal rule. . . .

Rules which make the wrongdoer liable for all the consequences of his wrongful conduct are exceptional and need to be justified by some special policy. Normally the law limits liability to those consequences which are attributable to that which made the act wrongful. In the case of liability in negligence for providing inaccurate information, this would mean liability for the consequences of the information being inaccurate.

I can illustrate the difference between the ordinary principle and that adopted by the Court of Appeal by an example. A mountaineer about to undertake a difficult climb is concerned about the fitness of his knee. He goes to a doctor who negligently makes a superficial examination and pronounces the knee fit. The climber goes on the expedition, which he would not have undertaken if the doctor had told him the true state of his knee. He suffers an injury which is an entirely foreseeable consequence of mountaineering but has nothing to do with his knee. . . .

Your Lordships might, I would suggest, think that there was something wrong with a principle which, in the example which I have given, produced the result that the doctor was liable. What is the reason for this feeling? I think that the Court of Appeal's principle offends common sense because it makes the doctor responsible for consequences which, though in general terms foreseeable, do not appear to have a sufficient causal connection with the subject matter of the duty. The doctor was asked for information on only one of the considerations which might affect the safety of the mountaineer on the expedition. There seems no reason of policy which requires that the negligence of the doctor should require the transfer to him of all the foreseeable risks of the expedition."

QUESTION

If one applies the 'but for' test to Lord Hoffmann's mountaineer example, what is the result? (cf. PETL art.3:101.)

NOTE

Lord Hoffmann may well be talking about liability and factual causation but two non-factual notions emerge from his discussion: they are the notions of deterrence and policy. These aims and policy aspects, when combined with various technical causal terms, only increase the complication, as the next extract illustrates.

Reeves v Commissioner of Police for the Metropolis **[2000] 1 A.C. 360, HL**

(For facts and further extract see p.377)

Lord Hobhouse (dissenting): ". . . My Lords, causation as discussed in the authorities has been complicated both by conflicting statements about whether causation is a question of fact or of law or, even, 'common sense' and by the use of metaphor and Latin terminology, eg, *causa sine qua non, causa causans, novus actus* and *volenti*, which in themselves provide little enlightenment and are not consistently used.

At one level causation is purely a question of fact. It is a question of fact whether event 'a' was a cause of event 'x'. To simplify, it is a factual question whether event 'x' would still have occurred if event 'a' had not. However facts are not that simple. Virtually every event will have a number of antecedent facts which satisfy such a factual test. The ordinary use of language then distinguishes between them, choosing some and discarding others. The presence of oxygen is a necessary cause of combustion yet it is not normally treated as being a cause. This is because it is part of the normal environment and therefore is disregarded when identifying the cause of some abnormal event. (In certain circumstances, oxygen is not or should not be part of the normal environment, e.g. in tanks used for the sea carriage of petroleum, in which case its presence would be identified as a cause.) The ordinary use of language makes a distinction, independent of any legal concept, between the normal and the abnormal in describing something as a cause.

This use of language is most easily observed in relation to physical events but is also applied to human conduct. Reasonable human responses to situations are not treated as causative; they are a normal consequence of the antecedent event and it is that event which is described as the cause. Thus the reasonable response of a rescuer to an accident caused by the negligence of another would not without more be described as a cause of an injury suffered by the rescuer. Similarly, to act reasonably on the faith of some misinformation is normally described as a consequence not as a cause. Human conduct, which is not entirely reasonable, for example, where it is itself careless, but is within the range of human conduct that is foreseeable and normally contemplated as not unlikely, may add a further cause of the relevant subsequent event but would not normally mean that an earlier relevant event ceased also to be a cause of that later event. Careless conduct may ordinarily be regarded as being within the range of normal human conduct when reckless conduct ordinarily would not.

Any disputed question of causation (factual or legal) will involve a number of factual events or conditions which satisfy the 'but for' test. A process of evaluation and selection has then to take place. It may, for example, be necessary to distinguish between what factually are necessary and sufficient causes. It may be necessary to distinguish between those conditions or events which merely provide the occasion or opportunity for a given consequence and those which in the ordinary use of language would (independently of any imposed legal criterion) be said to have caused the relevant consequence. Thus certain causes will be discarded as insignificant and one cause may be selected as the cause. It is at this stage that legal concepts may enter in, either in a way that is analogous to the factual assessment—as for 'proximate'; cause in insurance law—or, in a more specifically legal manner, in the attribution of responsibility (bearing in mind that responsibility may not be exclusive). In the law of tort it is the attribution of responsibility to humans that is the relevant legal consideration. . . ."

NOTES

1. A number of points emerge from this extract. Yet perhaps the most important at a technical level is that factual causation can be classified into various sub-categories depending upon the actual causal agency or event. Thus one important Latin tag is *novus actus interveniens* which gives expression to the idea of a new intervening cause. For example D negligently injures C but while C is being taken to hospital in an ambulance the ambulance driver carelessly crashes the vehicle causing further injury to C. Is D to be liable for this further injury

2. See also *Corr v IBC Vehicles Ltd* (p.378)

10.3.2 Intervention by a third party

One might start therefore with the causal situation where the new intervening event (novus actus interveniens) is by a third party.

The Oropesa **[1943] P. 32, CA**

This was an action for damages by the parent of one of the crew members of the *Manchester Regiment* who died when a lifeboat capsized. The *Manchester Regiment* had been involved in a collision with the *Oropesa* caused partly through the negligence of the *Oropesa*. The captain of the *Manchester Regiment* decided to confer with the captain of the *Oropesa* and set out, with various crewmembers including the claimant's son, in the fatal lifeboat. The owners of the *Oropesa* claimed they were not liable for the death because the act of the captain in setting out in the lifeboat had broken the chain of causation. This defence was rejected by the trial judge and an appeal to the Court of Appeal (Lord Wright, Scott L.J. and MacKinnon L.J.) was dismissed.

Lord Wright: ". . . If. . . the test is whether what was done was reasonable, there can be no question that the actions of both the master and the deceased were reasonable. Whether the master took exactly the right course is another matter. He may have been guilty of an error of judgment, but, as I read the authorities, that would not affect the question whether the action he took and its consequences flowed directly from the negligence of the *Oropesa*. . . . Having regard to the situation of the *Manchester Regiment* and those on board her, I think that the hand of the casualty lay heavily on her and that the conduct both of the master and of the deceased was directly caused by and flowed from it. There was an unbroken sequence of cause and effect between the negligence which caused the *Oropesa* to collide with the *Manchester Regiment*, and their action, which was dictated by the exigencies of the position. It cannot be severed from the circumstances affecting both ships. To that must be joined the duty which they were under in their positions as captain and sixth engineer.

There are some propositions which are beyond question in connection with this class of case. One is that human action does not per se sever the connected sequence of acts. The mere fact that human action intervenes does not prevent the sufferer from saying that injury which is due to that human action as one of the elements in the sequence is recoverable from the original wrongdoer. . . . The question is not whether there was new negligence, but whether there was a new cause. . . . To break the chain of causation it must be shown that there is something which I will call ultroneous, something unwarrantable, a new cause which disturbs the sequence of events, something which can be described as either unreasonable or extraneous or extrinsic. . . . Here it may be said that, even if the master of the Manchester Regiment was not doing quite the right thing, his mistake might be regarded as the natural consequence of the emergency in which he was placed by the negligence of the *Oropesa*. . . .

The real difficulty in the present case is the application of the principle, which is a question of fact. I agree entirely with Langton J in the way in which he has dealt with the question. I am not prepared to say in all the circumstances that the fact that the deceased's death was due to his leaving the ship in the lifeboat and to the unexpected capsizing of that boat prevented his death being a direct consequence of the casualty. It was a risk, no doubt, but a boat would not generally capsize in those circumstances. In my opinion, the appeal should be dismissed."

NOTE

The test applied was one of reasonableness. Such a test is not surprising given that factual causation was once a question for the jury. However 'reasonableness' in this context is not the same as in the duty of care question (cf. *Bolton v Stone*, p.140). The captain, in setting off in the small boat, may have been unreasonable in the sense that it could have been a careless thing to do (the present author's late father-in-law, a highly experienced merchant navy captain, decorated for bravery, who was a passenger on the *Oropesa* at the time of this accident, certainly thought it was pretty daft). But it does not follow that such duty of care unreasonableness is equivalent to causal unreasonableness. The tests are quite different.

10.3.3 Intervention by the claimant

The novus actus interveniens can result from the claimant's own act.

***McKew v Holland & Hannen & Cubitts Ltd* [1969] 3 All E.R. 1621, HL (Scotland)**

This was an action for damages by an employee against his employer in respect of two injuries, one sustained at work and one sustained while visiting a block of flats. In the second accident the plaintiff was descending some steep stairs when his leg gave way (a result of the first accident) and he tried to jump the rest of the way in order to land in an upright position. However he succeeded only in severely fracturing his ankle. The House of Lords (Lords Reid, Hodson, Guest, Upjohn and Viscount Dilhorne) held that the employer was not liable for this second injury.

Lord Reid: ". . . In my view the law is clear. If a man is injured in such a way that his leg may give way at any moment he must act reasonably and carefully. It is quite possible that in spite of all reasonable care his leg may give way in circumstances such that as a result he sustains further injury. Then that second injury was caused by his disability which in turn was caused by the defender's fault. But if the injured man acts unreasonably he cannot hold the defender liable for injury caused by his own unreasonable conduct. His unreasonable conduct is novus actus interveniens. The chain of causation has been broken and what follows must be regarded as caused by his own conduct and not by the defender's fault or the disability caused by it. Or one may say that unreasonable conduct of the pursuer and what follows from it is not the natural and probable result of the original fault of the defender or of the ensuing disability. I do not think that foreseeability comes into this. A defender is not liable for a consequence of a kind which is not foreseeable. But it does not follow that he is liable for every consequence which a reasonable man could foresee. What can be foreseen depends almost entirely on the facts of the case, and it is often easy to foresee unreasonable conduct or some other novus actus interveniens as being quite likely. But that does not mean that the defender must pay for damage caused by the novus actus. It only leads to trouble that if one tries to graft on to the concept of foreseeability some rule of law to the effect that a wrongdoer is not bound to foresee something which in fact he could readily foresee as quite likely to happen. For it is not at all unlikely or unforeseeable that an active man who has suffered such a disability will take some quite unreasonable risk. But if he does he cannot hold the defender liable for the consequences."

NOTES AND QUESTION

1. Compare the above decision with *Sayers v Harlow UDC* (1958) and *Wieland v Cyril Lord Carpets Ltd* (1969). Why was *Wieland* decided differently than *McKew*?

2. What is particularly important about Lord Reid's judgment in this case is that he clearly restates (i) the test as one of "reasonableness" and (ii) that this test is quite different

from "foreseeability". This latter test, as we shall see, is relevant only to remoteness of damage and not factual causation. The flexibility of the reasonableness test in factual causation is tested to the limit by the next case.

Reeves v Commissioner of Police for the Metropolis [2000] 1 A.C. 360, HL

This was an action for damages brought under the Fatal Accidents Act 1976 and Law Reform (Miscellaneous Provisions) Act 1934 against the police by a dependent of a man who had committed suicide while in police custody. The police were adjudged negligent but the judge held that the man, in taking his own life, was the sole cause of his damage. An appeal to the Court of Appeal was allowed, a majority holding that the claimant was entitled to full damages. A further appeal to the House of Lords (Lords Hoffmann, Mackay, Jauncey and Hope; Lord Hobhouse dissenting) was allowed: a majority held that the claimant was entitled to damages reduced by 50 per cent on the basis of contributory negligence.

Lord Jauncey: ". . . Mr Pannick submitted that the deceased's death was caused not by the negligence of the police officers but by the voluntary act of the deceased while of sound mind. This act broke the chain of causation between the Commissioner's breach of duty and the death. . . .

My Lords, I consider that this argument is flawed. Professor Glanville Williams in his *Joint Torts and Contributory Negligence* (1951) stated at para. 2–24 that:

'If a particular consequence of the defendant's wrongdoing is attributable to some independent act or event which supersedes the effect of the tortuous conduct, the defendant's responsibilities may not extend to the consequences of the supervening act or event.'

He went on to state that the *novus actus interveniens* 'must constitute an event of such impact that it rightly obliterates the wrongdoing of the defendant.' The reference to an independent act superseding the effect of the tortious conduct must, in my view, relate to an act which was outwith the contemplated scope of events to which the duty of care was directed. Where such a duty is specifically directed at the prevention of the occurrence of a certain event I cannot see how it can be said that the occurrence of that event amounts to an independent act breaking the chain of causation from the breach of duty, even although it may be unusual for one person to come under a duty to prevent another person deliberately inflicting harm on himself. It is the very thing at which the duty was directed. . .

The individual's right of self determination is irrelevant here for two reasons. In the first place it is not a defence to a breach of duty but rather an argument against the existence of a duty at all. If an individual can do to his own body what he wills, whether by positive act or neglect then there can be no duty on anyone else to prevent his so doing. In this case, however, it is accepted that the commissioner owed a duty of care to the deceased. In the second place the cases in which the principle has been recognised and to which your Lordships have been referred were cases in which prevention of injury to health or death would have involved an unlawful physical invasion of the individual's rights. In this case performance of the duty of care by closing the flap would have involved no invasion of any rights of the deceased. . . ."

Lord Hobhouse (dissenting): ". . . The attribution of human responsibility is often a complex exercise since it involves an examination of the legally relevant features of the consequence in question and the legally relevant features of the conduct complained of (eg *The Empire Jamaica* [1957] AC 386) in conjunction with or in contrast to other human conduct which may also be factually relevant. Legal criteria (maybe fact sensitive) have to be applied. At this level causation is a question of law. Now is not the time to enter upon an exhaustive examination of the legal criteria. For present purposes two categories are directly relevant.

Before examining these two categories, however, I would stress three points. First, a distinction is drawn between natural and human phenomena. Save in theologically inspired language now long discarded, responsibility is not attached to natural events. The only consideration to which they give rise is remoteness. Secondly, human conduct in contrast can have a double relevance, both to remoteness and to attracting legal and moral responsibility. But, for most purposes in the law, and in particular in the law of tort, all a plaintiff need prove is that the defendant's tort was a cause of the loss in respect of which the plaintiff claims. If two or more tortfeasors have each contributed to causing the plaintiff's loss, each of them is severally liable for that loss. Remoteness is, again, the only relevant consideration. Unless the conduct of one tortfeasor has been such as to take the consequence out of the scope of another's tortious duty and render it too remote, the liability of one does not preclude the claim of the plaintiff against each.

Thirdly and most importantly in the present context, there is a radical distinction between the conduct of the plaintiff and the conduct of third parties. To overlook this distinction will inevitably lead to error. At one level where it merely involves some lack of care or breach of duty it reduces but does not negative the plaintiff's right of recovery; this is the position (now) where there is contributory negligence. Failure to mitigate can be similarly analysed (though it can also be analysed pro tanto in terms of remoteness or causation). Where deliberate voluntary conduct of the plaintiff is involved in the knowledge of what the defendant has done, the plaintiff cannot disclaim responsibility for the consequence: he has caused his own loss. His conduct has a different impact to that of a third party. . . ."

QUESTION

If the majority had followed the dissenting opinion of Lord Hobhouse, would the police's duty of care towards the prisoner have been empty of content?

NOTE

Suicide does not automatically break the chain of factual causation.

Corr v IBC Vehicles Ltd [2008] 2 W.L.R. 499, HL

This was an action for damages under the Fatal Accidents Act 1976 by the wife of the victim of an industrial accident. The accident had resulted from the defendant employer's negligence and caused not just physical injury but very severe depression. Some years after the accident the victim committed suicide. The judge allowed a claim by the victim's estate but dismissed the action under the Fatal Accidents Act on the ground that the chain of causation between accident and suicide had been broken. The Court of Appeal allowed an appeal and a further appeal to the House of Lords (Lords Bingham, Walker, Mance and Neuberger; Lord Scott dissenting in part) was dismissed.

Lord Bingham: ". . . 15 The rationale of the principle that a novus actus interveniens breaks the chain of causation is fairness. It is not fair to hold a tortfeasor liable, however gross his breach of duty may be, for damage caused to the claimant not by the tortfeasor's breach of duty but by some independent, supervening cause (which may or may not be tortious) for which the tortfeasor is not responsible. This is not the less so where the independent, supervening cause is a voluntary, informed decision taken by the victim as an adult of sound mind making and giving effect to a personal decision about his own future. . . . In such circumstances it is usual to describe the chain of causation being broken but it is perhaps equally accurate to say that the victim's independent act forms no part of a chain of causation beginning with the tortfeasor's breach of duty.

16 In the present case Mr Corr's suicide was not a voluntary, informed decision taken by him as an adult of sound mind making and giving effect to a personal decision about his future. It was the response of a man suffering from a severely depressive illness which impaired his capacity to make reasoned and informed judgments about his future, such illness being, as is accepted, a consequence of the employer's tort. It is in no way unfair to hold the employer responsible for this dire consequence of its breach of duty, although it could well be thought unfair to the victim not to do so. . . .

(4) The unreasonable act issue

17 . . . [H]aving regard to the reasons I have given for holding the suicide of the deceased not to be a novus actus I would find it impossible to hold that the damages attributable to the death were rendered too remote because the deceased's conduct was unreasonable. It is of course true that, judged objectively, it is unreasonable in almost any situation to take one's own life. But once it is accepted, as it must be, that the deceased's unreasonable conduct was induced by the breach of duty of which the claimant complains, the argument ceases in my judgment to have any independent validity.

(5) The volenti issue

18 It is a salutary and fair principle that a tortfeasor cannot be held responsible for injury or damage to which a victim, voluntarily and with his eyes open, consents. But it is not suggested that Mr Corr consented in any way to the accident and injury which befell him on 22 June 1996. It is an argument addressed only to his suicide. But that was not something to which Mr Corr consented voluntarily and with his eyes open but an act performed because of the psychological condition which the employer's breach of duty had induced. I conclude, again, that this is an argument which has no independent validity. . . ."

QUESTIONS

1. In the Court of Appeal Ward L.J. said (at § 45): "Causation may be a matter of common sense but it also imports value judgments. As soon as the test is framed in terms of whether the action of the victim is 'unreasonable' as in *McKew v Holland & Hannen & Cubitts (Scotland) Ltd* [1969] 3 All E.R. 1621, then one is making a value judgment". Does this mean that all factual causation questions are, in the final analysis, policy rather

than purely factual questions? How might these value judgments impact upon the proof of factual causation?

2. Even if the law accepts that the claimant's suicide does not break the chain of factual causation, can it nevertheless be argued that the suicide is too remote as damage? (cf. below, p.402.)

3. Is the act of suicide part and parcel of the psychological damage?

4. What if a worker enjoys showing off to his mates and takes 'suicidal' risks while working in dangerous conditions?

McWilliams v Sir William Arrol & Co [1962] 1 W.L.R. 295, HL (Scotland)

This was an action for damages by a widow against the employer of her late husband. The House of Lords (Viscount Kilmuir L.C., Viscount Simonds and Lords Reid, Morris and Devlin) dismissed the claim.

Lord Devlin: "My Lords, the appellant is the widow of a steel erector who was killed by a fall in the course of his employment by the first respondents. She alleges that the employers were in breach of their duty at common law to the deceased in that they failed to provide him with a safety belt, and failed to instruct him to wear it. The courts below have held that the employers were in breach of their duty in failing to provide a safety belt, but that that was not the cause of the deceased's death since he would not have worn it if it had been provided. They have held also that there was no duty on the employers to instruct the deceased to wear it. . . ." [Lord Devlin went on to dismiss the appeal.]

Lord Reid: ". . . If I prove that my breach of duty in no way caused or contributed to the accident I cannot be liable in damages. And if the accident would have happened in just the same way whether or not I fulfilled my duty, it is obvious that my failure to fulfil my duty cannot have caused or contributed to it. No reason has ever been suggested why a defender should be barred from proving that his fault, whether common law negligence or breach of statutory duty, had nothing to do with the accident."

QUESTIONS

1. Did the deceased suffer the loss of a chance not to be killed? If so, what was the cause of the loss of this chance not to be killed? Could one raise a similar question in respect of *Barnett v Chelsea and Kensington Hospital Management Committee* (1969) (read in law report)?

2. Ought the employer to have been under a duty not only to supply safety belts but to ensure they were used? Would *McWilliams* be decided the same way today?

10.3.4 Intervention by nature

Sometimes the intervention is not by human hand but by an 'Act of God' or an 'Act of Nature'.

Carslogie SS Co v Royal Norwegian Government **[1952] A.C. 292, HL**

This was an action for damages by one ship owner against another in respect of damage to a ship arising out of a collision caused by the defendants' negligence. After the collision the claimant's ship was temporarily rendered seaworthy in England but she needed longer-term repairs in the USA. While crossing the Atlantic for these repairs she encountered heavy weather which rendered her once again unseaworthy. The claim for damages for the loss of use of the ship was unsuccessful in the House of Lords (Viscount Jowitt and Lords Normand, Morton, Tucker and Asquith).

Lord Morton: "My Lords, the *Heimgar* was detained in New York for nearly 50 days. At an early stage in the speech of counsel for the appellants, I asked whether it was common ground between the parties that, if the collision between the *Heimgar* and the *Carslogie* had never happened, the *Heimgar* would have been detained in New York for the same period of 50 days. The answer was in the affirmative. . . .

My Lords, I agree with this answer, and if it is the correct answer I can see no ground upon which the respondents can recover the damages which they claim for the detention of their ship. If the *Heimgar* had not encountered heavy weather on her voyage across the Atlantic, I entertain no doubt that the respondents could have recovered damages for her detention in New York for the period of 10 days which would have been required to repair the collision damage. In that event they would have lost the use of their profit-earning chattel for a period of 10 days and the negligence of the appellants would have been the cause of that loss; but in the events which happened the respondents have failed to prove that any loss of the use of their profitearning chattel resulted from the negligence of the appellants. . . ."

NOTES

1. See also *Performance Cars v Abrahams* (1961) (read in the law report).

2. These property cases (*Carslogie* and *Performance Cars*) can perhaps be seen as examples of the rule that a defendant must take his victim as he finds him. Normally this rule operates in favour of the claimant and so for example it is no defence that a victim has a particular susceptibility to injury ('egg-shell skull' principle) (see e.g. *Smith v Leech Brain & Co Ltd* (1962)). Equally an impecunious claimant might be able to claim special damages caused as a result of this impecuniousness (*Lagden v O'Connor*, p.450). In *Performance Cars* the rule operated in favour of the defendant in the second action: he had damaged an already damaged car and so the first damage absorbed the second so to speak. Yet much depends upon how the issue is framed. By focusing on the respray it is possible to say that this head of damage did not 'exist' when the second accident occurred. But, as we shall see later, if one attempts to extend this principle by analogy to personal injury damage, the courts may not be so generous to defendants because it is not so easy to isolate personal injury damage into discrete heads.

QUESTIONS

1. In *Carslogie* did the second (weather) damage obliterate the first?

2. What was the nature of the damage in issue in this case: was it physical damage to the ship or economic loss arising out of the loss of use of a profit earning thing?

3. What if the cause of action is not negligence but a strict liability tort?

Nichols v Marsland (1876) 2 Ex. D. 1, CA

This was an action for damages, based on *Rylands v Fletcher* (see p.243), brought by a county surveyor against a landowner in respect of damage to bridges caused by flooding. The defendant kept on her land ornamental pools containing large quantities of water and these pools burst their banks during a period of exceptionally heavy rainfall. The Court of Exchequer gave judgment for the defendant and this decision was confirmed by the Court of Appeal (Mellish L.J., James L.J., Cockburn C.J. and Baggallay J.A.).

> **Mellish L.J.** (delivering judgment of the court): ". . . Now, with respect to the first question, the ordinary rule of law is that when the law creates a duty and the party is disabled from performing it without any default of his own, by the act of God, or the King's enemies, the law will excuse him; but when a party by his own contract creates a duty, he is bound to make it good notwithstanding any accident by inevitable necessity. We can see no good reason why that rule should not be applied to the case before us. The duty of keeping the water in and preventing its escape is a duty imposed by the law, and not one created by contract. If, indeed, the making a reservoir was a wrongful act in itself, it might be right to hold that a person could not escape from the consequences of his own wrongful act. But it seems to us absurd to hold that the making or the keeping a reservoir is a wrongful act in itself. . . .
>
> It was indeed ingeniously argued for the appellant that at any rate the escape of the water was not owing solely to the act of God, because the weight of the water originally in the reservoirs must have contributed to break down the dams, as well as the extraordinary water brought in by the flood. We think, however, that the extraordinary quantity of water brought in by the flood is in point of law the sole proximate cause of the escape of the water. It is the last drop which makes the cup overflow."

QUESTION

1. Why should the public have to shoulder the risk of flooding caused by another landowner's acts of self-indulgence?

2. What does *Nichols* have in common with *Bradford Corp v Pickles* (p.72)?

10.3.5 Intervention by a rescuer

One particular form of causal intervention that raises a special policy question is where an intervener performs an act of rescue. For example, a passer-by dives into a river in an attempt to rescue the defendant who, through his (or a third party's) negligence, has got himself into difficulties. If the rescuer is injured or killed as a result of the rescue attempt, will the defendant, or his estate (if the defendant nevertheless dies), be liable to the rescuer or his or her dependants? Two possible arguments could be raised to deny liability. It could be argued that the claimant was the cause of his own injury or it could be said that he consented to the risk of injury. Not surprisingly the courts are slow to accept such arguments as the next case indicates.

Haynes v Harwood **[1935] 1 K.B. 146, CA**

This was an action for damages by a policeman against the owner of a van and horses whose employee had carelessly left the van unattended in the street. A passing boy threw a stone at the horses and they bolted. The policeman, realising that a woman and some children were in danger, managed to halt the horses but at the cost of personal injury to himself. The trial judge held in favour of the claimant and this decision was upheld by the Court of Appeal (Greer L.J., Maugham L.J. and Roche L.J.).

> **Greer L.J.:** ". . . If what is relied upon as novus actus interveniens is the very kind of thing which is likely to happen if the want of care which is alleged takes place, the principle embodied in the maxim is no defence. The whole question is whether or not, to use the words of the leading case, *Hadley v Baxendale*, the accident can be said to be "the natural and probable result" of the breach of duty. If it is the very thing which ought to be anticipated by a man leaving his horses, or one of the things likely to arise as a consequence of his wrongful act, it is no defence; it is only a step in the way of proving that the damage is the result of the wrongful act.
>
> There can be no doubt in this case that the damage was the result of the wrongful act in the sense of being one of the natural and probable consequences of the wrongful act. It is not necessary to show that this particular accident and this particular damage were probable; it is sufficient if the accident is of a class that might well be anticipated as one of the reasonable and probable results of the wrongful act. . . ."
>
> **Maugham L.J.:** ". . . In deciding whether such a rescuer is justified in putting himself into a position of such great peril, the law has to measure the interests which he sought to protect and the other interests involved. We have all heard of the reasonable man whom the law postulates in certain circumstances; the reasonable man here must be endowed with qualities of energy and courage, and he is not to be deprived of a remedy because he has in a marked degree a desire to save human life when in peril. So regarded, the present plaintiff was not acting unreasonably in the risks he took. . ."

NOTE

Maugham L.J. said that one has to balance the various interests in play. This is important in understanding the decision, for the horses were threatening members of the public; thus the novus actus interveniens was not just reasonable but admirable. If the horses had bolted into a field and were threatening no one the result might have been different: see *Cutler v United Dairies* (1933).

QUESTION

What if a member of the public, on seeing the horses running amok, had suffered severe psychological damage: could he or she have recovered damages from the defendant? Could he or she recover if the facts occurred today?

10.3.6 Overlapping damage

One of the more general problems that can emerge out of these *novus actus interveniens* cases is that of overlapping damage. D tortiously causes damage to C, but before judgment C suffers further damage which either aggravates the first damage or obliterates it completely. To what extent is D liable for this second damage? Where the damage is property damage two cases are important: *Carslogie SS Co v Royal Norwegian Government* (p.381) and *Performance Cars v Abrahams* (1961). And these decisions can be compared with art.3:104 of the *Principles of European Tort Law* (p.362). But what if the damage is personal injury?

Baker v Willoughby [1970] A.C. 467, HL

The claimant brought an action for damages against a car driver in respect of a leg injury. After the accident but before the trial the claimant was shot in the injured leg by robbers and as a result the leg had to be amputated. The car driver argued "that the second injury removed the very limb from which the earlier disability had stemmed, and that therefore no loss suffered thereafter [could] be attributed to the [car driver's] negligence". In other words "the second injury submerged or obliterated the effect of the first and that all loss thereafter must be attributed to the second injury" (Lord Reid). The trial judge rejected this argument, but it was accepted by the Court of Appeal. A further appeal to the House of Lords (Lords Reid, Guest, Donovan, Pearson and Viscount Dilhorne) was allowed.

Lord Reid: ". . . If it were the case that in the eye of the law an effect could only have one cause then the respondent might be right. It is always necessary to prove that any loss for which damages can be given was caused by the defendant's negligent act. But it is a commonplace that the law regards many events as having two causes: that happens whenever there is contributory negligence for then the law says that the injury was caused both by the negligence of the defendant and by the negligence of the plaintiff. And generally it does not matter which negligence occurred first in point of time.

I see no reason why the appellant's present disability cannot be regarded as having two causes,. . .

We were referred to a number of shipping cases where the question was who must pay for demurrage or loss of profit when a vessel damaged by two mishaps was in dock to have both sets of damage repaired at the same time. It would seem that much depends on which mishap rendered the vessel unseaworthy or no longer a profit-earning machine. I get no help from these cases because liability for personal injury cannot depend on which mishap renders the man 'unseaworthy' or 'not a profit-earning machine.' . . .

These cases [including *Performance Cars*] exemplify the general rule that a wrongdoer must take the plaintiff (or his property) as he finds him: that may be to his advantage or disadvantage. In the present case the robber is not responsible or liable for the damage caused by the respondent: he would only have to pay for additional loss to the appellant by reason of his now having an artificial limb instead of a stiff leg. . . ."

Lord Pearson: ". . . I think a solution of the theoretical problem can be found in cases such as this by taking a comprehensive and unitary view of the damage caused by the original accident. Itemisation of the damages by dividing them into heads and sub-heads is often convenient, but is not essential. . . ."

QUESTIONS

1. Was it right in *Baker* to make the defendant pay for the lost leg when there exists a state

scheme to compensate victims of violent crime (Criminal Injuries Compensation Scheme)?

2. Is *Baker* an example of the application of the theory of concurrent causes as defined in the *Principles of European Tort Law* art.3:102? If so, is the next case correct in saying that such a theory is often "unsatisfactory" (Lord Wilberforce)?

Jobling v Associated Dairies Ltd **[1982] A.C. 794, HL**

An employee brought an action for damages against his employer in respect of a back injury suffered at work in 1973 which reduced his earning capacity by 50 per cent. Before the trial, in 1976, the employee contracted a serious disease, quite unconnected with his work accident, which left him totally unfit to work. The House of Lords (Lords Wilberforce, Keith, Bridge, Edmund-Davies and Russell) held that the employer was liable to compensate the employee for reduced earning capacity only for the years between 1973 and 1976.

Lord Wilberforce: ". . . 1. Causation arguments. The unsatisfactory character of these is demonstrated by *Baker v Willoughby* [1970] A.C. 467. I think that it can now be seen that Lord Reid's theory of concurrent causes even if workable on the particular facts of *Baker v Willoughby* (where successive injuries were sustained by the same limb) is as a general solution not supported by the authority he invokes (*Harwood v Wyken Colliery Co* [1913] 2 K.B. 158) nor workable in other cases. . . .

In the present, and in other industrial injury cases, there seems to me no justification for disregarding the fact that the injured man's employer is insured—indeed since 1972 compulsorily insured—against liability to his employees. The state has decided, in other words, on a spreading of risk. There seems to me no more justification for disregarding the fact that the plaintiff—presumably, we have not been told otherwise—is entitled to sickness and invalidity benefit in respect of his myelopathy the amount of which may depend on his contribution record, which in turn may have been affected by his accident. So we have no means of knowing whether the plaintiff would be over-compensated if he were, in addition, to receive the assessed damages from his employer, or whether he would be under-compensated if left to his benefit. It is not easy to accept a solution by which a partially incapacitated man becomes worse off in terms of damages and benefit through a greater degree of incapacity. Many other ingredients, of weight in either direction, may enter into individual cases. Without any satisfaction I draw from this the conclusion that no general, logical, or universally fair rules can be stated which will cover, in a manner consistent with justice, cases of supervening events whether due to tortious, partially tortious, non-culpable or wholly accidental events. The courts can only deal with each case as best they can in a manner so as to provide just and sufficient but not excessive compensation, taking all factors into account. I think that this is what *Baker v Willoughby* did—and indeed that Lord Pearson reached his decision in this way: the rationalisation of the decision as to which I at least have doubts, need and should not be applied to other cases. In the present case the Court of Appeal reached the unanswerable conclusion that to apply *Baker v Willoughby* to the facts of the present case would produce an unjust result, and I am willing to accept the corollary that justice, so far as it can be perceived, lies the other way and that the supervening myelopathy should not be disregarded. If rationalisation is needed, I am willing to accept the 'vicissitudes' argument as the best available. I should be more firmly convinced of the merits of the conclusion if the whole pattern of benefits had been considered, in however general a way. The result of the present case may be lacking in precision and rational justification, but so long as we are content to live in a mansion of so many different architectures, this is inevitable. . . ."

QUESTIONS

1. Is this case an example of the application of the causal theory expressed in art.3:106 of the *Principles of European Tort Law*?

2. If the employee had been left totally unfit for work in 1976 as a result of being shot by robbers would the House of Lords have arrived at the same decision?

NOTE

Performance Cars has recently been confirmed not only as good authority but also as applicable to personal injury cases: *Halsey v Milton Keynes General NHS Trust* (2004). In this *Halsey* case the Court of Appeal said: "In the present case, the question is whether the second tortfeasor is responsible for the consequences of the first injury. To that question, the answer can only be: no. It is true that, but for the first accident, the second accident would have caused the same damage as the first accident. But that is irrelevant. Since the claimant had already suffered that damage, the second defendant did not cause it. This is not a case of concurrent tortfeasors" (§ 70).

10.3.7 Proof of causation

In order for a tortfeasor to be held liable for a particular type of damage the victim has to prove that the defendant is the actual cause of the actual harm in issue. Sometimes such proof can be difficult either because no definitive causal link can be established as a matter of, say, medical science or because there may be several possible defendants who might be the cause. For example, just because there is a statistically higher rate of cancer among those living near electric pylons this does not *prove* an actual causal connection between pylons and cancer (see *The Guardian* June 3, 2005, p.10). The problem of multiple defendants is illustrated by the next case.

Fairchild v Glenhaven Funeral Services Ltd **[2003] 1 A.C. 32, HL**

This was an action for damages by three appellants suffering from cancer (mesothelioma) as a result of being exposed to asbestos. The appellants had worked for more than one employer each of whom, in breach of a duty of care, had exposed the employees to asbestos; however the appellants could not prove which exposure had actually triggered the cancer and so the Court of Appeal dismissed their claims against all the tortfeasors on the ground of a lack of proof of causation. The House of Lords (Lords Bingham, Nicholls, Hoffmann, Hutton and Rodger) allowed the three appeals.

Lord Bingham: ". . .9. The issue in these appeals does not concern the general validity and applicability of that requirement, which is not in question, but is whether in special circumstances such as those in these cases there should be any variation or relaxation of it.

The overall object of tort law is to define cases in which the law may justly hold one party liable to compensate another. Are these such cases? A and B owed C a duty to protect C against a risk of a particular and very serious kind. They failed to perform that duty. As a result the risk eventuated and C suffered the very harm against which it was the duty of A and B to protect him. Had there been only one tortfeasor, C would have been entitled to recover, but because the duty owed to him was broken by two tortfeasors and not only one, he is held to be entitled to recover against neither, because of his inability to prove what is scientifically unprovable. If the mechanical application of generally accepted rules leads to such a result, there must be room to question the appropriateness of such an approach in such a case. . . .

Policy

33. The present appeals raise an obvious and inescapable clash of policy considerations. On the one hand are the considerations powerfully put by the Court of Appeal ([2002] 1 WLR 1052 at 1080, para 103). . . . The Court of Appeal had in mind that in each of the cases discussed in paras 14–21 above (*Wardlaw, Nicholson, Gardiner, McGhee*) there was only one employer involved. Thus there was a risk that the defendant might be held liable for acts for which he should not be held legally liable but no risk that he would be held liable for damage which (whether legally liable or not) he had not caused. The crux of cases such as the present, if the appellants' argument is upheld, is that an employer may be held liable for damage he has not caused. The risk is the greater where all the employers potentially liable are not before the court. This is so on the facts of each of the three appeals before the House, and is always likely to be so given the long latency of this condition and the likelihood that some employers potentially liable will have gone out of business or disappeared during that period. It can properly be said to be unjust to impose liability on a party who has not been shown, even on a balance of probabilities, to have caused the damage complained of. On the other hand, there is a strong policy argument in favour of compensating those who have suffered grave harm, at the expense of their employers who owed them a duty to protect them against that very harm and failed to do so, when the harm can only have been caused by breach of that duty and when science does not permit the victim accurately to attribute, as between several employers, the precise responsibility for the harm he has suffered. I am of opinion that such injustice as may be involved in imposing liability on a duty-breaking employer in these circumstances is heavily outweighed by the injustice of denying redress to a victim. Were the law otherwise, an employer exposing his employee to asbestos dust could obtain complete immunity against mesothelioma (but not asbestosis) claims by employing only those who had previously been exposed to excessive quantities of asbestos dust. Such a result would reflect no credit on the law. It seems to me, as it did to Lord Wilberforce in *McGhee* [1973] 1 WLR 1 at 7, that

> 'the employers should be liable for an injury, squarely within the risk which they created and that they, not the pursuer, should suffer the consequence of the impossibility, foreseeably inherent in the nature of his injury, of segregating the precise consequence of their default.'

Conclusion

34. . . . [I]t seems to me just and in accordance with common sense to treat the conduct of A and B in exposing C to a risk to which he should not have been exposed as making a material contribution to the contracting by C of a condition against which it was the duty of A and B to protect him. I consider that this conclusion is fortified by the wider jurisprudence reviewed above. Policy considerations weigh in favour of such a conclusion. It is a conclusion which follows even if either A or B is not before the court. It was not suggested in argument that C's entitlement against either A or B should be for any sum less than the full compensation to which C is entitled, although A and B could of course seek contribution against each other or any other employer liable in respect of the same damage in the ordinary way. No argument on apportionment was addressed to the House. . . . It would be unrealistic to suppose that the principle here affirmed will not over time be the subject of incremental and analogical development. Cases seeking to develop the principle must be decided when and as they arise. For the present, I think it unwise to decide more than is necessary to resolve these three appeals which, for all the foregoing reasons, I concluded should be allowed. . . ."

Lord Nicholls: "**36**. My Lords, I have no hesitation in agreeing with all your Lordships that these appeals should be allowed. Any other outcome would be deeply offensive to instinctive notions of what justice requires and fairness demands. The real difficulty lies is elucidating in sufficiently specific terms the principle being applied in reaching this conclusion. To be acceptable the law must be coherent. It must be principled. The basis on which one case, or one type of case, is distinguished from another should be transparent and capable of identification. When a decision departs from principles normally applied, the basis for doing so must be rational and justifiable if the decision is to avoid the reproach that hard cases make bad law. I turn therefore to consider the departure from the normal, and the basis of that departure, in the present appeals. . . ."

Lord Hoffmann: ". . . **60**. The problem in this appeal is to formulate a just and fair rule. Clearly the rule must be based upon principle. However deserving the claimants may be, your Lordships are not exercising a discretion to adapt causal requirements to the individual case. That does not mean, however, that it must be a principle so broad that it takes no account of significant differences which affect whether it is fair and just to impose liability.

61. What are the significant features of the present case? First, we are dealing with a duty specifically intended to protect employees against being unnecessarily exposed to the risk of (among other things) a particular disease. Secondly, the duty is one intended to create a civil right to compensation for injury relevantly connected with its breach. Thirdly, it is established that the greater the exposure to asbestos, the greater the risk of contracting that disease. Fourthly, except in the case in which there has been only one significant exposure to asbestos, medical science cannot prove whose asbestos is more likely than not to have produced the cell mutation which caused the disease. Fifthly, the employee has contracted the disease against which he should have been protected.

62. In these circumstances, a rule requiring proof of a link between the defendant's asbestos and the claimant's disease would, with the arbitrary exception of single-employer cases, empty the duty of content. If liability depends upon proof that the conduct of the defendant was a necessary condition of the injury, it cannot effectively exist. It is however open to your Lordships to formulate a different causal requirement in this class of case. The Court of Appeal was in my opinion wrong to say that in the absence of a proven link between the defendant's asbestos and the disease, there was no "causative relationship" whatever between the defendant's conduct and the disease. It depends entirely upon the level at which the causal relationship is described. To say, for example, that the cause of Mr Matthews' cancer was his significant exposure to asbestos during two employments over a period of eight years, without being able to identify the day upon which he inhaled the fatal fibre, is a meaningful causal statement. The medical evidence shows that it is the only kind of causal statement about the disease which, in the present state of knowledge, a scientist would regard as possible. There is no a priori reason, no rule of logic, which prevents the law from treating it as sufficient to satisfy the causal requirements of the law of negligence. The question is whether your Lordships think such a rule would be just and reasonable and whether the class of cases to which it applies can be sufficiently clearly defined.

63. So the question of principle is this: in cases which exhibit the five features I have mentioned, which rule would be more in accordance with justice and the policy of common law and statute to protect employees against the risk of contracting asbestos-related diseases? One which makes an employer in breach of his duty liable for the claimant's injury because he created a significant risk to his health, despite the fact that the physical cause of the injury may have been created by someone else? Or a rule which means that unless he was subjected to risk by the breach of duty of a single employer, the employee can never have a remedy? My Lords, as between the employer in breach of duty and the employee who has lost his life in consequence of a period of exposure to risk to which that employer has contributed, I think it would be both inconsistent with the policy of the law imposing the duty and morally wrong for your Lordships to impose causal requirements which exclude liability. . . ."

(For further extracts see p.45)

NOTE

This major decision of the House of Lords represents a triumph of justice over cynicism. The decision of the Court of Appeal whereby neither wrongdoer was to be liable because it could not be established which of the two actually caused the fatal illness raised a serious question about the quality of common law decision-making. One might note that in their search for justice the members of the House of Lords did not confine themselves to the common law; the Law Lords asked counsel to look at the civil law systems as well (see above p.45). Most textbooks in England on the law of tort rigidly confine themselves to common law precedents (although there are one or two exceptions); *Fairchild* ought to act as a wake-up call. Knowledge of tort law is no longer confined by European frontiers; indeed, it would seem from Lord Rodger's judgment (see p.45), that this knowledge is not confined by time-barriers either since he quotes extensively from Roman law. *Fairchild* is truly a leading case and one that will be celebrated by common lawyers and by civilians.

QUESTION

What was the actual damage suffered by the claimants in *Fairchild*?

Barker v Corus UK Ltd [2006] 2 A.C. 572, HL

This was an action for damages in negligence brought by the dependants of employees who had died as a result of being exposed to asbestos by various employers, many of whom had become insolvent. The defendants were the employers who were still solvent. The trial judge and the Court of Appeal held that the defendants were jointly and severally liable for all the damage (subject to a reduction for contributory negligence in one case) suffered by the employees. An appeal to the House of Lords (Lords Hoffmann, Scott and Walker and Baroness Hale; Lord Rodger dissenting) was allowed: liability was several only.

Lord Scott: "... **59** ... [T]he *Fairchild* defendants were not held liable for causing the eventual damage. In relation to none of them was it proved, nor could it be proved, that that defendant's breach of duty had caused the damage, and thereby brought about the fatal outcome. A defendant in a *Fairchild* type of case is held liable for having materially contributed to the risk of the eventual outcome. That this is so is, to my mind, apparent from the opinions delivered in *Fairchild* [2003] 1 AC 32 and is confirmed by Lord Hoffmann's references to *Fairchild* in *Gregg v Scott* [2005] 2 AC 176. . . . Liability is imposed by *Fairchild* on a negligent employer because that employer has, by allowing the victim to be exposed to the injurious agent in question, materially increased the risk that the employee will contract the disease or be afflicted by the condition attributable to that injurious agent. . .

60 . . . It is a well established principle in the law of tort that if more than one tortfeasor causes the damage of which complaint is made, and if it is not possible to attribute specific parts of the damage to a specific tortfeasor or tortfeasors in exoneration, as to those parts of the damage, of the other tortfeasors, the tortfeasors are jointly and severally liable for the whole damage. A pedestrian on the pavement injured by a collision between two cars both of whose drivers were driving negligently can hold either driver liable for his or her injuries. The apportionment of liability between the two negligent drivers is no concern of the victim.

61 If the *Fairchild* principle were based upon the fiction that each *Fairchild* defendant had actually caused the eventual outcome, the analogy with tortfeasors each of whom had contributed to an indivisible outcome would be very close. But *Fairchild* liability is not based on that fiction. It is based on the fact that each negligent defendant has wrongfully subjected the victim to a period of exposure to an injurious agent and has thereby, during that period, subjected the victim to a material risk that he or she will contract the disease associated with that agent. Each successive period of exposure has subjected the victim to a further degree of risk. If, in the event, the victim does not contract the disease, no claim can be made for the trauma of being subjected to the risk: see *Gregg v Scott* [2005] 2 AC 176. But if the victim does contract the disease the risk has materialised. If the degree of risk associated with each period of exposure, whether under successive employers or during self-employment or while engaged in domestic tasks, were expressed in percentage terms, the sum of the percentages, once the disease had been contracted, would total 100%. But the extent of the risk for which each negligent employer was responsible and on the basis of which that employer was to be held liable would be independent of the extent of the risk attributable to the periods of exposure for which others were responsible. The relationship between the various negligent employers seems to me much more akin to the relationship between tortfeasors each of whom has, independently of the others, caused an identifiable part of the damage of which the victim complains. The joint and several liability of tortfeasors is based upon a finding that the breach of duty of each has been a cause of the indivisible damage for which redress is sought. No such finding can be made in a *Fairchild* type of case and the logic of imposing joint and several liability on *Fairchild* defendants is, in my opinion, absent. Moreover, *Fairchild* constitutes an exception, perhaps an anomalous one, to the causation principles of tortious liability. It should not, therefore, be found to be surprising if consequential adjustments to other principles of tortious liability become necessary.

62 I would, therefore, hold that the extent of the liability of each defendant in a *Fairchild* type of case, where it cannot be shown which defendant's breach of duty caused the damage but where each defendant, in breach of duty, has exposed the claimant to a significant risk of the eventual damage, should be liability commensurate with the degree of risk for which that defendant was responsible. Ascertainment of the degree of risk would be an issue of fact to be determined by the trial judge. . .”

Lord Rodger (dissenting): “. . . **85** The new analysis which the House is adopting will tend to maximise the inconsistencies in the law by turning the *Fairchild* exception into an enclave where a number of rules apply which have been rejected for use elsewhere in the law of personal injuries. Inside the enclave victims recover damages for suffering the increased risk of developing mesothelioma (or suffering the loss of a chance of not developing mesothelioma) while, just outside, patients cannot recover damages for suffering the increased risk of an unfavourable outcome to medical treatment (or suffering the loss of a chance of a favourable outcome to medical treatment). On the other hand, if such a claim had been recognised outside the enclave, the patient would have been entitled to recover damages for the increased likelihood that he would suffer a premature death, whereas inside the enclave a victim who suffers an increased risk of developing mesothelioma cannot recover damages unless he actually develops it. Inside the enclave claimants whose husbands die of mesothelioma receive only, say, 60% of their damages if the court considers that there is a 60% chance that the defendant caused the death and no other wrongdoer is solvent or insured. Outside the enclave, claimants whose husbands are killed in an accident for which the only solvent defendant is, say, 5% to blame recover the whole of their damages from that defendant. . . .

90 Of course, it may seem hard if a defendant is held liable in solidum even though all that can be shown is that he made a material contribution to the risk that the victim would develop mesothelioma. But it is also hard-and settled law-that a defendant is held liable in solidum even though all that can be shown is that he made a material, say 5%, contribution to the claimant's indivisible injury. That is a form of rough justice which the law has not hitherto sought to smooth, preferring instead, as a matter of policy, to place the risk of the insolvency of a wrongdoer or his insurer on the other wrongdoers and their insurers. Now the House is deciding that, in this particular enclave of the law, the risk of the insolvency of a wrongdoer or his insurer is to bypass the other wrongdoers and their insurers and to be shouldered entirely by the innocent claimant. As a result, claimants will often end up with only a small proportion of the damages which would normally be payable for their loss. The desirability of the courts, rather than Parliament, throwing this lifeline to wrongdoers and their insurers at the expense of claimants is not obvious to me. . . .”

Baroness Hale: “. . . **126** . . . [I]n the *Fairchild* situation we have yet another development. For the first time in our legal history, persons are made liable for damage even though they may not have caused it at all, simply because they have materially contributed to the risk of causing that damage. Mr Stuart-Smith does not quarrel with the principle in *Fairchild*. He simply argues that it does not follow from the imposition of liability in such a case that each should be liable for the whole. I agree with the majority of your Lordships that indeed it does not follow. There is in this situation no magic in the indivisibility of the harm. It is not being said that each has caused or materially contributed to *the harm*. It can only be said that each has materially contributed to the *risk of harm*. The harm may be indivisible but the material contribution to the risk can be divided. There exists a sensible basis for doing so. Is it fair to do so?

127 In common with the majority of your Lordships, I think that it is fair to do so. On the one hand, the defendants are, by definition, in breach of their duties towards the claimants or the deceased. But then so are many employers, occupiers or other defendants who nevertheless escape liability altogether because it cannot be shown that their breach of duty caused the harm suffered by the claimant. For as long as we have rules of causation, some negligent (or otherwise duty-breaking) defendants will escape liability. The law of tort is not (generally) there to punish people for their behaviour. It is there to make them pay for the damage they have done. These *Fairchild* defendants may not have caused any harm at all. They are being made liable because it is thought fair that they should make at least some contribution to redressing the harm that may have flowed from their wrongdoing. It seems to me most fair that the contribution they should make is in proportion to the contribution they have made to the risk of that harm occurring. . . ."

QUESTIONS

1. Baroness Hale talks of fairness with respect to the defendants. But is it actually the defendants who pay or is it their liability insurance companies? Why is it fair to put the risk of the disease partly on the shoulders of those least able (in terms of salary and wages) to bear such a risk? Are the only people who have gained from this case the shareholders in insurance companies? Should such companies now pay a huge city bonus (say one million pounds) to each director who insisted on taking this case to the House of Lords?

2. What if it could be shown that all the defendants in the *Fairchild* and *Corus* situations had been in breach of their duties of care towards the claimants as a result of cost-cutting exercises?

3. A philosopher of science (G.G. Granger) makes a distinction with regard to scientific experiments between what he calls 'actual' and 'virtual' facts, scientists for the most part operating in a world of virtual fact. Do you think the same distinction could be said of judges? Do you think the law Lords in *Corus* were operating in a world of actual social fact or in a virtual world of fact that they themselves had created?

4. Has the result of *Corus* been reversed by statute? (See Compensation Act 2006 s.3.)

10.3.8 Loss of a chance

Barker v Corus indicates that the way of circumventing the difficulty raised in *Fairchild* is to rethink the nature of the damage. Instead of focusing on the physical harm itself one can ask if the tortuous behaviour of the defendant deprived the claimant of a chance of not contracting the damage in question. The starting point in English law of a loss of a chance damage is to be found in the contract case of *Chaplin v Hicks* (1911) where the defendant's breach of contract deprived the claimant of a chance of winning a competition. The Court of Appeal confirmed that the loss of a chance to win the beauty contest was a form of damage for which damages could be claimed. One can equally recall the *Spring* case.

***Spring v Guardian Assurance Plc* [1995] 2 A.C. 296, HL**

(See p.287)

Lord Lowry: ". . . Once the duty of care is held to exist and the defendants' negligence is proved, the plaintiff only has to show that by reason of that negligence he has lost a reasonable chance of employment (which would have to be evaluated) and has thereby sustained loss: *McGregor on Damages*, 14th ed (1980), pp 198–202, paras 276–278 and *Chaplin v Hicks* [1911] 2 KB 786. He does not have to prove that, but for the negligent reference, Scottish Amicable would have employed him. . . ."

QUESTIONS

1. C contracted dermatitis which he believed was caused by the hot and dusty conditions of his workplace. C sues D, his employer, for damages but cannot prove conclusively that his dermatitis was caused by D's workplace conditions. Can C claim, instead, that D's behaviour has deprived P of a chance of being free of dermatitis? (cf. *McGhee v NCB* (1973).)

2. C fell out of a tree and the resulting injury had, at the time of the actual accident, a 75 per cent chance of developing into a permanent disability. The hospital, however, carelessly failed to diagnose the correct problem and proper treatment was delayed increasing the chance of permanent disability to 100 per cent. Can C claim that the negligence of the hospital has deprived him of a 25 per cent chance of recovery from permanent disability? (cf. *Hotson v East Berkshire HA* (1987).)

3. Would your answer to questions 1 and/or 2 immediately above be different after the *Fairchild* case?

***Chester v Afshar* [2005] 1 A.C. 134, HL**

This was an action for damages by a claimant, who had reluctantly undergone a surgical operation to cure a back pain, against the surgeon in respect of serious neurological damage arising as a result of the operation. The claimant asserted that the surgeon had been negligent in not warning her of the small risk of neurological damage that accompanied such operations. The judge found as a fact that had the claimant been warned of the risk she would not have undergone the operation at the time she did; however he made no finding that she would never have had the operation. A majority of the House of Lords (Lords Steyn, Hope and Walker; Lords Bingham and Hoffmann dissenting) held that the claimant was entitled to damages.

Lord Steyn: ". . . **16**. A surgeon owes a legal duty to a patient to warn him or her in general terms of possible serious risks involved in the procedure. The only qualification is that there may be wholly exceptional cases where objectively in the best interests of the patient the surgeon may be excused from giving a warning. This is, however, irrelevant in the present case. In modern law medical paternalism no longer rules and a patient has a prima facie right to be informed by a surgeon of a small, but well established, risk of serious injury as a result of surgery.

17. Secondly, not all rights are equally important. But a patient's right to an appropriate warning from a surgeon when faced with surgery ought normatively to be regarded as an important right which must be given effective protection whenever possible.

18. Thirdly, in the context of attributing legal responsibility, it is necessary to identify precisely the protected legal interests at stake. A rule requiring a doctor to abstain from performing an operation without the informed consent of a patient serves two purposes. It tends to avoid the occurrence of the particular physical injury the risk of which a patient is not prepared to accept. It also ensures that due respect is given to the autonomy and dignity of each patient. Professor Ronald Dworkin (*Life's Dominion: An Argument about Abortion and Euthanasia*, 1993) explained these concepts at p 224:

'The most plausible [account] emphasizes the integrity rather than the welfare of the choosing agent; the value of autonomy, on this view, derives from the capacity it protects: the capacity to express one's own character—values, commitments, convictions, and critical as well as experiential interests—in the life one leads. Recognizing an individual right of autonomy makes self-creation possible. It allows each of us to be responsible for shaping our lives according to our own coherent or incoherent—but, in any case, distinctive—personality. It allows us to lead our lives rather than be led along them, so that each of us can be, to the extent a scheme of rights can make this possible, what we have made of ourselves. We allow someone to choose death over radical amputation or a blood transfusion, if that is his informed wish, because we acknowledge his right to a life structured by his own values.'

19. Fourthly, it is a distinctive feature of the present case that but for the surgeon's negligent failure to warn the claimant of the small risk of serious injury the actual injury would not have occurred when it did and the chance of it occurring on a subsequent occasion was very small. It could therefore be said that the breach of the surgeon resulted in the very injury about which the claimant was entitled to be warned.

20. These factors must be considered in combination. But they must also be weighed against the undesirability of departing from established principles of causation, except for good reasons. The collision of competing ideas poses a difficult question of law. . . .

23. It is true that there is no direct English authority permitting a modification of the approach to the proof of causation in a case such as the present. On the other hand, there is the analogy of *Fairchild v Glenhaven Funeral Services Ltd* [2003] 1 AC 32 which reveals a principled approach to such a problem. . . . The *Fairchild* case is, of course, very different from the facts of the present case. A modification of causation principles as was made in *Fairchild* will always be exceptional. But it cannot be restricted to the particular facts of *Fairchild* . . . .

24. Standing back from the detailed arguments, I have come to the conclusion that, as a result of the surgeon's failure to warn the patient, she cannot be said to have given informed consent to the surgery in the full legal sense. Her right of autonomy and dignity can and ought to be vindicated by a narrow and modest departure from traditional causation principles.

25. On a broader basis I am glad to have arrived at the conclusion that the claimant is entitled in law to succeed. This result is in accord with one of the most basic aspirations of the law, namely to right wrongs. Moreover, the decision announced by the House today reflects the reasonable expectations of the public in contemporary society. . . ."

Lord Hoffmann (dissenting): ". . . **31.** In my opinion this argument is about as logical as saying that if one had been told, on entering a casino, that the odds on No 7 coming up at roulette were only 1 in 37, one would have gone away and come back next week or gone to a different casino. The question is whether one would have taken the opportunity to avoid or reduce the risk, not whether one would have changed the scenario in some irrelevant detail. The judge found as a fact that the risk would have been precisely the same whether it was done then or later or by that competent surgeon or by another.

32. It follows that the claimant failed to prove that the defendant's breach of duty caused her loss. On ordinary principles of tort law, the defendant is not liable. The remaining question is whether a special rule should be created by which doctors who fail to warn patients of risks should be made insurers against those risks.

33. The argument for such a rule is that it vindicates the patient's right to choose for herself. Even though the failure to warn did not cause the patient any damage, it was an affront to her personality and leaves her feeling aggrieved.

34. I can see that there might be a case for a modest solatium in such cases. But the risks which may eventuate will vary greatly in severity and I think there would be great difficulty in fixing a suitable figure. In any case, the cost of litigation over such cases would make the law of torts an unsuitable vehicle for distributing the modest compensation which might be payable.

35. Nor do I agree with Professor Honoré's moral argument for making the doctor an insurer, namely that his act caused the damage. That argument seems to me to prove both too much and too little. Too much, because it is an argument for making a doctor the insurer of any damage which he causes, whether the patient knew of the risk or not. Too little, because it would excuse the doctor in a case in which he had a duty to warn but the actual operation was perfectly properly performed by someone else, for example, by his registrar. . . ."

QUESTION

Is Lord Steyn locating his decision within the law of persons (personality rights) rather than within the law of things (personal injury damage)? Does Lord Hoffmann appear to think this is the case?

NOTE

As Professor Waddams has observed (see above p.286), a differently constituted court may well have reached the opposite decision. This point is well illustrated by the next case.

Gregg v Scott **[2005] 2 A.C. 176, HL**

This was an action for damages for negligence brought by a patient against a doctor in respect of the latter's failure to diagnose an under arm lump as cancerous. By the time the patient had received a correct diagnosis, the cancer had spread into his chest leaving him with a poor chance of survival. The patient claimed that had he received the correct diagnosis from the defendant doctor his chance of survival would have been high, whereas it was now below 50 per cent. However statistical evidence, accepted by the trial judge as fact, indicated that even if he had received the correct diagnosis from the defendant his chance of survival would have been only 42 per cent and, given the relapses he had suffered, his actual chance was only 25 per cent. The trial judge held that although there had been a breach of duty by the defendant doctor, there could be no liability because on the balance of probabilities the claimant would not have survived even if treated promptly. The patient had, in other words, failed to show that he would have been, percentage-wise, in a materially different position from the position he would have been in had the defendant correctly diagnosed the lump. The House of Lords (Lord Hoffmann, Lord Phillips and Baroness Hale; Lords Nicholls and Hope dissenting) upheld this decision.

> **Lord Nicholls** (dissenting): ". . . **24**. Given this uncertainty of outcome, the appropriate characterisation of a patient's loss in this type of case must surely be that it comprises the loss of the chance of a favourable outcome, rather than the loss of the outcome itself. Justice so requires, because this matches medical reality. This recognises what in practice a patient had before the doctor's negligence occurred. It recognises what in practice the patient lost by reason of that negligence. The doctor's negligence diminished the patient's prospects of recovery. And this analysis of a patient's loss accords with the purpose of the legal duty of which the doctor was in breach. In short, the purpose of the duty is to promote the patient's *prospects* of recovery by exercising due skill and care in diagnosing and treating the patient's condition.

> **25**. This approach also achieves a basic objective of the law of tort. The common law imposes duties and seeks to provide appropriate remedies in the event of a breach of duty. If negligent diagnosis or treatment diminishes a patient's prospects of recovery, a law which does not recognise this as a wrong calling for redress would be seriously deficient today. In respect of the doctors' breach of duty the law would not have provided an appropriate remedy. Of course, losing a chance of saving a leg is not the same as losing a leg: see Tony Weir, *Tort Law* (2002), p 76. But that is not a reason for declining to value the chance for whose loss the doctor was directly responsible. The law would rightly be open to reproach were it to provide a remedy if what is lost by a professional adviser's negligence is a financial opportunity or chance but refuse a remedy where what is lost by a doctor's negligence is the chance of health or even life itself. Justice requires that in the latter case as much as the former the loss of a chance should constitute actionable damage. . . ."

> **Lord Hoffmann**: ". . . **90**. . . . [A] wholesale adoption of possible rather than probable causation as the criterion of liability would be so radical a change in our law as to amount to a legislative act. It would have enormous consequences for insurance companies and the National Health Service. In company with my noble and learned friends Lord Phillips of Worth Matravers and Baroness Hale of Richmond, I think that any such change should be left to Parliament. . . ."

Lord Hope (dissenting): ". . . **117**. The key to the decision in this case lies, I think, in the way in which the appellant's cause of action is identified. The description of it as a claim for the loss of a chance is invited by the approach which the pleader has taken to the issue of damages. The description is apt in cases where the claim is for an economic loss or the loss of something to which the claimant has a right, such as in *Chaplin v Hicks* [1911] 2 KB 786 and *Kitchen v Royal Air Force Association* [1958] 1 WLR 563. But that is not what this claim is about. It is, in essence, a claim for the loss and damage caused by the enlargement of the tumour due to the delay in diagnosis. It is for the loss and damage caused, in other words, by a physical injury which the appellant would not have suffered but for the doctor's negligence. The fact that there was a physical injury has been proved on a balance of probabilities. So too has the fact that, in addition to pain and suffering, it caused a reduction in the prospects of a successful outcome. I would hold that, where these factors are present, the way is open for losses which are consequential on the physical injury to be claimed too. I do not think that those consequences of the physical injury should be treated as if they were the product of a separate cause of action from the pain and suffering. I see the reduction in the prospects of a successful outcome as one element among several in the claim for which there is a single cause—the enlargement of the tumour. This was a physical injury, the avoidance or minimisation of which was within the scope of the doctor's duty of care when the appellant consulted him. . . ."

Baroness Hale: ". . . **195**. If it is more likely than not that the defendant's carelessness caused me to lose a leg. I do not want my damages reduced to the extent that it is less than 100% certain that it did so. On the other hand, if it is more likely than not that the defendant's carelessness did *not* cause me to lose the leg, then the defendant does not want to have to pay damages for the 20% or 30% chance that it did. A 'more likely than not' approach to causation suits both sides. . . .

223. Until now, the gist of the action for personal injuries has been damage to the person. My negligence probably caused the loss of your leg: I pay you the full value of the loss of the leg (say £100,000). My negligence probably did not cause the loss of your leg. I do not pay you anything. Compare the loss of a chance approach: my negligence probably caused a reduction in the chance of your keeping that leg: I pay you the value of the loss of your leg, discounted by the chance that it would have happened anyway. If the chance of saving the leg was very good, say 90%, the claimant still gets only 90% of his damages, say £90,000. But if the chance of saving the leg was comparatively poor, say 20%, the claimant still gets £20,000. So the claimant ends up with less than full compensation even though his chances of a more favourable outcome were good. And the defendant ends up paying substantial sums even though the *outcome* is one for which by definition he cannot be shown to be responsible.

224. Almost any claim for loss of an outcome could be reformulated as a claim for loss of a chance of that outcome. The implications of retaining them both as alternatives would be substantial. That is, the claimant still has the prospect of 100% recovery if he can show that it is more likely than not that the doctor's negligence caused the adverse outcome. But if he cannot show that, he also has the prospect of lesser recovery for loss of a chance. If (for the reasons given earlier) it would in practice always be tempting to conclude that the doctor's negligence had affected his chances to some extent, the claimant would almost always get something. It would be a 'heads you lose everything, tails I win something' situation. But why should the defendant not also be able to redefine the gist of the action if it suits him better?

225. The [claimant] in this case accepts that the proportionate recovery effect must cut both ways. If the claim is characterised as loss of a chance, those with a better than evens chance would still only get a proportion of the full value of their claim. But I do not think that he accepts that the same would apply in cases where the claim is characterised as loss of an outcome. In that case there is no basis for calculating the odds. If the two are alternatives available in every case, the defendant will almost always be liable for something. He will have lost the benefit of the 50% chance that causation cannot be proved. But if the two approaches cannot sensibly live together, the claimants who currently obtain full recovery on an adverse outcome basis might in future only achieve a proportionate recovery. This would surely be a case of two steps forward, three steps back for the great majority of straightforward personal injury cases. In either event, the expert evidence would have to be far more complex than it is at present. Negotiations and trials would be a great deal more difficult. Recovery would be much less predictable both for claimants and for defendants' liability insurers. There is no reason in principle why the change in approach should be limited to medical negligence. Whether or not the policy choice is between retaining the present definition of personal injury in outcome terms and redefining it in loss of opportunity terms, introducing the latter would cause far more problems in the general run of personal injury claims than the policy benefits are worth. . . .

226. Much of the discussion in the cases and literature has centred round cases where the adverse outcome has already happened. The patient has lost his leg. Did the doctor's negligence cause him to lose the leg? If not, did it reduce the chances of saving the leg? But in this case the most serious of the adverse outcomes has not yet happened, and (it is to be hoped) may never happen. The approach to causation should be the same for both past and future events. What, if anything, has the doctor's negligence caused in this case? We certainly do not know whether it has caused this outcome, because happily Mr Gregg has survived each of the significant milestones along the way. Can we even say that it reduced the chances of a successful outcome, given that Mr Gregg has turned out to be one of the successful minority at each milestone? This is quite different from the situation in *Hotson*, where the avascular necrosis had already happened, or in *Rufo v Hosking*, where the fractures had already happened. Mr Gregg faced a risk of an adverse outcome which happily has not so far materialised, serious though the effects of his illness, treatment and prognosis have been. The complexities of attempting to introduce liability for the loss of a chance of a more favourable outcome in personal injury claims have driven me, not without regret, to conclude that it should not be done. . . ."

QUESTIONS

1. Did the House of Lords decide this case on its actual facts or on some mathematical model supposedly representing the facts?

2. What is the present status of loss of a chance in personal injury cases in general? Is the 'principle' in *Gregg v Scott* to be limited to medical negligence cases? (cf. *Barker v Corus UK*, p.390.)

3. How would you characterise the reasoning in *Gregg*: (i) causal (mathematical); (ii) functional (policy); (iii) interpretative (meaning of 'loss'); or (iv) bits of all three?

4. Would justice be better served if all cases could be reduced to mathematical models?

5. Were the majority of the Law lords treating the claimant as if he should be grateful to be alive?

10.4 Remoteness of damage

Even if cause and connection can be established, as a question of fact, between tortuous act and damage a claimant can still fail if the court decides, as a question of law, that the damage is too remote. One of the main questions that have preoccupied the courts is the appropriate rule or test to be applied.

10.4.1 Directness test

The test established in the 19th century was one of directness. Once the defendant had been found to have committed a tort he was to be liable for all the damage directly flowing from the wrong. This test was confirmed in the case set out below.

***In re Polemis and Furness, Withy & Co* [1921] 3 K.B. 560, CA**

Bankes L.J.: "By a time charterparty dated February 21, 1917, the respondents chartered their vessel to the appellants. Clause 21 of the charterparty was in these terms. [The Lord Justice read it.] The vessel was employed by the charterers to carry a cargo to Casablanca in Morocco. The cargo included a quantity of benzine or petrol in cases. While discharging at Casablanca a heavy plank fell into the hold in which the petrol was stowed, and caused an explosion, which set fire to the vessel and completely destroyed her. The owners claimed the value of the vessel from the charterers, alleging that the loss of the vessel was due to the negligence of the charterers' servants. The charterers contended that they were protected by the exception of fire contained in clause 21 of the charterparty, and they also contended that the damages claimed were too remote. . . . To speak of 'probable' consequence is to throw everything upon the jury. It is tautologous to speak of 'effective' cause or to say that damages too remote from the cause are irrecoverable, for an effective cause is simply that which causes, and in law what is ineffective or too remote is not a cause at all. I still venture to think that direct cause is the best expression. Proximate cause has acquired a special connotation through its use in reference to contracts of insurance. Direct cause excludes what is indirect, conveys the essential distinction, which causa causans and causa sine qua non rather cumbrously indicate, and is consistent with the possibility of the concurrence of more direct causes than one, operating at the same time and leading to a common result. . .

In the present case the arbitrators have found as a fact that the falling of the plank was due to the negligence of the defendants' servants. The fire appears to me to have been directly caused by the falling of the plank. Under these circumstances I consider that it is immaterial that the causing of the spark by the falling of the plank could not have been reasonably anticipated. . . . Given the breach of duty which constitutes the negligence, and given the damage as a direct result of that negligence, the anticipations of the person whose negligent act has produced the damage appear to me to be irrelevant. I consider that the damages claimed are not too remote. . . ."

Warrington L.J.: ". . . The result may be summarised as follows: The presence or absence of reasonable anticipation of damage determines the legal quality of the act as negligent or innocent. If it be thus determined to be negligent, then the question whether particular damages are recoverable depends only on the answer to the question whether they are the direct consequence of the act. Sufficient authority for the proposition is afforded by *Smith v London and South Western Ry Co.* . . ."

Scrutton L.J.: ". . . To determine whether an act is negligent, it is relevant to determine whether any reasonable person would foresee that the act would cause damage; if he would not, the act is not negligent. But if the act would or might probably cause damage, the fact that the damage it in fact causes is not the exact kind of damage one would expect is immaterial, so long as the damage is in fact directly traceable to the negligent act, and not due to the operation of independent causes having no connection with the negligent act, except that they could not avoid its results. Once the act is negligent, the fact that its exact operation was not foreseen is immaterial. . . ."

NOTE

The method adopted by the judges in this case was to focus exclusively on the connection between act and damage. Once it was judged that the act (letting fall the plank) was careless, foresight was no longer relevant. Legal causation was closely intertwined with factual causation.

PROBLEM

John moves Camilla's bicycle without her permission so that John can park his own bike in the space where her bike was parked. In its new position, under a large tree, Camilla's bike is destroyed when the tree is struck by lightening. Is John liable to Camilla for the full value of the bicycle? What if Camilla missed an important job interview as a result of the destroyed bike: would John be liable in damages for the missed job?

10.4.2 Foreseeability text

The directness test came in for criticism and in 1961 it was rejected by the Privy Council.

Overseas Tankship (UK) Ltd v Morts Dock & Engineering Co (The Wagon Mound No 1) **[1961] A.C. 388, PC**

This was an action for damages by the owners of a wharf against the charterers of a ship from which oil had carelessly been discharged while the ship was in Sydney harbour. The oil had spread to the claimants' wharf and they halted their welding operations until assured by expert scientific opinion that oil on water would not ignite. Subsequently, when a spark from the claimants' welding fell on to a piece of floating rag, the oil did ignite and their wharf was destroyed in the ensuing fire. The Australian courts held that the destruction of the wharf was the direct but unforeseeable consequence of the spilling of the oil; they held the charterers were liable. The charterer's appeal to the Privy Council (Lords Reid, Radcliffe, Tucker, Morris and Viscount Simonds) was allowed.

Viscount Simonds: ". . . Enough has been said to show that the authority of *Polemis* has been severely shaken though lip-service has from time to time been paid to it. In their Lordships' opinion it should no longer be regarded as good law. It is not probable that many cases will for that reason have a different result, though it is hoped that the law will be thereby simplified, and that in some cases, at least, palpable injustice will be avoided. For it does not seem consonant with current ideas of justice or morality that for an act of negligence, however slight or venial, which results in some trivial foreseeable damage the actor should be liable for all consequences however unforeseeable and however grave, so long as they can be said to be 'direct.' It is a principle of civil liability, subject only to qualifications which have no present relevance, that a man must be considered to be responsible for the probable consequences of his act. To demand more of him is too harsh a rule, to demand less is to ignore that civilised order requires the observance of a minimum standard of behaviour. . . .

Their Lordships conclude this part of the case with some general observations. They have been concerned primarily to displace the proposition that unforeseeability is irrelevant if damage is "direct." In doing so they have inevitably insisted that the essential factor in determining liability is whether the damage is of such a kind as the reasonable man should have foreseen. This accords with the general view thus stated by Lord Atkin in *Donoghue v Stevenson*: 'The liability for negligence, whether you style it such or treat it as in other systems as a species of 'culpa,' is no doubt based upon a general public sentiment of moral wrongdoing for which the offender must pay.' It is a departure from this sovereign principle if liability is made to depend solely on the damage being the 'direct' or 'natural' consequence of the precedent act. Who knows or can be assumed to know all the processes of nature? But if it would be wrong that a man should be held liable for damage unpredictable by a reasonable man because it was 'direct' or 'natural,' equally it would be wrong that he should escape liability, however 'indirect' the damage, if he foresaw or could reasonably foresee the intervening events which led to its being done: cf *Woods v Duncan*. Thus foreseeability becomes the effective test. In reasserting this principle their Lordships conceive that they do not depart from, but follow and develop, the law of negligence as laid down by Baron Alderson in *Blyth v Birmingham Waterworks Co*. . . ."

NOTE

It has been said that the change of test from directness to foreseeability was more a change of name than a change of substance. But this is not strictly accurate. The change is one of method in that the focus is no longer on the *connection* between act and damage but on the *actor* as a 'reasonable man'. This is quite a different focal point giving rise to quite a different way of envisaging a factual situation (actional rather than causal). A 'reasonable man' is in effect now allowed to behave carelessly provided that his wrongful act does not give rise to any damage that a reasonable man might foresee. The problem of course is that the reasonable man ought not to indulge in careless behaviour in the first place (a point that seemed rather obvious to the judges in *Re Polemis*).

QUESTIONS

1. Does the foreseeability test apply only to the tort of negligence?

2. In a subsequent claim arising out of the same fire which destroyed the wharf in *The Wagon Mound (No 1)*, owners of ships moored alongside the wharf also sought damages

from the same defendants (*The Wagon Mound (No 2)* (1967)). Do you think this claim equally failed? If not, why not?

10.4.3 **Personal injury and foreseeability**

The test of foreseeability was, almost immediately, to give rise to new arguments for escaping from liability. Sometimes these worked, but sometimes they were unsuccessful as the next cases indicate.

Corr v IBC Vehicles Ltd **[2008] 2 W.L.R. 499, HL**

(For facts see p.378)

Lord Scott: "... **29** Authority ... discourages attempts to decide cases like the present by the application of a reasonable foreseeability test. The general rule is that in a case where foreseeable physical injuries have been caused to a claimant by the negligence of a defendant the defendant cannot limit his liability by contending that the extent of the physical injuries could not have been reasonably foreseen; the defendant must take his victim as he finds him. In *Smith v Leech Brain & Co Ltd* [1962] 2 QB 405, 415 Lord Parker CJ said:

'The test is not whether these employers could reasonably have foreseen that a burn would cause cancer and that [the victim] would die. The question is whether these employers could reasonably foresee the type of injury he suffered, namely, the burn. What, in the particular case, is the amount of damage which he suffers as a result of that burn, depends upon the characteristics and constitution of the victim.'

Smith v Leech Brain & Co Ltd did not involve psychiatric consequences of a physical injury, but *Page v Smith* [1996] AC 155 did. In *Page v Smith* the House held that where physical injury was a reasonably foreseeable consequence of the negligence the defendant was liable for psychiatric damage caused by the negligence even though physical injury had not in the event been caused and whether or not psychiatric damage as a consequence of the negligence was foreseeable. . . . *Page v Smith*, therefore, extended the rule as stated in *Smith v Leech Brain & Co Ltd* so as to include psychiatric injury. If a duty of care to avoid physical injury is broken and psychiatric injury is thereby caused, whether with or without any physical injury being caused, the negligent defendant must accept liability for the psychiatric injury. He must take his victim as he finds him. That this is so is a consequence of the House's decision in *Page v Smith*. That decision has been the subject of some criticism but not in the present case. If Mr Corr's psychiatric damage caused by the accident at work is damage for which his employers must accept liability, it is difficult to see on what basis they could escape liability for additional injury, self-inflicted but attributable to his psychiatric condition. If Mr Corr had not suffered from the clinical depression brought about by the accident, he would not have had the suicidal tendencies that led him eventually to kill himself. In my opinion, on the principles established by the authorities to which I have referred, the chain of causal consequences of the accident for which Mr Corr's negligent employers are liable was not broken by his suicide. For tortious remoteness of damage purposes his jump from the multi-storey car park was not, in my opinion, a novus actus interveniens. Mrs Corr is entitled, in my opinion, to a Fatal Accidents Act claim against his employers. . . ."

QUESTIONS

1. Is Lord Scott distinguishing between factual causation and remoteness of damage?

2. Ward L.J. in the Court of Appeal said that the "sad fact is that the awful event at the multi-storey car park on 23 May 2002 was a tragic accident which should be treated as such and not as an occasion for blame." Can the employers really be absolved of any blame in respect of this tragic event? Is it so unreasonable for the employers (in reality their insurance company) to pay for the upkeep of their late employee's family given that they destroyed not just part of his body but also his mental well-being?

3. What ought one to foresee: (i) the damage that actually occurs; (ii) the damage of the type that occurs; (iii) any possible damage?

NOTE

The rule that a tortfeasor must 'take his victim as he finds him' appeared (as Lord Scott indicates) not to have been suppressed by the foreseeability test. In *Robinson v Post Office* (1974) an employee, who cut his knee when he slipped off an oily ladder, brought an action for damages against his employer. The employee went to the doctor who administered an anti-tetanus injection but who carelessly failed to give a test dose; the employee was allergic to the serum and contracted encephalitis which left him partially handicapped. The employer admitted negligence but claimed they were not liable for the encephalitis. The Court of Appeal held that they were liable for the full damage. Orr L.J. said: "there was no missing link and the case is governed by the principle that the Post Office had to take their victim as they found him, in this case with an allergy to a second dose".

10.4.4 Typical damage

The foreseeability rule was at first to prove effective when it came to the type of damage suffered. Thus in one case the defendant negligently allowed his farm to become infested with rats with the result that an employee suffered what was then a very rare illness, namely Weil's disease contracted from rats' urine. Had the employee suffered illness from a rat's bite there would have been no problem with respect to liability, but the trial judge held the farmer not liable since Weil's disease was unforeseeable (*Tremain v Pike* (1969)). In other words "untypical damage" (an excellent expression fashioned by Tony Weir) may be unforeseeable. Much of course depends upon the question posed. Does one have to foresee the actual specie of damage which occurs or is foreseeability of the genus of damage enough? This question may now have been settled by the next case.

Jolley v Sutton London Borough Council **[2000] 1 W.L.R. 1082, HL**

This was an action for damages for personal injury against a local authority for negligence and for breach of the Occupiers' Liability Act 1957. The Court of Appeal held that the authority was not liable, but this decision was overturned by the House of Lords (Lords Browne-Wilkinson, Mackay, Steyn, Hoffmann and Hobhouse).

Lord Steyn: "My Lords, on 8 April 1990, in the grounds of a block of council flats owned and occupied by the London Borough of Sutton, Justin Jolley, then a schoolboy aged 14, sustained serious spinal injuries in an accident. It arose when a small abandoned cabin cruiser, which had been left lying in the grounds of the block of flats, fell on Justin as he lay underneath it while attempting to repair and paint it. As a result he is now a paraplegic. He claimed damages in tort from the council. At trial the claim was primarily based on a breach of the Occupiers' Liability Acts 1957 and 1984. After a seven day trial in 1998 Mr Geoffrey Brice QC, a Deputy High Court Judge, gave judgment for Justin but reduced the damages by 25 per cent by virtue of a finding of contributory negligence. The judge awarded damages in the sum of £621,710, together with interest: *Jolley v London Borough of Sutton* [1998] 1 Lloyd's Rep. 433. The council appealed. The Court of Appeal unanimously reversed the judge's conclusions on the merits and entered judgment for the council: *Jolley v Sutton LBC* [1998] 1 WLR 1546. . . .

The law

Very little needs to be said about the law. The decision in this case has turned on the detailed findings of fact at first instance on the particular circumstances of this case. Two general observations are, however, appropriate. First, in this corner of the law the results of decided cases are inevitably very fact-sensitive. Both counsel nevertheless at times invited your Lordships to compare the facts of the present case with the facts of other decided cases. That is a sterile exercise. Precedent is a valuable stabilising influence in our legal system. But, comparing the facts of and outcomes of cases in this branch of the law is a misuse of the only proper use of precedent, viz to identify the relevant rule to apply to the facts as found.

Secondly, Lord Woolf MR made an observation casting doubt on part of Lord Reid's speech in *Hughes v Lord Advocate* [1963] AC 837. The defendants left a manhole uncovered and protected only by a tent and paraffin lamp. A child climbed down the hole. When he came out he kicked over one of the lamps. It fell into the hole and caused an explosion. The child was burned. The Court of Session held that there was no liability. The House of Lords reversed the decision of the Court of Session. . . .

Lord Woolf MR observed that he had difficulty in reconciling. . . remarks [made by Lord Reid in *Hughes*] with the approach in *The Wagon Mound (No 1)* [1961] AC 388. It is true that in *The Wagon Mound (No 1)* Viscount Simonds at one stage observed, at p. 425E:

'If, as admittedly it is, B's liability (culpability) depends on the reasonable foreseeability of the consequent damage, how is that to be determined except by the foreseeability of the damage which in fact happened—the damage in suit?'

But this is to take one sentence in the judgment in *The Wagon Mound (No 1)* out of context. Viscount Simonds was in no way suggesting that the precise manner of which the injury occurred nor its extent had to be foreseeable. And Lord Reid was saying no more. The speech of Lord Reid in *Hughes v Lord Advocate* [1963] AC 837 is in harmony with the other judgments. It is not in conflict with *The Wagon Mound (No 1)*. The scope of the two modifiers—the precise manner in which the injury came about and its extent—is not definitively answered by either *The Wagon Mound (No 1)* or *Hughes v Lord Advocate*. It requires determination in the context of an intense focus on the circumstances of each case: see John Fleming, *The Law of Torts*, 9th ed, (1998), pp. 240–243.

Conclusion

My Lords, I would restore the wise decision of Mr Geoffrey Brice QC, the Deputy High Court judge. I would allow the appeal. I would further remit the case to the Court of Appeal to enable it to consider what course it should adopt on any application in regard to the determination of any issue relating to quantum of damages."

Lord Hoffmann: ". . . It is. . . agreed that what must have been foreseen is not the precise injury which occurred but injury of a given description. The foreseeability is not as to the particulars but the genus. And the description is formulated by reference to the nature of the risk which ought to have been foreseen. So, in *Hughes v Lord Advocate* [1963] AC 837 the foreseeable risk was that a child would be injured by falling in the hole or being burned by a lamp or by a combination of both. The House of Lords decided that the injury which actually materialised fell within this description, notwithstanding that it involved an unanticipated explosion of the lamp and consequent injuries of unexpected severity. . . .

I think that in a case like this, analogies from other imaginary facts are seldom helpful. Likewise analogies from real facts in other cases: I entirely agree with my noble and learned friend Lord Steyn in deploring the citation of cases which do nothing to illuminate any principle but are said to constitute analogous facts. In the present case, the rotten condition of the boat had a significance beyond the particular danger it created. It proclaimed the boat and its trailer as abandoned, res nullius, there for the taking, to make of them whatever use the rich fantasy life of children might suggest. . . ."

QUESTIONS

1. If Lord Hoffmann is right (genus and not species), does this mean that the decision in the Weil's disease case (*Tremain v Pike*) must now be in question?

2. Does *Jolley* go some way in resurrecting the directness test?

3. Is it really possible, in a case like *Jolley*, for counsel not to draw analogies with the facts of previous cases? How else do you argue the case in a precedent-based system given that the ratio decidendi always includes the material facts of the precedent?

4. In *Morris v Network Rail* (2004) Buxton L.J. asserted "no more in nuisance than in negligence is it possible to base a claim on liability in the air, in the sense that the defendant is liable for conduct, or for a state of affairs, just because it will foreseeably cause some harm to some person. What must be foreseen is relevant damage to this plaintiff or to a category of persons into which he falls, a requirement that subsumes the tests both of duty in fact and of remoteness of damage" (§ 34). Does this statement actually accord with Lord Hoffmann's view in *Jolley*? What does Buxton L.J. mean when he says that foreseeability subsumes the tests of duty in fact and of remoteness?

10.5 Damages

The final level that causation can operate is at the level of the remedy of damages. The details of this remedy will be pursued in the next chapter, but there are several rules which might usefully be discussed under the general heading of causation. These rules are contributory negligence, mitigation and remoteness of a particular head of damage.

10.5.1 **Contributory negligence**

Contributory negligence was once a question of factual causation: if the claimant was guilty of contributing by his own negligence to his damage this would amount to a complete novus actus interveniens isolating the defendant from liability (cf. *McWilliams v Sir William Arrol & Co*, p.380). This position was considered unjust and was alleviated by statutory intervention. The effect of this statute was to move contributory negligence from the level of factual causation to the level of damages. Contributory negligence is, on the whole, no longer a matter of liability but an issue of the amount of damages payable.

Law Reform (Contributory Negligence) Act 1945 (8 & 9 Geo VI, c.28)

"**1 Apportionment of liability in case of contributory negligence**.

(1) Where any person suffers damage as the result partly of his own fault and partly of the fault of any other person or persons, a claim in respect of that damage shall not be defeated by reason of the fault of the person suffering the damage, but the damages recoverable in respect thereof shall be reduced to such extent as the court thinks just and equitable having regard to the claimant's share in the responsibility of the damage. . .

4 Interpretation.

. . .

'damage' includes loss of life and personal injury . . .

'fault' means negligence, breach of statutory duty or other act or omission which gives rise to liability in tort or would, apart from this Act, give rise to the defence of contributory negligence.

NOTE

One question that has caused difficulty is whether the Act applies to breaches of contract. The next extract, in addition to giving a brief background to the 1945 Act, concludes that it does not, unless the facts also disclose a tort.

Barclays Bank Plc v Fairclough Building Ltd **[1995] Q.B. 214, CA**

Beldam L.J.: ". . . The common law rule that in an action in tort a plaintiff whose own fault contributed with the defendant's to cause his damage could recover nothing was perceived to be unfair and, as a result of the Law Revision Committee's Eighth Report (Contributory Negligence) (1939) (Cmnd 6032), the Law Reform (Contributory Negligence) Act 1945 was passed. Its purpose was to enable a court in actions of tort to apportion responsibility for the damage suffered by the plaintiff where there had been fault by both parties. . . .

In my judgment. . . in the present state of the law contributory negligence is not a defence to a claim for damages founded on breach of a strict contractual obligation. I do not believe the wording of the Law Reform (Contributory Negligence) Act 1945 can reasonably sustain an argument to the contrary. Even if it did, in the present case the nature of the contract and the obligation undertaken by the skilled contractor did not impose on the plaintiff any duty in its own interest to prevent the defendant from committing the breaches of contract. To hold otherwise would, I consider, be equivalent to implying into the contract an obligation on the part of the plaintiff inconsistent with the express terms agreed by the parties. The contract clearly laid down the extent of the obligations of the plaintiff as architect and of the defendant. It was the defendant who was to provide appropriate supervision on site, not the architect. . . ."

NOTE

The word 'fault' has also given rise to difficulties where the act of the claimant was intentional rather than careless.

Reeves v Commissioner of Police for the Metropolis **[2000] 1 A.C. 360, HL**

(For facts see p.377)

Lord Jauncey: ". . . Mr Blake QC for the plaintiff submitted that the act of suicide could not amount to contributory negligence on the part of the deceased inasmuch as it did not amount to fault by him within the meaning of section 4 of the Law Reform (Contributory Negligence) Act 1945. Section 1(1) of that Act provides that where A suffers damage 'as the result partly of his own fault and partly of the fault' of B, the damages recoverable may be reduced 'having regard to the claimant's share in the responsibility for the damage.' Fault is defined in section 4 as meaning 'negligence, breach of statutory duty or other act or omission which gives rise to a liability in tort or would, apart from this Act, give rise to the defence of contributory negligence.' Mr Blake contended that since an act which was intentional not only as to its performance but also as to its consequences would not have amounted to contributory negligence at common law it followed that the deceased's act of suicide was not 'fault' within the meaning of section 4. . . .

My Lords, no United Kingdom authority has been cited in support of Mr Blake's contention so far as the period before 1945 is concerned. This is perhaps not altogether surprising in view of the fact that the effect of contributory negligence at that time was identical to that of the defence of *volenti non fit injuria*. The authorities from New Zealand and the United States do not suggest that an act intentional both as to performance and consequences can never amount to contributory negligence. If the law is to retain the respect of the public it should where possible walk hand in hand with common sense. There are, of course, occasions where legislation both domestic and European appear to make this impossible but where there is no such legislative inhibition the law should be interpreted and applied so far as possible to produce a result which accords with common sense. To take an example A working beside a tank of boiling liquid which is inadequately guarded negligently allows his hand to come in contact with the liquid and suffers damage; B for a dare plunges his hand into the same liquid to see how long he can stand the heat. It would be bordering on the absurd if A's entitlement to damages were reduced but B could recover in full for his own folly. B's responsibility for the damage which he suffered is undeniable. I see no reason to construe section 4 of the Act of 1945 to produce such a result and I agree with the Lord Chief Justice that the word 'fault' in that section is wide enough to cover acts deliberate as to both performance and consequences. An individual of sound mind is no less responsible for such acts than he is for negligent acts and it is his share of responsibility for the damage which reduces the damages recoverable.

In this case the open flap was not a danger to an occupant of the cell acting normally with reasonable regard for his own safety. It only became a danger when it was deliberately used by the deceased as part of the mechanism whereby he strangled himself. The act of the deceased was accordingly a substantial cause of his own demise and any damages recoverable by the plaintiff should be reduced to reflect this.

Were I sitting alone I would have apportioned the blame as to one third to the commissioner and as to two thirds to the deceased. However, I understand that the majority of your Lordships favour a 50/50 division of responsibility and I do not feel inclined to dissent from that view.

In all the circumstances I would allow the appeal and make the same order as that proposed by my noble and learned friend Lord Hoffmann."

QUESTIONS

1. Does contributory negligence mean that a person owes a duty of care to him or herself? Or is it a duty owed to others? (cf. *Froom v Butcher* (1976)).

2. Will suicide always amount to contributory negligence?

Corr v IBC Vehicles Ltd **[2008] 2 W.L.R. 499, HL**

(For facts see p.378)

Lord Scott (dissenting on the contributory negligence issue): ". . . **30** . . . Section 5 of the 1976 Act applies where the deceased whose death has entitled the dependant to a Fatal Accidents Act damages action has died "as the result partly of his own fault and partly of the fault of any other person". In that event the damages recoverable by the dependant are to be reduced to the same proportionate extent as damages recoverable in an action brought for the benefit of the deceased's estate would have been reduced under section 1(1) of the Law Reform (Contributory Negligence) Act 1945. Here, too, I find it easier to examine the issue by supposing that Mr Corr had not died from his jump but had merely, if that is the right word, added to his physical injuries. Would he have been entitled to recover in full for those additional injuries, or would there have been a proportionate reduction to reflect the fact that the jump had been his own deliberate decision?

31 . . . Suppose, for example, that there had been people in the area on to which Mr Corr was likely to land if he jumped. If he had jumped in those circumstances and had in the process injured someone beneath, surely no court, faced with a claim by the injured person for damages, would have found any difficulty in attributing fault to his action. 'Fault' in section 4 of the 1945 Act includes: '[any] act or omission which gives rise to a liability in tort or would, apart from this Act, give rise to the defence of contributory negligence', and 'fault' in section 5 of the 1976 Act must bear the same meaning. So if the act of jumping in disregard for the safety of others would have constituted fault for tort purposes, it is difficult to see why that same act of jumping with the deliberate intention of terminating his own life should not also be so regarded. If, in jumping, Mr Corr had both injured someone else and also himself, it would seem to me highly anomalous to hold him liable in negligence in an action by the third party but not guilty of fault for contributory negligence purposes so far as his own injuries were concerned. . . ."

Lord Walker: ". . . **37** This appeal differs from the custodian cases in two important respects. The late Mr Thomas Corr was not, before the dreadful accident on the press line, a suicide risk; he was a happy family man. The appellant, IBC Vehicles Ltd, was not Mr Corr's custodian but his employer. IBC owed him various contractual, tortious and statutory duties, of which the most important for present purposes was to take reasonable care that he did not sustain personal injuries in the course of his work. Mr Corr did not suffer from depression, suicidal ideation or any other psychological disorder. There was no question of IBC owing him any special duty, before the accident, on account of any such disability. His severe clinical depression and feelings of worthlessness and hopelessness came after, and as a result of, the very serious physical injuries which he received in the accident. . . ."

Lord Neuberger: ". . . **69** In the end, I consider that the question to be addressed is the extent to which the deceased's personal autonomy has been overborne by the impairment to his mind attributable to the defendant. Where it has not been so overborne at all, the contribution, and hence the reduction in damages, may well be 50% (as in *Reeves's* case); where it has been effectively wholly overborne, there will be no reduction. In other cases, the answer will lie somewhere between those two extremes. In such cases, the question, while a relatively easy question to formulate, will, I strongly suspect, be a relatively difficult question to answer, at least in many circumstances. . . ."

QUESTIONS

1. Is the argument advanced by Lord Scott convincing from a functional point of view? Is someone who jumps off a building as a result of his mind being overborne by an impairment, and who injures another, actually guilty of 'fault'? Or does the law of tort just hold that he is in order to insure that the victim receives compensation?

2. If Mr Corr had hit and injured another person as a result of jumping off the building would his employer (assuming he was still technically employed) have been liable to this victim?

10.5.2 Mitigation of damage

The principle of mitigation of damage is explained in the next short extract.

Thomas v Countryside Council for Wales **[1994] 4 All E.R. 853, QBD**

Rougier J.: ". . . Under the normal law of contract and tort the fundamental basis for the measure of damages is compensation for pecuniary loss which directly and naturally flows from the breach . . . There is, however, a qualification that a plaintiff suing for breach of contract or, for that matter, for tort cannot call upon a defendant to pay the full direct consequences unless he himself has acted reasonably to mitigate the loss. It is sometimes loosely described as a plaintiff's duty to mitigate . . .

> If he wishes to claim the full measure of his loss, a plaintiff must act reasonably, but, as was recently pointed out in . . . *The Solholt*. . . a plaintiff is under no duty to mitigate his loss. He is completely free to act as he judges to be in his best interests. The significance of his failure to act in a reasonable manner is merely that he cannot then call upon the defendant to pay for losses which he might have avoided had he taken reasonable steps to do so. . . ."

NOTE

The idea that mitigation is no longer a question of 'duty' is valuable to the extent that it re-emphasises the causation aspect. Nevertheless to redefine it terms of an interest does nothing to change the normative aspect of the mitigation rule. A claimant who wishes to be compensated for losses 'has to' behave not just reasonably but, according to the next case, as the 'reasonable businessman'.

Darbishire v Warran [1963] 1 W.L.R. 1067, CA

The claimant brought an action for damages against another driver who had negligently caused serious damage to his Lea Francis shooting brake car. The County Court judge had assessed the value of the shooting brake at £80, but had allowed the claimant to recover damages of £180 because the claimant had had the shooting brake repaired at this cost. The defendant did not contest liability but argued that the claimant should be allowed to recover only the £80 (adjusted to £85) and not the £180. The Court of Appeal (Harman L.J., Pearson L.J. and Pennycuick J.) held that the claimant was not entitled to the cost of repairing the shooting brake.

> Pearson L.J.: ". . . For the purposes of the present case it is important to appreciate the true nature of the so-called 'duty to mitigate the loss' or 'duty to minimise the damage.' The plaintiff is not under any actual obligation to adopt the cheaper method: if he wishes to adopt the more expensive method, he is at liberty to do so and by doing so he commits no wrong against the defendant or anyone else. The true meaning is that the plaintiff is not entitled to charge the defendant by way of damages with any greater sum than that which he reasonably needs to expend for the purpose of making good the loss. In short, he is fully entitled to be as extravagant as he pleases but not at the expense of the defendant. . . .
>
> In my view it is impossible to find from the evidence that the plaintiff took all reasonable steps to mitigate the loss, or did all that he reasonably could do to keep down the cost. He was fully entitled to have his damaged vehicle repaired at whatever cost because he preferred it. But he was not justified in charging against the defendant the cost of repairing the damaged vehicle when that cost was more than twice the replacement market value and he had made no attempt to find a replacement vehicle. . . .
>
> . . .It is vital, for the purpose of assessing damages fairly between the plaintiff and the defendant, to consider whether the plaintiff's course of action was economic or uneconomic, and if it was uneconomic it cannot (at any rate in the absence of special circumstances, of which there is no evidence in this case) form a proper basis for assessment of damages. The question has to be considered from the point of view of a business man. It seems to me the practical business view is that if the cost of repairing your damaged vehicle is greatly in excess of the market price, you must look around for a replacement and you would expect to

find one at a cost not far removed from the market price, although unless you were lucky you might have to pay something more than the standard market price to obtain a true equivalent of a well-maintained and reliable vehicle."

QUESTION

Will the reasonable businessman test apply to all types of property damage?

NOTE

See also C&MC, pp.534–535.

11 Remedies

The Roman jurist Gaius, writing in the second century AD, stated that all law is about persons (*personae*), things (*res*) and actions (*actiones*). The latter category got lost from civilian private law in the 16th century thanks to the French humanist jurists who replaced 'actions' with 'obligations' (since they were associated in Justinian's *Digest*). The modern structure of civilian private law thus consists of the law of persons, the law of property and the law of obligations. However 'actions', or remedies, have not completely disappeared from English liability law. Of course the English forms of actions—trespass, debt, case, etc.—were a very different set of remedies from the Roman *actiones*, just as Chancery's remedies of injunction, specific performance, rescission etc. were only partly shaped by Roman thinking.

Remedies thinking remains vibrant, and useful, in the common law for several reasons. First, because the forms of action approach—that is to say thinking in terms of lists of categories of liability—never completely disappeared from the law of torts even after the abolition of the forms of action (see e.g. *Esso v Southport*, p.5 and **1.7**). Secondly, because common law remedies (debt and damages) and equitable remedies (injunction etc.) still act as institutional focal points for their own specific rules. There are thus textbooks devoted to damages, injunctions and specific performance.

A third reason why the remedy or *actio* remains active is that it is still a most useful perspective from which to view liability. This is particularly true when third parties are affected by a tortfeasor's infliction of damage on a victim. When a negligent car driver or employer carelessly kills or injures the father of a family do the other family members have an action against the tortfeasor? Does a child in the womb have an action against a tortfeasor who injures the mother? These questions can, of course, be seen in terms of substantive liability, yet starting out from the availability of an action is often a most helpful in terms of a structural analysis.

11.1 Actions and remedies

Remedies are thus important in that they act as a focal point for some fundamental practical questions. Who can bring an action and for what?

11.1.1 Types of remedy

As far as the tort lawyer is concerned, remedies can usefully be classified into three main groups: there are (i) monetary remedies; (ii) non-monetary remedies; and (iii) self-help remedies (and see further C&MC, pp.512–514). Very broadly, the monetary and non-monetary remedies reflect the difference between common law and equity; however the symmetry is not perfect. There are some equitable monetary remedies and the common law has long been prepared to order repossession of land.

Manchester Airport Plc v Dutton **[2000] 1 Q.B. 133, CA**

Laws L.J.: "I gratefully adopt the account of the facts set out in the judgment of Chadwick LJ. As there appears, the defendants or others (to whom I will compendiously refer as 'the trespassers') entered Arthur's Wood and set up their encampments before the grant of the licence by the National Trust to the airport company. Moreover it appears (and I will assume it for the purpose of the appeal) that the airport company has not to date gone into occupation of the land under the licence.

In those circumstances, the question which falls for determination is whether the airport company, being a licensee which is not de facto in occupation or possession of the land, may maintain proceedings to evict the trespassers by way of an order for possession. . . .

In my judgment the true principle is that a licensee not in occupation may claim possession against a trespasser if that is a necessary remedy to vindicate and give effect to such rights of occupation as by contract with his licensor he enjoys. This is the same principle as allows a licensee who is in de facto possession to evict a trespasser. There is no respectable distinction, in law or logic, between the two situations. An estate owner may seek an order whether he is in possession or not. So, in my judgment, may a licensee, if other things are equal. In both cases, the plaintiff's remedy is strictly limited to what is required to make good his legal right. The principle applies although the licensee has no right to exclude the licensor himself. Elementarily he cannot exclude any occupier who, by contract or estate, has a claim to possession equal or superior to his own. Obviously, however, that will not avail a bare trespasser.

In this whole debate, as regards the law of remedies in the end I see no significance as a matter of principle in any distinction drawn between a plaintiff whose right to occupy the land in question arises from title and one whose right arises only from contract. In every case the question must be, what is the reach of the right, and whether it is shown that the defendant's acts violate its enjoyment. If they do, and (as here) an order for possession is the only practical remedy, the remedy should be granted. Otherwise the law is powerless to correct a proved or admitted wrongdoing; and that would be unjust and disreputable. The underlying principle is in the Latin maxim (for which I make no apology), 'ubi jus, ibi sit remedium.'. . .

For all the reasons I have given, I would dismiss this appeal."

Kennedy L.J.: "delivered a judgment dismissing the appeal."

Chadwick L.J. (dissenting): ". . . It has long been understood that a licensee who is not in exclusive occupation does not have title to bring an action for ejectment. The position of a non-exclusive occupier was explained by Blackburn J. in *Allan v Liverpool Overseers* (1874) LR 9 QB 180, 191–192, in a passage cited by Davies L.J. in this court in *Appah v Parncliffe Investments Ltd* [1964] 1 WLR 1064, 1069–1070 and by Lord Templeman in the House of Lords in *Street v Mountford* [1985] AC 809, 818. . . .

That passage, as it seems to me, provides clear authority for the proposition that an action for ejectment—the forerunner of the present action for recovery of land—as well as an action for trespass can only be brought by a person who is in possession or who has a right to be in possession. Further, that possession is synonymous, in this context, with exclusive occupation—that is to say occupation (or a right to occupy) to the exclusion of all others, including the owner or other person with superior title (save in so far as he has reserved a right to enter). . . .

I would have allowed this appeal."

NOTE

This case is of interest because it raises a distinction that was fundamental to Roman law, namely the distinction between an *actio in rem* and an *actio in personam*. The former was a claim against a thing and was brought to enforce a property right while the latter was against another person and gave expression to liability in the law of obligations. The Romans, and indeed modern civil lawyers, kept the two types of claim strictly separate; English law, in contrast, seems to allow the two to become intermixed, which in turn causes conceptual difficulties when it comes to trying to isolate an English 'law of obligations' (dealing strictly with personal rights). The claimant was asserting a contractual right (*jus in personam*) against those occupying the land, yet he was effectively allowed to succeed in an *actio in rem*. In order to be able to assert a *jus in rem*, he would, as Chadwick L.J. pointed out, have to show that he was in possession (i.e. he had a real right or interest in the land) (see also P. Cane, *The Anatomy of Tort Law*, (Oxford: Hart, 1997), p.75).

QUESTIONS

1. Could the claimant in *Manchester* have sued for damages? If so, what would be the basis of its claim?

2. Would the claimant in *Manchester* be able, today, to seek some remedy or other under statute?

11.1.2 Legal subject (*persona*) and remedy (*action*)

When one focuses on the remedy (*actio*) it leads one to think about which persons (*personae*) are entitled to sue. Normally it is living people and fictional people (companies) who sue, but what if such people are either dead or unborn?

Law Reform (Miscellaneous Provisions) Act 1934 (24 & 25 Geo V c.41)

"1 Effect of death on certain causes of action

(1) Subject to the provisions of this section, on the death of any person after the commencement of this Act all causes of action subsisting against or vested in him shall survive against, or, as the case may be, for the benefit of, his estate. Provided that this subsection shall not apply to causes of action for defamation. . . .

(1A) The right of a person to claim under section 1A of the Fatal Accidents Act 1976 (bereavement) shall not survive for the benefit of his estate on his death.

(2) Where a cause of action survives as aforesaid for the benefit of the estate of a deceased person, the damages recoverable for the benefit of the estate of that person:—

> (a) shall not include—
>
>> (i) any exemplary damages;
>> (ii) any damages for loss of income in respect of any period after that person's death;. . ."

QUESTION

Does this Act create an artificial person (or ghost?) called an 'estate'?

NOTE

The 1934 Act keeps the *actio* alive in respect of the dead victim (for many claims), yet the victim's immediate family can also incur loss if the victim was the breadwinner. At common law they had no claim, but this was altered by statute.

Fatal Accidents Act 1976 (c.30)

"**1 Right of action for wrongful act causing death**

(1) If death is caused by any wrongful act, neglect or default which is such as would (if death had not ensued) have entitled the person injured to maintain an action and recover damages in respect thereof, the person who would have been liable if death had not ensued shall be liable to an action for damages, notwithstanding the death of the person injured.

(2) Subject to section 1A(2) below, every such action shall be for the benefit of the dependants of the person ("the deceased") whose death has been so caused.

(3) In this Act "dependant" means—

(a) the wife or husband or former wife or husband of the deceased;
(aa) the civil partner or former civil partner of the deceased
(b) any person who—

(i) was living with the deceased in the same household immediately before the date of the death; and
(ii) had been living with the deceased in the same household for at least two years before that date; and
(iii) was living during the whole of that period as the husband or wife or civil partner of the deceased;

(c) any parent or other ascendant of the deceased;
(d) any person who was treated by the deceased as his parent;
(e) any child or other descendant of the deceased;
(f) any person (not being a child of the deceased) who, in the case of any marriage to which the deceased was at any time a party, was treated by the deceased as a child of the family in relation to that marriage;

(fa) any person (not being a child of the deceased) who, in the case of any civil partnership in which the deceased was at any time a civil partner, was treated by the deceased as a child of the family in relation to that civil partnership;

(g) any person who is, or is the issue of, a brother, sister, uncle or aunt of the deceased.

(4) The reference to the former wife or husband of the deceased in subsection (3)(*a*) above includes a reference to a person whose marriage to the deceased has been annulled or declared void as well as a person whose marriage to the deceased has been dissolved.

(4A) The reference to the former civil partner of the deceased in subsection (3)(*aa*) above includes a reference to a person whose civil partnership with the deceased has been annulled as well as a person whose civil partnership with the deceased has been dissolved.

(5) In deducing any relationship for the purposes of subsection (3) above—

(a) any relationship by marriage or civil partnership shall be treated as a relationship by consanguinity, any relationship of the half blood as a relationship of the whole blood, and the stepchild of any person as his child, and

(b) an illegitimate person shall be treated as the legitimate child of his mother and reputed father.

(6) Any reference in this Act to injury includes any disease and any impairment of a person's physical or mental condition.

1A Bereavement

(1) An action under this Act may consist of or include a claim for damages for bereavement.

(2) A claim for damages for bereavement shall only be for the benefit—

(a) of the wife or husband or civil partner of the deceased; and

(b) where the deceased was a minor who was never married or a civil partner—

(i) of his parents, if he was legitimate; and

(ii) of his mother, if he was illegitimate.

(3) Subject to subsection (5) below, the sum to be awarded as damages under this section shall be £11,800.

(4) Where there is a claim for damages under this section for the benefit of both the parents of the deceased, the sum awarded shall be divided equally between them (subject to any deduction falling to be made in respect of costs not recovered from the defendant).

(5) The Lord Chancellor may by order made by statutory instrument, subject to annulment in pursuance of a resolution of either House of Parliament, amend this section by varying the sum for the time being specified in subsection (3) above."

QUESTIONS

1. Is s.1A really a compensatory damages provision or is it more like a statutory debt? What is the policy behind the section?

2. Does s.1A mean that bereavement is a very different head of damage from either severe psychological damage (nervous shock) or mental distress?

NOTE

The 1934 and the 1976 Acts deal with the physical disappearance of the human person and the effect that this disappearance has in the legal plan. A symmetrical problem arises with respect to 'persons' who have not yet come into existence, the most important of which, for tort lawyers, is the conceived but unborn child. It has been a general rule in all Western legal systems since Roman times that legal personality attaches to the human person only when they are born, although the law will strive to protect the interests of the unborn child. The complexity is reflected in the next extract.

Congenital Disabilities (Civil Liability) Act 1976 (c.28)

"1 Civil liability to child born disabled

(1) If a child is born disabled as the result of such an occurrence before its birth as is mentioned in subsection (2) below, and a person (other than the child's own mother) is under this section answerable to the child in respect of the occurrence, the child's disabilities are to be regarded as damage resulting from the wrongful act of that person and actionable accordingly at the suit of the child.

(2) An occurrence to which this section applies is one which—

   (a) affected either parent of the child in his or her ability to have a normal, healthy child; or
   (b) affected the mother during her pregnancy, or affected her or the child in the course of its birth, so that the child is born with disabilities which would not otherwise have been present.

(3) Subject to the following subsections, a person (here referred to as "the defendant") is answerable to the child if he was liable in tort to the parent or would, if sued in due time, have been so; and it is no answer that there could not have been such liability because the parent suffered no actionable injury, if there was a breach of legal duty which, accompanied by injury, would have given rise to the liability.

(4) In the case of an occurrence preceding the time of conception, the defendant is not answerable to the child if at that time either or both of the parents knew the risk of their child being born disabled (that is to say, the particular risk created by the occurrence); but should it be the child's father who is the defendant, this subsection does not apply if he knew of the risk and the mother did not.

(5) The defendant is not answerable to the child, for anything he did or omitted to do when responsible in a professional capacity for treating or advising the parent, if

he took reasonable care having due regard to then received professional opinion applicable to the particular class of case; but this does not mean that he is answerable only because he departed from received opinion.

(6) Liability to the child under this section may be treated as having been excluded or limited by contract made with the parent affected, to the same extent and subject to the same restrictions as liability in the parent's own case; and a contract term which could have been set up by the defendant in an action by the parent, so as to exclude or limit his liability to him or her, operates in the defendant's favour to the same, but no greater, extent in an action under this section by the child.

(7) If in the child's action under this section it is shown that the parent affected shared the responsibility for the child being born disabled, the damages are to be reduced to such extent as the court thinks just and equitable having regard to the extent of the parent's responsibility.

[. . .]

2 Liability of woman driving while pregnant

A woman driving a motor vehicle when she knows (or ought reasonably to know) herself to be pregnant is to be regarded as being under the same duty to take care for the safety of her unborn child as the law imposes on her with respect to the safety of other people; and if in consequence of her breach of that duty her child is born with disabilities which would not otherwise have been present, those disabilities are to be regarded as damage resulting from her wrongful act and actionable accordingly at the suit of the child."

QUESTIONS

1. Why did the Act simply not declare that a duty of care is owed to the unborn child? Are such unborn children owed such a duty at common law?

2. What if the "received professional opinion" is obviously wrong to any rational judge?

3. Is any exclusion clause in a contract between parent and defendant likely to be effective?

4. Is s.1(7) based on the principle that the sins of a parent ought to be visited upon the child?

5. Damages cannot, it seems, be claimed by a carer who is also a defendant (*Hunt v Severs* (1994), below p.437). In allowing a child to sue its mother does this amount to an indirect way in which a carer of the child (the mother) might get some damages?

PROBLEM

A medical centre negligently tells a pregnant woman, who has gone to the centre for tests, that she has not come into contact with any virus that is likely to impact on the health of her child. Had she been told the opposite, she would have terminated her pregnancy. In fact the woman had been exposed to a dangerous virus and as a result her child is born severely disabled. Can the child sue the medical centre claiming that it would have been better not to be born at all? In other words, can the child claim that his or her very birth is a form of damage in itself? If your answer to this question is 'no' for moral and (or) policy reasons, how would you explain to the child the morality of withholding compensation from him or her?

11.1.3 **Remedy (*actio*), right and interest**

The French Code of Civil Procedure states that the *actio* is available "to all those who have a legitimate interest in the success or rejection of a claim" (art.31). English law does not seem to have quite such a clear rule, but the notion of an interest is still of considerable importance in the law of actions. Normally the 'interest' dimension of a remedy is combined with the question whether or not the claimant has suffered damage.

***Revenue and Customs Commissioners v Total Network SL* [2008] 2 W.L.R. 711, HL**

(For facts and further extracts see p.117)

Lord Hope (dissenting in part): ". . . **27** It is not difficult to think of situations where the Commissioners could properly bring a claim of damages for loss sustained with regard to some interest that falls within the law's protection, such as damage to their buildings or their equipment. In *Inland Revenue Commissioners v Hambrook* [1956] 2 QB 641 the Revenue's claim for loss resulting from its being deprived of the services of a taxing officer due to a vehicle accident was dismissed. But this was because an action for that kind of loss did not lie where its relationship was with an established civil servant. In this case it is said that an action lies for loss sustained as a result of an unlawful means conspiracy. But can the amount sued for be said to be a loss sustained by the Commissioners for which they can sue in damages?

28 The Commissioners' duties and responsibilities are set out comprehensively in the statute. . . . The Commissioners are not authorised by the statute to carry on a business for profit. They have no commercial interests that need to be protected by the tort of conspiracy: see *Lonrho Ltd v Shell Petroleum Co Ltd (No 2)* [1982] AC 173, 189B-C per Lord Diplock. Their only function is to gather in and account to the Crown for VAT charged in accordance with the provisions of the Act. . . .

29 . . . There is, it may be said, a gap in the statute. But this does not mean that the Commissioners have suffered a loss for which they can sue in damages. All that can be said is that payment was made to Alldech which ought not to have been made. It is an amount that can be recovered as a debt due to the Crown from Alldech. It does not change its character as a debt due to the Crown because, when it is sought to be recovered from someone else, it is described as damages. It is an inescapable fact that the sums claimed as damages will become VAT for the purposes of the statute if and when they are paid to the Commissioners because they have no power under the statute to deal with those sums in any other way. But the Commissioners have no power to recover such a debt from strangers to the Act such as Total. In form the claim is one for damages, outside the scope of article 4 of the Bill of Rights. But in substance it is a claim for the recovery of VAT from a person who is under no liability to pay that tax under the statute. No provision for this is made in the Sixth Directive. Total do not need to invoke the protection of article 4. The issue is resolved by the terms of the statute. The statutory code precludes the claim. . . .

32 I do not think, with the greatest of respect, that it is an answer to say, as Lord Walker does, that the Commissioners regularly seek and obtain remedies against defaulting taxpayers which are not conferred on them expressly by statute or that the courts must be astute to deal with progressive techniques of tax avoidance when they are construing the taxing statutes. These points do not meet the fundamental objection that the purpose of this action is to recover VAT from a person who is not, for any of the purposes of VATA 1994, a taxpayer. Nor is it met by the example of cash representing collected taxes which was stolen from a vehicle belonging to the Commissioners while in transit. I agree that the Commissioners would have a civil remedy to reclaim the money if it could be traced to the robbers' bank account. But it would be recovered as a debt due by them to the Commissioners, not from a third party as damages. If the claim is properly to be seen as one for damages, the amount due would need to be assessed, as my noble and learned friend Lord Scott of Foscote points out. But the fact that techniques are available for the assessment of damages does not answer the question whether the Commissioners are in a position to make such a claim. . . ."

Lord Walker: ". . . **107** The Commissioners regularly present bankruptcy petitions and winding-up petitions against defaulting taxpayers of all sorts. In a winding up they can if necessary proceed against a receiver for misfeasance (*Inland Revenue Commissioners v Goldblatt* [1972] Ch 498). They do so in order to recover tax (not to 'levy' it). So far as I can see they have no express statutory power to seek these remedies, but it has never been doubted that they are available. Similarly (though your Lordships heard no argument on the point from either side) there does not appear to be any specific statutory power for the Commissioners to obtain a freezing order. But it was only by obtaining a freezing order in private law proceedings that the Commissioners were able to prevent the conspirators from removing their ill-gotten gains out of the jurisdiction. But for a freezing order, there would have been a severe loss to the Commissioners and to the general body of taxpayers. . . ."

QUESTION

Could it not be said that the tax authority represents the state? Does the state not suffer damage by illegal tax evasion?

NOTE

Although the majority of the House of Lords did not agree with Lord Hope on this damage point, his observations remain conceptually important in that they echo the civilian maxim which states 'no interest, no action' (*pas d'intérêt, pas d'action*). The Commissioners (according to Lord Hope) are not entitled to sue because they have not themselves suffered damage and thus do not have a 'sufficient interest'. But what if the claimant can show an interest in need of protection but no actual cause of action or right? The law of tort seems clearly to suggest that there will be no remedy, yet perhaps equity can help as the next case indicates.

Burris v Azadani [1995] 1 W.L.R. 1372, CA

This was an appeal by a man who had been imprisoned for failing to respect an injunction issued against him for his "intolerable history of harassment and molestation". The injunction had been obtained by the woman who had been the victim of this harassment. The Court of Appeal (Sir Thomas Bingham M.R., Millett L.J. and Schiemann L.J.) upheld the injunction.

Sir Thomas Bingham M.R.:

". . . The power of the High Court is found in section 37(1) of the Supreme Court Act 1981, which provides:

'(1) The High Court may by order (whether interlocutory or final) grant an injunction. . . in all cases in which it appears to the court to be just and convenient to do so.'

It is of course quite clear that the court cannot properly grant an injunction unless the plaintiff can show at least an arguable cause of action to support the grant, but subject to this overriding requirement section 37, as has often been observed, is cast in the widest terms.

If an injunction may only properly be granted to restrain conduct which is in itself tortious or otherwise unlawful, that would be a conclusive objection to term (c) of the 28 January 1994 injunction, since it is plain that Mr Azadani would commit no tort nor otherwise act unlawfully if, without more, he were to traverse Mandrake Road without any contact or communication with Miss Burris, exercising his right to use the public highway peacefully in the same way as any other member of the public. I do not, however, think that the court's power is so limited. . . .

Neither statute nor authority in my view precludes the making of an 'exclusion zone' order. But that does not mean that such orders should be made at all readily, or without very good reason. There are two interests to be reconciled. One is that of the defendant. His liberty must be respected up to the point at which his conduct infringes, or threatens to infringe, the rights of the plaintiff. No restraint should be placed on him which is not judged to be necessary to protect the rights of the plaintiff. But the plaintiff has an interest which the court must be astute to protect. The rule of law requires that those whose rights are infringed should seek the aid of the court, and respect for the legal process can only suffer if those who need protection fail to get it. That, in part at least, is why disobedience to orders of the court has always earned severe punishment. Respect for the freedom of the aggressor should never lead the court to deny necessary protection to the victim.

Ordinarily, the victim will be adequately protected by an injunction which restrains the tort which has been or is likely to be committed, whether trespass to the person or to land, interference with goods, harassment, intimidation or as the case may be. But it may be clear on the facts that if the defendant approaches the vicinity of the plaintiff's home he will succumb to the temptation to enter it, or to abuse or harass the plaintiff; or that he may loiter outside the house, watching and besetting it, in a manner which might be highly stressful and disturbing to a plaintiff. In such a situation the court may properly judge that in the plaintiff's interest—and also, but indirectly, the defendant's—a wider measure of restraint is called for. . . ."

QUESTIONS

1. Could the woman have sued the harasser for damages? (cf. above p.114)

2. Can a court issue an injunction whenever it thinks it 'just and convenient' to do so? If so, given that there is statutory power for a court to award damages in lieu of such an injunction (see *Jaggard v Sawyer* (1995), C&MC, p.557), can a court award damages whenever they think it just and convenient to do so?

11.1.4 **Remedies and damage**

As we have already suggested, interest can merge with damage. This merging is illustrated by the next case.

Rees v Darlington Memorial Hospital NHS Trust **[2004] 1 A.C. 309, HL**

This was an action for damages by a blind woman in respect of the birth of a healthy child born after she had undergone a sterilisation operation. She had undergone sterilisation because she felt that her disability would make the bringing up of a child particularly onerous. The operation had been negligently performed and the claimant sought damages for the costs of providing for the child. The judge held that the mother was not entitled to damages under this head, but the Court of Appeal allowed in part her appeal. On a further appeal, the House of Lords (Lords Bingham, Nicholls, Millett and Scott; Lords Steyn, Hope and Hutton dissenting) held that the claimant was not entitled to damages for the costs of bringing up a normal healthy child. However she was entitled to a conventional award of £15,000.

Lord Bingham: "1 My Lords, in *McFarlane v Tayside Health Board* [2000] 2 AC 59 a husband and wife, themselves healthy and normal, sought to recover as damages the cost of bringing up a healthy and normal child born to the wife, following allegedly negligent advice on the effect of a vasectomy performed on the husband. Differing from the Inner House of the Court of Session 1998 SLT 307, the House unanimously rejected this claim. A factual variant of that case reached the Court of Appeal in *Parkinson v St James and Seacroft University Hospital NHS Trust* [2002] QB 266: the mother, who had undergone a negligently performed sterilisation operation, conceived and bore a child who was born with severe disabilities. Following *McFarlane* the Court of Appeal held that the mother could not recover the whole cost of bringing up the child; but it held that she could recover the additional costs she would incur so far as they would be attributable to the child's disabilities. There was no appeal from that decision. The present case raises a further factual variant of *McFarlane*. The claimant in these proceedings (Ms Rees) suffers a severe and progressive visual disability, such that she felt unable to discharge the ordinary duties of a mother, and for that reason wished to be sterilised. She made her wishes known to a consultant employed by the appellant NHS Trust, who carried out a sterilisation operation but did so negligently, and the claimant conceived and bore a son. The child is normal and healthy but the claimant's disability remains. She claimed as damages the cost of rearing the child. The Court of Appeal (Robert Walker and Hale LJJ, Waller L.J. dissenting) held that she was entitled to recover the additional costs she would incur so far as they would be attributable to her disability: [2003] QB 20. The appellant NHS Trust now challenges that decision as inconsistent with *McFarlane*. The claimant seeks to uphold the decision, but also claims the whole cost of bringing up the child, inviting the House to reconsider its decision in *McFarlane*. . . .

7 I am of the clear opinion, for reasons more fully given by my noble and learned friends, that it would be wholly contrary to the practice of the House to disturb its unanimous decision in *McFarlane* given as recently as four years ago, even if a differently constituted committee were to conclude that a different solution should have been adopted. It would reflect no credit on the administration of the law if a line of English authority were to be disapproved in 1999 and reinstated in 2003 with no reason for the change beyond a change in the balance of judicial opinion. I am not in any event persuaded that the arguments which

the House rejected in 1999 should now be accepted, or that the policy considerations which (as I think) drove the decision have lost their potency. Subject to one gloss, therefore, which I regard as important, I would affirm and adhere to the decision in *McFarlane*.

8 My concern is this. Even accepting that an unwanted child cannot be regarded as a financial liability and nothing else and that any attempt to weigh the costs of bringing up a child against the intangible rewards of parenthood is unacceptably speculative, the fact remains that the parent of a child born following a negligently performed vasectomy or sterilisation, or negligent advice on the effect of such a procedure, is the victim of a legal wrong. The members of the House who gave judgment in *McFarlane* recognised this by holding, in each case, that some award should be made to Mrs McFarlane (although Lord Millett based this on a ground which differed from that of the other members and he would have made a joint award to Mr and Mrs McFarlane). I can accept and support a rule of legal policy which precludes recovery of the full cost of bringing up a child in the situation postulated, but I question the fairness of a rule which denies the victim of a legal wrong any recompense at all beyond an award immediately related to the unwanted pregnancy and birth. The spectre of well-to-do parents plundering the National Health Service should not blind one to other realities: that of the single mother with young children, struggling to make ends meet and counting the days until her children are of an age to enable her to work more hours and so enable the family to live a less straitened existence; the mother whose burning ambition is to put domestic chores so far as possible behind her and embark on a new career or resume an old one. Examples can be multiplied. To speak of losing the freedom to limit the size of one's family is to mask the real loss suffered in a situation of this kind. This is that a parent, particularly (even today) the mother, has been denied, through the negligence of another, the opportunity to live her life in the way that she wished and planned. I do not think that an award immediately relating to the unwanted pregnancy and birth gives adequate recognition of or does justice to that loss. I would accordingly support the suggestion favoured by Lord Millett in *McFarlane*, at p 114, that in all cases such as these there be a conventional award to mark the injury and loss, although I would favour a greater figure than the £5,000 he suggested (I have in mind a conventional figure of £15,000) and I would add this to the award for the pregnancy and birth. This solution is in my opinion consistent with the ruling and rationale of *McFarlane*. The conventional award would not be, and would not be intended to be, compensatory. It would not be the product of calculation. But it would not be a nominal, let alone a derisory, award. It would afford some measure of recognition of the wrong done. And it would afford a more ample measure of justice than the pure *McFarlane* rule. . . ."

Lord Steyn (dissenting): ". . . **46** Like Lord Hope I regard the idea of a conventional award in the present case as contrary to principle. It is a novel procedure for judges to create such a remedy. There are limits to permissible creativity for judges. In my view the majority have strayed into forbidden territory. It is also a backdoor evasion of the legal policy enunciated in *McFarlane*. If such a rule is to be created it must be done by Parliament. The fact is, however, that it would be a hugely controversial legislative measure. It may well be that the Law Commissions and Parliament ought in any event, to consider the impact of the creation of a power to make a conventional award in the cases under consideration for the coherence of the tort system. . . ."

Lord Hope (dissenting): ". . . **71** The award of a conventional sum is familiar in the field of damages for personal injury. Conventional sums are awarded as general damages for typical injuries such as the loss of a limb or an eye or for the bereavement that results from the loss of a child or parent in the case of a fatal accident. This is the means by which the court arrives, as best it can, at a figure for the damage suffered which is incapable of being calculated arithmetically: *Kemp & Kemp, The Quantum of Damages*, vol 1, para 1–003. The sum which it awards has been described by Lord Denning MR in *Ward v James* [1966] 1 QB 273, 303 as 'basically a conventional figure derived from experience and from awards in comparable cases': see also *Wright v British Railways Board* [1983] 2 AC 773, 777D, per Lord Diplock. The award is conventional in the sense that there is no pecuniary guideline which can point the way to a correct assessment: *Lim Poh Choo v Camden and Islington Area Health Authority* [1980] AC 174, 189G-H per Lord Scarman. But financial loss does not present the same problem. It is capable of assessment in money. So it has never been the practice to resort to a conventional sum as a means of compensating the claimant for that part of the loss that falls under the head of special damages. . . ."

QUESTIONS

1. Are the £15,000 damages awarded in this case compensatory? If so, what is the principle of compensation that underpins the award? (cf. Fatal Accidents Act 1976 s.1A, above p.416.)

2. Is Lord Hope right in assuming that the award is actually for financial loss?

3. Is this a policy decision? If so, what is the policy? (Reading in full the judgments of Lord Bingham and Lord Steyn, in the law report, will be valuable.)

11.2 Damages (1): general considerations

Statistically speaking, by far the greatest number of tort actions consists of personal injury claims. The remedy here is damages. This is a remedy that has attracted its own rules and principles and to explain the law in detail requires a textbook in itself. Separate monographs could be written on personal injury damages and on property damage claims. Thus damages actions can be classified into various different categories.

11.2.1 Compensatory damages

The basic principle of damages is to be found in the following extracts.

European Group on Tort Law, *Principles of European Tort Law* **(2003)**

"**Art. 10:101. Nature and purpose of damages**

Damages are a money payment to compensate the victim, that is to say, to restore him, so far as money can, to the position he would have been in if the wrong complained of had not been committed. Damages also serve the aim of preventing harm.

> **Art. 10:102. Lump sum or periodical payments**
>
> Damages are awarded in a lump sum or as periodical payments as appropriate with particular regard to the interests of the victim.
>
> **Art. 10:103. Benefits gained through the damaging event**
>
> When determining the amount of damages benefits which the injured party gains through the damaging event are to be taken into account unless this cannot be reconciled with the purpose of the benefit."

NOTE

These three principles more or less represent English law, as we shall see. The principle in art.10:101 is to be found in the next extract.

> *Livingstone v Rawyards Coal Co* **(1880) 5 App. Cas. 25, HL**
>
> **Lord Blackburn**: ". . . [W]here any injury is to be compensated by damages, in settling the sum of money to be given for reparation of damages you should as nearly as possible get at that sum of money which will put the party who has been injured, or who has suffered, in the same position as he would have been in if he had not sustained the wrong for which he is now getting his compensation or reparation."

NOTE

This principle was reformulated a century later by Lord Diplock who said "The general rule in English law today as to the measure of damages recoverable for the invasion of a legal right, whether by breach of a contract or by commission of a tort, is that damages are compensatory. Their function is to put the person whose right has been invaded in the same position as if it had been respected so far as the award of a sum of money can do so . . ." (Lord Diplock in *The Albazero* (1977), at p.841). However, much depends on the nature of the damage suffered.

QUESTION

Is there a difference between an award of damages for breach of contract and for tort?

> *Rees v Darlington Memorial Hospital NHS Trust* **[2004] 1 A.C. 309, HL**
>
> (For facts see above p.423)
>
> **Lord Scott**: ". . . 130 In applying this [*Livingstone*] principle there is often, however, a difference depending on whether the claim is a contractual one or a claim in tort. In general, where a claim is based on a breach of contract, the claimant is entitled to the benefit of the contract and entitled, therefore, to be placed in the position, so far as money can do so, in which he would have been if the contractual obligation had been properly performed. But where the claim is in tort, there being no contract to the benefit of which the claimant is entitled, the claimant is entitled to be placed in the position in which he would have been if the tortious act, the wrong, had not been committed. The difference in approach is often

important in cases where the claim is based on negligent advice or negligent misrepresentation. If the defendant was under a contractual obligation to give competent advice, the claimant is entitled to be put in the position he would have been in if competent advice had been given. But if the defendant owes no contractual obligation to the claimant and the case is brought in tort, the claimant must be put in the position he would have been in if no advice had been given at all. . . ."

NOTE

The measure of damages can be generally expressed in terms of protected interests. In contract there are normally three possible interests that will determine the basis of the compensation, depending on what the claimant can prove: (1) *expectation* interest; (2) *reliance* interest; or (3) *restitution* interest (see C&MC, pp.522–523). In tort the interest normally protected is one that might be termed the *restoration* interest. Sometimes, however, tort might protect the restitution interest (see, e.g. *Inverugie Investments Ltd v Hackett* (1995), p.26). Each of these general interests can in turn be sub-divided into particular interests (health, financial, reputation etc.).

QUESTION

What if the misrepresentation is fraudulent: is the victim better off suing in contract or in tort?

11.2.2 Damage, damages and interests

The basic principle is thus to translate 'damage' into 'damages'. However it has to be appreciated that the two are not synonymous; there are certain types of damage which the law will not compensate (see, e.g. *Best v Samuel Fox*, p.164). One key concept for translating damage into damages is, as we have just seen, that of an 'interest'. The harm suffered by a claimant is split into various heads of damage or particular interests; some of these interests—for example pure financial loss in some negligence cases—might be disregarded and this is why damage and damages are not symmetrical.

Christian von Bar, *The Common European Law of Torts*, (OUP, 2000), Vol.2, pp.4, 6–7 (footnotes omitted)

"1 The law of delict [tort] can only operate as an effective, sensible and fair system of compensation if excessive liability is avoided. It is important to prevent it from becoming a disruptive factor in an economic sense. No law based on rational principles can impose damages on each and every act of carelessness. . . .

3 We must therefore start by looking carefully at the term 'damage', the centrepiece of all delict law. European codifications have rarely attempted a detailed legal definition, whether general or particular, ie from a delict point of view. In English law damage is even defined separately for each tort. Here, damage as a general term represents the detriment the duty of care was intended to avoid. Damages, on the other hand, are the sum which the tortfeasor must pay to the injured party. Special damages (ie expenses incurred which can be, and

therefore have to be, proven) and general damages (the amount of which is determined by the judge) are distinguished. . . . Not everything considered as harm or loss by the individual, not even everything an impartial by-stander would qualify as harm or loss, merits compensation, even if negligently inflicted on another. . . . Therefore, someone who used to enjoy watching a specific type of bird which has stopped coming to the area due to environmental changes undeniably suffers considerable detriment. That this loss does not qualify as damage is undisputed in all European legal systems. . . ."

QUESTION

Is a system of law which gives much higher damages for the invasion of reputation than for serious personal injury one based on rational principles? (cf. *John v MGN Ltd*, below p.456.)

NOTE

The idea that damage is defined separately for each tort indicates, from a remedies position, how English tort law is concerned with protecting particular interests. This is why the notion of an 'interest' is so central to tort law. As the next extract shows, it brings together the various aspects of law, that is to say persons (legal subjects), things (assets) and actions (causes of action and remedies). One might note that French lawyers do not talk of *les dommages* (damages) but *les dommages-intérêts*.

Peter Cane, *Tort Law and Economic Interests*, 2nd edn (Oxford: OUP, 1996), pp.3–5 (footnotes omitted)

". . .[I]t is worth noting some nuances in the use of the word 'interest'. When we speak of someone having, for instance, a 'property interest', we mean that the person has some sort of claim over or right in some tangible or intangible thing; and when we speak of someone having a 'contractual interest' we mean that the person has some claim or right by reason of a contract. In such instances the word 'interest' is more or less synonymous with the word 'right' or 'claim'. . . . On the other hand, we often speak of a person's interests or of the public interest in a broader sense to mean simply objectives or states of affairs which are, or would be, to the person's or the public's advantage: for example, the public interest in the due administration of justice . . . While it is clear that both types of interest may be 'legal' in the sense of 'recognized and protected by law', interests of the former type are, on the whole, better protected than those of the latter type, at least in the sense that interests of the former type often constitute legal 'swords', whereas those of the latter type are often only effective as 'shields'. . . ."

NOTE

One should note Cane's distinction between the different meanings of 'interest'. Sometimes it is a *normative* (an 'ought') term almost interchangeable with the word 'right'; sometimes it is descriptive. In the law of damages it is descriptive in as much as it is used to divide up factual damage into different types (physical injury, mental injury, economic loss); yet it can be manipulated in the hands of some judges to have something of an 'ought' (normative) flavour ("the plaintiff has an interest that ought to be protected. . .").

Tony Weir, *A Casebook on Tort*, 10th edn (London: Sweet & Maxwell, 2004), p.6

"There are several good things in life, such as liberty, bodily integrity, land, possessions, reputation, wealth, privacy, dignity, perhaps even life itself. Lawyers call these goods 'interests'. These interests are all good, but they are not all *equally* good. This is evident when they come into conflict (one may jettison cargo to save passengers, but not vice versa, and one may detain a thing, but not a person, as security for a debt). Because these interests are not equally good, the protection afforded to them by the law is not equal: the law protects the better interests better: murder and rape are, after all, more serious crimes than theft. Accordingly, the better the interest invaded, the more readily does the law give compensation for the ensuing harm. In other words, whether you get the money you claim depends on what you are claiming it for. It would be surprising if it were otherwise."

NOTE

The law can give expression to the existence or non-existence of an interest in two ways. First, it can grant a cause of action directly to protect the interest in question; equally the absence of a cause of action suggests that the interest is not one that is to be fully protected. Secondly, it can give expression through the law of remedies. Certain types of mental distress may not give rise to a direct cause of action, but the distress may attract damages if the victim is able to establish liability through say negligence or breach of contract (see *Jackson v Horizon Holidays* (1975), C&MC, p.396 for an interesting case where a third party's interest was protected via the law of damages).

Geoffrey Samuel, 'The Notion of an Interest as a Formal Concept in English and in Comparative Law,' in Guy Canivet, Mads Andenas & Duncan Fairgrieve eds, *Comparative Law Before the Courts*, British Institute of International & Comparative Law, 2004, pp.263, 289 (footnotes omitted)

"[The] Roman contribution to the law of damages was of immense importance for two reasons. First, it provided a 'scientific' means of assessing compensation: damages would be payable only if an interest could be identified and valued. 'Interest', in other words, was the means by which one could link descriptive categories of harm to normative principles of what a defendant ought to pay. Secondly, it provided a means of giving concrete expression to intangible 'goods', such as loss of an expected profit, or intangible 'harms', such as depreciation of a collective group of objects through the destruction of a single item. 'Interest' in this sense became a form of property, an intangible thing (*res incorporalis*) that in turn endowed the whole idea of an obligation with its proprietary character. These ideas in turn helped transform the law of delict (tort) from a quasi-criminal law of actions, where a person who had caused harm paid a fine or penalty, to a law of actions founded on a relationship between two individuals where the idea was to re-establish harmony between two patrimonies. The development of the notion of an 'interest', in short, was virtually synonymous with the development of a sophisticated private law. . . ."

QUESTION

Does not the reduction of 'harms' and 'invasions' to 'interests' suggest that everything in the end has an economic value? Can interests such as liberty or privacy be traded?

11.2.3 **Non-compensatory damages**

Damages can also be non-compensatory. There are three categories: (i) exemplary damages which are awarded to punish a defendant; (ii) restitutionary damages which are awarded, not to compensate the claimant, but to deprive a defendant of an unjust profit (although exemplary damages may also be used to deprive a defendant of a profit as the next extract indicates); and (iii) nominal damages which are awarded in situations where either the claimant has suffered no recognisable damage or the court is of the view that the claimant merits such an award.

Rookes v Barnard **[1964] A.C. 1129, HL**

(For facts see p.102)

Lord Devlin: ". . . The first category [for an award of exemplary damages] is oppressive, arbitrary or unconstitutional action by servants of the government. I should not extend this category . . . Where one man is more powerful than another . . . he is not to be punished simply because he is the more powerful. In the case of the government it is different, for the servants of the government are also servants of the people and the use of their power must always be subordinate to their duty of service . . . Cases in the second category are those in which the defendant's conduct has been calculated by him to make a profit for himself which may well exceed the compensation payable to the plaintiff . . . Exemplary damages can properly be awarded whenever it is necessary to teach a wrongdoer that tort does not pay."

NOTE

The role of exemplary damages has been given further consideration by the House of Lords in a more recent case.

Kuddus v Chief Constable of Leicestershire **[2002] 2 A.C. 122, HL**

Lord Slynn: ". . . 2. The relevant pleaded facts are short. The appellant plaintiff told a police constable that he had come back to his flat where a friend had been staying to find that a lot of property was missing. The officer said that the matter would be investigated but some two months later he forged the plaintiff's signature on a written statement withdrawing the complaint of theft. Accordingly the police investigation ceased.

3. The defendant Chief Constable admits the forgery and that the officer's conduct amounts to misfeasance in a public office. He successfully contended, however, that exemplary damages are not recoverable for the tort of misfeasance by a public officer so that that part of the claim should be struck out. He accepts that there is a viable claim for aggravated damages for such misfeasance. . . .

27. So on the present appeal the question is whether the exemplary damages claimed are on the basis of facts which if established fall within the first category. For the purpose of the strike-out application, it is accepted that they do so fall. The claim is not excluded because it is not shown that a case on the basis of misfeasance in a public office had been decided before 1964. I would therefore allow the appeal. The claim for exemplary damages should

not have been struck out on the basis argued before the House. The question whether in principle the Chief Constable can be vicariously liable has not been argued and I do not think it right to discuss or to rule on it in this case."

Lord Nicholls: ". . . **50.** Exemplary damages are a controversial topic, and have been so for many years. Over-simplified, the matter may be summarised thus. Awards of damages are primarily intended to compensate for loss, whether pecuniary or non-pecuniary. Non-pecuniary loss includes mental distress arising from the circumstances in which the tort was committed, such as justified feelings of outrage at the defendant's conduct. Damages awarded for this type of loss are sometimes called aggravated damages, as the defendant's conduct aggravates the injury done. Sometimes damages may also be measured by reference, not to the plaintiff's loss, but to the profit obtained by the defendant from his wrongdoing: see the discussion in *Attorney General v Blake* [2001] 1 AC 268, 278–280.

51. Exemplary damages or punitive damages, the terms are synonymous, stand apart from awards of compensatory damages. They are additional to an award which is intended to compensate a plaintiff fully for the loss he has suffered, both pecuniary and non-pecuniary. They are intended to punish and deter. . . .

66. In *Rookes v Barnard* [1964] AC 1129, 1226 , Lord Devlin drew a distinction between oppressive acts by government officials and similar acts by companies or individuals. He considered that exemplary damages should not be available in the case of non-governmental oppression or bullying. Whatever may have been the position 40 years ago, I am respectfully inclined to doubt the soundness of this distinction today. National and international companies can exercise enormous power. So do some individuals. I am not sure it would be right to draw a hard-and-fast line which would always exclude such companies and persons from the reach of exemplary damages. Indeed, the validity of the dividing line drawn by Lord Devlin when formulating his first category is somewhat undermined by his second category, where the defendants are not confined to, and normally would not be, government officials or the like.

67. Nor, I may add, am I wholly persuaded by Lord Devlin's formulation of his second category (wrongful conduct expected to yield a benefit in excess of any compensatory award likely to be made). The law of unjust enrichment has developed apace in recent years. In so far as there may be a need to go further, the key here would seem to be the same as that already discussed: outrageous conduct on the part of the defendant. There is no obvious reason why, if exemplary damages are to be available, the profit motive should suffice but a malicious motive should not. . . ."

Lord Hutton: ". . . **79.** In my opinion the power to award exemplary damages in such cases serves to uphold and vindicate the rule of law because it makes clear that the courts will not tolerate such conduct. It serves to deter such actions in future as such awards will bring home to officers in command of individual units that discipline must be maintained at all times. In my respectful opinion the view is not fanciful, as my noble and learned friend Lord Scott of Foscote suggests, that such awards have a deterrent effect and such an effect is recognised by Professor Atiyah in the passage from his work on *Vicarious Liability* cited by Lord Scott of Foscote in his speech. Moreover in some circumstances where one of a group of soldiers or police officers commits some outrageous act in the course of a confused and violent confrontation it may be very difficult to identify the individual wrongdoer so that criminal proceedings may be brought against him to punish and deter such conduct, whereas an award of exemplary damages to mark the court's condemnation of the conduct can be made against the Minister of Defence or the Chief Constable under the principle of vicarious liability even if the individual at fault cannot be identified. . . ."

Lord Scott: ". . . **110**. Whatever may have been the position in 1964, when *Rookes v Barnard* [1964] AC 1129 was decided, or in 1972, when *Broome v Cassell & Co Ltd* [1972] AC 1027 was decided, there is, in my opinion, no longer any need for punitive damages in the civil law,. . .

122. Faced with the unattractive alternatives of leaving the cause of action test in place or removing it, I would, for my part, favour a pragmatic solution under which, on the one hand, the cause of action test were removed but, on the other, exemplary damages were declared to be unavailable in cases of negligence, nuisance and strict liability, and also liability for breach of statutory duty except where the statute in question had expressly authorised the remedy. In this way the main objections to the cause of action test would be met and tedious research into pre-1964 case law would be avoided but existing authority as to cases where exemplary damages cannot be claimed would be left broadly unaltered. It will be noticed that I have not included deceit among the nominate torts where, on authority, exemplary damages cannot be claimed. This is because if, which I regret, exemplary damages are to be retained and reformed, rather than abolished, deceit practised by a government or local authority official, or by a police officer, on a citizen ought, it seems to me, to be allowed in a suitable case to attract them. . . ."

[Appeal allowed.]

NOTE

Exemplary damages must be distinguished from aggravated damages: the latter are compensatory while the former are not.

QUESTIONS

1. Does the existence of exemplary damages mean that the separation between tort and criminal law is not yet complete?

2. Should exemplary damages be considered as one means of giving expression to constitutional rights? (cf. *Watkins v Home Office* (2006), above p.125.)

11.3 Damages (2): personal injury

As we have seen that physical health and bodily wholeness is an interest protected by the law of tort. Indeed, statistically, it is the most important interest since the great majority of tort claims are for personal injuries. The *summa divisio* within this broad interest is between the non-economic and economic (sub) interests associated with personal injury. (Note that in a number of the case extracts that follow in this section the facts are not given since they are not considered relevant to the subject matter of the judicial observation extracted.)

11.3.1 General introduction to personal injury damages

The general principle with respect to personal injury damages is given expression in the following code extract.

> **European Group on Tort Law, *Principles of European Tort Law* (2003)**
>
> "**Art. 10:202. Personal injury and death**
>
> (1) In the case of personal injury, which includes injury to bodily health and to mental health amounting to a recognized illness, pecuniary damage includes loss of income, impairment of earning capacity (even if unaccompanied by any loss of income) and reasonable expenses, including the cost of medical care.
> (2) In the case of death, persons such as family members whom the deceased maintained or would have maintained if death had not occurred are treated as having suffered recoverable damage to the extent of loss of that support.
>
> **Art. 10:301. Non-pecuniary damage**
>
> (1) Considering the scope of its protection (Art 2:102), the violation of an interest may justify compensation of non-pecuniary damage. This is the case in particular where the victim has suffered personal injury; or injury to his liberty, or other personality rights. Non-pecuniary damage can also be recovered by persons having a close relationship with a victim suffering a fatal or very serious non-fatal injury.
> (2) In general, in the assessment of such damages, all circumstances of the case, including the gravity, duration and consequences of the grievance, have to be taken into account. The degree of the tortfeasor's fault is to be taken into account only where it significantly contributes to the grievance of the victim.
> (3) In cases of personal injury, non-pecuniary damage corresponds to the suffering of the victim and the impairment of his bodily or mental health. In assessing damages (including damages for persons having a close relationship to deceased or seriously injured victims) similar sums should be awarded for objectively similar losses."

NOTE

The above European code provisions do not necessarily reflect with complete accuracy the present state of English law since damages for personal injury is a technical and complex topic. Yet this complexity makes it important to try to keep in mind the general principles that operate in this area together with an overview of the main interests protected. The next extract thus considers the broad approach to be adopted by the English courts.

433

Wright v British Railways Board **[1983] 2 A.C. 773, HL**

Lord Diplock: ". . . My Lords, claims for damages in respect of personal injuries constitute a high proportion of civil actions that are started in the courts in this country. If all of them proceeded to trial the administration of civil justice would break down; what prevents this is that a high proportion of them are settled before they reach the expensive and time-consuming stage of trial, and an even higher proportion of claims, particularly the less serious ones, are settled before the stage is reached of issuing and serving a writ. This is only possible if there is some reasonable degree of predictability about the sum of money that would be likely to be recovered if the action proceeded to trial.

The principal characteristics of actions for personal injuries that militate against predictability as to the sum recoverable are, first, that the English legal system requires that any judgment for tort damages, not being a continuing tort, shall be for one lump sum to compensate for all loss sustained by the plaintiff in consequence of the defendant's tortious act whether such loss be economic or non-economic, and whether it has been sustained during the period prior to the judgment or is expected to be sustained thereafter. The second characteristic is that non-economic loss constitutes a major item in the damages. Such loss is not susceptible of measurement in money. Any figure at which the assessor of damages arrives cannot be other than artificial and, if the aim is that justice metered out to all litigants should be even-handed instead of depending on idiosyncrasies of the assessor, whether jury or judge, the figure must be 'basically a conventional figure derived from experience and from awards in comparable cases'. . . .

As regards assessment of damages for non-economic loss in personal injury cases, the Court of Appeal creates the guidelines as to the appropriate conventional figure by increasing or reducing awards of damages made by judges in individual cases for various common kinds of injuries. Thus so-called 'brackets' are established broad enough to make allowance for circumstances which make the deprivation suffered by an individual plaintiff in consequence of the particular kind of injury greater or less than in the general run of cases, yet clear enough to reduce the unpredictability of what is likely to be the most important factor in arriving at settlement of claims . . ."

NOTES

1. The principle of a lump-sum award is now being increasingly modified by statute: see Damages Act 1996 s.2. This section allows a court in a personal injury action to award damages in the form of periodical payments, but the consent of the parties is required. It is likely that future legislation will remove this consent requirement.

2. English law approaches personal injury damages by reducing the damage to a number of categories. The *summa divisio* is between (i) pecuniary and (ii) non-pecuniary loss. Pecuniary loss is sub-divided into (a) expenses incurred in restoring the plaintiff back to a normal life or at least as normal as possible; (b) actual loss of earnings; and (c) loss of future earnings or earning capacity. Non-pecuniary loss is sub-divided into (a) pain and suffering and (b) loss of amenities. The pain and suffering (mental distress) applies to the victim and not the dependants, but one exception is to be found in the Fatal Accidents Act 1976 s.1A (p.416). There are some other categories that are of importance: in particular the problems caused by (a) collateral benefits and (b) death of the victim.

11.3.2 **Pecuniary loss**

Pecuniary damage can be defined as follows.

European Group on Tort Law, *Principles of European Tort Law* **(2003)**

"Art. 10:201. Nature and determination of pecuniary damage
Recoverable pecuniary damage is a diminution of the victim's patrimony caused by the damaging event. Such damage is generally determined as concretely as possible but it may be determined abstractly when appropriate, for example by reference to a market value."

QUESTION

Does English law employ the concept of 'patrimony'?

NOTE

The principle in art.10:201 may seem clear enough, but translating it into practice is another matter, as Lord Steyn has indicated.

Wells v Wells **[1999] 1 A.C. 345, HL**

This case involved several actions for damages for severe personal injuries where liability was admitted. The question to be decided was the rate of return on investment of damages. The House of Lords (Lords Lloyd, Steyn, Hope, Clyde and Hutton) held that an injured claimant was not in the same position as an ordinary prudent investor and was entitled to a greater security in respect of the damages sum to be invested. This security could be achieved through investment in index-linked government securities which the then current discount rate was 3 per cent.

Lord Steyn: ". . . The premise of the debate was that as a matter of law a victim of a tort is entitled to be compensated as nearly as possible in full for all pecuniary losses. For present purposes this mainly means compensation for loss of earnings and medical care, both past and future. Subject to the obvious qualification that perfection in the assessment of future compensation is unattainable, the 100 per cent. principle is well established and based on high authority: *Livingstone v. Rawyards Coal Co.* (1880) 5 App.Cas. 25, 39; *Lim Poh Choo v. Camden and Islington Area Health Authority* [1980] AC 175, at 187E, *per* Lord Scarman. The technique employed to achieve this result is to provide an annuity of an annual amount equivalent to the streams of future losses of earnings and cost of future expenses: *Hodgson v. Trapp* [1989] AC 807, *per* Lord Oliver of Aylmerton, at 826D-E.

It must not be assumed that the 100 per cent. principle is self evidently the only sensible compensation system. Judges have to a limited extent tried to control the size of awards for pecuniary losses in personal injury cases. Thus judges have in practice imposed a limit of 18 years in fixing a multiplier and, having done their sums in the context of the facts of a case, they have resorted to the so-called judicial discount for uncertainties. The first tendency is illustrated by *McIlgrew v. Devon County Council* [1995] PIQR 66, at 74, *per* Sir John May, and the second by the judicial discount applied in the case of Thomas. Moreover, the 100 per cent. principle has been criticised by commentators, notably in *Atiyah's Accidents, Compensation and the Law*, 5th ed. (1993) edited by Peter Cane, 1993. About the hundred per cent. principle Professor Atiyah states (at 131):

'. . .most other compensation systems, especially social security systems (and in other countries, worker's compensation laws) generally reject the 100 per cent. principle. Our own social security system generally pays benefits well below the full amount of lost earnings. Similarly, the New Zealand Accident Compensation Act provides for benefits of 80 per cent. of lost earnings; and the Australian Committee of Inquiry recommended benefits equal to 85 per cent. of lost earnings. Moreover, in most compensation systems there are minimum loss qualifications. Thus, no social security benefits are payable in this country for the first three days' loss of earnings; no criminal injuries compensation benefits are payable if the compensation would amount to less than £1,000, and so on.'

Clearly, such arguments are stronger in the case of loss of future earnings than in respect of the cost of future medical care. Rhetorically, Professor Atiyah asks 'why should different accident victims be compensated for the same injury on a scale which varies according to their previous level of earnings?' and 'if . . . two people are killed in similar accidents, what justification is there for compensating their dependants at different rates?': at pp. 127–129. The author gives two main reasons for rejecting the 100 per cent. principle. The first is the cost involved. The second is that it reduces the victim's incentive to return to work. The second consideration is not relevant to the appellants in the present appeals but may arguably be relevant in other personal injury cases. Not only do these arguments contemplate a radical departure from established principle, but controversial issues regarding resources and social policy would be at stake. Such policy arguments are a matter for Parliament and not the judiciary. . . .

Lord Clyde: ". . . In order to calculate the appropriate capital sum which will secure such an annuity one has to ascertain the appropriate rate of return which is appropriate for such a notional annuity. That depends upon the choice of investment to be adopted. Here one can only look to the markets for a solution. Between the rival suggestions put forward in the present appeals, namely investment in equities or investment in index-linked government stocks, it seems to me plain that the latter are the preferred choice. The problem which has been of concern in past years of meeting the risk of inflation, a problem which cannot reasonably be wholly disregarded for the future, is substantially met by the nature of an index-linked investment. . . . It was suggested that the present issues of index-linked government stock could not cover all the various periods which might be required in different cases. But the shortfall on an early maturity could reasonably be supposed to be covered by a cash investment from the remaining proceeds of the notional investment and in any event it may well be that future issues of index-linked stock will be made so that a greater variety of periods can be covered more precisely. . . ."

NOTES

1. The discount rate is now set by statutory instrument: see Damages Act 1996 s.1. The lower the discount rate, the higher the damages: See Weir, *Introduction to Tort Law* 2nd edn (OUP, 2006), p.211.

2. Calculating the future loss of earnings is not the only difficulty facing the courts. A severely injured claimant may well have to rely upon family members or friends.

Hunt v Severs **[1994] 2 A.C. 350, HL**

This was an action for damages by a pillion passenger against the driver of the motorcycle for severe personal injury arising out of the driver's negligence. The passenger claimed damages for the caring services rendered to her by the defendant driver who, after the accident, married the claimant. The House of Lords (Lords Keith, Bridge, Jauncey, Browne-Wilkinson and Nolan) held that, although damages could in principle be claimed by a victim for the cost of services rendered by a family member (the money to be held on trust by the victim for the carer), damages could not be claimed for a carer who was also the defendant.

Lord Bridge: "My Lords, a plaintiff who establishes a claim for damages for personal injury is entitled in English law to recover as part of those damages the reasonable value of services rendered to him gratuitously by a relative or friend in the provision of nursing care or domestic assistance of the kind rendered necessary by the injuries the plaintiff has suffered. The major issue which arises for determination in this appeal is whether the law will sustain such a claim in respect of gratuitous services in the case where the voluntary carer is the tortfeasor himself. . . .

The action was tried in April 1992 by Mr. David Latham Q.C., sitting as a deputy judge of the Queen's Bench Division [1993] PIQR Q43. He delivered judgment on 15 April 1992 awarding the plaintiff a total sum of £617,004 made up as follows:

	£
General damages for pain and suffering and loss of amenity	90,000
Special damages	90,094
Future loss	412,104
Interest on general damages	6,588
Interest on special damages	18,218
	£617,004

Included in the award of special damages was a sum of £4,429 representing the defendant's travelling expenses incurred in visiting the plaintiff while she was in hospital and a sum of £17,000 representing the value of the past services rendered by the defendant in caring for the plaintiff when she was at home. Included in the award for future loss was a sum of £60,000 representing the estimated value of the services which would be rendered by the defendant in caring for the plaintiff in future. The basis on which the judge approached the assessment of the several elements which went to make up the plaintiff's estimated future loss, subject to a number of detailed adjustments which it is unnecessary for present purposes to examine, was to apply a multiplier of 14 to the estimated future annual losses. . . . .

The law with respect to the services of a third party who provides voluntary care for a tortiously injured plaintiff has developed somewhat erratically in England. The voluntary carer has no cause of action of his own against the tortfeasor. The justice of allowing the injured plaintiff to recover the value of the services so that he may recompense the voluntary carer has been generally recognised, but there has been difficulty in articulating a consistent juridical principle to justify this result.

. . . I accept that the basis of a plaintiff's claim for damages may consist in his need for services but I cannot accept that the question from what source that need has been met is irrelevant. If an injured plaintiff is treated in hospital as a private patient he is entitled to recover the cost of that treatment. But if he receives free treatment under the National Health Service, his need has been met without cost to him and he cannot claim the cost of the treatment from the tortfeasor. So it cannot, I think, be right to say that in all cases the plaintiff's loss is 'for the purpose of damages . . . the proper and reasonable cost of supplying [his] needs.'. . .

Thus, in both England and Scotland the law now ensures that an injured plaintiff may recover the reasonable value of gratuitous services rendered to him by way of voluntary care by a member of his family. . . . I would think it appropriate for the House to take the opportunity. . . [of] adopting the view of Lord Denning M.R. in *Cunningham v Harrison* [1973] Q.B. 942 that in England the injured plaintiff who recovers damages under this head should hold them on trust for the voluntary carer.

By concentrating on the plaintiff's need and the plaintiff's loss as the basis of an award in respect of voluntary care received by the plaintiff, the reasoning in *Donnelly v Joyce* diverts attention from the award's central objective of compensating the voluntary carer. Once this is recognised it becomes evident that there can be no ground in public policy or otherwise for requiring the tortfeasor to pay to the plaintiff, in respect of the services which he himself has rendered, a sum of money which the plaintiff must then repay to him. . . .

The case for the plaintiff was argued in the Court of Appeal without reference to the circumstance that the defendant's liability was covered by insurance. But before your Lordships Mr McGregor, recognising the difficulty of formulating any principle of public policy which could justify recovery against the tortfeasor who has to pay out of his own pocket, advanced the bold proposition that such a policy could be founded on the liability of insurers to meet the claim. Exploration of the implications of this proposition in argument revealed the many difficulties which it encounters. But I do not think it necessary to examine these in detail. The short answer, in my judgment, to Mr McGregor's contention is that its acceptance would represent a novel and radical departure in the law of a kind which only the legislature may properly effect. At common law the circumstance that a defendant is contractually indemnified by a third party against a particular legal liability can have no relevance whatever to the measure of that liability. . . ."

QUESTIONS

1. It might seem perfectly logical within the two party structure (claimant–defendant) for the carer head of damages to be refused since, within this structure, the claimant would be obtaining money from the defendant which she would then have to pay back to the defendant. But the reality is that road accident claims involve three parties, the third-party being the defendant's insurance company. Ought the House of Lords to have

recognised this reality? Has Parliament recognised this reality (cf. Congenital Disabilities (Civil Liability) Act 1976 s.2, above p.418)?

2. A claimant is injured by the defendant's negligence and can no longer spend 77 hours a week looking after his disabled brother. He can only devote 35 hours of care, the rest being provided by his mother. Can the claimant sue for this loss? Can he also sue for loss of employment capacity given that he was unemployed before the accident only because he cared for his brother? (See *Lowe v Guise* (2002)).

NOTE

Hunt v Severs illustrates once again how the paradigm idea of one individual suing another (corrective justice) is an inadequate model, for it is not just the claimant victim who incurs damage; members of his or her family also suffer harm (cf. *Best v Samuel Fox*, p.164). Where the victim is killed outright as a result of a tort the family members who were dependent upon the victim have, thanks to statute, their own damages claims (Fatal Accidents Act 1976, p.416). But if the victim is not killed the family members will not have a claim, even if the victim's life is shortened. The objectives of a damages claim, where the victim is suing, thus can turn out to be wider than compensating the victim's own interests. A lump sum damages award must often reflect the interests of others. Where the victim's life is shortened as a result of the tort, the interests of the family are now given some expression in the law of damages (*Pickett v British Rail Engineering* (1980)).

11.3.3 Collateral benefits

A victim of an accident may receive money from a number of sources. He or she may have taken out private insurance or may benefit from money donated by the public or by friends or by a charity. If the victim sues a tortfeasor for compensation the question arises as to whether or not collateral benefits should be deducted from any damages awarded.

Hunt v Severs **[1994] 2 A.C. 350, HL**

(For facts see above p.437)

Lord Bridge: ". . . The starting point for any inquiry into the measure of damages which an injured plaintiff is entitled to recover is the recognition that damages in the tort of negligence are purely compensatory. He should recover from the tortfeasor no more and no less than he has lost. Difficult questions may arise when the plaintiff's injuries attract benefits from third parties. According to their nature these may or may not be taken into account as reducing the tortfeasor's liability. The two well established categories of receipt which are to be ignored in assessing damages are the fruits of insurance which the plaintiff himself has provided against the contingency causing his injuries (which may or may not lead to a claim by the insurer as subrogated to the rights of the plaintiff) and the fruits of the benevolence of third parties motivated by sympathy for the plaintiff's misfortune. The policy considerations which underlie these two apparent exceptions to the rule against double recovery are, I think, well understood; see, for example, *Parry v Cleaver* [1970] AC 1, 14, and *Hussain v New Taplow Paper Mills Ltd* [1988] AC 514, 528. But I find it difficult to see what considerations of public policy can justify a requirement that the tortfeasor himself should compensate the plaintiff twice over for the self-same loss. If the loss in question is a direct pecuniary loss (eg loss of wages), *Hussain's* case is clear authority that the defendant employer, as the tortfeasor who makes good the loss either voluntarily or contractually, thereby mitigates his liability in damages pro tanto. . . ."

QUESTIONS

1. What do you think are the public policy considerations which led to the "two well established categories" being ignored in assessing damages? (See *Parry v Cleaver* (1970)).

2. Does a victim of a tort, for measure of damages purposes, have to use the National Health Service or can the victim use private medical care? If the victim does use the NHS, can he or she nevertheless claim private medical expenses? (See Law Reform (Personal Injuries) Act 1948 s.2; Administration of Justice Act 1982 s.5.)

NOTE

A victim may be entitled to social security benefits simply as a result of his or her disability. The sums received are no longer deducted from damages but are recouped by the Secretary of State. The history of the various schemes is set out in the judgments below.

Wadey v Surrey CC [2000] 1 W.L.R. 820, HL

Lord Hope: "My Lords, these appeals, one from the Inner House of the Court of Session in Scotland and the other from the Court of Appeal, Civil Division, in England, both raise the same question. It is whether, in an action for damages for personal injuries, social security benefits received by the injured person that are disregarded in the assessment of special damages must be disregarded when interest is being calculated on those damages. All parties are agreed that this question should receive the same answer in Scotland and in England,. . .

The recovery of benefits—history

The original scheme for the recovery of social security benefits was set out in section 2(1) of the Law Reform (Personal Injuries) Act 1948. It had been recognised as a general principle by Beveridge that an injured person should not be compensated twice over for the same loss: *Social Insurance and Allied Services*, Cmnd. 6404 (1942), p. 101, para. 260. He suggested that this principle could be preserved if the claimant repaid the benefits to the Ministry when he was awarded damages or the benefits which he received were taken into account in the assessment of damages. When the Monkton Committee came to examine this issue the general principle was recognised, but there was disagreement as to how it was to be applied under the new scheme: *Departmental Committee on Alternative Remedies*, Cmnd. 6860 (1946), para. 38. The majority recommended that the general principle on which legislation should be framed was that the claimant should not recover more by way of damages and benefits than he could have recovered from either source alone: p. 18, para. 38. Two members dissented, on the view that the scheme for national insurance was very little different from private insurance so the claimant's benefits should be left out of account altogether in the assessment of damages.

Section 2(1) of the Act of 1948 appears to have been arrived at as a compromise between these two views. It provided that there was to be taken into account in the assessment of damages for any loss of earnings or profits accruing to the injured person from his injuries one half of the benefits which he had received during the period of five years beginning with the time when the cause of action accrued. But this system did not extend to the full range of welfare benefits. Only those specified in section 2(1) of the Act as amended from time to time were subject to the statutory rule that one half of the benefits received was to be offset in the calculation of damages. These were sickness benefit, invalidity benefit, non-contributory invalidity pension, severe disablement allowance, sickness benefit (formerly injury benefit) and disablement benefit. Attendance allowance and mobility allowance, family credit (formerly family income supplement), income supplement (formerly supplementary benefit), redundancy payments, reduced earnings allowance, statutory sick pay, and unemployment benefit were not subject to the statutory rule. In a series of decisions in both England and Scotland it was held that the whole of sums received in respect of benefits which were not subject to the rule must be deducted. This is in accordance with the general principle that damages are intended to be purely compensatory, and that what the court must measure is the net consequential loss and expense which has been incurred in arriving at the measure of the claimant's damages: see *Wilson v. National Coal Board*, 1981 SC (HL) 9; *Hodgson v. Trapp* [1989] 1 AC 807, 822A-823D *per* Lord Bridge of Harwich.

In the application of this scheme in assessing damages only one half of the listed benefits was regarded as compensation for the loss of income or loss of profits due to the accident. That half was taken into account in the calculation by deducting it from the loss of income or profits to arrive at the net loss. The other half was disregarded in the same way as if it had been received from charity or under a private insurance policy. Awards of interest followed the same pattern. The one half of the benefits which was taken into account in the calculation did not bear interest. As it had been deducted from the principal sum awarded as damages, it reduced by the same amount the net loss on which interest was to be payable. But the disregarded half bore interest along with the rest of the award. As Lord Sutherland said in *Wisely's* case at p. 918G, it was never suggested in Scotland that interest should not be payable on the whole of the loss of earnings so calculated even though the pursuer had received, during the relevant period, half of the benefits. In *Wadey's* case Simon Brown L.J. said at p. 1620H that *Jefford v. Gee* [1970] 2 Q.B. 130 made it plain that the plaintiff (whilst, of course, he received no interest on the moiety for which he gave credit against damages) did not have to give credit in the interest calculation in respect of his windfall receipt of the other moiety of the benefits paid.

The recommendation by Beveridge that the full amount of the benefits received by the injured person or his dependants as the result of an injury should be deducted in the assessment of damages was adopted when the whole subject of compensation for personal injury was considered by the Pearson Commission: *Royal Commission on Civil Liability and Compensation for Personal Injury*, Cmnd. 7054–1 (1978), ch. 13. It recommended that the full amount should be deducted, and this view was accepted in principle by the government: *Social Security Act 1975: Reform of the Industrial Injuries Scheme* Cmnd. 8402 (1981), ch. 8. But it was concluded that a workable scheme for the direct recovery of this amount from the injured person or his dependants would not be practicable in view of its cost and the large number of cases which were settled extrajudicially. It was not until 1989, when the Social Security Act 1989 was enacted, that a system was introduced for the recovery in full of the benefits received from the compensation paid to the injured person under a court order or an agreed settlement. . . .

The Scheme of the Act of 1997

The principal features of the scheme introduced by the Act of 1989 are reproduced in the Act of 1997. It enables the Secretary of State to recover the whole amount of any listed benefits paid to a person in consequence of any accident, injury or disease during the relevant period where that person also receives a compensation payment for that accident, injury or disease from a third party. The compensator is liable to pay to the Secretary of State the whole amount of the listed benefits received by the claimant for the relevant period. He is then entitled to deduct that amount from the compensation which he is to make to the injured party. But there are some important differences. Under the new scheme the reduction in respect of recoverable benefits is restricted to particular heads of the compensation payment, with the result that other heads—in particular damages for pain and suffering—are insulated from, or ring-fenced against, the deduction. According to a system of calculation which is set out in section 8 and Schedule 2, the only heads of compensation which are affected by it are those for loss of earnings, cost of care and loss of mobility during the relevant period against which are to be set the amount of any recoverable benefit which is attributed to those heads. There is no small payments limit under the new scheme, and a new procedure for appeals against certificates of recoverable benefit has been introduced. . . .”

Lord Clyde: “. . . The new regime was significantly different from the former scheme. Essentially while under the former scheme the wrongdoer or tortfeasor was relieved from paying the whole of the patrimonial loss, since one half of the benefits was to be set against the sum in the award, under the new scheme the Secretary of State is able to recover from the person paying the damages, referred to as the ‘compensator,’ a sum representing the benefits paid to the injured person and the compensator is then entitled to offset that sum against the amount which he is bound to pay to the injured person under the court’s order and is to that extent discharged from satisfying the order. Under the language of the Act a payment made to a person in consequence of an accident, injury or disease is a ‘compensation payment.’ By virtue of section 1(3) of the Act of 1997 voluntary payments as well as payments under a court order are included. For this purpose of the scheme the Act sets out in Schedule 2 various heads of loss which may be found within a compensation payment and a list of the particular benefits to which each head is to relate. Any of the benefits in the list which have been or are likely to be paid in respect of the accident, injury or disease, during a period defined in detail in section 3 and referred to as the ‘relevant period,’ constitutes a ‘recoverable benefit.’ In paying the person entitled to a compensation payment the compensator is entitled to offset against the heads of loss specified in Schedule 2 the recoverable benefits relative to each of those respective heads. . . .

What seems to me very evident from the new scheme is that a separation is being made between the court’s function in the assessing and awarding of damages and the quite distinct mechanism for the recovery of the recoverable benefits from the wrongdoer. The latter process is managed independently of the court. It operates after the court has made its order. It concerns particularly the time of payment to the pursuer, not the time of the making of any order or decree by the court. It affects not the terms of the order but the satisfaction of the order by the compensator. It has its own procedures for the resolution of disputes, which may involve reference to a medical appeal tribunal. Under section 14 of the Act and regulation 11 of the Social Security (Recovery of Benefits) Regulations 1997 (SI 1997 No. 2205) if it is found that the amount of the recoverable benefit has been over calculated and too much has been paid to the Secretary of State, then the balance is to be repaid by the Secretary of State to the compensator, the compensation payment is recalculated and the increase if any is paid to the person to whom the compensation payment was made. Nothing in that process touches upon the award made by the court. It is managed outwith the court processes. . . ."

QUESTION

1. If the state is entitled to recoup money paid to an injured person, why should a private insurance company not be able to do the same?

2. Is the Secretary of State's right to recover benefits a public or a private law right? Upon what principle do you think the right is based?

3. Ought the NHS to be able to recoup, from the tortfeasor, the cost of the medical services it provides to an injured claimant? What about a local authority that provides permanent care services to a seriously injured claimant?

Crofton v National Health Service Litigation Authority [2007] 1 W.L.R. 923, CA

The claimant was the victim of medical negligence and as a result suffered severe brain damage which meant that he would require lifetime care. In an action for damages for personal injury, the question arose as to whether direct payments made to the claimant by his local authority in respect of the lifetime care should be taken into account when assessing the quantum of damages. The judge held that they should and this decision was upheld by the Court of Appeal (May, Dyson and Smith L.J.J.).

Dyson L.J. (delivering the judgment of the court): ". . . **86** To summarise, the judge was right to hold that the council could and would make direct payments to meet the claimant's care needs despite the award of damages, and that these payments should be taken into account in the assessment of damages.

87 Once the judge decided that the council would make such direct payments, it seems to us that he was bound to hold that they should be taken into account in the assessment of damages. This point needs to be made because there is much to be said for the view that the tortfeasor should pay, and that the state should be relieved of the burden of funding the care of the victims of torts and that its hard-pressed resources should be concentrated on the care of those who are not the victims of torts. . . . It does not seem right, particularly where the care costs are very large, that they should be met from the public purse rather than borne by the tortfeasor.

88 Longmore LJ referred to the 'instinctive feeling that if no award for care is made at all, on the basis that it will be provided free by local authorities, the defendant and his insurers will have received an undeserved windfall'. The counter-argument is that, if the claimant does not have to give credit for benefits that he will receive from the state as a result of his personal injury, then on the law as it currently stands, he will make double recovery. To satisfy the "instinctive feeling", a change in the law would be necessary.

89 Such a change raises what is essentially a political question and, therefore, a matter for Parliament. Historically, the state provided many services to the victims of tortious accidents without charge and made no attempt to recoup the cost of those services from the tortfeasors. Recently, there has been an important change in respect of NHS hospital and ambulances services. Part 3 of the Health and Social Care (Community Health and Standards) Act 2003 (which came into force in January 2007) provides that any person who has made a compensation payment in respect of an injury to another person will be liable to pay relevant NHS charges for treatment and ambulance services provided to that person. This legislation does not affect the assessment of damages as between the claimant and the tortfeasor. We do not know whether this legislation signals a general change in the attitude of the legislature to the responsibilities of tortfeasors to pay for the costs presently imposed upon the public purse. We say only that we can see no good policy reason why the care costs in a case such as this should fall upon the public purse. We can see no good policy reason why damages which are about to be awarded specifically for the provision of care to the claimant, needed only as a result of the tort, should be reduced, thereby shifting the burden from the tortfeasor to the public purse. We recognise that the mechanism by which these ends could be achieved with justice might be complex and difficult. But, as we say, these are policy issues and are a matter for Parliament.

90 It is trite law that a claimant is entitled to recover the full extent of his loss. That involves asking what the claimant would have received but for the event which gave rise to the claim and which he can no longer get; and what he has received and will receive as a result of the event which he would not have received but for the event. The question then arises whether the latter sums must be deducted from the former in assessing the damages: *Parry v Cleaver* [1970] AC 1, 13. In *Hodgson v Trapp* [1989] AC 807, 819 Lord Bridge of Harwich said that it was "elementary" that if in consequence of the injuries he has sustained a claimant enjoys receipts to which he would not otherwise have been entitled, then prima facie those receipts are to be set against the aggregate of his loss and expenses in arriving at the measure of damages. To this basic rule there are certain well established exceptions, none of which is of application in the present case.

91 In principle, payments by third parties which a claimant would not have received but for his injuries have to be taken into account in carrying out the assessment of damages unless ggested that direct payments made by a local authority in the exercise of its statutory functions to make care arrangements under section 29 NAA and section 2 CSDPA may not in principle be taken into account. If the court is satisfied that a claimant will seek and obtain payments which will enable him to pay for some or all of the services for which he needs care, there can be no doubt that those payments must be taken into account in the assessment of his loss. Otherwise, the claimant will enjoy a double recovery. . . .

95 We would accept that there may be cases where the possibility of a claimant receiving direct payments is so uncertain that they should be disregarded altogether in the assessment of damages. It will depend on the facts of the particular case. But if the court finds that a claimant will receive direct payments for at least a certain period of time and possibly for much longer, it seems to us that this finding must be taken into account in the assessment. In such a case, the correct way to reflect the uncertainties to which Tomlinson J referred is to discount the multiplier. We did not understand Mr Taylor to contend otherwise. . . .

110 We cannot conclude this judgment without expressing our dismay at the complexity and labyrinthine nature of the relevant legislation and guidance, as well as (in some respects) its obscurity. Social security law should be clear and accessible. The tortuous analysis in the earlier part of this judgment shows that it is neither. . . ."

QUESTION

Why could the problem outlined in paragraph 88 of Dyson L.J.'s judgment not be solved by recourse to the law of restitution (unjust enrichment)? In other words, why cannot the supplier of the service to the victim sue the tortfeasor on the ground that the supplier is providing a benefit that the tortfeasor ought to be providing? (cf. *Receiver for Metropolitan Police District v Croydon Corporation* (1957)).

11.3.4 **Non-pecuniary loss**

General damages for pain and suffering and loss of amenity are, as we have seen, awarded to a victim suffering personal injury. This interest can be seen as a species of mental distress, but what if the victim is permanently unconscious?

H West & Son Ltd v Shepard [1964] A.C. 326, HL

The question that arose in this case was whether a person who had been reduced to permanent unconsciousness by the tortious act, or was otherwise unaware of his or her condition, could recover damages for loss of amenity. A majority of the House of Lords (Lords Tucker, Morris and Pearce; Lords Reid and Devlin dissenting) held that awareness of the loss was not a factor to be taken into account in awarding personal injury damages for non-pecuniary loss.

Lord Pearce: ". . . The loss of happiness of the individual plaintiffs is not, in my opinion, a practicable or correct guide to reasonable compensation in cases of personal injury to a living plaintiff. A man of fortitude is not made less happy because he loses a limb. It may alter the scope of his activities and force him to seek his happiness in other directions. The cripple by the fireside reading or talking with friends may achieve happiness as great as that which, but for the accident, he would have achieved playing golf in the fresh air of the links. To some ancient philosophers the former kind of happiness might even have seemed of a higher nature than the latter, provided that the book or the talk were such as they would approve. Some less robust persons, on the other hand, are prepared to attribute a great loss of happiness to a quite trivial event. It would be lamentable if the trial of a personal injury claim put a premium on protestations of misery and if a long face was the only safe passport

445

to a large award. Under the present practice there is no call for a parade of personal unhappiness. A plaintiff who cheerfully admits that he is happy as ever he was, may yet receive a large award as reasonable compensation for the grave injury and loss of amenity over which he has managed to triumph I venture to think that an alteration of the current principles of assessing damages for personal injury would be an embarrassment to a practice which in spite of its difficulties does in the main produce a just result. Common law courts should not lightly abandon a method of estimation that works reasonably well and achieves a certain amount of precision, for a method that is nebulous, variable and subjective. . . ."

Lord Morris: ". . . My Lords, leaving aside for the moment the question as to whether the amount is, as an amount, excessive I can see no fault in the approach of the learned judge. It is necessary to have in mind the matters for which he was awarding these general damages. Accepting the estimate as to the plaintiff's expectation of life, damages were to be given to cover a period of over seven years. At the age of 41 everything that life held for her was taken away from her. For a period of about seven years instead of having life's activities and amenities she will have mere existence but little else, save that, to the extent that I have described, she may have the torment of a realisation of her helplessness. If in some degree she has processes of thought she has the agony and frustration of being unable to convey her thoughts or to give them expression. All these matters constitute grave and sombre deprivations for which in my view she is entitled to receive substantial compensation."

Lord Reid (dissenting): ". . . To my mind there is something unreal in saying that a man who knows and feels nothing should get the same as a man who has to live with and put up with his disabilities, merely because they have sustained comparable physical injuries. It is no more possible to compensate an unconscious man than it is to compensate a dead man. The fact that the damages can give no benefit or satisfaction to the injured man and can only go to those who inherit the dead man's estate would not be a good reason for withholding damages which are legally due. But it is, in my view, a powerful argument against the view that there is no analogy between a dead man and a man who is unconscious and that a man who is unconscious ought to be treated as if he were fully conscious.

It is often said that it is scandalous that it should be cheaper to kill a man than to maim him, and that it would be monstrous if the defendant had to pay less because in addition to inflicting physical injuries he had made the plaintiff unconscious. I think that such criticism is misconceived. Damages are awarded not to punish the wrongdoer but to compensate the person injured, and a dead man cannot be compensated. Loss to his estate can be made good, and we can give some compensation to those whom he leaves behind. Perhaps we should do more for them—but not by inflating the claim of the dead man's executor, for then the money may go to undeserving distant relatives or residuary legatees or even to the Treasury if he dies intestate and without heirs. And it is already the case that it may benefit the defendant to injure the plaintiff more severely. If he is injured so severely that he can only live a year or two at most the damages will be much less than if he is less severely injured so that he may survive for many years. And that brings me to the other matter of loss of expectation of life. . . ."

Lord Devlin (dissenting): ". . . I can see no distinction, logical or otherwise, between sudden death and death preceded by a period of unconsciousness, long or short. The injury that mortifies the limbs and cuts off the faculties has in both cases the same effect on the power of enjoyment; in each case the deprivation is absolute. Death is often preceded by some period of unconsciousness. For how long must the period last in order that the victim's estate may benefit by the higher measure? For days, for weeks or for months? I find it, with respect, repugnant to common sense and to justice that if the victim dies at once the estate benefits only by a few hundreds but if the body is kept alive and inert when the mind is dead, the amount should grow and grow until it reaches a sum such as £15,000. . . ."

QUESTIONS

1. What if a victim of a tort knows that he is going to die within a year or so because of the accident for which the tortfeasor is responsible: should the victim be awarded damages for this knowledge? If so, should he be awarded damages for the foreshortening of his life even if he does not know it has been foreshortened?

2. A victim is reduced to a living vegetable as a result of the defendant's negligence and a judge in the family division decides that it is in the victim's 'best interests' that the hospital no longer artificially keeps the victim alive (*Airedale NHS Trust v Bland* (1993)). What are the implications for the law of damages?

3. The Law Commission has recommended that the amount awarded for pain and suffering should be increased. Can Parliament only implement this recommendation or can the judges do it?

Heil v Rankin **[2001] Q.B. 272, CA**

These were actions for damages in which the claimants disputed the awards made for pain and suffering and loss of amenity. The Law Commission in its *Report on Damages for personal Injury: Non-Pecuniary Loss* (1999, Law Com No 257) had recommended substantial increases in the damages to be awarded under these non-pecuniary heads. The Court of Appeal (Lord Woolf M.R. and Beldam L.J., Otton L.J., May L.J. and Nelson J.) held that the awards should be increased in the case of awards currently above £10,000 but not to the levels recommended by the Law Commission.

Lord Woolf M.R. (delivering judgment of the Court): ". . . **1.** In June 1995 the then Lord Chancellor announced the Law Commission's ('Commission') sixth programme of law reform. The programme included an examination of: 'the principles governing and the effectiveness of the present remedy for damages for monetary and non-monetary loss, with particular regard to personal injury litigation'. A matter for specific consideration was 'the award of damages for pain and suffering and other forms of non-pecuniary loss'.

2. In January 1996 the Commission published a Consultation Paper (No. 140) Damages for Personal Injury: Non-Pecuniary Loss. This was followed by the publication of the Commission Report (No. 257) which was ordered by the House of Commons to be printed on 19 April 1999. Included among the recommendations was a recommendation that the level of damages for non-pecuniary loss for personal injuries should be increased. The recommendation was set out in the Summary of Recommendations contained in the report in the following terms:

'(1) Damages for non-pecuniary loss for serious personal injury should be increased. We recommend that:

(1) in respect of injuries for which the current award for non-pecuniary loss for the injury alone would be more than £3,000, damages for non-pecuniary loss (that is for pain and suffering and loss of amenity) should be increased by a factor of at least 1.5, but by not more than a factor of 2;

(2) in respect of injuries for which the current award for non-pecuniary loss for the injury alone would be in the range £2,001 to £3,000, damages for non-pecuniary loss (that is for pain and suffering and loss of amenity) should be increased by a series of tapered increases of less than a factor of 1.5 (so that, for example, an award now of £2,500 should be uplifted by around 25 per cent).

(3) Finally, if the increases recommended by us are not implemented until over a year after publication of this report, the recommended increases should be adjusted to take into account any change in the value of money since the publication of this report. (paragraphs 3.40 and 3.110)'

. . .

48. In summary, our conclusion is. . . that it is appropriate for the Court to consider the Commission's recommendation. What is involved is part of the traditional role of the courts. It is a role in which juries previously were involved. Now it is the established role of the judiciary. It is a role which, as a result of their accumulated experience, the judiciary is well qualified to perform. Parliament can still intervene. It has, however, shown no inclination that it intends to do so. If it should decide to do so then the fact that the courts have already considered the question will be of assistance to Parliament. Until Parliament does so, the courts cannot avoid their responsibility. While a public debate on this subject would no doubt be salutary, the contribution which it could make to the actual decision of the Court is limited. The Court has the report of the Commission. It also has the other material which the parties have placed before it. It is in as good a position as it is likely to be to make a decision in the context of the present appeals. We see no reason to accede to Mr Havers' submission that we should postpone doing so. To postpone would be to neglect our responsibility to provide certainty in this area as soon as it is practical to do so. . . ."

QUESTION

1. Is this case an example of judicial activism?

2. Is the Law Commission now a source of English law?

11.3.5 Damages arising out of death

Where the victim is killed as a result of the tort, two potential claimants can sue. There is the estate of the victim which survives as a legal subject thanks to legislation (see above p.415) and there are the dependants.

Fatal Accidents Act 1976 (c.30)

"**3 Assessment of damages**

(1) In the action such damages, other than damages for bereavement, may be awarded as are proportioned to the injury resulting from the death to the dependants respectively.

(2) After deducting the costs not recovered from the defendant any amount recovered otherwise than as damages for bereavement shall be divided among the dependants in such shares as may be directed.

(3) In an action under this Act where there fall to be assessed damages payable to a widow in respect of the death of her husband there shall not be taken account the re-marriage of the widow or her prospects of re-marriage.

(4) In an action under this Act where there fall to be assessed damages payable to a person who is a dependant by virtue of section 1(3)(*b*) above in respect of the death of the person with whom the dependant was living as husband or wife or civil partner there shall be taken into account (together with any other matter that appears to the court to be relevant to the action) the fact that the dependant had no enforceable right to financial support by the deceased as a result of their living together.

(5) If the dependants have incurred funeral expenses in respect of the deceased, damages may be awarded in respect of those expenses. . . .

4   Assessment of damages: disregarded benefits

In assessing damages in respect of a person's death in an action under this Act, benefits which have accrued or will or may accrue to any person from his estate or otherwise as a result of his death shall be disregarded."

QUESTION

What is the policy consideration behind s.3(3)?

NOTE

In *H v S* (2003) Kennedy L.J. said (at § 29) "In my judgment, in the light of the authorities, the position is reasonably clear. Where, as here, infant children are living with and are dependant on one parent, with no support being provided by the other parent, in circumstances where the provision of such support in the future seems unlikely, and the parent with whom they are living is killed, in circumstances giving rise to liability under the Fatal Accidents Act 1976, after which the other parent (who is not the tortfeasor) houses and takes responsibility for the children, the support which they enjoy after the accident is a benefit which has accrued as a result of the death and, pursuant to section 4 of the 1976 Act, it must be disregarded, both in the assessment of loss and in the calculation of damages".

11.4 Damages (3): non-personal injury damage

It might be thought that calculating damages for damage other than personal injury harm would be relatively straightforward. Sometimes it can be, but there are many situations where the

449

calculation can prove extremely difficult and sometimes controversial. Damages for intangible harm to reputation is one obvious example. Yet even physical damage to property can prove difficult when the thing damaged is, for instance, a profit-earning chattel. Physical damage is not the only type of interference with another person's thing; wrongful use and complete deprivation are other forms of harm.

11.4.1 **Property damage**

The economic consequences of damage to property can prove difficult in a range of situations.

Lagden v O'Connor **[2003] 1 A.C. 1067, HL**

This was an action for damages by the owner of a car damaged by the negligence of the defendant. The unemployed claimant was unable to afford to hire a replacement car while his was off the road and so he signed an agreement with a credit company whereby it provided the claimant with a car, at no cost to him personally, recouping the money from the defendant's insurance company. Such a car hire arrangement was more expensive than if the claimant had been able to hire a car himself from a hire company. The defendant admitted liability but disputed the cost of the credit company charges. The trial judge and the Court of Appeal held that the impecunious claimant was entitled to damages for the credit hire package since he had no other option; an appeal to the House of Lords (Lords Nicholls, Slynn and Hope; Lords Scott and Walker dissenting) was dismissed.

Lord Nicholls: ". . . 6 My Lords, the law would be seriously defective if in this type of case the innocent motorist were, in practice, unable to obtain the use of a replacement car. The law does not assess damages payable to an innocent plaintiff on the basis that he is expected to perform the impossible. The common law prides itself on being sensible and reasonable. It has regard to practical realities. As Lord Reid said in *Cartledge v E Jopling & Sons Ltd* [1963] AC 758, 772, the common law ought never to produce a wholly unreasonable result. Here, as elsewhere, a negligent driver must take his victim as he finds him. Common fairness requires that if an innocent plaintiff cannot afford to pay car hire charges, so that left to himself he would be unable to obtain a replacement car to meet the need created by the negligent driver, then the damages payable under this head of loss should include the reasonable costs of a credit hire company. Credit hire companies provide a reasonable means whereby innocent motorists may obtain use of a replacement vehicle when otherwise they would be unable to do so. Unless the recoverable damages in such a case include the reasonable costs of a credit hire company the negligent driver's insurers will be able to shuffle away from their insured's responsibility to pay the cost of providing a replacement car. A financially well placed plaintiff will be able to hire a replacement car, and in the fullness of time obtain reimbursement from the negligent driver's insurers, but an impecunious plaintiff will not. This cannot be an acceptable result.

7 The conclusion I have stated does not mean that, if impecunious, an innocent motorist can recover damages beyond losses for which he is properly compensatable. What it means is that in measuring the loss suffered by an impecunious plaintiff by loss of use of his own car the law will recognise that, because of his lack of financial means, the timely provision of a replacement vehicle for him costs more than it does in the case of his more affluent neighbour. In the case of the impecunious plaintiff someone has to provide him with credit, by incurring the expense of providing a car without receiving immediate payment, and then incur the administrative expense involved in pursuing the defendant's insurers for payment.

8 In your Lordships' House the appellant sought to derive assistance from *Owners of Liesbosch Dredger v Owners of SS Edison (The Liesbosch)* [1933] AC 449 and Lord Wright's much discussed observations, at pp 460–461, regarding not taking into account a claimant's want of means when assessing the amount of his loss. For the reasons given by my noble and learned friends, Lord Hope of Craighead and Lord Walker of Gestingthorpe, these observations, despite the eminence of their source, can no longer be regarded as authoritative. They must now be regarded as overtaken by subsequent developments in the law.

9 There remains the difficult point of what is meant by 'impecunious' in the context of the present type of case. Lack of financial means is, almost always, a question of priorities. In the present context what it signifies is inability to pay car hire charges without making sacrifices the plaintiff could not reasonably be expected to make. I am fully conscious of the open-ended nature of this test. But fears that this will lead to increased litigation in small claims courts seem to me exaggerated. It is in the interests of all concerned to avoid litigation with its attendant costs and delay. Motor insurers and credit hire companies should be able to agree on standard enquiries, or some other means, which in practice can most readily give effect to this test of impecuniosity. I would dismiss this appeal."

Lord Hope: ". . . **32** In *Harbutt's "Plasticine" Ltd v Wayne Tank and Pump Co Ltd* [1970] 1 QB 447 the plaintiffs' factory, which was in an old mill, was destroyed by fire as a result of defects in the design of equipment supplied by the defendants and its having been switched on and the plant left unattended. A new factory had to be built. The plaintiffs had no other option if they were to continue their business of making plasticine. They were not allowed to rebuild the old mill, so they had to put up a new factory. A question was raised as to the measure of damages. The defendants said that it should be limited to the difference in the value of the old mill before and after the fire and that the plaintiffs should not be allowed the cost of replacing it with a new building. This argument was rejected. . . .

34 Of course, the facts in these two cases were quite different from those in this case. But I think that the principles on which they were decided are of general application, and it is possible to extract this guidance from them. It is for the defendant who seeks a deduction from expenditure in mitigation on the ground of betterment to make out his case for doing so. It is not enough that an element of betterment can be identified. It has to be shown that the claimant had a choice, and that he would have been able to mitigate his loss at less cost. The wrongdoer is not entitled to demand of the injured party that he incur a loss, bear a burden or make unreasonable sacrifices in the mitigation of his damages. He is entitled to demand that, where there are choices to be made, the least expensive route which will achieve mitigation must be selected. So if the evidence shows that the claimant had a choice, and that the route to mitigation which he chose was more costly than an alternative that was open to him, then a case will have been made out for a deduction. But if it shows that the claimant had no other choice available to him, the betterment must be seen as incidental to

> the step which he was entitled to take in the mitigation of his loss and there will be no ground for it to be deducted. . . ."

NOTES AND QUESTIONS

1. Is the *Liesbosch* (1933) (read in the law report) still of any relevance to the law of damages?

2. Is this case an example of the application of the principle that a tortfeasor must take his victim as he finds him?

3. Certain heads of damage (e.g. loss of profit) can sometimes be refused on the ground of remoteness (see e.g. *Spartan Steel* (1973), p.159) or mitigation (see *Darbishire v Warran* (1963), p.410) or indeed causation (*The Liesbosch* (1933)). Does *Lagden* fall under one of these grounds or is it based on some independent principle?

4. In *Spartan Steel* (1973) (see p.159) Lord Denning M.R. said (at p.35): "I do not like this doctrine of 'parasitic damages'. I do not like the very word 'parasite'. A 'parasite' is one who is a useless hanger-on sucking the substance out of others. 'Parasitic' is the adjective derived from it. It is a term of abuse. It is an opprobrious epithet. The phrase 'parasitic damages' conveys to my mind the idea of damages which ought not in justice to be awarded, but which somehow or other have been allowed to get through by hanging on to others. If such be the concept underlying the doctrine, then the sooner it is got rid of the better." Lord Denning was commenting upon counsel's attempt to attach, in the negligence action, the claim for the loss of profits to the claim for the physical damage to the metal. Does Lord Denning's comment indicate the power of metaphor in legal reasoning?

5. In *The Mediana* (1900) Earl of Halsbury L.C. said this (at p.117): "Now, in the particular case before us . . . the broad proposition seems to me to be that by a wrongful act of the defendants the plaintiffs were deprived of their vessel. When I say deprived of their vessel, I will not use the phrase 'the use of the vessel'. What right has a wrongdoer to consider what use you are going to make of your vessel? More than one case has been put to illustrate this: for example, the owner of a horse, or of a chair. Supposing a person took away a chair out of my room and kept it for 12 months, could anybody say you had a right to diminish the damages by showing that I did not usually sit in that chair, or that there were plenty of other chairs in the room? The proposition so nakedly stated appears to me to be absurd." Is it absurd for a defendant to claim that a person would not have used the property even if it had not been damaged? Imagine that C has three cars, one of which is damaged by D's negligence: can C claim in court that he has been deprived of the means of getting to work and has had to run up large taxi bills?

11.4.2 Damages for trespass to property

See *Inverugie Investments v Hackett* (p.26).

QUESTION

With regard to the Earl of Halsbury's comment above, would it be absurd to award full loss of use damages (as if it were mid summer) to a deck-chair hiring company at a seaside resort deprived of the use of a few of its deckchairs during the winter season?

11.4.3 **Damages for trespass to the person**

Where a defendant causes deliberate personal injury the normal rules applicable to personal injury damages will obviously apply. However many trespass claims are brought against the police and thus involve, also, an invasion of the claimant's constitutional rights. Awards are often made by juries, but judges have been given statutory power to modify any awards (see *John v MGN Ltd*, p.456)

Thompson v Commissioner of Police of the Metropolis **[1998] Q.B. 498, CA**

This case involved two actions for damages against the police. In the first case the claimant had been awarded by the jury £1,500 compensatory and £50,000 exemplary damages for false imprisonment and malicious prosecution. In the second case the claimant had been awarded £20,000 compensatory (including aggravated) and £200,000 exemplary damages for trespass. The Court of Appeal (Lord Woolf M.R., Auld L.J. and Sir Brian Neill) substituted an award of £10,000 compensatory and £25,000 exemplary damages in the first case and reduced the award of exemplary damages, in the second case, to £15,000.

Lord Woolf M.R.: "This is the judgment of the court. In a number of recent cases members of the public have been awarded very large sums of exemplary damages by juries against the Commissioner of Police of the Metropolis for unlawful conduct towards them by the police. As a result these two appeals have been brought by the commissioner. The intention is to clarify the directions which a judge should include in a summing up to assist the jury as to the amount of damages, particularly exemplary damages, which it is appropriate for them to award a plaintiff who is successful in this type of action. As similar appeals are pending any guidance given by us on this subject should influence the outcome of those appeals in addition to providing guidance for the future. . . .

. . . Part of the claim can have, as in both of these appeals, a personal injury element which makes the experience in ordinary personal injury cases directly relevant. A difference in the awards for compensation for the same injury, ignoring any question of aggravation, cannot be justified because the award is by a jury in a small minority of cases (the false imprisonment cases) while in the majority of cases (the other personal injury cases) the award is by a judge. If this court would intervene in one situation it should do so in the other. There is no justification for two tariffs. Furthermore even where what is being calculated is the proper compensation for loss of liberty or the damaging effect of a malicious prosecution the analogy with personal injuries is closer than it is in the case of defamation. The compensation is for something which is akin to pain and suffering. There is also recognition today that the uncertainty produced by the lack of consistency as to the damages which will be awarded in cases of this sort results in increased costs.

We have already referred to what was said in his judgment in *John v MGN Ltd* [1997] QB 586 by Sir Thomas Bingham MR as to the effect of excessive awards of damages in defamation cases on the public perception of civil justice. In this category of case the reaction could understandably be stronger since the excessive awards are being paid out of public money (though police forces other than the Metropolitan do take out insurance) and could well result in a reduction in the resources of the police available to be used for activities which would benefit the public. The Law Commission's Consultation Paper to which we have already made reference considers whether the power to award aggravated and exemplary damages should be abolished. The Law Commission's provisional views expressed in their consultation paper is that the power should be retained. However it is counterproductive to give juries an impossible task. It must at present be very difficult for a jury to understand the distinction between aggravated and exemplary damages when there is such a substantial overlap between the factors which provide the sole justification for both awards. The extent to which juries fluctuate in the awards which they make (which the present appeals demonstrate) indicates the difficulties which they have. On the other hand there are arguments which can be advanced to justify the retention of the use of juries in this area of litigation. Very difficult issues of credibility will often have to be resolved. It is desirable for these to be determined by the plaintiff's fellow citizens rather than judges, who like the police are concerned in maintaining law and order. Similarly the jury because of their composition, are a body which is peculiarly suited to make the final assessment of damages, including deciding whether aggravated or exemplary damages are called for in this area of litigation and for the jury to have these important tasks is an important safeguard of the liberty of the individual citizen.

As the Court of Appeal has usually the responsibility for determining the level of damages when it allows an appeal its decisions should indicate what is the appropriate level for damages in these actions. A standard will be established with which jury awards can be compared. This will make it easier to determine whether or not the sum which the jury has awarded is excessive. To not provide juries with sufficient guidance to enable them to approach damages on similar lines to those which this court will adopt will mean the number of occasions this court will be called on to intervene will be undesirably frequent. This will be disadvantageous to the parties because it will result in increased costs and uncertainty. It will also have adverse consequences for the reputation of the jury system. It could be instrumental in bringing about its demise. . . .

(5) In a straightforward case of wrongful arrest and imprisonment the starting point is likely to be about £500 for the first hour during which the plaintiff has been deprived of his or her liberty. After the first hour an additional sum is to be awarded, but that sum should be on a reducing scale so as to keep the damages proportionate with those payable in personal injury cases and because the plaintiff is entitled to have a higher rate of compensation for the initial shock of being arrested. . . .

(6) In the case of malicious prosecution the figure should start at about £2,000 and for prosecution continuing for as long as two years, the case being taken to the Crown Court, an award of about £10,000 could be appropriate. If a malicious prosecution results in a

conviction which is only set aside on an appeal this will justify a larger award to reflect the longer period during which the plaintiff has been in peril and has been caused distress. . . .

(10) We consider that where it is appropriate to award aggravated damages the figure is unlikely to be less than a £1,000. We do not think it is possible to indicate a precise arithmetical relationship between basic damages and aggravated damages because the circumstances will vary from case to case. In the ordinary way, however, we would not expect the aggravated damages to be as much as twice the basic damages except perhaps where, on the particular facts, the basic damages are modest. . . .

(13) Where exemplary damages are appropriate they are unlikely to be less than £5,000. Otherwise the case is probably not one which justifies an award of exemplary damages at all. In this class of action the conduct must be particularly deserving of condemnation for an award of as much as £25,000 to be justified and the figure of £50,000 should be regarded as the absolute maximum, involving directly officers of at least the rank of superintendent. . . .''

QUESTIONS

1. From the citizen's point of view, does it matter whether his or her constitutional rights are invaded by a constable or a by superintendent?

2. What is the object of the award of damages in false imprisonment and malicious prosecution cases: is it the invasion of the constitutional right or the mental distress of the victim? (cf. *Watkins v Home Office* (2006), p.125.)

11.4.4 Damages for nuisance

Private nuisance is a tort that attaches to land and thus damages are measured prima facie with reference to the *res* (thing) rather than to the persons (*personae*) who occupy the property.

Hunter v Canary Wharf Ltd [1997] A.C. 655, HL

(See p.232)

Lord Hoffmann: ". . . I cannot. . . agree with Stephenson L.J. in *Bone v Seale* [1975] 1 WLR 797, 803–804 when he said that damages in an action for nuisance caused by smells from a pig farm should be fixed by analogy with damages for loss of amenity in an action for personal injury. In that case it was said that "efforts to prove diminution in the value of the property as a result of this persistent smell over the years failed." I take this to mean that it had not been shown that the property would sell for less. But diminution in capital value is not the only measure of loss. It seems to me that the value of the right to occupy a house which smells of pigs must be less than the value of the occupation of an equivalent house which does not. In the case of a transitory nuisance, the capital value of the property will seldom be reduced. But the owner or occupier is entitled to compensation for the diminution in the amenity value of the property during the period for which the nuisance persisted. To some extent this involves placing a value upon intangibles. But estates agents do this all the time. The law of damages is sufficiently flexible to be able to do justice in such a case: compare *Ruxley Electronics and Construction Ltd v Forsyth* [1996] AC 344.

There may of course be cases in which, in addition to damages for injury to his land, the owner or occupier is able to recover damages for consequential loss. He will, for example, be entitled to loss of profits which are the result of inability to use the land for the purposes of his business. Or if the land is flooded, he may also be able to recover damages for chattels or livestock lost as a result. But inconvenience, annoyance or even illness suffered by persons on land as a result of smells or dust are not damage consequential upon the injury to the land. It is rather the other way about: the injury to the amenity of the land consists in the fact that the persons upon it are liable to suffer inconvenience, annoyance or illness.

It follows that damages for nuisance recoverable by the possessor or occupier may be affected by the size, commodiousness and value of his property but cannot be increased merely because more people are in occupation and therefore suffer greater collective discomfort. If more than one person has an interest in the property, the damages will have to be divided among them. If there are joint owners, they will be jointly entitled to the damages. If there is a reversioner and the nuisance has caused damage of a permanent character which affects the reversion, he will be entitled to damages according to his interest. But the damages cannot be increased by the fact that the interests in the land are divided; still less according to the number of persons residing on the premises. . . . Once it is understood that nuisances 'productive of sensible personal discomfort' (*St. Helen's Smelting Co. v Tipping*, 11 HL Cas 642, 650) do not constitute a separate tort of causing discomfort to people but are merely part of a single tort of causing injury to land, the rule that the plaintiff must have an interest in the land falls into place as logical and, indeed, inevitable. . . ."

QUESTIONS

1. Does it really make sense to say that the victim of a nuisance is the land rather than the people on it?

2. An occupier of a terraced house deliberately plays loud music at 3am in the morning in order to annoy the families on each side of him. In one family several children do badly in their GCSE exams probably as a result of the noise; in the other family only one child does badly in the exams probably as a result of the noise. If you were the solicitor acting for both the victim families would you advise them that each family could only be awarded more or less the same amount of damages?

11.4.5 Damages for defamation

Invasion of a person's reputation interest has given rise to particular difficulties in the law of damages as the next extract indicates.

John v MGN Ltd [1997] Q.B. 586, CA

In an action for damages for defamation against *The Sun* newspaper, the entertainer Elton John was awarded £75,000 compensatory and £275,000 exemplary damages by a jury. The Court of Appeal (Sir Thomas Bingham M.R., Neill L.J. and Hirst L.J.) reduced the figure to £25,000 compensatory and £50,000 exemplary damages.

Sir Thomas Bingham M.R.: ". . . The successful plaintiff in a defamation action is entitled to recover, as general compensatory damages, such sum as will compensate him for the wrong he has suffered. That sum must compensate him for the damage to his reputation; vindicate his good name; and take account of the distress, hurt and humiliation which the defamatory publication has caused. In assessing the appropriate damages for injury to reputation the most important factor is the gravity of the libel; the more closely it touches the plaintiff's personal integrity, professional reputation, honour, courage, loyalty and the core attributes of his personality, the more serious it is likely to be. The extent of publication is also very relevant: a libel published to millions has a greater potential to cause damage than a libel published to a handful of people. A successful plaintiff may properly look to an award of damages to vindicate his reputation: but the significance of this is much greater in a case where the defendant asserts the truth of the libel and refuses any retraction or apology than in a case where the defendant acknowledges the falsity of what was published and publicly expresses regret that the libellous publication took place. It is well established that compensatory damages may and should compensate for additional injury caused to the plaintiff's feelings by the defendant's conduct of the action, as when he persists in an unfounded assertion that the publication was true, or refuses to apologise, or cross-examines the plaintiff in a wounding or insulting way. Although the plaintiff has been referred to as 'he' all this of course applies to women just as much as men.

There could never be any precise, arithmetical formula to govern the assessment of general damages in defamation, but if such cases were routinely tried by judges sitting alone there would no doubt emerge a more or less coherent framework of awards which would, while recognising the particular features of particular cases, ensure that broadly comparable cases led to broadly comparable awards. This is what has happened in the field of personal injuries since these ceased to be the subject of trial by jury and became in practice the exclusive preserve of judges. There may be even greater factual diversity in defamation than in personal injury cases, but this is something of which the framework would take account. . . .

. . . A series of jury awards in sums wildly disproportionate to any damage conceivably suffered by the plaintiff has given rise to serious and justified criticism of the procedures leading to such awards. This has not been the fault of the juries. Judges, as they were bound to do, confined themselves to broad directions of general principle, coupled with injunctions to the jury to be reasonable. But they gave no guidance on what might be thought reasonable or unreasonable, and it is not altogether surprising that juries lacked an instinctive sense of where to pitch their awards. They were in the position of sheep loosed on an unfenced common, with no shepherd. . . .

Following enactment of section 8(2) of the Courts and Legal Services Act 1990 and the introduction of RSC, Ord 59, r 11(4) in its present form the Court of Appeal was for the first time empowered, on allowing an appeal against a jury's award of damages, to substitute for the sum awarded by the jury such sum as might appear to the court to be proper. . . .

. . .[T]here is continuing evidence of libel awards in sums which appear so large as to bear no relation to the ordinary values of life. This is most obviously unjust to defendants. But it serves no public purpose to encourage plaintiffs to regard a successful libel action, risky though the process undoubtedly is, as a road to untaxed riches. Nor is it healthy if any legal process fails to command the respect of lawyer and layman alike, as is regrettably true of the assessment of damages by libel juries. We are persuaded by the arguments we have heard that the subject should be reconsidered. . . .

In the passage from the judgment of the court in the *Rantzen* case [1994] QB 670. . . the Court of Appeal essentially adopted the approach of Lord Hailsham LC in *Broome v Cassell Co Ltd* [1972] AC 1027 in concluding that there was no satisfactory way in which conventional awards in actions for damages for personal injuries could be used to provide guidance for an award in an action for defamation. Much depends, as we now think, on what is meant by guidance: it is one thing to say (and we agree) that there can be no precise equiparation between a serious libel and (say) serious brain damage; but it is another to point out to a jury considering the award of damages for a serious libel that the maximum conventional award for pain and suffering and loss of amenity to a plaintiff suffering from very severe brain damage is about £125,000 and that this is something of which the jury may take account. . . ."

QUESTIONS

1. Have the awards of damages in defamation cases been brought under control?

2. Could the amounts awarded in defamation cases ever give rise to human rights issues?

11.4.6 Damages for deceit

Damages awarded in the tort of deceit for fraudulent misrepresentation may be more generous than would be the case if the misrepresentation had been negligent. See *Smith New Court Securities Ltd v Scrimgeour Vickers Ltd* (p.322).

11.4.7 Damages for breach of a human right

Under the Human Rights Act 1998 damages may be awarded (s.8) for an unlawful act which breaches a Convention right (s.6(1)).

Anufrijeva v Southwark LBC **[2004] Q.B. 1124, CA**

This case concerned a number of actions for damages against public authorities under s.8 of the Human Rights Act 1998 by persons seeking asylum in the UK. The claimants argued that the authorities had breached their rights under art.8 of the Convention for the Protection of Human Rights and Fundamental Freedoms to respect for their private and family life. The Court of Appeal (Lord Woolf C.J., Lord Phillips M.R. and Auld L.J.) held that on the facts of each claim there had been no breach of art.8 but that, had there been such a breach, modest damages could have been awarded.

Lord Woolf (delivering judgment of the court): ". . . **50** As we shall see, whereas damages are recoverable as of right in the case of damage caused by a tort, the same is not true in the case of a claim brought under the HRA for breach of the Convention. The language of the HRA and the jurisprudence of the Court of Human Rights make this clear. . . .

57 Section 8(4) of the HRA requires the court to take into account the principles applied by the Court of Human Rights when deciding whether to award damages and the amount of an award. Both the decisions of that court and the HRA make it plain that when damages are required to vindicate human rights and to achieve just satisfaction, damages should be awarded. Our approach to awarding damages in this jurisdiction should be no less liberal than those applied at Strasbourg or one of the purposes of the HRA will be defeated and claimants will still be put to the expense of having to go to Strasbourg to obtain just satisfaction. The difficulty lies in identifying from the Strasbourg jurisprudence clear and coherent principles governing the award of damages. . . .

59 Despite these warnings it is possible to identify some basic principles the Court of Human Rights applies. The fundamental principle underlying the award of compensation is that the court should achieve what it describes as restitutio in integrum. The applicant should, in so far as this is possible, be placed in the same position as if his Convention rights had not been infringed. Where the breach of a Convention right has clearly caused significant pecuniary loss, this will usually be assessed and awarded. . . . The problem arises in relation to the consequences of the breach of a Convention right which are not capable of being computed in terms of financial loss. . . . .

72 An infringement of a Convention right may have similar consequences to a tort giving rise to a claim under our domestic law-indeed the same act may constitute both a tort and a breach of a Convention right. . . Where a breach of article 5(4) results in a patient continuing to be detained in a hospital where he would otherwise have been released, the consequence of the breach bears close comparison with the consequences of the tort of false imprisonment. Should the English court, when awarding damages under the HRA, use the damages awarded for the tort of false imprisonment as a model?. . .

74 We have made plain that the discretionary exercise of deciding whether to award compensation under the HRA is not to be compared to the approach adopted where damages are claimed for breach of an obligation under civil law. Where, however, in a claim under the HRA, the court decides that it is appropriate to award damages, the levels of damages awarded in respect of torts as reflected in the guidelines issued by the Judicial Studies Board, the levels of awards made by the Criminal Injuries Compensation Board and by the Parliamentary Ombudsman and the Local Government Ombudsman may all provide some rough guidance where the consequences of the infringement of human rights are similar to that being considered in the comparator selected. In cases of maladministration where the consequences are not of a type which gives rise to any right to compensation under our civil law, the awards of the ombudsman may be the only comparator.

75 We have indicated that a finding of a breach of a positive obligation under article 8 to provide support will be rare, and will be likely to occur only where this impacts severely on family life. Where such a breach does occur, it is unlikely that there will be any ready comparator to assist in the assessment of damages. There are good reasons why, where the breach arises from maladministration, in those cases where an award of damages is appropriate, the scale of such damages should be modest. The cost of supporting those in need falls on society as a whole. Resources are limited and payments of substantial damages will deplete the resources available for other needs of the public including primary care. If

459

the impression is created that asylum seekers whether genuine or not are profiting from their status, this could bring the HRA into disrepute. . . ."

QUESTIONS

1. Is an action for damages under s.8 HRA 1998 a true claim in tort or is it a rather different type of substantive claim? (See *R. (Greenfield) v Home Secretary* (2005), § 19.)

2. Is this case authority for the proposition that the measure of damages in the law of obligations should take account not only of the claimant's interests but also those of the defendant?

11.5 Debt and similar claims

The great majority of claims in tort are damages actions by a victim against a single tortfeasor. Yet on occasions damage can be attributable to more than one wrongdoer and when this is the case the victim is entitled to claim the whole of his damages from any single defendant (unless the 'damage' is split up and apportioned causally to different actors: *Rahman v Arearose* (2001); *Barker v Corus* (2006), p.390). However the defendant who pays is entitled under statute to reclaim, provided certain conditions are fulfilled, contribution, if not a complete indemnity, from other tortfeasors. These claims are not really damages actions since they are based more on the principle of unjust enrichment. Conceptually therefore it might be better to see such claims for specific amounts as recourse 'debt' actions (although whether they are technically debt claims is open to discussion: *R (Kemp) v Denbighshire Local Health Board* (2007), at §§ 82–86).

Civil Liability (Contribution) Act 1978 (c.47)

"**1 Entitlement to contribution**

(1) Subject to the following provisions of this section, any person liable in respect of any damage suffered by another person may recover contribution from any other person liable in respect of the same damage (whether jointly with him or otherwise). . . .

(3) A person shall be liable to make contribution by virtue of subsection (1) above notwithstanding that he has ceased to be liable in respect of the damage in question since the time when the damage occurred, unless he ceased to be liable by virtue of the expiry of a period of limitation or prescription which extinguished the right on which the claim against him in respect of the damage was based. . . .

2 Assessment of contribution

(1) Subject to subsection (3) below, in any proceedings for contribution under section 1 above the amount of the contribution recoverable from any person shall be such as may be found by the court to be just and equitable having regard to the extent of that person's responsibility for the damage in question.

(2) Subject to subsection (3) below, the court shall have power in any such proceedings to exempt any person from liability to make contribution, or to direct that the contribution to be recovered from any person shall amount to a complete indemnity. . . .

6 Interpretation

(1) A person is liable in respect of any damage for the purposes of this Act if the person who suffered it (or anyone representing his estate or dependants) is entitled to recover compensation from him in respect of that damage (whatever the legal basis of his liability, whether tort, breach of contract, breach of trust or otherwise). . . ."

NOTE

The background to this statute is explained in the next two extracts.

Rahman v Arearose **[2001] Q.B. 351, CA**

Law L.J.: ". . . **18** The reason for the rule that each concurrent tortfeasor is liable to compensate for the whole of the damage is not hard to find. In any such case, the claimant cannot prove that either tortfeasor singly caused the damage, or caused any particular part or portion of the damage. Accordingly his claim would fall to be dismissed, for want of proof of causation. But that would be the plainest injustice; hence the rule. However, the rule was a potential source of another injustice. A defendant against whom judgment had been given, under the rule, for the whole of the claimant's damages had at common law no cause of action against his fellow concurrent tortfeasor to recover any part of what he had to pay under the judgment; so that the second tortfeasor, if for whatever reason he was not sued by the claimant, might escape scot free. Hence the 1978 Act and its predecessor the Law Reform (Married Women and Tortfeasors) Act 1935. It provides a right of contribution between concurrent tortfeasors. The expression 'same damage' in section 1(1) therefore means (and means only) the kind of single indivisible injury as arises at common law in a case of concurrent torts. . . ."

QUESTION

The facts of the above case are interesting both from a contribution and a causation point of view. The claimant had been attacked by two youths while working in the King's Cross branch of Burger King and subsequently had to undergo an eye operation as a result. However the operation was negligently performed and the claimant lost the sight in that eye. In addition to the hospital's negligence, the employer had also been at fault in not providing the employee with sufficient security at his workplace. This loss of an eye was not the only damage suffered; there was also pain and suffering, loss of future earnings and severe psychological harm. Should each defendant (employer and hospital) be separately liable for the whole of the claimant's damage or should each defendant be liable only for parts of the overall damage? (Read the case in the law report.)

Dubai Aluminium Co Ltd v Salaam [2003] 2 A.C. 366, HL

Lord Hobhouse: ". . . 71 In a simple case, say, injury to a passenger arising from a collision between two cars, both to blame, no problem arises. The court apportions the liability between the two drivers. But where, as in the present case, there has been a conspiracy to defraud involving a number of individuals, complications can arise. Only some of them may be before the court; some may be beyond the practical reach of the law; some may be insolvent; the routes by which liability has arisen may differ.

72 Section 2 of the statute requires the court to order contribution in an amount which is 'just and equitable having regard to the extent of that person's responsibility for the damage in question', the 'person' being the person being ordered to contribute and the 'damage in question' being the damage suffered by the victim for which the persons claiming and paying contribution were both liable. The concept of what is just and equitable corresponds to the restitutionary principles applied elsewhere in the law, for example, contributions between sureties or between insurers. The right to a contribution arises from the fact that one person has borne a disproportionate burden which it is just that another should share (or even bear in full, section 2(3)). Likewise responsibility includes both the degree of fault and the causative relevance of that fault. The power given to the court is principled but not otherwise restricted. It is this power which the court must use to solve any problems and arrive at a just and equitable outcome. . . ."

QUESTION

What is meant by 'the same damage' in s.1(1) of the 1978 Act?

Birse Construction Ltd v Haiste Ltd [1996] 1 W.L.R. 675, CA

This was an action for damages by a reservoir construction company (Birse) against consulting engineers (Haiste) in respect of the building of a defective reservoir for a water company (Anglian). Birse assumed responsibility for the defective reservoir and agreed to build a new reservoir at its own expense for Anglian. Haiste in turn brought a statutory contribution claim against a third party (Newton), an employee of the water company who was advising on the reservoir project, on the basis that the third party had been negligent and in breach of contract. The question arose as to whether the damage suffered by Anglian in having a defective reservoir was the 'same damage' as the damage suffered by Birse in having to build, at its own expense, a new reservoir. The Court of Appeal (Sir John May, Roch L.J. and Nourse L.J.) held that they were not the same since one was physical damage while the other was economic loss.

Roch L.J.: "I agree. A person liable for damage suffered by another may recover contribution from any other person liable in respect of the same damage under section 1(1) of the Civil Liability (Contribution) Act 1978, subject to the following provisions of the section. The liability of the person claiming contribution, Haiste, and the liability of the person from whom contribution is claimed, Mr Newton, does not have to be joint (section 1(1)), nor does the legal basis of the liability of Haiste have to be the same as the basis of the liability of Mr Newton: see section 6(1) of the Act.

The word 'damage' in the phrase 'the same damage' in section 1(1) does not mean 'damages.' This is demonstrated by other sections of the Act, for example section 2(3). By section 6(1) "damage" is the harm suffered by the 'another person,' to use the phrase in section 1(1), for which that person is entitled to recover compensation; it is not the compensation which is recoverable although in cases of purely financial loss it may be commensurate with it.

For there to be an entitlement to claim contribution the damage for which the person who claims contribution and the person from whom contribution is claimed has to be the same damage, that is to say the sufferer must be the same person or some person representing his estate or dependants. This is because the person who is entitled to recover compensation for the damage has to be the person who suffered the damage. I disagree with Judge Cyril Newman QC that this interpretation of the Act requires the addition of section 1(1) of the Act of words that are not there. In my view, this is the correct construction to be placed on section (1) when the Act is construed as a whole.

The damage suffered by Anglian in this case was the physical defects in the reservoir. The damage suffered by Birse was the financial loss of having to construct a second reservoir for Anglian. Anglian and Birse did not suffer the same damage. Consequently, I, too, would answer the question raised in the summons in the negative."

QUESTION

Did Anglian suffer physical damage or did it suffer only financial loss in not getting as good a 'product' as it expected under the construction contract? If Anglian's damage was only financial would this mean that it was the same damage as that suffered by Birse?

NOTE

This right to contribution is not unproblematic and can, on occasions, give rise to unfortunate results in terms of loss spreading, one reason being that the central concept is fault. When fault (tort) finds itself in the same arena, so to speak, as unjust enrichment (restitution), one concept tends to lose out: see e.g. *Lister v Romford Ice Co* (1957) (p.63); and for a brief but perceptive discussion see Weir, *Introduction to Tort Law* 2nd edn (OUP, 2006), pp.117–122. As Weir observes, the 1978 Act "permits a party who should bear the loss through his liability insurance to throw this loss or part of it onto a person, public or private, who would never have been sued by the primary victim" (ibid., pp.120–121).

11.6 Injunctions

Although the normal claim in a tort action is for damages, there are occasions—for example where the cause of action is harassment or nuisance—when the remedy of damages is insufficient. What is required is a court order to prohibit the defendant from continuing his activity. Such a remedy is the injunction, but being equitable (that is to say it was developed by the Court of Chancery) it brings into play its own particular principles that attach to the *actio* itself (see

C&MC, p.570; *Miller v Jackson* (1977), above p.15; *Burris v Azadani* (1995), p.421). Note that interlocutory (emergency) injunctions are subject to special principles that can make them particularly valuable as a means of developing existing, or even new, causes of action. But note also that *Manchester Airport Plc v Dutton* (2000) (p.414) is not an injunction case; it was an order for repossession of land. Could the claimant in the case have sought repossession by injunction? Statute is now of importance in that 'Anti-social behaviour' injunctions are available in some kinds of nuisance cases thanks to legislation: see e.g. Housing Act 1996 ss 153A-153D.

11.7 Self-help

There are occasions when a victim of a tort can 'take the law into his own hands' and use self-redress. However this "is a summary remedy, which is justified only in clear and simple cases, or in an emergency" (Lloyd L.J. in *Burton v Winters* (1993) at p.1082). Perhaps the most famous example of self-help is self-defence, which of course is a self-redress remedy used to resist a trespass. And this self-help resistance often arises in constitutional 'rights' cases: can a person unlawfully arrested escape conviction for assaulting a police officer on the basis that the assault was justified as self-defence?

> ### *R v Self* [1992] 1 W.L.R. 657, CA
>
> **Garland J.:** ". . . This matter comes before the court by leave of the single judge on a point of law. There is one point central to the appeal. It is this. Since the appellant was acquitted of theft neither Mr Frost nor Mr Mole were entitled by virtue of section 24 of the Police and Criminal Evidence Act 1984 to effect a citizen's arrest. If they were not entitled to do that then this appellant could not be convicted of an assault with intent to resist or prevent the lawful apprehension or detainer of himself, that is to say his arrest. . .
>
> The view of this court is that little profit can be had from taking examples and trying to reduce them to absurdity. The words of the statute are clear and applying those words to this case there was no arrestable offence committed. It necessarily follows that the two offences under section 38 of the Offences against the Person Act 1861 could not be committed because there was no power to apprehend or detain the appellant.
>
> It follows also, that that being the law, as this court sees it, the convictions on counts 2 and 3 must be quashed and this appeal allowed."

QUESTIONS

1. Could the defendant now sue Mr Frost and Mr Mole for damages in tort?

2. What if the defendant had been arrested by a policeman? (cf. *Police and Criminal Evidence Act 1984* s.25.)

3. Under what circumstances could Mr Frost and Mr Mole have lawfully arrested the defendant? (cf. *Police and Criminal Evidence Act 1984* s.24.)

NOTE

However any force used must not be excessive.

Revill v Newbery **[1996] Q.B. 567, CA**

This was an action for damages by a burglar injured when shot by the owner of a shed into which he was trying illegally to enter. The Court of Appeal (Neill L.J., Evans L.J. and Millett L.J.) upheld an award of damages suitably reduced for contributory negligence.

Neill L.J.: ". . . Each case must depend on its own facts. There may well be cases where in order to frighten a burglar away a gun is discharged in the air and the burglar is injured because unexpectedly he is on the roof. That, however, is not this case. I have carefully considered what weight should be given to the fact that the defendant thought that the intruder was at the window rather than at the door. I have come to the conclusion, however, that the judge was entitled to treat the discharge of the gun not merely as a warning shot but as a shot which was likely to strike anyone who was in the vicinity of the door. Although the intruder may have been at the window a person in the defendant's position could reasonably have anticipated that if the window were shuttered, as it was, the intruder might move to the door. The hole through which the gun was discharged was at body height and, as I understand it, the gun was fired more or less horizontally.

It is right to emphasise, as did the judge, that the defendant certainly did not intend to hit the plaintiff. Nevertheless I am satisfied that on the facts of this case the judge was entitled to find that the plaintiff was a person to whom the defendant owed some duty and that the defendant was in breach of that duty. The finding of a substantial proportion of contributory negligence was more than justified.

I would dismiss the appeal."

Millett L.J.: "For centuries the common law has permitted reasonable force to be used in defence of the person or property. Violence may be returned with necessary violence. But the force used must not exceed the limits of what is reasonable in the circumstances. Changes in society and in social perceptions have meant that what might have been considered reasonable at one time would no longer be so regarded; but the principle remains the same. The assailant or intruder may be met with reasonable force but no more; the use of excessive violence against him is an actionable wrong.

It follows, in my opinion, that there is no place for the doctrine ex turpi causa non oritur actio in this context. If the doctrine applied, any claim by the assailant or trespasser would be barred no matter how excessive or unreasonable the force used against him.

I agree that, for the reasons given by Neill LJ, the judge was entitled to find that the defendant's conduct was not reasonable. It was clearly dangerous and bordered on reckless. I would dismiss the appeal."

QUESTIONS

1. Is the defendant liable to the claimant in the tort of trespass or negligence?

2. Is this case authority for the proposition that one should never try to defend oneself, one's family or one's property against a burglar, for there is always a risk that one will have to pay him or her damages?

3. Why is it not possible to say that a burglar who enters another's property takes the risk of the householder behaving, perhaps out of fear, irrationally?

4. A householder shoots and kills a professional burglar. The wife of the burglar sues the householder for damages under the Fatal Accidents Act 1976. Can she claim compensation for the 'earnings' that her late husband would have made from his 'professional' activity had he not been wrongfully killed?

NOTE

Abatement is a self-help remedy against a nuisance, see: FH Lawson, *Remedies of English Law* 2nd edn (London: Butterworths, 1980), at p.28.

FURTHER QUESTION

What if a person mistakenly believes that he is being attacked by another: will such a mistake undermine the defence of self-defence?

Ashley v Chief Constable of Sussex Police **[2008] 2 W.L.R. 975, HL**

Lord Scott: "... **17** ... It is urged upon your Lordships that the criteria for self-defence in civil law should be the same as in criminal law. In my opinion, however, this plea for consistency between the criminal law and the civil law lacks cogency for the ends to be served by the two systems are very different. One of the main functions of the criminal law is to identify, and provide punitive sanctions for, behaviour that is categorised as criminal because it is damaging to the good order of society. It is fundamental to criminal law and procedure that everyone charged with criminal behaviour should be presumed innocent until proven guilty and that, as a general rule, no one should be punished for a crime that he or she did not intend to commit or be punished for the consequences of an honest mistake. There are of course exceptions to these principles but they explain, in my opinion, why a person who honestly believes that he is in danger of an imminent deadly attack and responds violently in order to protect himself from that attack should be able to plead self-defence as an answer to a criminal charge of assault, or indeed murder, whether or not he had been mistaken in his belief and whether or not his mistake had been, objectively speaking, a reasonable one for him to have made. As has often been observed, however, the greater the unreasonableness of the belief the more unlikely it may be that the belief was honestly held.

18 The function of the civil law of tort is different. Its main function is to identify and protect the rights that every person is entitled to assert against, and require to be respected by, others. The rights of one person, however, often run counter to the rights of others and the civil law, in particular the law of tort, must then strike a balance between the conflicting rights. Thus, for instance, the right of freedom of expression may conflict with the right of others not to be defamed. The rules and principles of the tort of defamation must strike the balance. The right not to be physically harmed by the actions of another may conflict with the rights of other people to engage in activities involving the possibility of accidentally causing harm. The balance between these conflicting rights must be struck by the rules and principles of the tort of negligence. As to assault and battery and self-defence, every person has the right in principle not to be subjected to physical harm by the intentional actions of another person. But every person has the right also to protect himself by using reasonable force to repel an attack or to prevent an imminent attack. The rules and principles defining what does constitute legitimate self-defence must strike the balance between these conflicting rights. The balance struck is serving a quite different purpose from that served by the criminal law when answering the question whether the infliction of physical injury on another in consequence of a mistaken belief by the assailant of a need for self-defence should be categorised as a criminal offence and attract penal sanctions. To hold, in a civil case, that a mistaken and unreasonably held belief by A that he was about to be attacked by B justified a pre-emptive attack in believed self-defence by A on B would, in my opinion, constitute a wholly unacceptable striking of the balance. It is one thing to say that if A's mistaken belief was honestly held he should not be punished by the criminal law. It would be quite another to say that A's unreasonably held mistaken belief would be sufficient to justify the law in setting aside B's right not to be subjected to physical violence by A. I would have no hesitation whatever in holding that for civil law purposes an excuse of self-defence based on non existent facts that are honestly but unreasonably believed to exist must fail. This is the conclusion to which the Court of Appeal came. . . .

19 I have found it helpful to consider also the somewhat analogous defence of consent. Consent is, within limits, a defence to a criminal charge of assault. It is relevant in physical contact games but is also frequently put forward as a defence where allegations of sexual assault, whether of rape or less serious varieties, are made. If the consent relied on had not been given but was honestly believed by the assailant to have been given, the accused would be entitled, as I understand it, to an acquittal. An honest belief that could not be rebutted by the prosecution would suffice. But why should that suffice in a tort claim based upon the sexual assault? It would surely not be a defence in a case where the victim of the assault had neither expressly nor impliedly consented to what the assailant had done for the assailant to say that he had honestly albeit mistakenly thought that she had, unless, at the very least, the mistake had been a reasonable one for him to have made in all the circumstances. So, too, with self-defence. . . .

20 . . . I would start with the principle that every person is prima facie entitled not to be the object of physical harm intentionally inflicted by another. If consent to the infliction of the injury has not been given and cannot be implied why should it be a defence in a tort claim for the assailant to say that although his belief that his victim had consented was a mistaken one none the less it had been a reasonable one for him to make? Why, for civil law purposes, should not a person who proposes to make physical advances of a sexual nature to another be expected first to make sure that the advances will be welcome? Similarly, where there is in fact no risk or imminent danger from which the assailant needs to protect himself, I find it difficult to see on what basis the right of the victim not to be subjected to physical violence can be set at naught on the ground of mistake made by the assailant, whether or not reasonably made. If A assaults B in the mistaken belief that it is necessary to do so in order to protect himself from an imminent attack by B, or in the mistaken belief that B has consented to what is done, it seems to me necessary to enquire about the source of the mistake. If the mistake were attributable in some degree to something said or done by B or to anything for which B was responsible, then it seems to me that the rules relating to contributory fault can come into play and provide a just result. If the mistake were attributable in some degree to something said to A by a third party, particularly if the third party owed a duty to take care that information he gave was accurate, the rules relating to contributions by joint or concurrent tortfeasors might come into play. But I am not persuaded that a mistaken belief in the existence of non-existent facts that if true might have justified the assault complained of should be capable, even if reasonably held, of constituting a complete defence to the tort of assault. . . ."

EXERCISE

An armed police officer suddenly sees a car approaching, at a very excessive speed, a group of women and children holding an illegal sit-down demonstration against the Iraq war. It is obvious that unless he intervenes the car will kill and injure many of the demonstrators. The officer draws his gun and shoots dead the driver, the car careering off into a shop front causing much damage to the shop and its stock. If sued for damages by (a) the wife of the dead driver and (b) the insurance company of the shop owner (subrogated to his rights), will the defence of self-defence be available to the police?

11.8 Final word

The great temptation is to conclude a book on tort by referring, favourably or critically, to its function or its internal structure. Does tort achieve what it is supposed to achieve? (And what is it supposed to achieve?) Is it a philosophically coherent subject or an incoherent mess? (And so on.) This temptation has been resisted in this present student book—not, it must be said at once, because these functional or structural questions are irrelevant (they are not). The temptation has been resisted because one of the most difficult aspects of tort is arguably its reasoning methodology.

Stephen Waddams, *Dimensions of Private Law*, (Cambridge: Cambridge University Press, 2003), pp.222–223, 231, 233 (footnotes omitted)

". . .[W]riters have denounced aspects of the law as chaotic and disorderly: if only the reader would join in accepting a few simple principles and in discarding a few anomalous decisions (the argument proceeds) order might be achieved. A common method has been to propose a scheme, to invite the reader to infer from a selective use of past decisions that there is historical support for it, to imply that adoption of the scheme will lead in the future to desirable consequences, and then to 'explain' (as showing the hidden operation of the scheme) those non-conforming decisions where the same result could have been reached on a conforming basis, and to condemn the rest as exceptional and unprincipled. This method has been very common in legal writing, but from a historical perspective it has limitations: it tends to assume what is sought to be proved, to marginalize inconvenient material, and to confuse the assessment of the past with a judgment of what is desirable for the future. . . .

A single-minded search for precision in private law tends to be self-defeating as new terminology is devised, and concepts and sub-concepts are multiplied and then further refined, in an attempt to accommodate awkward cases. It has. . . encountered judicial resistance, and has led to warnings that 'a preoccupation with conceptualistic reasoning' may lead to 'absurd' conclusions. Such warnings do not indicate a rejection of concepts, or of reason, or of classification; they signal a recognition that in law, as elsewhere, strict adherence to principle (admirable in itself) may, 'if relentlessly pursued' in a single dimension of a complex question, ultimately impede, rather than assist, sound judgment.

. . . The result has not been perfect order. But it does not follow that it has been chaos."

NOTES

1. See Lord Steyn in *Att-Gen v Blake* (2001) (above p.58) and in *Lister v Hesley Hall* (2002) (above p.272, para.16 of his judgment).

2. These wise words from one of the common law's leading professors might be born in mind each time one reads a tort textbook or article. See the further extract from Professor Waddams in C&MC, pp 104–105.

FINAL QUESTIONS

1. Are appeals to policy more frequent in the judgments in tort cases than in contract, land law and trust cases? If so, why do you think this is?

2. Does 'tort' gain its normative force from: (i) legal history; (ii) black-letter positive rules; (iii) moral philosophy; (iv) social policy; (v) economic policy; (vi) tort's own internal symmetry; (vii) a mixture of philosophical, social, political and economic arguments brought to bear on particular factual situations; (viii) analogies with the facts of previous cases; (x) the personal beliefs and ideologies of judges; (x) or some other source?

3. Is the source of tort law to be found in: (i) judgments and statutes; (ii) textbooks on the law of tort; or (iii) arguments of counsel?

4. What if the law of tort took as its starting point *activities* rather than individual *acts*: would the cases in this book be very different?

5. Consider the extract from JA Jolowicz on p.85 and imagine that his proposal appeals to the government. First, draft a statute putting his proposal into effect. Secondly, consider how the following cases might have been decided if Professor Jolowicz's proposal was law: *Esso Petroleum v Southport Corporation* (1953–56) (p.5); *Roe v Minister of Health* (1954) (p.356); *The Wagon Mound (No 1)* (p.400); *Hughes v Lord Advocate* (1963); *Rigby v Chief Constable of Northamptonshire* (1985) (p.371); *Pitts v Hunt* (1991) (p.370); *Marcic v Thames Water Utilities* (2004) (p.239).

6. To what extent are 'constitutional rights' seen as an interest to be specifically protected by the law of tort?

7. Is it true to say that English law now has a special regime for horses but not for motor vehicles (cf. *Welsh v Stokes* (2008) ([2008] 1 WLR 1224))?

Index

LEGAL TAXONOMY

FROM SWEET & MAXWELL

This index has been prepared using Sweet and Maxwell's Legal Taxonomy. Main index entries conform to keywords provided by the Legal Taxonomy except where references to specific documents or non-standard terms (denoted by quotation marks) have been included. These keywords provide a means of identifying similar concepts in other Sweet & Maxwell publications and online services to which keywords from the Legal Taxonomy have been applied. Readers may find some minor differences between terms used in the text and those which appear in the index. Suggestions to *taxonomy@sweetandmaxwell.co.uk*.

(All references are to paragraph number)